MW01250484

HARRY BRELSFORD'S SMB SERIES

Advanced
WINDOWS SMALL
BUSINESS SERVER 2003
Best Practices

SMB Nation Press

SMB Nation Press
P.O. Box 10179
Bainbridge Island, WA 98110-0179
206-824-1127

10 9 8 7 6 5 4 3 2

Printed in the United States of America

ISBN: 0-9744858-07-2

Cover Design: Alyssa Johnson
Editors: Vicky McCown, Melinda Spencer, Christy Jobe
Indexing: Judith Gibbs
Interior Layout: Stephanie Martindale

Contents

SECTION ONE: SBS 2003 Deployment

Chapter 1

Chapter 2

Chapter 3
SBS 2003 Licensing 3-1

SECTION TWO: SBS 2003 Utilization

Chapter 6
Exchange Server 2003: Advanced Topics 6-1
by Michael Klein

Chapter 7
Windows Sharepoint Services: Advanced Topics 7-1
by Jonathan Hassell

Chapter 9
Using Microsoft SQL Server 2000 with Small Business Server 2003

SECTION THREE: SBS 2003 Security

Chapter 11

Chapter 12
Advanced SBS 2003 Security:
Part 2: ISA Server 2004 12-1

by Beatrice Mulzer with Dr. Thomas Shinder

SECTION FOUR: SBS Advanced Topics

Chapter 13
System Monitoring 13-1

Chapter 15

About The Authors

Harry Brelsford

An SBSer since the very start of the product (early 1997), Harry lives with his family on Bainbridge Island just outside Seattle, Washington and enjoys many friendships with folks at the Microsoft Corporation. The author of 11 books and lead author on this book, Harry has enjoyed serving real world customers as a small-medium business technology consultant for the past 15-years including acting as the advisor to Peace Corps on its 76-country worldwide SBS deployment. Harry holds an MBA and several industry certifications including the MCSE. An adjunct college instructor for 12-years, Harry finally left the classroom when his wife suggested his two boys would like to ski and bike on the weekends! Harry enjoys delivering his worldwide HP-sponsored one-day SMB Nation workshops in over 60 cities per year spanning 25 countries. His annual SMB Nation conference is held in the Seattle area each September and you can sign up for his free SMB Technology Watch newsletter at www.smbnation.com. Finally, Harry holds the SBS-MVP designation common to several other writers in this book.

Andy Goodman

Andy has been involved with the computer industry since the mid 1970's. He owns and operates DownHome Computers a small computer shop in Kernersville, NC, USA focused on Small Business IT solutions and of course SBS. He is a MS System Builder and an Intel IPD. Andy has been involved with SBS since the early days of 4.0 in 1997. Along with hosting the SBS Forum on SBS for MCP Magazine he also does a monthly SBS chat for MCPmag.com. In his spare time he writes how to articles for a number of e-zines as well as his own site www.SBS-Rocks.com. Andy has been involved with the user group community since the early 90's and been on the board of a number of groups, such as Bay Area NT Group, NT Engineering Association, Silicon Valley Computer Society to name a few. Andy is also the founding father of the Triad SBS Group a consultants group focused on SBS (www.TriadSBSgroup.org) in North Carolina.

Bea Mulzer

Jack of all trades and hasn't mastered a thing, Beatrice holds certifications like MCSE's, MCT and MSU (a.k.a. Make Stuff Up) and keeps busy bicycling, running and swimming. She avoids having to get a real job by consulting to local businesses on SBS with a niche in litigation technology. Beatrice practices results-based consulting with the long term relationship in mind. One of her latest accomplishments was getting a $5 Million settlement for one of her clients supported on an SBS network diligently used for trial preparation. Having the incurable malady of truly caring for her customers and constantly biting off more than she can chew has proven to be a successful methodology for growing her business and expertise.

She has taught the academic Microsoft Official Curriculum at local college campuses and delivered numerous Microsoft Hands-on-Labs including Small Business Server throughout the United States. Beatrice has been published in Microsoft Certified Professional Magazine and writes the monthly Certification and Education column for Reseller Advocate Magazine. She has developed training curriculum for Microsoft as well as delivered Web Casts.

When she is not deep-sea fishing, kayaking or having lunch with clients, you will find her supporting local non-profits, volunteering at functions or raising money for cures of cancer and MS (that is multiple sclerosis, not Microsoft…). Beatrice is a member of the Better Business Development Board of the Cocoa Beach Area Chamber of Commerce, the Microsoft Small Business Advisory Council and a member of the Space Coast Triathletes.

Her motto: Life is too short to take yourself seriously ☺ Beatrice currently resides in Cocoa, Florida with her two Labradors and Mimi the cat.

Chris Angelini

Chris Angelini was raised in Bakersfield, CA, where he returned after graduating from UCLA in 2004 to found Texpert Consulting. His writing career dates back to 1998 when, as a freshman, he consciously chose computers over a life of collegiate debauchery. He has since contributed content to nearly 20 influential technology-related web sites, Smart Computing, Computer Power User, Reseller Advocate Magazine, PC Upgrade, Computer Source Magazine, and Computer Gaming World, in addition to being quoted on news.com and The Wall Street Journal. Outside of technology, Chris' interests include sailing, hunting, investing, and his family.

Frank Ohlhorst

Frank came to CRN in 1999 and has held the positions of Technical Editor and Senior Technical Editor and CRN's Technology Editor prior to being named Director of CRN Labs. Frank is responsible for overseeing the CRN Test Center and associated staff, generating product reviews, features, supplements and special reports. Frank also speaks at industry conferences, hosts round tables, technology panels and is a frequent contributor to CMP Media's Netseminar series. Frank focuses on Enterprise Networking, Security technologies, Wireless networking and solutions aimed at the small and medium business market

Prior to CRN, Frank was employed for 7 years with the U.S. Department of Energy, where he was a network manager responsible for overseeing a multi-site heterogeneous network and associated staff. Frank was also responsible for network security, evaluating, implementing and managing hardware and software solutions, managing Intranet and Internet connectivity and a multi-site SQL-based workflow systems.

Before his employment with DOE, Frank spent several years operating his own computer consulting business, providing custom software and networking solutions, and has developed vertical market software for many businesses, including local government and non-profit organizations.

Frank is also a frequent guest on Dave Graveline's "In to tomorrow" radio show and has also appeared on "lets talk computers." Frank has contributed to several other technology publications and has authored several white papers.

Frank has been active in the IT industry since 1984 and has held positions with both consulting firms and corporations. Frank holds several industry specific certifications, Including Novell's CNE, Microsoft MCP, Comptia A+ and N+ certifications.

Jeff Middleton

An author's bio page typically reads the more distant third person, repeating "he was…" until you believe it's an obituary in progress. The voice of a conversation is what I expect most people know of me, my first person voice online. In six years as an SBS MVP, I've posted far in excess of 10,000 pages of comments to the Small Business Server newsgroups hosted by Microsoft.

This is my official first "you can buy it in a bookstore" writing effort. I've written professionally for years, both technical documentation and consulting reports. I'm also handy with database, spreadsheet, and language programming. The VAR/Systems Integrator business I began 15 years ago originally reflected my passion for cool tools in videographics and animation, and it built a staff of five after as many years. I changed direction, and for the past nine years chose a simpler lifestyle over larger scale business, became a one-man band for small business solutions. I sold my first six SBS installs the month it debuted, discovered the newsgroups soon after. From that I found a place we share the passion for helping each other within a worldwide community. It's redefined my life, and my career. I can work from anywhere in the world, and I don't work alone anymore as long as I have web access.

Grey Lancaster introduced me to Harry on my first visit to Microsoft Redmond. I wouldn't be an SBS MVP if not for my respect for Grey's example of what one person can do for the world. More than thirty SBS MVPs now share such efforts to the community, and among each other. Three of them include Susan, Wayne and Andy, each a great friend who played a significant role in my opportunity to contribute to this book along side them. I can't possibly explain the debt I owe to all the SBS MVPs for their skills and inspiration. For testing my ideas on Swing Migration, showing me what to improve, and persuading me to start SBSmigration.com as a new business, YCST. These are some of my best friends around the world, literally.

I owe much in the year past to Harry for sharing his opportunities with me. David Allinson of Microsoft Australia has my thanks for the month I had there to present the content from the migration chapter to Microsoft partners. Finally, the global friendships I recall from this past year are woven together with threads of memories about Lyn, and her dedication to global friendships. That is my dedication for this book connecting so many friends in a global community. Contact me at YCST@SBSmigration.com.

Jonathan Hassell

Jonathan Hassell is an author, consultant, and speaker residing in Charlotte, North Carolina. His work is seen regularly in Windows IT Pro Magazine, SecurityFocus, PC Pro, and Microsoft TechNet Magazine. He speaks around the world on topics including networking, security, and Windows administration.

Kevin Royalty

Kevin Royalty (MCSE, SBS) is the Chief Consulting Officer for Solution Net Inc (www.solution-net.com), a consulting firm in Cincinnati Ohio. He sits on the advisory board for CincyTechUSA, an arm of the Greater Cincinnati Chamber of Commerce, as well as the Information Technology Advisory Team, an arm of the Northern Kentucky Chamber of Commerce. He is the current president of the Cincinnati Networking Professionals' Association (CiNPA) www.cinpa.org, a large group of IT Professionals that meet once a month to discuss technology. He chairs the SBS Special Interest Group (SIG) in CiNPA as well, a subgroup that caters to all the Consultants and Administrators of SBS networks in the area. At the formation of the SBS SIG, the group of 9 consultants represented an installed base in the Cincinnati market of 138. As this chapter was being written, the membership was approximately 30 and growing as word spreads.

Lawrence Rodis

President and Chief Technology Officer, Strategic Resource Consulting Group L.L.C.

Analytical, precise and attentive to detail, Mr. Rodis is known for his proficiency in all aspects of computer technology and information management. He has been recognized for his diverse background in strategic planning, mission critical 24x7 systems, implementations and networking, client server computing and supplier management.

Educationally, Mr. Rodis holds a Masters of Arts in Organizational Management and a Bachelor of Science in Computer Science. He has earned the Microsoft Certified Professional (MCP) designation, and under his direction, Strategic Resource Consulting Group gained the Microsoft Certified Partner (MCP) status in 1999. In 2004 with the introduction of competencies for the Microsoft Certified Partner program SRCG earned the Network Infrastructure Competency.

Mr. Rodis serves as a consultant to a number of educational, nonprofit, and professional service organizations. He has been implementing Microsoft Small Business Server since founding his company in 1999. Prior to founding SRCG, he worked at Intel where he provided management, strategy and project management expertise in implementing network infrastructure at their worldwide manufacturing locations

In addition to his leadership of Strategic Resource Consulting Group L.L.C., Mr. Rodis teaches undergraduate and graduate level technology courses for the University of Phoenix, Nevada Campus.

Lawrence is the father of three wonderful children and a fabulous wife. In his spare time he is following in his children's footsteps and is pursuing his Black Belt in Taekwondo.

Michael Klein

Michael Klein founded Computer Directions, Inc., a New York based computer and management consulting firm, in 1987. Computer Directions is a full service organization that offers its clients one-stop shopping, a single phone call for all their computer needs so that they can concentrate on their business. Some of the services include accounting software, network installation, Internet connectivity, e-mail setup, remote access, and Web site design.

Mr. Klein also uses his broad business and management background to focus not only on the computer equipment, but the entire business as well. He works with his clients to use technology to find bottom-line benefits, such as increasing sales, reducing expenses, improving the quality of life, and exceeding customer expectations.

Prior to Computer Directions, Mr. Klein was an internal consultant improving productivity and profitability for both Chase Manhattan Bank and American Express. He also served as an officer of Chemical Bank in their Emerging Technology Group.

Mr. Klein has been mentioned several times in the computer industry trade press during this past year for his findings regarding Windows Server 2003. He was named Small Business Consultant of the month in June 2004. He was selected by Microsoft to become a member of their Small and Medium Business Advisory Council. He is frequently asked by major software vendors to test, provide feedback, and help shape the direction of their new products. Recent examples include: Microsoft Small Business Server, Microsoft Internet Security and Acceleration Server, Peachtree Accounting Software, and Timeslips. Because of his expertise and background, Mr. Klein has been called upon to help with forensic investigations and expert witness testimony. He is also a frequent lecturer.

Mr. Klein holds a BS in Computer Engineering from the University of Rochester, an MS from Polytechnic University, an MBA in Finance and an MBA in Marketing from Adelphi University. He can be reached at Info@ComputerDirectionsInc.com.

Steven Banks

With over eight years hands on experience in the Internet and computer technology fields, Steve, the founder of the Puget Sound Small Business Server User Group and President of Banks Consulting Northwest Inc. (www.banksnw.com), is a Microsoft Certified Professional in Windows 2000 and Small Business Server 2003, holds certification from SonicWALL as a Certified SonicWALL Security Administrator and is a recipient of the Microsoft Most Valuable Professional award (Windows Server Systems - Small Business Server). Prior to entering the Internet industry, Steve sold consumer electronics for seven years in the Puget Sound region. Steve has collaborated with Microsoft, Forbes and Hewlett-Packard on white papers and case studies focusing on TechNet, Small Business Server 2000, and Windows Small Business Server 2003. Banks Consulting Northwest has also participated extensively in Microsoft's Technology Adoption Program, helping to gather feedback and real world user experiences of Microsoft solutions in the small business space. If you live in the Puget Sound region and are looking to increase your involvement with the SBS Community to better your skills as a business supporting Small

Business Server, contact Steve at http://groups.msn.com/pssbs to join the Puget Sound Small Business Server User Group!

Susan Bradley

Susan started her career in computing with IBM 8088 computers and Compaq "luggable" portables. To this day she is convinced that her right arm is longer than her left arm because she lugged those dang "luggables" for an entire summer at an audit job. Now she practically has an RJ45 connection growing out of her body. ;-) A fellow CPA turned her on to this new fangled product called Small Business Server 4.0 [see the power of word of mouth marketing] and when the consultant she hired obviously did not use any of the wizards [be careful that your customer may actually read the product documentation, unlike you], she went in search of community resources and found the SBS communities. When she was ready to upgrade to Small Business Server 2000, she interviewed Microsoft Gold Certified partners who tried to talk her out of SBS [she now knows to go find mere Registered partners as they are better SBSers]. Her passion is Security and she has received the SANS Global Security Essential Certificate, and AICPA's Certified Information Technology Professional credential as well as being a beta exam tester and receiving the "SBS MCP", the MCP for Designing, Deploying, and Managing a Network Solution for a Small- and Medium-Sized Business.

Susan is a Small Business Server and Security MVP—Most Valuable Professional—a title bestowed by Microsoft on independent experts who do not work for the company. Known as the "SBS Diva" for her extensive command of the bundled version of Windows Server 2003, she's a partner in a CPA firm and spends her days cajoling vendors into coding more securely.

Wayne Small

With over 25 years in the IT industry, Wayne Small, MCSE 2000, MCSE+I, is one of Microsoft's 30 Microsoft Small Business Server focused Most Valuable Professionals (MVP) worldwide and hosts one of the leading non Microsoft sources of information for Small Business Server, www.sbsfaq.com. He has been an International guest speaker at a number of conferences in 2003 and 2004 covering both business and technical topics. He has also participated in various road shows focused on Small Business Server for Microsoft Australia. Wayne is also the Owner and Technical Director of successful Sydney based IT Integration company - Correct Solutions. Correct Solutions supports small to medium businesses with complete IT solutions. The company has been involved in the Small Business Server product since its inception in 1997.

Dedication

Rightfully dedicated to all of the SBSers located around the world!

Acknowledgements

Where to begin? Thanks to:

- Nancy Williams at SMB Nation. All authors involved in this project were able to meet Nancy and work closely with her on completing this book. Nancy drove people to new heights!

- HP: David Sinclair, Marc Semadeni, Andy Bauman helped move this book forward.

- Microsoft: Sharon Erdman, Eric Ligman and countless others!

- Reviewers who pitched in: Fred Fulenwider, Dean Calvert, Les Connor, Javier Gomez

- Bang Printing: Justin and the gang.

- And all the rest!

Foreword to Harry Brelsford's SMB Series

To live free, make an impact, enjoy your work, and make a profit. Those are the primary life goals of most any SMB consultant you are likely to meet. The trick is that an SMB consultant can't get too hung up on any one of those four issues, because the secret to happiness is to balance those often conflicting needs, rather than letting any one of them dominate at the expense of the other three.

Of course, this is all much easier said than done, so it takes an extraordinary individual to be a successful SMB consultant. Unlike their mercurial customers, the SMB entrepreneur needs to combine patience with business insight to help guide their customers through a labyrinth of technology choices that can easily aggravate a class of customers who are keenly aware "time is money."

The simple truth is the SMB owner is the most challenging customer in the IT industry because, more often than not, their business can flourish or expire thanks to the right or wrong technology decision. Alas, nothing in this industry is ever as straightforward as it seems, so a nervous SMB owner who is typically worried about making payroll can easily be led astray. And once that happens, a torrent of frustration and recrimination is quickly unleashed squarely on the head of the SMB consultant.

All too frequently this leads to the tarring of all SMB consultants in the same way a few bad lawyers or journalists can cast aspersions on an entire profession. Of course, there are times when the misstep of a consultant does lead to some debacle, but the root cause of that disaster is usually ignorance rather than malfeasance. All told, the vast majority of SMB consultants are a credit to the industry.

Whether an SMB consultant created their practice as a deliberate act to advance their careers or as an unintended consequence derived from events beyond their control, everybody needs a helping hand. So we at CRN applaud the publishing of a book that seeks to increase the number of savvy SMB consultants in the world, which will reduce the number of failed IT projects and consulting practices while simultaneously increasing the value proposition of technology itself.

It's important to remember that the technology industry as a whole would not exist as we know it today if it were not for the SMB consultants serving as its evangelists for countless products. More often than not, it is the SMB market leading the way in terms of bringing new technology innovations to market. That becomes even more apparent when you consider the challenges of the SMB owner. With fewer resources and people, the SMB owner frequently needs to compete for business against larger rivals by being more adroit. And in the absence of larger rivals, there's always the need to be more efficient, because the cardinal rule of business is "Revenue drives growth."

The only way to achieve those twin goals is to reduce the steps it takes to execute a business process and increase revenue per employee. And the quickest way to do that is to maximize a technological edge before any one else does.

Of course, most SMB owners are not technological gurus. So they turn to trusted SMB consultants to get them through the all-too-often daunting tasks associated with investing in technology. For the industry as whole, this means the SMB consultant is the primary way the word gets out about which products work and which don't. Without the guidance of the SMB consultant, billions of dollars spent on technology marketing would fall on the deaf ears of SMB owners too busy to appreciate the lasting impact any given technology can have on their business.

So here's a salute to the SMB consultant. For the most part, they make a good living and enjoy being masters of their own domain. But more often than not, they are typically underappreciated and undervalued by vendors who are more focused on the name on the check than the actual person who got them the deal.

We can only hope that with the publishing of more books such as this one, it will become easier for a larger number of people to form their own SMB consulting practices. Lest we forget, it is the SMB consultant who truly forms the bulwark of this industry and, as such, we are invested in their success.

Yours very truly,
Michael Vizard,
Editor In Chief, CRN

Michael Vizard joined CMP Media's CRN, the newsweekly for builders of technology solutions, as editor in chief in August 2002. In this role, Mr. Vizard is responsible for the strategic vision of the newsweekly, ensuring editorial coverage goals are met by evolving the reporting and editorial beats to accommodate readers' information needs.

Mr. Vizard has more than 15 years of computer technology and publishing experience. In 2001 and 2002, Mr. Vizard was voted one of the Top 30 Most Influential Technology Journalists by Technology Marketing. He was also named one of the Top 15 media influencers in the trade press category. Prior to joining CRN, Mr. Vizard spent seven years as editor in chief of InfoWorld Media Group, where he was responsible for managing strategic editorial partnerships, the day-to-day management of InfoWorld's editorial department, and leading the content of InfoWorld Online.

Prior to joining InfoWorld, Mr. Vizard had been an editor at PC Week, Computerworld, Digital Review, and ebn. Mr. Vizard holds a degree in journalism from Boston University.

Preface

Welcome to *Advanced Small Business Server 2003 Best Practices*! This book is an advanced guide to Microsoft Windows Small Business Server 2003 (SBS 2003), an attractively priced product that's offered in two editions in the current release (standard and premium). SBS 2003 combines the key infrastructure and application elements that small businesses prize.

Of course, I'm preaching to the choir! As experienced SBSers (fans, users, and sometimes abusers of SBS), you the various readers of this text already know the basics about SBS 2003. Perhaps you learned about SBS 2003 at a class or seminar. Or maybe you've installed it for your own use. More likely you've deployed SBS for one or more clients. Lastly, you might be very experienced with a prior version of SBS and thus are confident in rocketing right into this advanced SBS 2003 text (welcome aboard!).

Respecting your status as an intermediate or better user of SBS, this book won't retell the basic SBS 2003 story already covered in my introductory book, *Windows Small Business Server 2003 Best Practices*. However, visit www.microsoft.com/sbs if you want to learn more about the SBS product.

And now, assumptions about your SBS 2003 product awareness safely made, let's move forward and set expectations for this book (after all, that is the basic job of a preface, you know!).

What This Book Is About

This book is about taking your skill as an SBSer to the next level—to an advanced level. The next sections describe how this book will help you get to that level.

Advanced Topics

The topics in this book address the sorts of advanced issues you're likely to consider after having gained some experience with SBS 2003. The discussions herein also reflect contemporary topics of the day, things that have emerged since the October 2003 release of SBS 2003 at the Microsoft Worldwide Partner Conference in New Orleans, Louisiana. As you might imagine, subjects that were initially important have since been upstaged by other issues that are even more important and more current and that warrant advanced discussion. While building up a stockpile of advanced SBS topics and factoids to present to you within the covers of this book, my writing team and I looked both in the mirror and into the steely eyes of our clients; we scoured newsgroups, we read e-mails sent to us from users very much like yourself, and we even overheard interesting conversations within the Redmond hallways of Microsoft itself!

A Winning Writing Team

Please forgive, I think I mentioned my writing team without first personally introducing them. Meet the team with my words (also see the individual author bios early in the Front Matter of this book).

- Harry Brelsford. That's me, of course! I'm responsible for the Preface, Chapter 1 covering introduction and advanced planning topics, and also Chapter 3 on licensing issues.

- Chris Angelini. A hardware guru who has penned tons of articles focusing on hardware, Chris authored Chapter 2 of this text.

- Steven Banks. An all-around SMB consultant with the proper balance of business and technical skill sets, Steven's status as a reseller and Microsoft partner made him uniquely qualified to handle Chapter 3 on licensing.

- Andy Goodman. A long-time SBSer who is also an SBS MVP, Andy is well qualified to tackle the advanced SBS deployment issue, which he's done in Chapter 4 of this book.

- Frank Ohlhorst. The technology editor at CRN magazine, Frank is an experienced SBSer. Because his duties at CRN include running the test lab, Frank is in the unique position for Chapter 5 to discuss third-party tools for SBS 2003.

- Michael Klein. With his well-established New York City SBS consulting practice focused on the legal community, Michael is all about fostering strong communications with his clients. Ergo, he was the natural choice for knocking out an advanced Microsoft Exchange Server 2003 chapter, Chapter 6.

- Jonathan Hassell. A long-time SBS writer, Jonathan is a multi-trick pony, with his current book on "hardening Windows" doing very well. Because he wrote a book a couple of years ago on SharePoint technologies, Jonathan was selected for Chapter 7 of this book, the advanced Microsoft Windows SharePoint Services chapter.

- Wayne Small. A "tall poppy" from down under, Australian SBS MVP Wayne Small was selected to write Chapter 8 because of his overriding excitement about the mobility features of SBS 2003. His experience as an SBS professional is evident.

- Alan Shrater. A renascence man in the SBS community, Alan is an accountant (CPA), developer (Microsoft SQL Server), and networking consultant based in Colorado. Alan was charged with the task of telling the story of advanced SQL Server 2000 in SBS 2003, which he's accomplished while keeping a keen eye focused on "business purpose." Alan wrote Chapter 9 of this book.

- Kevin Royalty. The first words that come to mind with regard to Kevin are "extensive experience!" Kevin stepped up to write Chapter 10 on advanced faxing topics.

- Susan Bradley. The queen of the SBS newsgroups (Microsoft and Yahoo!), Susan was ready, able, and willing to share her advanced knowledge of SBS-related security in Chapter 11, from which we will all benefit.

- Thomas Shinder. A world-renowned security author in the Microsoft Internet Security and Acceleration (ISA) Server area, Thomas is a big fan of SBS and he has taken this book to the next level by focusing his efforts on ISA Server 2004, which is available to SBS 2003 premium owners! Thomas co-authored Chapter 12.

- Bea Mulzer. She is the Queen Bea of SBS and hails from Florida. She is well-know for striking a balance between complex technical issues and business matters in the SBS community. Bea co-authored Chapter 12.

- Lawrence Rodis. Larry comes from the big leagues (enterprise-level) where he learned first-hand the importance of network monitoring and appropriate responses. Thank God Larry embraced SBS many years ago and is a kind soul who likes to share his knowledge freely, which he has done here in Chapter 13.

- Jeff Middleton. I have saved the introduction of perhaps the most esteemed contributor for last. If you've ever posted to the Microsoft-supported SBS newsgroups, you've bumped into Jeff, who was one of the very first SBS MVPs. Jeff has written two world class chapters for this book, Chapter 14 on disaster recovery and Chapter 15 about migration.

You can learn more about each writing team member by reviewing their individual biographies in the front matter of this book.

In fact, I should explain how this team came into being. While on walkabouts in Australia, while peddling a bike through parts of Europe, and even while enjoying a simple respite on my beloved Bainbridge Island outside Seattle—always and forever while pondering SBS life—I concluded that the only way to write an advanced SBS text that would be truly meaningful would be to assemble a world class team of writers such as has seldom been assembled before. As a result, I gathered a writing team for this book that is the New York Yankees of the SBS world! (For those overseas readers who are perhaps unfamiliar, the

New York Yankees are a dominant baseball team in Major League Baseball in the USA and Canada.)

Given that advanced topics by their very nature tend to be specializations, it serves that no one person could successfully write an entire advanced book, worthy of five-star reviews on Amazon.com, about a product as broad and diverse as SBS. This book is the combined effort of a team of subject matter experts who have bared their analytical SBS souls in the chapters that follow, delivering substantial and practical information based on each writer's individual area of expertise. I'm delighted that such an outstanding team has taken time from their busy schedules to come together and contribute in many ways to the betterment of all SBSers.

The gathered effort of this superstar writing team had but one ultimate goal—that you would come out the winner! Let's face it. You have paid good money for this book. We the writing team have done our best and we hope that this book will meet your needs and exceed your expectations.

Presentation

My role during the creation of this book has in many ways been like being the conductor of an SBS symphony. Having assembled a first-class orchestra of SBS virtuosos, it was then my responsibility to bring order to individual fine works, in order to create a magnificent concerto through which to present the collective SBS expertise! I applied the following guiding principles as I led this effort:

- Individual acknowledgement. The beginning of each chapter notes which member of the writing team authored the words that follow. Not only do these acknowledgements allow you to applaud the proper persons; they also allow you to glean something about each writer, a contextual insight into what each author has written. Certainly the writer from Manhattan Island in New York City might have a much different perspective about SBS than does the laid-back mellow dude on Bainbridge Island (hey, that's me!). Why? Because there's a big difference between a "New York minute" and the slow pace of life on Bainbridge Island, and clients are likely to have different demands as a result.

- Academic freedom. As the publisher of this volume, I not only encouraged the expression of personal and professional opinions in the contributed works, but I also lead the march in defending the rights of the writers to express such sentiments! Write on!

- First person. In the ongoing effort of SMB Nation Press to avoid ever publishing "another boring computer book" dominated by corporate communication standards that originate from the Dark Ages, I nudged all of the writing team members to write in the first person. I wanted them to be able to write from their hearts, presenting you with the authority and credibility of their firsthand experience. Also, it was with great pleasure that I allowed, even encouraged, bragging! I encouraged the writers to point you to other books they've written for other publishers, because it's likely that the chapters these excellent writers have contributed here will wet your appetite for more of their existing works.

- Consistent tone. My job has been to take the diverse writing styles of multiple authors and attempt to lay down a consistent tone throughout this book, to improve readability without compromising the expressive freedoms of the writers. (And I thought writing an entire book as a solo author was hard!) Seriously, my goal has been for this book not to appear as a collection of individual white papers but as a coordinated and collective work.

- Real World. Some publishers seem to suffer from tunnel vision, only presenting information related to Microsoft offerings while ignoring all other third-party applications that might be beneficial to customers. They also seem to steer clear of offering war stories from the trenches. Not so this book! Within these pages you'll find a refreshing real-world view of advanced SBS that includes war stories as well as third-party product information to assist you.

- Third-party view of Microsoft. As third-party writers who aren't financially beholden to Microsoft for our day jobs, we (the writing team) provide an essential outsider's view of Microsoft and the SBS product. This third-party perspective perhaps is even one of the reasons why you selected this book over (or in addition to) other materials such as Microsoft SBS-related white papers.

- Less Humor and No Dogs! An advanced SBS book necessarily addresses important and serious issues related to the SBS product. Unlike my introductory and intermediate SBS books that incorporate humor and Springer Spaniels Limited (a sample company for the storyline), this book deemphasizes the humor to appeal to the more serious-minded SBSer who is seeking SBS advanced answers.

- Make Love, Not War. This book represents at its core the ability for SBSers of all types, such as the diverse team of writers who contributed to this volume, to come together to work for a common, meaningful end—in this case to provide you, the reader, with an interesting and useful advanced text!

How This Book Is Organized

Not surprisingly, this book is organized into sections that reflect the book's mission. While the devil is in the details (and those details are outlined in the Table of Contents), following is the general organizational context of the sections in this volume.

Section One: SBS 2003 Deployment

The fact of the matter is that everyone regardless of skill level, even those of you who are hardened SBSers, should honor the "essentials" discussed in the first five chapters of this text. The first chapter touches on advanced SBS 2003 planning issues that are current and relevant today. This is followed by a strong chapter about hardware issues that affect SBS and small businesses. Next, a chapter about licensing, a subject about which an entire book could be written. Then comes a chapter about advanced setup and deployment, picking up on these issues where other SBS 2003 books leave off. Finally, the section about essentials closes with a chapter that highlights third-party tools you can use for advanced administration of SBS.

Section Two: SBS 2003 Utilzation

After you have your SBS 2003 infrastructure solidly in place, it's natural to commence the ascent to the application level. SBS delivers several critical applications such as Exchange, Windows SharePoint Services, and SQL Server. Section Two, consisting of Chapters 6 through 10, discusses these applications at length, and also explores functionality specific to SBS including the Remote Web Workplace feature and the many faxing options available in SBS.

Section Three: SBS 2003 Security

Could you really have an advanced technology book without a security section? The answer of course is nada, nyet, NOT! Two of the great security gurus in the industry have teamed to deliver the two chapters in this section (Chapters 11 and 12) that provide two different viewpoints on security. This is the "payoff section" for many readers, the primary reason many of you purchased this book— and I can assure you that you won't be disappointed.

Section Four: SBS 2003 Advanced Topics

This section addresses an area related to advanced SBS 2003 that, during the early planning stages of this book, particularly represented a dearth for available information. Readers were screaming for more guidance about monitoring, migration, and disaster recovery. The writers assigned to the chapters in this section (Chapters 13–15) were eager to respond to this unmet need, and the result is what will prove to be another "payoff section" for many readers.

Who Should Read This Book

The readership of this book will fall into a few identifiable categories.

- Gurus. You're much of the reason we came together as a team of SBS experts to write this book. This book is for you!

- Consultants. Advanced SBSers who are consultants will want to use this book to get a leg up on your professional peers and to better serve your customers.

- Channel Partners. In addition to consultants (which includes Microsoft Partners), independent software vendors (ISVs) and distributors also constitute part of the channel. A surprisingly strong readership group, channel partners who read this book are those of you who are seeking to learn more about the SMB space in order to deliver much needed services and solutions to eager SBSers!

Who Shouldn't Read This Book

- Inexperienced SBSers. The SBS community is affirming, open, accepting and even downright warm and huggy, so all SBSers including newbies are welcomed with outstretched arms. However, you have to learn to walk before you can run, and this book is clearly a marathon manual. So if you are a newbie, you might consider picking up my introductory and intermediate SBS texts before you delve into this digest. You'll be happier for having done so, getting the SBS fundamentals firmly in place before then climbing higher, flying faster, and driving farther with this volume.

- End-user customers. Of course anyone in business blesses the very customers who contribute to their cash flow. I'm no exception. But customers potentially could be mis-served by this book, arming themselves with just enough information to be dangerous. If you're a customer or end user who has inadvertently purchased this book, please e-mail my office at sbs@smbnation.com so we can recommend an SBS consultant in your area to help you be more successful with SBS. We have a worldwide list of SBSers who would love to hear from you and lend a helping hand.

Forward!

Enough said. Time to dig deep into the good stuff. Let's move forward together to Chapter 1, after one final thought.

Unless you've lived in a cave, you know that all software ships with bugs and vulnerabilities. Microsoft, even with its billions in cash and buildings full of brilliant technologists, is accused in this respect more than most. Well, I've got news for you—just as millions of lines of software code might have one or two commas out of place, so too might books! All technology books ship with bugs (often reflecting the bugs in the underlying product), and unfortunately this book will be no exception.

Another fact of life with both software and books is this: the developers of the software and the authors of the book would both probably change about a hundred things if they were given a second go and enough time. The problem, of course, is that software would never ship and books would never publish, and in the end you would be deprived of great works in both camps.

If you spot a bug or have a suggestion about how to improve a future revision of this book, please drop a note to sbs@smbnation.com. We'll be sure to reply! Also—monitor our Web site at www.smbnation.com for frequent updates to the book!

Cheers, mates....harrybbbbb

Harry Brelsford
Publisher, SMB Nation Press
Bainbridge Island, Washington, USA
February 2005

Section ONE
SBS 2003 Deployment

CHAPTER 1

Introduction and Planning
BY Harry Brelsford

CHAPTER 2

Understanding Hardware in the SBS Environment
BY Chris Angelini

CHAPTER 3

SBS 2003 Licensing
BY Harry Brelsford WITH Steven Banks

CHAPTER 4

Advanced Setup and Deployment
BY Andy Goodman

CHAPTER 5

Using Third-Party Tools to Boost SBS 2003 Performance
BY Frank Ohlhorst

CHAPTER 1
Introduction and Planning
BY Harry Brelsford (Bainbridge Island, WA)

Welcome to the first chapter of the world's first *advanced* book about Microsoft Windows Small Business Server 2003 (hereafter referred to as SBS)! We begin by taking the current pulse of the world of SBS, and then go on to bring to light some critical planning issues for you to consider. We will be discussing many important topics across the pages of this book. This chapter provides the introductory and planning discussion components that precede the more technical discussion.

As of This Writing

As of this writing, following are some of the beats I've noted about the current pulse of SBS 2003, both for the product and its surrounding culture.

- SBS 2003 is both a bundle of joy as well as a bundle of Microsoft solutions that sit atop the Microsoft Windows Server 2003 (standard edition) operating system. For a closer look at the specific components that are included in SBS 2003, such as Microsoft Exchange Server 2003, see www.microsoft.com/sbs. Of course, as an experienced user you already know that SBS 2003 comes in two flavors, standard and premium.

- A three day Microsoft Official Curriculum (MOC) course for SBS 2003 is available that addresses the broader area of small and medium business (SMB) networking. Feedback from some folks who've attended this course indicates that it provides plenty of technical depth, balanced with practical business education. Personally, I support the course as a genuine attempt by Microsoft to balance the technical and business realities of working with SBS 2003. However, be aware that some course attendees who went hoping to be exposed to the "C" code underneath SBS 2003 commented that the course was "too light." You be the judge.

- Microsoft also offers a certification exam for SBS 2003 that, like the MOC course, balances the technical and business aspects of using this product. Some folks like the exam; some folks don't. For more information about the MOC course or the certification exam, visit www.microsoft.com/learning.

- The SBS marketing and development team apparently felt that the SBS 2003 setup process is relatively straightforward, so they did not make a setup video for partners, and only provided a thin manual and setup configuration checklist in the product box. If you would like step-by-step procedures for setup of SBS 2003, these are provided in my introductory text, *Windows Small Business Server 2003 Best Practices*.

- Microsoft has been enjoying much success with this release of SBS (earlier versions were less successful by comparison), and the company has created some interesting and enticing incentives related to the product. For example, there have been bundled promotions for SBS 2003 involving Microsoft Business Solutions Retail Management System, and also Customer Relationship Management (CRM) 1.2. (You'll find more information about this bundle in the next section.) Note that Microsoft expected to enjoy a 100 percent sales increase with SBS 2003 over the previous release. These sales goals have been exceeded, according to unnamed sources.

- Additions. There have been additions to the SBS 2003 product during its life to date. For example, if you own the premium edition, you are eligible to receive a copy of Microsoft's BizTalk Server software.

- Subtractions. Several components have been removed from the product and are not part of SBS 2003. The Shared Modem Service failed the 2002 internal Microsoft security review and consequently was removed from the SBS 2003 product. Also, the Microsoft Exchange product team removed the internal instant messaging capability from Exchange Server 2003 (this capability was present in Exchange 2000 Server).

BEST PRACTICE: I devote more than forty pages of my introductory text, *Windows Small Business Server 2003 Best Practices*, to introducing SBS 2003. As an advanced SBSer, you're already well familiar with the introductory stuff, so I won't repeat it here. However, if you do desire a refresher on introductory and intermediate topics, my earlier volume is just what you need. Otherwise, let's march on ahead and continue our review of the current SBS landscape.

What's Working

In surveying SBSland for this chapter, I looked at existing client sites, spoke to other SBS consultants, heard from readers of my previous SBS books, touched base with numerous stakeholders (such as SBS MVPs and members of the SBS product team at Microsoft), and talked at length with attendees at my SMB Nation Summit workshops. Following is the consensus regarding what's working with SBS 2003.

The Product

Everyone agrees that the SBS 2003 product is working very well, and there is widespread satisfaction with this, the fourth major release. Clients are confident both of the stability of the product and also of the smooth interaction between the application and the operating system. Absolutely no one is begging for more features, because they are satisfied with the features and functionality that are native to SBS 2003. The product has found its footing, and now SBSers can turn their attention to other matters. For example, the efficient setup cycle takes attention away from the deployment internals of SBS 2003 and allows you to focus on the future (such as "Now what do I do with this new network?").

The Price

Small businesses are frugal, tending toward great price sensitivity with every purchase, and buying SBS 2003 is no exception. Recognizing this (as well as other product design considerations), Microsoft has offered both a standard and a premium edition. The bottom line from consumers is that price still sells SBS more than anything else.

The Promotions

In my travels, what SBSers gush over most are the successful SBS 2003 promotions. This includes the Microsoft Customer Relationship Management (CRM) 1.2 and SBS 2003 bundle, which is described (as of this writing) at http://members.microsoft.com/partner/solutions/business/crm/sbspromo.aspx, and which you can see in Figure 1-1.

Figure 1-1:

Now you have something to "do" with your SBS 2003 network! Put a business application such as Microsoft CRM 1.2 on top of it, to get some real work done. Note that while this figure illustrates the U.S. promotion, the promotion is actually worldwide.

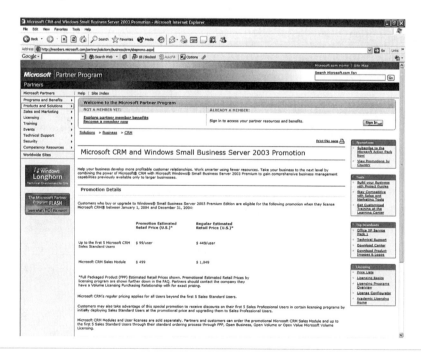

BEST PRACTICE: Go with the flow! While some SBSers are struggling to find their way as mere network installers, others are thriving with SBS 2003 because they have taken advantage of SBS as a powerful infrastructure and have added more "stuff" to it. For example, Scott Colson is an SBSer who has created a consulting niche with CRM 1.2. He told me he turned away two gigs because his staff was too busy with the CRM niche to have time to perform the other work. Sounds like the kind of SBSer you might want to shadow!

The Placement

The idea of product "placement" has several connotations. You can view product placement from a geographic perspective: for example, as of the time this book went to press, SBS 2003 is once again doing very well in Australia. There is also, of course, the product placement in which Microsoft has made SBS 2003 a channel play instead of a consumer play. From Microsoft's perspective, growing the width of the channel and enjoying double-digit product growth is something that is going very well right now. And there is the notion of retail placement. Microsoft is now selling SBS 2003 "on the shelf" in the USA at Best Buy and Sam's Club. This is a blessing and curse as the retail placement increases brand awareness but can penalize the SBS consultant when customers perform self-installs. Microsoft Germany will also pursue a retail strategy in 2005 with a large German retailer.

What's Not Working

Hindsight is always twenty-twenty, or so the saying goes. Given the chance to redo certain things, of course you and I and even the short-order cook at the local eatery would probably do so! I preface the following discussion with that dose of reality because, while SBS 2003 is doing very well in the marketplace, there have been and continue to be areas for possible improvement.

- **What Wasn't Working but Is Now**. You might recall that, upon product release, the client access licenses (CALs) for SBS 2003 were very difficult to obtain. There was apparently a distribution snafu that continued into early 2004, but this has since been resolved. Not only is it possible to purchase all the CALs you need—you can also read all about them in Chapter 3 of this book.

- **Extensive Usage of Microsoft Windows SharePoint Services (WSS).** No, I'm not talking turkey here (a passing reference to the WSS dynamic-link library malady of late November 2003, which is described and resolved in my introductory SBS 2003 book). Rather, I'm speaking about the lack of WSS excitement and acceptance as we approach the one year birthday of SBS 2003. WSS is a great component, so why aren't more SBSers truly using it? Hopefully Chapter 7 of this book will get you fired up and turned on about WSS!

- **BizTalk Bump in the Road.** Microsoft introduced BizTalk Server 2004, an electronic data interchange (EDI) product, into SBS 2003 premium edition (see the CRN article at www.crn.com/showArticle.jhtml ?articleID=18842296&flatPage=true for details), but it seems that someone forgot to tell the SBS community. Very few SBSers are using BizTalk.

- **Microsoft Office Small Business Edition (SBE) 2003 and SBS.** On paper, it looked simple: sell one SBS server machine, and that in turn will sell several workstations with Windows XP Professional and Office SBE 2003. Unfortunately, what works on the whiteboard doesn't always work in the real world. Office SBE 2003 has not experienced the SBS 2003 sales boost that was anticipated. Oh sure, attempts have been made to jump-start this relationship, and I was even retained by a Microsoft vendor to create the SBS 2003 and Office SBE 2003 hands-on lab that was delivered at the Microsoft Worldwide Partner Conference (WWPC) in Toronto in July 2004 (the hands-on lab was well-attended, by the way!). But much more work remains to get folks excited about Office SBE 2003. Stay tuned.

- **Customer Demand Generation.** While the accountants at Microsoft are reasonably satisfied due to the success of SBS 2003, some SBSers would, quite frankly, like more clients to serve. Microsoft's channel-focused strategy assumes that SBS consultants will serve as a virtual SBS sales force for Microsoft. Microsoft itself does little customer advertising that truly generates a demand for SBS consultants; many of you reading this book already know this. But let me point you to a fascinating study from Yankee Group, released in July 2004, which calls Microsoft to task for NOT DOING ENOUGH to generate demand for SBS 2003. A portion of the study is displayed in Figure 1-2.

Figure 1-2

While applauding SBS 2003 success, study author Laura DiDio from Yankee Group strongly asserts that Microsoft's SBS demand generation efforts could be improved. The white paper also does a great job of introducing SBS 2003 from a business viewpoint.

BEST PRACTICE: Download the Yankee Group study from www.smbnation.com using the SBS and SMB Consulting Working Papers link. Read it!

Right before the publication of this book, there is an important update to share regrading customer demand generation. Microsoft Ireland and Microsoft Germany are planning to engage in customer-facing demand generation in 2005. These subsidiaries will run radio ads and print ads. Here is to being hopeful this demand generation strategy will work!

Advanced Discussion: The Small Business Server Space

There are some real nuggets of gold in "them thar" SBS hills that I want to share with you.

United Kingdom SBS Breakfasts

Necessity is the mother of invention, and John Coulthard, Director of Small Business at Microsoft UK, is one heck of an inventor! He has directed an effort to equip Partners with a seminar-in-a-box that is essentially a turnkey SBS breakfast sales presentation. The formula is simple. Use John's kit to create a breakfast event for prospective SBS customers. These prospects will hopefully convert to paying customers for you. During the life of SBS 2003 so far, this is the most impressive Microsoft program I've personally witnessed. Figure 1-3 displays the Web page http://www.microsoft.com/uk/partner/box/default.aspx where you can download this sales kit for free.

Figure 1-3

A visit to this site is a must *to help you do more SBS business.*

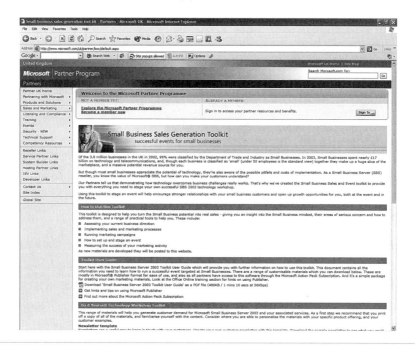

SBS User Groups

One thing that's bringing order to the fragmented and heterogeneous small business space where SBS 2003 plays is the formation of SBS user groups. In the U.S. alone as of this writing, there are over 25 SBS user groups, and you can find five such groups in Australia. The purpose of these groups is to provide a place for like-minded SBSers to gather in a regular and grassroots fashion. Within these groups, the members discuss not only the proverbial technical issues of the day, but also relevant business issues. In fact, one SBS user group, the Technology Wizards out of Portland, Oregon, focuses on the business side of the SBS 2003 experience and on generating more good business for its membership—which they accomplish by running print and radio advertisements. Figure 1-4 shows the home page for the Technology Wizards, including a sample advertisement in the lower left.

Figure 1-4

The Technology Wizards are filling the customer demand generation void by running customer-facing advertisements for SBS 2003. Good stuff!

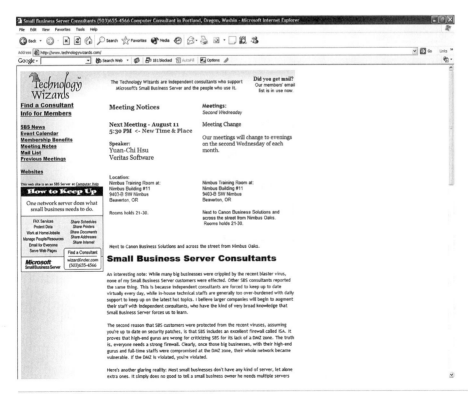

You can find an official "roll call" of SBS user groups at www.microsoft.com/windowsserver2003/sbs/community/usergroups.mspx. This roll call is also shown in Figure 1-5.

Figure 1-5

You are not alone as an SBSer! You can bond with other like-minded technologists by participating in a user group near you. (By the way, user group members have been known to receive free stuff and toys from Microsoft! Hint-hint.)

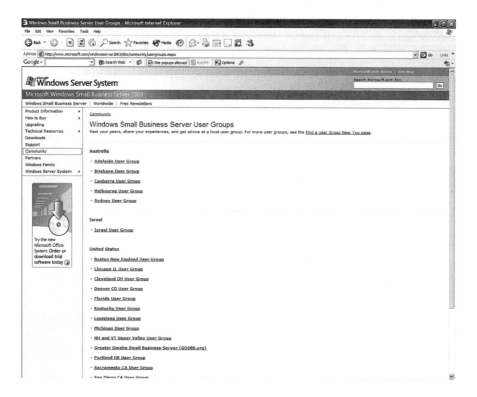

BEST PRACTICE: My book *SMB Consulting Best Practices* spends the better part of almost 700 pages defining the SMB and SBS consulting marketplace. So as not to diminish the value of the material offered in this earlier volume, I defer to it for discussion about the current SBS marketplace. You can purchase this business-related book from www.smbnation.com.

Planning

Planning is important in any technology implementation, and SBS 2003 is no exception. In my research for this section, I scoured the earth for updated planning topics so as to not simply repeat the material in my other SBS 2003 books.

Re-visiting the Basics

Every Olympic athlete or weekend warrior knows that proper planning prevents poor performance (these are "the five Ps"). Like so much of SBS 2003 discussion, you can evaluate planning for SBS 2003 in the context of two different dimensions, the business and the technical.

Business

From the business side, the ongoing challenge in the planning arena is to get customers either to plan out their own implementations or else to hire an SBS consultant to do so. This challenge continues even as I pen this advanced text a full year into the life of SBS 2003!

Marketplace

Microsoft has come a long way in a very short time in learning about the small business marketplace. The Yankee Group study I mentioned earlier provides an excellent summary of the small business marketplace and Microsoft's current awareness. Data released in mid-2004 from another research house, AMI, summarized succinctly that small businesses are thrifty (okay, cheap) and most fall into a minimalist or pragmatic category when it comes to adopting technology. Read into this what you may, but the AMI research had the average USA small business spending somewhere around $1,000 per year on technology. And while this might seem depressing to the SBS consultant who is seeking a leg up financially and is hoping to make heaps of money installing SBS, let me keep your hope alive by continuing this discussion!

Notes:

The beacon for SBS optimism is the TS2 event series put on by Microsoft in over 600 USA cities each year, for SBS consultants and other small business technology service providers and aficionados (details at www.msts2.com). The August 2004 TS2 content had a slide asserting a contra-cost argument that suggests a small business could suffer losses by not having an efficient and stable SBS 2003 network installed (Figure 1-6).

Figure 1-6
When small businesses balk at technology spending, introduce the "cost of doing nothing" argument as shown here.

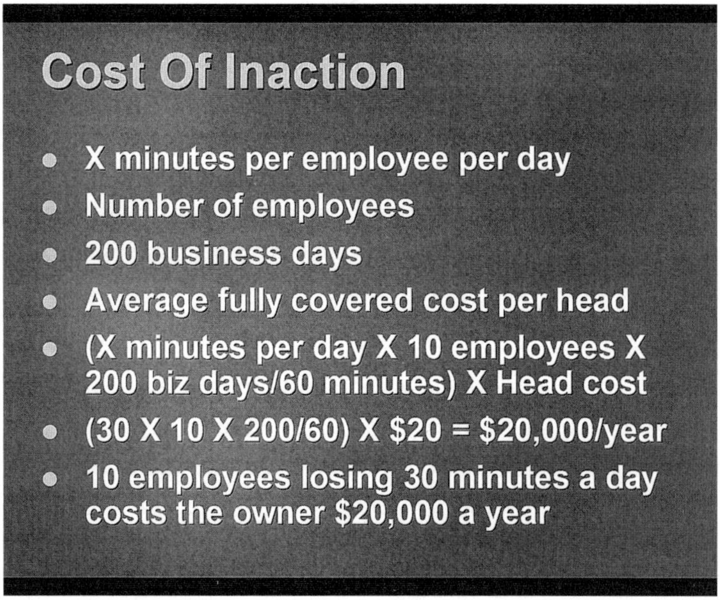

Let's Get Coffee!

Delving deeper into advanced SBS 2003 planning topics, I again had to look no further than the excellent Fall 2004 TS2 presentation (which you can download from the TS2 site link in the previous section). The context is refreshingly casual and really conveys the typical way that many SBSers initially plan an SBS network with a customer—over a cup of joe at the local espresso café!

A little background is in order before I present a couple of critical coffee house slides. The TS2 mission in the PowerPoint deck was to encourage SBS consultants to elevate themselves to become trusted technology advisors (a subject that is the crux of my *SMB Consulting Best Practices* book). That's followed by some introductory sales discussion about initial cold calls, first introductions, and so on. Then we get into the good stuff, as shown in Figure 1-7, that establishes early SBS-related consulting boundaries. If not set early with a customer, these boundaries will end up shifting, resulting in scope creep.

Figure 1-7

Of special note is the competency establishment point. Your technical expertise, such as that gained from this advanced SBS 2003 book, will equip you to better serve SBS customers.

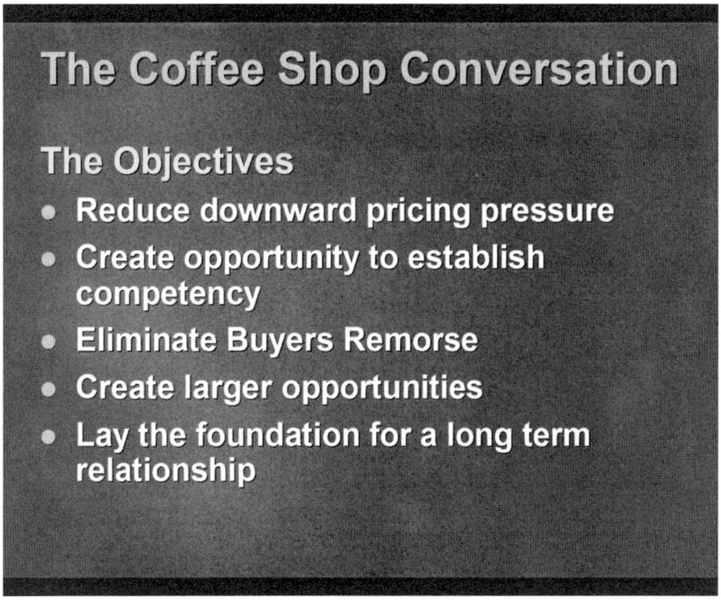

The Coffee Shop Conversation

The Objectives
- **Reduce downward pricing pressure**
- **Create opportunity to establish competency**
- **Eliminate Buyers Remorse**
- **Create larger opportunities**
- **Lay the foundation for a long term relationship**

Perhaps the most important planning slide in the whole coffee shop scenario is next, in Figure 1-8. This MBA-type flow diagram really cuts to the chase and highlights several planning points.

- Pain and Frustration. Like it or not, the basis for nearly all technology projects is to eliminate customer pain or frustration. The top of Figure 1-8 speaks to this with the "Listen for Frustration" box and the "Prioritize Hot Buttons" circle.

- Information Gathering. Notice that the middle of Figure 1-8 has you engaging in information gathering activities that are both business-related and technical in nature. All good consultants instinctively do this whether they are involved in technology or not. Even an in-house technologist would want to honor these formal planning steps, or suffer the consequences!

• Money. Money is an important driver in any technology discussion. Enough said. See the "Determine Financial Impact" button in Figure 1-8.

• Timing and Follow-up. Having gathered sufficient information from a customer, you can create your Statement of Work (SOW) and return at a future date to present it. This step is recommended even if you're an SBSer in the "do it yourself" category (not all SBSers are consultants, of course!).

Figure 1-8
Honor this time-tested technology sales and planning flow chart and you'll do well with SBS!

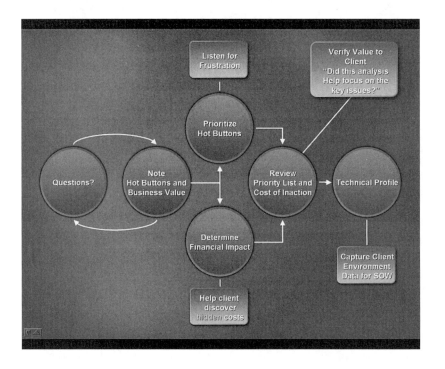

The money discussion continues in Figure 1-9 with a darn good break out of soft and hard costs for SBS sites. Even though it's unlikely all of these points would apply to the discussion at every SBS site in the planning phase, many points do, such as the "Cost of downtime" bullet.

Figure 1-9

Take a moment to revisit how SBS, properly implemented, will affect these business cost areas. Hopefully the impact will be favorable!

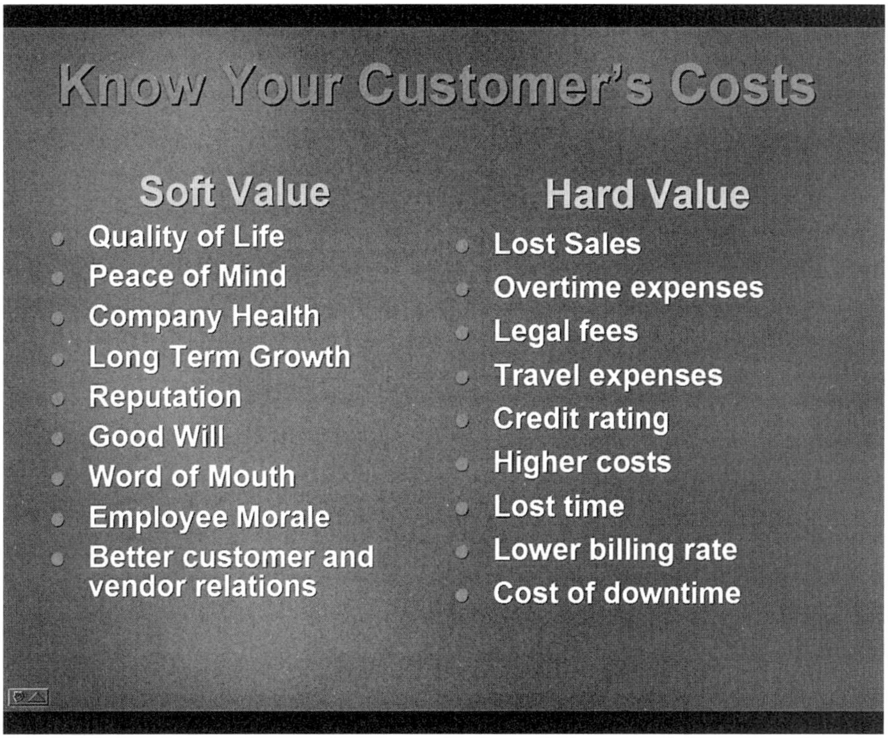

Notes:

Finally, Figure 1-10 summarizes the coffee shop planning approach and puts it in its proper perspective—that this is only the start of the planning process, the first meeting! From the coffee shop experience, an SBSer will have a better idea of what SBS can do for end users (the customers). More importantly, the emphasis is placed on next steps and not on making hasty commitments. Planning takes the form of several steps and much more time than we typically acknowledge.

Figure 1-10

You've only just begun the ongoing technology planning cycle at the coffee shop. Fortunately, planning for SBS isn't as difficult as complex enterprise roll outs!

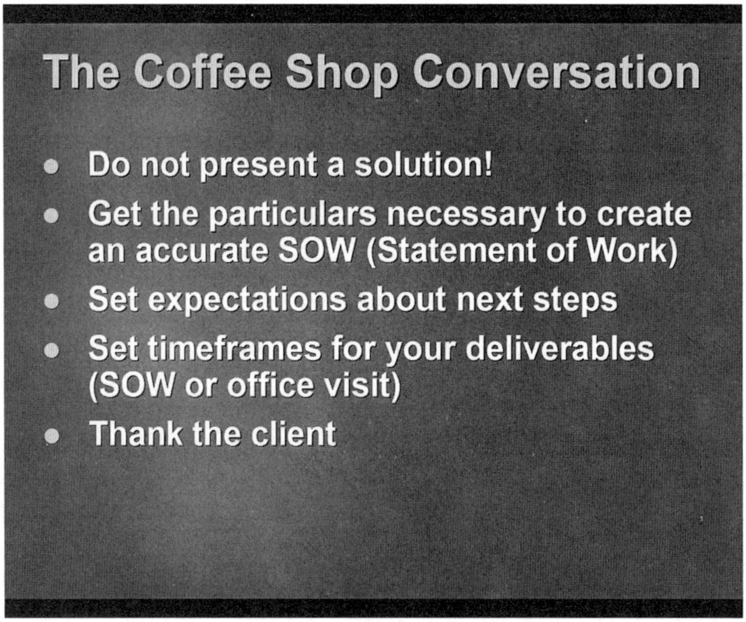

The Coffee Shop Conversation

- Do not present a solution!
- Get the particulars necessary to create an accurate SOW (Statement of Work)
- Set expectations about next steps
- Set timeframes for your deliverables (SOW or office visit)
- Thank the client

Licensing

No business planning is complete without casting an eye toward the current licensing model surrounding SBS 2003. I don't even pretend this book can keep up with the ever-changing world of Microsoft licensing, although we have attempted to do so in Chapter 3. Hilton Travis, a reader from Australia, was especially excited about the licensing discussion, in particular the client-side licensing mix. Hilton found that, with regard to providing SBS to customers, the licensing issues extend well beyond the server machine itself. The point that I want to make here is that licensing is an evergreen component in the SBS planning cycle: it's always an issue. And there is some true ROI here. By having your licensing all in order, you not only avoid jail time (as in under-subscribing your licenses) but you also avoid overpaying for licenses (an over-subscribed scenario).

Bill Leeman, long-time SBSer and reader, posted this practical planning advice on the SBS Yahoo! Newsgroup with respect to licensing. (See Appendix A for SBS Resources). Bill writes:

```
Just thought I'd pass this along as it's the first time
it's ever happened to me. Got a call from another
consultant friend of my bosses who needed help with an
SBS 2K3 install. Went onsite and proceeded to get ready
and opened the sealed envelope from MS licensing and
then broke the shrink-wrap on the SBS2K3 standard Open
Business kit. Lo and behold no Disc 1!!! Since SBS
doesn't make use of the eOpen site for the base product
(only the CAL's) I couldn't use a different Disc 1 with
this clients key. So make sure you check your kits early
just in case.

--Bill Leeman
```

Recasting Business Operations

My past writings on SBS and SMB consulting have emphasized how SBS can radically alter the landscape of a business after it has been properly introduced. Suddenly stick-in-the-mud reluctant owners are asking to implement network-based faxing (native to SBS 2003), the SBS 2003 mobility features, and so on. Heck, as I researched this chapter, the hot topic I bumped in to was implementing Voice over IP (VOIP) technology in small businesses running SBS!

Reader Terry Constable wanted expanded discussion on the business use of SBS 2003 mobility features and running line-of-business applications remotely. Terry writes:

> I have run into situations where I have a client that wants to deploy
> SBS, but also needs access to a parent corporation's resources as well.

One of these was a broker (transportation not investment) for a larger company and wanted SBS but also needed access to Exchange and LOB apps from parent. It ended up easy to solve with VPN, but Tony Su and others brought up security considerations, especially since the folks on the other end were an NT 4.0 environment with very lax security. Being a transportation/distribution-centric specialist, I see a lot of this kind of thing, smaller companies that act as local agents for big conglomerates; so it might be an issue that others see as well.

The other situation I'm pondering now is a small manufacturing company that is being spun off from it's parent corporation which currently hosts their e-mail and ERP software, as well as having a sales office in the parent company's HQ building. I am going to have to connect the sales folks at MotherCompany to SBS server at SpinoffCompany, retain the link to the MotherCompany ERP system until SpinoffCompany implements their own system (they are in no big hurry either), and work with an IT staff 800 miles away to migrate exchange data into SBS. I don't know how that sounds to you, but it's the most complicated job I've faced in my short career; especially since Spinoff Company has determined that they want a DSL line for their SBS e-mail and Internet, but are also going to retain a fraction T-1 point-to-point with MotherCompany for the ERP system. This brings up DNS and network design issues that are outside the usual design of an SBS network. I was planning to post a question about that on the Yahoo group, or e-mail Tony Su or Tom Shinder directly looking for some expert advice.

I don't know if either of these situations interests you, but I thought they are definitely advanced setups; which is good because it is forcing me to learn new and interesting things. Looking forward to seeing the new book, I'm in the midst of doing a re-read on SBS 2003 Best Practices for a couple of my weaknesses and anything I missed the first time around. I won't be able to make SMB Nation this year, but I hope to make the Miami workshop with a little luck.

Keep up the great work!

Terry Constable
Constable Consulting
Portsmouth, VA

Gotcha covered, Terry, and thanks for surfacing your real world SBS planning concern.

Going Canadian, Eh?

In late 2004, Microsoft Canada created a technical assessment form for use by its small business partners with a twist: financial incentive. If you, the budding Canadian SBSer, completed the technology assessment form as part of your SBS business planning process with a new customer, you were eligible to receive a rebate from Microsoft Canada. Nothing talks like money, eh?

Technical

As a reader with the qualifications to ply an advanced book, you already know many of the technical issues involved with SBS 2003 planning, such as product limitations like the lack of trust relationships between multiple domains. And you're likely well versed in the technical planning basics such as conducting a site survey (the number of wall jacks, desk placement, etc.), highlighted in my introductory SBS book. So what new technical planning issues may be on the SBS 2003 horizon? Read on.

Security

Top of the list is ongoing security planning—that is, before, during, and after an SBS 2003 deployment! That's what Susan Bradley, Beatrice Mulzer and Dr. Thomas Shinder have taken on in the security section later in this book. What I want to do right here and right now is show you the current TS2 slide that summarizes the TS2 lengthy and excellent security seminar (Figure 1-11).

Notes:

Figure 1-11

TS2's take on SBS-related security.

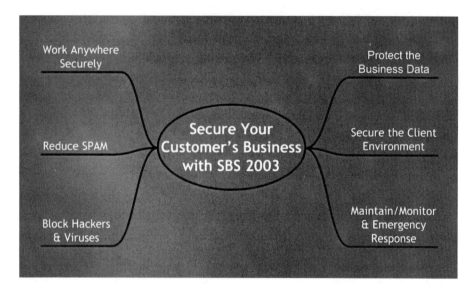

In Figure 1-11, six key security areas have been identified that apply to all small businesses running SBS 2003. While some are obvious areas of concern, you might have missed one or two of these points save for this illustration. In particular, note the point about data protection. A reader, Brian Kruse, specifically asked that this area be addressed in this book. I think Brian will be pleased with the treatment afforded to the subject of backups in Jeff Middleton's disaster recovery chapter, Chapter 15.

Windows XP Professional Service Pack 2

One issue coming quickly to the forefront as of this writing is how the Microsoft Windows XP Service Pack 2 (SP2) release will play in SBS 2003 environments. There is at least one known potential issue involved with this release, concerning the use of the Windows XP personal firewall behind the SBS 2003 server. This issue concerns the personal firewall contained in Windows XP SP2. There are two schools of thought on its proper role on a client computer joined to an SBS 2003 network. On the one hand, it would appear that you might not need the firewall on such a client computer that is networked and sits behind either the RRAS or ISA Server firewall that is native to SBS 2003. But on the other hand, the alternative is to use the personal firewall for even greater protection. Susan

Bradley, a proponent of this second method, revisits this discussion in Chapter 11, which she kindly wrote for this book.

I'll admit, when asked by Harpert Bramervaer, an enthusiastic SBSer from the Netherlands about this issue, I originally suggested the first alternative of not using the Windows XP SP2 personal firewall for a client computer on the SBS 2003 network. My gut reaction was that SBS 2003 provided sufficient protection from external threats. However, in discussing this with Brad Walton, a small business field representative in Microsoft's Dallas office, I was corrected! What if the threat originated internally on the SBS LAN and wasn't subject to the firewall protection offered by SBS 2003? What resulted was one humble Harry who needed to revise his answer for Harpert in Holland! So while there are two alternatives with respect to the personal firewall configuration, I'd like to side with Susan and suggest you indeed invoke the personal firewall. See her chapter for more good stuff on this topic!

To obtain the most current SBS 2003 technical news, such as the latest on the XP SP2 matter, visit the Microsoft TechNet site at www.microsoft.com/technet and search for common terms like "Small Business Server."

Small Business Server 2003 Service Pack 1

Imagine it's the Fall of 2004 and you are on the SBS development team in Building 43 at Microsoft's Redmond campus. You're working madly to bring together the components needed to get SP1 for SBS 2003 out the door. Your biggest challenge is to make sure you've incorporated all the separately released fixes for the underlying Windows Server 2003 operating system and the numerous applications included in SBS 2003. Then, after all that, you're making final decisions about what additional functionality, such as Microsoft ISA Server 2004, should be released as part of SP1. Congratulations. You're living in the "here and now" as SBS 2003 SP1 is being developed and this chapter is being written. Please visit www.smbnation.com for book errata and newsletter articles that will expand on SBS 2003 SP1 well after this book goes to print.

Microsoft CRM 1.2

As I alluded to earlier in the chapter, CRM 1.2 is hot! Show me a happy SBS user successfully running their business on SBS 2003, and I can likely show you a CRM 1.2 candidate. Scott Colson, who I mentioned earlier, says the fact of the matter is that the infrastructure deployment (SBS 2003) is the easy part in a combo SBS 2003\CRM 1.2 scenario. A CRM implementation, clearly more complex than an SBS 2003 deployment, requires the business owner to sit down and start to draw out meaningful relationships between customers and opportunities. For more information on SBS 2003 and CRM 1.2, visit the following link for back issues of my SBS 2003 newsletter: www.smbnation.com/newsletter/Issue3-6-march2004.htm.

BizTalk

Something mentioned briefly earlier in this chapter is that Microsoft's electronic data interchange (EDI) product is known as BizTalk Server. While traditionally sold to large enterprises to facilitate business transactions with vendors and partners, in 2004 there was a product announcement that tied BizTalk Server to SBS 2003. It essentially goes down like this. If you own SBS 2003 premium edition, you can complete a registration form on Microsoft's SBS site (www.microsoft.com/sbs) and receive a free copy of the low-level version of the BizTalk Server product (there are different versions). While writing this section, I spoke with Mark Fredrickson, an SBSer who is helping customers implement BizTalk Server (and who delivered a BizTalk speech at the SMB Nation 2004 conference), to get a current assessment about how much traction BizTalk Server has in the SBS community as of late Summer 2004. The answer was that it has very little traction. I and other SBSers always knew the deployment of BizTalk in the small business segment would be a small niche at best, and the marketplace has behaved accordingly. So I then followed up with Microsoft's BizTalk Server team to learn even more, and they admitted that new product strategies are being developed to get the SBS community more excited about BizTalk Server. So standby because this is an evolving story, but you can read a past article in my SBS newsletter at www.smbnation.com/newsletter/Issue3-7-april2004.htm.

SQL Server 2000

I think the case can be made for upfront planning and discussion surrounding the SBS 2003 premium edition database component, SQL Server 2000. While historically only ten percent of SBS customers even bothered to install SQL Server 2000 (in the SBS 2000 era), today that number is increasing. If you want SQL Server 2000, simply purchase the SBS 2003 premium version to get it and deploy it. Today there is better boundary definition between those who care about SQL Server 2000 and those who don't.

The reality is that once you realize what SQL Server 2000 is about, including its powers and capabilities, your eyes are truly opened to a world full of possibilities. This includes many of the topics a leading SBSer, Alan Shratter, has written about in the SQL Server 2000 chapter included in this book (Chapter 9). Personally, I see SQL Server 2000 as opening up a whole new world of possibilities when it comes to installing Line of Business (LOB) applications such as ERP systems, manufacturing systems, and the like. So I put the question back to you: wouldn't the deployment of LOBs on SBS 2003 require significant upfront planning? The answer is YES!

Upgrades

It's a fact of life that not all SBS 2003 installations are fresh. One key planning area for SBSers is upgrades and migrations. Tavis Patterson from Michigan contributed the following real world planning insights at my request.

Couple of things that I can come up with regarding advanced planning topics on a couple of installs.

1. A non profit that is only about 7 people in the HQ wanted to upgrade to SBS 2003. They had SBS 4.5 and were using Outlook Express with POP3 for email. On our proposal we submitted that we would transfer the domain to no-ip as they were using a dynamic IP DSL account. Also we would be using SMTP straight to the server for the benefits of email. All of this was approved by the on site technical contact and the executive director of the non profit. Little did we know that in the middle of the migration when we called to start the transfer of the DNS information we found out that they had about a 100 people using their domain name for paid email access on their public web site hosting agency along with about a dozen different servers and various mailing list programs as well. Needless to say the web site company was not wanting to change the DNS registration and we didn't want to accept the risk as well. This was all news to us as we didn't expect anything of this magnitude for a small office. Perhaps a little more due diligence would have found the problem or perhaps not.

So what was the resolution? We implemented the POP3 Connector and instead of using mail.xxx.org for the address for VPN and RWW we used xxx.redirectme.org (a no-ip.com domain). They can't have the benefits of SMTP mail now but this did get us to where we needed to be and the more important thing is that the nonprofit is very happy with the results.

2. In doing an SBS 4.5 migration lately the biggest factor that has to be understood in planning is where do I cut off the use of the whitepaper that Microsoft publishes for migrating from 4.5 to 2003. We have found that at about 10 users and below just throw the whitepaper away and start from scratch. It's much easier to recreate users and start fresh than follow every little detail of things such as ADMT when those smaller offices never have enforced group policies or group security and just want to access their "company data". As a solution provider those advanced topics come much after the install and well into a maintenance plan.

Just a couple of items that I've seen lately.

Thanks.

Tavis Patterson

TAZ Networks

517.579.0578

Jeff Middleton writes extensively about upgrades in the migration chapter of this book (Chapter 15).

Small Business Server 2005 (or Later?)

Lord only knows what the future holds with respect to SBS. As of the time this chapter is being written, there is to be an SBS 2005 release (or at least SBS 2003 R2). A few of us gamblers bet that'll slip to the year 2006 (I would guess early 2006). I'm not sure what SBS 2005 will contain, and I even question if anything else, save for a PBX telephony application, should be added to SBS. But in the context of planning, you must recognize that SBS will be upgraded in either the year 2005 or shortly thereafter. So you need to consider what that means to you, the SBSer. Should you wait for the next release for both yourself and your consulting clients? (A classic technology delay tactic in business, eh?) Or does the SBS 2003 release more than meet the needs marketplace and you'll charge full steam ahead and perhaps bypass the next upgrade? All of these (and more unspoken futuristic issues) are fair game in the planning cycle.

Extending Existing SBS 2003 Technologies

Advanced uses of SBS 2003 include extending native applications such as SharePoint. And while discussion of some of this area occurs in this book, the "extending SBS 2003" arena is so huge that I'm working on another book specifically on that topic. I and a team of SBSers are writing a book about extending SBS 2003 that will be out in early 2005 and that will allows SBSers and their respective stakeholders to go to the next level (extending SBS 2003). For that volume, Scott Colson is doing three chapters about CRM on SBS, and Amy Luby is writing two chapters about the Microsoft Retail Management System on SBS. We'll also have chapters on Office 2003, BizTalk Server, numerous line-of-business applications, and business analysis and business intelligence tools.

I thought the Fall 2004 TS2 presentation, which I've cited several times previously, had an especially forward looking view of building the small business technology infrastructure beyond SBS 2003, as shown in Figure 1-12. This figure also reiterates the "extending" points I was trying to make in the last paragraph.

Figure 1-12
The SBS 2003 growth pyramid.

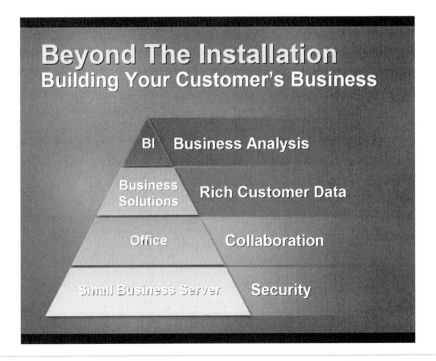

Here the idea is to take advantage of a secure SBS 2003 network by laying Office 2003 functionality, line-of-business functionality, and even hardcore business analysis and business intelligence functionally on top of SBS 2003. That's all harder than it looks, but you get the point.

The SBS 2003 Franchise Manual

As reported in my SBS 2003 monthly newsletter, Microsoft is offering its business partners a series of information technology (IT) solutions at absolutely no charge (that's the "F" word, otherwise known as FREE!). These solutions integrate Microsoft products with complementary partner technologies, to address real world business IT problems that customers face. Each solution covers planning, building, operating, and supporting an IT infrastructure, and includes messaging, collaboration, and file and print services. The solutions are designed to address four different levels of IT need, on scale as follows.

- Peer-to-Peer Networking with Windows XP. This solution is designed for businesses with up to ten users in a server-less environment, and is targeted primarily to do-it-yourself audiences.

- Small IT Solution. This solution is for five to fifty users in an environment with a server. It is targeted primarily to Microsoft Partners serving small businesses, and to generalist IT audiences.

- Medium IT Solution. This solution is also targeted primarily to Microsoft Partners and to generalist IT audiences, but it offers the flexibility that's needed for a setting with 50 to 250 users.

- Large IT Solution. This solution is designed for settings with 250 to 500 users, and it addresses enterprise-level requirements, such as scalability and round-the-clock operations. It is targeted primarily to professional IT audiences.

The Small IT Solution provides detailed, step-by-step guidance for implementing a small business infrastructure in entry-level server-based computing. It provides core technology for e-mail messaging, local and remote client networking, and file and print services. You can download this solution from http://

members.microsoft.com/partner/solutions/infotech/default.aspx, as shown in
Figure 1-13.

Figure 1-13

*This small business IT guidance, based on SBS 2003, is your franchise
operations manual for successfully deploying SBS 2003 the exact same way
every time you set up an SBS site—without any usurious franchise fees!*

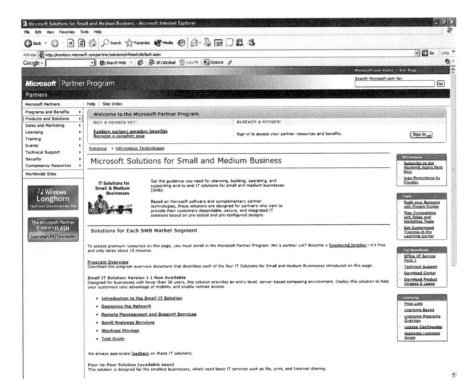

BEST PRACTICE: The new solutions that are coming available to
small and medium businesses will be the basis for my worldwide
SMB Nation Summit workshop tour in 2005.

Notes:

Summary

In this chapter I made a commitment, beloved reader, to provide you with SBS 2003 general and planning topics that go beyond the introductory information in my previous SBS 2003 books. I've done my best to honor that promise, and now its time to move on to discussing truly hard-core, gnarly SBS 2003 matters. Now you're armed with additional foundational knowledge from this chapter, some of which perhaps you already knew, but also some of which hopefully provided you with new insights about the world of SBS 2003. The next few chapters focus on fundamental SBS infrastructure issues.

CHAPTER 2
Understanding Hardware in the SBS Environment
BY Chris Angelini (Bakersfield, CA)

Generally when you talk to someone with a technical background, they quickly make it apparent whether their proficiency is in hardware or software; very rarely is it in both. Put two self-proclaimed software nuts in a room and they'll banter for hours. Likewise with the hardware aficionados. Mixing hardware and software, however, is like mixing oil and water. In the case of the hardware and software gurus, it's not that they don't like each other; they just speak two different languages.

Yet deploying SBS 2003 requires the happy marriage of both software smarts and enough familiarity with hardware to ensure a long life of smooth operation. It could certainly be a two-person job if it needed to be, but there's no reason to shy away from leveraging hardware as a means to generate revenue. It's all a matter of understanding the technology from a low-enough level to explain its benefits and to zero in on the best components to create value. Moreover, taking the figurative hardware bull by the horns will help during your SBS planning stage, especially when it comes time to order hardware and have it all installed.

Fortunately, advances in technology over the past few years have driven the performance and functionality of hardware through the roof, while prices have fallen dramatically. It's now entirely possible to build a mid-range server, complete with RAID, multi-threading, redundant power, and Gigabit Ethernet, for less than two thousand dollars. For business owners looking at technology that will persist over the next five years, today's hardware scene is all about choices and saving money.

Server versus Workstation

First things first, though. In order to make life a little easier when it comes time to make important design decisions, let's define the server and workstation environments. It's important to draw a distinction here because your server will be built with certain needs in mind, in turn necessitating particular hardware configurations. Meanwhile, workstations (commonly referred to as clients) are tasked with different responsibilities than the server and are built accordingly. It's safe to say that your server will be the most expensive piece of hardware you buy, and the workstations will cost substantially less.

Serving Up SBS

Your server will generally, in a small to medium business (SMB) environment, host SBS 2003 as a singular entity, unless you need an additional domain controller (DC) or application server. Your server needs sufficient horsepower to ensure that the operating system will run satisfactorily. This usually means investing in server-class hardware, although I've done work in smaller businesses where an Intel Pentium 4 client machine worked well enough as a dedicated server.

Regardless of the base platform you choose for building the server, consider a few imperatives. For example, the server is a mission-critical piece of your SBS puzzle. Every minute that it's down, someone, somewhere, is losing money and is bound to be upset. Thus it goes without saying that your server must be reliable, from its processor and motherboard to its I/O subsystem and software. But accidents do happen, mechanical parts break, and unfortunately software does crash from time to time, which is why it's also imperative to have a server backup strategy in place for keeping information current and for minimizing loss.

Fortunately you can take an active part in preventing unwanted server down time. Until the electric company can give you a written guarantee that the power will never go out, you will undoubtedly want to buy some sort of battery backup for the server. The extra 10 or 20 minutes afforded by battery power just might mean the difference between a graceful shutdown and a less favorable situation. You can take your power-delivery preparedness (or paranoia, depending how you want to look at it) a step further by banking on redundant power supplies.

In the unlikely but statistically inevitable event that one power supply fails, the second will ensure that operation persists without interruption.

Another topic that's hot now and that will only get hotter in the future is the issue of security. When your server is the system that's closest to the wild and wooly Internet, it's hard to feel safe, even with two NICs (network interface cards), the RRAS basic firewall, and an external hardware firewall. Even with these precautions in place, you should perhaps devote a little more energy to security by looking within the confines of your establishment. To begin, think about your valuable data. If it's backed up on tapes or discs that are on location, your backup data isn't truly redundant. At least once a week, make complete backups and take them elsewhere, somewhere safe from theft or fire. Then there's also the issue of employee access. Configuration of permissions is an important part of implementing SBS 2003 on the software side. However, it's prudent to also think about measures to keep your server and backups *physically* safe from tampering. Keep these issues in mind as you draw up your battle plan for SBS deployment, because you'll find that maximizing security is one of the best ways to gain your customer's trust.

Buying a Better Workstation

Relatively speaking, workstations have it easy. SBS accommodates up to 75 CALs, meaning that up to 75 workstations can be logged in to Microsoft Windows Server 2003 at any given time across a wide range of operating systems. Naturally, those clients aren't usually responsible for the same information load that a server handles, and they don't need the same beefy power redundancy, I/O subsystems, or manageability features of a server. However, this isn't an invitation to skimp on those features. Processing power is cheaper than ever and I can guarantee that recycling old Pentium or Pentium II machines will cost more in lost productivity than it will save in initial investment. If you're going to deploy SBS in an environment with mixed hardware—systems that span different generations of hardware and software—identify a cutoff point according to the recommended list that follows, and replace anything that falls below that benchmark.

SBS 2003 Minimum and Recommended Requirements

Microsoft's responsibility as a developer is to ensure that its software works on the widest selection possible of available hardware, allowing a broad audience to enjoy SBS 2003. Thus, the minimum system requirements for SBS 2003 leave the door open to almost any computer from the preceding several years that still works. In the pages to come I'll spend some time critically analyzing platform performance, to identify crucial sweet spots in balancing budget against an enjoyable user experience.

Table 2-1

Requirement	Minimum	Recommended
CPU speed	300 MHz	550 MHz or faster
RAM	256 MB	384 MB or higher (4 GB max)
Hard disk	4 GB of available hard disk space.	4 GB of available hard disk space.
Drive	CD-ROM	CD-ROM or DVD-ROM
Display	VGA or hardware that supports console redirection.	Super VGA (800 × 600) or higher resolution monitor.
Other devices	· Hardware that supports console redirection. · Ethernet network interface card from the Windows Server Catalog.	· Keyboard and Microsoft Mouse or compatible pointing device. · Two Ethernet network interface cards from the Windows Server Catalog.
Additional items and services required for Internet access	· Internet access and payment of a separate fee to a service provider, for some server functionality. Local and/or long-distance telephone toll charges may apply.	· Internet access and payment of a separate fee to a service provider, for some server functionality. Local and/or long-distance telephone toll charges may apply. · Broadband or high-speed modem Internet connection.

	· Broadband or high-speed modem Internet connection.	
Additional items required for networking	· Dedicated Class 1 fax modem to use fax service.	· Dedicated Class 1 fax modem to use fax service. · Pocket PC Phone Edition 2003 or Smartphone 2003 for Outlook Mobile Access. · Windows XP Professional or Windows 2000 Professional for client operating systems.

Microsoft's minimum system requirements for SBS 2003 actually are *very* minimal. A 300 MHz processor, falling in the Pentium II or AMD K6-II families, takes us all the way back to 1998. Needless to say, that's ancient technology that has no business being used in a modern server or workstation—especially when you consider that with the speed at which hardware falls in price, it's actually very easy to buy even newer, faster components on the cheap. Even the recommended 550 MHz processor represents Intel's very first Pentium III. While I've had clients abide by the more general Microsoft Windows XP recommended hardware guide, a week of the frustratingly slow performance that results is enough to sell them on the need for a more robust machine.

Similarly, systems with the minimum recommended 256 MB of RAM are also somewhat antiquated. Windows XP Professional Edition itself is slow enough on a client system with that much memory, so even if SBS 2003 will run with just 256 MB of RAM, it doesn't mean you should try it. Unfortunately, the recommended 384 MB isn't much better; but never fear, my personal suggestions are coming in the next section.

In both the minimum and recommended hard drive capacity categories, you'll need at least 4 GB. Let me tell you, though, that 4 GB of storage space costs less today than a super-sized value meal at your local fast food restaurant, when you consider the price per gigabyte of less than one dollar. Make sure that you have at *least* 4 GB—but trust me, you'll want more. Besides, there are plenty of high-capacity drives that offer great performance at an affordable price tag.

While we're discussing storage, note that the minimum CD-ROM requirement actually is reasonable for installing SBS 2003 and any supplemental applications. Microsoft suggests stepping up to a DVD-ROM drive, but really there's little reason to do so unless you anticipate buying the DVD version of SBS 2003 or watching movies on your server. Actually, there's an even better alternative to DVD-ROM, which we'll talk about in the next section.

Among the other SBS 2003 requirements, you'll need at least VGA graphics and an Ethernet NIC or two. We'll spend more time on both topics in the pages to come. These are simply the bare necessities.

The *Real* SBS 2003 Recommended Hardware Guide

In an ideal world, SBS would run well on a platform built strictly around Microsoft's recommended hardware list. But that's the sweet, sugar-coated version of the story. In reality, you'll want much more muscle. In this section I'll set you on the right track given today's hardware scene.

Building the Best Server on a Budget

Capable hardware is relatively inexpensive, as I mentioned earlier, so it doesn't pay to scrimp—especially when you can actually extend the useful life of your server and client machines by investing in more powerful components. For example, an entry-level HP ProLiant ML 110 server starts at under $500 and includes a 2.6 GHz Celeron. It's hard, though, to make valuations on clock speed alone these days, because Intel and AMD have both given up using actual frequencies in their product names. AMD instead uses a model rating for its desktop products and an arbitrary number scheme for its server chips, while Intel uses a similar number scheme for the Pentium 4; only its Xeon family is still sold on the basis of operating frequency. But I digress.

The point is that even a $500 server is significantly more sophisticated than anything on the SBS 2003 recommended hardware list, and I'd be reluctant even to use a 2.6 GHz Celeron (Intel's value desktop solution) when more capable hardware is readily available. There's an old saying, that nobody ever got fired for buying an IBM machine. The same holds true for Intel processors. But I'm going to go out on a limb here and tell you that the smart buy isn't necessarily the one from the biggest blue-chip manufacturer. Rather, when you buy, choose the components that offer the most value today. While large enterprises seek warmth under the blankets of big names, know that plenty of companies recognized AMD's innovation early on and adopted Opteron for their custom 64-bit environments.

So when it comes to choosing a server platform, I'd recommend looking either to **Intel's Xeon** at 2.8 GHz and higher, or to **AMD's Opteron 240** and higher. Both products, though not inexpensive, support up to dual-processor configurations for ample expansion and more than enough performance in SBS 2003. However, there *are* other servers available for under $1000 that still have the Xeon chip, such as HP's ProLiant ML330.

After sinking a fair dime into a modern processor, you might be tempted to leave an entry-level server with its preconfigured 256 MB of system memory. But keep in mind that SBS 2003 requires 256 MB and Microsoft actually recommends at least 384 MB. Memory isn't the high-end commodity that it once was, though, so try to make room in the budget for at least **1 GB of RAM**, or 512 MB at the bare minimum. Because most platforms utilize dual-channel configurations, a pair of 512 MB modules will put you at the ideal capacity and in most cases will leave at least two more slots for expansion, should you desire an extra gigabyte or two down the road. Using two modules will also guarantee peak performance. I've seen more than one name-brand server sporting a single memory module, which cuts theoretical bandwidth in half (from 5.3 gigabytes per second to 2.6 gigabytes per second on Intel's E7525 chipset with DDR333 memory).

The goal here is balance, so erring on the side of overabundance will keep your server's proverbial gears well oiled. And if you're looking for a point of reference, I've been running 1 GB of RAM for well over a year now in my workstation, and it's as responsive as ever.

When it comes to hard drives, there's no such thing as too big. There is such a thing as too expensive, though, so you'll want to weigh performance against capacity. Enterprise-level SCSI hard drives (10,000 to 15,000 RPM) are naturally the most popular, by virtue of their speed and phenomenal reliability ratings. But I don't consider them to be necessary implements, especially in smaller applications where a mail server might be doing double duty as a file server for five to ten client systems. In those cases, I'm a big proponent of Serial ATA hardware, which is significantly easier to install and configure than older SCSI technology, plus is much cheaper.

This doesn't mean that you should sacrifice redundancy. Most of Intel's server and workstation boards include at least some form of Serial ATA RAID support, and standalone RAID cards now offer up to Serial ATA RAID 5 for peak performance and data security. Maxtor's near-line MaXLine III, for example, is available in capacities up to 300 GB, with massive 16 MB buffers and a 1,000,000 hour mean time between failures (MTBF). Suddenly the recommended 4 GB of storage space doesn't seem like much, does it? A more mainstream recommendation for businesses with low I/O throughput would be a simple **pair of 160 GB drives in a RAID 1 mirroring configuration** for data redundancy. The result is reasonably fast and relatively secure, and is substantially less expensive than an exotic hot-plug SCSI array. More demanding applications could use the extra performance of a RAID 5 array.

> BEST PRACTICE: One of Microsoft's most basic requirements for SBS 2003 is a CD-ROM drive, or they optionally recommend the use of a higher-capacity DVD drive. Either option works just fine, but I've also had luck using a **DVD writer** as an alternative backup device. Some of the best 16x drives write at 22.8 megabytes per second and finish 4.7 GB discs in less than six minutes. While media is somewhat expensive and is only usable once, many backup applications are fully capable of recognizing and spanning entire hard drives over 4.7 GB optical discs. Consider optical backup if you anticipate the need to locate individual files, which is much easier with an optical disc than with the slower access time of a tape drive.

While we're on the subject of backup, Microsoft's list doesn't really emphasize the importance of saving your information on a regular and consistent basis. My personal business server has a 146 GB SCSI drive for primary storage, a

160 GB external USB 2.0 drive for primary backup, and a DVD±R/RW drive as a secondary backup. This might sound excessive, but I have lost all of my data on more than one occasion and on more than one system as a result of negligence, and I'm not going to let it happen again.

My own business operation doesn't call for tape backup, but that's something you'll surely want to consider for a larger business. **Tape backup** offers a few benefits over optical storage and even external hard drives. For starters, tape can cost mere cents per gigabyte—a fraction of the price you can expect to pay for other, perhaps more convenient solutions. Tape also enjoys a wide range of capacities, between 4 GB and 500 GB uncompressed, making it easy to run daily incremental backups or more thorough and complete backups, depending on your strategy. Then there's the fact that tapes are rewritable, shock-resistant, and durable, lasting up to 30 years. If you choose tape in favor of a disk drive, make the backup procedure easy by buying a drive with enough capacity to do the job in one cartridge.

The other option is an **external disk drive**, which is gaining popularity as the prices for hard drives fall. My favorite backup routine is to run Dantz Retrospect 6.5, tuned especially for SBS 2003, in full backup once a week, with incremental saves (that is, only data that has changed) scheduled every night while I'm asleep. The drive itself is harder to move offsite, but I appreciate the speed of USB 2.0 connectivity and the lower initial investment, since a tape drive can cost many times more than an external hard drive.

Another critical subsystem is communications. Now, the de facto standard for integration on server motherboards is one or two Gigabit Ethernet controllers. But while Gigabit Ethernet is fast and relatively inexpensive, it requires a lot of cabling work in offices that aren't already wired with CAT5e (remember that CAT5 was designed for Fast Ethernet at 100 Mbps, not for Gigabit). If you don't need the copious throughput of Gigabit (often it isn't necessary), you can still get reasonable performance over a 100 Mbps (megabits per second) connection.

Recently I've had a few customers inquire about **wireless networking**, referring to any one of the three broadcast standards for transmitting data over the air from a router or access point to receiving clients. The benefits of wireless are numerous, such as reduced installation costs, flexibility to reorganize the office without losing network connectivity, room for growth should you add workstations in the future, and competitive performance. After having weighed the perceived shortcomings of wireless, including security issues and reliability, I've implemented a handful of wireless small business networks, with great results. As such, wireless ranks right up with Gigabit-done-right on my recommended list.

If you're worried about a display adapter that can fulfill the SBS 2003 recommended 800x600 resolution, you don't need to be. Nearly all server motherboards include an **integrated graphics processor** with somewhere between 4 MB to 8 MB of RAM. However, you might need an inexpensive monitor (a sleek 15" LCD would work well). I'll briefly cover graphics a little later, for those of you who anticipate connecting a graphics or engineering workstation to your SBS servers.

Finally, pay some mind to power delivery on your server. While a traditional power supply might suffice, dedicated servers (such as HP's ProLiant ML 350) boast a pair of redundant units that are designed to maintain operation even if one should fail. The extra security of a redundant power supply goes one step beyond a UPS system and two steps past your everyday surge protector, to reduce the average down time of your network. That's not to say that those other power components aren't necessary. A UPS is imperative, not because it allows you to continue computing when the power goes out, but rather because it facilitates a smooth and graceful server shutdown. Client systems that are only plugged in to surge protectors might not be so lucky, but your server is key. Look for UPS hardware that includes management software, such as **APC's PowerChute Business Edition** which enables unattended shutdown of up to 25 protected servers and workstations.

Table 2-2

Select Hardware Reminder List	
Select a modern processor	Either Intel's Xeon DP or AMD's Opteron 240 and higher work well in medium-sized servers. A Pentium 4 or Athlon 64 would also work.
Choose memory capacity	Modern platforms employ dual-channel memory. Opt either for

	512 MB or 1 GB of RAM split across two modules.
Storage	Regardless of whether you choose SATA or SCSI, protect against hardware failure by using a striped array.
Backup	Spend time evaluating the benefits of tape drives, external hard drives, and optical storage. Choose the option that best fits your application.
Networking	Just because Gigabit Ethernet is the flavor of the day, don't rule out wireless networking in environments that seem particularly suited for it.
Graphics	Unless you're configuring a workstation, don't worry about discrete graphics. Most server motherboards include an older, stable graphics chip.
Other considerations	In order to maximize uptime, I recommend battery backup and redundant power supplies, on top of the standard data backup routines.

The Five-Minute Workstation Buyer's Guide

The subject of workstation configuration is outside the realm of SBS 2003 and as a result, client systems don't receive their due attention. However, it would be a shame to do a stellar job of deploying SBS only to realize poor overall performance due to bottlenecked workstation hardware.

In most instances, the systems connecting to your SBS server won't be nearly as powerful as the server itself. All the same, evaluate the requirements of each machine in a small business environment to determine where you can save money and where you should spend it. For example, if you have a CAD artist who could use a professional graphics adapter, plenty of RAM, and the best processor available, spend extra money there and cut back on other, less critical workstations.

A simple baseline for inexpensive hardware that will resist aging for a couple of years is an Intel Pentium 4 2.4 GHz processor, 256 MB of RAM (I'd be more likely to say 512 MB if you are concerned about running demanding software), an inexpensive discrete graphics card (which will generally deliver better image quality than an integrated processor), 80 GB Serial ATA hard drives, CD-RW drives (they're so inexpensive), USB 2.0 connectivity, a NIC capable of at least 100 Mbps (wireless is optional), a surge protector, and 17" CRT monitors.

The sky's the limit when it comes to a true graphics or an engineering workstation, but you'd probably be fine with at least a 3 GHz Pentium 4 or Athlon 64 3000+, 1 GB of RAM, an NVIDIA Quadro FX 1300 or so, an 80 GB system drive, and a 200 GB drive for storing projects. Complement the workstation hardware with an appropriate display, especially if the system will be running some sort of high-end application.

Understanding the Hardware Landscape

What makes an Opteron better than a Xeon, or vice versa? Truth be told, each processor architecture, memory technology, and platform design lends itself to particular environments. Understanding hardware's strengths and weaknesses is key to making the right infrastructure choices.

Today's Processor Technology

Don't feel bad if you aren't up to speed on the latest processor architectures. Both Intel and AMD are continually making adjustments to optimize for this or that, and it's a full-time job keeping up with their advancements. Fortunately, despite divergent names, AMD's Opteron and Athlon 64 families are built using very similar blueprints, as are Intel's Xeon and Pentium 4 processors.

AMD Opteron

For the sake of alphabetical convenience, let's start with AMD and its now-popular Opteron—centerpiece for many higher-end servers and workstations, such as HP's ProLiant DL145. The Opteron is available in several different models: the 100 series, for use in single-processor systems; the 200 family, capable of dual-processing; and the 800 series, with support for up to eight-way configurations.

There are actually quite a few reasons why the Opteron is attractive in a small business environment. To begin, it offers perhaps the most compelling performance at its price inflection point, due to a number of distinct architectural features.

- Before the Opteron emerged, processors communicated with RAM through another motherboard component called a north bridge, which housed the platform's memory controller. AMD sought to minimize the latency overhead associated with the north bridge by integrating a memory controller directly on the processor die. In cutting out the figurative middle-man, AMD maximized real-world memory bandwidth and increased the Opteron's responsiveness. The Opteron supports up to two channels of DDR400 memory for up to 6.4 gigabytes per second of bandwidth.

- The Opteron also boasts large caches (the small, temporary data repositories located on the processor). Whereas Intel's Xeon comes with 16 KB of L1 (level one) data cache and enough storage to hold 12,000 micro-ops, the Opteron features 64 KB each of L1 data and instruction cache. It also comes with 1 MB of L2 (level two) memory, similar to the latest models of Intel's Xeon.

- In single-processor computers, all of the front-side and memory bus bandwidth is focused to just the one processor. But when you start adding extra processors, there needs to be a coordinated effort to manage traffic between each CPU. Intel's Xeon employs a shared bus, where only one processor can control the bus at a time, reducing effective throughput to each processing core. In contrast, the Opteron resides on a point-to-point bus. Each processor has a dedicated path to system memory, resulting in greater overall bandwidth in multi-processor systems. As a result, the Opteron is considered to be highly-scalable—a great attribute for growing businesses.

- One of AMD's principal selling points is 64-bit computing, supported by both its Opteron and Athlon 64 processors. Now, the most notable benefit of a 64-bit chip is the ability to address, or recognize, more than 4 GB of RAM, which today's 32-bit processors cannot do. However, in order for a system to run in 64-bit mode, it requires a compatible processor, BIOS, operating system, and set of device drivers. Because Windows Server 2003 is a 32-bit operating system, the Opteron won't employ the benefits of 64-bit processing. In all honesty, few small businesses need more than 4 GB of RAM anyway, but it's nice to know that the Opteron leaves the door open for a future migration to 64-bit technology. Note that Microsoft's plans for 64-bit SBSing (a future release of SBS that would natively support 64-bit processing) are not known as of this writing. This type of information is reported, as it becomes available, in the free SBS newsletter that you can sign up for at www.smbnation.com.

• In a small business environment with limited on-site IT support, a low-maintenance infrastructure is invaluable, and that includes a secure back-end that won't succumb to malicious viruses propagated through security vulnerabilities. AMD's Opteron includes a special hardware bit that prevents the execution of code in what's called a "buffer overrun." AMD claims that its Enhanced Virus Protection technology, used in conjunction with Windows XP Service Pack 2 (or Windows Server 2003 SP1), would have protected systems against the MSBlaster and Slammer bugs.

• Beyond its most attractive features, the Opteron also supports the MMX, SSE, and SSE2 instruction sets pioneered by Intel. Figure 2-1 illustrates the basic layout of Opteron's core, and how the chip is able to work so efficiently.

Figure 2-1

With its on-die memory controller and HyperTransport connection, Opteron enjoys low latency and high performance. Image courtesy of AMD.

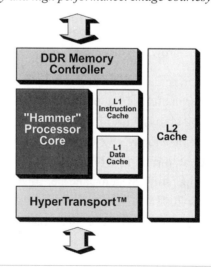

For all of its advanced features, the underlying platform infrastructure for the Opteron is maturing more slowly than Intel's competing Xeon. AMD doesn't devote a lot of its time to chipset development, so most workstations rely on core logic from either NVIDIA or VIA, AMD's most prominent chipset partners. Emerging technologies, such as PCI Express, aren't yet prevalent in either chipset manufacturers' products. Fortunately, PCI Express graphics cards and high-speed networking products aren't yet necessities in small business servers or clients. A stable, integrated graphics processor works wonders, and any number of Gigabit Ethernet products should suffice in the networking department.

AMD Athlon 64

As I mentioned previously, the Opteron shares a number of common features with the Athlon 64, its desktop counterpart. It has the same integrated memory controller, similar caches (with a couple of exceptions), 64-bit computing extensions, the Enhanced Virus Protection feature, and built-in support for the most popular extended instruction sets, such as SSE and SSE2. Because the chip only runs in single-processor configurations, the whole debate about shared versus point-to-point buses doesn't apply here.

The Opteron's nomenclature is admittedly obscure (Opteron Model 250 doesn't say a whole lot about what the chip can do or how it compares to Intel's wares). Anticipating a more mainstream audience for its Athlon 64, AMD employed a different naming scheme. Each model is differentiated by a relative performance rating, such as 3800+ or 3500+, which roughly corresponds to Intel's own Pentium 4 frequencies. An Athlon 64 3400+, for example, actually operates at 2.2 GHz and competes with Intel's 3.4 GHz Pentium 4.

Along with its somewhat simpler rating system, the Athlon 64 differs from the Opteron in a couple of regards.

- When AMD first introduced the Athlon 64, it fit into a 754-pin socket. Those processors featured 1 MB of L2 cache, like the Opteron, but only supported one channel of DDR memory, effectively cutting the available bandwidth in half. Over time, AMD improved the platform and eventually released a 939-pin version of the processor, simulta-neously adding a second channel of DDR memory and cutting the L2 cache down to 512 KB. Today's Athlon 64 comes in both 939-pin and 754-pin varieties, with a number of clock speed and cache memory variations. Just remember that platforms centering on the new 939-pin interface will generally yield higher performance, despite the smaller L2 cache.

- As processors evolve, they naturally get more complex. Shrinking lithography processes and ambitious manufacturers, eager to cram more features onto tiny processor dies, invariably lead to components that consume lots of power and dissipate plenty of heat. The Athlon 64 includes a feature called Cool'n'Quiet, which dynamically throttles the processor clock frequency according to computing demands. When an Athlon 64 system is under heavy load, the processor runs at full speed, and when it idles, Cool'n'Quiet reduces its speed, cutting back on both power consumption and heat. This is an especially useful feature, particularly in small spaces that are intolerant to heat buildup.

- There's one aberration in the Athlon 64 family—AMD's Athlon 64 FX. Functionally similar to the Opteron, the FX is a high-end enthusiast component destined for the very fastest desktop machines. It features an unlocked clock multiplier, a boon to enthusiasts dedicated to tweaking their hardware. Overall, it isn't of interest to SMBs; simply be aware of this top-dollar flagship and its intended audience.

The Athlon 64 suffers from the same slow platform development as the Opteron, though the most modern chipsets really don't lack any features other than PCI Express connectivity. Even still, don't expect to see many Athlon 64-based servers. AMD's desktop processor is most at home in a high-end workstation or client machine, such as a content creation or graphics rendering system.

Intel Xeon

The Xeon family has a distinguished heritage, beginning in 1998 with the 400 MHz Pentium II Xeon. Today's Xeon is much more diverse, available in several different configurations, operating at a wide range of speeds, and supporting varying features. The uppermost models are very similar to their desktop Pentium 4 counterparts, manufactured on a 90 nanometer (nm) lithography process and armed with 1 MB of L2 cache memory. Of the few differences between the Xeon and Pentium 4 processor families, dual-processing support is perhaps the Xeon's most notable attribute. Incidentally, Intel's Xeon family is one of the last of the modern processors to rely on its clock frequency for naming purposes.

The NetBurst micro-architecture on which the Xeon is centered has been a topic for debate since it emerged in 2000. Right from the start it was designed to be highly scalable by virtue of its incredibly long execution pipeline. And while that vision has only partially materialized, there's little doubt that Intel is a bona fide veteran in the server and workstation space, with the experience to build solid server hardware. Though the previous incarnation of Intel's Xeon was ill-prepared to compete with the Opteron, recent changes have infused the Xeon with much-needed horsepower.

- Because Intel employs a shared bus architecture, dual-processor systems are sensitive to front-side bus performance. The latest Xeon chips support an 800 MHz front-side bus, enabling throughput of up to 6.4 GB per second. Of course, the shared bus isn't an issue in single processor configurations.

- AMD might be planning to manufacture processors with two cores midway through 2005, but Intel already has technology for augmenting performance in particularly taxing situations. Hyper-Threading Technology enables the Xeon to execute threads in parallel, encouraging more efficient utilization of the processor's execution resources. It isn't quite the same as using two physical processors; however, Windows Server 2003 will recognize a Xeon with Hyper-Threading as two logical chips. A dual-processor setup will accordingly identify four logical processors. Bottom line—regardless of how it works, Hyper-Threading effectively improves overall responsiveness in a multi-tasked environment.

- Marketing folks get knocked around for unnecessarily complicating simple concepts with silly names. DBS (Demand Based Switching) is a prime example of why. Essentially SpeedStep technology in different colored wrapping paper, DBS allows the Xeon to run at lower clock speeds with a reduced operating voltage during periods of light load. The result is diminished power consumption, resulting in less thermal output, and quieter operation. The cumulative power savings is quantifiable in a larger business environment, but most SMBs won't notice a significant reduction in their electricity bills.

- Under extreme pressure from the AMD64 initiative, Intel reluctantly added 64-bit extensions to the Xeon family in the form of EMT64 (Extended Memory 64 Technology). The raw mechanics of Intel's implementation must be fairly similar, because 64-bit applications designed to run on the Opteron should also be compatible with Intel's EMT64. But of course, since Windows Server 2003 is a 32-bit operating system, 64-bit computing isn't yet an issue for SBS 2003. As I mentioned though, it's good to have that sort of hardware flexibility should the need for 64-bit arise in the future.

There's also a new chipset, the E7525, to complement Intel's reworked Xeon processor. In addition to supporting Xeon's architectural revisions, it introduces new memory and serial I/O technologies, though there's still support for older PCI and 64-bit PCI-X technologies through the 6700PXH PCI hub. Figure 2-2 shows the four components that are required for the Xeon architecture to function properly, including the processor itself, the E7525 workstation MCH, the ICH5-R (named 82801ER), and the 6700PXH PCI hub.

Figure 2-2

The E7525 platform is designed for high-end workstations that require Xeon's power. Image courtesy of Intel.

The serial I/O bus used on the E7525 is called PCI Express and is designed to work around some of the bottlenecks imposed by the parallel PCI bus to which we've grown accustomed. For example, PCI uses a shared bus topology for communication amongst devices populating the bus. Though initially relatively simple and inexpensive, PCI gets much more complicated as you tweak it for extra performance, as many powerful server-class components tend to do. High-end 133 MHz 64-bit PCI devices (such as SCSI RAID cards) are significantly more expensive due to strict manufacturing requirements and complex board designs. Bottom line—while it delivered ample performance back in 1993, the parallel nature of today's PCI bus limits its scalability.

In contrast, PCI Express employs a point-to-point topology, where each device is directly connected to a shared switch that routes bus traffic, and uses a serialzed approach to establish communication between connected devices. That is, rather than move data in multiple streams, PCI Express utilizes a single stream that moves much faster and is more scalable than a parallel connection. Each stream is capable of transmitting up to 2.5 gigabits per second of data in each direction at the same time. Even more impressive, up to 32 streams (referred to as lanes) can be aggregated into a single, 128 gigabit link. That's 16 gigabytes per second of bandwidth compared to one gigabyte per second for a 64-bit, 133 MHz PCI-X device.

Those figures only illustrate the scalability of PCI Express. Intel's E7525 chipset offers one x16 PCI Express connection, accommodating the latest generation of graphics cards (ideal in high-end workstations) and one configurable x8 interface that is divisible into two x4 slots. What might all of that PCI Express connectivity be used for, you ask? Well, the x16 slot is exclusively for use with a graphics card, and the x8 interface could, for instance, support a pair of Intel's 82571EB Gigabit Ethernet controllers plus its 6700PXH PCI-X bridge for a SCSI RAID card. The permutations will undoubtedly multiply as more PCI Express devices emerge.

Intel Pentium 4

The Pentium 4 dates back to 2000, when Intel gave its micro-architecture an overhaul in order to procure more operating frequency from its processors. The Pentium 4 began its life at 1.5 GHz, a figure that has more than doubled since then, thanks to lots of work under the chip's proverbial hood.

That doesn't necessarily mean that the chip's performance has multiplied. The latest incarnation of the Pentium 4, centering on a 90 nm manufacturing process, employs a longer execution pipeline, which makes it a little less efficient. But there's also a laundry list of new features that overshadow that minor drawback.

- The previous Pentium 4 processor came with 512 KB of L2 cache and 8 KB of the faster, more expensive L1 data cache. The latest implementation actually boasts a full 1 MB of L2 and 16 KB of L1 memory. The larger repositories are just about enough to make up for Pentium 4's elongated pipeline.

- One of Intel's unquestionable strengths is the way it rallies software developers to its causes. Perhaps you've heard of the SSE2 instruction set, supported by the original Pentium 4 and designed to enhance a number of operations that center on multimedia. On its own, SSE2 is worthless. However, applications that are properly optimized to recognize SSE2 are able to benefit from the performance increases that are inherent to the instruction set. But that's old news; even AMD's Athlon 64 supports SSE2. The latest Pentium 4 features SSE3, a small upgrade consisting of 13 new instructions that improve the efficiency of processing complex arithmetic, video encoding, graphics, and thread synchronization.

- The Xeon is a server-class processor, and as such it emphasizes performance over stability. Intel's E7525 chipset, Xeon's core logic backbone, consequently supports up to DDR2 memory at 400 MHz. The performance-oriented Pentium 4 goes a bit further, with sanctioned support for DDR2 memory at 533 MHz, with some motherboard manufacturers advertising 600 MHz memory and above.

Most of the Pentium 4 features are shared in common with the Xeon. Both processors boast very similar core architectures for processing information, related value-added features such as Hyper-Threading and support for the SSE3 instruction set, and platforms with like-minded capabilities like the 800 MHz front side bus and the prominence of PCI Express.

Then there's Intel's reputation for reliability. While AMD has made fantastic strides in improving its image as a corporate contender, there's little doubt that Intel still rules the roost. It then goes without saying that Pentium 4 client systems generally go over well, especially given the integration options of Intel's latest chipsets.

Figure 2-3

The 925X chipset is intended for desktop workstations, enabling all of Intel's best technology. Image courtesy of Intel.

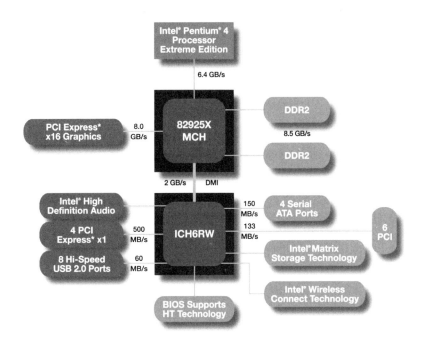

The top-end platform is Intel's 925X, a performance juggernaut that features a 775-pin socket to accommodate the latest Pentium 4 processors. DDR2 memory support is of course included, as is a PCI Express x16 slot for the latest graphics cards. According to Intel representatives, Accelerated Graphics Port (AGP) is on the outs, making PCI Express the latest in a series of new selling points.

There's also expanded Serial ATA support through Intel's new ICH6 controller hub that features an important second-generation feature called Native Command Queuing (NCQ). Especially in servers and workstations, NCQ improves performance by intelligently managing data requests, though it requires compatible core logic on both the controller and the hard drive. One variant of the ICH6, bearing a –R suffix, adds RAID 0 and RAID 1 support for either enhanced performance or extra I/O security. Finally, the ICH6-W features wireless networking, though it requires an add-on PCI card to expose wireless functionality.

Processor Summary

At the end of the day, there are two principal products for servers—AMD Opteron and Intel Xeon—and two processors that are more oriented for client machines— AMD Athlon 64 and Intel Pentium 4. Now, a Pentium 4 works just fine in server environments, and an Opteron would perform superbly in a graphics workstation, so don't feel constrained by each manufacturer's target applications. Just keep in mind that a Pentium 4 server and its complementary platform won't sport the same manageability and reliability features as a higher-end Xeon machine. At the same time though, smaller businesses won't always tax the Pentium 4 anyway.

When you choose the processor for your SBS 2003 server, keep three things in mind: budget, expected load, and headroom. Of course, you should only buy what you can afford, so don't go over the top if it isn't necessary. Further, businesses with only 20 client systems won't need the raw horsepower that shops three times that size would require. But if you project significant growth in the next five years, it's easier to buy the better hardware today rather than have to replace your server a few years down the road.

Notes:

Table 2-3

Processor Feature Summary List				
	AMD Opteron	Intel Xeon	AMD Athlon 64	Intel Pentium 4
Memory Controller	On-die, up to DDR400, ECC memory required.	Off-die, up to DDR2-400, ECC memory required.	On-die, up to DDR400, unbuffered.	Off-die, up to DDR2-533, unbuffered.
Cache	128 KB L1, 1 MB L2.	16 KB L1 data, 12,000µop L1 instruction, 1 MB L2.	128 KB L1, 1 MB L2.	16 KB L1 data, 12,000µop L1 instruction, 1 MB L2.
Bus Type	Point-to-point	Shared	Point-to-point	Shared
64-bit extensions	Yes, AMD64.	Yes, EMT64 (only Xeons supporting 800 MHz FSB).	Yes, AMD64.	Some, EMT64.
Other features	Highly scalable architecture, Enhanced Virus Protection, SSE, SSE2.	DBS, Hyper-Threading, advanced platform support, SSE2, SSE3.	Cool'n'Quiet, Enhanced Virus Protection, SSE, SSE2.	Hyper-Threading, advanced platform support, SSE2, SSE3.

Making the Most of Memory Technology

Configuring a server or workstation is almost an art form. It requires a delicate balance between each component in order to optimize performance across the entire platform. In other words, why waste several thousand dollars on multiple gigabytes of memory if you're using an 800 MHz Pentium III? In such a scenario, the processor invariably is going to bottleneck performance and no amount of RAM will change that, especially in an SBS 2003 environment where one machine performs numerous duties.

Along the same lines, it's important that a Xeon or Opteron server have enough memory to avoid idle time. But it can be just as much of a challenge to buy for either platform as it is to buy for your cousin on the East coast who you see once a year at Christmas. To begin, both platforms require a special type of module called "registered memory," which sacrifices some speed in the name of augmented reliability. Moreover, both processors interface with 128-bit memory buses for optimal performance. Because modern modules are 64-bits wide, it takes two identical pieces to populate the bus, in what is called a "dual-channel" configuration.

Because Opteron's memory controller is located on the processor die itself, the chip enjoys very low latencies when accessing system memory. Unfortunately, that also means that adding support for cutting-edge memory technologies is more difficult. It's of little consequence, though, as the Opteron performs very well with up to DDR400 RAM. Verify that whatever server you choose, it comes with registered modules installed in pairs.

Intel's Xeon differs in that it supports the latest memory technology, DDR2, but doesn't enjoy the same degree of throughput as Opteron. Xeon is also optimized for dual-channel operation with either DDR2 400 memory (400 referring to the frequency in megahertz) or DDR333. By virtue of its off-die controller, Xeon is more readily upgraded to forward-looking memory technologies.

The Pentium 4 is subject to many of the same constraints as Xeon, its pricier sibling, minus the registered memory requirement. It employs a 128-bit memory bus that interfaces with two modules rated at up to DDR2 533 speeds, yielding a maximum of 8.5 GB per second of bandwidth. Real-world numbers won't ever get that high due to latencies in accessing the memory and the fact that the Pentium 4's bus only moves at 800 MHz, transferring 6.4 GB per second. But it's still highly flexible, with backward compatibility for DDR2 400, DDR400, and DDR333 modules.

AMD's Athlon 64, on the other hand, has the same integrated memory controller as the Opteron, and as such is limited to DDR400, DDR333, or DDR266 modules. It apparently doesn't matter though, as AMD's own representatives claim that the processor is very sensitive to memory latency and its current support yields better performance than even the latest DDR2 memory technologies.

BEST PRACTICE: Be especially diligent when it comes to outfitting your server and workstations with memory. Most vendors aren't specific in their use of single-channel and dual-channel implementations, and while the price difference isn't significant (a single 1 GB module will cost roughly the same as two 512 MB modules), performance is impacted significantly. Whenever possible, be sure you're utilizing your hardware to its fullest potential with dual-channel memory.

Making Sense of the Storage Scene

If you look at a hierarchy of storage performance, at the top you'll see the ultra-fast temporary registers that are within all processors, several levels of temporary cache, then system memory, and then persistent storage—hard drives—at the very bottom. While hard drives are the slowest data repositories in the storage chain of command, they also offer the most value per megabyte (or more commonly, gigabyte) of capacity, and several new and upcoming technologies promise to alleviate some of bottlenecks that hard drives traditionally impose.

One reason that hard drives are so slow is that, unlike cache or system RAM which are strictly electrical components, magnetic drives are mechanical in nature, using moving parts that need to operate with utmost precision. Moreover, the basic drive operation has gone more or less unchanged for years: the drive receives read and write requests from the chipset, the requests are sent to the drive's onboard buffer, and they are then executed by the drive's controller. But changes are now being made, both inside and outside of hard drives themselves, to improve both performance and flexibility alike.

Serial ATA

Serial ATA is a connecting technology that facilitates communication between chipsets and storage devices such as hard drives and optical drives. It's characterized by a four-wire interface cable—miniscule by comparison with the unwieldy 80-conductor IDE cables of yesteryear. Consequently, it's much easier to route cables and maximize airflow in systems with multiple Serial ATA hard drives.

Beyond the appeal of its physical implementation, Serial ATA facilitates faster data transfer (up to 150 MB per second), even if today's hard drives aren't able to keep pace with the interface itself. More important, Serial ATA maintains backward compatibility with parallel ATA drives, so you can make the transition on your workstations and low-end server without worrying about interoperability.

The second generation of Serial ATA promises more features for the server market. The interface will begin by offering 3 Gbps of throughput, or a maximum of 300 MB per second. Performance is further improved with the implementation of Native Command Queuing (NCQ), a technology that facilitates the reordering of commands for organization in the most efficient manner, most effective in non-sequential transfers. Hot-plug support is planned as well.

With so many new enterprise-level features trickling down to mainstream drives, it's immediately tempting to tap Serial ATA for use in servers. Just keep in mind that Serial ATA is still intended for desktop use, where duty cycles hover around eight hours a day, five days a week. Serial ATA drives don't tolerate rotational vibration well, they transmit in half-duplex mode (meaning that data can only move in one direction at a time), and they don't include the same internal data integrity checks as those built into the SCSI and SAS devices I discuss next.

Serial ATA in an SBS environment carries with it the benefit of reduced cost, high performance in ideal conditions, and excellent reliability in the context of a RAID 5 disk array. However, it does bear a few caveats, mainly that Serial ATA drives aren't as reliable as SCSI, error-recovery occurs at the controller level rather than the drive level, and the addition of hot-spares adds to cost. Bottom line, though— if you're looking to save some money on storage, Serial ATA is a phenomenal alternative to costlier SCSI arrays, for a smaller SBS server.

SCSI and Serial Attached SCSI (SAS)

SCSI dates back to 1986, when it materialized as an 8-bit bus running at 5 MHz. Since then it has slowly matured up to 320 MHz, amplifying issues with its parallel bus that transfers multiple streams of data concurrently. However, attenuation, signal reflections, and cross-talk now prevent further evolution of parallel SCSI technology. So naturally the door is open for Serial Attached SCSI (SAS), another serial technology that is more attuned to the needs of enterprise customers than is Serial ATA. Figure 2-4 illustrates the improved connecting mechanisms of Serial ATA and SAS.

Notes:

Figure 2-4

Keying between the power and data ports differentiates Serial ATA and Serial Attached SCSI (SAS). Image courtesy of Maxtor.

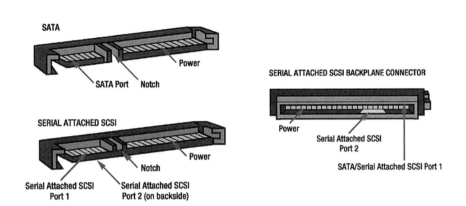

SAS takes over where Serial ATA left off by adding full duplex communication, a dual-port interface, and maximum cable lengths of 10 meters. As you can see in Figure 2-4, the connectors for Serial ATA and SAS are very similar, the latter featuring a filled keyway to prevent an SAS drive from plugging in to a Serial ATA interface. The second port sits on the opposite end of the drive, for access to the drive from two independent sources. SAS supports expansion through edge expanders, which accommodate up to 64 SAS or SATA ports, though you almost certainly won't need to worry about that degree of expansion even if you do dabble with SAS at some point.

In addition to the robust expandability of SAS, SAS drives are able to offer greater reliability and performance than their Serial ATA counterparts. Serial ATA maintains respectable throughput in environments without rotational vibration, but drops off quickly when confronted with the subtle vibrations associated with random actuator movement from nearby drives. SAS, on the other hand, is largely immune to reasonable levels of rotational vibration. And while the newest Serial ATA drives are blessed with 1,000,000 MTBF ratings, SAS drives sport even higher ratings under more grueling duty cycles.

Hard drive manufacturer Maxtor recently illustrated the flexibility of both SAS and Serial ATA by demonstrating the two technologies working together in a three terabyte array with an LSI Logic host bus adapter (HBA) and Vitesse expander. In a recent discussion with representatives who oversaw the demonstration, I confirmed that SAS will work natively with Windows Server 2003, and thus with SBS.

Network Attached Storage (NAS)

An increasingly popular storage medium that doesn't tax your SBS server or its clients is the Network Attached Storage (NAS) device. Think of an NAS device as a dedicated file server, only instead of employing general-purpose hardware, it uses highly integrated, embedded subsystems to minimize cost, maximize reliability, and perform its duty of delivering data to clients as efficiently as possible.

NAS systems operate independently of your SBS machine and are accessed over the network, just like any other client with shared resources. But because they are specialized, NAS devices generally cost less than configuring a separate server, and are often more scalable as well. The resulting benefits include simplified management, cross-platform data-sharing, and reduced load on your primary server.

NAS is particularly attractive to SMBs with moderate file-sharing requirements and enough network bandwidth to make centralized storage feasible. On the other hand, if you don't work with a lot of collaborative information, an NAS appliance might be unnecessary.

> BEST PRACTICE: Be sure to check Microsoft's Windows Server Catalog at www.microsoft.com/windows/catalog/server/ to verify that Windows Server 2003 supports the device that you're eying.

Hard Drive Summary

When considering a hard drive purchase, once again you're faced with a decision between cost and performance. Serial ATA has it benefits, as does SAS. Fortunately, both technologies, with all of their inherent benefits, should maintain price parity with the parallel interconnects they replace.

One area where you might notice a difference between Serial ATA and SAS is in the cost of controllers. Because Serial ATA is predominantly a desktop interface, most modern platforms include native support. And in an attempt to integrate the most compelling feature set, several vendors include RAID 0 and

RAID 1 capabilities as part of the package. For example, Intel's ICH6-R I/O controller features Matrix RAID technology, to turn two Serial ATA hard drives into separate RAID 0 and RAID 1 arrays by using a pair of partitions on each. It's tricky stuff to be sure, but it emphasizes the value that chipset manufacturers are putting into their Serial ATA offerings. Expect to pay several hundred dollars extra for a server with SCSI capabilities and 10K- or 15K-RPM drives.

Networking Basics

Though not an active part of building a server or configuring a workstation, implementing a fully functional network with ample bandwidth capabilities is nevertheless an important part of your SBS deployment. As they say during marriage counseling (or so I hear), communication is of utmost importance in a healthy relationship, and the same holds true for networked devices in the office.

Gigabit Ethernet: Been There, Done That

It doesn't get much more vanilla than Gigabit Ethernet these days. If you're chuckling to yourself remembering back to when 10 Mbps adapters seemed fast, keep in mind that nowdays almost every mid-range motherboard and above includes an integrated Gigabit Ethernet adapter as a value-add. Moreover, you can find Gigabit Ethernet switches for less than $100.

The most difficult step in installing a Gigabit network is running the cable. "But wait," you say, "I already have copper CAT5 running all over the place— I don't need new cable." Fair enough—test the line for crosstalk, continuity, and signal loss. If it passes all three exams, your existing cabling will probably suffice. More often than not, though, you'll want at least CAT5e to realize the best performance with Gigabit. Just remember that older cable, poor splices, and runs that exceed CAT5's 100m limit will all degrade performance.

Even your platform will have a big impact on network throughput. PCI Gigabit cards in your workstations might operate without issue, mostly because they probably won't be pushing the PCI bus very hard, but this same kind of card on a server could be choked for bandwidth by its aging bus and an inundation of network requests. The advent of PCI Express is already seeing a new generation of Gigabit adapters with wider pipes over which to communicate. Plus, specialized Gigabit applications (such as NVIDIA's nForce3 250 Gb on-chipset solution) realize in excess of 800 MB per second of bandwidth thanks to well-engineered avoidances of PCI.

Wireless: Exoticism and Trepidation

You already have enough to worry about when it comes to dealing with security, so why add another potential point of entry into your network by going wireless? It's all about risk mitigation, baby. Twice I've proposed a network topology to clients who, say, run an architectural firm from the top floor of their house, or who live in the back room of their storefront (both true scenarios). After looking at wired and wireless designs, both clients chose to shed the cables in favor of proprietary variants of 802.11g that deliver performance close to a 100 Mbps wired connection. Despite their initial nervousness about broadcasting invoices through the air, I walked the clients through the wireless setup wizards to enable Wi-Fi Protected Access (WPA), and verified that the processors in their wireless gear would support an upgrade to 802.11i, the upcoming standard for wireless security.

In both instances the clients highly valued flexibility, expandability, and availability. The architect wanted online access from his bedroom downstairs without having to run cable through the house, while the businessman wanted room for growth, responsive performance, and the ability to connect from his room across the shop. An 802.11g router with a four-port 100 Mbps switch was more than enough for each client, saving money that one client instead used for LCD displays and that the other client used for deluxe small form-factor platforms.

Networking Summary

Wired or wireless, Gigabit or 100 Mbps, new cable or old—decisions, decisions. To help you better evaluate your networking hardware situation, take a look at the current implementation, if there is one. Make a list of what the new setup will need to achieve, and take note of how many of those goals the current network may fulfill. If it looks like you might need to scrap the old and lay bigger pipes to contend with expanding throughput, go back to your list and determine how wired or wireless would suit your needs. Consistently large file transfers across the network favor Gigabit, while flexibility and ease of implementation make wireless attractive.

BEST PRACTICE: It's important to map out how you'll install your network, and though it wouldn't seem so, this is especially true if you choose wireless. For example, if you connect a wireless router or firewall to the Internet and directly attach your SBS server, with two Ethernet cards for added security, realize that broadcasting a wireless signal might be providing unauthorized access around the server's firewall and back into your network. Instead, consider connecting a broadband modem to your server's external NIC and connecting a wireless access point to the internal NIC so you're better protected from external attacks.

Betting on Backup

I'm preaching to the choir here, but it bears repeating that your server, no matter how robust, needs to be backed up on a regular basis. Traditionally, most servers have included some sort of tape backup for archiving information nightly. But the rapid evolution of optical technology has witnessed a spirited adoption of single-layer and dual-layer DVD writers, and the proliferation of inexpensive hard drives has also encouraged high-capacity external drives that connect over USB 2.0 or IEEE 1394 buses. What backup device you choose should depend on your storage needs.

Note that backup matters are discussed further in Chapter 15 of this book (including discussion of advanced disaster recovery). The introductory SBS book of this series, *Windows Small Business Server 2003 Best Practices*, discusses the basic SBS 2003 backup routine in Chapter 11. You can purchase that volume at www.smbnation.com.

Sticking to Tape

While groundbreaking advancements in tape backup devices are few and far between, tape remains one of the most convenient mediums for storing valuable information. It costs less per gigabyte than optical discs and removable hard drives, and it often stores more data to boot.

The most economical tape drives are of the Direct Attached Storage (DAS) variety; as opposed to LAN-based solutions, they physically connect to your server. DAS devices are characterized by simple manageability, broad software support, economical acquisition, and peak utility in smaller offices.

Within the family of DAS tape drives there are a number of tape technologies, spanning a broad array of performance and price points. One of the most popular technologies, with capacities up to 40 GB, is the Digital Audio Tape (DAT) format. Unfortunately, DAT drives interface exclusively with SCSI controllers, a factor that adds to their cost. They also top out at a data rate of 4.8 MB per second, which is relatively slow next to other more advanced designs. For example, the Digital Linear Tape (DLT) format is characterized by more capacity, faster transfer rates, and enhanced reliability. In its most advanced form, DLT is able to hold 70 GB of compressed data moving at 20 MB per second. But like DAT, DLT is limited to use with a SCSI controller.

Perhaps a more attractive solution is an external USB 2.0 Advanced Intelligent Tape (AIT) drive that balances reasonable capacity (90 GB, compressed) with moderate performance (roughly 4 MB per second) and a price tag under $1,000. Just remember that tape is almost exclusively an archival medium, so pay particular attention to specifications such as access times, which often range right up to 30 seconds. Compare that to the millisecond ratings for external hard drives and it quickly becomes apparent why the two mediums each excel in their own different respects.

Optical Options

CD and DVD writers don't boast the flexibility of a tape drive, but they do facilitate quick and easy backup for document folders and multimedia files. Due to the extreme rotational velocity of 52x CD-R drives (the fastest available), CD writing technology probably won't evolve much beyond its current speed. DVD±R/RW drives continue to accelerate however, managing to write 4.7 GB of information in just over five minutes. If you're looking for a versatile medium that enjoys compatibility with an array of other devices (try plugging that tape cartridge into your laptop or a client's workstation), a DVD writer might be the most economical backup solution.

> BEST PRACTICE: If you're looking for true portability and aren't necessarily concerned with capacity, invest in a USB flash drive— one of those little keychain devices that hold between 32 MB and

> 1 GB of data. I carry one with me everywhere; it's great for storing documents, music, and the latest driver updates. While it isn't an answer to your SBS backup problem, you never know when the extra storage might come in handy.

The freshest idea in the optical drive market is the dual-layer DVD. Capable of storing 8.5 GB of information, many of the dual-layer drives are priced under $100. Unfortunately, media is still rare and prohibitively expensive, though proliferation of DVD+R DL hardware should help drive the price down over time. Don't count on using a series of dual-layer discs for running a complete backup; rather, it's a technology to keep your eye on for now.

External Hard Drives

The championing of high-speed peripheral-to-PC interconnects, such as USB 2.0 and IEEE 1394, has enabled an impressive array of external hard drives that feature excellent performance, massive capacity, availability through random access (for when you need to find just one file), respectable portability, and best of all, a reasonable price tag.

A number of tape drives have also made the jump to USB connectivity, which is convenient for servers that don't have SCSI controllers, especially entry-level servers. However, I maintain that an external hard drive together with flexible backup software is a good alternative to tape. I use Seagate's 160 GB external repository for weekly backups of a 146 GB Cheetah 10K.6 SCSI drive. Using Dantz Retrospect 6.5, I'm able to run automated, incremental backups of all files, including those that are in use. Even the network clients I select are monitored and protected by Retrospect's network support. The large capacity means that the backups all run unattended and without the need to rotate media, as I'd have to do with a tape drive. Further, at the greater than 50 MB per second transfer rate, incremental backups only take a few minutes.

Backup Summary

I'm of the opinion that high-speed external hard drives are the backup medium of choice for SMB applications, in part because they're less expensive than the combined cost of a tape drive and media. Tape is still an excellent choice too, but I'm from a generation that perceives tape as an archaic medium, despite its clear merits. And, while optical media has its place in the hierarchy of backup devices, it's probably a better secondary solution, with good interoperability across a wider range of drives.

The backup strategy that I encourage involves two external drives, which are physically rotated on a nightly basis. Attached to the USB 2.0 port on your SBS machine, each drive is conveniently swapped each day before you leave the office. The backup application, scheduled to update overnight, brings the replacement drive up to date with the day's work. If a disaster were to strike, you'd essentially lose one day, but would still have the previous day's backup set for a recent restoration. There's no switching of media, keeping track of multiple cartridges, or investing in extraneous hardware.

For a more advanced discussion of backup, see Chapter 15 later in this book.

Right-Sizing SBS Hardware

With a thorough understanding of what's happening in today's server hardware world, you're better equipped to make the appropriate buying decisions based on features and capabilities. However, the real art involves "right-sizing" a hardware configuration to the needs of each customer. A wise man by the name of Roger Otterson, one of the driving forces behind the San Diego Small Business Server Group (www.sandiegosbs.org), explained right-sizing as the ability to evaluate a business' needs and, based on a rough budget (which gets even more complicated if the customer doesn't have any idea what they should be spending), propose a complete package that covers all of the bases for that entity. According to Roger, one of the most difficult aspects of right-sizing is that businesses often aren't sure exactly what they need. The customer might have a raw feeling with regard to price and performance, akin to buying a new car and knowing the difference between a Toyota Corolla and a Lexus LS430, but it's the job of the technically-minded consultant to synthesize knowledge and an understanding of the customer. That means shedding the medium-business IT mentality of buying an entire Lexus fleet. Instead, maximize the potential of something less expensive, to fit within the confines of a small business budget.

In other words, a business with 10 client workstations running a standard suite of Windows Server 2003, Microsoft Exchange, Microsoft Outlook, Microsoft Windows SharePoint Services, and perhaps a Microsoft SQL Server database, probably won't tax a dual-processor server with a SCSI RAID array. Moreover, suggesting a $700 server, adding $300 for a pair of external hard drives, $600 for software, and another $500 for additional network hardware might very well turn off your customer, leaving them with an impression of you akin to the stench of a car salesman angling for a big commision.

There is no hard and fast equation for determining what hardware a server that's communicating with 5, 10, 25, or 50 clients will need to function smoothly. Perhaps the easiest way to make that valuation is to consider the benefits of each platform—Xeon versus Pentium 4, and Opteron versus Athlon 64—and determine which features are imperative. If the business with 20 client machines doesn't need DBS or EMT64, and doesn't anticipate doubling in size over the next few years, there isn't any need for a Xeon. Going the Pentium 4 route will save hundreds of dollars. If the customer plans on turning their server off every night, if they won't be running an enterprise database application, and if they don't plan on serving large files to each client on a regular basis, there probably isn't any need for SCSI hard drives either. Investing in Serial ATA will yield more capacity, comparable speeds in light-load environments, and modest reliability, and again will save hundreds of dollars. Finally, if an office is already wired for 100 Mbps Ethernet and Gigabit isn't explicitly required, you can surely save even more money by sticking to the older standard.

Selling SBS Hardware

Let's stick with the car salesman analogy for a minute while we talk about how to sell your customer on the hardware needed for their deployment. Say that you know all there is to know about Audi's 2000 S4 and you're trying to sell a lease return. Each customer that looks at the vehicle remarks about its attractive body, its luxurious yet unpretentious styling, and the beautiful interior. "That's not all," you say. "Take a look under the hood. Here you see two turbochargers that augment the 2.7L engine to 250 horsepower. If you replace the stock programming with an aftermarket chip to increase the boost pressure, you can hit 320 horsepower easily. Just replace these diverter valves, add more robust piping here to make it more reliable, and swap out the standard Audi hose over there. This thing's a beast. Pushing 20 lbs of boost, you'll fly by every Mustang GT and will look good doing it, too."

While it's obvious that you know your Audi in this scenario, your customer didn't and is now overwhelmed by all of the noise you've fed into what could have been an informational dialogue leading to the sale of a great car. Similarly with hardware, if you start gushing about how the Opteron's point-to-point bus gives it better scalability characteristics than Xeon, or about the benefits of dual-channel memory controllers, you'll quickly move into the arena of techno-babble instead of technology-oriented sales.

Keep in mind that the presentation itself is completely different from the process of understanding today's hardware landscape or of right-sizing. By this point you've done your homework, learning what each piece of server hardware does and how it interacts with other components. You've "right-sized," determining just how much server is needed to deliver acceptable SBS performance, and you've compiled a list of components, including the server, a backup solution, software, and a maintenance plan, using your knowledge of hardware and an understanding of the customer's needs. Now it's time to explain the package in a way that the customer can easily understand.

For example, suppose a small business with five client computers wants to use an SBS server to organize collaborative projects between graphic artists, handle e-mail, and do some file sharing. They're hoping $1,500 will be enough for hardware, so you determine that a 2.6 GHz Pentium 4 machine with dual 120 GB Serial ATA hard drives in a RAID 1 configuration would offer a respectable balance between performance, data security, and price. Add in a pair of external hard drives plus backup software, and SBS 2003. You're probably coming in a little high on price, but at least you can suggest areas to cut back if it's absolutely necessary.

In essence, you just synthesized your knowledge of hardware into a marketable package—something that small and medium businesses want and need. You propose the "right-sized" SBS 2003 package to your customer, extolling the benefits of Intel's Pentium 4 not for its peppy 800 MHz front side bus Hyper-Threading Technology, but because it's fast and it won't cost them much money at all. The storage subsystem is easy for you to configure; that doesn't matter to the customer, though. A RAID 1 array ensures the safety of your customer's data in the event of a drive failure, and the capacity guarantees enough storage space for years to come. The two external hard drives are easy to use as backup devices and, rotated properly, ensure true data redundancy. You don't even need to mention the performance of USB 2.0 or your opinion of hard drives versus tape drives. Simply present the package and explain its benefits as they pertain to the customer.

A Server Case Study: HP's ProLiant ML 350 G4

You'll find that there are numerous differences between servers (even with entry-level machines) and desktop PCs. The most obvious differences are apparent by examining a server chassis. HP has provided a fourth-generation ProLiant ML 350 to model the server's innards and to give you a more tangible idea of how the hardware I've already discussed works together in an SBS environment. Figure 2-5 shows the front of the server, opened to expose its highly-accessible drive bays.

Figure 2-5

HP's ML 350G4 offers plenty of room for storage expansion. My test platform included three SCSI drives built in.

Visual Inspection

The ProLiant ML 350 is based on a free-standing tower design. Rack mount servers are also available from HP, though they are generally used in multi-server deployments. In its fully configured form, the ML 350 weighs more than 75 pounds. The server's steel construction is the biggest contributor to this weight; however, a rugged drive bay populated with Ultra320 SCSI disks and two 700 W power supplies also add to the system's heft.

With the ML 350's door open, notice the CD-ROM and floppy drives mounted up top, with spare 3.5" bays covered. Power and Unit Identification (UID) buttons are located just below, with indicator lights sandwiched between. The lower half of the system's front side is equipped with bays for SCSI drives. The example here features three 36.4 GB disks in a RAID 5 configuration.

Trotting around to the system's back side reveals redundant power supplies for uninterrupted operation, twin PS/2 ports for mouse and keyboard connectivity, one serial port, a single parallel port, a 15-pin VGA connector, two USB 2.0 ports, and an RJ-45 connector that interfaces with the platform's integrated Gigabit Ethernet controller. The 120 mm fan mounted on the server's back panel pushes up to 220 cubic feet per minute out of the chassis, easily dealing with whatever thermal output might be generated by the 15,000 RPM hard drives and dual-processors contained within. The obvious byproduct of that airflow is significant fan noise. Fortunately, the cooling system is variable, so the fan only spins at full speed when it needs to. Figure 2-6 shows the 120 mm fan relative to the server's back panel. Figure 2-7 shows the server's modular power supplies, which serve to prevent hardware-related down time.

Notes:

Figure 2-6

Cooling and connectivity. The back of the ML 350 looks like your typical computer system, save for the redundant power supplies.

Figure 2-7

If one of the 700 W power supplies were to fail, you'd simply pull it out and replace it, while the other kept the server running.

Cracking open the side cover unveils the ProLiant in one of its default configurations: a single 3.2 GHz Xeon with EM64T and an 800 MHz front side bus, 512 MB of registered DDR333 memory, HP's Smart Array 641 Controller, and a motherboard centering on Intel's E7520 chipset. There's clearly room for another processor, should an upgrade prove necessary. Further, populating an additional memory slot with 512 MB of memory would boost memory bandwidth on the dual-channel platform up to 5.3 gigabytes per second, a significant improvement over its existing 2.7 gigabytes per second. The motherboard itself provides four PCI-X slots, a pair of PCI Express connectors (one each of x4 and x8), an integrated dual-channel Ultra320 SCSI controller, and the ATI Rage XL graphic accelerator. Figure 2-8 is a candid of the ATI Rage XL included with HP's ML 350. Figure 2.9 shows the server's expansion possibilities.

Figure 2-8

Though it isn't a 3D powerhouse, the Rage XL is an inexpensive graphics accelerator that delivers a stable platform for integrated display support.

Figure 2-9

There's plenty of room to upgrade the ML 350. Notice the vacant processor socket, the three empty memory slots, PCI Express, and the PCI connectors.

Up and Running

In our case study using the ProLiant ML 350, now that we've completed our visual inspection we can plug everything in and fire up the server for its initial configuration. There are actually two setup routines to check out, though both should be preconfigured when the machine ships. The first setup is the initial BIOS sequence, which is accessible by pressing the appropriate function key when prompted. Figure 2-10 shows the welcome screen that appears when you enter the ML 350's primary system BIOS. Figure 2-11 includes a list of settings that are available after clicking System Options. Figure 2-12 displays all of the installed PCI devices, enabling a quick hardware lookup without opening the server's chassis. Figure 2-13 shows the order of boot devices, which can be shuffled around to boot from different devices. Finally, Figure 2-14 shows where you can enable a custom POST message to display on the server as it starts up.

Figure 2-10

If you're used to working in a desktop machine's BIOS, this shouldn't be too difficult. The welcome screen gives you relevant information about the server, and a list of available options.

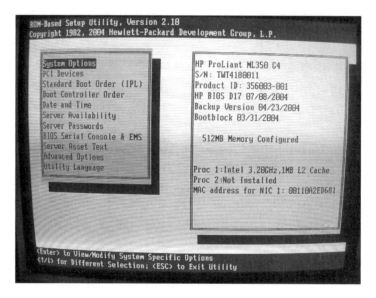

Figure 2-11

Whereas most workstations give you multiple options for configuring hardware, most of the choices here consist of enabling and disabling features.

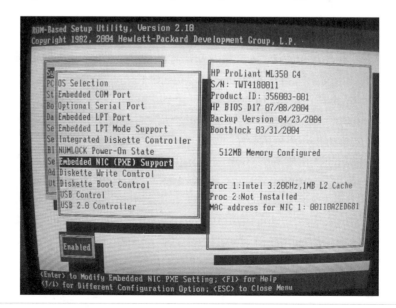

Figure 2-12

Other screens are purely informational, such as this list of installed PCI devices.

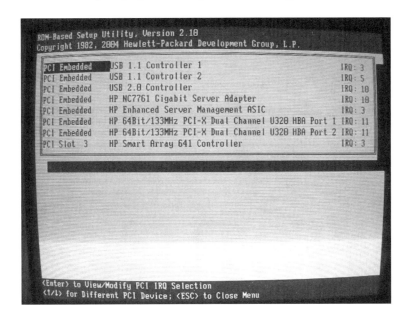

Figure 2-13

If you have multiple boot devices, the boot menu allows you to reorder them in the proper order. You can even boot from the network!

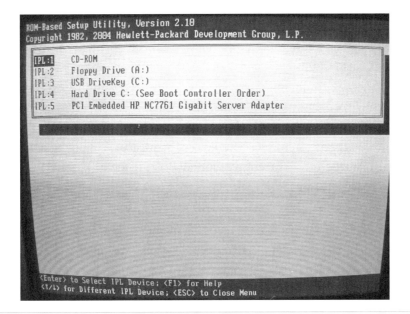

Figure 2-14

Add a custom message in the message field, such as the name of your consultancy and its phone number. Or, a simple "Welcome to SBS 2003" will suffice.

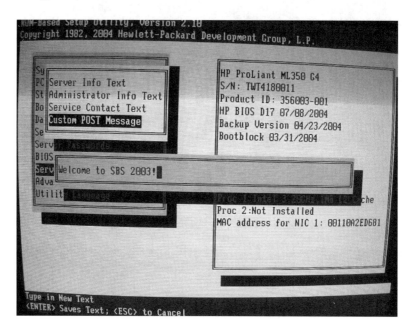

Server BIOS files are far less configurable than those of your everyday desktop. You'll generally see a few details about the installed hardware, and will be presented with a handful of options for switching components on and off. The ML 350's first BIOS screen conveys the software version, memory capacity, and processor information. Delving one level deeper into System Options generates a list of relatively low-level features that you can toggle. A PCI device list identifies connected peripherals, and a boot-order menu allows you to shuffle bootable devices around for an optimal boot sequence. Without belaboring the system BIOS, additional screens provide controls for setting thermal thresholds, employing Hyper-Threading Technology, and customizing welcome messages.

The RAID controller card has its own BIOS as well, which you can use to view connected SCSI drives and configure them to your liking. As you can see from the figures, the HP ProLiant ML 350 features the three previously mentioned 36 GB drives in a RAID 5 configuration for 67.8 GB of total capacity. If there were an additional drive, it might be designated a spare, should one of the three primary drives fail. Figure 2-15 shows the options you have available upon entering the RAID card's own BIOS file. Figure 2-16 is the View menu, which displays the current status of the ML 350's RAID 5 array. Figure 2-17 displays a breakdown of each drive in the array, and its current health status.

Figure 2-15

With only three options, it isn't difficult to create, monitor, and delete RAID arrays. The toughest part is deciding what RAID technology to use.

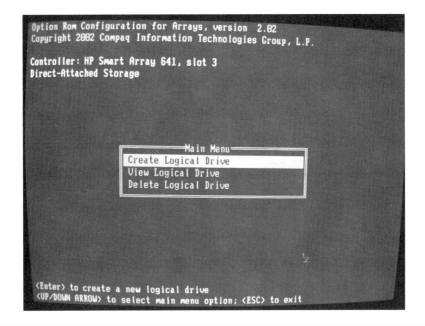

Notes:

Figure 2-16

The overall drive status page reports on the array's status. Explore further by hitting the Enter key for a breakdown of each drive in the RAID array.

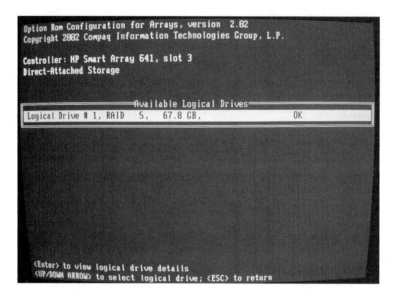

Figure 2-17

In the event of a failure, this menu let's you know which drive to replace, because the drive's health would no longer be 'OK.'

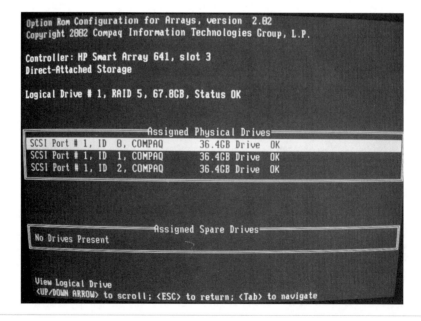

Windows, Meet Hardware. Hardware, Windows.

With all of the BIOS-level options set, the installation of SBS 2003 may commence. However, just because SBS employs the latest Windows Server 2003 operating system doesn't mean all of your hardware will work seamlessly. If you see an error like the one in Figure 2-18, Windows Server isn't loading the proper driver for your disk controller. In the case of the error in this figure, I was forced to visit HP's Web site, override the default driver that Windows identified, and proceed until I was greeted with the screen in Figure 2-19, which told me the array had been recognized.

Figure 2-18

Disk controller cards that were manufactured after Windows Server 2003 came out generally aren't supported. Not loading the appropriate driver results in the RAID array not being detected.

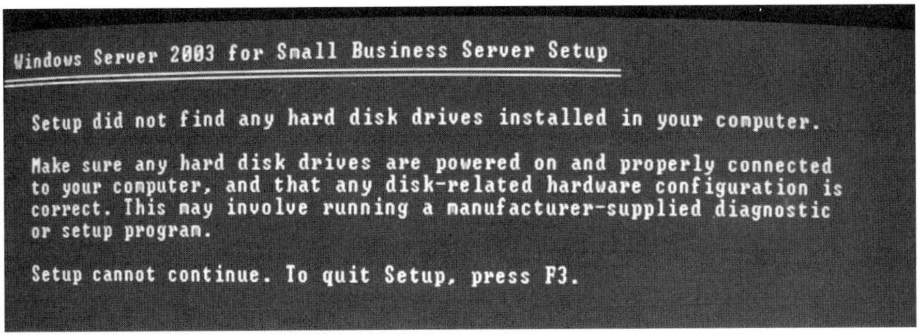

```
Windows Server 2003 for Small Business Server Setup

Setup did not find any hard disk drives installed in your computer.

Make sure any hard disk drives are powered on and properly connected
to your computer, and that any disk-related hardware configuration is
correct. This may involve running a manufacturer-supplied diagnostic
or setup program.

Setup cannot continue. To quit Setup, press F3.
```

Notes:

Figure 2-19

After loading the HP driver by hitting F6 as Windows Setup initialized, I was able to continue the setup routine.

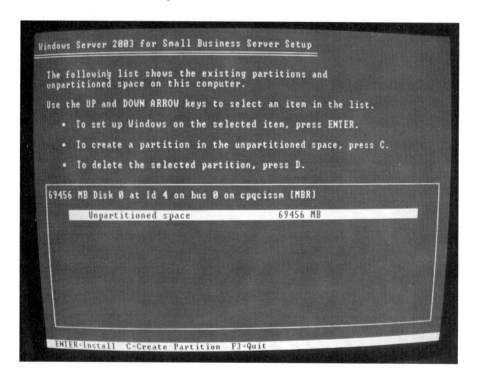

Even after you complete the Windows Server installation, there's a chance that hardware won't function properly. For example, in Figure 2-20, SBS Setup claims that it can't continue without an Ethernet adapter, despite the integrated Gigabit NIC that is already enabled. It took another visit to HP's Web site on another system to download the proper driver required for connectivity.

Notes:

Figure 2-20

Even after Windows is installed, install all necessary drivers to ensure there aren't any snags in the SBS 2003 setup script.

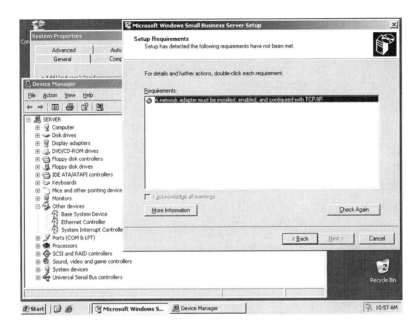

BEST PRACTICE: Rather than be surprised every time Windows fails to identify a component, visit your server manufacturer's Web site before starting the SBS installation. Download relevant drivers and software utilities and burn them onto a CD, if possible. Be sure to keep the drivers for your hard drive controller on a floppy disk, since CD support isn't yet available and a number of newer hard drive controllers aren't supported by the Windows Setup routine.

Hardware Management

Because it's important to maintain the health of the server, HP's ProLiant comes with a number of software applications that you won't find on a desktop machine. Consider a comparison between a Formula 1 race car and an old work truck. The race car sports a lot more in the way of telemetry to monitor its high-speed, low-drag status as it runs lap after lap around the track. The truck, outfitted with a consumer engine and driven more conservatively, doesn't need all of that fancy instrumentation.

HP's "telemetry package" is comprised of several separate applications that come together to provide the following: proactive notification of problems before those problems turn into unscheduled down time; Web browser-based management agents for monitoring server and client instrumentation; simplified initial server setup; and, in some of the more advanced servers, integrated remote management functionality.

Systems Insight Manager

The backbone of HP's management package, Systems Insight Manager compliments the management features of Windows Server 2003 to deliver fault, configuration, performance, and asset management for both HP servers and connected clients. The idea here is to consolidate support for a breadth of hardware platforms and software infrastructures, in order to minimize the amount of maintenance dirty work with which you're forced to contend. In the SMB environment, you probably won't need to rely heavily on Systems Insight Manager, though the application's software baseline feature might prove useful for keeping important software updates uniform across clients on your network.

SmartStart

Remember those Windows installation screens a few pages back where I demonstrated (with matter-of-fact setup errors) the caveats to using cutting-edge hardware? Well, SmartStart alleviates those problems with ProLiant support packs—optimized drivers that are distributed in operating system–specific bundles. A number of system maintenance utilities are also included under the SmartStart banner.Finally, there's an online component of SmartStart that includes notifications of updated firmware and driver software.

Integrated Lights-Out (iLO)

One of the most exciting features of HP's higher-end server families (a number of the DL-class machines and HP's ML 370, for example) is Integrated Lights-Out (iLO) Advanced, a remote management package built onto the server itself. Learning about this package while writing this chapter was akin to hitting pay dirt. Finally with this package I see hardware in the SBS equation being addressed from a wholistic systems approach, because this technology (as well as the RILOE II technology that I discuss in the next section) adds hardware-level mobile management to the picture, to a limited degree.

Especially useful for businesses that don't have the budget for dedicated IT, iLO allows you to take remote control of a properly equipped server at the hardware level, before it even boots into Windows Server 2003. The embedded iLO processor enables a virtual graphical remote console with full control of the troubled server's video, keyboard, and mouse, including the ability to remotely boot from a local floppy or CD-ROM drive recognized as virtual media.

Once the server is booted into Windows, iLO hands off management responsibilities to Terminal Services, part of Windows Server 2003. The remote desktop functionality provided by Terminal Services is very similar to iLO's graphic console, granting you control over the remote server for off-site service.

Naturally, iLO has tremendous implications for those of you who preside over SBS networks and their clients. Not only does it enable further reach (you won't need to drive two hours to service those distant clients), saving both time and money, but clients with iLO-equipped servers will enjoy less down time, since you as the consultant can be more responsive. And, when a new service pack or security bulletin hits the wires, you can apply updates remotely using iLO's virtual media feature.

Visit http://h18013.www1.hp.com/products/servers/management/riloe2/ supported-servers.html, HP's iLO Advanced Support page for a list of compatible servers.

Remote Insight Lights-Out Edition II (RILOE II)

Those servers that are not equipped with iLO may attain similar functionality through Remote Insight Lights-Out Edition II (RILOE II), a PCI-based hardware solution. The principal difference between the two, according to Ray Nix with HP's embedded management marketing department, is that because RILOE II is based on its own graphics chip and PowerPC processor, it provides enhanced console performance. (Ray was very helpful when I was researching this functionality, for which I thank him!) Moreover, once the server loads Windows Server 2003, it is no longer dependant on Terminal Services, opening up the possibility of accessing the server from Red Hat or SUSE Linux, as well.

The RILOE II kit includes the card itself, an external power adapter, power cables, a keyboard and mouse adapter, the virtual power button cable, and support CDs. The power adapter enables uninterrupted access to the RILOE board, even when the server is turned off. Or, you can elect to connect RILOE to an internal motherboard header, which serves the same purpose, enabling the Virtual Power Button for graceful shutdowns and startups. Support for virtual media is another invaluable addition. Using a floppy or CD image located anywhere on the network (it doesn't necessarily have to be localized), you can install applications, including the all-important patches and security updates, can perform disaster recovery of failed operating systems, and can deploy an entirely new installation, all through the 128-bit encrypted graphical console. Figure 2-21 shows the naked RILOE II board in all of its glory.

Figure 2-21

RILOE II is a full-length PCI card that includes all of the necessary functionality to enable remote management.

The RILOE II card features its own 10/100 Mbps network interface for dedicated access to the server, and can provide real-time Simple Network Management Protocol (SNMP) notifications in the event of a server problem. Moreover, RILOE is even accessible through wireless and dial-up connections through an iPAQ Pocket PC with its own special browser interface. And if you don't have access to the SMB's LAN or WAN, RILOE supports access over a standard 56k modem using a modem gateway or Microsoft's Remote Access Service (RAS). Unfortunately, I find that the access limitation reduces the RILOE II card's viability somewhat in an SBS environment because the bandwidth of a 56k connection isn't sufficient to perform a remote operating system deployment or large Service Pack update from localized virtual media. I'd recommend weighing the cost of RILOE with its real-world benefits.

As with iLO, RILOE II maximizes productivity through reduced server down time for SMB clients, minimal on-site interaction (of course, any hardware upgrades will have to be physically performed), and cost savings on both sides of the equation. Fortunately, the card has come down in price since it initially debuted, and can now be added for about $400.

> BEST PRACTICE: At $400, RILOE II is still a notable investment, so be sure to evaluate its usefulness on a case by case basis. Most SMBs aren't going to be running WANs. As a result, the amount of management that RILOE II would enable will likely be dictated by the bandwidth of the connection used to access the card.

Summary

Though it might be tempting to leave hardware "strictly up to the experts" at any number of system integrator or original equipment manufacturers from whom you buy, there's real value in learning about today's technologies, platforms, and architectures. After all, if we all followed the now-outdated recommended hardware list for SBS 2003, we'd be searching in vain for 500 MHz processors and building handicapped $300 servers. To put hardware in a more real-world context allows us to anticipate the performance we'll need for any given application, and to make decisions based on our customers' projected growth, desired budget, and available resources.

As you work, not only will you find that a more complete knowledge of hardware helps in configuring effective servers and workstations—it also helps turn that inward-facing expertise into the outward-facing ability to right-size an SBS installation and sell hardware effectively. Both right-sizing and selling are managed manifestations of your inner-geekdom, polished to a salesman's shine and made as user-friendly as possible.

It's easy to tell when someone doesn't understand much about hardware. They'll often oversell to compensate, erring on the side of too much power...and spending too much money in the process. That's where you come in, trained in the ways of servers and ready to build the right one for each application, from 5-person offices to 50-employee businesses. Between reading up on the hardware scene, learning how to right-size, and selling effectively, you are now better prepared to approach some of the other advanced SBS 2003 topics.

CHAPTER 3
SBS 2003 Licensing

BY Harry Brelsford (Bainbridge Island, WA)

WITH Steven Banks (Port Orchard, WA)

In speaking with SBSers around the world, this licensing chapter has been eagerly anticipated. Why? Because even on a good day, licensing topics surrounding SBS 2003 are bewildering and maddening! This chapter is divided into three sections to bring order to the licensing discussion:

- **Case Study - Alaskan fishing company**. This is a sample company I use to draw out many licensing issues.

- **Microsoft Licensing Frequently Asked Questions (FAQ) review**. Believe it or not, many of the answers to your licensing questions already exist online. I will also discuss Terminal Services licensing (which is very important to Canadian readers according to my research) and member server licensing. You will also learn about per server licensing at the server application-level.

- **More Microsoft-centric licensing topics**. You'll learn about the Ligman lease, the non-existent downgrade scenario, and other facts that are stranger than fiction in this section.

Case Study—Alaskan Fishing Company

One of the most popular slides in the morning session of my worldwide SMB Nation Summit workshops concerns an Alaskan fishing company that I've served with pleasure over the years. And as you will see, this fishing company serves as an example to convey many of the complexities surrounding SBS 2003 licensing. Let's get started!

Figure 3-1

The Alaskan fishing company.

The Question

The question I pose to the workshop audience is simple and might not normally prompt deeper scrutiny:

> *"Just to clarify…my fishing company has 900 employees. But we have only 30 computers. Will SBS 2003 work for me?"*

Such a simply question results in a surprisingly complex set of answers about SBS 2003 licensing, as you will see.

The Simple Answer

The first answer is YES! This Alaskan fishing company could indeed utilize SBS 2003 to provide networking capabilities to its 30 computers. This would be accomplished using device Client Access Licenses (CALs). The Alaskan fishing company would purchase 25 such device CALs (note that SBS 2003 ships with five universal CALs by default that can assume "device" licensing status). So you might be inclined to say "end of story" and leave it there. But really, we need to delve deeper into device CALs before causing analytical turbulence by introducing more CAL types.

As the simple scenario stands, 30 PCs attached to the SBS 2003 network can operate as full network citizens and enjoy all the rights bestowed upon those devices under the licensing terms and conditions set forth by the Microsoft Corporation. The device CALs deployed by the Alaskan fishing company would allow:

- All 900 employees to be entered into the Active Directory database as user objects in SBS 2003. Ideally, you would do this via the Add User Wizard that is accessed from the To Do List. Active Directory is explained by author Jeff Middleton in Chapter 15; adding users is mentioned to some extent in Chapter 4 by Andy Goodman.

- All 900 employees could have an SMTP e-mail address as part of being added to Active Directory in SBS 2003. This would allow these employees to send and receive e-mails with the Alaskan fishing company's Internet identity (i.e., alaskanfishingcompany.com).

- You could place one or more of the 30 PCs in the lunchroom of the Alaskan fishing company for the boat-based employees to use when they are in port. Imagine these employees queued up to use a PC while waiting for their paychecks. The only bizarre thing about this example would be that the line to utilize the computer might be very long and slow, as folks would likely have to read six months of accumulated e-mail.

- Finally, the 30 device CALs would support the 30 PCs referenced in this storyline. But a greater number of users could certainly share those 30 computers, as my example implies.

The Complex Answer

Let's introduce some complexity into this example. First, take a step back in recent history to understand the current context of CAL licensing. Microsoft is a very large company with over 60,000 employees worldwide! SBS 2003 is a product suite that touches many different groups at Microsoft and requires deft coordination to even get the product out the door in a timely manner. Microsoft as a whole is trying to standardize its products to provide a consistent "Microsoft customer experience." This standardization would affect the user interface (UI) of its applications and operating systems, and require consistent language in print and on-screen help systems (these are communication standards). Believe me, knowing what I know about Microsoft via my personal relationships, this is a very tall order!

Back to SBS 2003 CALs. Microsoft has correctly determined that SBS 2003 should not have "unique" licensing that is inconsistent with the underlying Windows Server 2003 operating system. Makes sense! So I can weave a personal tale of SBS lore that better explains this concept. When Microsoft was madly preparing to launch SBS 2003 in New Orleans on October 9, 2003, its SBS development and marketing team resources were stretched incredibly thin. Yours truly was engaged by the Microsoft SBS marketing team to write several of the public-facing Web pages over a weekend just before the product launch. One page that I was assigned to write was about SBS 2003 licensing. I wondered aloud about mastering and writing Microsoft Web page content on this seemingly complex topic with such a tight deadline. My manager put me at ease when he explained that SBS 2003 CALs are simple: SBS CALs are precisely the same as the CALs of the underlying operating system for the first time in history. Just use the same basic wording as the CAL page for Windows Server 2003. Whew! That was easy to understand.

> BEST PRACTICE: When in doubt or confused about SBS 2003 CALs, just return to your "roots." Up until SBS 2003, we only had device licensing with the SBS product and, quite frankly, we all got along just fine. After you realize that the old-fashioned form of licensing still exists, you could certainly expand your horizons that give credence and consideration to the new user CALs that are discussed next.

One final point on device CALs. The device CALs are assigned to a specific device. So Computer#1 has a specific device CAL assigned to it. So does Computer#9 in the organization. Once a device CAL is assigned to a specific computer (or other computational device), that CAL can't be rotated to another device in a round robin fashion.

User CALs

Okay—time to introduce user CALs, the new client-side licensing paradigm revealed in the SBS 2003 timeframe. User CALs are assigned to a user, and this user can utilize any number of devices on the SBS 2003 network. For example, a software development firm might have 50 employees and each employee has three computers and a SmartPhone (which is a "device" when remotely connected to the SBS 2003 network). So it behooves a software development company that has a high ratio of devices to users to utilize user CALs. In this example, the software development firm would need a user CAL for each of its 50 employees (50 in all), even though the total number of devices used by these employees may be significantly greater than 50.

Now allow me the privilege of weaving this user CAL discussion into the Alaskan fishing company scenario (which, of course, is not in the software development business as per the paragraph above). Suppose that the Alaskan fishing company has 10 executives who have desktop PCs at work, PCs at home, and laptops for mobility purposes while traveling. This suggests three devices per executive, on average. On the one hand, the Alaskan fishing company could make sure that they purchased three device CALs per executive to remain "legal," for a total of 30 device CALs. But that, of course, would be economically inefficient and financially silly. Rather, the Alaskan fishing company should purchase ten user CALs for the ten executives. But what about other employees of the company who need to use a computer?

Mix and Match

To meet the needs of all employees of the Alaskan fishing company, the company could mix and match SBS 2003 CALs, for a total of ten user CALs and 20 device CALs. There are still 30 CALs in total, but the CAL composition now appears different than originally presented. Now the ten executives laden with multiple devices could compute away with impunity and not fear a visit from the SBS software police, and other employees would have appropriate access to the company's other network devices. You get the point.

BEST PRACTICE: Mixing and matching SBS 2003 device and user CALs is akin to the linear programming problems you solved in the quantitative sciences series (the ole "quant" series) you completed in your University education. You'll recall that linear programming is all about optimal resource allocation decisions. CALs are a resource and should be efficiently allocated. Some users can benefit from user CALs, given the nature of their work habits, etc. Other users are better off with device CALs. Ideally, you'll minimize licensing costs while obtaining the optimal mix of CALs, given your employees' device usage patterns.

In Figure 3-2, observe the probable mix and match scenario for the Alaskan fishing company.

Figure 3-2
Mix and match time, baby!

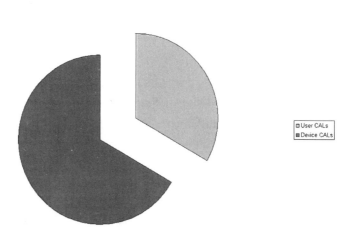

Alaskan Fishing Company CAL Allocation

□ User CALs
■ Device CALs

BEST PRACTICE: User CALs make great sense when the number of devices exceeds the number of users. In contrast, device CALs make the most sense when the number of users exceeds the number of devices.

Specific User CAL Assignments

Slow down just a second, my fellow Microsoft partner! What about the user CAL point that surfaced earlier, about a CAL being assigned to a specific user? Is that to say something like user CAL number seven is assigned to Barry Jones, the CEO of the Alaskan fishing company? Yes it is! User CALs are assigned to a specific person. You would be wrong to assume that you could purchase a handful of user CALs and then let ANY EMPLOYEE pluck user CALs from the licensing pool when needed (such as when traveling and remotely accessing the SBS 2003 network). It doesn't work that way. *User CALs are not allocated in a round robin fashion, mate!*

> BEST PRACTICE: Here's another simple rule of thumb you can employ in the madness surrounding purchasing the proper licenses: any user who will utilize Remote Web Workplace (RWW) to access their desktop computer back at work will need a user CAL. That is because the external PC being used to access the SBS 2003 network is considered an external device and the internal PC is also considered a device. Granted—you could purchase two device CALs, but that would be unnecessarily expensive.

However, and read closely, there is a situation where a user accessing the SBS 2003 network via RWW could use a device CAL. That would occur when the device is the user's laptop that she takes with her (the device CAL would be assigned to the laptop) and the user <u>does not</u> access another computer on the internal SBS 2003 network (e.g., she only accesses the RWW interface).

Alaskan Fishing Company—Frequently Asked Questions

Running around the world and delivering my SMB Nation Summit workshops is a great way for me to gather feedback that I can reuse in future lectures and even book chapters! So, in the past when I've told this story in lecture, I'm often peppered with questions such as the following:

- **Why not just purchase a user CAL for every employee of the Alaskan fishing company and be done with it?** The answer is that SBS

2003 has a 75 CAL limit. Beyond that, the company would need to migrate to the full Microsoft server products.

- **What if a fisherman on a boat wants to access the network from the boat via satellite and has a bona fide CAL (e.g., a device CAL for the one PC on the boat)?** This would be legal as this example stands. However, the cost of satellite time makes this infeasible.

- **Suppose a fisherman only wants to access Outlook Web Access (OWA) from an Internet Café in Dutch Harbor, Alaska. He doesn't need a CAL for this form of access, right?** Wrong! The use of OWA requires network authentication, and this requires a CAL.

BEST PRACTICE: Now would be a great time to review Microsoft's baseline CAL discussion at http://www.microsoft.com/windowsserver 2003/sbs/howtobuy/CALs.mspx. I want to make sure you're adequately equipped to proceed with this chapter and the Alaskan fishing company example as it gets more complex.

Initial Licensing State

Microsoft's more recent SBS 2003 brochures have improved greatly since their earlier counterparts were published. The one-page product sheet now clearly describes the initial licensing state and how more licenses can be purchased. I suspect this document has evolved over time to reflect the cumulative feedback from partners. So, here are da' facts related to the Alaskan fishing company scenario. Kindly note the yet-again modified storyline that forces you to comprehend this increasingly complex example.

Changing Tides

I want to throw a twist in the story just to make sure I've got your attention. The Alaskan fishing company has now determined that there are really only five executives who travel. And after a hissy-fit and much fuss that bombarded the SBS computer consultant from the rough-and-tough fishermen with biceps like Popeye (a popular fictional cartoon character in the Western world), another

PC was purchased for the lunchroom to provide common Internet access. So the question is, what type(s) of CALs should be purchased and in what quantities?

The answer, of course, starts simple and grows increasingly complex. If you've correctly followed the original scenario plus the modified details, you would quickly conclude that the SBS 2003 network at the Alaskan fishing company needs 31 CALs. And you'd likely propose the following license allocation:

- **User CALs**—The company needs five user CALs for the five traveling executives.

- **Device CALs**—The company needs 26 device CALs for the other computer devises in use at the company's office and on its fishing boats.

Okay. So far you are correct. However, it is not possible to get just 31 CALs because cumulative CAL counts must be divisible by the following numbers: 5 or 20. Why? Because CALs are sold in packs of 5 or 20, as illustrated in Figure 3-3. In a moment I'll make the finer distinction between the user and device CAL SKUs (product identification number).

Figure 3-3

CDW is a popular distributor for SBSers to patronize!

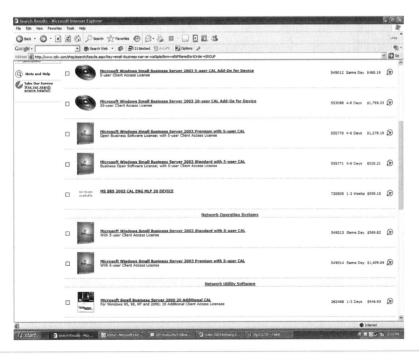

Visit www.microsoft.com/technet for the latest updates for any Microsoft product.

> BEST PRACTICE: Consider other popular distributors as well to both sell and help you manage your licensing. Softwareone.com is a resource that allows you to "outsource" your licensing activities.

Knowing what you now know, how would you make the proper and prudent CAL purchase for the Alaskan fishing company? The best you could do is purchase 35 CALs, and I would suggest the following combination: 30 device CALs and 5 user CALs. In the next section, I'll discuss the possibility of changing needs and licensing requirements. But for now, assume you agree and you've made this purchase.

An interesting digression and SBS licensing factoid bears mention here. If we were dealing with the "other SBS" from Provo Utah (that is Novell's Small Business Suite product), we'd be in a better position with respect to purchasing 31 CALs. The "other SBS" allows licenses to be purchased individually. Personally, I wish Microsoft would adopt this practice of single CAL purchases.

Modified Licensing State

So what if things change at ye' olde' Alaskan fishing company, mates? What if three additional white collar executives show their true colors as bona fide road warriors and are out pounding to pavement as high class fish mongers? Is the SBS 2003 licensing framework flexible enough to accommodate such organizational changes? I submit that the answer is yes. Here's why.

Universal CALs

When you purchase SBS 2003, either premium or standard edition, five CALs are included in the purchase price. The first five CALs that are included with the initial SBS product purchase are called universal CALs and can be assigned as either user, device CALs or a combination of both. The choice is yours.

Additional and Future CAL Purchases

A growing customer such as the Alaskan fishing company would likely be required to purchase additional CALs so that its SBS 2003 network functions legally. You can purchase either the device or user CALs in the quantities you deem necessary (as long as that number is in multiples of 5 or 20!). Here are the

SKU numbers as of January 2005 to help you understand the world of SBS licensing from the nuts and bolts viewpoint (Figure 3-4).

Figure 3-4

Note closely the CAL SKU numbers. These SKU numbers change depending on the licensing program (Retail/Full Packaged Product, Open, Open/ Software Assurance).

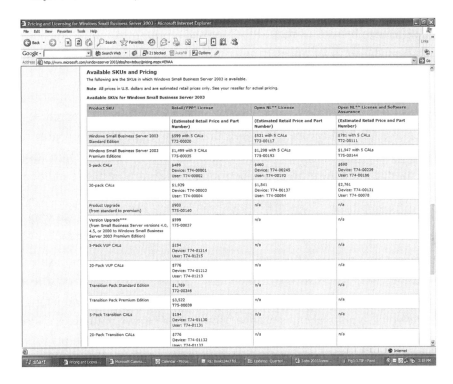

An interesting tidbit to know is that the underlying "bits" associated with the CALs are the same regardless of whether you elect device or user CAL status. In reality, when you purchase additional CALs, you receive an activation code, which you enter into SBS. Only after you've entered this code will your CAL count increase.

So, assume the Alaska fishing company made the following CAL purchases:

- **Five user CALs**—I suggest that these be allocated from the five universal CALs included in the SBS 2003 product itself, which would be the T75-00035 SKU from Figure 3-4. This assumes the Alaskan fishing company purchased SBS 2003 premium edition at the retail level.

- **Device CALs**—These would be purchased as three items. First, you would purchase one 20-device CAL SKU at the Retail/FPP level (T74-00003). Second, you would purchase two copies of the five-user device CAL product (T74-00001).

The above purchase order should add up to 35 CALs, which supports the 31 users/devices in the Alaskan fishing company.

The difference between Retail/FPP, Open and Open/Software Assurance will be discussed later in the chapter.

Switch-a-Roo

As stated above, the first five CALs included with your SBS 2003 purchase are universal CALs and can be either user or device CALs. That's probably real clear. However, with Software Assurance (discussed near the end of this chapter), there exists a one-time provision to perform a switch-a-roo with the additional, incremental CALs when you re-subscribe to Software Assurance. . It appears you could change from device to user or user to device. But you can only do this once under Software Assurance when you renew your agreement.

But what about the rest of us with respect to the CAL switch-a-roo. Note the guidance from Microsoft is mixed here. At http://www.microsoft.com/WindowsServer2003/sbs/techinfo/overview/licensingfaq.mspx, the language reports you can not make this change. However, at http://www.microsoft.com/windowsserver2003/sbs/howtobuy/CALs.mspx, the langugage reports that you can make this change. Monitor the book erratta at www.smbnation.com for an update on this subject as changes are made to the CAL licensing program. This is a kind way of saying that, as of this writing, we don't have an exact answer yet!

You're Fired!

Moving forward, imagine a business malady has struck the Alaskan fishing company. It seems the Chief Financial Officer (CFO) who is an executive with a user CAL and the bookkeeper (who used a device CAL) were embezzling funds. They were conspiring and sneaking cash out of the business in the belly of fish carcasses. The security guards didn't catch them for months.

Once these culprits were found out and terminated, an interesting issue was raised. How are the CALs handled? I've already told you that the user CAL is assigned to a specific individual and can't be allocated in a round-robin fashion. Device CALs are assigned to a specific device in a similar manner. So the answer is this: it shouldn't matter! The CALs are effectively reassigned under this termination scenario. The new CFO and bookkeeper can simply assume these CALs and proceed with using the SBS 2003 network. See page 3-23 for more.

Enforcement!

So how are the CALs actually enforced? Simple. CALs are enforced by authentication which can be users, devices and some processes. Such is the state of licensing in the SBS 2003 timeframe.

Microsoft Licensing FAQs

This is an interesting section. Most of the content in this section is taken from Microsoft's Web site regarding licensing questions, found at http://www.microsoft.com/WindowsServer2003/sbs/techinfo/overview/licensingfaq.mspx. But this isn't simply a "reprint" or copy-and-paste operation to fill pages in a chapter. Nope. In most cases, I add context to specific question and in the process, I hope to add value for you in understanding the madness surrounding SBS 2003 licensing.

Here's an interesting historical note regarding this FAQ Web page. In the fall of 2003, I participated as one of the USA hands-on lab instructors for the SBS 2003 road show. We were peppered with licensing questions in city after city. We consistently fed those answers back to the SBS marketing and development team in Redmond, and that resulted in much of the content on the licensing FAQ page that is explored below!

This section is divided into the following two discussions:

- General Licensing

- Transition Pack Licensing. This relates to the "transition pack" used when a company exceeds 75 CALs and needs to migrate to the full Microsoft server products.

General Licensing

Q. What is the difference between a Windows Small Business Server 2003 license and a Windows Small Business Server 2003 client access license (CAL)? Why do I need both?

A. The Windows Small Business Server 2003 license gives you the right to install and use the server software. The Windows Small Business Server 2003 CAL gives you the right to have a device or user access the server software.

Harry's Viewpoint: This is an important distinction between the server application license and the client license. A server license relates to the legal mumbo jumbo associated with the actual server-based operating system or program running on the server machine. The client-side CAL relates to a user having the legal right to access the server from the network. The importance of this specific dialog is that you must purchase CALs above and beyond the server-side application and operating system.

Q. Are my CALs for Small Business Server 2000 still valid after I upgrade to Windows Small Business Server 2003?

A. If you purchased Software Assurance for your Small Business Server 2000 CALs, then you will receive free upgrades to Windows Small Business Server 2003 CALs. If you did not purchase Software Assurance, you must purchase new CALs when you upgrade to Windows Small Business Server 2003.

Harry's Viewpoint: Software Assurance is discussed later in this chapter. The rest of us must purchase CALs (either new or upgrade CALs).

Q. How can I obtain CALs for Small Business Server 2000 or previous versions of the product now that Small Business Server 2000 CALs have been discontinued?

A. You will need to purchase Windows Small Business Server 2003 CALs, apply your downgrade rights, and then contact your reseller to order fulfillment media at a nominal fee. You need to order the fulfillment media separately since Windows Small Business Server 2003 CAL packs do not contain the floppy disk that is necessary to deploy licenses on Small Business Server 2000. The Small Business Server 2000 floppy disk also works with previous versions of Small Business Server.

Harry's Viewpoint: I distinctly remember this question. The context was an SBSer who had a client who was not yet ready to upgrade to SBS 2003 but needed more SBS 2000 CALs.

Q. Are Windows Small Business Server 2003 CALs (whether per user or per device) by concurrent connections?

A. No, CALs are per user or per device. They are not concurrent.

Harry's Viewpoint: You can never use the word "concurrent" in the context of SBS 2003 licensing. This means the CALs are assigned to a specific user or a specific device. This point is the result of my being misquoted in one of Brian Livingston's popular Windows columns (www.briansbuzz.com). I was quickly corrected by Microsoft's PR agency, Wagner Edstrom, and I've since removed the word "concurrent" from my vocabulary.

Q. I purchased Software Assurance for my Small Business Server 2000 installation and CALs. Am I eligible to receive Windows Small Business Server 2003 Premium Edition?

A. Yes. If you purchased Small Business Server 2000 Software Assurance, you are eligible to receive an upgrade copy of Windows Small Business Server 2003 Premium Edition. If you purchased Software Assurance through a reseller or computer manufacturer, contact the media fulfillment center at 800/248-0655 to order your upgrade. For more information about Software Assurance, contact your reseller or see the Microsoft Web site.

Harry's Viewpoint: This clearly supports the case for Software Assurance. See further discussion later in the chapter.

Q. Does the price of Windows Small Business Server 2003 CALs vary depending on whether I buy the standard edition or the premium edition? What is the price for CALs?

A. CALs cost the same for the standard edition and the premium edition of Windows Small Business Server 2003. For more information about the offerings of both editions of Windows Small Business Server 2003, see Pricing and Licensing for Windows Small Business Server 2003.

Harry's Viewpoint: This topic came up numerous times in the seminars and workshops. It seems there is a case of economic injustice here because the SBS 2003 standard edition contains less server-side functionality then the

SBS 2003 premium edition (premium contains SQL Server 2000, ISA 2000/ 2004, and FrontPage 2003). YET THE CALs COST EXACTLY THE SAME. WHAT GIVES WITH THAT?!?!? (Yes—I'm yelling for effect).

Q. Does Windows Small Business Server 2003 use floppy disks to activate new CALs, like previous versions did?

A. Windows Small Business Server 2003 does not use floppy disks to distribute or install CALs. CALs are now activated over the Internet using unique activation codes, similar to how Terminal Services CALs are purchased and installed. As an alternative, you can call a local telephone number to activate CALs.

Harry's Viewpoint: Microsoft eliminated the licensing diskette, which I consider a positive step. It eliminates the pain-in-the-ass step of remembering the order you applied the CAL diskettes in SBS 2000 and earlier time frames. See an article I wrote on the old SBS 2000 CAL diskettes in one of my early newsletters at: http://www.smbnation.com/newsletter/Issue1-9.htm (go to the bottom of the newsletter). There is also a Microsoft KBase article on SBS 2000 licensing diskette installation order (Q247944).

Q. My server does not have a connection to the Internet. How can I activate the CALs that I purchased?

A. Run the Windows Small Business Server 2003 Add Licenses Wizard, and choose to activate your CALs by calling a local telephone number.

Harry's Viewpoint: Given that most of SBS's sales are to non-USA (overseas) countries and SBS's best future prospects are in emerging countries, this is an important FAQ! Of course, as SBS-MVP and contributing author Susan Bradley correctly pointed out, you're missing out on the "cool stuff" in SBS 2003 without an Internet connection.

Q. What is the difference between a device CAL and a user CAL?

A. A device CAL permits one device (used by any user) to access the server software. A user CAL permits one user (using any device) to access the server software.

Harry's Viewpoint: This is an excellent explanation. Note that a user CAL will apply to a specific user and a device CAL applies to a specific device.

Q. Why is Microsoft offering both user CALs and device CALs for Windows Small Business Server 2003?

A. Microsoft offers both user and device CALs for Windows Small Business Server 2003 to ensure that customers can implement a licensing plan that enables users to access the network using not only laptops and desktop computers, but also remote devices such as Pocket PCs and SmartPhones.

Harry's Viewpoint: This topic was discussed earlier in the chapter, but note that remote devices such as Pocket PCs and SmartPhones are mentioned here. That is very important to understand!

Q. Can I use a device CAL and a user CAL on the same server?

A. Yes, device and user CALs can both be used on the same server. But for easier managing and tracking, we strongly recommend that you buy either user CALs or device CALs, not both.

Harry's Viewpoint: This is the mix-and-match discussion that was presented earlier in the chapter. I don't know why Microsoft states you should buy one form of CAL or the other but not both! Rumor has it Microsoft is viewing this from a simple logistics point of view.

Q. Is there a difference in price between user CALs and device CALs?

A. No, user CALs and device CALs cost the same.

Harry's Viewpoint: Enough said!

Q. Can I switch between user CALs and device CALs?

A. If you have Software Assurance for your Windows Small Business Server 2003 CALs, you can switch between user CALs and device CALs, or vice versa, when you renew your Software Assurance contract. If you do not have Software Assurance for your Windows Small Business Server 2003 CALs, then you cannot switch.

Harry's Viewpoint: See the earlier discussion about the Alaskan fishing company and its CAL switching.

Q. How many Windows Small Business Server 2003 CALs are needed when using Terminal Server in application sharing mode?

A. Adding a second server (Terminal Server in application sharing mode) does not alter the Windows Small Business Server 2003 CAL requirements. You will need a Windows Small Business Server 2003 CAL for each user or device that authenticates on the Windows Small Business Server 2003 network. We specifically prohibit multiplexing as a means of reducing the CAL requirement. In addition, you will also need Terminal Server CALs for each Terminal Server user. For more information on Terminal Server licensing, see Licensing Terminal Server in Windows Server 2003.

Harry's Viewpoint: This Q and A on Terminal Services (TS) is well presented. Note that the context is TS running on a second server (I highly recommend a member server). It is not possible for TS to run in application sharing mode on the SBS 2003 server machine. More TS issues are discussed later in this chapter.

> BEST PRACTICE: Remember that TS CALs are TOTALLY separate from any prior SBS CAL discussion and if you owned a copy of Windows XP prior to April 23, 2003, you are grandfathered TS CALs and do not need to purchase additional TS CALs for those specific computers. Note that April 23, 2003 was the release date of Windows Server 2003 in San Francisco, California.

Q. Does Windows Small Business Server 2003 provide a mechanism to track and display how many user or device CALs are in use?

A. Windows Small Business Server 2003 does not provide a mechanism to track or display CALs. We strongly suggest, however, that you choose one CAL type (user/device) for your Windows Small Business Server 2003 installation. Windows Small Business Server 2003 will display only the number of CALs that have been activated.

Harry's Viewpoint: This is a major disappointment in SBS 2003 and I discuss this more in the More Microsoft-centric Licensing Topics section later in the chapter. You're asked to comply with fairly rigorous licensing terms and conditions yet not given the best tools to do so!

Q. Can I upgrade or migrate from Small Business Server 2000 to Windows Small Business Server 2003 Standard edition and still use Microsoft SQL Server and/or Microsoft ISA Server?

A. Windows Small Business Server 2003 is built, sold, and licensed as an integrated server platform. Customers who purchase a new license for Windows Small Business Server 2003 Standard Edition are only licensed for the server applications that come as part of that edition. If you install that over the top of a Small Business Server 2000 installation, you will not be licensed to use either SQL Server 2000 or ISA Server 2000. Windows Small Business Server 2003 has a version upgrade SKU T75-00037 that is priced at $599 US to specifically address this scenario.

Harry's Viewpoint: I agree with Microsoft on this one. The whole idea between the two versions of SBS 2003 was to give the customer more choices in selecting the right fit. It seems appropriate to me that users shouldn't be able to bring forward SQL Server 2000 or ISA Server 2000 and pull a fast one by running it on the standard edition of SBS 2003. Nadda! By the way, there isn't explicit blocking code in SBS 2003 standard edition that would prevent you from bringing forward SQL Server 2000 and ISA Server 2000 from the SBS 2000 timeframe, but to do so would be illegal! Note the last sentence above about the upgrade SKU (which is a good thing!). And in the real world, it would be insane, at the insanely low upgrade price, not to go from SBS 2000 to SBS 2003 premium edition.

Q. I have noticed that the Server Management console shows the maximum usage number in the licensing section. Why?

A. Windows Small Business Server 2003 shows a rough indicator of the maximum usage since the system was last restarted. This is intended as a simple indicator that allows you to evaluate if further CALs are required.

Harry's Viewpoint: This is the high water mark indicator and I'll be flat out honest with you: it's not that useful.

Q. Are the five CALs that came with the server license per device or per user?

A. For these first five CALs you get to choose. At the top of the CAL End User License Agreement (EULA) in the retail packaging, you can choose to allocate these CALs (up to a maximum of five) to either user or device. Again, we strongly recommend that you choose one type for your Windows Small Business Server 2003 installation.

Harry's Viewpoint: This confirms my discussion earlier in the chapter, but Microsoft's recommendation for selecting just one type of CAL class for the total licensing scenario is bogus.

Q. Do I need a CAL for Outlook Web Access or Remote Web Workplace?

A. Regardless of how you connect to the Windows Small Business Server 2003-based server, you need either device CALs or user CALs. If you have chosen device CALs, then your use of Outlook Web Access or Remote Web Workplace will consume a CAL.

Harry's Viewpoint: This is an excellent point. The use of OWA or RWW requires a CAL!

Q. When I buy a 20-CAL pack, can I split it into 16 per users and 4 per device CALs?

A. There are separate device CAL packs and user CAL packs. You choose at purchase time. Please see Pricing and Licensing for Windows Small Business Server 2003.

Harry's Viewpoint: Microsoft's answer is mildly confusing but basically you wouldn't be able to create this division from a 20-CAL pack.

Q. Which mode do I select for licensing?

A. You choose the mode when you purchase additional CALs and when you install the server for the first 5 CALs.

Harry's Viewpoint: This election for additional CALs is made by virtue of selecting the CAL SKU to purchase.

Q. How do I know which mode I have selected?

A. For the first 5 CALs that come with the server, you should complete the CAL license document. There is a field for writing in whether you would like to choose per user or per device CALs. For CAL add-on packs there are separate SKUs for per user and per device.

Harry's Viewpoint: This is lame! The above statement is telling you that your universal CAL election is made with handwriting on a piece of paper, not via an elegant licensing management tool. Arrggg...

Q. How does multiplexing affect licensing?

A. Multiplexing does not reduce the number of CALs required for Windows Small Business Server 2003. For example, using a Terminal Server-based server does not reduce the number of Windows Small Business Server 2003 CALs required.

Harry's Viewpoint: This is true because your SBS 2003 network authentication, even before you utilize TS, would require an SBS 2003 CAL.

Q. How do I know I am in compliance?

A. You will need to maintain records of what you have purchased, and how you have assigned the first 5 CALs that come with the server. Windows Small Business Server 2003 does not provide an automated way to track CAL use.

Harry's Viewpoint: This about says it all. No licensing management tool is provided inside SBS 2003 and the burden is placed on you to keep track of your own CALs and associated compliance.

Q. How do I buy licenses for Windows Small Business Server 2003?

A. For pricing and licensing information, see Pricing and Licensing for Windows Small Business Server 2003 at the Microsoft Web site.

Harry's Viewpoint: The Server Management console, shown in Figure 3-5, also allows you to learn about purchasing additional CALs from prized vendors. However, I still find Manage Client Access Licenses to be a lame tool.

Figure 3-5

Information about licensing can be found here. See the Purchasing Licenses link for information about purchasing additional CALs.

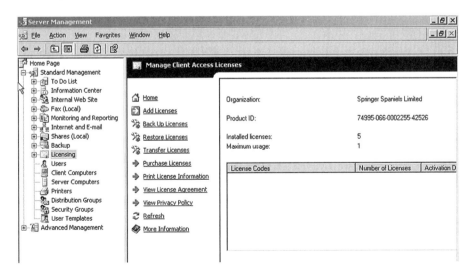

Q. How do I add licenses for Windows Small Business Server 2003?

A. After you have obtained your CAL add-on packs, you use the Server Management console to enter the product key that ships with the CAL pack.

Harry's Viewpoint: This is very easy to do. Have fun!

Q. Can I apply the CALs on multiple servers?

A. The product key that ships with the CAL pack can only be used with one server.

Harry's Viewpoint: This makes sense. SBS's fundamental design paradigm, in its heart of hearts, is a single server and this is consistent with that sentiment that SBS CALs would only apply to a single SBS server. Additional SBS servers on other separate domains would require additional unique CALs.

Q. I want to have additional Windows-based servers in my Windows Small Business Server 2003 domain. Do I need CALs for those servers?

A. Your Windows Small Business Server 2003 CALs cover you for any additional Windows-based servers in the domain. You do not need to buy additional CALs for them.

Harry's Viewpoint: This is a KEY POINT. The SBS CALs act as CALs for the underlying network operating system (NOS) when additional Windows servers are introduced. This is a good thing!

Q. Does the Windows Small Business Server 2003 CAL allow me to access other Exchange or SQL servers on the network?

A. The Windows Small Business Server 2003 CAL only covers you for the single Windows Small Business Server server machine and any additional Windows Server System servers. Additional CALs will be required for Exchange, terminal server, or SQL servers in the network.

Harry's Viewpoint: This is correct. If you want to add more Microsoft server applications on additional servers, you would need new application-level CALs for those servers. I liken this to an example I use in lecture. If you wanted to add an Oracle database application on a member server, do you really think your SBS 2003 CAL would cover that licensing requirement? Nope!

Q. Do accounts such as the administrator account and service accounts need a CAL?

A. If you choose per user CALs and then install third-party applications that create accounts, you will need a single CAL for each.

Harry's Viewpoint: This is a little known factoid about SBS 2003 licensing and very important to know! Susan Bradley notes that mileage may vary here and she has not seen any of her applications consume a CAL on an SBS 2003 network.

Q. Is each per user license tied to a specific user?

A. If you choose per user CALs, then each Windows Small Business Server 2003 user will consume a CAL, and that CAL is tied to that specific user. You can re-allocate a user CAL if that reassignment is permanent. You can also temporarily re-assign it if the user or device is disabled or on leave.

Harry's Viewpoint: Point made and case closed. This mirrors the example of the fired CFO and bookkeeper with the Alaskan fishing company.

Q. Is each per device license tied to a specific device?

A. If you choose device CALs, then each device that accesses the Windows Small Business Server 2003 server will consume a CAL. You can re-allocate that CAL if you retire a device.

Harry's Viewpoint: This reiterates the earlier point in this chapter that a device CAL is tied to a specific device.

Q. If I have selected to be licensed in one mode for Windows Small Business Server 2003, am I then restricted to that mode for member servers as well?

A. Yes, your choice of licensing mode applies to any member servers within the Windows Small Business Server 2003 domain.

Harry's Viewpoint: Betcha didn't know this one. A strange but true fact of SBS 2003 licensing. SBS 2003 supports per user/per device mode and the other member servers must honor that fact. And the official Microsoft documentation says to use per user or device to ensure that you don't have errors in your log files such as error 202 in the event logs.

Q. Can I use the SQL Server component for Web-based business applications?

A. Yes, new with Windows Small Business Server 2003 is the ability for you to use the SQL Server component for an unlimited number of un-authenticated users. As long as you are un-authenticated, you also do not need a Windows Small Business Server 2003 CAL.

Harry's Viewpoint: This is a common question regarding e-commerce functions using SQL Server 2000 in an SBS 2003 environment. Take heed. Also note that we have friendlier SQL Server 2000 licensing terms and conditions than the standalone SQL Sever 2000 product.

Q. If I bought Windows Small Business Server 2003 from an OEM, where do I go to get additional CALs?

A. You can purchase additional CALs from any sales channel you prefer (retail, open, OEM) and use those CALs with a server purchased through the OEMs. You can also get additional CALs through some OEMs. Contact your OEM for more information on your CAL purchase options.

Harry's Viewpoint: This is another common question. If you purchased an HP server, you could purchase your additional CALs from HP.

Q. Does Windows Small Business Server 2003 Standard Edition have downgrade rights in volume licensing?

A. No, only Windows Small Business Server 2003 Premium Edition can be downgraded to Small Business Server 2000.

Harry's Viewpoint: This is a somewhat academic discussion because you wouldn't want to revert back to SBS 2000 unless you had a line of business application that was incompatible with SBS 2003, eh?

Q. Does my company qualify for Live Communication Server 2003 licenses as part of our Small Business Server Software Assurance purchase?

A. If your company is licensed for Small Business Server (server license and CALs) with Software Assurance on a product that was signed and valid as of October 1, 2003, then you are entitled to an equivalent number of Live Communications Server 2003 CALs and/or server licenses at a nominal media fulfillment fee. Contact your Microsoft reseller for more details about how to take advantage of this offer.

Harry's Viewpoint: This speaks towards the restoration of the Instant Messaging function found in SBS 2000 as part of Exchange 2000 Server BUT which was removed in SBS 2003 when Exchange Server 2003 eliminated IM functionality. This is a peace offering from Microsoft. Also note that once you get the LCS, you are welcome to install it on any server in the SBS 2003 network (e.g. a member server). It doesn't have to be installed on just the SBS 2003 server machine.

Transition Pack Licensing

Q. What is the Windows Small Business Server 2003 Transition Pack?

A. The Windows Small Business Server 2003 Transition Pack provides a way for customers to grow out of Windows Small Business Server 2003 into the standard line of server products. The transition pack contains both technology and licensing components.

Harry's Viewpoint: Enough said.

Q. Why would I buy the Windows Small Business Server 2003 Transition Pack?

A. You would purchase the transition pack for the following reasons:

- You need more than 75 users or devices.

- You want to separate the Windows Small Business Server components (for example, Windows Server 2003, Exchange Server 2003, or SQL Server) onto separate server machines.

- You want features available only in the enterprise editions of Windows Server System, such as SQL Server 2000 Enterprise Edition or Exchange Server 2003 Enterprise Edition.

Harry's Viewpoint: This above list succinctly outlines why you would want to upgrade to the full Microsoft server products from SBS 2003. Note that you lose some SBS-specific functionality such as the ability to use Remote Web Workplace or some of the SBS wizards.

Q. How much does the Windows Small Business Server 2003 Transition Pack cost?

A. It depends on which version of Windows Small Business Server 2003 you have, and how many Windows Small Business Server 2003 CALs you are licensed for. The transition pack includes several SKUs, one for each edition of Windows Small Business Server 2003 (standard or premium), and transition

CALs to transition the number of Windows Small Business Server CALs for which you are licensed. The pricing has been designed so that you are not penalized for starting with Windows Small Business Server 2003. For example, the pricing for the Windows Small Business Server 2003 Standard Edition Transition Pack is $1,769 US. For each of the transition pack SKUs, this is calculated based on the cost of what you transition to, minus what you have paid for Windows Small Business Server licenses.

Harry's Viewpoint: What the above discussion avoids stating is that, after you purchase the transition pack, you are "rolled back" to five CALs regardless of the number of SBS 2003 CALs you previously purchased (e.g., 35 SBS 2003 CALs). You would then need to purchase all new transition CALs. This is illustrated in Figure 3-6, which shows the transition pack and its associated CALs.

Figure 3-6

Note the distinction here between the transition pack and the transition pack CALs.

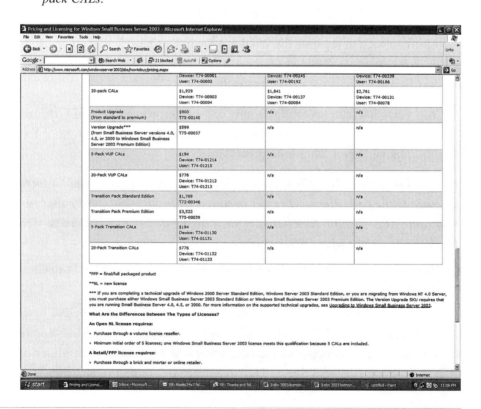

Q. How can I purchase the Windows Small Business Server 2003 Transition Pack?

A. See Pricing and Licensing for Windows Small Business Server 2003.

Harry's Viewpoint: This is at www.microsoft.com/sbs.

Q. From a technical standpoint what does the Windows Small Business Server 2003 Transition Pack do?

A. The server transition pack removes all of the Windows Small Business Server 2003 limits (such as 75 CALs, no Active Directory trusts, and CAL enforcement). The CAL transition packs are a license only.

Harry's Viewpoint: This makes the point that the transition pack has both an economic relationship (a financial path to upgrade to full Microsoft server applications) and a technical relationship to SBS 2003.

Q. From a licensing standpoint what does the Windows Small Business Server 2003 Transition Pack do?

A. From a licensing perspective, the transition pack converts your Windows Small Business Server licenses into standard licenses for the server components in the edition of Windows Small Business Server you have (standard or premium). For example if you had previously purchased Windows Small Business Server 2003 Standard Edition with one pack of 20 additional CALs, the transition pack SKUs would convert your licenses to 1 Windows Server 2003 Standard Edition license and 1 Exchange Server 2003 Standard Edition license, with 20 Windows Server 2003 CALs and 20 Exchange Server 2003 CALs, respectively.

Note: CAL packs only include Windows Server 2003 CALs and Exchange Server 2003 CALs, regardless of whether you purchase the premium or standard editions. The Premium Transition Pack, however, includes standalone licenses for SQL Server.

Harry's Viewpoint: This discussion isn't clearly stating that you would need to purchase 20 transition CALs in order for this scenario to work.

Q. What do I have after I have purchased and installed the Windows Small Business Server 2003 Transition Pack?

A. After you have purchased the transition pack SKUs, you are licensed for the standard versions of the Windows Server System products. For example, if you purchased the standard edition of the transition pack, you will have Windows Server 2003 and Exchange Server 2003. If you purchased the premium edition of the transition pack, you will have Windows Server 2003, Exchange Server 2003, ISA 2000 Server, and SQL Server 2000.

Note: CAL packs only include Windows Server 2003 CALs and Exchange Server 2003 CALs, regardless of whether you purchase the premium or standard editions. The Premium Transition Pack, however, includes standalone licenses for SQL Server.

Harry's Viewpoint: This is good discussion clarifying product content in the transition pack.

Q. How do I install the transition pack?

A. For the server transition pack SKU, simply run the Setup program from CD 1 on your Windows Small Business Server server machine.

Harry's Viewpoint: You perform something akin to a "mock install" for the transition pack to complete its duties.

Q. Does the transition pack move any of the server components to another physical server?

A. No, the transition pack simply removes the Windows Small Business Server 2003 limits and converts your licenses.

Harry's Viewpoint: While the above statement is true, you are allowed to install the server applications on other server machines. This is a key point because it is the transition pack that allows you to depart from the "all applications on one server" mentality of SBS 2003. Note that you would need to acquire the "normal" media for the server products to effectively install said server applications on separate servers.

Q. Should a system failure occur, how do I reinstall one of the server components?

A. If you need to reinstall or move one of the server components and you do not already have a media kit, you should obtain one from your nearest reseller.

Harry's Viewpoint: This is a basic disaster recovery statement. See Chapter 14.

Q. After using the transition pack, can I continue to use the Windows Small Business Server wizards and tools?

A. Once the transition pack process is complete, the Windows Small Business Server wizards and tools are still available (however keep in mind that while they are still there as per http://seanda.blogspot.com/2005/01/what-happens-when-i-grow-past-75.html if you reinstall as you are not "going through SBS" you lose Remote Web Workplace and all other SBS wizards). You can continue to use the standard Microsoft Management Console (MMC)-based tools for your server administration needs until you reinstall Windows Small Business Server.

Harry's Viewpoint: This is a way to sneak cool SBS 2003 management functionality into a larger organization.

Q. Running Small Business Server 2000, how can I grow beyond 50 users now that the Small Business Server 2000 Migration Pack has been discontinued?

A. You will need to upgrade to Windows Small Business Server 2003. If you grow beyond 75 users, you also will need to purchase the Windows Small Business Server 2003 Transition Pack. The Small Business Server 2000 Migration Pack is no longer available.

Harry's Viewpoint: Enough said!

FAQ Conclusion

During February 2004, at the SMB Nation Summit in Melbourne, Australia, the entire workshop was disrupted by a licensing rebellion, where the attendees got distracted with this licensing topic. The Microsoft employee proceeded to walk the entire workshop through the above Licensing FAQs and an important discovery was made: the online Microsoft licensing FAQs for SBS are AWESOME and answered everyone's questions. Granted, some attendees didn't always agree with the answer, but an answer existed! Heck, there was even a motion on the floor that a workshop dedicated to SBS licensing be conducted at a future date. Hmmm......

More Microsoft-Centric Licensing Topics

This section is a buffet of SBS licensing factoids. Some of these facts are stranger then fiction. Let's start with a couple of points about the legacy SBS 2000 era to provide context and move on to the modern SBS 2003 release.

Honoring the SBS 2000 Legacy

There are some interesting licensing topics regarding SBS 2000 you might be interested in. Did you know that…

- SBS 2000 contained a licensing bumper of five CALs. That means an SBS 2000 server with 15 purchased CALs would actually authenticate 20 logons.

- SBS 2000's only serious "bug" in my humble opinion was the badly behaved License Logging Service when this product version was first released. Basically what happened was users weren't properly "logged out" at the end of a computing session and the SBS 2000 server effectively ran out of CALs. This was fully described in one of my early SBS newsletters at: http://www.smbnation.com/newsletter/Issue1-2.htm.

Moving Forward with SBS 2003

There are some interesting licensing quirks with SBS 2003 worth noting.

The Great Upgrade CAL Caper

SBS 2003 was released on October 9, 2003 in New Orleans. But somewhere in the madness, a licensing oversight occurred and the version upgrade CALs (VUP) weren't available until, by my estimation, early 2004. In fact, when I upgraded my real estate brokerage client in January 2004, I still couldn't purchase the VUP CALs. Because of the time sensitivity related to this client's upgrade, we had to proceed and purchase the much more expensive retail CALs. This beloved client effectively overpaid for its CALs even though it qualified for the VUP CAL edition. Ouch! And Microsoft had no way to refund the difference to this customer (e.g., turn in the retail CALs for the VUP CALs later). Double ouch!

Here are the VUP CALs that are now available:

5-Pack VUP CALs:
- Device: T74-01214

- User: T74-01215

20-Pack VUP CALs
- Device: T74-01212

- User: T74-01213

Canada and Terminal Services CALs

My January 2005 workshop in Toronto revealed an interest factoid. Apparently, 95 Canadian partners complained to the Microsoft Canada SBS partner manager about SBS 2003 not running TS in application sharing mode, which was a real hindrance for customers. The Microsoft Canada SBS manager remedied the situation by offering five free TS CALs for the affected customers, as seen in a Microsoft Canada slide deck in Figure 3-7.

Figure 3-7

It's good to be Canadian if you want to receive five free TS CALs. This is not a worldwide offer; it is only offered in Canada.

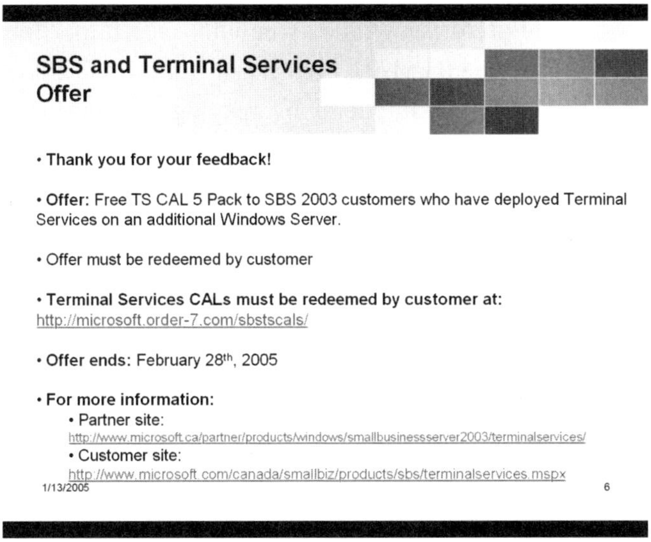

Granted, by the time you read this, the offer will have expired. But it's interesting nonetheless that the use of Terminal Services as a remote worker solution has so much traction in Canada.

> BEST PRACTICE: Refer to Chapter 8 in my Small Business Server 2000 Best Practices book for a generic Terminal Services licensing discussion that is still germane. And see Brian Livingston's series of articles on Terminal Services licensing at www.brianlivingston.com. Another great resource for TS licensing is Brian Madden's page: http://www.brianmadden.com/subject.asp?ID=25

And did I forget to say that running TS in application sharing mode on an SBS server is totally insane?!?!?

No Real Licensing Management Tool
When asked to contribute to the wish list of features to be included in a future SBS release, you probably will join me in asking for a real licensing management tool. There simply isn't a pretty Microsoft Management Console (MMC) snap-in or other tool to manage CALs and determine who or what is assigned which CAL. Please revisit Figure 3-5.

Implicitly Overpaying For Outlook 2003
Oliver Rist, a columnist for InfoWorld, raised an interesting argument in his November 7, 2003 Enterprise Windows column (see http://itproductguide beta.infoworld.com/article/03/11/07/44enterwin_1.html and Figure 3-8). He suggested that many folks are implicitly overpaying for their SBS CALs with respect to Outlook 2003. Why? Because many people acquire Outlook 2003 when they get Office 2003, such as when they buy a new PC with Office 2003 pre-installed or simply purchase Office 2003 directly. He's got a valid point and perhaps we need yet another CAL SKU sans Outlook 2003.

Notes:

Figure 3-8

Oliver Rist took a fresh look at SBS 2003 and surfaced an interesting licensing discussion!

External Facing Windows SharePoint Sites

At the Toronto SMB Nation Summit workshop in January 2005, a lively SBS licensing discussion was had during the afternoon discussion. Newly minted SBS MVP Jeff Loucks correctly schooled the attendees that an external facing Windows SharePoint Services (WSS) site would require a CAL for a user to access. The ramifications of this are significant. The reason for an external-facing WSS site is to work closely with customers, vendors, and the like. But can you imagine purchasing a CAL for each of these external parties? Nope!

A question was asked during a workshop as to whether this policy regarding licensing and an external WSS site would change? Perhaps in the future if you join me in providing vocal feedback to Microsoft at its TS2 events (www.msts2.com), hands-on labs, Partner events and other public forums!

Underselling SBS 2003

Something I want to make crystal clear in this chapter is that sometimes a misunderstanding about SBS licensing results in lost SBS opportunities for SBS consultants. If you didn't know better and didn't closely follow the Alaska fishing company example, you might not sell SBS into large companies (over 75 employees) when, in fact, SBS would fit just fine. Don't let employee head count discourage you from considering SBS for larger companies. That's where device licensing might help, just like it did for the Alaska fishing company!

The Ligman Lease

Nearly everyone agrees that SBS 2003 is awesome, myself included. But one of the hurdles many small businesses hit when trying to implement SBS 2003 is the lack of money to fund such an important technology implementation. Time after time you'll hear a customer comment that they love the idea of SBS 2003 but have no idea how to pay for it.

Enter Eric Ligman stage left! Eric is a fulltime Microsoft employee in the Chicago office who has really poured his heart and soul into the SBS community. He developed an impressive leasing solution using Microsoft's Open Value licensing program where a customer could get SBS 2003 premium, software assurance, BizTalk (Microsoft's electronic data interchange program), CRM 1.2 (as of this writing) at the five CAL level for under $100 USD per month or just over $3.00 USD per day (the price on a double latte coffee drink!). You can learn more on this specific money-saving opportunity to slide SBS 2003 into the small business via one of my old SBS newsletters at http://www.smbnation.com/newsletter/Issue3-9-june2004.htm (see the article about Eric Ligman near the bottom). Eric's excellent site should also be visited at www.mssmallbiz.com.

> BEST PRACTICE: The example above features Microsoft's Open Value licensing arrangement. Other SBSers have shared with me private sector SBS-based leasing arrangements that they have constructed with firms such as Studebaker Worthington, CITI and local banks (e.g. American Marine Bank). You are encouraged to find the right financial fit to introduce SBS in a small business.

No Mas! No Downgrade Scenario

When Microsoft ships a version of SBS, as you might imagine, it takes more work and effort than meets the eye. Imagine combining a buffet of "BackOffice" server applications, the underlying network operating system and some super duper SBS-specific tools and getting said bundle out the door in working form! You can appreciate that your SBS development team works hard as rapidly as possible to make this happen.

Now for the primary point of this section. SBS will never ever ship on the same day as the underlying operating system upgrade. Witness:

- The underlying Windows 2000 Server operating system shipped in February 2000 at a launch in San Francisco, California. SBS 2000 shipped in February 2001 at the Atlantic City, NJ launch site. This constituted a 12-month lag between the operating system release and the subsequent same-version SBS release.

- The underlying Windows Server 2003 product shipped in late April 2003 in San Francisco, California. SBS 2003 was released on October 9, 2003 in New Orleans at the Worldwide Partners Conference. And even then, you couldn't physically purchase SBS 2003 standard edition in the USA until late October 2003 (around Halloween). You couldn't really purchase SBS 2003 premium edition until late November 2003 (around Thanksgiving). This constituted a 6-month lag between the operating system release and the subsequent same-version SBS release.

The point is that, even under the best of circumstances, SBS will always lag the core operating system release date by about six months (even though internal goals at Microsoft would suggest that some day the lag time could be shortened to 90-days—dream on!).

So what happened with both SBS 2000 and SBS 2003 is that good small business citizens, seeking a modern network solution, either couldn't or wouldn't wait for the SBS release after the core operating system had been released. That is, these small businesses purchased during the "lag time" between operating system and subsequent SBS release. Ouch!

Imagine if you were one of these small businesses and you trotted out and purchased Windows Server 2003 in July 2003. Perhaps you didn't know that SBS 2003 was mere months away from shipping. Or perhaps you knew that but couldn't wait! Nonetheless, you purchased the underlying operating system when the SBS 2003 product would have been a better technology fit. Is there any recourse for you to obtain SBS 2003 at a reduced price or event free?

The answer is NO! Microsoft considers moving a customer from the underlying Windows Server 2003 product to SBS 2003 to be a downgrade scenario and that isn't supported. What? Is this some form of double-speak? Here is the reasoning for this. Windows Server 2003 is approximately $999 USD. SBS 2003 standard edition is $599 USD. The SBS solution is effectively cheaper than the original operating system purchase and would be a downgrade scenario. It is not supported (I'm just the message carrier here).

Moving forward, what if the small business customer proceeded to purchase the SBS 2003 product after purchasing the Windows Server 2003 product. What are the ramifications?

- The small business customer would need to purchase SBS 2003 without any pricing discounts.

- The small business customer would need to purchase SBS 2003 CALs without any pricing discount

- The small business customer might consider redeploying the Windows Server 2003 machine as a member server on the SBS 2003 network in order to continue to utilize that specific SKU. This might be a great use of a member server running Terminal Services in application sharing mode!

Software Assurance

Two of the true ladies of technology, Laura DiDio and Susan Bradley, have weighed in with their respective opinions on Microsoft's Software Assurance program. Laura DiDio from Yankee Group conducted a Software Assurance survey and wrote a report, which is summarized at http://www.eweek.com/article2/0,1759,1675761,00.asp and shown in Figure 3-9.

Figure 3-9

DiDio's study summarized here.

And Susan Bradley offered these insights for this chapter (Susan has written Chapter 11 for this book).

Notes:

Why is Software Assurance a good thing...
by Susan Bradley

Software assurance "locks" in flexibility. Small businesses need that flexibility.

Let's look what SA gave me on SBS 2000:

- I have Communication Server because of the SA I had on SBS 2000.

- I got the upgrade to SBS 2003 automatically.

- Now that I am on SBS 2003 Software Assurance, I can ensure that I will receive all updates to the SBS platform for the next three years.

- I have "cold server rights," meaning that I can install the OS on a spare system that sits in the corner "just in case."

- I get sent the media automatically.

- I can spread the payments over three years.

- My CAL codes are handled and kept on a site just in case something happens.

If I add SA to an OEM version of SBS, I then get the right to move the install to a different piece of hardware. VERY key for firms that might need to have a bigger, better server later. Remember that OEM software is tied to the hardware.

Next, I don't have to worry about budgeting or planning for the next system. I know that I will get the updates. In my business, we're just used to subscription models in software and thus, for me, it made perfect sense.

Is it a bit of a leap of faith? Yes, but it very obviously worked out VERY much in my favor when I signed up for SA on SBS 2000. I'm betting that it will make perfect sense again in three years.

http://www.mssmallbiz.com/MS%20Small%20Biz%20Shared%20Documents/SBS%20Std%20Why%20Open%20Value.pdf.

What Are the Differences Between Types of Licenses?

As promised earlier, here are the differences between Open, Retail/FPP, and Software Assurance licenses, according to Microsoft's SBS Web site.

Licensing Requirements

An Open New License (NL) license requires:

- Purchase through a volume license reseller.

- A minimum initial order of five licenses. One SBS 2003 license meets this qualification because five CALs are included.

A Retail/FPP license requires:

- Purchase through a brick and mortar or online retailer.

- No minimum purchase.

A Software Assurance license requires:

- Enrollment in the Microsoft software assurance program.

Licensing Benefits

Benefits of an Open NL license include:

- Savings over an FPP license.

- Capability to track your licenses using the eOpen website instead of having to manage them as paper licenses.

Benefits of a Retail/FPP license include:

- Fully legal and licensed software that requires no qualifications to purchase.

Benefits of Software Assurance include:

- New version rights. You can get the latest versions of software as they are released, without waiting for special budget approvals and at no additional cost.

- eLearning. Online training offers you convenience and flexibility. Susan Bradley reports the eLearning is only for Office and not the server-side components.

Next Steps?

Licensing, like security, is never ending and constantly evolving. So while this chapter was written at a fixed point in time, it will age and you'll need to continue to educate yourself on licensing matters. Here are some suggested next steps.

- Read Microsoft SBS Licensing FAQs. Even though the current (as of January 2005) FAQs were explored in this chapter, you can bet that site will be updated continuously. So please take a moment to visit http://www.microsoft.com/WindowsServer2003/sbs/techinfo/overview/licensingfaq.mspx.

- Bookmark Eric Ligman's Small Biz site for the page that specifically provides licensing resources at http://www.mssmallbiz.com/Lists/Licensing%20ResourcesTraining/AllItems.aspx.

- Attend Microsoft TS2 events. This is Microsoft's channel-facing seminar series outreach that you can attend quarterly. Visit www.msts2.com.

- Attend SMB Nation events (annual, workshops). SMB Nation presents a third-party view of Microsoft matters. Stay current at www.smbnation.com.

- And don't forget to visit Microsoft's licensing site or call the licensing hotline telephone number: http://www.microsoft.com/licensing/default.mspx and 1-800-426-9400 (option 4).

Notes:

- Align yourself with independent licensing experts and distributors. Softwareone.com is shown in Figure 3-10.

- Pray that Microsoft never implements other technology licensing programs like Computer Associates "power points" licensing for its UniCenter product. Here licensing is based on the processor power inside the computer.

Figure 3-10

Softwareone.com is SBS friendly.

Summary

Whew! I've had enough. Licensing is certainly one of those topics that could be an entire book and often is. Just visit your local law library and look in the intellectual property study section! This chapter presented SBS 2003-related licensing topics from a case study, FAQ, and detailed factoid framework. Let's move on to Chapter 4 and discuss advanced setup and deployment matters.

CHAPTER 4
Advanced Setup and Deployment
BY Andy Goodman (Winston-Salem, NC)

Small Business Server 2003 prides itself on a rapid, seamless setup and deployment approach. In the introductory book about SBS 2003 from SMB Nation Press, *Small Business Server 2003 Best Practices*, a great deal of timber (that's pages) was dedicated to the step-by-step setup and deployment of SBS 2003; in fact, those areas constituted over 25 percent of the entire book. This chapter picks up where that book left off, without making you suffer through a repeat of the basic setup and deployment steps. In other words, in this chapter I offer you the tips and tricks that I find useful in my day-to-day life of installing and supporting SBS. I've assumed that readers of this chapter have set up SBS 2003 previously and are ready to learn about the complex procedures described here.

> BEST PRACTICE: If for some reason you need to revisit the basic SBS 2003 setup and deployment steps, I provide an extensive graphical walk-through on my Web site:www.SBS-Rocks.com/ articles.htm. A review of that material might make for a great "compare and contrast" view of how I set up SBS 2003 versus how the setup occurred in Harry's *Small Business Server 2003 Best Practices* introductory book.

SBS 2003 Setup Specifics

In this section, I impart my sage wisdom as it applies to the following SBS setup phases:

- Installation midpoint,

- Partitioning,

- Protecting certain files, and

- Volume shadow copy restore.

Installation Midpoint

The following tip will ring true for many of you. I like to stop an SBS 2003 installation after the base Windows Server 2003 operating system installation, at the exact moment after the second reboot when I'm presented with the Continue Setup dialog box. Why? A lot of my SBS 2003 installs are on server machines that I have built myself, because I'm a system builder. Being an Intel Product Dealer (IPD), I have had a lot of Intel-sponsored system builder training, and one point Intel always emphasizes is the importance of the "order of installation" of the hardware and software drivers. So I always take advantage of this midpoint break in the SBS 2003 installation procedure to get all the current hardware and software drivers installed.

> BEST PRACTICE: The "order of installation" law is especially true for **motherboard .inf** files before the Sound , Video and Lan Drivers. The inf which actually is a setup Information file is what contains the details windows needs to install hardware and software. If you turn on hidden files and search for **.inf** you will find hundreds of them on you computer. You can also right click on them to install the associated driver or program.. If you are wondering why this is so important, if you don't install the motherboard inf's before the rest of the components, windows does not know how to talk to the motherboard chipsets. According to Intel, if you get these out of order on some systems, the only repair is a re-install of the OS!

Next, I launch the Device Manager in Windows (available from System in the Control Panel or by right clicking "My Computer" and choosing Manage) and verify that there are no yellow exclamation points or red checkmarks (the "X" character) that would signal some type of driver failure (including the drivers you just loaded). Obviously, if you have hardware failure issues, including those directly related to the drivers, there is no sense in going any further until you have resolved those issues.

TCP/IP Networking

At the midpoint in the installation, you can decide what Transmission Control Protocol\Internet Protocol (TCP/IP) subnet addressing you are going to use on your SBS 2003 network. For many customers, accepting the default 192.168.16.x network is acceptable.

> BEST PRACTICE: As a reader of this book, you are probably an SBS consultant who "eats your own dog food," meaning that you use SBS 2003 for your clients' networks as well as your own. If this is the case, you should set up your own network on a subnet that is different from that of your clients (such as 192.168.32.x) to make your own SBS 2003 network unique compared to that of your customers, who I assume will be configured as the default 192.168.16.x. This uniqueness is evident by viewing the difference in the third octet position of the TCP/IP address (remember that SBS 2003 is using a Class C subnet mask of 255.255.255.0). Uniqueness between networks is important because, when you use a virtual private network (VPN) to access a customer's SBS 2003 network from your existing SBS 2003 network, the internal TCP/IP subnet cannot be the same as the subnet of the accessing network. The networks must have unique internal TCP/IP subnets so you, as the SBS consultant, can fully access the internal network at the customer site.

Source File Copy

Another thing I like to do at the midpoint of the SBS 2003 installation is to copy all of the SBS Setup CD source files to my Library partition (I describe my partitioning schema in the next section). This allows me to run the rest of the SBS 2003 setup from the hard drive, rather than from the CD drive. I can't tell you how many times I've been performing a remote repair over the weekend or late at night for an SBS customer and have needed source files from one of the SBS Setup CDs but there was no one on-site at the customer's location to put the proper SBS CD into the CD drive for me. So now I don't even think twice about it; I just copy the SBS Setup CD source files to the hard drive where these files are always within my easy reach.

Partitioning Tips

Ok, so you buy a new server from a hardware original equipment manufacturer (OEM) and it comes with SBS 2003 pre-installed. At first blush you might ask, "What could be better?" For many customers, this is a good fit. But there *are* some partitioning issues that you should be aware of.

The first issue you will run in to is that when the hardware OEM builds the server, they typically create only one big partition and then "dump" SBS 2003 onto it. For them this is efficient, plus they don't have to maintain the SBS 2003 system going forward—you do!

> BEST PRACTICE: In all fairness, some hardware OEM vendors such as Hewlett Packard allow you to specify multiple partitions as part of your purchase process. That's good news, but be advised that even when you can specify multiple partitions, you cannot tell the manufacturer where to put the Users Shared Folders folder (share name: users) or the Microsoft Exchange-related databases (although you can move these later).

So let's take a moment to see why I think having a single partition is not such a great idea. To start with, today's hard drives range from around 150 to 250 Gigabytes (GB) of storage. Have you ever run the Chkdsk utility on a 250 GB drive? If not, take my advice and send the users on your client's network home because this disk utility job is going to take a few hours.

Reasons to Partition

You may find it valuable to partition in order to:

- Improve performance.

- Isolate fragmentation.

- Isolate files that need protection from a utilities, such as anti-virus or defragmenter applications.

- Separate data and system files for easier disaster recovery.

- Isolate files that you want to protect with Volume Shadow Services (VSS).

I recommend the following partitions:

- **System partition.** At least 10 GB. Use this partition to store core operating system files. On a average system I build this is a 32 Gb partition

- **Data partition.** At least 30 GB. Use this partition to store company data and User Data. This partition will have VSS enabled.

- **Library partition.** At least 10 GB. Use this partition to store source files (I mentioned this earlier in the chapter).

- **Swap partition.** I usually make a 7.68Gb C: Drive and put the swap file and log files on it. If you have multiple physical drives use the fastest one for this partition.

- **System Data partition to hold the Exchange and SQL databases**

Partitions and Performance

How about performance? As you probably already know, if you split up your load between different physical drives, performance will be better. But even if all you have is a single mirror or a single RAID 5 array, you can use some tricks to speed up data access and make maintenance quicker.

I'm sure some of you just jumped to your feet and started yelling at me through the book. Sit down and take a breath—there's a method to my apparent madness. When you talk about drive partitioning and different types of RAID arrays, people are ready to defend their point of view to the death. So keep in mind that what I am about to share with you is not law; it is just my opinion of what works for me and my customers. As they say, your mileage may vary!

Partitions and Fragmentation

Here's another topic that seems to rile people up: fragmentation. Some folks will tell you that they never defragment their drives, while others will tell you they are constantly doing it. Fragmentation is a fact of life with today's file systems. But it can be kept to a minimum by careful partition placement of the files that fragment the most. On an SBS server, this means locating the page file and the log files on a separate partition. That will keep most of the fragmentation isolated and also keep the disk heads from swinging widely back and forth across the disk (which is the slowest part of disk reads and writes). This also assists in the quest for improved performance.

People have asked about this issue at the SBS forum that I moderate for the Microsoft Certified Professional Magazine (www.mcpmag.com). Let me expand on what I mean about placement of log files. I'm not talking about the event viewer logs; I'm talking about the logs for Exchange Server, Microsoft Internet Information Services (IIS), Microsoft Internet Security and Acceleration (ISA) Server, Routing and Remote Access Service (RRAS), and Microsoft SQL Server. These are very active files that are constantly being updated with new information. In the next few sections I explain how to move these log files from their default locations so you can relocate them to a different partition. The following procedures are provided below:

- Moving Exchange Server Transaction Log Files

- Relocating IIS Log Files

- Relocating ISA Server Log Files

- Relocating RRAS Log Files

- Moving SQL Server Log Files

Moving Exchange Server Transaction Log Files

To move the Exchange Server transaction log files:

1. Log on to SBS 2003 as the administrator.
2. Launch the Server Management console.

3. Under **Advanced Management**, your domain name (Exchange), **Servers**, right-click **First Storage Group** and select **Properties** on the context menu.

4. On the **First Storage Group Properties** dialog box, in the **Transaction log location** field, set the location for the Exchange Server transaction logs.

   You can use the Browse button to navigate to a new location.

5. Click **OK** and the Exchange Server transaction log files will be moved to the new location.

   When you click **OK**, a dialog box will appear warning you that the Exchange Server store will need to be dismounted for a few minutes.

Relocating IIS Log Files

To change the location to which IIS log files are written:

1. Log on to SBS 2003 as the administrator.

2. Launch the Server Management console.

3. Under **Advanced Management, Internet Information Services, Your Computer Name**, right-click **Web Sites** and select **Properties** on the context menu.

4. In the **Web Sites Properties** dialog box, select the **Web Site** tab and click **Properties**.

5. When the **Logging Properties** dialog box appears, move the IIS log files to the **Log file directory** field.

Note that this procedure does not move existing IIS log files. Instead, it creates a new location for future log files. Move existing log files manually from the default location at %Systemroot%\system32\LogFiles.

> BEST PRACTICE: To make your IIS log files easier to read, select the **Use local time for naming and rollover** check box.

Relocating ISA Server Log Files

There are three different ISA Server log files. To change the location to which these ISA Server log files are written:

1. Log on to SBS 2003 as the administrator.

2. Open the **ISA Management Console** by clicking **Start**, selecting **All Programs**, Microsoft ISA Server and finally ISA Management.

3. Expand **Servers and Arrays**, your computer name, and **Monitoring Configuration**, and click **Logs**.

4. Right-click **Packet Filters** and choose **Properties** from the context menu.

5. On the **Packet filters Properties** dialog box, click **Options**.

6. On the **Options** dialog box, click the **Other folder** radio button and click **Browse** to manually set the storage location you would like (See Figure 4-1 for an illustration of this procedure).

7. Repeat this procedure until you have changed the location for all three ISA Server logs. The 3 three log files are Packet filters, ISA Server Firewall service, ISA Server Web Proxy Service.

Note that this procedure does not move existing ISA Server log files; it merely establishes the location for future log files. If you want to move old ISA Server log files, you must do so manually. You can find these log files in the original ISA Server installation directory in a subfolder called ISALogs (the default directory is typically "C:\Program Files\Microsoft ISA Server\ISALogs").

Figure 4-1

Relocating the ISA Server log files.

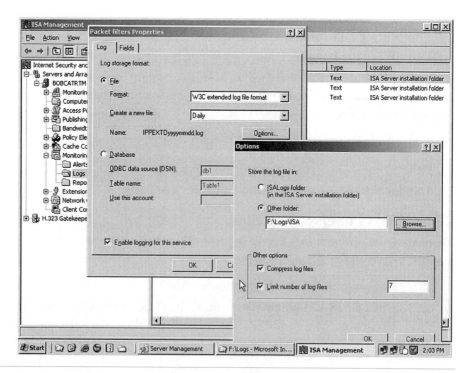

Relocating RRAS Log Files

To change the location to which the RRAS log files are written:

1. Log on to SBS 2003 as the administrator.
2. Launch the Server Management console.
3. Open **Advanced Management**, expand **Computer Management (Local)**, **Services and Applications**, **Routing and Remote Access**, and click **Remote Access Logging**.
4. In the right pane, right-click **Local File** and select **Properties** from the context menu.
5. On the **Log File Properties** dialog box, select the **Log File** tab.
6. Click **Browse** to set the location for the log files.

   The Browse button here displays a dialog box that does not include a New Folder button, so you will need to create the new folder ahead of time (for example, on the Library partition).

Note that this procedure does not move existing RRAS log files; it merely establishes the location for future log files. To move existing RRAS log files, you must manually copy them from the default location of %Systemroot\System32\LogFiles.

Moving SQL Server Log Files

Moving SQL Server log files is somewhat complex, so rather than trying to explain it all here, I would like to point you to Microsoft Knowledge Base Article 224071 "Moving SQL Server databases to a new location with Detach/Attach". Note, however, that one step is missing from the article concerning how to start the SQL Command Interface. Assuming you are going to move the SharePoint files, here is the command: **osql –E –S computername \SharePoint**. Be sure to replace "computername" with your actual computer name.

Protecting Certain Files

Some files just need to be left alone; they should not be scanned for viruses, defragmented, or touched at all during normal operations. For me the easiest way to remember which files are untouchable is to put those files on their own partition. This way I can just exclude that partition from any utility that needs to run. What files am I talking about? I'm referring to the Exchange Server databases, SQL Server databases, and MSDE databases.

As Jeff Middleton explains in greater detail in Chapter 15, your disaster recovery chores are much more manageable if you separate your data files from your system files. By not having your data intertwined with your system files, the data is much more portable if you lose a server. Even without a catastrophic loss, disaster recovery is less complicated when certain file types, including data files, are compartmentalized.

Volume Shadow Copy Restore

As part of its data protection paradigm, SBS 2003 uses Volume Shadow Copy Restore, which is a really cool technology that allows users with Windows XP Professional workstations to recover accidentally deleted files or prior versions of the files. By default it is enabled on the partition that holds the users share.

Not only does Volume Shadow Copy Restore use space for its copies of deleted data, it also uses some overhead to keep track of all this information. So if you have the default SBS 2003 OEM single partition installation, Volume Shadow Copy Restore will try to maintain a shadow copy of the entire server, at least to the copy limits that you configure in the SBS 2003 backup wizard (discussed in *Windows Small Business Server 2003 Best Practices*). My solution, which is the same as that suggested in the introductory book, is to create a separate partition for the users share data. That is why earlier in this chapter you saw a partition named DATA. Bottom line: this will save you storage space and keep you from wasting hard disk reads and writes.

Post-SBS 2003 Setup

This section presents some advanced computer connection tips you might consider after SBS 2003 is installed on the server machine and you proceed with the deployment. When it works, the Connect Computer page is wonderful, The page is actually called Network Configuration, but everyone calls it the Connect Computer page because of how you access it. You access this page from a workstation that is attempting to join the SBS 2003 network by typing http://servername/connectcomputer. This is so much better than having to make that "magic" disk used in prior SBS versions where you had to run around, putting said magic disk in each computer. However, when the Connect Computer page doesn't work, this functionality is frustrating because it is very hard to troubleshoot. Described below are some HandyAndy workarounds to try in the event you hit a roadblock:

- Run IPCONFIG

- Add to a new workgroup

- Add a user

- Synchronize client computer time

- Synchronize logon time

- Keep server time sync'd

Run IPCONFIG

Assuming you've physically connected to the local area network (LAN) segment (don't laugh—its easy to overlook), try this. Run the IPCONFIG command on the errant workstation and verify it is getting an IP address from the SBS 2003 server machine. In the perfect world of SBS 2003, this should be a 192.168.16.x IP address. If it is not, you've got some basic network troubleshooting to do because obtaining an IP address from the SBS 2003 server machine is a low-level function.

One way this address-leasing problem reveals itself is in the IPCONFIG output. If you are getting a 169.x.x.x automatic address generated natively by Windows XP Professional, then clearly the IP address is not coming from the SBS 2003 server machine and you need to resolve your network issues first. This will be a true test of your skills as a competent SBSer.

On the other hand, if you *are* getting a valid IP address from the SBS 2003 server machine, run the IPCONFIG /ALL command to verify that the IP address lease is a "rich fully featured" lease wherein the SBS 2003 server is the only DNS entry for the client machine. We want the name resolution activity facilitated by the SBS 2003 DNS services to be first in line. You do not want name resolution activity initially going to an external DNS server on the Internet because they can not resolve internal names.

Add to a New Workgroup

Next in your client connection troubleshooting, try adding the workstation to a new workgroup (do this from Control Panel, Network). If the client computer is still not properly joining the SBS 2003 domain, reboot the workstation two more times. I know it sounds absurd, but it has worked a number of times. Our industry is the only place where you can do the same thing over and over and expect different results, and no one thinks you're nuts.

Add a User

Here again, fact is stranger than fiction. Try only adding one user to the client computer machine in the Connect Computer phase. I have had a few experiences where I could not add multiple users while running the Connect Computer routine, but when I tried adding only one user, it worked fine. Also, although it shouldn't be necessary, try running the Connect Computer routine as the administrator, which means you have the rights of the Domain Admins security group.

Synchronize Client Computer Time

If other approaches to connect the client computer to the SBS 2003 domain fail, there is a good chance your workstation is too far out of time synchronization with the SBS 2003 server. Time can be a real issue on the domain. Check the time on the server and, if necessary, set it manually to match the server time. Do this on the workstation by double-clicking on the clock icon in the bottom right corner of the screen. You can also check the time service on the server and make sure it is running.

> BEST PRACTICE: If you chose the "Router" option when you ran the Configure Email and Internet Connection Wizard, the time service was turned off. Why? Because some routers are dial on demand; the time service would cause the router to excessively dial up the ISP, resulting in a potentially expensive connection pattern. So, if you need the time service running, perhaps as part of your client computer troubleshooting approach, you have to set the time service to start automatically in the services console.

Speaking of time synchronization, this is as good a time as any to mention that if you are using ISA Server 2000 in SBS 2003, you need to open up port 123 UDP using the following procedure so the time service can "get out" and sync with an external time source.

1. Logon to the SBS 2003 as the administrator.
2. Click **Start**, **Programs**, **Microsoft ISA Server**, **ISA Management Programs**, **Microsoft ISA Server**, and select **ISA Management**.
3. In the ISA Management console tree, expand **Servers and Arrays**, expand **servername**, expand **Access Policy**, and right-click on **IP Packet Filter**.
4. Click **New**, **Filter**. Name the new filter **Time** and click **Next**.
5. Select **Allow packet transmission** and click **Next**.
6. In the **Filter Type** dialog box, select **Custom**.
7. Set the **IP protocol** to **UDP**.
8. Set the direction to **Send receive**.
9. Set the **Local port** to **Fixed port** and the **Port number** to **123**.
10. Set the **Remote port** to **Fixed port** and set it to **123**.

The property sheet for the time filter you just created in shown in Figure 4-2.

Notes:

Figure 4-2
*Notice the procedure settings are properly reflected on the Time Properties,
Filter Type page.*

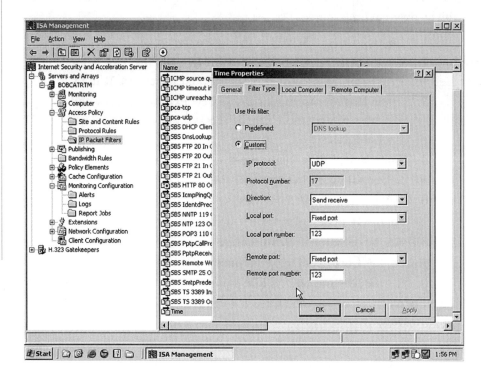

11. Click **OK**.
12. Accept the default selection of **Default IP addresses for each exter-
     nal interface on the ISA Server computer** and click **Next**.
13. In the **Apply this packet filter to** window, select **All computers** and
     click **Next**.
14. Review the summary information and click **Finish**.
It is that easy.

> BEST PRACTICE: A lot of SBSers think you need to create a protocol
> rule to achieve the functionality presented above. You don't! Protocol
> rules allow the client machines to get out and access the Internet.
> We want internal client computers to synchronize with the SBS 2003
> server machine so a protocol rule is not needed.

Synchronize Logon Time

I also like to synchronize all my workstations at login. Note that this is not necessary for Windows XP Professional client computers anymore because internal XP technology automatically performs the time synchronization function.

To time-synchronize non-Windows XP Professional client computers, I modify the SBS_LOGIN_SCRIPT.bat file located in %systemroot%\SYSVOL\sysvol\ %domainname%\scripts directory of the SBS 2003 server machine. This file has one line by default. Modify this line by adding the word **call** to the begining of the line. and then add the following as the second line.

call net time /set /yes.

Make sure your server is getting it's time synchronized from someplace trustworthy, I use time.windows.com. To accomplish this, run the following commands once at the SBS 2003 server machine console:

net time /setSNTP:time.windows.com

net stop w32time

net start w32time

In the first line, notice that there is a reference to time.windows.com, which is an externally verifiable time source. But you don't have to use time.windows.com; you may use any time source you like. You can also use a list of time servers by separating them with semicolons. For more information on setting an authoritative time source, see Knowledge Base Article# 216734: How to configure an authoritative time server in Windows 2000. Don't worry it applies to Windows 2003 also.

Keep Time

SBSer Steve Carmeli shared a time problem that you might find interesting. His D-Link router was sending out a time synchronization command that was preventing his domain from syncing. I don't have the exact specifications on his network, but all signs point to this as another example of why you shouldn't run SBS 2003 with a single network adapter card. Spend the extra few dollars to buy a second network adapter card and save yourself some grief. (This is another way of saying you should make the SBS 2003 server machine the lord of your network.) Here is Steve's story.

> *I finally started installing SBS this week. After I was done installing it, I couldn't log on. Why? SBS kept telling me that the server's clock was out of sync with the network clock! Well, while I'd only read through to Chapter 3 in the SBS Best Practices book (I'd read through the consulting best practices book), I'd never read that, and it didn't make any sense to me. I reinstalled twice but never really checked the time when it came up during the install. Finally, on the third install, I compared the time on the server on Windows Install with my workstation and, sure enough, they were out of sync by over an hour. Well, I adjusted the server on the Windows install, but that still didn't fix it; I still couldn't log on. I rebooted and caught the setup features of the PC before Windows started and, sure enough, the Windows install didn't change the server's clock. I adjusted the server's clock, rebooted and this time I could log on.*

> *It turns out that the clock in my router and the clock in my server were set to different times. When I set them to the same time, then the server allowed me to log on.*

> *But note that was with the D-Link router, which I returned. I had nothing but problems with that router and that would be something I'd write in the knowledgebase. The Linksys router, though more expensive, and though I had to wait much longer for tech support, worked the first time.*

> *Steve Carmeli*

Notes:

Group Policy Tips

Let's move on and discuss Group Policy, which is an area that didn't get any air time in the introductory SBS 2003 book in this series (*Small Business Server 2003 Best Practices*). Provided here are discussions about:

- Creating new group policy objects,

- Group policy and software update services, and

- GPO exception or override.

Working with Group Policies has changed. Where you used to be able right click an object such as an OU or the Domain and select **Properties** and the **Group Policy** tab, that is no longer the case. If you try, you will get **You have installed the Group Policy Management snap-in, so this tab is no longer used**. Instead the **Group Policy Management Console** will open. This console will make seeing the effects of your policies much easier. But actually editing a policy may take you a little bit to figure out.

I poked around the Group Policy Management snap-in for quite some time trying to figure out how to actually change a Group Policy Object (GPO). It seemed like everything I clicked on was a view, but not editable. Here is the solution. All you have to do is right-click on the GPO or the shortcut to that GPO and choose **Edit** from the context menu that appears. It is always so simple once you figure it out!

Creating New GPOs

It's time for a little Group Policy 101. Let's make sure we understand how GPOs work. First of all, GPOs have to be connected to a container. Valid containers for GPO's are:

- Sites,

- Domains, and

- Organizational Units (OUs).

With SBS 2003, you will work mostly with OUs and the Domain Container. To be brutally honest, sites are more of an enterprise concept and don't really relate to the world of SBS 2003.

No matter where you create your GPO, the actual policy code will reside in the sysvol directory on the domain controller at **%systemroot%\SYSVOL\ domain\Policies**.

What you actually put in the container OU or Domain is a link to the GPO. You can have more than one link to the same policy because they are re-useable (another author in the GPO field refers to this as "tattooing"). GPO relationships follow the hierarchical OU tree downward, unless you specifically block the GPO from being applied. That is, a nested child OU will inherit the GPO functionality of a parent OU.

This section covers the following procedures:

- Creating a new OU

- Internet Explorer GPO trick

- Logoff command

Creating a New OU

Let's start out by creating a new OU to hold the link to a new GPO:

1. Logon to SBS 2003 as the administrator.
2. Launch the **Server Management** console.
3. Expand **Advanced Management,** select **Active Directory Users and Computers**, expand the domain name object, expand the **MyBusiness** OU, and expand **Users**.
4. Right-click on the **SBS Users** OU and select **New, Organizational Unit** from the context menu.
5. Title your new OU as **LimitThese** then click **OK**.

Now you will use the Group Policy Management snap-in:

1. In the **Server Management** console under **Advanced Management**, select **Group Policy Management**.
2. Expand **Forest, Domains, your domain name, MyBusiness, Users**, and **SBSUsers**.

3. Right click on the new OU you created above, **LimitThese**. Select **Create** and **Link a GPO Here** and name the new GPO **NoRegeditNoRun**.

BEST PRACTICE: When possible, I like to use a name that will remind me about what the GPO does. For a look at the power of GPOs, complete this quick exercise:

Right-click on the **NoRegeditNoRun** GPO and select **Edit** from the context menu. As you can see, there are two main sections: Computer Configuration and User Configuration. Take a moment and observe the thousands of GPO settings available. It is here you start to see the power that Group Policy can put in your hands via GPOs.

4. Expand **User Configuration, Administrative Templates** and click **Start Menu and Taskbar**.
5. Scroll down to **Remove Run menu from the Start Menu**. Double-click on this setting to open it.
6. Click the **Enabled** radio button.
   You can click the **Explain** tab for a detailed explanation of the settings. Kudos to the Microsoft team that wrote this excellent on-line help!
7. Click **OK**.
8. Find and select the heading titled **System**. On the right-side pane open **Don't run specified Windows applications**.
9. Click the **Enabled** radio button.
10. Click **Add** and enter **regedit.exe** in the text field.
11. Click **Add** again and enter **regdt32.exe** in the text field.
12. Click **Add** again and enter **cmd.exe** in the text field.
13. Click **Show**. The **Show Contents** dialog box appears, similar to Figure 4-3.
14. Click **OK** twice and close the Group Policy Object Editor snap-in.

Notes:

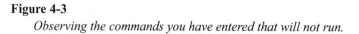
Figure 4-3

Observing the commands you have entered that will not run.

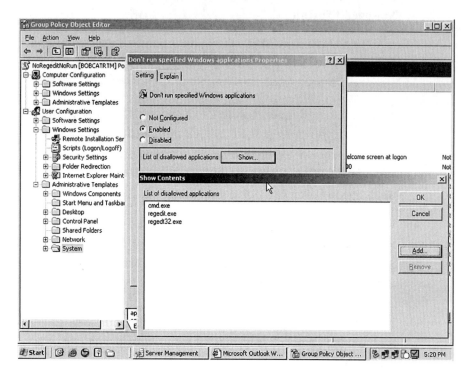

So what does the new GPO do at this point? Nothing. We have not put any users into the NoRegedtNoRun OU we created, so perhaps I just gottcha with that trick question, huh? But once users have been placed in the OU, they will be impacted by the GPO (the Run command will not be available from the Start menu on their desktop computer). Additionally, the users will not be able use registry editor or the command prompt.

> BEST PRACTICE: A note of caution: be careful! You can really hurt yourself with group policy, so go lightly until you get a feel for it. Be especially careful that you don't put yourself or the administrator in the OU that you just created. Why? Because you will find it difficult to administer your network with the above-cited functionality disabled.

Always test your GPO on a temporary user to make sure it performs as expected, before turning it loose on your network. Go ahead and create a temporary user in the new OU. Log on to a workstation as that new user to see the effect of the policy. Log off and log back on as the administrator. See why we put our GPO in the user section instead of the computer section? It is very important to think about what it is you are trying to control. Also keep in mind that most user settings are applied at logon, whereas most computer settings are applied at boot-time.

Internet Explorer GPO Trick

Here is a tip that will help you win the hearts of your clients. People like to see their names in important places, so put the client's company name on the title bar of Internet Explorer. How, you ask? With a GPO that will edit the Default Domain Policy:

1. Assuming that the **Group Policy Object Editor** (Figure 4-3) is still open, expand the **User Configuration** section.
2. Select the **Windows Settings, Internet Explorer Maintenance**, and **Browser User Interface**.
3. Double-click on **Browser Title** object, select **Customize Title Bars**, and enter the client's company name.
4. Click **OK**.

Notes:

You should get a result like that shown in Figure 4-4. When a user opens a page in Internet Explorer, note the top of the window where "provided by SMBNation" has been added to the default title.

Figure 4-4
Customizing the Internet Explorer title bar using a GPO.

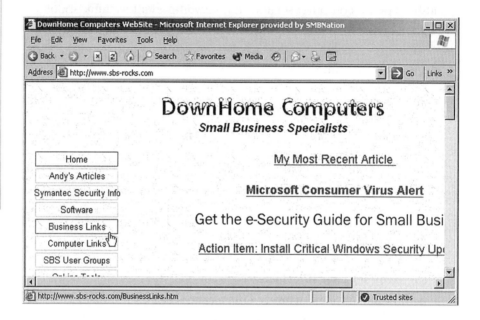

Logoff Command

You should also consider adding the logoff command to the Start menu to benefit your users.

1. While you are in the Default Domain Policy in the **Group Policy Object Editor**, select **User Configuration**, **Administrative Template**, and then click **Start Menu and Taskbar**.
2. On the right side, double-click **Add Logoff to the Start Menu** and check **Enabled**.
3. Click **OK**.

Now close the Group Policy Object Editor. Since these changes were made to the default domain policy, everybody will get these changes the *next* time they log into the network.

Group Policy and Software Update Services

While we are talking about Group Policy, let me mention that you should be using Software Update Services (SUS) to keep your client machines updated with security patches. I only mention it here because it is administered with—you guessed it—a Group Policy. You will need to download SUS or the yet-to-be released (as of this writing) Windows Update Services (WUS) at: www.microsoft.com/windowsserversystem/sus/default.mspx.

SUS Server-Side

The initial setup is pretty straightforward. Run the setup executable and provide an installation path. Once SUS is installed, you perform administrative tasks using a Web page with the following URL: //servername/susadmin. You need to configure only a few settings to get the SUS server-side operational. Set these under the "Set options" link on the welcome page, as seen in Figure 4-5.

Figure 4-5

Configure SUS on the Set options page.

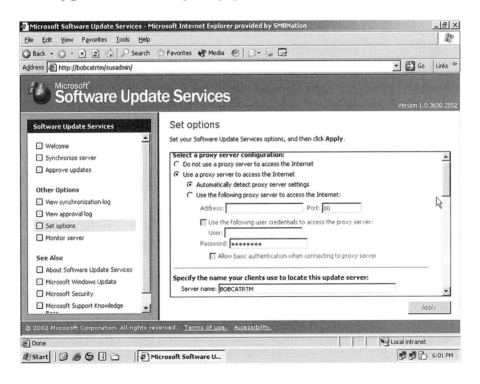

SUS setup will automatically set the proxy option and put in the SBS 2003 server name. Then you must decide where your server will synchronize SUS content. Some consultants prefer to run a SUS server in their consulting office and have their customer's SUS servers synchronize from the consultant's office instead of Microsoft itself. You can also choose to have SUS automatically approve new versions of Microsoft updates or to ask for approval (which is my personal preference). Another option allows you keep a copy of the updates locally or have each client machine pull them down from Microsoft. You can greatly reduce your bandwidth demands by keeping a local copy of the updates on your server. Another option allows you to select which languages you would like to support.

If you look closely at Figure 4-5, you will see the **Synchronize server** link on the left. Here you have the option of a one-time immediate synchronization or configuring a schedule to automatically synchronize. The first synchronization is very time consuming (as of Fall 2004, 239 updates for the English language needed to be downloaded!). After you synchronize your server, you need to select the **Approve updates** page and select which updates you want to be applied to the clients. There is no "approve all" button, so you will need to select the desired updates one at a time. I found a rapid way to approve these individual updates: Select the first update you want to approach and then hit Tab, Tab, SpaceBar. Keep repeating and if you get to an update you don't want to apply, hit Tab instead of SpaceBar. That is all there is to setting up the server side of SUS!

SUS Client-Side

And now for Group Policy! The SUS client-side configuration is handled through GPOs. If you are running Windows 2000 Service Pack 2 (SP2) or Windows XP without Service Pack 1 (SP1), you will need to download the new SUS client at the Microsoft download URL (www.microsoft.com/windowsserversystem/sus/default.mspx). If your desktops are more current, you already have the new SUS client. When the SUS server was installed, the Administrative Template was added to allow you to create or edit SUS settings.

To automatically update the client computers with approved updates, follow this procedure:

1. Logon to SBS 2003 as the administrator.
2. From the Start menu, launch **Server Management**.
3. Expand **Advanced Management, Group Policy Management, Forest, Domain, yourdomain**.
4. Right-click on **Small Business Server Client Computer** and select **Edit**.

   The **Group Policy Object Editor** will appear.
5. Expand **Computer Configuration, Administrative Templates, Windows Components** and select **Windows Update**.

   Four options need to be configured for SUS to automatically update the client computers.
6. Select **Configure Automatic Updates.** Check the radio button for **Enabled**.

   Select the frequency you would like it to check with your server

   Select the install time

   When satisfied click **next**
7. Click **Enabled**. Complete the URL for your SUS server in the form of http://Servername.

   Populate the Update and Statistics server fields with the same URL since the SBS 2003 server machine will perform all of these roles.
8. Click **Next Setting** and configure the client update schedule.

   The default is five minutes. There is one caveat if your users are running with Local Administrator rights (which Susan Bradley will warn you about in her Security chapter): the updates will not be automatically applied. Instead, the updates will generate a system popup message indicating that updates are available. The user has to click **OK** to download and install the updates. Until these updates are installed, NO FURTHER UPDATES will install!
9. Click **Next Setting**, where you will make a decision about client computer automatic reboots after updates are applied.

   As much as I would like to tell you to leave this disabled, I have found it causes a lot of turmoil with the users to have machines unexpectedly rebooting in the middle of their projects. So it is probably better to enable this option, which effectively disables the automatic reboot. Remember: if you are confused by any of the choices, just use the Explain tab on each policy settings page to get more information.

GPO Exception or Override

As powerful as a GPO can be in the affirmative, an exception GPO can be just as powerful and useful by effectively denying some behavior. I'll give you an example of an exception or override GPO. One of my clients had his users creating all sorts of local user accounts on the desktops when I arrived as the new SBS consultant. This local user malfeasance caused potential security holes in their SBS network. When I pointed this out to the guy in charge, he asked if I could lock down the system so we could control who logged onto which client computer. I created a neat little GPO that forced everyone to logon with a domain account, which prevented local logons. Note that work was performed in the SBS 2000 timeframe and can't be exactly replicated in SBS 2003, so kindly accept the above discussion as explanatory in nature.

To create an exception GPO:

1. Logon to the SBS 2003 server machine as the administrator.
2. From the Start menu, launch **Server Management**.
3. Expand **Advanced Settings** and **Group Policy Management**.
4. Expand **Forest, Domains, yourdomain, MyBusiness, Users, SBSUsers**.
5. Right-click on the new OU you created earlier in this chapter titled **LimitThese**.
6. Select **Create and Link a GPO Here** and name the new GPO **OverRideNoRegeditNoRun**.
7. Right-click on this new GPO and choose **Edit** from the dropdown list.
8. Expand **User Configuration, Administrative Templates** and click **Start Menu and Taskbar**.
9. Double-click **Remove Run menu from the Start Menu**. Select the **Disabled** radio button and click **OK**.
10. Under **Administrative Templates**, select **System**.
11. In the right pane, double-click **Don't run specified Windows applications**. Select the **Disabled** radio button.

12. Click **OK** twice and close the **Group Policy Editor**.

13. Right-click this newly created GPO and select **Enforced**.

14. Under **Advanced Management** in **Server Management**, **Group Policy Management**, **Forest**, **Domains**, **yourdomain**, **Group Policy Objects**, click the **OverRideNoRegeditNoRun** GPO.

15. Click the **Scope** tab in the right pane.

16. Under **Security Filtering**, click **Remove** to remove **Authenticated Users**.

    This is shown in Figure 4-6.

Figure 4-6
Authenticated Users will be removed in the Security Filtering section.

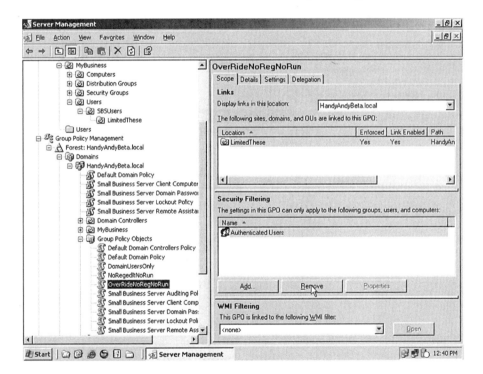

17. In the Security Filtering section, click **Add**.

18. In the **Enter the Object name to select** field, type **Administrators**, click **Check Names**, and then click **OK**.

You have now created an exception GPO.

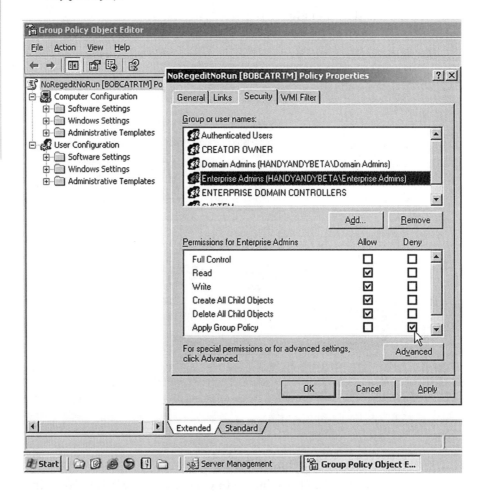

BEST PRACTICE: If all you want to do is keep a specific GPO from
being applied to a user or group, the easiest way is to remove the
Apply Group Policy permission from the GPO itself. Do this on the
Security tab of the GPO property sheet, as seen in Figure 4-7.

Figure 4-7

*Select Deny for Apply Group Policy as a permission restriction. You will receive
a warning message relating to a Deny selection (the warning is that Deny is
very powerful).*

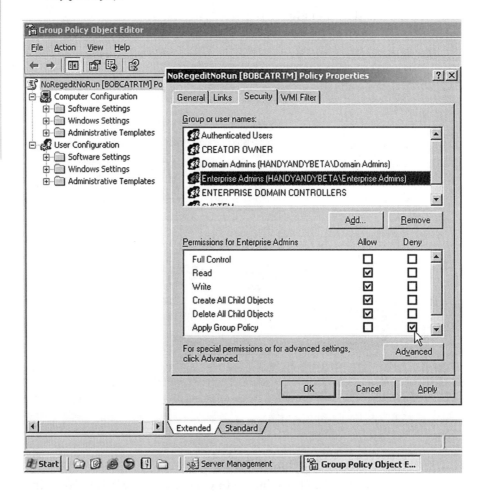

Software Installation Options

Microsoft's SBS development team was especially focused on the client computer with this release. This section discusses ways to install software on client computers.

You have several choices when it comes to getting software deployed out to the client computer desktops. Right off the bat, you can rule out sticking the CD into each computer or copying the software to the server and then going to each computer and running Setup. Realistic options for deploying SBS to client computers are:

- Using SBS 2003's Set Up Client Application Wizard.

- Pushing out the software with a GPO.

These options are described below. Some may also opt to use a third-party product such as Executive Software's SiteKeeper or Symantec's Client Migration, but I do not describe those options here.

Using SBS 2003's Set Up Client Application Wizard

Let's use the ISA Firewall client for this demonstration.

1. Logon to the SBS 2003 server as the administrator.
2. From the Start menu launch **Server Management**.
3. Select **Client Computers**.
4. Select **Assign Applications to the Client Computers**.
5. Click **Edit Applications**.
6. Click **Next**.
7. Click **Add**.
8. In the **Application name** field type **Microsoft ISA Client**.
9. In the **Location of setup executable for this application** field, type **\\computername\mspclnt\setup.exe /s**.
10. Click **OK** and acknowledge the warning message regarding the need to use Domain Users, Read and Execute permissions on the folder containing the installation files

That is all there is to setting up the server side, next I will show you how to deploy it.

Pushing Out Software with a GPO

This section demonstrates how to install Microsoft Office XP using a GPO. I want to show you how to deploy a software package so everyone gets precisely the same installation.

To prepare for this example, I have run the administrative installation of Office XP to get the software planted on the server and ready to be deployed by the GPO (see the Microsoft Office site at www.microsoft.com/office for more details on an administrative installation). I have also shared out this server-side installation directory with the share name of OfficeXP and given the Domain Users group the read and execute permissions. This process is slightly different for each version of Office, so be advised that my example applies to Office XP. Note that you can deploy client software based on the user or computer being a member of a security group and a member of an OU.

Follow this procedure to create a GPO at the domain level and use the security filtering to limit which computers will have Office XP installed:

1. Logon to the SBS 2003 server machine as the administrator.
2. From the Start menu launch **Server Management**.
3. Expand **Advanced Management**, **Group Policy Management**, **Forest**, **Domains** and right-click on your domain name.
4. Choose **Create and Link a GPO Here** from the context menu. Name the GPO **OfficeInstall.**
5. Right-click on the **OfficeInstall GPO** in the right pane and choose **Link Disabled**.

   This will save any settings we change from being applied before we are ready.
6. Right-click the **OfficeInstall GPO** again and choose **Edit** from the context menu. The Group Policy Object Editor will launch.
7. Expand **Software Settings** under **Computer Configuration** and right-click **Software installation**, then select **New**, **Package**.

   You must put the complete network path into the Microsoft Installer Information (MSI) file in the **Look in** field. If you forget and put in a local path such as "C:\MySoftware," it will not work. The installation runs from the local machine and your files won't be there. Drill down from My Network Places to find your network installation share and enter it as a Uniform Naming Convention (UNC) path.

Tuning the GPO

In this procedure, you will learn how to tune the GPO.

1. Click **Open**, select the **Advanced** radio button, and click **OK**.
2. Leave the default name for the package and click the **Deployment** tab. Select the check box titled **Uninstall this application when it falls out of the scope of management**.

   This will allow you to easily remove the application from the client computer if necessary. Take a moment to observe the other settings available. This is very powerful stuff and well worth the time it takes to learn about it.
3. Since we're not going to use any of those other settings for our demonstration, click **OK**.
4. Close the **Group Policy Object Editor**.
5. Under **Standard Management** in the **Server Management** console, click **Security Groups**.
6. Click the **Add a Security Group** link on the right pane and name the new security group **OfficeXPComputers**.
7. In the **Description** field enter **Computers to Receive Office Installation** then click **Next**.
8. On the **Group Membership** dialog box, click **Next** without adding any members.

   The member we want does not appear on the list.
9. Click **Finish**.
10. Double-click **OfficeXPComputers** and click the **Members** tab.
11. Click **Add**, click **Object Types**, and select the **Computers** checkbox.

    Here is where you add the client computers where you want to have software installed.
12. Click **OK**.

Controlling Where the GPO is Applied

In this procedure, you will control where the GPO is applied.

1. In **Server Management**, under **Advanced Settings**, **Group Policy Management**, **Forest**, **Domains**, **yourdomain**, **Group Policy Objects**, click the **OfficeInstall** GPO.

2. Select the **Scope Tab** on the right pane. In the **Security Filtering** section, click **Remove** to remove **Authenticated Users**.

3. Click **Add**. In the **Enter the object name to select** field, enter **OfficeXPComputers** (the security group we created earlier) then click **OK**.

We are ready to put our new policy into effect.

4. In **Server Management** under **Advanced Settings**, **Group Policy Management**, **Forest**, **Domains**, click on your domain name. In the right pane, right-click **OfficeInstall** and choose **Link Enabled** from the context menu.

5. In the **Do you want to change the Link Enabled setting for this GPO Link(s)?** warning dialog box, click **OK**.

6. Open a Command Prompt window (**Start**, **Run** and type the **CMD** command in the **Open** field) and enter the following command: **gpupdate /target:computer /force**.

   This will ensure our GPO handiwork is updated in Active Directory.

7. Reboot one of the client computers that will get the Office XP installation and watch what happens!

   You will hopefully see a message box before the desktop is displayed saying **Installing managed software Microsoft Office XP with...** and the installation will proceed. Cool huh?

By using this GPO-based method to install your applications, you can keep your fleet of client computer desktops consistent with the same installed application library. Everything is the same on each client computer! Another benefit is that since these are managed applications, you can easily maintain a consistent patch level across the SBS 2003 domain for the application by updating the GPO.

Windows XP Service Pack 2

While this chapter was being written, Windows XP Service Pack 2 (SP2) was released. Benefits of Windows XP SP2 are discussed below.

Specific Fixes Addressed by SP2

Security Center

Located in the Control Panel, Security Center provides a central location for viewing security status, changing security settings, and learning more about security issues. Security Center runs as a background process that constantly checks on the state of these three important security components:

- **Windows Firewall**. Using a firewall is important regardless of the type of Internet connection. The Windows Firewall component is turned on by default.

- **Automatic Updates**. Checks are performed to monitor the current status of the Automatic Updates feature (discussed more below).

- **Virus Protection**. Security Center looks for the presence of antivirus software, and checks to see if it is turned on and is up-to-date.

Pop-up Blocker

Turned on by default in Internet Explorer, this functionality stops most unwanted pop-up windows from appearing. If a Web site opens a pop-up window that is blocked by Internet Explorer, the Internet Explorer Information Bar notifies the user and a sound plays. The user can elect to allow the pop-up.

Internet Explorer Add-Ons

A security feature, the Internet Explorer Add-on Manager allows the user to view and control the list of add-ons that can be loaded by Internet Explorer. This functionality also provides an easy way to detect and disable add-ons.

Automatic Updates

When you install Windows XP Professional SP2, you are prompted to turn on the Automatic Updates capability. That means the computer will routinely check for updates that can help protect the computer against the latest viruses and other security threats.

Easier wireless configuration

The improved wireless support offered in Windows XP Professional SP2 simplifies the process of discovering and connecting to wireless networks. A dialog presents more information about the type of network, wireless network name, signal strength, and support for the latest standards (WiFi Protected Access and Wireless Provisioning Services). I discuss this more below.

Local Group Policy Security Settings

Windows XP Professional SP2 delivers 609 new GPO settings specific to security configurations.

Outlook Express Improvements

Attachments can be isolated in Outlook Express so they cannot harm the computer. The Outlook Express privacy updates capability helps reduce unwanted e-mail by limiting the possibility of your e-mail address being validated by potential spammers.

Drilling down

In this section, I will drill down into three Windows XP SP2 topics: the cool new wireless configuration, issues surrounding line of business (LOB) applications and a specific SBS 2003 patch.

New Wireless Setup Process

Those annoying Wired Equivalent Privacy (WEP) keys that we all love to type have been reduced to a manageable condition. Now when you set up a wireless network under Windows XP SP2, you enter the first key followed by the rest of the network setup info. The Wireless Network Wizard collects all the information and records it onto a USB Flash Drive, which you can take around to the rest of the laptops or wireless desktops (see Figure 4-8).

Figure 4-8

Is that cool or what? Check out the USB flash drive option!

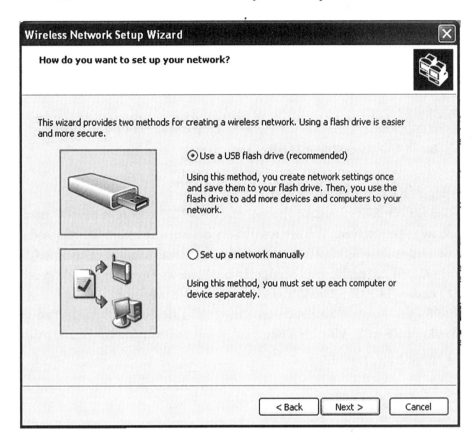

The information is written to the flash drive. When you plug the USB device into the next computer running Windows XP SP2, it will automatically configure the wireless settings for you.

When you plug the USB device back into the original computer, it writes the entire configuration back to the computer. When you want to add another computer later, all the information is already available.

LOB Applications

Reports coming from SBS users around the world indicate that some LOB applications are rendered broken and otherwise unusable when SP2 is applied to a Windows XP client computer. It appears there is merit to these apoplectic warnings and you must keep your IT administrator guard up. Among heaps of examples, there is a proven case of Symantec's Norton anti-virus software breaking after SP2 was applied to a Windows XP client computer.

> BEST PRACTICE: You will need to test Windows XP SP2 on a test client computer before deploying it to your entire fleet of client computers. It's the only sane way to assure yourself that SP2 won't break a mission critical LOB!

SBS 2003-specific Fix

Windows XP SP2's standard firewall and SBS 2003 networks have an issue that must be resolved. The Microsoft SBS development team has released a Knowledge Base article (Update for Windows Small Business Server 2003: KB 872769) that enables and configures the Windows Firewall in Windows XP SP2 on an SBS 2003 network. You are encouraged to check the SBS Community Site for up-to-date information on SBS 2003-specific topics that relate to Windows XP SP2. Visit http://www.microsoft.com/windowsserver2003/sbs/community/default.mspx.

Summary

This chapter covered a lot of real estate related to server machine setup and client computers on an SBS 2003 network. Tips related to the core SBS 2003 started things off, followed by an overview of post-SBS 2003 network setup troubleshooting. You even learned how to keep time. A core part of the chapter delved deeply into Group Policy. Next up was what I hope was a valuable section on software installation options. We wrapped things up with a discussion about Windows XP SP2 in SBS 2003 environments.

CHAPTER 5
Using Third-Party Tools to Boost SBS 2003 Performance
BY Frank Ohlhorst (Manhasset, NY)

Pack your bags! We're going on a voyage to a land where Microsoft doesn't rule—third-party land! What is third-party land, you ask? It's an environment where you use products other than those produced by Microsoft! Why would anyone want to go to this mysterious land? It's simple!

While SBS 2003 is full of useful features, several areas could use improvement, and that, my friends, is actually a good thing! If you are a Value Added Reseller (VAR), those improvements can lead to profits and offer your customers security and value. As an end user, the improvements described in this chapter solve problems and can extend the overall value of SBS 2003.

This chapter focuses on four main areas of SBS 2003 functionality that can be improved with third-party software or appliances. These are:

- Backup solutions,

- Dynamic ISP addresses,

- Spam,

- Other nuisances.

Backup Solutions

One of the first rules of IT is backup. Let me repeat that: Backup, Backup, Backup! Now more than ever, reliable, current backups are crucial. Thanks to worms, viruses, ill-behaved applications, and poorly deployed patches, having good backups is more than just a good idea; it's a requirement!

Traditionally, backup has revolved around tape and specialized backup software. Tape is not a feasible option for most businesses because it:

- Is expensive when you consider today's storage requirements.

- Takes too much time to do a complete backup.

Don't get me wrong; tape still has its place in many businesses. But we now have better, faster ways to complete backups: imaging and disk-to-disk (D2D) technology. Let's go through the steps of using imaging and D2D technologies to backup a typical small business server running SBS 2003.

Imaging

First, let's clarify what imaging is and how it can help your business. Many of you are familiar with products like Symantec's Ghost, which pretty much created the imaging market some 12 years ago. Ghost's claim to fame was its ability to "take a snapshot" of a hard drive and store all of the hard drive's data to a single file. This is a great concept, especially as it relates to backup. Now let's fast forward to the present day and see how that simple concept behind Ghost has evolved into a complete, instant backup and recovery solution.

Hardware Requirements

The first item we need to address is hardware. When it comes to protecting data, I'm a belt and suspenders type of guy; that is, I'll put into place as many backup technologies as possible. First off, I always set up RAID Level 1 on a server (Drive Mirroring) and if the budget allows, I throw a third hard drive into the system (more on that later). Despite my tirade on tape, I still like the versatility tape can offer for archival and off site backups. We can also add a few other elements to the mix, such as Firewire, USB 2.0, and a portable external hard disk.

My demo system employs those elements. For this section of our solution, I selected an HP Proliant ML110 server with 1 Gbyte of Ram, Pentium 4 2.8Ghz (with hyper threading), and three Maxtor 80Gbyte EIDE. I then added a Belkin

USB2.0/ Firewire PCI Card, an Iomega USB 2.0 REV Drive (external hard disk unit), and just for fun, an external Exabyte VXA-2 packet tape drive with Firewire. Of course, the operating system (OS) is SBS 2003 Standard edition.

Imaging Products

With the hardware out of the way, I started to consider what imaging products would meet my needs. Two came to mind: V2I Protector from Symantec and Acronis True Image Server.

V2I Protector, now called Symantec Live State Recovery, is designed primarily for the enterprise market. Small business users may not need all of the capabilities and complexities associated with Symantec Live State Recovery; True Image Server is a better and more economical choice for small business, so that's what I focus on in this chapter.

True Image Server

Key features of True Image Server include:

- Bootable rescue media,

- Support for a variety of drive partitions,

- Data compression,

- The ability to browse images, and

- Drive duplication.

The first step is to download and install the product, which is a straightforward process that we won't describe here.

Now let's get into how we use True Image Server. After the installation, one of the first things you will want to do is create bootable rescue media (an emergency recovery disk set). Here it helps to have a writable CD drive in your server, which is cheap and offers another way to perform backups. Better yet, put a DVD/CDRW drive in your server and you can benefit from installing SBS 2003 from the DVD (which is much faster) and create backup CDs.

True Image Server will create a bootable CD with a complete recovery environment. You can also choose to write the rescue disk out to 1.44 floppies, but that's not efficient—you'll need at least six disks!

The main interface, shown in Figure 5-1, offers an intuitive look at exactly what you can accomplish with True Image Server. Note the scheduling and image processing options.

Figure 5-1

Main interface

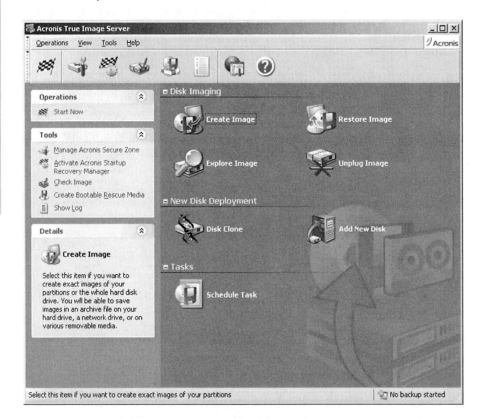

Notes:

One of the first things we want to do is create an image of our SBS server using the Create Image Wizard.

1. Select what partition you want to image.

   As you can see in Figure 5-2, we have our C: Drive partition and another drive available at E: (that will be our third hard drive and destination).

Figure 5-2

Drive partitioning

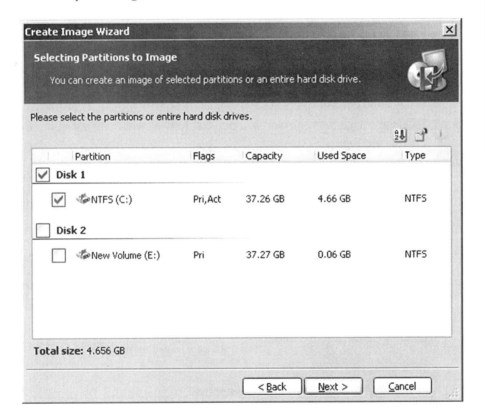

2. Select a destination.

   You may want to create a directory structure that you can use to store multiple images. This is also when you can use that fancy portable drive you selected. You can name the image something important if you like or just go by the date and time stamp of the file .

3. The first time around, you'll need to complete a full image.

Later on you can append changes to the image and speed up the whole backup process. (Tip: Use the speedy append option as a quick way to back up the server before applying a patch or installing new software.)

4. Choose the level of compression for your image file. The level of compression has a direct impact on both speed and file size, so click the various options to get estimates before proceeding.

5. Password protect the image for added safety.

BEST PRACTICE: Always use passwords when saving an image to removable or portable media. That way, if a disk or tape goes missing, your data is protected from prying eyes.

6. You can add comments for the image archive.

   A good description is always a plus!

7. True Image Server gives you one last look at what you are going to do (see Figure 5-3).

Figure 5-3

Final look.

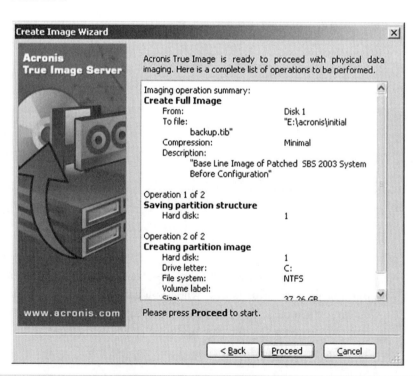

After completion, our image lives where we told it to, as shown in Figure 5-4. In a nutshell, that's the whole imaging process!

Figure 5-4

Completing the imaging process.

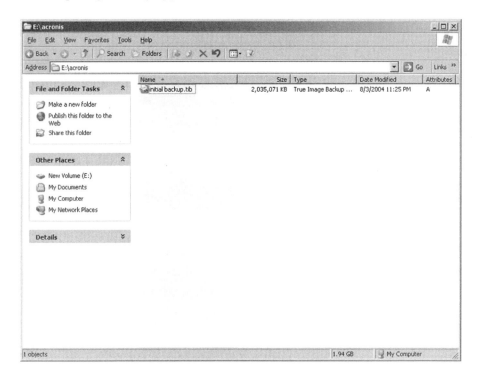

BEST PRACTICE: You should setup a schedule to create an image every night, and save it to that third internal drive I told you about. Better yet, save three or four images there; this way, you can go back a few days if you need to recover from a worm or virus. Also, consider backing up archival data to tape. Once a month or week or quarter, use SBS 2003's built in backup utility to copy image files over to your tape drive. Store those tapes off site!

Also consider copying images or creating images on that removable hard drive each day. You can then throw that drive in your car's glove box for an up-to-date daily offsite backup (think flood, theft, fire, earthquake, or any other disaster). And don't forget to keep a copy of the recovery CD off site also. That way, if your office burns down, just pick up another server or similar machine, boot off your recovery CD with that removable drive plugged in, and you're up and running in a short time!

Disk-to-Disk Technology could be an efficient and economical replacement for traditional tape-based backup. D2D really shines when combined with an imaging-based backup utility, where the speed and storage capacity offered by D2D offer a major advantage. That said, D2D technology can also be used with traditional file-by-file backups (such as the backup program bundled with SBS 2003), but that is an area where tape may prove to be easier to manage.

Dynamic DNS: A Static Problem with a Dynamic Solution

Navigating the Internet is much like navigating the seas; without proper charts, you would soon be lost. In Internet terms, ports of call are referred to as domain names (such as www.overhere.com). For a domain name to work, it has to:

- Be registered with an Internet Register (think Network Solutions or someone like that),

- Be set up in the domain name server system, and

- Have that friendly domain name (or Uniform Resource Locator – URL) tied to an IP address.

Seems pretty simple, right? But let's throw a monkey wrench into the works, and let's call that monkey wrench a Dynamic IP address!

As you may already know, SBS 2003 offers some great remote features; all you have to do is connect to your server over the Internet to use these features. That can be a simple process when you have a URL associated with the IP address assigned by your Internet Service Provider (ISP). But what happens when your ISP changes the IP address on you (a process that is all too common with many of today's broadband purveyors)? Having your IP address change all the time is bad enough, but throw some blocked ports into the mix and you really have a lack of connectivity.

To help SBS 2003 function under this burden, consider installing a Dynamic DNS service or port forwarding, which involves working through the problem at the broadband router level. Each of these options is described in detail below.

Dynamic DNS

Dynamic DNS works by watching what your assigned public IP address is and then updating the name servers to correspond with any IP address assigned by your ISP. There are quite a few Dynamic DNS providers out there and most work by a subscription-based model, where you run a small client application on your server to keep the IP addresses up to date. A few of these providers are Tzolkien's TZO, no-ip.com, dynDNS.org, and ZONEEDIT.com. Personally, I have had good luck with Tzolkien's TZO service, which I discuss in detail below.

TZO

TZO offers both a software client and a comprehensive online management system. What's more, TZO allows you to redirect both Web and email traffic if ports 80 and 110 are blocked by your ISP.

First things first: TZO is not a free service. Prices start at around $39 per year for a basic Dynamic Domain Name System (DDNS) account. Also, you may have to make some changes to Internet Information Services (IIS) and/or your broadband router to use the service. I'll cover that stuff as we go through setting up the product.

First off, you'll need to set up an account with TZO by visiting TZO.com and selecting your service level and payment options. (You can also try TZO for 30 days free by following the links on TZO.com).

After you have an account, download the TZO client and install it on your server. Some routers have the TZO service client built in. Check on TZO.com for more details. Installation and activation of the TZO client is straightforward and wizard driven. There are two versions of the client: a full version, which adds a ton of features, and a light version that does just the basics. For an SBS 2003 server, the light version will do just fine.

1. After installing the TZO client, you'll need to input a registration key. If you are using the 30-day free trial, you'll need to click "I Need a Trial Key" and register for a temporary key.
2. Enter the email address associated with the registered key.
3. Tell the TZO service what to do and how often to do it (see Figure 5-5). The default calls for a 10-minute update interval, but you can choose the interval to best suit your needs.

Figure 5-5
TZO service frequency.

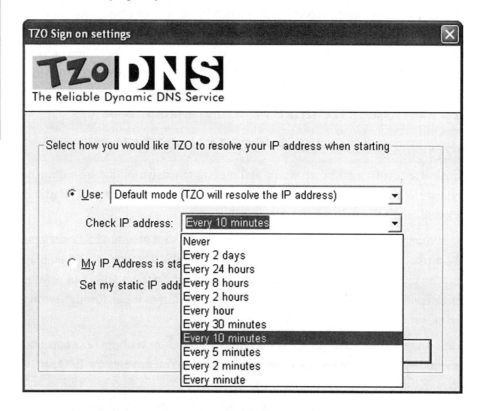

After TZO is properly set up, the client will contact the service and register the external IP address with TZO.

Notes:

4. Check the status on the client (see Figure 5-6).

Figure 5-6

Client status check.

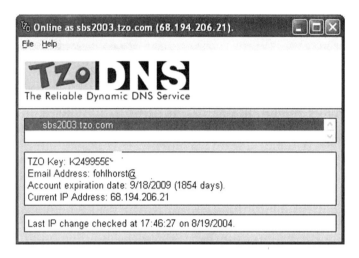

5. Once everything is set, you can play with the service's various options, such as port redirection, email options, and auto fail-over, using the TZO control panel (see Figure 5-7).

Figure 5-7

Service options.

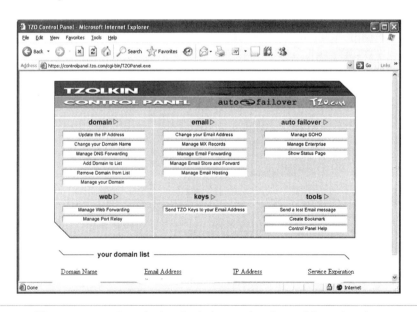

You'll want to pay special attention to the Web forwarding option (see Figures 5-8 and 5-9), which is where you allow TZO to redirect Web requests to a port other than 80.

Figure 5-8

Web forwarding options.

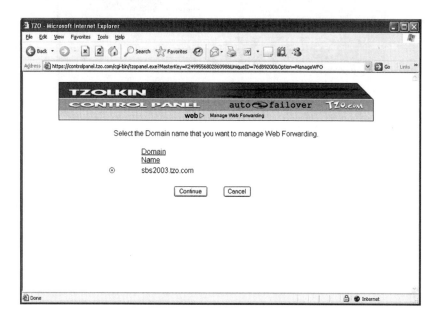

Figure 5-9

More Web forwarding options.

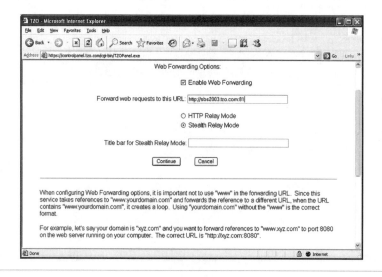

6. You can also set some start and exit options on the client side (see Figure 5-10).

Figure 5-10

Start options

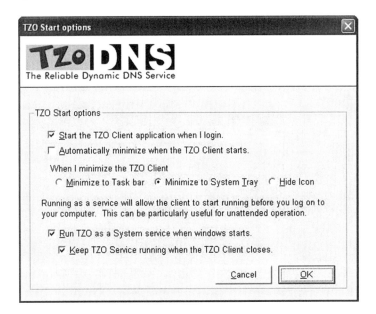

We're now all done with Dynamic DNS and port redirection, right? Well, I saved the best part of the configuration for last: what you need to do to SBS 2003 for it to accept traffic on the alternate port.

Port Forwarding

But before we get into that, let's consider another option – not changing a thing on SBS 2003 and making all of this happen at the broadband router level! You did install a hardware firewall, right? Or, at the very least, you installed a router? (If not, shame on you!) If so, make sure you can do port forwarding. Most of the major broadband gateways/routers support that. One of my personal favorites, the DLink DI-784, makes this a snap.

Simply go to the Advanced administration tab (see Figure 5-11) and add a virtual server that takes external traffic on port 81 (or whatever port you told TZO to redirect to) and have that go on over to port 80 on the internal network on your server's external NIC card. Whew! I know it sounds complicated, but in this case, a picture is worth a 1,000 words.

Figure 5-11

Advanced administration tab.

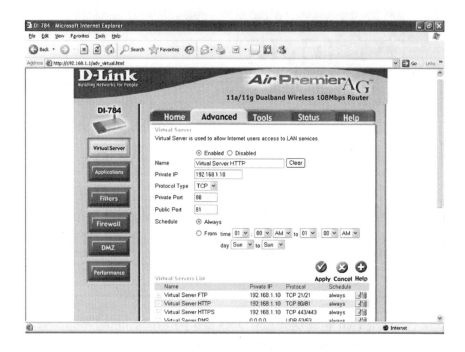

But what happens if your router doesn't support port forwarding or, worse yet, you plugged your server directly into your broadband connection (for viewers of the popular "Lost In Space" TV show, you'll appreciate the Will Robinson warning: your server is open to attack!). Well, we just have to take the time to teach IIS how to listen on a new port.

1. To make that happen, you'll need to launch IIS Manager from Start, Administrative Tools.

Notes:

2. Once in the manager, navigate to your Web site, right click on the site, and select the manage option.

   In Figure 5-12, the port number assignment (the default) is 80. Just change that to your new port number and viola! You're in business!

Figure 5-12

Changing the port number.

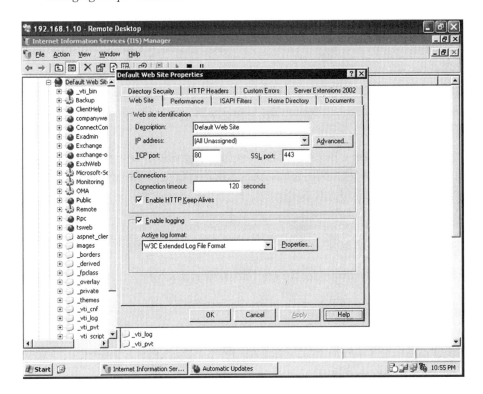

Now that the fog has cleared around the Dynamic IP address dilemma, you can see how easy it is to overcome ISP-introduced problems. Never give up, never surrender. Turn to the Web to find your solutions!

Spam, Spam, Spam!

Too often, you might find yourself uttering these immortal words from Monty Python: "Spam! I don't want *any* spam!" Spam has quickly become the scourge of the Internet, even rendering email inboxes useless in extreme cases. While there's no single best way to eliminate spam altogether, some solutions are a good fit for SBS 2003.

You can fight spam at the desktop level with a product such as Norton Anti-Spam. While that may effectively kill spam, it still allows it into the local area network (LAN), which can clog up the Microsoft Exchange mail store, so let's eliminate desktop-based solutions from our discussion here. (Of course, feel free to add a desktop solution on top of a network solution to offer a one-two whammy against spam.) This section focuses on network anti-spam solutions that integrate with Microsoft Exchange.

There are several key features to look for in a network anti-spam solution, the first of which is tunable filtering. Right off the bat, installers and end users alike should be able to:

- Build a white list, which is a list of acceptable emails from authorized senders. A white list helps to cut down on false positives (email marked as spam that really isn't).

- Regularly update black lists, which are lists of known spammers. Black lists help to block spam before it enters your LAN.

- Check a spam folder for mail marked as spam.

- Fine-tune individual settings.

All of the tunable filtering considerations listed above are addressed by GFI MailEssentials. GFI MailEssentials for Exchange/SMTP is a software-based anti-spam solution that integrates with Microsoft Exchange. It's one of my favorites. What's more, you can download a trial version of the product for free and give it a try.GFI MailEssentials. This product is sold based on the number of mailboxes in the LAN and starts at a surprisingly low price of $295 for 10 mailboxes. The initial price also includes a year's worth of updates, which help to keep your anti-spam solution in tiptop shape.

Using MailEssentials

Integrators will find the installation straightforward (make sure you have sufficient room on the server for the product and for spam mail storage). Also, processing speed helps; any filtering product will put a load on the server, so make sure your server is up to it!

Now for the meat of our discussion: software features and why they matter. I took the liberty of gathering some screen shots of GFI's product to demonstrate the power behind it and also for you to use as a sales tool for selling MailEssentials.

First off, GFI offers a simple interface (see Figure 5-13) that let's you easily navigate between white lists, black lists, and so on.

Figure 5-13

GFI interface.

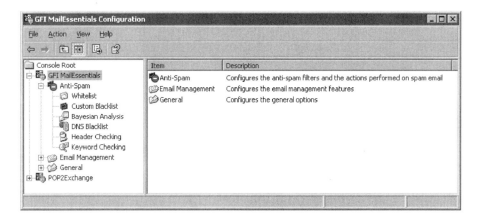

Select the Actions tab to define what your system should do with spam (see Figure 5-14). You can delete or move spam, or even forward it to another account. More importantly, you can auto move spam to a junk mail folder with Microsoft Exchange 2003.

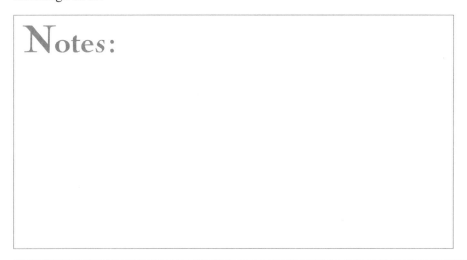

Notes:

Figure 5-14
Action tab.

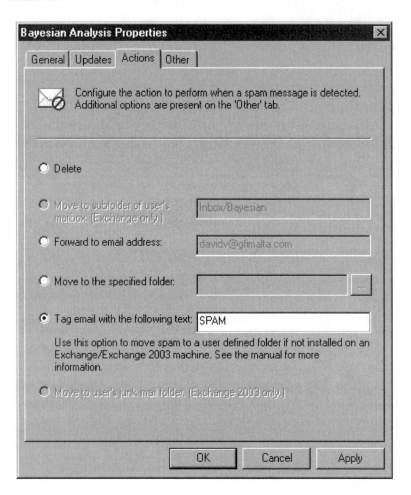

Notes:

Select the General tab to define how MailEssentials should learn which email is acceptable. The product can add to a user's white list automatically using two different methods listed here.

Where does all the spam go and what can a user do with it? The answer comes with tight integration with Outlook, as shown in Figure 5-15. What's more, with Exchange 2003, spam can be moved right over to a junk mail folder, automatically!

Figure 5-15

Outlook integration.

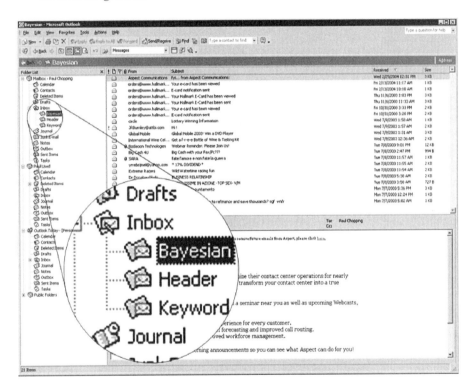

Notes:

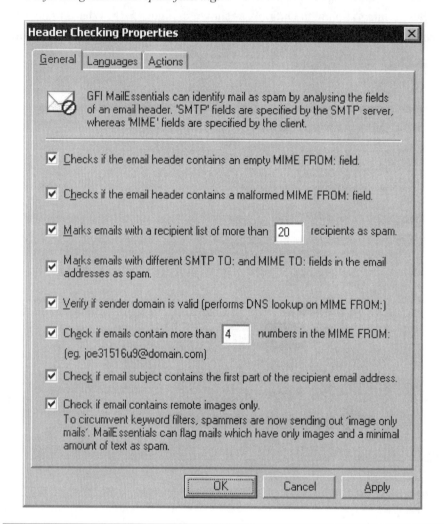

You can direct MailEssentials to perform additional spam filtering by scanning the header for additional information (see Figure 5-16).

Figure 5-16

Performing additional spam filtering.

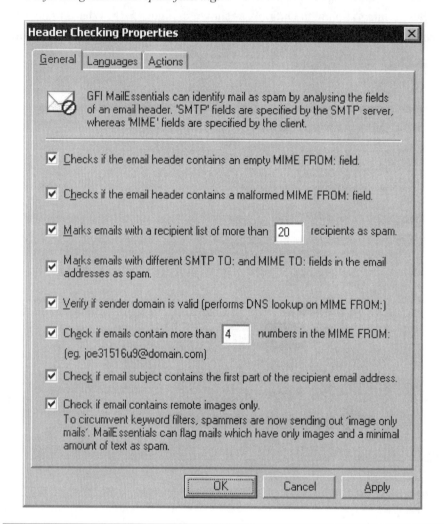

Notes:

A white list proves to be a key feature for preventing false positives. MailEssentials makes that quite easy (see Figure 5-17).

Figure 5-17
White list capability.

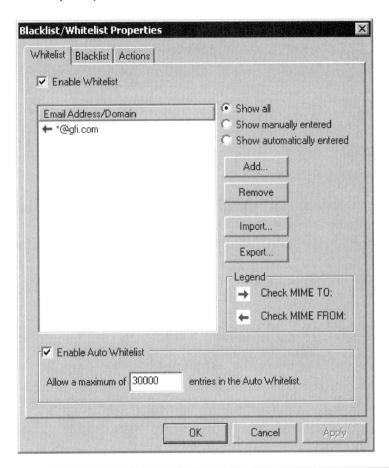

Notes:

How can you prove to your customer that a spam filtering solution is worth the expense? That's simple; just turn to the integrated reporting capabilities to show what's been accomplished (see Figures 5-18 and 5-19).

Figure 5-18

Integrating reporting capability.

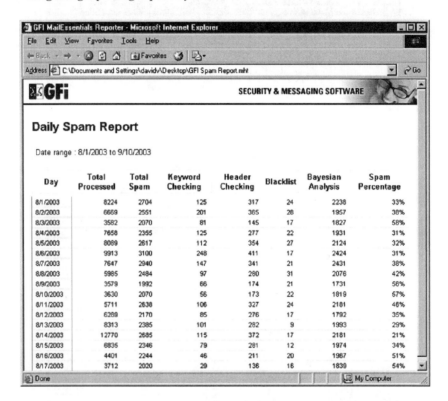

Daily Spam Report

Date range : 8/1/2003 to 9/10/2003

Day	Total Processed	Total Spam	Keyword Checking	Header Checking	Blacklist	Bayesian Analysis	Spam Percentage
8/1/2003	8224	2704	125	317	24	2238	33%
8/2/2003	6669	2551	201	365	28	1957	38%
8/3/2003	3582	2070	81	145	17	1827	58%
8/4/2003	7658	2355	125	277	22	1931	31%
8/5/2003	8089	2617	112	354	27	2124	32%
8/6/2003	9913	3100	248	411	17	2424	31%
8/7/2003	7647	2940	147	341	21	2431	38%
8/8/2003	5985	2484	97	280	31	2076	42%
8/9/2003	3579	1992	66	174	21	1731	56%
8/10/2003	3630	2070	56	173	22	1819	57%
8/11/2003	5711	2638	106	327	24	2181	46%
8/12/2003	6269	2170	85	276	17	1792	35%
8/13/2003	8313	2385	101	282	9	1993	29%
8/14/2003	12770	2685	115	372	17	2181	21%
8/15/2003	6835	2346	79	281	12	1974	34%
8/16/2003	4401	2244	46	211	20	1987	51%
8/17/2003	3712	2020	29	136	16	1839	54%

Notes:

Figure 5-19

Another reporting view.

Other Nuisances

With spam out of the way, we should be all set! But wait, spam is only the tip of the iceberg in a sea of computer nuisances! What about viruses, worms, security breaches, denial of service attacks, and so on? An SBS 2003 server connected to the Internet 24/7 can bring scary things home to roost in your system. Sure, our broadband router offers some protection and our newly installed spam filter offers a little more protection, but what about the rest of the dangers out there, specifically viruses and worms? Oh my!

A ton of solutions are out on the market, many of which install on the server, some of which install at the desktop, and others that function in a completely different fashion: the appliance!

Appliance-Based Security Solutions

Some of you may wonder why you would want to use an appliance in a small business environment and not go with the usual software-based anti-virus solution. Well, there are several reasons:

- First, most software-based solutions don't offer protection against zero-day worm attacks! A zero-day attack is when a new worm or virus is released into the wild, and none of the software-based signatures have been updated to combat it.

- Second, anti-virus solutions are notorious for increasing the load placed on a CPU and have a notable impact on server performance.

- Third, with software-based solutions, the battle against the virus or worm occurs on the server, whereas an appliance prevents the malicious code from even reaching the server.

Now, with my tirade about why appliances are better out of the way, some of you may wonder why I don't recommend an appliance for handling spam. Simply put, when you perform spam filtering at the appliance level, you lose a lot of the control associated with a good spam-fighting product. Users are often forced to access a Web console on the appliance to change settings, revise white lists, and even access their junk mail folder. This inconvenience can create a lot of angst for the typical small business user.

You should look for several features when choosing an appliance-based security solution. The first consideration is how well the appliance protects against worms and viruses. Next on the list is a firewall. (I know we spoke about using a broadband firewall for protection earlier, but in selecting the proper appliance, you can ditch that broadband firewall. Think of the security appliance as a broadband firewall on steroids!) That firewall should incorporate intrusion prevention and offer stateful packet inspection (SPI).

With these considerations in mind, we have greatly narrowed the field of potentially useful appliances. Throw in a couple of other elements, such as price and support, and we can choose the best appliance to deploy. My favorite is the Fortigate series of anti-virus firewalls (from Fortinet), discussed in detail below.

Fortigate Series of Anti-Virus Firewalls

The Fortigate series of anti-virus firewalls starts at just $495 for the 10-user Fortigate-50a. Of course, you can scale up to larger models to handle larger implementations. The appliance is ASIC-based (Application-Specific Integrated Circuit), running custom FortiOS software. Browser-based wizards make setup and management a snap. All of the menus are concise and offer a logical flow for management.

For most implementations, the Fortigate-100 (shown in Figure 5-20) would be the best choice. At a MSRP of $1,395, the unit bundles network-based anti-virus capabilities with a SPI firewall, VPN server, Web filtering, and dynamic intrusion prevention. The Fortigate-100 also offers a DMZ port that can be used for Web servers or other devices that are exposed to the Internet.

Figure 5-20
The Fortigate 100.

Once installed, it is quite easy to manage the Fortigate unit. The well-defined status console lets you know what's going on at a quick glance (see Figure 5-21).

Notes:

Figure 5-21

Fortigate status console.

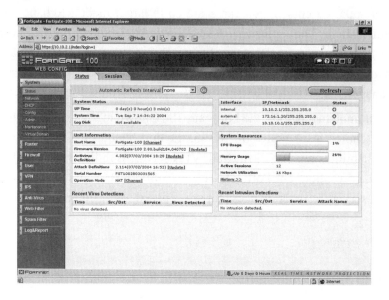

That level of ease extends to formerly complex settings; please note how easy it is to manage network settings, as illustrated in Figure 5-22.

Figure 5-22

Managing network settings.

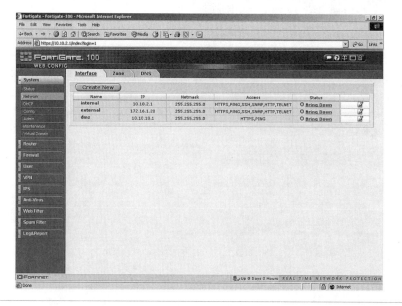

Armed with the above information, securing a SBS 2003 network with an appliance should become a "no-brainer. Installers will find the largest obstacle to overcome is still the budgetary hurdle. It simply comes down to "How much is your data worth?"

Summary

In this chapter, I have described some of my favorite third-party software and appliances that address shortcomings in SBS 2003. By implementing these solutions, you can reassure your customers that their systems are:

- Regularly backed up using various (and helpfully redundant!) media,

- Responsive and flexible in the face of changing ISP addresses, and

- Safe from Internet attacks and spam.

By beefing up your customers' systems with other-than-Microsoft products, you are enhancing the solid features of SBS 2003 while effectively shoring up your system against current SBS 2003 deficiencies.

Section TWO
SBS 2003 Utilization

CHAPTER 6
Exchange Server 2003: Advanced Topics
BY Michael Klein (New York, NY)

Introduction

"There are three kinds of men:
The ones that learn by reading.
The few who learn by observation.
The rest of them who have to pee on the electric fence for themselves."
—Will Rogers

I have studied karate for many years. In karate, you learn form (referred to as "Kata" in Japanese styles or "Hyung" in Korean styles) which is a predetermined sequence of moves. Most of these forms are hundreds of years old. Each time I studied the exact same form with a different master, I found I learned something completely different. One master would stress the power behind the moves, another the beauty, another the history, another speed, another endurance, another the practical applications, and so on. Who thought there could be such a difference in teaching and interpreting the exact same material?

What does this have to do with Small Business Server? Everything! Isn't Microsoft Exchange Microsoft Exchange? Not exactly.

Although the core is the same, there are subtle differences. A typical book on Microsoft Exchange will cover items such as site replication and front end/back end servers. These just do not exist in the SBS world. Yet other items, such as the Internet Connection Wizard, exist only in the SBS world.

There are also important differences in environment. For example, a Fortune 500 company will be running the Exchange Enterprise edition with several Exchange experts on staff to monitor and tune it. In the SBS world, we have a limited-sized mail database (more on this later) and unattended operation. The bottom line is that we have to be able to get the Exchange Server to run reliably, with minimal maintenance, since SBS sites do not have the luxury of a full-time Exchange administrator on staff.

The Importance of Exchange

"Mr. Watson, come here, I want you."
–Alexander Graham Bell to his assistant Thomas Watson, 1876

In the computer industry we talk about the "Killer App." First heard during the mid-1980s, this phrase was used to describe Lotus 1-2-3 when demand for that product became the major reason people bought IBM PCs. A "Killer App" is a program that drives sales. Just think of the old advertising slogan "You gotta get this thing!"

E-mail is the "Killer App" of the Internet Age. The following table, which appeared in *VarBusiness Magazine* in November 1997, highlights the phenomenal acceptance of e-mail.

Table 6-1

Internet e-mail growth

Year	Millions of Users	Millions of Messages/Day
1992	5	10
1996	40	100
2001	135	500
2005*	170	5000

* Projected

Recent data shows that typical corporate e-mail users receive 81 messages a day and send 29. They receive 9.6 MB of data per day, which is projected to rise to 46 MB by 2005.[1] When asked, "Which Internet technology will most impact your business?" 94% of the respondents responded, "E-mail."[2] To underscore the phenomenal growth of e-mail, consider this: From 1998 to

2002 the number of pages faxed fell by 50% [3]. Why? It takes only a few seconds to receive a 50-page e-mail, but an hour to receive the same document via fax. Then if you want to work with the document, you must rekey the information. Not so with e-mail.

Not only is e-mail a "Killer App," but it is a driving force behind SBS sales for one very good reason: cost. Exchange Server Standard Edition alone runs $699 USD. SBS Standard Edition, which includes Exchange Server Standard Edition plus Windows Server 2003, Shared Fax Service, Sharepoint Services, etc., and 5 client access licenses, costs only $599 USD. Which would you buy?

From my experience, Exchange is also a source of the majority of support calls. This is due to a number of reasons:

- **Widely used**—Accounting software may be used by only handful of people, but everyone uses e-mail.

- **Visable**—If your printer is down, you may be the only one to notice, but if your e-mail is down, the whole world notices. It is the modern-day equivalent of losing all your telephone lines.

- **Accessible to outsiders**—Not only is Exchange accessible to the outside world, it is downright under attack from the outside.

And, since problems with e-mail can affect sales and result in frustrated clients of your clients, end users want e-mail problems fixed yesterday.

A big part of this chapter will be to show you how to keep Exchange running with a minimum of effort, how to avoid problems, how to repair the most common problems, and how to include some Exchange-related business tips along the way. This will be real life.

Installation

"Default: the option selected by a computer when the user is too lazy to choose."
—William Safire

Your first encounter and our first step along the road to a trouble-free Exchange Server is the installation. Let's revisit the default installation and see if we can add to the out-of-box experience.

Preinstallation

*"A poorly planned project takes four times longer to complete than expected,
whereas a well-planned project takes twice as long."*
–Laurence Peter, Peter's Planning Principle

I have yet to encounter a client who only uses e-mail internally. A big advantage
of e-mail is the ability to send a message to anyone around the world nearly
instantly. But to connect Exchange Server to the Internet, you need to know a
few things before you install SBS. Here is the checklist:

- **Domain Name**—Talk to your client. Does he already have a domain
  name such as xyz.com? If not, you will need to register one in order to
  send and receive e-mail on the Internet. I typically work with the client
  to develop three possible domain names, then prioritize them. Domain
  names must be unique. Because of the Internet's wild popularity, domain names go fast, so there is no guarantee the client's first choice
  will be available. There will be more on domain name registration later
  in this chapter.

- **Connection Type**—How will you be connecting to the Internet? There
  are different types of connections. Will it be broadband or dial-up? If
  it's broadband, will it be cable, DSL, or fractional T1? Does the client
  presently have the Internet line? If not, sign up. Depending on the ISP,
  this can take from several days to several weeks.

- **Public IP Type**—Will the public IP address be static or dynamic?
  What's the difference? With a static IP, the address will be a fixed,
  permanent number, always the same. You will get this number from
  the ISP. With a dynamic IP, the IP number is temporary, the same way
  we assign workstations temporary IP numbers via DHCP. While this
  is fine for outbound activities like Web surfing, it creates difficulties
  for inbound services like e-mail and remote access. To get an idea
  what this would be like, imagine that every time you picked up your
  telephone, you were given a different telephone number. You could
  call out all you wanted, but your ever-changing phone number would
  make you a moving target no one could ever find. There is a way

around this problem: using a dynamic DNS service such as TZO. More on this later in the chapter.

Note: There are only a limited number of public IP numbers available. Given the mad dash to the Internet, these numbers are being gobbled up. One of the really nice things about SBS is that you only need a single public IP to communicate with everything on your network, such as the mail server, remote workstations, VPN, etc. Previously, you would have needed multiple public IP numbers, and ISPs tend to be very stingy when it comes to handing these out.

- **Domain Name Hosting and DNS**—Will the ISP provide DNS services? People refer to you by your domain name, but the Internet operates by IP address. DNS converts the domain name into the IP number. If you want mail to arrive at your server, someone is going to have to provide you with domain name hosting and DNS service. Ask your ISP whether they provide this service. If they do, get the names and IP numbers of their name servers. Also ask if they can spool your e-mail in case your Internet line or your server is down. This is a great backup, ensuring that all mail is received. If they do not provide DNS services, then you can use a dynamic DNS service as previously mentioned.

- **Router**—Will your ISP be providing a router? If so, how are changes made to it? If your server has one network card or if you have a dynamic IP address, then a router is required. If you have two network cards and a static IP address, then you do not need a router, although, in my opinion, it is still recommended. A router performs numerous functions, such as adding a layer of protection through a facility called Network Address Translation (NAT), allowing a single Internet connection to be shared by multiple workstations and interfacing your network with the particulars of the ISP's line. For example, some ISPs use a system called PPPoE that turns off the line after a few minutes if there is no activity. Most routers have the ability to send out a very small message once a minute to keep the line always on and available (sometimes referred to as a "heartbeat" or "keepalive").

Routers are not expensive. If your ISP does not provide a router, you can buy a basic router from a company like Linksys or Netgear. They start around $50. Since a router provides some basic firewall capabilities, ports are closed unless they are explicitly opened. If you do use a router, you will need to open ports to allow the server to receive incoming traffic. These ports may include: 4125, 3389, 1723, 500, 444, 443, 110, 25 and others depending on which SBS services you are making available over the Internet.

Even if the ISP provides the router, it is often locked, and you cannot program it yourself. If this is the case, you will need to contact the vendor's tech support department to make the changes for you.

- **Blocked Ports**—Ask the ISP if they are blocking any ports. If they are blocking inbound port 25, you will not be able to receive e-mail. I'll explain a solution for bypassing this blockage later in this chapter.

- **ISP's Outgoing Mail Server**—What is the name of the ISP's outgoing mail server? Although your server can directly send mail to the recipient's mail server, you may find it is refused by the recipient because of their antispam measures. If this occurs, it may be necessary to forward all your outgoing mail to your ISP's mail server. This is absolutely essential if you are connecting via a dynamic IP address. Note a cross-reference for this discussion area is page 4-25 in the introductory\intermediate *Small Business Server 2003 Best Practices* (SMB Nation Press).

- **Exchange Databases and Logs**—You need to determine where to put the Exchange data files on the file server. The Exchange software can go on the C: drive, but what about the data and logs? Although you can put them on the C: drive, this partition tends to be small. You may not have control over the size of the C: drive, since it may be predefined by the hardware vendor. It is best to put these files on a separate partition. Not only does this provide better room for growth, but it will help with performance as well, since both Windows Server and Exchange Server are intensive programs. Putting the Exchange database on a different drive and/or partition can help spread out the workload and alleviate bottlenecks. That part is fairly straightforward. Where to put the databases and logs, however, is a hotly debated issue. This topic is covered in Chapter 4: Advanced Setup and Deployment, written by Andy Goodman. He also has included the procedures for moving the database and log files to a different drive if your server came preinstalled with these files on the C: drive.

Remember, this is the preinstallation or planning stage. Our goal is to collect this vital information we will be using later on. Now moving on to the actual installation stage.

Installation Stage

Basic installation was covered very well in Harry's book, *Small Business Server 2003 Best Practices* (SMB Nation Press), and you'll find additional deployment information in Chapter 5 of this book written by Andy Goodman. However, but I have one observation to share that you might find surprising: You may not want to install Outlook 2003 at all.

Outlook 2003 offers many benefits, however there are two drawbacks to its installation if your client is running a version of Microsoft Office prior to 2003. (And if your client is running Office 2003, you don't need to install Outlook 2003, do you?) Although Outlook will work, you will lose both interactive spellchecking (seeing the errors underlined in red) and the ability to use Word as your mail editor, because Outlook 2003 will only integrate with Word 2003 and not talk to prior Word versions, such as Word XP (aka Word 2002). This drawback has surprised and frustrated a few end users after upgrading to SBS 2003, so you want to first ask your client which Outlook version is preferred. Some clients may actually choose to stay on a previous version of Outlook to retain that functionality.

Notes:

Post-Installation

Got Milk?
(ubiquitous advertising slogan)

When you first get a container of milk, it smells sweet and tastes good. You can't say the same thing two weeks later. Milk, although nourishing and good for you, spoils quickly.

The same can be said about some of the information in this section. I am referring to a few of the adjustments and hotfixes that must be applied after installation. In an ideal world, we could just install the SBS disks and be done. But we live in the real world. And while the information here is both important and necessary, it will spoil quickly. Why? Because this information is time-sensitive. The patch that you need to install today may not be necessary tomorrow, since Microsoft does periodically update the code it delivers.

Service Packs

"You can't keep trouble from visitin', but you don't have to offer it a chair."
–Gladiola Montana

After you install the server, you are presented with the "To Do" list. One of the first tasks in this list is to run the Configure E-mail and Internet Connection Wizard via the Connect to the Internet task. When you do, you will automatically be connected to the Windows Update Web site to download the latest security updates and software patches for Windows from Microsoft. Installing the latest updates is critical. But, be aware: At the present time, Windows Update does not update Microsoft Exchange. You will have to update Exchange for yourself.

There has always been some confusion as to whether you could install patches released for an individual program, such as Exchange, or had to wait for patches released by the SBS team itself. Yes, any patch, service pack, or hotfix released for a component program, such as Exchange, can be installed on an SBS server. In fact, if you go to the Microsoft Web site and check the SBS downloads page, you will notice that the links actually take you back to the exact same download location as the individual program.

To see what patches are available for your SBS server, please use the following link: http://www.microsoft.com/windowsserver2003/sbs/downloads/default.mspx.

Exchange Server 2003 SP1

Rather than installing a slew of individual patches, a service pack will let you accomplish the same thing with a single install. Since SBS 2003 was released, the Microsoft Exchange group has released Service Pack 1. This is available for download from http://www.microsoft.com/exchange/downloads/2003/sp1.asp. (Note: You must first download from Microsoft and install patch KB831464 to fix an IIS 6.0 compression issue. Exchange SP1 will not install unless this has already been applied.) Not only does SP1 contain the previous Exchange hotfixes, it also includes a recovery storage group wizard, incremental snapshot support for Volume Shadow Copy Services, and improved performance on multiprocessor systems, as well as other additions. It is well worth your while to download and install.

As I said in the introduction, Exchange is not always Exchange. SP1 offers a prime example. While Service Pack 1 resolves many issues for Exchange, it also introduces several of its own into the SBS integration. For example, after you install SP1, you will find that you cannot log on to OWA or OMA with your username. You must use domain\username. You will also find the monitoring tools in Windows Small Business Server repeatedly send a critical alert warning you that STORE.EXE is consuming more memory than usual. But there is a solution: Download and install Q843539 from Microsoft's Web site. This patch will resolve these issues.

Office 2003 SP1

Outlook is also a critical part of your message system. Because Outlook is considered part of Microsoft Office, to patch Outlook you must install the latest Microsoft Office Service Pack, which currently is Office 2003 SP1. You can also go to http://office.microsoft.com and click on **Check for Updates** (this is run from a workstation and not the server).

Note: Office 2003 SP1 does not load Q331320, which is required to add support for RPC over HTTP (see *SBS 2003 Best Practices*). So you will still need to download and install this separately (unless you have Windows XP Service Pack 2 installed).

Microsoft Hotfixes

While service packs save time and work, they are not released all that frequently. If there is a known issue, why wait for the next service pack to get the fix? Remember, our aim is to prevent the fire rather than put one out. This is where you need to install a hotfix. A hotfix is designed to solve a specific problem and is released much faster than a service pack. Since it addresses only a single issue, you may find it necessary to install several hotfixes. At press time, Microsoft had the following hotfixes listed for Exchange:

- Update to Fix Outlook Web Access – KB 831464

- Update for Microsoft Connector for POP3 Mailboxes Causing Unexpected Outbound Messages – KB 835734

- Update for Microsoft Connector for POP3 Mailboxes Consuming 100% of CPU While Downloading Messages – KB 833992

- Vulnerability in Exchange Server 2003 Could Lead to Privilege Escalation – KB 832759

- Update to Fix Inetinfo.exe Process Failure – KB 827214

As I mentioned earlier, this information changes fast. So please check the following for a list of the latest available hotfixes: www.microsoft.com/exchange/downloads and www.microsoft.com/windowsserver2003/sbs/downloads/default.mspx

> BEST PRACTICE: You should check for current hotfixes not only as part of the installation, but on a regular and ongoing basis. As I said in the introduction, one of our goals is to prevent problems ("...better to prevent a fire than to rush into a burning building to put it out"). If there are known issues and Microsoft has the fix available, then install it and prevent the problem. Both you and your clients will be happier.

Fire Prevention: Other Important Fixes

"The secret of success is to know something nobody else knows."
–Aristotle Onassis
The next two items also fall into the fire prevention category.

The /3GB Switch

It turns out that if you run Exchange Server 2003 on a Windows Server 2003 box (which describes all Small Business Servers) on a server with 1 GB or more (which virtually all are), there is a *mandatory* switch that must be added to the system startup file BOOT.INI. Without this switch, the Exchange Server will slowly consume all available memory, leaving the Windows Server with insufficient resources to run.

For example, a server with 2 GB of physical RAM that does not have the /3GB switch in the BOOT.INI file will run out of memory when the STORE.EXE virtual address space reaches 2 GB. See TechNet Article 823440 for more details.

Microsoft also recommends that the /Userva=3030 switch be used in conjunction with the /3GB Switch. See TechNet Article 810371 for more details.

To fix this problem, follow these steps:

1. Log on to the file server as **Administrator** or equivalent.
2. Click **Start**, then **Run**.
3. Type **c:\boot.ini** and press **ENTER**.
4. Windows Windows Notepad will start and open the BOOT.INI file.
5. You must change the line that starts the Small Business Server to add the new switches.

Notes:

Here is a sample of a corrected BOOT.INI file:

```
[boot loader]

timeout=30

default=multi(0)disk(0)rdisk(0)partition(2)\WINDOWS

[operating systems]

multi(0)disk(0)rdisk(0)partition(2)\WINDOWS="Windows Server
2003 for Small Business Server" /fastdetect /3GB /Userva=3030
```

Notes on the above sample:

- Because of the width of the page, the last line has wrapped onto a second line for display purposes only. Please make sure that yours is entered all on one line.

- The BOOT.INI file, by default, has its attributes set to hidden, system, and read-only. If that is the case, you will not be able to save the file after you make your changes. You must cancel out of the Notepad editor, start **Windows Explorer**, navigate to **c:\BOOT.INI**, right-click on the file, and select **Properties**. You can then clear the hidden, system, and read-only attributes. You can now reenter the Notepad to make your change and save your file. Remember to reset the changed attributes after you have edited the file.

- The above file is a sample. Due to differences in your hard drive configuration, some of the information in your BOOT.INI and the one above might be slightly different.

The Shutdown Fix

In both the Standard and Premium Editions of SBS, there is an error in the registry that can cause services, such as Exchange, to corrupt data when the server is shut down or rebooted. Fortunately, the registry entry can be corrected manually.

The errors arise because the SBS 2003 installation routine incorrectly configures the length of time to wait to zero before the server kills services during shutdown. This doesn't allow enough of a time lag for data to be saved properly in some cases. For additional information, refer to Microsoft Knowledge Base Article 839262.

To fix this problem, the registry value that controls this should be set to 120000 (milliseconds) and must use the registry's REG_SZ data type. Follow these steps:

1. Log on to the file server as **Administrator** or equivalent.
2. Click **Start**, then **Run.**
3. Type **Regedit** in the Open box and press **ENTER**.
4. Locate and then click the following registry subkey: **HKEY_ LOCAL_MACHINE\SYSTEM\CurrentControlSet\Control**
5. Right-click the **WaitToKillServiceTimeout** value, click **Delete**, then click **Yes** to confirm the removal of the registry value.
6. In the left pane of Registry Editor, right-click **Control**, point to **New**, and then click **String Value**.
7. Create the following registry value:

   Value name: **WaitToKillServiceTimeout**

   Value type: **REG_SZ**

   Value data: **120000** (make sure the "Base" option is set to Decimal first)
8. Close the Registry Editor and then restart the computer.

BEST PRACTICE: It is always a good practice to first back up the registry before making any changes. To do this click **Start**, then **Run**. Type **Regedit** and press **ENTER**. Click **File** and **Export**. Select **All for Export Range**, enter a filename, and click **Save**.

The Memory Fragmentation Fix

Imagine that you need to write a note. You have a piece of loose-leaf paper, but instead of it being a single sheet measuring the standard 8½" x 11", it is cut up into pieces each the size of a postage stamp. While you have the same total space as the loose-leaf page, that space is too fragmented to be usable.

The same type of problem exists with the memory in a file server. Instead of having one large block of memory, you have numerous small pieces of memory scattered about. This is called "memory fragmentation." On an Exchange Server, this can lead to poor performance and system instability.

The following fix is only intended for servers that have one gigabyte of memory or more. If that's the case, then do the following:

1. Log on to the file server as **Administrator** or equivalent.
2. Click **Start**, then **Run**.
3. Type **Regedit** in the Open box and then press **ENTER**.
4. Locate and then click the following registry subkey: **HKEY_ LOCAL_MACHINE\SYSTEM\CurrentControlSet\Control\ Session Manager**
5. Create a DWORD value called **HeapDecommitFreeBlock Threshold**.
6. Double-click the **HeapDecommitFreeBlockThreshold** value and enter a value of **262144** in decimal (**0x00040000** in hex).
7. Locate and then click the following registry subkey: **HKEY_ LOCAL_MACHINE\SYSTEM\CurrentControlSet\Control\Session Manager\Memory Management**
8. Double-click on **SystemPages** in the right pane.
9. Set this to **Zero**.
10. Close the Registry Editor and restart for the changes to take effect.

Cool Tools

"One only needs two tools in life: WD-40 to make things go, and duct tape to make them stop."
–G. Weilacher

Microsoft had intended to release an updated version of Exchange in 2006 code-named "Kodiak" but has abandoned that plan. Instead, they will be releasing some of the features individually as they are developed. You will need to monitor Microsoft's Exchange Web site for these new tools at www.microsoft.com/ exchange/downloads.

The first of these is the Intelligent Message Filter, known as IMF. We will be discussing the IMF later in this chapter.

There is also a collection of useful utilities that can help manage and administer an Exchange Server. I was going to recommend several to download; however, now that is not necessary. Microsoft has released ExAllTools.exe, which contains 31 separate Exchange tools packaged in a single bundle.

The following tools are included as shown in Table 6-2:

Table 6-2
  Cool Tools

Utilities included with ExAllTools	
Tool	**Description**
Planning and Architecture	
Application Analyzer 2003 Lotus Notes	Compile raw data about your Lotus for Notes applications and view an executive summary report.
Jetstress	Verify the performance and stability of your disk subsystem by simulating disk I/O load on an Exchange test server before putting your server into a production environment.
Load Simulator 2003	Simulate the performance load of MAPI clients with this benchmarking tool, which enables you to test how an Exchange 2003 server responds to e-mail message loads.
Deployment	
Exchange Deployment Tools	Find out the steps you should take, the diagnostic tools you should use, and the Setup links to help you successfully install Exchange 2003 (requires Exchange 2003 SP1).
LegacyDN	Change Exchange 2000 and Exchange 2003 organization names and administrative group names on critical system objects. You can also use this tool to view or change legacyExchangeDN values.
Management Pack Configuration Wizard	Configure test mailboxes, message tracking, and monitoring services in the Exchange 2000 and Exchange 2003 Management Packs with this graphical user interface.

Tool	Description
Operations	
Address Rewrite	Rewrite return e-mail addresses on outgoing messages sent from a non-Microsoft mail system to Exchange and destined to external or Internet addresses.
ArchiveSink	Archive message and log recipient details and other information about messages sent to or received by your server running Exchange.
Authoritative Restore	Force a restored directory database to replicate to your other servers after restoring from a backup by using this tool.
Auto Accept Agent	Automatically process meeting requests for resource mailboxes. The agent checks the availability of the resource mailbox based on the resource schedule (not free/busy) and accepts or declines new or updated meeting requests.
Badmail Deletion and Archiving	Delete or archive files automatically in the Badmail directory of specified Simple Mail Transfer Protocol (SMTP) virtual servers.
DNS Resolver	Troubleshoot e-mail delivery problems due to DNS issues by simulating the SMTP service internal code path and reading diagnostic messages.
E-Mail Journaling Advanced Configuration	Augment the current Exchange archiving features and capture recipients on expanded distribution lists, BCC recipients, and other message details.
Error Code Lookup	Determine error values from decimal and hexadecimal error codes in Microsoft Windows operating systems.
Exchange Management Pack	Get specialized monitoring for Exchange 2003. The Management Pack for Microsoft Operations Manager includes a health check for servers running Exchange 2003 and raises an alert for states that require intervention.

Tool	Description
Exchange Server Domain Rename Fixup	Repair Exchange attributes in Active Directory database after using the Microsoft Windows Server 2003 domain rename tool. All Exchange servers in the renamed forest must be running Exchange 2003 SP1. See Jeff Middleton's Chapter 15 for more discussion on this area.
Exchange Server Stress and Performance 2003	Use this highly scalable tool to simulate large numbers of client sessions by concurrently accessing one or more protocol servers.
GUIDGen	Generate globally unique identifiers (GUIDs) with this tool.
Information Store Viewer (MDBVU32)	Browse storage, address book, and other Messaging Application Programming Interface (MAPI) providers by executing MAPI calls specified by a user.
MTA Check	Look for message transfer agent (MTA) database consistency and perform repairs.
Outlook Web Access Web Administration	Administer Microsoft Outlook Web Access with this Web-based tool.
SMTP Internet Protocol Restriction and Accept/ List Configuration	Programmatically set Internet Protocol (IP) restrictions on an SMTP virtual Deny server.
Up-To-Date Notifications Troubleshooting	Solve common notification issues and test e-mail message delivery to specified devices with this troubleshooting tool.
WinRoute	Get a visual representation of the Exchange routing topology and the status of the different routing components.
Migration and Upgrade	
AUTD Binding Cleanup	View and remove existing AUTD event registration items (bindings) on an individual as well as a bulk level.
Exchange Server Profile Update	Update Outlook profiles after moving mailboxes across Exchange organizations or administrative groups.

Tool	Description
Importer for Lotus cc:Mail Archives	Import cc:Mail archive files to folders in an Exchange 2003 mailbox store or to one or more personal folder (.pst) files.
Mailbox Merge Wizard (ExMerge)	. Extract data from mailboxes on one Exchange server and then merge that data into mailboxes on another Exchange server with the help of this tool.
Interoperability	
Inter-Organization Replication	Replicate public folder and free and busy information between Exchange organizations.
Security and Protection	
Add Root Certificate	Add a custom root certificate onto your Microsoft Windows Mobile-based Pocket PC.
Disable Certificate Verification	Disable the Secure Sockets Layer (SSL) certificate check that is performed on a server running Exchange ActiveSync.

Source: www.microsoft.com/exchange/downloads/2003/default.mspx

Stop the Press!

"Accuracy in the press is important; the newspaper has to hit the porch."
-Charles Osgood

Boy, I always wanted to say that. Now I can.

Late in the production process of this book, Microsoft has released a tool for Exchange that is so good, I just had to get it into this book. It is the Exchange Server Best Practices Analyzer Tool. It is free and can be downloaded from http://www.microsoft.com/exchange/downloads/2003/exbpa/default.asp.

This is one of those items that will help us on our mission to prevent problems. "It's a kind of an engineer-in-a-box that shows how to best set up and configure Exchange," says Wayne Ashton, a group product manager for Exchange. It will proactively examine the health of your Exchange Server and look for known problems. The Best Practice Analyzer Tool gathers 1200 settings from your Exchange server, compares them to a Microsoft rules database, can make recommendations for improvements, and will let you know where your server deviates from Microsoft's best practices guidelines. Microsoft claims that it takes about five minutes to scan a single Exchange server, but my server scanned in a little over a minute.

You'll find using Exchange Server Best Practices Analyzer Tool to be extremely worthwhile. Microsoft plans to eventually include it as a feature built into Exchange.

Internet E-Mail

Before we discuss the setup and troubleshooting of Internet e-mail, a little background is in order. Let's take a brief, simplified view of this process. Just how does e-mail get to you? How does it work?

The Internet works by IP addresses. Every device connected to the Internet has a unique address in the form x.x.x.x where x is a number between 0 and 255. An example would be 214.59.153.48. Although this is fast and efficient for a computer, it becomes unwieldy for people, especially for those who work with more than a handful of sites.

The HOSTS File

In the early days, when the Internet was still small, the HOSTS file was invented to handle this problem. It was a simple ASCII text file that contained a list of IP numbers and computer names. The user could then refer to other computers by some recognizable name and the computer would look up its IP number in the HOSTS file. A sample HOSTS file would look like this:

216.34.32.23   www.yahoo.com

111.111.11.11   www.smbnation.com

HOSTS files are still in use today. In Windows 2000 and XP, this file is located in the c:\Windows\System32\Drivers\ETC folder. Unfortunately, this file has recently come under attack. Some spyware programs will create or alter the HOSTS file. Consider a spyware operator who operates an advertising Web site at 213.34.213.23 and changes the HOSTS file to look as follows:

213.34.213.23   www.google.com

213.34.213.23   google.com

213.34.213.23   www.yahoo.com

213.34.213.23   yahoo.com

In this case, if you were to open Internet Explorer on this workstation and enter www.google.com you would not go to google.com. Instead, you would go to his Web site thinking it was Google. In fact, unless you change the HOSTS file, you never will get to Google. Some spyware programs will make hundreds of entries to block all the popular search engines.

But you can also use this trick to your advantage. The IP address 127.0.0.1 is a special one. It is called the "loopback address" and points back to the workstation you are on. I have actually used this to block sites I do not want people to go to. For example:

127.0.0.1   www.napster.com

BEST PRACTICE: Set your HOSTS file to read-only to make your workstation more secure. Right-click on the **HOSTS** file in Windows Explorer and select **Properties**.

While a HOSTS file was a simple, workable solution in the early days of the Internet, it could not keep pace with the explosive growth of the Internet. Consider having to load on each workstation a list of every Web site and mail server on the Internet. First, the file would be huge and, second, the file would never be accurate. Since servers are constantly added, removed, or moved to a new location on the Internet, maintaining and distributing the HOSTS file would be a monumental task. Out of this problem the Domain Name System or DNS was born.

DNS to the Rescue

The Domain Name System is implemented as a hierarchical and distributed database containing various types of data, including host names and domain names. The names in a DNS database form a hierarchical tree structure called the domain namespace. Domain names consist of individual labels separated by dots.

Consider the example www.ComputerDirectionsInc.com. In this case: **.com** is the top-level domain. Other top-level domains include .edu, .org, .net, .gov, .mil, and codes for countries such as .ca for Canada. **ComputerDirectionsInc** is the second level domain; **www** is the hostname.

Each of the top-level domains is managed by a registrar. A registrar is an entity responsible for the distribution of domain names to customers. If you want your e-mail addressed to MKlein@ComputerDirectionsInc.com, you would need to contact a registrar to request the domain name ComputerDirectionsInc.com. If the name ComputerDirectionsInc.com is not already in use, they will issue you that name. The name will be yours for a period of time, depending on what you request and pay for. At the end of that time you will have the option to renew that name. If you do not renew, the name will go back into the available pool of names and someone else can register it.

Until 1999, one company was authorized to issue domain names for the .com space. That company was Network Solutions. In recent years this has opened up and other companies such as Tucows and Register.com can issue domain names such as .com, .net, and .org. However, given Network Solutions' dominance in the market, our discussions will be based around them and their Web site.

If you go to www.NetworkSolutions.com, you will be able to click on "WHOIS." You can then enter a domain name and query the Network Solutions' database to see how it is defined. This is also a useful tool when attempting to troubleshoot e-mail problems. A sample listing follows in Table 6-3:

Notes:

Table 6-3

Network Solutions information

```
Information at Network Solutions
Domain Registration for MYCOMPANY.COM
Registrant:
My Demo Company, Inc. (MYCOMPANY-DOM)
 235 Park Avenue 11th Floor
 New York, NY 10003
 US
 Domain Name: MYCOMPANY.COM
 Administrative Contact:
  Torres, Felix (FTS79) ftorres@MYCOMPANY.COM
  My Demo Company, Inc.
  235 Park Avenue
  11th Floor
  New York , NY 10003
  212-555-4400 (FAX) 212-555-3042
 Technical Contact:
  Klein, Michael (MK13995) mklein@COMPUTERDIRECTIONSINC.COM
  Computer Directions
  80 Birch Hill
  Searingtown , NY 11507
  516-621-7218 (FAX) 516-621-7228
 Billing Contact:
  Accounts, Payable (PAB404) AP@MYCOMPANY.COM
  MY Demo Company, Inc.
  235 Park Avenue
  11th Floor
  New York , NY 10003
  212-555-4400 (FAX) 212-555-0621
 Record last updated on 14-Mar-2001.
 Record expires on 13-Dec-2007.
 Record created on 12-Dec-1997.
 Database last updated on 16-Nov-2001 05:08:00 EST.
 Domain servers in listed order:
 NS1.MYISP.NET   198.4.75.100
 NS2.MYISP.NET   169.132.133.1
```

So Network Solutions can grant you a domain name. They can make sure that no two people try to use the same name, but they still don't know where you are on the Internet. There is still a missing link in this chain: your ISP. Since they installed your Internet line and assigned you an IP address, they must know your IP address. Whoever can get to them can get to you.

This is where the distributed part of the system comes into play. The last two lines in the above diagram listed under the section "Domain Servers in listed order" points to whoever will provide your DNS services. This is typically your ISP and was information we collected from them during the preinstallation phase. They will provide you at least two servers known as the primary and secondary servers. You can list additional servers should your ISP have them. This is to ensure that if one of your ISP's domain servers should have a problem, there is a backup available to provide for uninterrupted service.

So now someone can find your ISP. They are much closer, but they are still not home yet. Your ISP provides lots of Internet lines for lots of customers. Just how does someone know which is your mail server on your SBS box? By the DNS records your ISP creates.

DNS Records

Just what are DNS records? There are several types as seen in Table 6-4:

Table 6-4
   DNS record types

Common DNS Resource Records		
Description	**Record Type**	**Purpose**
Start of Authority	SOA	Always the first record and begins the DNS definition. It contains the domain name. It also contains basic properties that affect timing, renewal, and expiration.
Name Server	NS	Lists name servers in use for this domain and any subdomains.
Host	A	Used to assign a DNS domain name to an IP address.
Mail Exchanger	MX	Used to define the address of a mail server.
Alias or Canonical Name	CNAME	Used to create more than one name for a host server.
Pointer	PTR	Used for reverse DNS.

Let's look at some of these in action. Here is a sample of the DNS records used by MYCOMPANY.COM as seen in Table 6-5:

Table 6-5
Sample DNS information for MYCOMPANY.COM

Sample DNS Information at the ISP

```
;Start of Authority (SOA) record
mycompany.com.   IN SOA ns1.myisp.net. postmaster.myisp.net. (
     20040105 ; serial # (date format)
        10800 ; refresh (3 hours)
         3600 ; retry (1 hour)
       604800 ; expire (1 week)
        86400) ; TTL (1 day)
@       IN    MX 10 mailserver.mycompany.com.
@       IN    MX 20 mailspool.myisp.net.
@       IN    NS  ns1.myisp.net.
@       IN    NS  ns2.myisp.net.
mailserver    IN    A  169.132.112.154
www           IN    A  169.132.41.179
```

Notes:

- It can take many lines to define all the DNS records for a domain name. The use of the symbol @ in the records indicates that we are continuing to define the same name from the start of the section

- This is a partial DNS listing for discussion purposes only. Other DNS records may be required.

The MX records contain the addresses of the mail exchange system(s) for this domain. Please note that this is the public IP address. It is not the private IP address, such as 192.168.x.x, that you used for your SBS server.

Since we want to send an e-mail message to mycompany.com, we would look up the MX record for the mycompany.com domain. The MX record states that mail goes to mailserver.mycompany.com. We look for an A record for mailserver. We found it! We see that their mail server is at IP address 169.132.112.154.

Please note there are two MX records. Remember when we defined a secondary domain server so that we would have a backup in case there was a problem with the primary? Well we can do the same thing with our mail servers. The number before the address in the MX record is the preference. The MX record with the lowest preference number is used first. If the sender is unable to establish contact with that server, it will then attempt to contact the server on the MX record with the next lowest value. In our case that is mailspool.myisp.net.

> BEST PRACTICE: The ISP in this example provides e-mail spooling. Think of it like print spooling, but for e-mail. If our server is down or if our Internet line is unavailable, they will spool, or hold onto, our mail until we come back up. It is an easy way to make sure that mail is not lost.

Do not be overly concerned by the syntax and structure of the DNS records. The goal is not to make you a DNS maven or guru who can create and maintain all these records. You will not have to do that, but you do need to know they exist. If they are not set up correctly or if you have a problem receiving mail, you need to be able to understand the process so you can deal with your ISP's technical support to resolve the problem.

Dynamic DNS

One other note: The previous discussion was based on a static IP address. Given the low cost, a large percentage of SBS sites will be using DSL and Cable Internet access. Overwhelmingly, these come with a dynamic IP address. If you have a dynamic IP address, your IP address can, and will, change. As soon as that happens, your DNS A record will no longer point to the correct IP address and your mail delivery will stop. There is, however, a solution; a dynamic DNS service. This is available from companies such as Tzolkin Corporation (www.tzo.com), Dynamic Network Services (www.dyndns.org), No-IP.com (www.no-ip.com), and Deerfield.com (www.dns2go.com). These companies offer solutions to this and other roadblocks you may encounter when attempting to connect your mail server on the Internet. We will be covering some of these problems later in this chapter. These companies provide an invaluable service.

GUEST COLUMN

Typical Dynamic DNS Solutions in the Small Business Server Environment

Eric McIntyre, Vice President, Tzolkin Corporation

What is Dynamic DNS?

Dynamic DNS (DDNS) is a simple way of assigning a domain name to an IP address. In order to run a server on the Internet, you need to have a domain name to point to an IP address where the server resides. To find this server, the IP address should be static, or never change. In the past, a static IP address was needed; but now, with DDNS, your IP address could change multiple times in a day. Since many broadband Internet providers assign DHCP or Dynamic IP addresses to the majority of their customers, it is nearly impossible to provide a reliable server on a dynamically assigned IP address without dynamic DNS.

How does it work?

This is where DDNS comes in. Dynamic DNS software typically runs on a router or PC that is connected to the broadband modem. This DDNS software is constantly listening to the assigned IP address of the broadband modem. When the DDNS software notices that the IP address has changed, the domain name is automatically updated. This "IP check" can happen as often as every minute, and keeps the Domain name in "synch" with the IP address—even if it is dynamically assigned and constantly changing! Dynamic DNS is a very inexpensive alternative compared to a static IP, and since most broadband ISPs do not offer static IP options, this is the only way to run any type of server on a dynamic IP. In order to run your own e-mail server on a dynamically assigned broadband connection, you need to use a DDNS service. The DDNS software is typically installed on your SBS server or somewhere on your network where the SBS server resides. If your IP address on the broadband connection changes, your MX (Mail Exchange) records are automatically updated to the new IP address instantly.

How can I protect my e-mail?

Operating your own mail server on a broadband connection is only as reliable as your broadband connection, and in many cases could result in lost e-mail if your broadband connection goes offline. This is where an e-mail backup such as the TZO Store and Forward service can be very helpful. If your ISP has connection problems, e-mail directed to your IP will bounce back to the sender as undeliverable. These undeliverable messages can have a detrimental effect on your business.

The TZO Store and Forward service provides a simple solution to this problem by offering a primary MX record that receives all e-mail destined for your server, stores that e-mail temporarily, and then attempts to deliver that e-mail to your mail server directly. If your mail server is up and responding, the TZO Store and Forward servers deliver the e-mail. If your broadband connection is down, or your mail server is undergoing maintenance or is offline, the TZO Store and Forward servers will queue up your mail and store it as long as your server is offline. A service such as this offers a much more reliable mail server and prevents lost e-mails. This Store and Forward service also offers the ability to deliver your e-mail on a port other than the standard SMTP port 25—just in case your ISP blocks port 25 inbound.

What if e-mail is blocked outbound?

Many ISPs are also implementing outbound SMTP port blocking. This is used when sending mail from your server. This recent blocking of port

25 is due to the massive increase in SPAM/UCE e-mail and is difficult to work around if you run your own server. TZO offers a unique service for outbound mail called OMR, or Outbound Mail Relay. This mail relay service gives you the ability to use TZO as a "smart host" to deliver your e-mail to the proper destination. If your ISP blocks outbound SMTP e-mail on port 25, the TZO OMR service can accept your e-mail on a port such as 2525 and will then deliver the e-mail to the intended recipient.

Knock, Knock

So now the sender's mail server knows your IP address and where you are on the Internet. The message is knocking at your door, but can it come in? Probably not because there still may be a little more work to do before a message can be received.

(The rest of our discussion in this section will be based on the diagram below, which is Figure 1. Although your IP addresses and network devices may be different, the process and the discussion would be very similar.)

In the following diagram, knowing the public IP address would only get you to the external interface of the router. E-mail uses a protocol known as the Simple Mail Transfer Protocol or SMTP. SMTP communications operate via TCP port 25. Routers, by design, have their inbound ports closed. So if we want to receive e-mail, port 25 needs to be opened. Specifically, we want to forward port 25 to 10.0.1.2. That means any Internet traffic that reaches the external interface on the router on port 25 will be sent to 10.0.1.2, which is the external interface of the SBS server.

If your router was supplied by your ISP, you probably do not have access to reprogram it. You will have to contact their tech support and ask them to forward port 25 traffic to 10.0.1.2.

If you supplied your own router, you will need to do this yourself. This is typically done by opening Internet Explorer from one of the workstations, entering the IP address of the router 10.0.1.5 in our example, and entering the router's password. You will now be in the router's control panel. If the router were a Linksys, which is a very popular router for small businesses, you would:

1. Click on **Applications and Gaming** and then **Port Range Forward**. You would then see a chart to fill in for this information.

2. Click on **Enable** and then **Save Settings**.

This is the same screen to use should you want to open other ports for remote access. Again, routers are different, so check the documentation that came with your specific router.

Figure 6-1

Sample Network Diagram

Sample Network Diagram

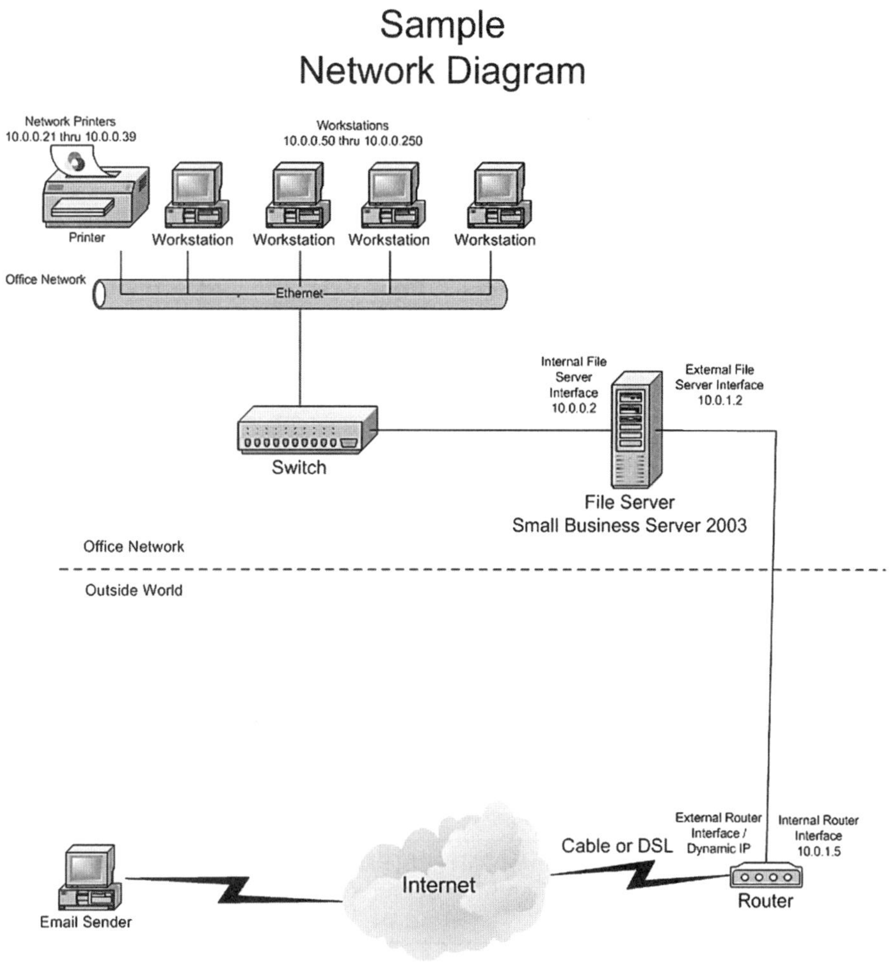

Can We Talk?

Once port 25 is open and the sender's mail server has the recipient's IP address, it can now begin a conversation with the recipient's mail server. And it does literally that starting with hello, though it spells it as HELO. Table 6-6 summarizes the SMTP commands used in the conversation between the two mail servers:

Table 6-6
SMTP Summary

SMTP command	Function
HELO	Sent by a client to identify itself, usually with a domain name.
EHLO	Enables the server to identify its support for Extended Simple Mail Transfer Protocol (ESMTP) commands.
MAIL FROM	Identifies the sender of the message; used in the form MAIL FROM:.
RCPT TO	Identifies the message recipients; used in the form RCPT TO:.
TURN	Allows the client and server to switch roles and send mail in the reverse direction without having to establish a new connection.
ATRN	The ATRN (Authenticated TURN) command optionally takes one or more domains as a parameter. The ATRN command must be rejected if the session has not been authenticated.
SIZE	Provides a mechanism by which the SMTP server can indicate the maximum size-message supported. Compliant servers must provide size extensions to indicate the maximum-size message that can be accepted. Clients should not send messages that are larger than the size indicated by the server.
ETRN	An extension of SMTP. ETRN is sent by an SMTP server to request that another server send any e-mail messages that it has.
PIPELINING	Provides the ability to send a stream of commands without waiting for a response after each command.

SMTP command	Function
CHUNKING	An ESMTP command that replaces the DATA command. So that the SMTP host does not have to continuously scan for the end of the data, this command sends a BDAT command with an argument that contains the total number of bytes in a message. The receiving server counts the bytes in the message and, when the message size equals the value sent by the BDAT command, the server assumes it has received all of the message data.
DATA	Sent by a client to initiate the transfer of message content.
DSN	An ESMTP command that enables delivery status notifications.
RSET	Nullifies the entire message transaction and resets the buffer.
VRFY	Verifies that a mailbox is available for message delivery; for example, vrfy ted verifies that a mailbox for Ted resides on the local server. This command is off by default in Exchange implementations.
HELP	Returns a list of commands that are supported by the SMTP service.
QUIT	Terminates the session.

Source: Microsoft Exchange Server 2003 Transport and Routing Guide—Part 5—Transport Internals

Now let's look at that conversation in Table 6-7. By using a program called TELNET, which is built into Windows, I can connect to a mail server and issue the above commands. I am, in essence, manually playing the role of mail server. By issuing a few simple commands, I am able to connect, state who I am, state who the recipient is, enter my message, and have it delivered.

Notes:

Table 6-7

E-mail conversation

```
220 computerdirectionsinc.com Microsoft ESMTP MAIL Service, Version:
6.0.3790.211ready at Mon, 20 Sep 2004 00:59:25 -0400
ehlo aol.com
250-computerdirectionsinc.com Hello [10.0.10.61]
250-TURN
250-SIZE
250-ETRN
250-PIPELINING
250-DSN
250-ENHANCEDSTATUSCODES
250-8bitmime
250-BINARYMIME
250-CHUNKING
250-VRFY
250-X-EXPS GSSAPI NTLM LOGIN
250-X-EXPS=LOGIN
250-AUTH GSSAPI NTLM LOGIN
250-AUTH=LOGIN
250-X-LINK2STATE
250-XEXCH50
250 OK
mail from: bob@aol.com
250 2.1.0 bob@aol.com....Sender OK
rcpt to: vendors@computerdirectionsinc.com
250 2.1.5 vendors@computerdirectionsinc.com
data
354 Please start mail input.
This is a test message into my vendor mailbox.The input ends with a line
that has a single period in it—like this.
.
250 Mail queued for delivery.
quit
221 Closing connection. Good-bye.
Connection to host lost.
C:\>
```

You can see how simple and easy this is. If you look closely at the above, you will actually see a dialog that you can read between the two servers. Underneath it all, it is really quite simple. Also, as you could imagine, using TELNET to mimic a sending server, being able to issue command, and seeing the response can be very helpful when troubleshooting e-mail problems.

Yet, the above should also give you a reason for concern. If you look carefully, you will notice I issued the command **mail from: bob@aol.com** and the Exchange Server responded with **Sender OK**. Then my message was accepted and delivered. There is just one problem: I am not Bob from AOL. As you can see, it is very easy to forge e-mail and hide the true sender. The Internet was built on trust and openness. Unfortunately, unscrupulous people are now taking advantage of this. More on this later in the chapter.

Putting It All Together

"This can easily be done by a 10-year-old with 30 years of experience."
—Unknown

Now that you have a good overview of the process, let's go through the details to set it up on your server. In the previous section, I provided you with a preinstallation checklist and you collected a lot of information. Now let's put it all together. Here is how to connect your Exchange Server to the Internet.

Contact the ISP

Follow these simple steps.

- Determine what line speeds are available and their cost. Make a selection that best fits your needs and budget.

- Gather the following information from the ISP:

    o   Will the Internet line be a static or dynamic IP address?

    o   If the IP address will be static, determine whether they will provide DNS services. If so, get the names and IP addresses of their name servers to use with Network Solutions or other registrar. These are used by the outside world when trying to find you on the Internet. If the line is d ynamic, you are going to need to order a dynamic DNS service.

o　If the ISP is providing DNS services, do they offer e-mail spooling services and at what cost?

o　Determine whether the ISP will provide a router. Even if it isn't necessary, a router is recommended. If so, who will make the pro- gramming changes to it?

o　Determine which ports, if any, the ISP blocks and in which direc- tion. If port 25 is blocked inbound, you will not be able to receive e-mail. There is a solution: an e-mail relay/forwarding service from a dynamic DNS provider. More about this later.

o　Determine the name of the ISP's outgoing mail server.

o　Determine the IP addresses of the ISP's primary and secondary DNS Servers. These are used, for instance, by your staff when Web browsing. If someone were to open Internet Explorer and enter google.com, these are the servers that would return the IP address of 216.239.39.99. These addresses are also required when running the CIECW.

Order the Network Line

Depending upon the type of line, it may take several weeks to get this installed, which is why you want it to be one of the first things you do. Some ISP's are moving to self-installation, which can dramatically reduce this waiting period, but this is only applicable in situations where a line is already present in an office. For example, if you are using DSL from your local telephone company and your server is already located near the correct telephone line, then this can save a considerable amount of time. Otherwise, you will have to wait.

Dynamic DNS

If you have a dynamic IP number, contact a dynamic DNS service like TZO.com to get their name server information. You will need this in the next step when you obtain your domain name from the registrar. You will not be able to sign up with the dynamic DNS service now since you do not yet own a valid, registered domain name. Over time this step becomes unnecessary. I have done so many SBS servers that I know TZO's domain servers are ns.tzo.com and ns2.tzo.com by heart.

Domain Name

Obtain your domain name from Network Solutions or another registrar. If you do not yet have a domain name, now is the time to create it. To do this with Network Solutions:

1. Go to **www.networksolutions.com** or **www.netsol.com**.
2. On their home page, enter the desired domain name in the box number 1. Choose your extension, such as .com, in box number 2.
3. Click on **Search**. In a few moments you will find out whether the name is taken or available. If the name is already in use, go back and try another. This is why I ask my clients for several possible names.
4. If the name is available, click on **Continue**. You will have several more screens that ask for information, such as contact name and address, the time period you want to register the name for, and credit card information.

Now the name is yours, but you still need to enter the name server for whoever will be hosting your domain name.

1. Once you are in the **Domain Details** screen, you will see a field entitled **Domain currently points to.** Click the **Edit** button next to it.
2. You will next see a box labeled **Move DNS to a New Name Server.** Click the **Continue** button in that box. You can now enter the name servers that point to your DNS provider. If your server will have a static IP, point your entry with Network Solutions to the name servers you got from your ISP. If your server will have a dynamic public IP address, point your entry with Network Solutions to the name servers you got from the dynamic DNS service.

Although it takes only a few minutes to sign up, it can take two days or so for the information to propagate through the Internet. I typically do this several days before I am scheduled to install a new server. By the time I show up on site, everything is all set to go.

Dynamic Versus Static IP

If you have a dynamic IP address, it's time to call back the dynamic DNS service such as TZO.com. Since you now have a valid, registered domain name, you can complete their sign-up process and subscribe to their service. You may also need to sign up for additional services.

- To prevent mail from being bounced if your Internet line or mail server is down, sign up for an e-mail spooling service.

- If port 25 is blocked inbound by your ISP, sign up for a mail relay/ forwarding service.

- If port 25 is blocked outbound by your ISP, sign up for an outbound mail service. (If your ISP blocks port 25 outbound, they may still have it opened to their mail server. If this is the case, then you do not need a dynamic DNS service. You can use the ISP's mail server as your smart host).

If you have a static IP number, contact your ISP and have them create your DNS records including your MX record. Also make sure they enable your e-mail spooling if they offer it.

Connect to the Internet

Consider the following when connecting to the Internet:

- Determine your IP scheme. Assign IP numbers to the internal and external network cards on the file server. And if you don't have two network cards on the server, why not?

- If necessary, purchase and connect the router.

- Program the router. Assign an IP address to the internal router interface. Open port 25 and any other ports you might need, such as the port listed earlier for remote access. Forward any traffic on these ports to the external network card of your SBS server. If the router was supplied by your ISP, you may need to contact them to program it.

- Connect the Internet line to the router.

BEST PRACTICE: Be safe! As we will discuss, connecting to the Internet can be dangerous if you are unprotected. Make sure you have antivirus software in place before connecting. Once you do connect, patch Windows and Exchange server as was previously discussed. Also, be sure to get the latest antivirus definitions available. If you are running SBS 2003 Premium Edition, then check the chapter on ISA server for its setup and configuration.

Configure Server

If necessary and not already done, move Exchange databases and logs off the C: drive. See Chapter 4: Advanced Setup and Deployment for details on this.

Sending E-mail

Decide whether mail will be sent via DNS or smart host. Historically, everything was sent via DNS. Your mail server would resolve the address of the recipient's mail server via DNS and then send the mail directly to the recipient's mail server. With smart host your server sends all the outgoing mail to another mail server, typically your ISP's outgoing mail server, which then delivers the mail to the recipient. Why not send it directly to the recipient? Because many ISPs and mail servers refuse the mail due to increased security measures. Spam and scams are getting out of hand. If you don't adhere to their rules, your mail will be refused.

An example can be found at http://postmaster.aol.com/guidelines/standards.html, which contains a long list of rules to comply with for AOL to accept your mail. One states that AOL will not accept mail if your server has a dynamic IP address. This one rule eliminates a large percentage of SBS sites from sending mail directly to AOL, and there are other rules as well. AOL is fairly typical. If in doubt, it is safer and easier to use a smart host.

Cablevision, one of the cable companies in my region, now blocks all outbound port 25 traffic except to their outgoing mail server. If they are your ISP, you must use a smart host if you want to send e-mail.

If you do opt to use DNS for delivery, make sure whoever provides your DNS also creates a PTR record so that recipients can perform a reverse DNS lookup.

With standard DNS, you provide a domain name and you are returned an IP address. With reverse DNS, you provide the IP address and the domain name is returned. This can be compared to the inbound message to see if the sender is really who they say they are. It is a good way to cut down on spam.

Configure E-mail and Internet Connection Wizard

Run the Configure E-mail and Internet Connection Wizard (CEICW) on the SBS server. This is where it all comes together. This was done at length in Chapter 4 of *Small Business Server 2003 Best Practices* (SMB Nation Press), but that example was based on DNS for delivery. Let's discuss how to configure delivery using a smart host.

When you run the CEICW, you will come to a screen entitled **E-mail Delivery Method** which gives you two choices. If you select the first option, **Use DNS to route e-mail,** the server will send the mail directly to the recipient's mail server via DNS. If you choose the second option, **Forward all e-mail to e-mail server at your ISP**, you will send mail via a smart host. There is space below this option to enter your ISP's outgoing mail server as the smart host. It's that easy.

If using a dynamic DNS service, download and install their client software on the file server. This program typically checks your public IP address every minute or so. It then reports this information back to your dynamic DNS provider's server, which automatically updates your DNS records, keeping them current and correct. Even if your IP address changes, people can still find you on the Internet.

Test

Send a test e-mail to someone outside your network and see if it is received. Then respond and see if that message can find its way through the Internet and into your mailbox. If any of these tests fail, see the troubleshooting section later in this chapter.

Success!

That's it. You are done. You may find that you can skip some of the steps if they are already completed. For example, a client might already have an Internet line, so there would be no need to order another one. Or, maybe the client has an existing domain name, which means you don't need to register a new one. However, you may have to update the records to point to the correct name server.

ISP Port Issues

I would like to address one situation you may encounter while setting up e-mail that has become fairly common: an ISP blocks port 25. While I have mentioned this previously, let me now show you how to set up your Exchange server so you can still receive e-mail.

Overview

Each IP address has around 64,000 ports. Even if an ISP blocks some ports, thousands of other ports are still open. Instead of receiving mail on port 25, couldn't you use another port? Yes you can!

The key to this is a dynamic DNS service. I have been using TZO for many years on all my clients who have a dynamic IP address. I am going to use their service in our example. They have a service called E-mail Store and Forward, which receives mail on port 25 and will forward it along any port number you choose. As an example, let's use port 2525.

You will need to open port 2525 along the rest of the route. This includes the router and either RRAS for SBS Standard Edition or ISA for SBS Premium Edition. Finally, you need to instruct Exchange to listen for mail on port 2525.

The beauty of this solution is that the sender does nothing different nor even knows what is happening. She sends on 25 and you receive on 2525. It is completely transparent.

The Process

This section will walk you through the procedures.

Dynamic DNS Service

Complete the following:

1. Sign up with TZO for their Store and Forward service or equivalent product from another dynamic DNS service.

2. Double-click on the **TZO icon** in the system tray.

3. Click on **TZO Control Panel.**

4. Once in the TZO Control Panel, click on **Manage Email Store and Forward.**

5. Enter 2525 for **Use the port**.

6. Click on **Continue.**

7. Once this is done, you will temporarily stop receiving mail, since the rest of the system still needs to be programmed for the new port. Do not worry. The e-mail is being spooled and all mail will be delivered once you are finished with the setup.

Router

Forward port 2525 traffic on your router to the file server's external network card. This was 10.0.1.2 in the sample network diagram. The exact procedure will vary with the make and model of your router.

Open Port on Server

If you are running SBS Standard and using RRAS:

1. From the SBS server, click on **Start,** then **Programs, Administrative Tools,** and **Routing and Remote Access.**

2. Expand your server name **(local),** then expand **IP Routing.**

3. Select **NAT / BASIC Firewall.**

4. Right-click on your external network card in the panel on the right and select **Properties.**

5. Click on **Services and Ports** tab.

6. Click **Add.**

7. Enter a description such as **Redirected E-mail.**

8. Select **TCP** for the **Protocol**.

9. Enter 2525 for **Incoming Port.**

10. Enter 127.0.0.1 for **Private Address.**

11. Enter 2525 for **Outgoing Port.**

12. Click **OK.**

If you are running SBS Premium and using ISA:

1. From the SBS server, click on **Start,** then **Programs, Microsoft ISA Server,** and **ISA Management**.

2. Expand **Servers and Arrays,** then choose your server name, **Policy Elements,** and **Protocol Definitions**.

3. Click on **Create a Protocol Definition**.

4. Enter **Redirected E-mail** for **Protocol Definition Name** and click **Next.**

5. Enter **2525** for **Port Number**.

6. Enter **TCP** for **Port Type**.

7. Enter **Inbound** for **Direction** and click **Next**.

8. Select **No** for **Do you want to use secondary connections?** and click **Next**.

9. Click **Finish**.

10. Click on **Publishing, then Publish a Server**. The New Server Publishing Rule Wizard starts.

11. Enter **E-mail** on **Redirected Port for Server Publishing Rule Name** and click **Next**.

12. Enter **10.0.0.2** for **IP Address of Internal Server**.

13. Enter **10.0.1.2** for **External IP Address** and click **Next**.

14. Select **Redirected E-mail** for **Apply the rule to this protocol** and click **Next**.

15. Select **Any request** for the **Client Type.** Click **Next**.

16. Click **Finish**.

17. Click on **Access Policy,** then **IP Packet Filters** and **Create a Packet Filter.** The New IP Packet Filter Wizard starts.

18. Enter **Redirected E-mail** for **IP Packet Filter Name.** Click **Next**.

19. Select **Allow packet transmission.** Click **Next**.

20. Select **Custom** for **Filter Type.** Click **Next**.

21. Select **TCP** for **IP Protocol**.

22. Select **Inbound** for **Direction**.

23. Select **Fixed Port** for **Local Port**.

24. Enter **2525** for **Port number**.

25. Select **All Ports** for **Remote Port**. Click **Next**.

26. Select **Default IP addresses** for each external interface on the ISA Server computer for **Apply this packet filter to**. Click **Next**.

27. Select **All remote computer**s for **Apply this packet filter to.** Click **Next**.

28. Click **Finish**.

Within Exchange Server 2003, perform the following:

1. From the SBS server, click on **Start,** then **Programs, Microsoft Exchange,** and **System Manager**.
2. Expand **Servers,** then select **Servername, Protocols,** and **SMTP**.
3. Right-click on **Default SMTP Virtual Server** and select **Properties**.
4. On the **General** tab, click **Advanced**.
5. Click **Add**.
6. Use **All Unassigned** for **IP Address**.
7. Enter **2525** for **TCP port**.
8. Click **OK**.

War Story

It was barely 48 hours after I had finished writing the above procedure when I walked into my office and noticed that I had not received one piece of e-mail overnight. That's strange, I thought. I asked around and neither had anyone else. After a little checking, I determined that my inbound port 25 had been blocked by my ISP. They hadn't even given any advanced notice. Time to take my own advice: I followed the above instructions to redirect my inbound port 25 to another port. Harvey Mackay wrote a book entitled *Beware the Naked Man Who Offers You His Shirt*. I can assure you the above directions work—and I am fully clothed.

> BEST PRACTICE: Some routers can receive traffic on one port and send it on another. So, it could receive traffic on port 2525 on the external network and send it along port 25 on the internal network. If your router supports this feature, you do not have to reconfigure SBS to listen on another port. Leave it set to the default of port 25. The router will listen for e-mail on a different, non-blocked port and convert the traffic back to port 25. No reconfiguring necessary!

Notes:

GUEST COLUMN

Getting POPPED by the POP3 Connector

Harry Brelsford, CEO, SMB Nation, Inc.

God bless real-world clients. It's the lessons learned in the field of SBS consulting that not only provide book fodder but add to our experience base and make us better consultants. Such was the case in 2003 when I served a well-respected newsletter publisher running SBS 2003 who insisted on using the POP3 connector. This customer wanted to retain his multiple POP3 accounts for some very important business reasons, including brand identity consistency and system continuity. He saw the POP3 connector as a way to keep his existing POP3 accounts and have e-mail continue to safely arrive—even if his SBS 2003 server machine wasn't functional because of a power outage, etc. In this power outage example, the ISP would continue to receive the e-mail.

The lessons learned were:

- ***The POP3 Connector doesn't forward e-mail to a Public Folder.*** *The newsletter publisher wanted incoming e-mail from his 160,000 readers to be placed into a Public Folder where staff could respond to the e-mails in a timely manner. The POP3 Connector provides a screen where you select which Active Directory user account that is Exchange Server 2003 e-mail-enabled would receive the incoming POP e-mail. However, even though a Public Folder is SMTP-enabled in Exchange Server 2003, it is not an official Active Directory object and thus won't appear as a mapping option when using the POP3 Connector. FYI—the use of a Public Folder to receive the readers' incoming e-mails was considered mandatory.*

- ***The POP3 Connector can not interact with an Active Directory contact object.*** *The next idea was to have the POP3 Connector map to an Active*

Directory contact object (again, one that was Exchange Server 2003 SMTP e-mail-enabled) which would then forward the incoming POP e-mail to a Public Folder. No cigar again, mate! The POP3 Connector will not interact with an Active Directory contact object.

- **Mary Hartman, Mary Hartman!** *The final solution was to create a fictitious humanoid masquerading as an Active Directory user object that was Exchange Server 2003 SMTP e-mail-enabled. This Active Directory user account, which could use a silly name like Mary Hartman (from Norman Lear's popular madcap 1980s late-night TV sitcom), would then forward the e-mail to the Public Folder. Madness indeed!*

- **There is no way to "parse" incoming POP e-mail via the POP3 connector to distribute the e-mail to different accounts depending on subject matter.** *So what if the subject line told the whole truth and nothing but the truth relating to the reader's inquiry? Would a keyword like "subscribe" redirect the POP e-mail to a different SMTP-based e-mail account (ultimately another Public Folder using the Mary Hartman forwarding method described above)? Was there a way to invoke a rule at the POP3 Connector level to accomplish this? The answer was no!*

- **The POP3 Connector maintains a one-to-one relationship between the POP account and Active Directory user accounts that are SMTP e-mail-enabled.** *The POP Connector didn't provide an easy interface to have multiple POP e-mail accounts flow into a single Active Directory user account that was SMTP e-mail-enabled. It required multiple one-to-one entries.*

- **Some Public Folder oddities can't be blamed on the POP3 Connector.** *Public Folders don't notify you that a message has arrived, been read, or remains unread. Enough said and enough sadness at the customer site over this one. For staff to utilize Public Folders as a real customer service tool, they needed to know when e-mail arrived and whether it had or had not been read. Boo-hoo!*

So there you have Harry's baptism by fire with the POP3 connector. Kindly note that I still view the POP3 Connector as a transition and migration tool whereby a business can retain its POP3 accounts until it is ready to fully exploit the SMTP e-mail system inherent in Exchange Server 2003. I know that many SBSers agree with this sentiment.

Cheers....harrybbbbb

PS—The Microsoft online document surrounding the POP3 Connector, which is presented in the CEICW (aka Internet Connection Wizard), is excellent this time. If that documentation doesn't answer your questions or meet your POP3 Connector needs, please use the SBS resources mentioned in Appendix A, such as the SBS Yahoo! Groups, to post your specific POP3 question and await your answer!

PPS—And just who was this newsletter publisher? Visit www.briansbuzz.com to see for yourself! Tell him Harry sent you when you sign up for his well-received technology newsletter.

The 16 GB Wall

"640K ought to be enough for anybody."
–Bill Gates, 1981

Every time I use that quote, people chuckle. Hindsight is, of course, 20/20. Yet, what once seemed huge to Bill Gates, now seems tiny in retrospect to all of us.

Remember the floppy? Remember how over the years, hard drive capacity went from 5 meg to 80,000 meg and the standard amount of RAM on a computer grew from 640KB to 512 MB? Yet the 1.44 floppy floundered. It stagnated. It started at 1.44 MB and 10 years later, it was still at 1.44 MB. Well, we face a similar situation when it comes to Microsoft Exchange.

The first version of SBS was labeled SBS 4.0, not only because it was based on NT 4.0, but also with the knowledge that people are leery of buying version 1.0 of anything. When this first version of SBS was released, the maximum database size of the Exchange database was 16 GB. Years later and now on its fourth version, SBS still offers only 16 GB. The original designers no doubt thought, to paraphrase Bill Gates, "A 16 GB Exchange database ought to be enough for anybody."

Well, for many SBS sites, it isn't. Why? First, the maximum number of users on an SBS box has increased to 75. Next, the average message size has grown. Finally, and what is most significant, each person is using e-mail more than ever before. The volume of messages per day is growing exponentially. Since the Exchange database needs free space to function, we must be more vigilant to protect against exceeding this 16 GB limit.

Misconception Clarification

First, let me clear up two common misconceptions regarding the 16 GB limit.

Misconception #1: This is an SBS-imposed limit.

Not true. The limit comes from Exchange Server. Anyone running Exchange Server Standard Edition will face the same 16 GB limit.

Misconception #2: The 16 GB limit applies to both the public and private combined.

This is also false. The limit is separate. So the Public Information Store can be 16 GB and the Private Information Store can also be 16 GB.

Note: Although the database can be as large as 16 GB, there is a practical limit of 2 GB on the size of an individual mailbox. This is primarily caused by the size limits of the .pst and .ost files.

A little background is in order. All your individual user mailboxes are stored in a single database called the Private Information Store. There is also a single database for all your shared public folders called the Public Information Store. Each of these databases can be 16 GB.

Now if we dig a little deeper, we will see each of these databases is in fact made up of two files: an .edb and an .stm. This is important since, if you want to know how much space you are using, you will have to add them together. Let's look at an example in Table 6-8:

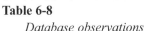

Table 6-8

Database observations

```
D:\Exchsrvr\MDBDATA>dir
 Volume in drive D is Company Data
 Volume Serial Number is 0CE6-50B0
 Directory of D:\Exchsrvr\MDBDATA09/19/2004 10:23 AM  <DIR>      .
09/19/2004 10:23 AM   <DIR>          ..
09/19/2004 04:38 PM               8,192    E00.chk
07/30/2004 07:20 PM           5,242,880    e00.lnw
09/19/2004 10:23 AM           5,242,880    E00.log
09/19/2004 10:23 AM           5,242,880    E00005E3.log
09/19/2004 02:00 AM           5,242,880    E00tmp.log
09/13/2004 09:15 PM       1,116,807,168    priv1.edb
09/14/2004 09:17 PM         503,324,672    priv1.stm
09/18/2004 11:28 PM         724,639,744    pub1.edb
08/14/2004 11:33 AM           6,299,648    pub1.stm
02/20/2004 11:16 AM           5,242,880    res1.log
02/20/2004 11:16 AM           5,242,880    res2.log
08/15/2004 09:55 PM           7,753,728    tmp.edb
      12 File(s) 2,390,290,432 bytes
       2 Dir(s) 87,205,908,480 bytes free
D:\Exchsrvr\MDBDATA>
```

The Exchange databases are kept in the mdbdata folder. The Public Information Store is made up of both the pub1.edb and the pub1.stm files. In the example above, the pub1.edb is 724 MB and the pub1.stm is 6 MB. Together they consume 730 MB. There is plenty of breathing room.

The Private Information Store is made up of both the priv1.edb and the priv1.stm files. In the example above, the priv1.edb is 1,117 MB and the priv1.stm is 503 MB. Together they consume 1,620 MB. Again, the information store is well within limits.

If your site is a heavy user of e-mail, this is something you might need to check regularly.

Avoiding Bump and Grind

So now that you know about the limit, how do you guard against bumping up against it?

First you need to know that the problem of exceeding the limit is not a product of the message, but the attachment. A typical e-mail message from one of my clients might range from 1K to 5K. Yet, these same clients might attach a database, PDF, scanned image, or log file attachment that may be many megabytes in size.

The potential to exceed the 16 GB limit is not only dependent on the number of users, but the industry in which they work as well. One client of mine, a public relations company, regularly e-mails high-resolution graphics files that are 10 MB or more to its outside printing service. I have small clients who constantly have space problems and large clients who never do. So you can see how it's important to know your clients, their business, even their personalities if you want to effectively assess their needs in this area.

There is one good piece of news. To help control the size of the database, Exchange supports single instance message storage. If a message is sent to more than one mailbox in the same database, only one copy of the message is stored in one mailbox. The other mailboxes contain pointers back to the one stored message. Imagine if a message with a 5 MB attachment is sent to 10 people; if each person stored the message, 50 MB would be consumed. With the single instance storage, only 5 MB is consumed. That represents a tremendous savings.

Monitoring

"You can see a lot by observing."
 —Yogi Berra

Our premise is that it is better to prevent a problem rather than to solve one. How do you keep from hitting the 16 GB wall? By monitoring the space. You will never know you have a space problem unless you look. But how do you monitor the space?

You have several tools at your disposal to watch the space in use. The first set are big picture tools available to the System Administrator:

- **Exchange\MDBData folder**—This was discussed earlier. Use Windows Explorer to navigate to the folder where Exchange keeps the databases and see how large they are. Remember to add the .edb and the .stm files together. This is easy and only takes a few seconds. Yet it only tells you how much total space is in use, not what or who specifically is consuming the space.

- **Read the Server Usage Report**—This is one that only we in the SBS world are lucky enough to get. If you enabled Monitoring on the server's To Do List, and you should have, then you will be getting Server Usage Reports every two weeks. The report contains a section called Mailbox Size. This shows the starting mailbox size, ending mailbox size, and rate of change by user over a two-week period. You can see at a glance who is consuming the space. You can also easily zero in on any dramatic changes. Since it is listed by user, it does not contain any information about public folder space.

- **Exchange System Manager**—This is the traditional Exchange way in which to view the space in use by each folder. Separate screens list the size of each public and private folder. The information can be sorted by any column title. Clicking on the **Size** (KB) column title is an easy way to see all the largest consumers of space.

  To view the private mailboxes, click on **Start**, **Programs**, **Microsoft Exchange**, **System Manager**, **Servers**, your server name, **First Storage Group**, **Mailbox Store**, and then **Mailboxes**. The folder size information will be on the right-hand side of the screen. Note that it shows both the folder size and the number of items. You could have lots of items and consume very little space. You could have one item and consume a huge amount. It is the folder size that is the real concern.

  For public folders, click on **Start**, **Programs**, **Microsoft Exchange**, **System Manager**, **Servers,** your server name, **First Storage Group**, **Public Folder Store,** and then **Public Folders**.

The previous tools are for the System Administrator. Here are a few in Outlook that are available to users as well:

- **Folder Size**—How much space does your mailbox use and which of your folders use the most space? Outlook will tell you. To check this, right-click on the top of the user's **Mailbox** in the folder list, click on **Properties** and then **Folder Size**. You will see the total size and a list of each folder with the space it uses. It is easy to see which ones are the space hogs. This also works on public folders.

- **Message Size**—Typically, the biggest drain on space will be a user's Inbox. If you want the users to manage this space, it would help if they could see how much a particular message is consuming. Along with the sender, subject, and time, a good practice is to add a column displaying the size of each message.

Prevention

"Lots of folks confuse bad management with destiny."
–Kin Hubbard

Given the mandate that it is better to prevent a problem than fix it, how do you prevent running into the 16 GB wall?

Keep only important messages

This one should go without saying. Many users are pack rats. They treat their Inbox as a file cabinet. And, if their Inbox is bad, their Sent Items folder is worse. It is out of sight and out of mind.

BEST PRACTICE: Not only is this a space issue, but a productivity issue as well. Think of a messy desk where you can't find anything. Time management experts will tell you when you initially touch a paper, piece of mail, or e-mail you should take some type of action. That action could be to file it, delete it, forward it (i.e., delegate it), or act on it. Don't keep sifting through the same information again and again. To impress this upon clients, I use a mnemonic that I learned from Ray Ozzie of Lotus Notes fame. I remind them of the OHIO Principle: "only handle information once."

Remove attachments

As we said earlier, it isn't the messages, but the attachments that are the problem. It is possible to keep the message, but either delete the attachment or move it to your hard drive.

1. Once you open a message, right-click on the attachment.
2. If you select **Save as** and enter a filename, you can save the attachment to your hard drive or a folder on the file server.
3. If you right-click and select **Remove**, you can keep the message but eliminate the attachment.

    This can be easily done to messages in the Sent Items folder since the source of the attachment would be a file already on your server.

Block large inappropriate attachments

In many companies there is simply no valid business reason why someone would need to receive an .mp3, .mpg, .avi, etc., type attachment. So why let them in? One easy way to do this is via the CEICW.

1. Click **Start**, **Server Management**, select **To Do List** then **Connect to the Internet**.
2. Follow the screens as has been previously described until the **Remove E-mail Attachment** window appears.
3. Click **Add…**, add the types of attachments to block, and then complete the wizard as normal.

Use the public information store

In most companies I find the public folders woefully underused. It gives you an additional 16 GB of storage and doubles how much information you can keep in Exchange.

BEST PRACTICE: There is another reason to use public folders; it encourages the sharing of information. To quote John Donne, "No man is an island." Yet, most businesses have islands of information trapped in their e-mail systems. Bill can't see the messages Sue sent to Client X. Sue can't see the messages Bill received from Client X. If someone wants to know what is happening with Client X, there may be bits and pieces of communications locked away in the Sent Items and Inboxes of a dozen employees.

One way around this problem is to create a public folder for each client or customer. Each e-mail sent or received is dragged into their public folder. Once a firm adopts this approach, there are huge benefits. First, the users' mailboxes become smaller and more organized. Second, the firm now takes advantage of an additional 16 GB of storage. Finally, and most important, you have one spot to go to check all communications with the client. Whether sent or received, whether from Bill, Sue, or Bob, there is no guesswork, wasted time, or missing information. Anyone can see the status of the client or what was promised. Appropriate security can be applied to the public folder to keep unauthorized people out.

Besides, wasn't the sharing of information the whole purpose in getting a server anyway?

Move Data to a PST file

You can create a PST file and move completed, inactive, or large messages to the PST. Please keep in mind that PST files can't be shared.

More Ideas!

The previous ideas are good, but they rely on the cooperation of your users. End users, as you will find out, are the least reliable part of your network. Here are a few facilities that are a little more automatic.

Notes:

Use Quotas

You can limit the size of each user's mailbox. In fact, out-of-the-box SBS limits each user to a 200 MB mailbox. Warning messages are sent to the user starting at 175 MB. At 200 MB, the user can no longer send and receive e-mail. Pretty effective! If you want, you could also set this to merely issue warnings.

The maximum number of users on an SBS server is 75. If each of these users has a 200 MB limit, that totals 15 GB, which is just under the 16 GB limit. You can change this limit to suit your needs. You can set a single number for the entire company or vary this on a user-by-user basis.

To do this for the entire company:

1. Click **Start,** then **Programs**, **Microsoft Exchange**, **System Manager**, **Servers**, your server name, and **First Storage Group**.
2. Right-click on the **Mailbox Store**, then **Properties** and the **Limits** tab. Now enter the desired values.

The British scholar C. Northcote Parkinson gave us Parkinson's Law, which states that work expands to fill the time allotted for its completion. Parkinson's Law of Data states that data expands to fill the space available for storage. This holds true for mailbox space as well. Give someone 200 MB, and he will fill it. Give him 300 MB, and he will fill that. So, if you do need to relax the quota for an individual, do so sparingly.

To change the limit for an individual user:

1. Click **Start, Server Management**, then **Users**, followed by a double-click on the desired user.
2. Click on the **Exchange General** Tab, then **Storage Limits**.
3. Uncheck **Use mailbox store defaults**, then enter the desired values for this user.

Delivery Restriction

Not only can you limit the size of a mailbox, you can also limit the size of incoming and outgoing messages. When I examine my own Inbox, I see that the typical size of an e-mail message from one of my clients is about 5K. I could store 40,000 such messages in the 200 MB of space allotted to me. That's a lot of messages. The cause of the space problem isn't the message, but the attachments, which can be huge. The largest tend to be jokes, songs, porn, or other nonessential material. Exchange will allow you to limit the maximum allowable size for a message sent and for a message received. You can institute limits that will allow normal business messages to be delivered, while inappropriate materials won't get through.

To do this by user:

1. Click **Start, Server Management**, then select **Users**.
2. Double-click on the desired user, then select the **Exchange General** tab.
3. Click on **Delivery Restrictions**. Enter the desired value for the maximum sending size and the maximum receiving size.

To do this for the entire company:

1. Click **Start,** then select **Programs, Microsoft Exchange, System Manager**, and **Global Settings**.
2. Right-click on the **Message Delivery**, then **Properties** and the **Defaults** tab. Now enter the desired limits.

BEST PRACTICE: There are some businesses that *do* need to receive large files from their clients. For example, CPAs typically receive accounting databases from their clients which can be quite large. Instead of transferring these via e-mail, consider setting up an FTP site. Files transferred via FTP are outside of Exchange and, as such, do not apply towards your Exchange database limits.

AutoArchive

You can set each folder in Outlook to automatically archive or delete data over a certain age. To set the default AutoArchive rules in Outlook 2003, click on **Tools, Options, Other**, and **AutoArchive.** Be aware that if you choose archive, by default, Outlook creates the archive .pst file on the C: drive. You may want to change this. Servers typically have mirrored hard drives or a raid system. Servers also have backup. Not so for many workstations. If your .pst file is going to contain important company data, make sure it is protected.

You can also set different rules for each folder. To do this, right-click on any folder in a mailbox and select **Properties** then the **AutoArchive** tab. You can now choose to delete old items, use the default AutoArchive rule, enter a custom AutoArchive rule, or even disable AutoArchive completely on this folder.

> BEST PRACTICE: One easy way to reclaim space is to set the Deleted Items folder and the Junk E-mail folder to automatically delete. I am reminded of a user at one of my clients who didn't want a cluttered Inbox, so they quickly deleted their e-mail. They then used their Deleted Items folder as a working file cabinet. They wouldn't be very happy if we automatically emptied their Deleted Items. So it is best to ask your users first.

While this gives us tremendous control, it is quite laborious to institute. Imagine going to each desktop to start Outlook to set the rules for each folder. In the words of former President Ronald Reagan, "Hard work never killed anyone, but why take the chance?" There has got to be a better way.

There is. It is called the Mailbox Manager. From the server you can create a rule or a series of rules for your organization. It not only allows you to monitor the age of messages, but also their size. It is similar to the Mailbox Cleanup in Outlook, but it can be run in a centralized managed fashion.

To define this:

1. Click **Start**, then **Programs, Microsoft Exchange, System Manager**, and **Recipients**.
2. Right-click **Recipient Policies**. Click **New**, then **Recipient Policy**, then select **Mailbox Manager Settings**. Click **OK**.
3. You now need to enter a **Descriptive Name**. Click on **Modify** to select the mailboxes this rule will apply to. Click on the **Mailbox Manager Settings (Policy)** tab.
4. Here you can decide what to do when processing a mailbox and a message is beyond the policy limit. The choices are **Generate report only**, **Move items to Deleted Items folder**, **Move items to System Cleanup folder**, or **Delete immediately**. You can also set the maximum age and message size for items in each of the folders. From this screen you can also elect to notify the user by e-mail and even tell her how many messages were processed. Click **OK**.

While most of the mailbox processing options are pretty straightforward, the System Cleanup option needs a little explanation. When this option is used, a top-level folder called System Cleanup is created. Under this, a copy of your existing mailbox hierarchy is created. As items are removed from the original folder, they are placed in a folder with the same name under the System Cleanup folder. The next time the Mailbox Manager is run, the System Cleanup folder and its contents are permanently deleted. This means if the Mailbox Manager is run on the weekend, the users have until the next weekend to do something with the items they want to keep before they are gone for good.

Now that you have defined your mailbox rules, you need to schedule this to run.

1.   Click **Start**, then **Programs, Microsoft Exchange, Exchange System Manager**, and **Servers.**
2.   Right-click on your server name, select **Properties**, then the **Mailbox Management** tab. This tab will let you determine when to run the cleanup, whether to generate a detail or summary report, and to whom to e-mail the report.

If you want to run the mailbox management immediately:

1.   Click **Start**, then select **Programs, Microsoft Exchange, Exchange System Manager**, and **Servers**.
2.   Right-click on your server name and **Start Mailbox Management Process**.

Enact antispam measures

People are getting more and more spam. If you reduce the amount of the spam, you reduce the size of the mailbox. You will see how to do this later in this chapter.

Limit the size of public folders

The public folder information store, like the mailbox information store, has a 16 GB limit. As users add to these folders, you may encounter space problems. Like user mailboxes, these can have quotas too.

To set a default limit for all public folders:

1.   Click **Start**, then select **Programs, Microsoft Exchange, Exchange System Manager, Servers**, your server name, and **First Storage Group**.

2. Right click on **Public Folder Store**, then **Properties** and **Limits**. Now enter your limits. Notice there is a field called **Maximum item size** on this screen. This is a great way to enforce posting items that have small or no attachments.

Limits can also be set on each individual public folder. To do this:

1. Click **Start**, then select **Programs**, **Microsoft Exchange**, **Exchange System Manager**, **Folders**, and **Public Folders**.

2. Traverse to the desired folder. Right-click on the folder and select **Properties** and then the **Limits** tab. Now enter your limits. You can also use permissions on a public folder to limit who can add into the folder.

Please consider the nature of your client's business and each user's job responsibilities before enacting any of the above. For example, you may have users who have valid business reasons to send and receive large e-mails. You don't want to do anything to hamper their ability to perform their job.

Hitting the Wall

"A skeptic is a person who, when he sees the handwriting on the wall, claims it is a forgery."
—Morris Bender

I once received an emergency call from a 25-person accounting firm whose mail server would not start. Upon examination I found that the information store would not mount because there was insufficient space on the server's C: drive. Where did all the space go? It was consumed by their Exchange database, which had just gotten too big. Don't let this happen to you.

You've tried to prevent it, you've monitored it, and still the database has reached 16 GB anyway. Now what?

Database Diet

It's time to put the database on a serious diet. How many people say they are starting a diet tomorrow and tomorrow never comes? Either they talk about it or they only make a half-hearted attempt. Well, they won't lose weight unless they get serious and neither will your database. It's time to get real.

While you may have run into trouble getting people to listen before, they will definitely pay attention now. People hate it when mail delivery stops. Trust me, they will be eager to help.

What do I mean by getting serious? Let me give you an example. Early in my career, I worked on mainframes for American Express. I had to—PCs hadn't been invented yet. We had a similar problem with insufficient space on the hard drive used by our IBM mainframe. I printed a list of all the files on the drive. I sent it around to all the programming staff with a note saying we were low on space and asking them to mark what could be deleted. When I got it back only a handful of items were marked. Not enough to put a dent into my space problem.

I decided to change my focus and get serious. I sent around the same list of files a second time, again with a note. However, this time the note said that all files would be deleted the following Monday except those files specifically marked to keep. What a difference! Problem solved.

When asked why he robbed banks, Will Sutton replied, "Because that's where the money is." So where do we start? With the worst offenders. Use the items from the monitoring section above to isolate what is consuming the space and attack these folders. It's not the number of messages, but the total space consumed. Revisit the items in the previous section on prevention. Try them again, but more aggressively. Have users review their Inbox and Sent folders, deleting what is nonessential. The Junk E-mail folders should also be emptied.

Now that you have removed all this information, the problem is solved? Right? Wrong!

Deleted Items

First, you need to empty the Deleted Items folders since they also consume space. Then you need to compress the database. It turns out that deleting messages doesn't reduce the size of the database file (.edb and .stm combined) on the server's hard drive. Even with an exhaustive cleanup, you won't see the file size decrease unless you run a compression.

There are two types of compression: online and offline. Online compression runs daily and performs an internal cleanup of the database, but it does not change the file size of the database. E-mail users will have complete access to their mailboxes while an online compression is running. It is best to schedule it to run at a different time than your normal system backup. The time is controlled by right-clicking on a **Store**, selecting **Properties** and the **Database** tab, then setting the **Maintenance interval**.

Offline Compression

An offline compression is needed to solve the 16 GB problem. It runs from the command prompt via the eseutil /d command. ESE stands for Extensible Storage Engine.

The offline compression will physically shrink the file size of the database. When it runs it creates a temporary empty database, copies data records one at a time from the live database into the temporary, discards any unused or deleted pages, then deletes the old database, and finally replaces the temporary database as the live database. When it is done, you have a new, more compact database file.

Since it uses a second, temporary database, you need to make sure your hard drive has enough space for two copies of your database before you run the compression. If there isn't enough space on that drive, you can put the temporary file in another location using a /t parameter.

To Run:

1. From Start, go to **Programs**, **Microsoft Exchange**, **Exchange System Manager**, **Servers**, your server name, and **First Storage Group**.
2. Right-click on **Mailbox Store**.
3. Click **Dismount Store**.
4. Go to a command prompt. Click on **Start,** then **Run** and type **CMD.** Click **OK**.
5. Type **cd C:\Program Files\Exchsrvr\bin**, then press **ENTER**.
6. Type **Eseutil /d "c:\program files\Exchsrvr\mdbdata\priv1.edb" /td:\temp.edb**, then press **ENTER**.

This example assumes your database location is on drive C:. It also put the temporary database in the root of drive D: in a file called temp.edb. If you have enough space on drive C:, the /t switch is unnecessary.

The eseutil can only run against one information store at a time. You will need to run this twice if you want to compress both the public and private information stores. The public information store is typically located in Exchsrvr\mdbdata\Pub1.edb. Make sure you have a good backup before you run this utility.

If you do reach the 16 GB limit, you will find that the mailbox store will not mount even with ample disk space remaining. You will probably see Event IDs 445 and 1112 in the application event log. How can you clean the store if you can't even get into it?

Temporary 1 GB

There is a little known way to add a temporary 1 GB of space so you can remount the mailbox store, remove unnecessary content, and defragment the database back within the 16 GB limit. The extra 1 GB is temporary. The database will revert back to a 16 GB limit the next time Exchange is started. This only works once, so if your database reaches 17 GB, you are out of luck. Because of this, it is a good idea to temporarily stop the SMTP service to prevent additional mail from being delivered while you are attempting to clean up. This would only add to your space problem. Please refer to KB Article 828070 "Exchange Server Mailbox Store Does Not Mount When the Mailbox Store Database Reaches the 16-GB Limit" for further details.

Still not enough?

"There is never enough time unless you're serving it."
–Malcolm Forbes

What if you do the above and you still have a space problem? Here are two solutions.

The first comes from a company called MADSolutions. MAD is for Messaging and Directory Services. They have a program called Attachment Executive that solves the 16 GB problem in a unique way.

Notes:

GUEST COLUMN

E-mail Management Server 2005 keeps Exchange databases below the 16 Gigabyte limit!

Steve J. W. Geisel, President, MADSolutions

GeiselS@MADSolutions.com

Key areas to focus on:

• Delete specific attachments but leave the message intact and place the filename in the message for reference

• Move large attachments out of Exchange and put them in user's home directories or another network location, but leave a hyperlink in the message for easy access

• Archive really old messages on an ongoing automated basis

Deleting attachments that make your database size grow unnecessarily

The attachments in users' Sent Items folders more often than not can contribute to 50% of the storage problem. These attachments are unnecessary. Documents, presentations, graphics, spreadsheets, etc., users send to others have to come from somewhere. Deleting attachments in users' Sent Items folders after the messages are 14 or 30 days old helps users keep their mailbox size under control and prevents it from growing so quickly. Users, however, will want a record that they sent the file. Using Exchange's built-in utilities will not help. With E-mail Management Server, the deleted attachments are replaced with the name of the attachments so users still have the information for their reference.

Move large attachments out of Exchange databases and put them elsewhere

Move attachments out of Exchange and to less costly Windows 2000 or 2003 file servers. When E-mail Management Server moves attachments, a hyperlink to the attachment is placed in the message. Users simply click on the link just like they would have clicked on the attachment. Most won't even know the difference.

Archive really old messages on an ongoing automated basis so databases don't keep growing

Most users don't really need to keep e-mail over a year old in their mailbox. Have E-mail Management Server 2005 automatically move messages out of users' mailboxes and into a personal folder file once they reach a certain age. You can ensure that as each day goes by and new mail comes in, really old mail is being moved out. Meaning: New messages in. Old messages out! This helps ensure that Exchange Databases are taken care of every day.

An evaluation version is available at http://www.MADSolutions.com/EM/Main.htm

Enterprise Edition

If all else fails, there is always the Enterprise Edition of Exchange. It allows for up to four storage groups and five databases per storage group. Each database can be 8 terabytes in size. This is a massive amount of storage.

Unfortunately, it also comes with a healthy price tag. Where Small Business Server Standard Edition is $599 USD, Exchange Server Enterprise Edition is $3999 USD. But wait, there's more! You would have to buy a separate server, load it with Windows 2003 Server at $999 USD, and then purchase Client Access Licenses at $67 USD for each of your users. The cost can add up fast.

In a small business, the goal is to keep costs down. So it is best to keep things simple. If you can use one of the other solutions, you'll find it easier and less expensive.

Protecting Your Exchange Server

"A word to the wise ain't necessary; it's the stupid ones who need the advice."
–Bill Cosby

While we can get into a heated debate over how to put out a fire, we would all agree it is best to prevent the fire in the first place. The same is true with recovering an Exchange database. It is better not to have the problem in the first place. Consider the following protective measure discussion.

Server Hardware

Exchange is only as reliable as the foundation on which it is built. If you want to prevent database problems, you need a server that is dependable and trustworthy. For starters, make sure that the server running Exchange has adequate physical resources to get the job done. Do not skimp on the CPU, hard drive, and memory.

Next, go back to the basics you have seen quoted throughout this book. You need: mirrored hard drives or RAID, ample free disk space, an uninterruptible power supply, antivirus software, and some type of backup device. Make sure your server isn't too old and that it is patched. You want a safe, reliable server.

Backup

In prior versions of SBS, you needed to use a third-party backup. Although SBS came with NT Backup built in, it had serious limitations and just wasn't viable. All that has changed. The backup that comes built into SBS 2003 is dramatically improved and quite capable.

That said, if you have the budget, there is still a place for third-party backups. They offer facilities above and beyond those included within the built-in backup.

For example, with the built-in backup, if you have a problem you must restore the entire database. With a third-party backup, such as Veritas Backup Exec, you can restore an individual user's mailbox. The program performs what is called a "brick-level backup," which allows you to back up and restore individual mailboxes. Other advanced features include the ability to eject tapes when the backup is done, flexible scheduling with the ability to skip holidays, and the ability to e-mail backup results and logs.

Be careful though. Not all backup programs will be able to properly back up and restore the Exchange database. You will need to get one that is Exchange-aware, meaning one specifically designed for SBS or one that includes an Exchange backup agent.

Monitoring

Run the SBS Monitoring Configuration Wizard to enable monitoring on your server. This wizard is your tireless friend and will keep an eye on the server even if you can't. It can be a first alert if there is a problem that arises with your Exchange Server. I list at least two recipients for the monitoring reports. The first is my firm, so I will know if my client has a problem. The other is someone on staff at the client site who becomes my single point of contact for computer-related issues. This can be either a business owner, an office manager, or an IT person, if they have one. If you own a Blackberry or Smart Phone, you can also forward these alerts to enjoy 24-hour coverage.

One of the reports produced by SBS monitoring is the daily Server Performance Report. Due to the wide variations in servers, it is impossible for me to provide you with specific numbers to use when reading this report. The key is to determine a baseline or normal reading for your server. If you look at these reports over several days, you can determine what a normal value should be for your server. When you receive and analyze a subsequent daily report, you are looking for numbers that differ from the norm. From an Exchange perspective, here are several items to examine when you receive a daily Server Performance Report in your mailbox:

- **Free Disk Space**—Make sure both the drive containing the Exchange databases as well as the drive with the operating system, normally C:, have sufficient free space.

- **Memory In Use**—For the best performance, make sure the amount of memory in use is less than the amount of physical memory installed in the server. This number is listed as the Amount of RAM in the Server Specifications section. Do not count your swap file as part of your RAM.

- **Disk Busy Time**—This is another performance reading. The lower the number, the better.

- **Store.exe**—Expect to see Store.exe as the top program in terms of memory usage. You will need to determine its normal value for comparison in subsequent reports.

- **Auto-Started Service Not Running**—Check that all the Exchange services are running.

- **Critical Alerts**—Research and resolve any alerts that are Exchange-related.

The other report produced by SBS monitoring is the Server Usage Report which is created every 14 days. We previously discussed monitoring the Mailbox Size, its rate of change, and users who are near their mailbox quota. One critical area to watch is the number of external e-mails sent. More about this later.

Also be sure to check the standard Windows Event Logs, particularly the Application event log. You need to check these even with the SBS Monitoring reports.

Threats

If you followed the instructions given a few pages ago, you were able to connect your SBS server to the Internet. The good news is that you are now able to communicate with the rest of the world. The bad news is that you are now also under attack.

In the good, old, innocent days, our job was to deploy systems. Now, the nature of the job has changed. To borrow a phrase from the local police department, our job is now "to protect and defend." It's become a jungle out there.

To understand one of the reasons why, let's talk about making a chocolate cake. Previously, it took tons of skill and experience to learn how to make a decent cake. I have often heard baking described as chemistry that tastes good. A person needed to study for years to learn about the ingredients, the handling, the mixing, and the baking. They also needed the proper equipment to make a cake. Obviously, few people ever learned to make a good cake.

Then along comes Duncan Hines. Just about everything you need is in the box, including not only the ingredients, but the skill as well. All you have to do is add one egg and a little water. If you cook it for 10 minutes too long or 5 minutes too short, the cake is still edible. No experience, training, or special equipment is necessary. To make a delicious chocolate cake no longer requires a master baker. Millions of people can now make a cake.

The same thing is true, unfortunately, with Internet threats. In the old days, not many people had the skill or tools to make something like a virus. Now virtually anyone can. There are Web sites, newsgroups, and chat rooms filled with information. Tips, techniques, and pieces of code are easily available. All they need to do is add water.

The Internet has made it easy. A search of "Virus Creation" on Google returned 875,000 hits including Web sites and books at Amazon.com. There is even a college course on the subject taught by Dr. John Aycock at the University of Calgary. There is a world of information that is easily available to the people who want to hurt your system.

How bad is it?

- An August 2004 report from the SANS Institute stated that the average unpatched, unprotected Windows PC lasts less than 20 minutes on the Internet before it is compromised. A year before the survival time was approximately 40 minutes. It is bad and going to get worse before it ever gets any better.

- There are now 1,740 known unpatched security flaws in Windows and other operating systems. In 1999, there were only 417[4].

- On average, an organization received 11 attacks per day.[5]

- *The New York Times* reported that as of June 30, 2004, there were more than 10,000 documented threats to Windows.[6]

Microsoft promotes their three steps to safer computing: use an Internet firewall, download Windows updates, and use up-to-date antivirus software. I like to add a fourth: Use anti-spyware software.

The firewall will be addressed by Beatrice Mulzer and Dr. Thomas Shinder in Chapter 12.

We had already discussed service packs and hotfixes earlier in this chapter, though I would like to add one item. A common misconception is that hackers find a hole and then Microsoft scrambles to release a patch. The reality is that Microsoft releases a patch, hackers review the documentation, and then write a program to exploit the hole. Why does this work if the patch is available from Microsoft? Because many people either do not patch at all or do not do so promptly. The hackers rely on this time for their exploit to be effective. Symantec reports that the average time between a public disclosure of a vulnerability and the release of an exploit for it is only 5.8 days.[7] You need to patch promptly.

For example, the Klez virus, which caused havoc in April 2003, exploited a problem that was first identified in Microsoft Security Bulletin MS01-020 on March 29, 2001[8]. Although people had two years to download and install the fix, Klez was still able to cause $13.9 billion in damages.[9]

This brings us to the topic of viruses.

Viruses

"If I had my way, I'd make health catching instead of disease."
–Robert Ingersoll

Viruses started back in the early 1980s. They tended to be harmless jokes programmers would play on each other to demonstrate their programming prowess. By 1986, the first viruses were being released into the wild and attacking Microsoft operating systems. Back in the dark ages, the original viruses spread via floppy. It would take weeks or months for a virus to spread. So, it was easy to get the updated antivirus definitions before the actual virus ever got to you.

The Internet has changed all that. The Internet has proven to be the most efficient means ever devised for stealing music, accessing porn, and spreading viruses. To see its impact, just consider Table 6-9:

Table 6-9

Infection speed

Speed of Infection				
Virus Name	Year	Type of Virus	Time to Become the Most Prevalent	Virus Damage to Networks
Jerusalem, Cascade, Form	1990	EXE file, boot sector	3 years	$50 million for all viruses over 5 years
Concept	1995	Word Macro	4 months	$50 million
Melissa	1999	E-mail-enabled Word Macro	4 days	$93-$385 million
Love Bug	2000	E-mail-enabled VBScript	5 hours	More than $700 million in less than one week

Source: Congressional Testimony May 10, 2000, Peter S. Tippett, Chief Scientist, ICSA.NET

This explosive growth is being fueled by e-mail and the availability of cheap, high-speed broadband. What had previously taken years, now takes only hours. The virus can get to you before the news of its existence ever does.

Not only are they increasing in speed, viruses are also increasing in number. Symantec documented 4,496 new Windows-based viruses and worms alone for the first half of 2004. This is a 450% increase over the same period in 2003[10]. One in 12 e-mails carried viruses in the first six months of 2004.

You simply don't have time to react. You must have your defenses set up, running, and automatically updating 24/7/365.

E-mail provides another benefit to virus creators. It allows them to easily hide, or spoof, their identity. This is important to a virus creator. People believe a virus's primary mission is to destroy. It is not. Its primary mission is to spread. If it doesn't spread, it can't destroy.

Say you received an e-mail from Joe@abc.com and it contained a virus. You would call Joe, tell him he is infected, and Joe would remove the virus. The virus wouldn't get very far, would it? If Joe originated the virus and used his real e-mail address, it would be similar to his sending a kidnapping note and putting his real return address on the envelope. It wouldn't be long before the police would be knocking on his door. When sending ransom notes, a phony return address—or none at all—is essential.

Viruses use the same approach. To spread successfully, they must use a phony return address. As demonstrated earlier when I became Bob@aol.com, this is very easy to do on the Internet due to its trusting nature. If you receive a virus-infected e-mail from Joe@abc.com, it's not necessarily from Joe. You really have no idea who sent it. The real infected computer is free to continue sending and infecting other computers.

This also explains one frequent question I get from my clients. The question goes, "I just received a notice from someone saying I sent them an e-mail that is virus-infected. I've never sent an e-mail to this person. What's going on?" The message being sent is virus-infected. The receiver has antivirus software that blocks the message and sends a message back to the sender that the message is infected. Due to the forged sender, the alert goes to the wrong person. My client is clean and never sent the message. The infected person is still unknown and unaware.

> BEST PRACTICE: It's best to configure your antivirus software so it does not send antivirus alerts back to the sender. Although antivirus software allows you to do so, you now see this is useless. It adds extra work for your server, it creates additional traffic for the Internet, and the notice will go to someone who had nothing to do with it. In a way it becomes a nuisance, like spam, to the "sender."

This also brings to light another problem. Many users incorrectly believe they are safe because they only open e-mail from people they know. This simply is not the case anymore. I ask myself the following questions before I open any e-mail:

- Do I know the recipient?

- Am I expecting an e-mail from that person?

- Does it have an attachment?

- Is this message in the normal scope of my communication with that person? That is, I wouldn't expect my banker to send me naked photos.

- Is the message written generically, such as "You gotta see this!" or "Please review." The more detailed and specific it is, the less likely it is to be a virus. A virus isn't going to say, "Michael, I spoke to Tom and he would like all three of us to meet in October to discuss setting up a wide area network with our office in Columbus, Ohio."

- Does the message have spelling and grammatical mistakes?

This list has saved me from disaster many times. Yet, if a virus is new or the sender hasn't taken adequate antivirus measures, you can still get an e-mail from someone you know and have it infected with a virus.

You also need to let your users know about hoaxes. Some of these have become as dangerous as a virus itself. For example, you receive an e-mail warning saying something like "This is the worst virus ever! It cannot be detected by any known antivirus scanner and will cause certain destruction." It then gives the name of a file and asks you to see if it is on your computer. If it is, then your computer is infected. The e-mail tells you to delete the file and then e-mail everyone you know to warn them as well.

It turns out that the file they ask you to check is part of Windows, so everyone is guaranteed to find it. If you remove the file, you are damaging your own computer. This is simpler to create than an actual virus. Instead of writing a program to delete the files on your computer and spread to other computers, the hacker is getting you to do the dirty work yourself. And they don't have worry about any antivirus software. Since the hoax e-mail doesn't contain an actual virus, it won't be stopped by any antivirus programs. Symantec has a database of known hoaxes that can be referenced at http://www.sarc.com/avcenter/hoax.html. Another good site is http://hoaxbusters.ciac.org/.

Now let's see what we can do at the server to prevent the virus from even getting to the user.

Exchange Antivirus

"In business, it's always easier to stay out of trouble than to get out of trouble."
–Unknown

Getting rid of viruses is like getting rid of cockroaches; you must kill them all or you're just wasting time. If just one gets in, you have a big problem on your hands. So, you must protect all points of entry. This includes all workstations, the file server, and the single biggest point of entry for viruses: the mail server.

Antivirus software on the mail server must perform two functions. It must prevent the server from getting infected and it must prevent the virus from being passed to a user's mailbox. The typical antivirus programs people know are file-level scanners. This includes most programs you find on the shelf at your corner retail store. These file-level antivirus programs cannot properly interact with the Exchange Server. In fact, they can cause a severe failure in the Exchange database and can also cause -1018 errors (you'll see these in the Application event log). Given the unique characteristics of the information store, you will need an antivirus program written explicitly for Microsoft Exchange. I use Symantec Mail Security, which is part of the Symantec Antivirus Corporate Edition. Trend Micro also makes a very good Exchange antivirus scanner.

Exchange 2003 supports the Virus Scanning Application Program Interface or VSAPI 2.5. This allows the antivirus company to interact with the Exchange database on a low level interface. It guarantees that no e-mail can be accessed before it is scanned. Given the constant flow of e-mail being sent and received, in addition to the server's other normal workload, scanning a message isn't always as easy as it sounds. To deliver on its guarantee, the VSAPI offers three scanning modes:

- Proactive—Messages are scanned as soon as they reach the information store. If the server is busy, there may not be time for proactive scanning.

- On demand—This is scanning when a document is requested. If the document wasn't proactively scanned or if the virus definitions have updated since the proactive scan, the message will be scanned on-demand with high priority.

- Background scanning—This scans the entire contents of the information store. This is helpful to detect viruses that might have arrived before the antivirus definition to detect it. You can find and remove it before the message is opened.

While you must have an Exchange-aware antivirus program, it is also important to also have a normal file-level antivirus program installed given all the other functions performed by an SBS server. How can the two coexist and prevent the corruption and code -1018 error we just discussed? The key is to exclude the Exchange folders from the file-level backup. This is easy to do.

To prevent problems on Exchange 2003, exclude the following folders from the file-level antivirus program on the server:

- Exchange databases and log files (default location: Exchsrvr\Mdbdata)

- Exchange MTA files (default location: Exchsrvr\Mtadata)

- Exchange temporary files: Tmp.edb

- Exchange Message Tracking log files (default location: Exchsrvr\server_name.log)

- Virtual server folders (default location: Exchsrvr\Mailroot)

- Site Replication Service (SRS) files (default location: Exchsrvr\Srsdata)

- Internet Information Service (IIS) system files (default location: C:\windows\System32\Inetsrv)

- Working folder for message conversion .tmp files. (default location: Exchsrvr\Mdbdata)

- The temporary folder that is used in conjunction with offline maintenance utilities such as Eeseutil.exe. By default, this folder is the location from which you run the executable, but you can configure this folder when you run the utility.

- The folder that contains the checkpoint (.chk) file

File-level antivirus software can safely scan the following folders:

- Exchsrvr\Address

- Exchsrvr\Bin

- Exchsrvr\Conndata

- Exchsrvr\Exchweb

- Exchsrvr\Res

- Exchsrvr\Schema

It is also possible to protect against viruses by running the antivirus software on a separate SMTP scanner. This would be a server between your Exchange Server and the Internet. All incoming mail would have to pass through it before arriving at your Exchange Server. It has the advantage of putting less of a load on the Exchange Server and any garbage is removed before it gets to your mail server. Given the cost factor, this is not typically used in an SBS environment.

Remember that this will only scan your Exchange e-mail. If your users have personal or other e-mail accounts out on the Internet, the mail is delivered directly to their workstation and the Exchange antivirus will not detect it. This includes POP3 mail and Web-based e-mail from Yahoo or Hotmail. This is one reason why you still need to run an antivirus program on each workstation.

The Window of Opportunity for a Virus

You have installed antivirus software on the Exchange Server. You are running managed antivirus on the all workstations. You have also installed a file-level antivirus scanner on the SBS server. You have guarded all the points of entry. You are also checking and downloading updates on a frequent basis. So, you are safe, right? Wrong!

Once a virus is released, it will circulate for a while before someone realizes that something is wrong. They will then have to submit a sample to one of the antivirus vendors. The vendor will have to isolate the virus, develop an antidote, update their antivirus database, and publish it to the Internet. The new definitions will sit on their Web site until you run your next scheduled download. Even with antivirus software, there will always be a window of opportunity for a new virus to gain entry—no matter how frequently you update. Remember how quickly viruses are now spreading. What can we do?

Attachment Blocking

E-mail attachments are the main way in which viruses spread. If we block attachments, we have a good way to protect against a virus that may arrive before the antivirus definition. It turns out that we do not need to block all attachments, merely the ones that contain executable code. Since most end users never e-mail executable code, this is a fairly painless solution.

It is also easy to do. Attachment blocking can be enabled as part of the Configure E-mail and Internet Connection Wizard. Microsoft has preloaded the extensions of 50 of the most common virus carrying attachments into this list for you. Table 6-10 displays the attachments that SBS blocks by default:

Table 6-10

SBS Attachment Blocking

Default Attachments Blocked by SBS

Ext	Description
.ade	Microsoft Access project extension
.adp	Microsoft Access project
.app	FoxPro-generated application
.bas	Microsoft Visual Basic class module
.bat	Batch file .chm Compiled HTML Help file
.cmd	Microsoft Windows-NT Command script
.com	Microsoft MS-DOS program
.cpl	Control Panel extension
.crt	Security certificate
.csh	Unix shell script
.exe	Program
.fxp	FoxPro file
.hlp	Help file
.hta	HTML program
.inf	Setup Information
.ins	Internet Naming Service
.isp	Internet Communication settings
.js	JScript file
.jse	JScript Encoded Script file
.ksh	Unix shell script
.lnk	Shortcut

.mda	Microsoft Access add-in program
.mdb	Microsoft Access program
.mde	Microsoft Access MDE database
.mdt	Microsoft Access add-in data
.mdw	Microsoft Access workgroup information
.mdz	Microsoft Access wizard program
.msc	Microsoft Common Console document
.msi	Microsoft Windows Installer package
.msp	Microsoft Windows Installer patch
.mst	Microsoft Windows Installer transform; Microsoft Visual Test source file
.ops	FoxPro file
.pcd	Photo CD image; Microsoft Visual compiled script
.pif	Shortcut to MS-DOS program
.prf	Microsoft Outlook profile settings
.prg	FoxPro program source file
.reg	Registration entries
.scf	Windows Explorer command
.scr	Screen saver
.sct	Windows Script Component
.shb	Shell Scrap object
.shs	Shell Scrap object
.url	Internet shortcut
.vb	VBScript file
.vbe	VBScript Encoded Script file
.vbs	VBScript file
.wsc	Windows Script Component
.wsf	Windows Script file
.wsh	Windows Script Host Settings file
.xsl	XML file that can contain script

This list can be altered. Extensions can be added to or removed from this list. Attachments that match your criteria can either be completely removed or saved to a folder.

Also note that this only blocks attachments from external senders. This has no effect on e-mail sent between two users on the local network.

Here's another idea. If you receive a message with an attachment you are uncertain about, just wait. Yes, wait. I know this doesn't seem very high-tech, but this will give your antivirus provider some time to work. For example, if you get a suspicious e-mail at 5:30 pm, leave it until the next morning. If your server gets updates every two hours, you will receive eight updates by the next morning. If it is a virus, you should have received a valid database and antidote by then. If the attachment hasn't been removed or blocked by then, it is probably safe to open. In fact, some antivirus vendors are looking at the possibility of quarantining all inbound messages for a user-defined period of time just for this reason.

Here are a few other antivirus recommendations:

- Keep your definitions up-to-date—Set the antivirus software to update as frequently as possible.

- Scan everything—Do not limit it to just .exe or similar "program" type files.

- Be aware—Configure alerts so that you will be notified if there is an outbreak.

- Know your renewal dates—I am often reminded of people that buy a mail-order PC that comes with a trial version of an antivirus program good for 90 days. At the end of the 90 days, very few people renew, yet they still walk around with a false sense of security. They feel safe because they have antivirus software installed. The software is only as good as the definitions are. Monitor your subscription renewal date, so you don't let it lapse. It is imperative that you continue to receive your antivirus updates.

- Always keep your guard up—Enable real-time scanning on workstations and the Exchange Server.

- Background scan—I like to background scan both information stores once a day. Since the server is constantly getting new definitions, this may catch new strains of viruses that had previously slipped in undetected.

This list is not final. Virus writers are creative. They are always coming up with new and different techniques to try and damage your system. This is a constant and never-ending battle.

Finally, not all threats are transmitted by e-mail. Some, for example, scan blocks of IP addresses looking for open ports. So be sure to use this in conjunction with a good firewall.

Viruses are an ever-present danger. Given a section of this size, it is impossible to cover all aspects of this problem. Given the importance of virus protection, I urge you to check the following resources. The first two are great "how to" guides from Microsoft that are free to download.

The Antivirus Defense-in-Depth Guide—http://www.microsoft.com/technet/security/guidance/avdind_0.mspx

E-security Guide for Small Businesses—http://www.microsoft.com/smallbusiness/gtm/desktopsecurity/pdf.mspx

Microsoft Knowledge Base Article "823166—Overview of Exchange Server 2003 and antivirus software"

Microsoft Knowledge Base Article "285667—Understanding Virus Scanning API 2.0 in Exchange 2000 Server SP1"

Microsoft Knowledge Base Article "245822—Recommendations for troubleshooting an Exchange Server computer with antivirus software installed"

The following documents can be found at office.microsoft.com:

- Best practices for protection from viruses

- How Outlook helps to protect your computer from viruses

Spam

"Like almost everyone, I receive a lot of spam every day, much of it offering to help me get out of debt or get rich quick. It's ridiculous."
–Bill Gates

The Problem

Viagra, pharmaceutical drugs, insurance, bootleg software, porn, mortgages, etc. Arrgh!

Junk e-mail. The formal name is "unsolicited commercial e-mail" or UCE, but everyone tends to use a four-letter word to describe it. Spam.

The British comedy troupe Monty Python had a famous skit about a restaurant specializing in dishes involving lots of spam. A group of Vikings sitting in the corner would sing "Spam, Spam, Spam, lovely Spam. Wonderful Spam!" so loudly that it would drown out the waitress and all other conversations in the restaurant.

Junk e-mail has reached that level. It is something that keeps repeating and repeating to the point of annoyance. It's so loud, you can't hear other conversation. That is, spam occurs at such a high volume that you cannot see or find your real e-mail.

Windows Secrets Newsletter is a great publication from Brian Livingston. In his September 24th, 2004, issue he quoted the following statistics:

- Spam exceeded 70% of all e-mail in July 2004.

- About 60% of all spam is now sent via zombie-infected machines.

- Comcast sends out 800 million daily e-mails a day, 700 million of which are spam.

- There were 1,974 phishing attacks reported in July 2004. This is growing at more than 50% each month. Antiphishing.org puts monthly growth at 52%.

An article in the September 27th issue of *Network World* independently reports similar numbers. The article reports spam levels in the 70% to 80% range and growing. In 2001, spam only accounted for 8% of all e-mail[11].

The Cost

"E-mail fatigue—mental exhaustion caused by receiving a large number of e-mail messages each day."
–www.wordspy.com

Spam offers marketers a great deal. It is easy, fast, and cheap. Putting together a marketing campaign using traditional mail can take weeks or months. Marketers must have their piece designed, sent to a professional printer for layout, returned for proofing, updated, signed off, printed in volume, folded, and stuffed into envelopes. Then they have to pay for postage, mail the pieces, and wait for their delivery. This takes a lot of time and money. With e-mail, the spammer can send a message to thousands of people, quickly, at little expense. Given the extremely low cost, they can get a miniscule response and still make money. With junk snail mail, the direct response industry states that 1% is typical and 2% is a great response rate. With spam it only takes a .001% response rate to be profitable. Given the economics, is it any surprise that spam is spreading like wildfire?

For a recipient like you, spam is a whole other story. While there is virtually no cost to the sender, there is a high cost to the recipient. As the level of spam increases, each of the following is adversely affected:

- Reduces Internet bandwidth—The more messages that flow into your mail server, the less bandwidth is available, and the slower the Internet line becomes for everyone.

- Reduces available hard drive space—The additional messages will consume additional hard drive space. It also increases the size of the information store which adds to the 16 GB problem.

- Reduces server performance—The additional messages will consume additional CPU cycles to process. The more spam, the slower the server becomes.

- Causes more housekeeping—Spam creates work. Like a houseful of teenagers who leave their dirty clothes and dishes wherever they want, spam leaves a mess that you have to clean up. You spend valuable time removing the unwanted messages and reclaiming the space.

- Loss of employee productivity—This is the biggest cost of all. An article in the June 9th, 2004 issue of *eWeek* reports that spam is costing companies $1,934 per employee per year just for lost productivity only, based on 29 spam messages per day and a wage of $30 per hour[12]. This doesn't include the costs for the other items mentioned above.

How Do Spammers Find You?

"You want your Inbox to be UCEless."
–www.wordspy.com
Spammers will get your mail address by any means they can. This includes:

- from mailing lists and Web sites to which you subscribe.

- from your newsgroup postings.

- from your chat sessions.

- from spambots that crawl the Web looking for anything including an @ sign on a Web page. It then scrapes the e-mail address and follows the links to related sites looking for more addresses. Think of how Google crawls the Internet indexing all words; this is a similar technique that merely looks for e-mail addresses.

- from your domain registration.

- from Internet white and yellow pages.

- from your Web browser. Try www.privacy.net/analyze to see what can be discovered about you by merely visiting a Web site.

- from e-mail lists the spammer buys. On June 23, 2004, an employee of AOL was arrested for stealing the entire subscriber list of 90 million e-mail addresses and selling it to a spammer[13,14].

Even if they have only your domain name and not the actual mailbox, spammers still may have enough to send you spam. One technique used by spammers is called a "dictionary attack." A spammer may send thousands of e-mails generating the recipients by using a dictionary of names and typical mailbox addresses. They will flood your server with e-mail to Abby, Abigail, Adele, Adriana, Agnes, Amanda, Amelia, Amy, etc. They also include e-mails to all known Microsoft system accounts. Typically these e-mails will include a Web beacon, also known as a Web bug—generally transparent, invisible graphic images, usually 1 pixel by 1 pixel in size, used to monitor the recipient's behavior. They can send information back to the spammer's server, including: the IP address of the computer that opened the e-mail, the name of the person who opened the e-mail, the time the Web bug was viewed, and the type of browser used to view the Web bug. Using this beacon, they can determine which e-mails went to nonexistent accounts and which were opened by a real person. This is used to fine-tune their list.

There ought to be a law against this!

"Lawyers earn more from problems than solutions."

–Unknown

Have you ever heard someone say, "There ought to be a law against this"? Well, with spam there is! It is called the Controlling the Assault of Non-Solicited Pornography and Marketing or Can-SPAM Act of 2003. It went into effect on January 1, 2004. Did you notice the big difference it made? Well, neither did I. The legislation, no matter how well-intentioned, had no impact, because it is easy for the spammers to hide their identity, move their servers outside the United States, or use a zombie.

What is a zombie? It's a computer that contains a hidden program that enables the machine to be controlled remotely. The spammer might load a program on one of your workstations so that it will send the spam. You do the dirty work for him. As spammers become known, people will attempt to block e-mail from their servers. No one would suspect spam coming from you.

Time for a war story. I was called in to the office of a new client who had an existing SBS 2003 server. The network was configured so poorly it reminded me of those hidden picture puzzles that ask the reader: "How many mistakes can you find in this picture?" One item I noted was the SBS Monitoring had never been enabled. Before I left, I turned it on. Two weeks later I received their first usage report and found that one of their employees had sent 465,532 e-mails in two weeks! This workstation had been infected, turned into a zombie, and was sending out e-mail for some spammer. The SBS Usage Report made this simple to find. To fix zombies and other spyware programs, I suggest using Spybot, Adaware, and HijackThis. Workstation and browser security settings were also far too lax at this office. For more information on this, please see Chapter 11 which is Susan Bradley's take on security.

> BEST PRACTICE: Exchange 2003 initially sets the number of recipients per message to 64,000. This is unnecessary in the SBS environment. This can be set to a much lower number, although SMTP standards prevent this number from being set less than 100. The number you use will be dependant upon the nature of your business, typically in the 100 to 1000 range.

To change this value:

1. From Start, click on **Programs**, then **Microsoft Exchange**, **System Manager**, **Servers**, your server name, **Protocols**, and **SMTP**.

2. Right-click on **Default SMTP Virtual Server**, select **Properties**, then the **Messages** tab.

3. Enter the desired value for **Limit number of recipients per message to:**

In the early days, a lot of spam was sent through an open relay. A spammer would remotely connect to your mail server and state that the recipient of the e-mail was a person who was not on the local network. Your mail server would accept the mail from this outside source and then forward it along to the intended recipient. It is analogous to criminals who buy a legitimate business to launder their money. This would allow spammers to hide their identity and the original source of the e-mail. Most companies never realized their mail servers were being used from the outside or just thought the server was a little slow. In the early days, I would telnet into the Exchange Server and issue the SMTP commands to test for an open relay. This is no longer necessary. A much easier way to is use a Web site, such as www.abuse.net/relay.html or www.ordb.org/submit, to test your server. Open relays no longer cause a problem in the SBS world since Exchange Server 2003 blocks open relaying by default. Spammers, though, are a creative bunch and they keep inventing new ways to send their junk and mask their identity.

> BEST PRACTICE: Make sure all accounts have good-quality passwords and locks after a reasonable number of incorrect password attempts. At an insurance client of mine, I actually found spammers attempting to relay even though SBS 2003 blocks open relay. Once spammers would connect, they would have to authenticate before the Exchange Server would accept any mail from the outside. They would take a few guesses at a system account and then move on to the next system account before they would lock-out the account. They tried ten accounts and couldn't get in. They tried again in two weeks. Then two weeks after that. They never got in and never

came back. If they could have guessed a password, they would have been able to use my client's server to send spam. So make sure you have good, strong passwords.

What Can Be Done?

"Every solution breeds new problems."
–Murphy's 10th law

There is no simple answer. It has become a game of cat and mouse. We have a problem with spam, we develop a solution, the spammers find a way around the solution, and we have a spam problem again. It is a vicious circle.

Table 6-11 below identifies the four situations that can occur when receiving a piece of e-mail:

Table 6-11

Spam Assessment

		Is it Spam?	
		No	**Yes**
Is the Message Blocked?	**No**	Quadrant 1 Real mail that is allowed in.	Quadrant 2 Spam that slips through.
	Yes	Quadrant 3 Real mail that is blocked. These are false positives.	Quadrant 4 Spam this is correctly identified and blocked.

If your antispam rules are too tight, you will find yourself in Quadrant 3 with too many false positives. Too many real messages will be denied access. If you use antispam measures that are too loose, you will find yourself in Quadrant 2 still with too much spam. Part of the problem is the delicate balance we are trying to strike.

A server-based solution would be best. The user never sees the message. It also reduces impact on server performance and other system resources.

There has been no shortage of solutions to deal with spam. Here are just a few[15]:

- **Keyword searches**—This is a list of banned words. As mail arrives, it is compared against the list. If a message contains the banned words, the message is blocked. This is easy to implement, but requires work to maintain the list. More important, this is easy for the spammers to circumvent. Viagra becomes V1agra or v.i.a.g.r.a. or v_i_a_g_r_a. Spammers can also put non-viewable HTML tags between the letters so there are virtually an infinite number of ways to spell a single word. Recently, spammers have been sending messages with no text. The message is contained in a graphic image so there are no keywords to match against.

- **White lists**—This is a list of known good senders. Unfortunately, you would need to know the sender and add that person to the list before you could receive a message. This works well for correspondence with repetitive clients, but not for new clients, prospects, or one-time communications.

- **Black lists**—Sometimes referred to as a "block list" or "junk list." This is a list of e-mail addresses from which you no longer want to receive mail. E-mails from anyone on this list will be blocked or delivered to a special folder, such as a Junk E-mail folder. But this approach suffers from an Achilles heel that spammers can easily exploit: Black lists work only if the spammer is sending from a fixed location. Since getting a new e-mail address is easy, spammers can constantly change their sending address. The address you add to your black list today may not be the address they send from tomorrow.

- **Hashes/Signatures**—This is a similar approach to what is used for viruses. A database is made of known spam messages. Each message is reduced to a hash code or signature. Once this database is downloaded, all incoming messages are compared to it and any matches are blocked. Spammers have found that if they insert random words or characters into the message, it will produce a different hash code, and they can defeat this system. Antispam software vendors are looking at ways to use "fuzzy logic" to get around this problem. They hope to develop software that either eliminates the noise spammers add to messages or matches on the significant characteristics of the message.

- **Reverse DNS**—This attempts to verify that senders are really who they say they are and will block forged e-mail. Where standard DNS turns a domain name into an IP address, reverse DNS turns an IP address into a domain name. When a piece of e-mail is received, the IP address of the incoming message is reversed and turned back into a domain name. If this domain name does not match that of the incoming message, the message is deemed a forgery and blocked. The weakness with this approach is that it may also block real mail from a sender who does not have reverse DNS configured or whose reverse DNS is configured incorrectly. Senders must have their ISP configure reverse DNS and add the necessary PTR record before your server will allow their mail in. This creates problems for sites using a dynamic IP number, since their IP can, and will, change. These sites will need to forward their mail to their ISP's outgoing mail server to correctly authenticate for reverse DNS.

BEST PRACTICE: There is an option on the Default SMTP Virtual Server called "Perform reverse DNS lookup on incoming messages." This option has caused so much confusion that Microsoft released Knowledge Base Article 297412 to help clarify things. Most people see it and believe that enabling this feature will block e-mail that fails a reverse DNS lookup. This is wrong. This option merely performs the reverse DNS lookup and adds the host name to the header of the e-mail. It does not block any messages.

This option can be found by:

1. From Start, click on **Programs**, then **Microsoft Exchange**, **System Manager**, **Servers**, your server name, **Protocols**, and **SMTP**.

2. Right-click on **Default SMTP Virtual Server**.

3. **Click Properties, then the Delivery tab and Advanced.**

- **Realtime Blackhole List or RBL**—This is a list of known spammers or open relays and the IP addresses of these servers. When the Exchange Server receives an inbound message, the sender is checked against the RBL. If the sender is listed, the mail is refused. There are many Web sites that provide RBLs and you can check a message against multiple lists. This approach has several limitations:

* No list is 100 percent accurate, up-to-date, and foolproof. As previously mentioned, spammers frequently change their e-mail address.

* Spammers have begun to use other techniques, such as zombies, so the e-mail doesn't originate from their known locations.

* Instead of blocking a single IP number, an RBL provider may block a range of IP addresses. This means that innocent senders may be incorrectly included on a list and you would not be able to receive their messages.

- **Challenge / Response**—An approved white list is created. If a message is received from a sender who is not on the white list, the message is held and a challenge is issued. The challenge is an e-mail message back asking the sender to confirm. If no response is received, the message is not delivered. If a response is received, then the message is delivered and the sender is added to the white list. Typically the challenge includes solving a captcha. "Captcha" is an acronym that stands for "Completely Automated Public Test to tell Computers and Humans Apart" and are tasks that are trivial for humans but nearly impossible for computers to solve. The challenge may contain an image such as a stretched, distorted word and ask the sender to type the word and send it back. If a spammer sends thousands of messages, they cannot respond to all the challenges. This does slow down the initial e-mail. I have seen people send an e-mail and leave on vacation not expecting to receive a challenge. Senders who are not computer savvy may need some hand-holding to get this to work.

Notes:

The Intelligent Message Filter

"Any sufficiently advanced technology is indistinguishable from magic."
–Arthur C. Clarke

Another approach, called Bayesian filtering, looks at the entire message, not just keywords. This includes headers, HTML codes, IP addresses, words, word pairs, and phrases, which it compares to its database. It gives good scores to items that typically appear in legitimate mail and bad scores to items that typically appear in spam. It makes a final evaluation by looking at the items at the extremes. How many items does it consider? If the number of items used for scoring is too low, let's say two, then one wrong word can determine the results. If the number of items used is too high, such as perhaps 100, the spammer could simply include several paragraphs from a novel to bring the score back to "innocent." After much testing, it turns out that the optimal number of items to use in scoring e-mail is approximately 15. How does it know each item's probability? It takes an analysis of a tremendous number of previous e-mails where the messages have been classified either as spam or as legitimate, then builds lists of good and bad mail attributes and probabilities automatically.[16]

The resulting filter offers a number of advantages. Bayesian filters:

- are effective and accurate.

- have a low rate of false positives.

- automatically learn and can adapt to new spamming tactics dynamically.

- need no adjustments, as they are self-tuning black boxes.

- are difficult for spammers to trick.

Bayesian filters are, however, more CPU-intensive than other spam-prevention methods.

Microsoft has released a Bayesian-type filter for Microsoft Exchange. The "Intelligent Message Filter" or IMF is available free of charge. It is based on their patented SmartScreen Technology for probability-based content filtering which was developed by their R&D arm, Microsoft Research. SmartScreen can track over 500,000 e-mail characteristics it "learned" from analyzing millions of e-mails submitted by Hotmail subscribers.

IMF scans messages after they pass through any other Exchange filters, but before a message is allowed into the information store. These other filters could be a connection, recipient, or sender filter. It only examines SMTP-based e-mail. It will not scan POP3 mail.

Figure 6-2

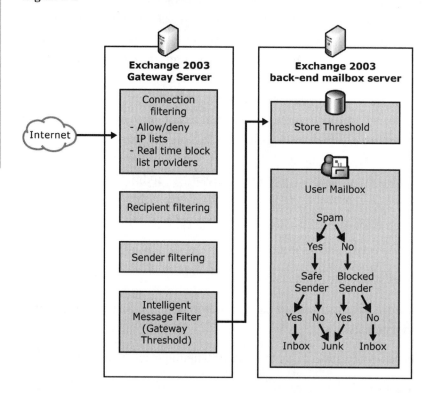

Source: Microsoft Exchange Intelligent Message Filter Deployment Guide

IMF then processes each message, examines its characteristics, and determines its raw score. The score is converted into a number between 1 and 9 called the Spam Confidence Level or SCL. The higher the number, the greater the likelihood the message is spam.

The IMF controls are very simple. There is a user-specified value which is a gateway blocking threshold. All messages with an SCL rating greater than or equal to this number can be rejected, deleted, archived, or allowed at the server. There is a second user-specified value which is a Junk E-mail threshold. All messages with an SCL rating greater than or equal to this number are delivered to users' Junk E-mail folder instead of their Inbox unless the sender is on the Safe Sender list. In this case, the message will be delivered to their Inbox.

Setting the numbers is easy. Knowing what numbers to use is a little trickier. If you set the numbers too low, legitimate mail can be blocked. If you set these numbers too high, you might still get too much spam. The numbers used will also vary from business to business. I have a client who receives e-mail all day long about women, 36DD bras, and panties and none of it is spam or inappropriate. They are a successful public relations firm specializing in women's fashions and these are vital messages. This probably wouldn't be the case in a pediatrician's office.

In general, most people would rather err on the side of caution. They would prefer to allow a few extra pieces of spam than block a potentially important message. Most people start high and gradually lower the SCL until an acceptable level is found.

One way to speed the fine-tuning process is to configure Outlook to display the SCL. You and your users will be able to see how the messages are being scored and determine the correct settings much faster than by trial and error.

Another way is to use the Windows Performance Monitor. The IMF installation program adds the MSExchange Intelligent Message Filter performance object into the Performance Monitor. This adds 16 counters, such as total messages assigned to a specific SCL rating, total messages archived, the total number of messages scanned, and the percentage of the total messages that were determined to be spam. This can provide a wealth of information about the mix of mail you receive and the correct settings for the IMF thresholds.

Notes:

IMF Installation

Contrary to popular belief, IMF is not part of Exchange SP1. In fact, SP1 is not even a prerequisite. IMF is its own separate download and can be installed on any Exchange 2003 server. It can be downloaded free of charge from http://www.microsoft.com/exchange/downloads/2003/imf/default.asp. There is also a wealth of additional documentation here as well as the Intelligent Message Filter Deployment Guide. Click on the **Exchange Intelligent Message Filter** link and then **Download** to get the installation package ExchangeIMF.MSI. To install:

1. From the SBS Server, double-click on the **ExchangeIMF.MSI** you downloaded.
2. The Welcome screen appears. Click on **Next**.
3. The End User License Agreement screen appears. Click **I agree**, and then **Next**.
4. The components screen appears. Both components should be selected by default so simply click **Next**.
5. IMF now installs.
6. Click **Finish** when done.

Note: IMF may not install correctly if the NetBIOS name of your SBS Server is 15 characters long. There is a hotfix available. Please refer to Knowledge Base Article 873434 for more information.

Now that the IMF is installed, we need to set its configuration options. To do this:

1. From Start, click on **Programs**, then **Microsoft Exchange, System Manager**, and **Global Settings.**
2. Right-click on **Message Delivery.** Select **Properties** and then the **Intelligent Message Filtering** tab. This brings you to the main IMF control screen.
3. **Enter the gateway threshold value.** This is the SCL rating at which a message is classified as spam at the server. As discussed, this number will vary by company and may take some experimentation. It is safer to start high and slowly reduce the gateway threshold value.
4. **Enter the gateway action.** There are four possible choices:
   o **No action**—There is no action taken at the gateway. The message is accepted and assigned its SCL rating. The message will be

delivered to the user's Inbox or Junk E-mail folder based on the Junk E-mail threshold value.

o **Reject**—The message is rejected by Exchange. The sender's server may issue a non-delivery report.

o **Delete**—The message is accepted by Exchange and then automatically deleted. Neither the sender nor the recipient is notified that the message has been deleted.

o **Archive**—The message is accepted, but it is not delivered to the recipient's mailbox. Instead, the message is placed in an archive folder which gives the recipient the opportunity to check and recover false positives. The archive defaults to exchsrvr\mailroot\vsi 1\UCEArchive, which is located under C:\Program Files\ unless it was changed during SBS installation. The messages are stored in .EML format and can be opened with Outlook Express or Notepad. If you do discover a message incorrectly classified as spam and placed into the archive, you can correct this by moving the message to the exchsrvr\mailroot\vsi 1\Pickup folder where the message will be processed and delivered. Several notes on archiving:

- The archive folder can fill quickly. You need to closely monitor the free space on the drive storing the archive and periodically clear out the folder.

- Should you need to change the archive to another folder or drive, this can be accomplished via REGEDIT. Go to HKLM\Software\Microsoft\Exchange\ContentFilter and create a new String value or Reg-SZ entry called "ArchiveDir." Then set this value to the new directory path of the folder where you want the archived messages to be stored.

- Until you determine the proper threshold values, it is safer to archive than to reject or delete.

- A false positive can lead to a support call from a user who needs to have her document retrieved from the archive. To minimize support calls and get the document in the hands of the recipient ASAP, it may be necessary to show someone on-site how to do this. If confidentiality is not an issue, one possibility is to move the archive folder into a user-accessible share. Obviously, use this with caution, but it can save on a lot of support calls. An other approach is to take "No Action" at the server and only use the Junk E-mail threshold until you are certain of the appropriate threshold settings.

- There is a better way to process the contents of the archive folder. It is a program called IMFAM. More on this shortly.

5. **Enter the Junk E-mail threshold**—This is the SCL rating at which a message is delivered to a user's Junk folder instead of their Inbox. If it is set equal to or greater than the gateway threshold, then it will have no net effect, since the gateway will have already blocked these messages. So it is best to set this to a number less than the gateway threshold. Again, this will take some experimentation to determine the best value for you.

6. Click **OK**.

Note: Any time you change an SCL threshold you must restart the Microsoft Exchange Information Store service for the change to take effect.

Finally, you need to enable the filter. To do this:

1. From Start, click on **Programs**, then **Microsoft Exchange**, **System Manager**, **Servers**, your server name, **Protocols**, and **SMTP**.

2. Right-click on **Intelligent Message Filtering**. Select **Properties.**

3. Click the checkbox for the **Default SMTP Virtual Server**. Normally on an SBS server you will find only one entry. If your ISP blocked port 25 and you had to configure Exchange to listen for mail on another port, you will see the Default SMTP Virtual Server listed more than once. This is normal. You can enable IMF to filter mail on multiple virtual servers.

4. Click **OK.**

That's it. You're all done.

Optional IMF Steps

There are two optional steps I would recommend.

James Webster, a Software Test Engineer of the Exchange Transport Team, has developed the Intelligent Message Facility Archive Manager or IMFAM, which greatly simplifies managing and processing the contents of the archive folder. It allows you to review each message and then delete, resubmit, copy to the clipboard, or report the message as spam to an RBL provider.

The IMF Archive Manager can be downloaded from http://workspaces .gotdotnet.com/imfarchive. To set it up:

1. Double-click on **IMFFilterManager.exe** that was downloaded.
2. The Browse for Folder screen appears. Navigate to the archive folder and click **OK.** This is typically C:\program files\exchsrvr\mailroot\vsi 1\ucearchive. Note: if you install IMFAM immediately after you install the IMF itself, you may not see the archive folder. It is not created when IMF is installed, but when it needs to add a message to it.
3. Another Browse for Folder screen appears. This time navigate to the **Pickup** folder and click **OK.** This is typically C:\program files\exchsrvr\mailroot\vsi 1\pickup.

If you run IMFAM, you will notice that there is no SCL value on the archived messages. There is a registry change that will override IMF's default behavior.

1. From Start, click **Run** then **Regedit**.
2. Navigate to **HKLM\SOFTWARE\Microsoft\Exchange**.
3. Right-click on **ContentFilter**.
4. Click **New – DWORD Value**.
5. Type **ArchiveSCL** for the registry value.
6. Right-click on **ArchiveSCL**. Select **Modify**.
7. Enter **1** for value data and click **OK**.

The other optional but recommended step is to configure Outlook to display the SCL. This, like IMFAM, is from James Webster of the Microsoft Exchange Group. For this to work, you need to create an Outlook configuration file. This file is too detailed to go into here, so I am going to direct you to two possible sources.

The first is straight from the horse's mouth. James has the necessary information in the Exchange Group blog, entitled "You Had Me At EHLO." The link for displaying the SCL in Outlook is http://blogs.msdn.com/exchange/archive/2004/ 05/26/142607.aspx. You can copy the information from the Web page and paste it into Notepad and then save it as SCL.CFG.

The other source is the great Web site www.smallbizserver.net run by Mariette Knap and Marina Roos. They have the SCL.CFG file ready and waiting to be downloaded at www.smallbizserver.net/default.aspx?tabid=121. You may need to register to be able to download.

Here is how to put it all together:

1. Create or download the **SCL.CFG** file.
2. Move this file to the **C:\Program Files\Microsoft Office\Office11\forms\1033 folder**. The 1033 is the language ID and it may be different for you.
3. Start Outlook 2003. From the menu select **Tools**, **Options**, the **Other** tab, **Advanced Options**, **Custom Forms**, and **Manage Forms.**
4. Click **Install.**
5. Navigate to the **SCL.CFG** file from above. Click **Open** then **OK**. This will install the form into your Personal Forms Library.
6. Click the **OK** button several times to return to the main Outlook screen.
7. Go to the **Inbox** or any folder where you want to see the SCL. Right-click on the column heading and select **Field Chooser**.
8. Pull down the scroll bar and select **Forms....**
9. The **Select Enterprise forms for this folder** screen appears. Select **Personal Forms**, then highlight **SCL Extension Form** and click **Add**.
10. Drag and drop the **SCL property** into your column headings**.**

Other Protections

"A million here and a million there, and pretty soon you're talking real money."
–Senator Everett McKinley Dirksen

The IMF is so good it's easy to forget there are other facilities in Exchange to combat spam. Even if one of these methods stops only a small amount, every little bit helps. Use a number of them at the same time and incoming spam will have multiple hurdles to overcome. Together they can create a very effective defense.

Let's discuss connection, recipient, and sender filters which were depicted in the IMF diagram a few pages back.

Connection Filter

You can create a filtering rule that will block connections from IP addresses found on a Realtime Block List. The Exchange Server will determine the IP address of the sender and then query the RBL provider to see if they are listed.

To create a Connection Filter, do the following:

1. From Start, click **Programs**, **Microsoft Exchange**, **System Manager**, and **Global Settings**.
2. Right-click on **Message Delivery**, then select **Properties**.
3. Select the **Connection Filtering** tab, then click **Add.**
4. Enter a descriptive name for this Connection Filter in the **Display Name** field.
5. In the **DNS Suffix of Provider** box, type the DNS suffix for your RBL provider. For spamhaus, you can use **sbl.spamhaus.org** and/or **xbl.spamhaus.org**.
6. If you want a specific error message, enter that in the **Custom Error Message to Return**. Otherwise a standard error message will be generated which says "<IP Address> has been blocked by <Connection Filter Rule Name>." There are three variables that can be used for this message: %0 represents the connection IP address, %1 represents the name of the Connection Filter rule, and %2 represents the name of the block list provider.
7. Click **Return Status Code** if you want to specify a custom return code. The default is to match the filter rule to any return code.
8. Click **OK** twice.

BEST PRACTICE: You can use multiple RBL providers. I like to use several for added effectiveness. You would repeat the above instructions and create a rule for each RBL that you are checking. They are processed in the order listed. A good list of RBL providers can be found at www.email-policy.com/spam-black-lists.htm. This list also contains other valuable information such as the return codes and whether there is any cost to use the provider.

If this should incorrectly block people with whom you need to communicate, you can place them on an exception list which bypasses the RBL to solve this problem. You can add the exceptions by a single IP address or range of IP addresses using the **Accept** button available on the **Connection Filtering** tab. You can also add exceptions by domain name using the **Exception** button. Wildcards are accepted. So to bypass RBL checking for anyone from my company, you would click the **Exception** button on the **Connection Filtering** tab, click **Add**, enter *@ComputerDirectionsInc.com for the recipient, and then click **OK**.

Using the **Deny** button you can create your own black list[17]. If a sender doesn't appear on a black list, and you do not want to receive e-mail from him, add that sender to your own Deny List.

Once a Connection Filter is created, you will need to enable it. To do this:

1. From Start, click **Programs**, **Microsoft Exchange**, **System Manager**, **Servers**, your server name, **Protocols,** and **SMTP**.
2. Right-click on **Default SMTP Virtual Server** and select **Properties**.
3. On the **General** tab, click **Advanced**.
4. Highlight the IP address/port you want filtered, then click **Edit**. In SBS there is typically only one entry on this screen unless your ISP blocked port 25, in which case you will see two.
5. Click to select **Apply Connection Filter** then click **OK**.
6. Restart the SMTP Virtual Server. To do this, right-click on the **Default SMTP Virtual Server** and select **Stop**. Once it has stopped, right-click again on the **Default SMTP Virtual Server** and select **Start**.

Recipient Filtering

Recipient Filtering allows you to block mail based on its destination. Although you can list individual recipients, there is a very powerful option which lets you stop e-mails to recipients that do not exist within your organization. You can actually check as to whether the recipient exists in the Active Directory before the message is accepted. This is a great defense against a dictionary attack by spammers and it takes only seconds to set up. It also saves the Exchange Server and antivirus software considerable work in processing the flood of messages from a dictionary attack.

To create a Recipient Filter, do the following:

1. From Start, click **Programs**, **Microsoft Exchange, System Manager**, and **Global Settings**.
2. Right-click on **Message Delivery**, then select **Properties**.
3. On the **Recipient Filtering** tab, click to select **Filter recipients who are not in the Directory**.

Once the Recipient Filter is created, you will need to enable it. To do this:

1. From Start, click **Programs**, **Microsoft Exchange**, **System Manager**, **Servers**, your server name, **Protocols**, and **SMTP**.
2. Right-click on **Default SMTP Virtual Server**, then select **Properties**.
3. On the **General** tab, click **Advanced**.
4. Highlight the IP address/port you want filtered, then click **Edit**. In SBS there is typically only one entry on this screen unless your ISP blocked port 25, in which case you will see two.
5. Click to select **Apply Recipient Filter** and then click **OK**.
6. Restart the SMTP Virtual Server.

Recipient filters only apply to anonymous connections. It does not affect authenticated users.

Sender Filters

We can also filter by the sender. To get to the Sender Filter controls, do the following:

1. From Start, click **Programs**, **Microsoft Exchange**, **System Manager**, and **Global Settings**.
2. Right-click on **Message Delivery**. Select **Properties**.
3. Select the **Sender Filtering** tab.

From this tab you can add e-mail addresses of senders you want to block. Wildcards are permitted. So if you want to stop receiving e-mail from joe@AnnoyingSales.com, click **Add** and enter his e-mail address. You can also enter *@AnnoyingSales.com to block mail from anyone at his company.

There is an option to **archive filtered messages**. If you check this box, any messages from blocked senders will be placed into the exchsrvr\mailroot\vsi 1\filter folder. If you decide to use archiving, you must review and clear this folder on a regular basis.

Another useful option in combating spam is to **filter messages with blank sender.** If a message arrives and the From line is blank, the message will be refused.

Finally, there is a choice to **drop connection if the address matches the filter** or to **accept messages without notifying sender of the filtering**. They cannot both be selected at the same time.

Once the sender filter is created, you will need to enable it. To do this:

1. From Start, click **Programs**, **Microsoft Exchange**, **System Manager**, **Servers**, your server name, **Protocols**, and **SMTP**.
2. Right-click on **Default SMTP Virtual Server** and select **Properties**.
3. On the **General** tab, click **Advanced**.
4. Highlight the IP address/port that you want filtered, then click **Edit**. In SBS there is typically only one entry on this screen unless your ISP blocked port 25, in which case you will see two.
5. Click to select **Apply Sender Filter**, then click **OK**.
6. Restart the SMTP Virtual Server.

Outlook Spam Protection

You can also look to Outlook on the desktop for help in your war on spam. Outlook 2003 contains Junk e-mail Options, which are good tools in your arsenal. Please note that these run at the workstation, not on the server. To minimize performance and bandwidth issues, Microsoft wants this run in cached Exchange mode. If you aren't using this, do the following:

1. From Start, click **Settings**, **Control Panel**, **Mail**, **E-mail Accounts**, **View or change existing e-mail accounts**, and **Next**.
2. Highlight **Microsoft Exchange Server** and select **Change**.
3. Click to select **Use Cached Exchange Mode**, **Next**, and **Finish** to enable this mode. The change will take effect the next time you start Outlook 2003.

Once back inside Outlook, click **Tools**, then **Options**, the **Preferences** tab, and **Junk E-mail** to get to the controls for Junk E-mail processing. You will see several tabs where you can specify:

* Safe Senders

* Blocked Senders

* Safe Recipients

* Blocked Top-Level Domains

* Blocked Encodings

While building allow and deny lists should be old hat to you by now, here are three tips that can make them even more effective:

- On the **Safe Senders** tab, enable **Also trust e-mail from my Contacts** and **Automatically add people I e-mail to the Safe Senders List**. These will populate the safe list quickly and painlessly, help reduce the number of false positives, and lead to happier clients.

- On the International tab, use **Blocked Top-Level Domain List** and **Blocked Encodings List.** When I first mention this to people, they are surprised. Most small businesses are local and do not conduct international business. That is exactly why they can be so effective. How many real messages have you ever received from Liberia or Nigeria? Any messages I have ever received from an .lr or .ng top-level domain is a variation on the "419" fraud scheme where an alleged "official" is going to cut me in for millions of dollars. Also, a growing portion of spam is coming from overseas. This is especially true as spammers move abroad to protect themselves from recent antispam legislation. You can use the Blocked Top-Level Domain to restrict the top level to only those countries with which you or your client does business. You can use Blocked Encodings to limit messages in foreign character sets. However, if your client does business or has family in Limnos, Greece, for example, you will need to create exceptions to these restrictions, so it is best to check with your client before you implement any of these filters. It may help to think of the top-level domain and the encodings like IP ports. Why keep them open if they are not used? (Note: If you do not see the International tab, then you will need to download and install Service Pack 1 for Microsoft Office.)

- Show users how to add a message to the blocked senders list. One key difference between blocking an e-mail address in Outlook versus the sender filtering done at the server is that this is under the user's control. So to take best advantage of Outlook's Junk filters, be sure to show users how to fine-tune their safe sender and blocked sender lists.

On September 14, 2004, Microsoft released an update to the Junk E-mail Filter that has a more current definition of the messages that should be considered as junk e-mail. This is available for download. See Knowledge Base Article 870765 for more details. Expect Microsoft to keep updating the Junk E-mail Filter on a regular basis to keep pace with the spammers. So be sure to check periodically for an updated filter.

Outlook 2003 can also block Web beacons by default. If you need to adjust these settings, click on **Tools**, **Options**, the **Security** tab, and **Change Automatic Download Settings**.

No discussion of spam would be complete without discussing the user. Some basic tips can go a long way to help control spam:

- Get a second e-mail address. Free ones are available from Hotmail or Yahoo! or Google. Use it for non-business matters. It can also be used anytime you have to disclose your e-mail, such as a newsletter. Consider this e-mail address disposable. As soon as the spam level gets too high, delete the account and get another free account.

- Guard your e-mail address. Think of it like an unlisted phone number and only give it to people who really need it. If at all possible, don't post your address online. If you must post, mung the address. "Mung" is an acronym for "mash until no good." Instead of posting BobM@mycompany.com, use BobM at mycompany.com or BobM<AT>mycompany.com. A human reading it will be able to interpret the e-mail address, but a program crawling the Internet looking for a valid e-mail address would skip Bob's munged address.

BEST PRACTICE: I carry two types of business cards: one with my e-mail address on white stock and one without on a grayish stock. If I am at a trade show and there is a fish bowl raffle, I use the one without my e-mail address. If I meet a new prospect, I make sure to use the business card with my e-mail address.

- Use caution when surfing the Web. Before you offer any information to a Web site, read their privacy statement. How will they be using your information? Will they be divulging your information to a third party? When asked, many times I submit a phony e-mail address. If you do have to give your real e-mail address, opt out of everything you do not need to help keep your mail to a minimum. One final idea is to change your middle initial when giving your name at a Web site. It won't cut down on the amount of e-mail you get, but it is fascinating to see how quickly your name is passed around and to whom, since you now have a way to track it.

- Don't answer spam. This just confirms that your e-mail address is real and current. Recent e-mails have been known to use return receipts to ascertain which e-mails reach their targets. Also be careful with out-of-office auto-replies which also proves your existence to a spammer. Then there's the subject of unsubscribing. The standard rule of thumb is never attempt to unsubscribe. Here I slightly differ. If the unwanted e-mail comes from a reputable company, then unsubscribing does work. If the e-mail is for ridiculously cheap software, then do not attempt to unsubscribe. If you feel your user will not be able to tell the difference between these, then have them stick with the simple, tried and true rule of "never unsubscribe."

Third-Party Solutions

If all that isn't enough, you can always consider a third-party solution. Be careful of users who attempt to tackle the spam problem themselves. They tend to buy a program in the checkout lane at the corner store. Retail products tend to be POP3-based and will not handle SMTP-based e-mail.

Third-party solutions fall into two categories: internal and external. The internal variety runs as an add-on to your SBS server while the external solution is more of a service bureau that scans and cleans the e-mail before it is delivered to your network. Internal solutions are available from companies such as MailFrontier and Cloudmark. You could outsource your spam filtering to a company such as Postini or Advascan. Also check your antivirus software. Many vendors are starting to incorporate antispam features into their antivirus software.

For the long term, the industry is looking at various solutions. Several possible ideas being examined are based on sender authentication, such as digital signatures and sender-ID, which is similar to a caller-ID for e-mail[18]. Another idea is to charge a small fee for each sent e-mail. A penny per e-mail wouldn't add significant cost for the typical SMB, but it would prevent major spammers from sending out 2,000,000 messages per day. Ironically, although the Do Not Call list has been very successful for telephones, it will not be implemented for spam. In June 2004, the Federal Trade Commission decided against the idea. In the words of Chairman Timothy Muris, "Under current technology, any do-not-spam list would become a do-spam list[19]."

For additional information, the following documents are available at Microsoft.com:

- Best practices to help prevent spam

- What you need to know about phishing

- Identify fraudulent e-mail and phishing schemes

- Exchange Intelligent Message Filter Deployment Guide

Troubleshooting

"The way out of trouble is never as simple as the way in."
–Ed Howe

Troubleshooting Internet E-mail

Think of the relay race in the Olympics. At the starting line a runner is given a baton. He runs a distance and hands off the baton to the next runner. This repeats until the last runner crosses the finish line.

The same principle is at work here. A message is sent and then passed from computer to computer, from service to service, until it reaches its destination. If there is a problem with the message, your first indication may be when an end user says, "Someone sent me an e-mail two hours ago and I still haven't received it." Solving the problem isn't as difficult as figuring out which runner dropped the baton. Considering all the components that touch an e-mail along its travels, isolation is the key. Troubleshooting e-mail problems can be pressure-packed, given its vital nature to many businesses. No sooner do I walk into a client's office than I am beseeched by a chorus of "Is it fixed yet?" This is where a backup MX or an e-mail spooling service can alleviate some of the pressure.

Notes:

Fact Finding

"Facts do not cease to exist because they are ignored."

–Aldous Huxley

First, you need to assess the situation. The following table (Table 6-12) contains some simple tests you can perform or questions you can ask an end user who is on-site:

Table 6-12

Troubleshooting Questions

Basic Troubleshooting Questions	
Questions	**Notes**
Is the server running?	It sounds funny, but you would be surprised how often this happens. If this is the case, reboot the server and e-mail will be back up and running in a few minutes.
Do you have basic Internet access?	Open Internet Explorer and go to a Web site. I like to use a site that has frequently changing information with the date and time on the page, such as www.cnn.com. This ensures that the page is live and not in the browser's cache. If there is no Internet access, then check the router and Internet line itself.
Can you send internal e-mail? Can you receive internal e-mail? Can you send e-mail over the Internet? Can you receive e-mail over the Internet?	If you can send e-mail internally but not externally, then it might be a blocked port 25 or a problem with the smart host. If you cannot receive Internet e-mails, then look to the registrar, such as Network Solutions, DNS issues, blocked inbound port 25.
Does Outlook work? Can you open existing messages?	If you are unable to enter Outlook, this can indicate a problem with the Information Store.
Do many people have the problem or is it just one person?	This helps isolate whether the problem is isolated to a user or workstation.
Does the same problem exist when accessing OWA?	This helps eliminate Outlook and the workstation as potential sources of the problem.

I also like to set up a batch file which tests each leg of the route a message will follow to look for any problems. With a single mouse click, an end user can find if and where there is a problem communicating with the Internet. By the time a client calls me, he already knows where and what the problem is. It will, in order:

- Ping the Server's Internal NIC

- Ping the Server's External NIC

- Ping the Router's Internal NIC

- Ping the Router's External NIC (if it is a static IP)

- Ping the ISP's gateway (if it is a static IP)

- Ping 216.168.224.111 (this is the IP address of Network Solutions)

- Ping netsol.com (this is the domain name of Network Solutions)

The following is a sample program to accomplish this. Please note this is based on the sample network diagram earlier in this chapter that also had a dynamic IP address for its Internet connection. It will need to be adapted to your specific network configuration and IP scheme. Also be aware that many devices, such as routers, may not respond to a ping. You will need to try this and, if necessary, remove this test from the batch file before turning it over to a user.

```
@echo off
REM*******************************************************************
REM *****Written by Michael Klein - Computer Directions, Inc.*****
REM *****  Copyright 2003 - Computer Directions, Inc. - All rights Reserved*****
REM *******************************************************************
cls
 echo Now Testing 10.0.0.2 - The File Server internal interface
 ping 10.0.0.2
 if errorlevel == 1 goto :errIn
 echo.
 echo The test to the File Server Internal Interface was successful
 echo.
 echo.
 echo ————————————————————————————
rem *****************************************************************
 echo Now Testing 10.0.1.2 - The File Server external interface
 ping 10.0.1.2
 if errorlevel == 1 goto :errOut
```

```
 echo.
 echo The test to the File Server External Interface was successful
 echo.
 echo.
 echo ———————————————————
rem ****************************************************************
 echo Now Testing 10.0.1.5 - Is router accessible?
 ping 10.0.1.5
 if errorlevel == 1 goto :errRtr
 echo.
 echo The test to the Router was successful
 echo.
 echo.
 echo ———————————————————
rem ****************************************************************
 echo Now Testing 216.68.224.111 - Is the Internet accessible?
 ping 216.68.224.111
 if errorlevel == 1 goto :errNet
 echo.
 echo The test to the Internet was successful
 echo.
 echo.
 echo ———————————————————
rem ****************************************************************
 echo Now Testing netsol.com - Is DNS working?
 ping netsol.com
 if errorlevel == 1 goto :errDNS
 echo.
 echo The test to the Internet was successful
 echo.
 echo.
rem ****************************************************************
 echo All tests were successful
goto end
:ErrIn
 echo I cannot see 10.0.0.2 - Please check the internal interface of the File Server
goto end
:ErrOut
 echo I cannot see 10.0.1.2 - Please check the external interface of the File Server
goto end
:ErrRtr
 echo I cannot see 10.0.1.5 - Please check your Router
 goto end
:ErrNet
 echo I cannot access the Internet - The problem appears to be with the Cable / DSL / T1 line.
 goto end
:ErrDNS
 echo I cannot access Netsol.com - The problem appears to be with DNS
 goto end
:end
 Pause
```

There are additional items to check, but they require access to the server and are too technical for the typical end user. You will need either a savvy end user or remote access, if you are not on-site. These additional items include:

- Check that all Exchange services are running. If necessary, start any services that may have stopped. By default there are five services that should be running:

  o Microsoft Exchange Information Store

  o Microsoft Exchange Management

  o Microsoft Exchange Routing Engine

  o Microsoft Exchange System Attendant

  o Simple Mail Transfer Protocol (SMTP)

  There will be a sixth service called the Microsoft Connector for POP3 Mailboxes if you are using the POP3 connector. To check the services, click **Start**, **Server Management**, then **Advanced Management**, **Computer Management (Local)**, **Services and Applications**, and **Services.** The services will be displayed in the right pane.

- Check the server's event logs—Check the System Log in addition to the Application Log. Are there any errors that have been posted to the event logs? If so, research and resolve. To check the event logs, click **Start, Server Management**, then **Advanced Management, Computer Management (Local)**, **System Tools**, and **Event Viewer.**

- Check the message queues—Check whether there are messages accumulating in the queues. To do so, click **Start**, then **Programs**, **Microsoft Exchange**, **System Manager**, **Servers**, your server name, and **Queues.** The details will be displayed in the right pane.

Sending Issues

Problems sending e-mail tend to be less frequent than problems receiving e-mail. It is a simpler process with fewer things to go wrong, but that doesn't mean things can never go wrong. Here are a few tests and fixes.

Sending Directly to Recipient

If you are not using a smart host and instead are sending mail directly to the recipient via DNS, make sure that your reverse DNS has been set up correctly. To verify this, I use www.dnsstuff.com. This is a great Web site that offers a battery of tests and information. On their home page is a Reverse DNS lookup test. Enter the static public IP address of your network and see if it correctly resolves back to your domain name. If it reports "Unknown" or that the domain name doesn't match your domain name, your mail will be rejected and you have found the source of your problem. If you do not know your static public IP address, it is displayed on the bottom of the www.dnsstuff.com home page or you can use ipid.shat.net.

Next, test that port 25 is open outbound. Let's say that you are attempting to send e-mail to joe@xyz.com. From a command prompt, issue the command **TELNET SERVER1.XYZ.COM 25** (where server1.xyz.com is the Fully Qualified Domain Name and server1 is the mail server). Note: You can identify the mail server with the following command nslookup -q=mx xyz.com and the Mail Exchange (MX) record will have the lowest number (highest priority) and the name associated with it (server1.xyz.com). You should see a response similar to:

220 xyz.com Microsoft ESMTP MAIL Service, Version: 6.0.3790.211 ready at Mon, 4 Oct 2004 02:02:47 -0500

If you do not, then you need to run this test against several other domains. You want to be certain that the problem is your outbound port 25 and not xyz.com's inbound port 25. If your outbound port 25 is blocked, then you will need to use a smart host or an outbound mail relay service.

Note: Your Telnet response will vary slightly based on the recipient's mail software, date, and time.

Sending via Smart Host

If sending e-mail via a smart host, then verify the smart host information from your ISP. Rerun the CEICW using the smart host information and try sending again. If this still fails, test your access to the smart host. From a command prompt, issue the command **TELNET smart host 25**. For example, if the smart host was mail.optonline.net, the command would be **TELNET mail.optonline.net 25**. You should see a response similar to:

220 smart host Microsoft ESMTP MAIL Service, Version: 6.0.3790.211 ready at Mon, 4 Oct 2004 02:02:47 -0500

If you do not, contact your ISP. It could be a problem on their end. Also, some ISPs are beginning to institute authorization procedures in order to accept your mail. There are procedures later in this chapter on how to add the required user ID and password to your outgoing mail.

Sending Either Way

Whether sending directly or via smart host, send test e-mails to several recipients on different mail servers. Do any get through? For those that don't, is anything returned to you? If so, what information does it contain?

Have you been blacklisted? Could the recipient's mail server refuse to accept your e-mail because it thinks you are a spammer? Run a Spam Database Lookup, available on the home page of www.dnsstuff.com, to see if you have been blacklisted.

You can also use Telnet to connect to another mail server and manually issue native SMTP commands. You saw an example of this earlier in this chapter. Simply issue an SMTP command and monitor the other system's response to it. If there are any problems, you will see them firsthand.

Reception Issues

Now, here are a few suggestions to help you deal with those pesky reception problems:

- From a workstation on the network, go to a command prompt and issue the command **TELNET x.x.x.x 25** where x.x.x.x is the internal IP address of the server. You should see a response similar to the following:

220 YourDomainName.com Microsoft ESMTP MAIL Service, Version: 6.0.3790.211 ready at Mon, 4 Oct 2004 02:02:47 -0500

If you are unable to connect to the Exchange Server, the problem is normally somewhere on your server. Start by restarting the Exchange services and any third-party Exchange antivirus services. If necessary, restart the file server.

Note: Your Telnet response will vary slightly based on your domain name, date, time, and patch level.

- From a workstation outside the network, go to a command prompt and issue the command **TELNET z.z.z.z 25** where z.z.z.z is the external, public IP address of the router. If you have a dynamic address, then use http://ipid.shat.net or http://www.dnsstuff.com to first ascertain your network's public IP address. You know from your previous test that the mail server works internally, so if this test fails, the problem is connectivity. Make sure port 25 is opened on the router and traffic is directed to the external network card on the file server. Check that RRAS is configured correctly. You would also check ISA if you are running SBS Premium Edition. If you are running an external firewall, check connectivity through that device as well.

BEST PRACTICE: When troubleshooting sending and receiving issues, it really helps to have remote access to another workstation outside your network. This could be via Remote Web Workplace, Remote Desktop Connection, or Terminal Server. You can open that workstation in one window and a local copy of Outlook in another. You can then test sending and receiving between the two separate networks without ever leaving your seat.

If this is not available, you can always use Hotmail, Yahoo mail, Google's Gmail, AOL, etc. These will let you send and receive, but you will not be able to perform some items like a Telnet test.

- If you have a dynamic IP and are using a dynamic DNS service, make sure their client program is running. If this program isn't running, you will not receive mail. If you are using a store and forward service, make sure the port you are listening on matches the port they are forwarding on.

- Next check that Network Solutions is set up correctly. Go to www.netsol.com, click on **WHOIS,** enter your domain name, and verify the results. Are the domain servers correct? Have you changed this information recently? Changes can take 24 to 48 hours to take effect.

What is the expiration date? I once had a client who could not receive e-mail. My investigation uncovered that the domain name had expired with Network Solutions. Why? It turned out that the contact listed had left the company, so the renewal e-mails went to a nonexistent mailbox. No one ever saw them.

- The next stop after we check Network Solutions is the ISP. Previously, I would have listed several different tests for you to perform manually. Not anymore. The easy way to check this is to use the Web site www.checkdns.net. It not only reports on the DNS settings, but it tests them as well. It can show whether the DNS records are correctly configured, the ISP's name servers are operational, the MX records exist, or port 25 is blocked. It will also show you a transcript when it connects and issues SMTP commands to your Exchange Server. It is a great Web site.

BEST PRACTICE: Watch out if you change to a new ISP. I had a client who was using a large ISP and changed to a new ISP. The old ISP didn't remove the DNS records when the client left. My client was unable to receive e-mail from anyone who was still connected to the old ISP. It was as if he had moved to a new house but the mailman kept delivering his mail to his old house. One way to test for this is with a TRACERT command, which is included with Windows. If you go to a command prompt and issue the command TRACERT DomainName or TRACERT IPAddress, you will get a report that shows every system between your computer and the destination. You can see if it is resolving correctly or going to a wrong destination.

- One other area to check are all the filters you may have in effect to protect you. This includes connection filtering, sender filtering, antivirus filtering, Intelligent Message Filter, antispam filtering, and junk filters. Many of these filters, like IMF, may have archive folders where you can check for missing incoming e-mails. If you are using an RBL, you should also check whether the sender is blacklisted. Most RBL providers have a lookup or you can use www.dnsstuff.com and click **Spam database lookup** to check over 150 spam databases.

Internet Message Headers

What They Are

There are two parts to an e-mail message: the body and the header. The body is the portion everyone is familiar with. It is the content, such as the note you type. The header is the tracking information. It contains the sender and the recipient. Each system that touches the message along its journey adds its name, along with the date and time it was processed. Header information can provide valuable information when troubleshooting. Unfortunately, header information can also be forged.

How to View Them

Right-click on a message in your **Inbox**, then select **Options**. The information is displayed in the **Internet headers** box. Alternatively, if you have opened and are viewing a message, click **View** and then **Options**. The information is again displayed in the **Internet headers** box. The information in this box can be copied and pasted into other applications, such as Word or Notepad, should you need to print it. Below is a sample Internet header.

```
Microsoft Mail Internet Headers Version 2.0
Received: from nhm1.nethealthmon.com ([207.202.238.212]) by
computerdirectionsinc.com with Microsoft SMTPSVC(6.0.3790.211);
Tue, 21 Sep 2004 12:37:47 -0400
Subject: RE: Chapter Update
Date: Tue, 21 Sep 2004 09:36:16 -0700
MIME-Version: 1.0
Content-Type: multipart/related;
        type="multipart/alternative";
        boundary="——_=_NextPart_001_01C49FF9.8914FD46"
Message-ID:
<0A1E6CACCE28BA4AB267BE52BAA719C120FFB9@nhm1.nethealthmon.com>
X-MS-Has-Attach: yes
X-MimeOLE: Produced By Microsoft Exchange V6.0.6249.0
X-MS-TNEF-Correlator:
Content-class: urn:content-classes:message
Thread-Topic: Chapter Update
thread-index: AcSf81WHe8ow0PSUTAyLoE7rtEngPAABiVRw
From: "Harry Brelsford" <harryb@nethealthmon.com>
To: "Michael Klein" <MKlein@computerdirectionsinc.com>
Return-Path: harryb@nethealthmon.com
X-OriginalArrivalTime: 21 Sep 2004 16:37:47.0705 (UTC) FILETIME=[53EED290:01C49FF9]
```

How to Read an Internet Header

The contents of an Internet header will vary based on a number of factors, including the sender's e-mail software, the route the message follows, and what the message contains.

The basic information such as To, From, CC, and Subject are pretty self-explanatory.

The Date statement contains the date and time the message is sent. The time is supplied by the sender and is only as accurate as the sender's clock. To merely say that a message was sent at 9:39, though, isn't enough, since people can use the e-mail from anywhere in the world. 9:39 in New York is 8:39 in Chicago, is 7:39 in Denver, etc. To solve this problem, all e-mail messages give the time both in the originating time zone and relative to Greenwich Mean Time (GMT). Greenwich Mean Time is also known as Universal Time (UTC).

In the example above, Harry sent me an e-mail. Harry's SBS server is on Bainbridge Island just outside of Seattle. He is in the Pacific time zone. Pacific Daylight Time (PDT) is seven hours behind GMT which is why -0700 appears after the time 09:36:16. On some systems you may see it listed as -0700 (PDT).

The Reply To: statement contains the address to use when someone presses the reply button. The example above uses its close cousin, the Return-path: statement. Normally this is the same as the From: address. An example where this may not be the same is with a Blackberry device. The Blackberry has its own e-mail address provided by the telco carrier. This creates a problem. You would never know whether responses would be sent to Outlook or the Blackberry. You would have two places to check for new incoming messages instead of one. It would be better if all the responses were sent to Outlook where they would also be backed up. On many devices, such as the Blackberry, you can. In this case the From: address and the Reply To: address would be different.

An e-mail message may also contain X-headers, which are user-defined headers. They can be inserted by e-mail software or the message transfer agent.

Next is the Received statement, and this is where things get interesting. Each machine that processes the e-mail message adds a Received line. This becomes the history of the message as it moves through the Internet. In our example above, we see that the message was sent directly from nhm1.nethealthmon.com, whose IP address is 207.202.238.212, to ComputerDirectionsInc.com. My server is running version 6.0.3790.211 of Microsoft's SMTP Service (or SMTPSVC) program.

Notice the timestamp at the end of the Received line: 12:37:47 -0400. It did not take three hours to deliver the message. My SBS server is in New York, which is four hours behind GMT. Let's see how long it took to actually deliver the message.

First, convert all the times to GMT. The message was sent at 9:36:16 -0700, which translates to 16:36:16 in GMT time. It arrived at 12:37:47 -0400 or 16:37:47. Now subtract the time it was sent (16:36:16) from the time it arrived (16:37:47) to find that the message took 1 minute and 31 seconds to deliver.

Here's a visual example of the explanation above:

	Local Time	Difference From GMT	Time in GMT
Arrived:	12:37:47	-0400	16:37:47
Sent:	9:36:16	-0700	16:36:16
Time to Deliver			1:31

Here's another example:

```
Received: from saf.tzo.com ([216.235.248.73]) by
computerdirectionsinc.com with Microsoft SMTPSVC(6.0.3790.211);
    Sat, 18 Sep 2004 17:19:54 -0400
Received: from 151.204.161.194 by saf.tzo.com
    id 2004101817125643785 for Info@computerdirectionsinc.com;
    Sat, 18 Sep 2004 21:12:56 GMT
```

This is a little more involved since we have more than one Received statement. Each system that processes the message along its journey adds a Received line, so we can tell this message didn't come to us directly. We read them in reverse order, from the bottom up.

In this case, we can see that the message was sent from 151.204.161.194 and went to saf.tzo.com. This is TZO's store and Forward Service. I use this e-mail spooling service as a backup should my mail server be unavailable. That day I was installing upgrades onto my server and it was down for about 15 minutes for a reboot. The message did not bounce. We can see from the second received statement that TZO's Store and Forward Service (saf.tzo.com at 216.235.248.73) delivered the message to my server 6 minutes and 58 seconds later.

Now, here are two important examples about the real world use of Internet headers.

Unspoofing a Virus

Kevin and Rob are both employees at one of my clients whose offices are about 20 feet apart. Kevin got an e-mail from Rob. When he opened it, he discovered that the message had been replaced with a virus notification. Kevin then proceeded to receive a tidal wave of these messages. The client was concerned that the virus had entered the company's network. I was able to use the Internet header to prove conclusively that Rob wasn't infected and to stop new incoming viruses.

Since a message sent from one person to another within the same office never gets to the Internet, it will not have any Internet headers. When I opened the message Kevin got from Rob, the Internet header should have been blank. It wasn't. What I saw was:

```
Received: from 67.125.69.46 by myclient.com with Microsoft
SMTPSVC(5.0.2195.5329);
        Tue, 14 Sep 2004 12:37:47 -0700
```

The received statement in the header showed that the message was sent from 67.125.69.46 and from somewhere in the Pacific Time Zone. I then went to www.dnsstuff.com to run a WHOIS on 67.125.69.46. These were the results:

WHOIS results for 67.125.69.46

Generated by www.DNSstuff.com

```
Country: UNITED STATES
NOTE: More information appears to be available at PIA2-ORG-ARIN.
Using 6 day old cached answer (or, you can get fresh results).
Hiding E-mail address (you can get results with the E-mail address).

OrgName:  Pac Bell Internet Services
OrgID:    PACB
Address:  208 Bush St. #5000
City:     San Ramon
StateProv: CA
PostalCode: 94104
Country:  US
NetRange:  67.112.0.0 - 67.127.255.255
CIDR:      67.112.0.0/12
NetName:   PBI-NET-10
```

```
NetHandle: NET-67-112-0-0-1
Parent:    NET-67-0-0-0-0
NetType:   Direct Allocation
NameServer: NS1.PBI.NET
NameServer: NS2.PBI.NET
Comment:   ADDRESSES WITHIN THIS BLOCK ARE NON-PORTABLE
RegDate:   2001-10-16
Updated:   2003-03-07
TechHandle: PIA2-ORG-ARIN
TechName:  IPAdmin-PBI
TechPhone: +1-800-648-1626
TechEmail: **********@sbis.sbc.com

OrgAbuseHandle: APB2-ARIN
OrgAbuseName:  Abuse - Pacific Bell
OrgAbusePhone: +1-800-648-1626
OrgAbuseEmail: *****@pacbell.net

OrgNOCHandle: SPBI-ARIN
OrgNOCName:  Support - Pacific Bell Internet
OrgNOCPhone: +1-800-648-1626
OrgNOCEmail: ******@pacbell.net

OrgTechHandle: PIA2-ORG-ARIN
OrgTechName:  IPAdmin-PBI
OrgTechPhone: +1-800-648-1626
OrgTechEmail: **********@sbis.sbc.com
```

The IP address was owned by Pacific Bell. I contacted their abuse department using the above phone number. They were able to turn off the viruses at the source and put an end to the problem.

BEST PRACTICE: This works with spam as well as viruses. If you get undesirable mail, view the header and determine the sender's IP address from the Received statement. Now use Connection Filtering to refuse a connection from the offending IP address. You can also contact the abuse department of the sender's ISP. They, in turn, will contact the sender. Many times the sender is completely unaware of the infection.

The Real CSI-NY

Because of my background and the fact that so many of my clients are attorneys, I have often been called to provide forensic services and appear as an expert witness in court. I was called in to help defend someone who was charged with sending a threatening e-mail to another party. The "victim" produced a printout of an e-mail, including the Internet headers, in which my client threatened to kill him. He was immediately granted an order of protection from the court. My client claimed he didn't do it. My client's attorney called me and asked whether I could do anything to prove his innocence. I then asked to see a copy of the e-mail.

There it was. The threatening note. The Internet gobbledy-gook. It looked convincing. I could see how a layperson would believe it. Yet, when I looked carefully, I found lots wrong. Here are a few examples:

- The sending IP was listed as 622.15.127.227. However, that couldn't possibly be true, for 622.15.127.227 is not a valid IP address.

- The sending server was listed as version 3.5.2378. This did not match the version of Exchange my client was running in his office.

- One of the timestamps was listed as 17 Feb 2002 09:54:55 -0700 (EST). This also was impossible. My client's mail server is in New York, which is in the Eastern Standard Time zone, noted as -0500 or 5 hours behind Greenwich Mean Time (GMT). -0700 would put the sending mail server somewhere in the Mountain Standard Time zone, such as Colorado.

And there were more errors, but you have seen enough to get the idea. There were just too many mistakes. It couldn't have been sent through the Internet. It had to be a forgery.

Apparently, the "victim" took a previous e-mail from my client, then cut and pasted the old header onto a new note he typed. He had changed some of the information on the header, printed it, and presented it in court. Since he really didn't understand Internet headers, he must have just guessed what to change.

Armed with this information, I was able to go back into court with the attorney. Once this information was presented, the "victim" recanted and the order of protection was removed. I was able to restore my client's good name and reputation all because I knew how to read an Internet header.

Other Troubleshooting Tools

Diagnostic Logging

If you are still having trouble isolating a problem, maybe a little more information would help. Increase the level of diagnostic logging. This will post more information to the event log.

To change the logging level:

1. From Start, click **Programs**, **Microsoft Exchange**, **System Manager**, and **Servers**.
2. Right-click on your server name, select **Properties,** and then the **Diagnostics Logging** tab.
3. On the left side of the window, select the desired service. If you would like more information on these services, click **Help** and then **Set Diagnostic Logging Properties.** You will get a list of all the services with a brief description of each.
4. A list of categories will appear on the right. Select the desired category and increase the logging level from **None** to **Minimum**, **Medium**, or **Maximum**. You may need to select multiple categories.

The diagnostic messages will be posted to the application log. Although you may be tempted to go directly to the maximum setting, it may be better to start with a lower setting. The maximum setting can generate a flood of entries. Trying to find the right one to help solve your problem can be like trying to find a needle in a haystack. Remember to lower the logging level when the problem has been resolved.

Virtual Server Logging

You can use protocol logging to get a detailed log of all the incoming and outgoing SMTP commands that are processed for each message. This is another good way to generate information to help resolve a problem.

To turn on the logging:

1. From Start, click **Programs**, **Microsoft Exchange**, **System Manager**, **Servers**, your server name, **Protocols**, and then **SMTP**.

2. Right-click on **Default SMTP Virtual Server**, then click **Properties** and the **General** tab.

3. Click on **Enable logging** and select **W3C Extended Log File Format.** The W3C Extended Log File Format is the default format and is an ASCII file. Although there are other formats, this has the advantage of letting you control what information is included in the log file.

4. To see this, click on **Properties**, and then the **Advanced** tab. You will see a window with extended logging options. This is a long list of data items that can be included in the log with a checkbox for each.

To view a log, open Windows Explorer and navigate to the C:\Windows\system32\LogFiles\SMTPSVC1 folder. The logs will be named EX*.log and typically have the year, month, and day as part of the file name such as ex040915.log.

Message Tracking

When Message Tracking is enabled, each Exchange component handling a message reports its activities to a log file maintained by the System Attendant. As a message is received, processed, and delivered, each step of its journey through Exchange will be posted to this log. Viewing this log will allow you to trace the steps a message takes as it flows through Exchange.

To enable Message Tracking:

1. From Start, click **Programs**, **Microsoft Exchange**, **System Manager**, and **Servers**.

2. Right-click your server name, then **Properties**, and the **General** tab.

3. Select **Enable subject logging and display**, then click **Enable message tracking**, **Remove log files**, and then **Accept the default of 7 days.**

4. Click **OK**.

Since a single message may have multiple entries at different times as it flows through Exchange, Microsoft has made a tool to help search and report on a message. This query tool is called the Message Tracking Center. To access it:

1. From Start, click **Programs**, **Microsoft Exchange**, **System Manager**, **Tools**, and **Message Tracking Center.**

2. In the right pane will be a query screen. Here you can enter data such as date/time ranges, sender, or recipient to filter the database.

3. Once you enter your criteria, click **Find Now.** The results will be displayed in the bottom of the query windows. Once you find a message of interest, double-click and you will see the history of the message as it was processed by Exchange.

Repairing a Database

"I created Ctrl—Alt—Delete, but it was Bill Gates and Windows that made it famous."
–David Bradley, on retiring after 28 years as an IBM Engineer

When a computer problem occurs, there are usually two general approaches:

- The "get your hands dirty" approach—Open the hood of the car, roll up your shirt sleeves, dive in, and get your hands dirty. If you have the expertise, parts, and the right tools, you can solve the problem.

- The "I know it worked yesterday" approach—Grab a backup and travel the time machine back to a point before the problem existed and everything still worked properly.

The "I know it worked yesterday" is typically the easier approach. Yet, because of the importance of e-mail, its high volume, and its rapidly changing nature, people are reluctant to turn back the clock to solve a problem. This is especially true for sites using the built-in SBS backup, since a problem with a single message or mailbox means you must roll back every mailbox in the entire firm.

Jeff Middleton has an entire chapter on the "I know it worked yesterday" approach (See Chapter 14). His chapter on recovery is excellent, but I did want to mention several tools that are Exchange-specific just in case you need to "get your hands dirty."

The first tool is one we have seen before. It is ESEUTIL—a single program that performs a wide array of repair functions. I tend to think of it as a Swiss Army knife, because there is a tool in there for just about every situation. It runs from the command line and the first parameter controls its function. ESEUTIL can do the following as shown in Table 6-13:

Table 6-13

ESEUTIL Functions

ESEUTIL		
Function	**Command Line Switch**	**Description**
Functions that Only Read the Database		
Integrity	/g	It verifies the integrity of the database. It looks for errors, but it does not repair them. If the database is in "dirty shutdown" state, a recovery should be run before the integrity option is attempted.
Checksum	/k	This calculates a checksum for each database page and compares it to the value stored for that page in the database. Checksums can also be calculated for the checkpoint file, streaming file, and log files. If the database is in a "dirty shutdown" state, it is not possible to verify checksums.
File Dump	/m	This displays information about the database, log files, and checkpoint files. The /m switch itself has several options depending upon what you want to display. The most common is /mh which displays header information.
Copy File	/y	This makes a copy of a database, streaming file, or log file.
Functions that Read and Write to the Database		
Defragment	/d	This performs an offline database compaction. It defragments the database by moving pages into contiguous blocks in a new, temporary database. Unused or deleted pages are discarded. The old database is deleted and the temporary database becomes the new main database.
Recovery	/r	A database file is inconsistent if there is information in the cache that has not yet been physically written to the file. This is caused by a "dirty shutdown" in which the database is stopped abruptly. A recovery plays back any uncommitted transactions and applies them to the database to return it to a consistent state. This is known as a "soft recovery."
Restore	/c	This brings the database to a consistent state by performing a "hard recovery.[20]" This is typically run after the restoration of an online backup. A "hard recovery" applies patch file data into the log file replay process where a "soft recovery" does not. Exchange 2000 SP2 and later no longer use patch files.[21]

Repair	/p	This repairs a corrupted or damaged database. After successfully running a repair, you must then run the following: • ESEUTIL /d. • ISINTEG -fix -test alltests. Running a repair can cause data loss, so this should be done only as a last resort. You should also back up the database before running a repair.[22]

ESEUTIL is run from the command line and can be found in the \Program Files\Exchsrvr\bin folder. Each of ESEUTIL's functions requires additional parameters. Running ESEUTIL with no parameters will display a help screen which gives the full syntax of each of its functions.

ESEUTIL inspects and fixes the low-level structure of the database and its pages. It does not look at higher level data content, such as mailboxes and public folders. To do that, we need another tool. This tool is the Information Store Integrity Checker or ISINTEG.

ISINTEG inspects and fixes a long list of items, including folders, mailboxes, attachments, ACL lists, and timed events.[23] It also checks the links between tables and even looks for orphaned objects. Although you can run individual tests, it is possible to run all tests in one command. The format of this command is: ISINTEG -fix -test alltests.

ISINTEG, like ESEUTIL, is an offline utility that runs from the command line and resides in the \Program Files\Exchsrvr\bin folder. You may need to run this several times until it finds and fixes zero errors.[24] This can take some time depending on the speed of your server and the size of your database. Make certain to back up the database before running ISINTEG since it may cause data loss.

If you are upgrading from Exchange 5.5 or earlier, you will be happy to learn that the ISINTEG -patch command is no longer required.[25]

Another useful tool is MTACHECK. When messages are destined for another system, the Exchange information store submits the mail to the message transfer agent (MTA). The MTA accepts the mail, adds it to the work queue, and temporarily stores it in a file called DB*.dat file in the \Program Files\Exchsrvr\MTAData folder. When the message is processed, it is removed from the work queue and the DB*.dat file is marked for reuse. The MTACHECK detects and corrects message transfer agent (MTA) database consistency problems between the work queue and the DB*.dat files. It can remove corrupted or inconsistent messages from the queue[26].

This tool is not included with the SBS installation. Either download it individually from the Microsoft Web site or as one of the tools inside of the ExAllTools.exe described earlier in this chapter. You will need to copy the MTACHECK.EXE file to the \Program Files\Exchsrvr\bin. It is a command line utility and it runs very quickly.

These are powerful tools, but do not use them indiscriminately. The information stores are valuable and fragile. Incorrect use could make a bad situation worse. Although you now have familiarity with the tools and their functions, you should consult with Microsoft's Knowledge Base for your specific error code or problem before attempting any repair.

The Exchange Survival Guide

"It is not the strongest of the species that survives, nor the most intelligent that survives. It is the one that is most adaptable to change."
–Charles Darwin

Here it is—a list of frequent problems, support calls, and situations you may encounter in your daily life as an Exchange administrator.

Exchange Issues

Problem: Can I assign more than one name to a mailbox?

Solution: Yes, you can assign multiple e-mail addresses to a single mailbox. I will often create e-mail addresses such as Info@mycompany.com, Sales@mycompany.com, and Accounting@mycompany.com and assign them to individuals in addition to their normal e-mail address. Although you can have multiple e-mail addresses, you will need to select one as the primary. The primary e-mail address will appear in outgoing e-mail in the From: field. When viewing a user's e-mail addresses, the primary e-mail address will be depicted in bold in the display window. To create the additional addresses:

1. From Start, select **Server Management** then **Users.**

2. Double -click on the selected User. Then click the **E-mail Addresses** tab, **New**, **SMTP Address**, and **OK.**

3. Enter the new address.

BEST PRACTICE: Sometimes you won't get e-mail because people misspell your e-mail address. I have seen no shortage of ways to spell my last name: Klien, Kleine, Kline, Klyne, Cline, Clyne, etc. I list these as aliases to my mailbox. I will also add combinations such as MKlein, Mklien, MKline, Mike, Michael. E-mail is important to me. I want to be sure I get all of it. Creating multiple names for my mailbox makes this easy.

Problem: Can I host more than one domain name? I own company 1 .com and company 2 .com. I need to use both.

Solution: Yes. To configure an Exchange Server to receive mail for multiple domains:

1. From Start, click **Programs**, then **Microsoft Exchange** and **System Manager**.

2. Click to expand the **Recipients** container.

3. Click **Recipient Policies**.

4. Double-click on **Default Policy.**

5. Click the **E-Mail Addresses** tab, click **New**, and then add any additional Simple Mail Transfer Protocol (SMTP) addresses that you want the Exchange-based computer to host.

6. If necessary, select which address is the primary address.

7. Restart the Microsoft Exchange Information Store service. Remember, there may be setup necessary beyond your Exchange Server to make this work. For example, you may need to update your domain name definition with your registrar. You may also need to have your ISP set up the DNS MX records for the additional domain name. If you are using dynamic DNS, you will need to sign up for service on the additional domain name.

Problem: How do I know what service packs have been installed and what version of Exchange I am running?

Solution:

1. From Start, click **Programs**, then **Microsoft Exchange**, **System Manager**, and **Servers.**
2. Right-click on your server name, then **Properties.** The version number and service pack level are now displayed.

Problem: How do I control how a user can access Exchange?

Solution:

1. From Start, select **Server Management** then **Users.**
2. Double click on the selected User. Then click the **Exchange Features** tab. This will bring you to a screen which shows each of the methods available to connect to Exchange, such as Outlook Web Access, POP3, IMAP4, and Outlook Mobile Access. You can then enable or disable an individual feature as needed.

Problem: I am locked out of a public folder. Employee X created a public folder and is no longer at the company. She is listed as the owner.

Solution: Most people attempt to assign folder security through Outlook. That won't work in this case. You need to use the System Manager from the file server to solve this problem. To regain control of the folder:

1. From Start, click **Programs**, then **Microsoft Exchange, System Manager, Folders,** and **Public Folders.**
2. Right-click on the desired folder, select **Properties**, then the **Permissions** tab.
3. Click **Client Permissions.** From here, select the users and/or groups and their corresponding permissions. Make sure that at least one existing user is deemed owner of the folder. This person can assign any future permissions from Outlook at his desk.

Problem: How do I forward e-mail to an outside mailbox such as AOL, Hotmail.com, or Yahoo.com?

Solution: This used to be a much more popular request before the introduction of SBS's remote access features like Outlook Web Access, but it is still used and important. Many companies use subcontractors who are not given access into the server or have people who have another mailbox as their primary mailbox and don't want to have to check both mailboxes. I have also used this to forward e-mail to a Blackberry device. There are two steps to accomplish this. The first creates a contact with an external e-mail address. The second forwards the e-mail for a user to that contact. Here is the process:

- Step One: From Start, select **Server Management, Advanced Management, Active Directory Users and Computers**, your company.local, **MyBusiness**, and **Users.** Right-click **SBSUsers,** select **New,** and then **Contact**. Enter a name for the external contact and click **Next**. Click **Modify, SMTP Address**, and **OK**. Enter the forwarding e-mail address, click **OK, Next**, and **Finish**.

- Step Two: From Start, **Server Management**, then **Users.** Double-click on the desired User. Then click the **Exchange General** tab, **Delivery Options**, and **Forward to**. Click **Modify** and then select **Contact** created in the above step. You also have a choice at this point to deliver mail to one or both mailboxes. You do need to be careful when forwarding. A few years back, before remote access was built into SBS, a client decided to forward his Exchange mailbox to a Hotmail type account while he was on a nearly three-week vacation. About two weeks in, that mailbox filled. It would refuse to accept any new message, sending it back with a header indicating the mailbox was filled to capacity. Unfortunately, when the message was returned, Exchange saw it as another incoming message and again sent it to the filled external mailbox, which would again return it. The message became a "hot potato" being passed back and forth. And, this would happen with each message. It literally turned into his own denial of service attack until the forwarding was turned off. So, be careful about forwarding to external mailboxes, especially small ones.

BEST PRACTICE: If you are an outside consultant, use e-mail forwarding to send any e-mail received at an SBS administrator's mailbox at a client to your office. You may not be on-site every day. If there is an important alert, renewal notice, etc., it will be sure to get to you in a timely fashion.

Problem: Can Outlook be installed on the file server?

Solution: While this would be nice from a support standpoint, don't do it. It turns out that there are incompatibilities in the MAPI sub-systems that are installed by Exchange Server and Microsoft Outlook on Server.[27] There are two alternatives. First, you can use Outlook Web Access on the server. Second, you can use Remote Web Workplace or Remote Desktop Connection to connect to a workstation on the network for a full version of Outlook.

Problem: My ISP requires a user ID and password to access their outgoing mail server.

Solution:

1. From Start, Click **Programs**, **Microsoft Exchange**, **System Manager**, and **Connectors**.
2. Right-click on **SmallBusiness SMTP connector**, then **Properties**, the **Advanced** tab, **Outbound Security**, **Basic Authentication (password is sent in clear text)**, and **Modify**.
3. Enter the user, password, and password confirmation. Then click **OK**.

Problem: One of my employees receives inappropriate e-mail and/or e-mail from friends. We cannot turn off their e-mail since they still need it for use within the office.

Solution: If external e-mail is becoming a problem for an employee, create a Recipient Filter. This will prevent e-mail from being accepted for that person by the Exchange Server, but will not affect internal e-mail. To do this:

1. From Start, Click **Programs**, then **Microsoft Exchange**, **System Manager**, and **Global Settings**.
2. Right-click on **Message Delivery**, then select **Properties**.
3. Click on the **Recipient Filtering** tab. Click **Add.**
4. Enter the person's e-mail address. Click **OK**.

Once the Recipient Filter is created, you will need to enable it. To do this:

1. From Start, click **Programs**, then **Microsoft Exchange**, **System Manager**, **Servers**, your server name, **Protocols**, and **SMTP**.
2. Right-click on **Default SMTP Virtual Server**, then select **Properties**.
3. On the **General** tab, click **Advanced**.
4. Highlight the IP address/port you want filtered, then click **Edit**. In SBS there is typically only one entry on this screen unless your ISP blocked port 25, in which case you will see two.
5. Click to select **Apply Recipient Filter** and **OK**.
6. Restart the SMTP Virtual Server.

You could also accomplish this in another way:

1. Click **Start, Server Management** and then **Users**.
2. Double-click the desired User. Then click the **Exchange General** tab and **Delivery Restrictions.**
3. Click to select **Accept Messages From authenticated users only.**

If you need to grant the Internet access, but you just want to block access from a handful of friends or inappropriate senders, use the sender filtering discussed earlier.

Problem: Can we block the ability for someone to send Internet e-mail, but still allow that person to send internally?

Solution: Yes.

1. From Start, click **Programs, Microsoft Exchange, System Manager,** and **Connectors**.
2. Right-click **on SmallBusiness SMTP connector**, then **Properties** and **Delivery Restrictions**.
3. Click **Add** under **Reject Message from**.
4. Enter the user's name and click **OK.**

Problem: I set up an Out-of-Office reply at my workstation. I had one of my co-workers test it and it worked, but none of my clients received it. What is wrong?

Solution: By default, Out-of-Office replies to the Internet are disabled. This is a security measure, since many companies do not want outsiders knowing employee whereabouts. Out-of-Office replies also confirm to spammers that their message has reached a valid mailbox. If you do wish to allow this in your company, do the following:

1. From Start, click **Programs, Microsoft Exchange, System Manager, Global Settings,** and **Internet Message Formats**.
2. In the **Details** pane, right-click on **Default** and select **Properties.** The default domain is "*."
3. Click on the **Advanced** tab.
4. Click to select **Allow out-of-office responses.**

Problem: What should we do about e-mail when someone leaves our company?

Solution: Many times I have seen people at a company so eager to delete the departing employee's network account that they forget to consider the implications on their e-mail. There may be new, incoming communications from customers that are vital to a business's continued operations, such as new sales orders. If this is the case, then you may want to assign the mailbox name to another employee in the same department. The procedures for this were given in the first item in this section entitled "Can I assign more than one name to a mailbox?"

You may also want someone to review the contents of the departed employee's mailbox for important information. There may be important names and addresses in Contacts, items still to be completed in Tasks, etc. These should be copied elsewhere before the account is deleted.

I also do not recommend to my clients to autoforward e-mail for former employees. If the employee does ask to have e-mail forwarded, it is better to have someone on staff review and decide what is appropriate to forward. You don't want to be sending new sales orders to an employee who left to work for the competitor across town.

Problem: Our shared company phone book is a free-for-all. We need to have tighter controls on it.

Solution: If your company phone book is out of control, then limit access to read-only for most people and read/write only for those who need to update and maintain the phone book. To do this:

1. From Start, click **Programs**, **Microsoft Exchange**, **System Manager**, **Folders**, and **Public Folders**.
2. Right-click on the company contacts folder, select **Properties**, then the **Permissions** tab, and then **Client Permissions.**
3. Click on **Default** and set the **Permission Role** to **Reviewer.**
4. For each user who will maintain the contacts, click **Add...**, select each name from the list, click **Add**, click **OK**, click on the name again, and set the **Permission Role** to **Editor** or higher, then click **OK**.

Problem: Why isn't there any bad mail in the BadMail folder?

Solution: The BadMail folder typically contains mail that is received by the server but is undeliverable. By default, this is in the Exchsrvr\Mailroot\vsi 1\Badmail folder. This folder can fill quickly, especially if you are the target of a dictionary attack.

In the past, policing the BadMail folder and its collection of .BAD, .BDP, and .BDR files was a manual process. In fact, Exchange would keep adding mail to the BadMail folder until the hard disk filled to capacity. A good Exchange administrator would make sure to clean it out on a frequent basis to prevent this from happening. This is why they are so surprised when they look and find that the BadMail folder is empty. So what happened to all the undeliverable mail?

It turns out that this is one nice side effect of Exchange 2003 Service Pack 1.[28] By default, undeliverable mail is no longer written to the BadMail folder. It is automatically deleted. This means you can now take a vacation and not have to worry that the folder will consume all the available disk space and crash the server. If you do want to keep receiving BadMail, you are going to need to use Regedit and add a few registry keys. But the real question is: Why?

Problem: Is it possible to turn off non-delivery reports (NDRs) to the Internet?

Solution: Yes. In fact, there is something called an NDR spam attack. Each message will have the intended spam victim in the sender's field and a fictitious recipient in your domain in the recipient field. A spammer will send thousands of these messages into your server. Your server will determine that the recipient doesn't exist and send an NDR e-mail back to the "sender" who is the ultimate spam victim. The NDR message is more likely to slip through antispam measures and more likely to be read by the victim. To disable NDRs:

1. From Start, click **Programs**, **Microsoft Exchange**, **System Manager**, **Global Settings**, and **Internet Message Formats.**
2. In the Details pane, right-click on **Default** and select **Properties.** The default domain is "*."
3. Click on the **Advanced** tab.
4. Deselect **Allow non-delivery reports**. Click **OK**.

Notes:

Outlook Issues

Problem: How do I let another person have access to my mailbox?

Solution: This is a very common request. For example, I travel; how do I allow my secretary into my Inbox? This is done in two steps. First, grant the person security to access your folders. Then, have that person add your mailbox to his Outlook. To do this:

1. Start Outlook on your workstation. Right-click on the folder you want to share, then click **Properties, Permissions,** and click **Add...,** select the user from the list, and click on **OK**. Then grant them the appropriate level of access. This could range from read-only access of messages and information to the ability to edit and delete information as well.

2. Next, go to the workstation of the person who wants access. Start **Outlook** and click **Tools, E-mail Accounts, View or Change Existing Accounts,** and **Next**. Highlight **Exchange Server** and click **Change, More Settings,** the **Advanced** tab, and **Add.** Enter name of first user whose mailbox is being shared. Click **OK**.

You might find it easier to first switch to Folder list view (Click **Go**, then **Folder List** from the top menu bar in Outlook) to see all the folders and then to assign permissions. You should grant access to the Mailbox—User name root folder using the same procedure as in Step 1 above. Permissions assigned to a folder do not flow down to the subfolders.

Problem: Why are my messages or appointments one hour off?

Solution: This is typically caused by the workstation not correcting for daylight savings time. To correct:

1. From Start, click **Settings, Control Panel, Date and Time**, and the **Time Zone** tab.

2. Click to select **Automatically adjust clock for daylight savings changes**.

There is one other possibility. Check that the workstation is set to the correct time zone. To correct:

1. From Start, click **Settings, Control, Panel, Date and Time**, and the **Time Zone** tab.

2. Select the correct time zone.

Problem: I received a message "A program is trying to access e-mail addresses you have stored in Outlook. Do you want to allow this?"[29]

Solution: If you are synchronizing your Palm Pilot, you may get this message when it attempts to read your contacts to move them onto your PDA. In this or similar cases, you can allow access for a short duration, such as five minutes.

If this message appears unexpectedly, then it is typically a virus. This is a security precaution built into Outlook to keep you from spreading the virus to everyone you know and love. If you are at all uncertain, it is safer to say no.

Problem: How do I send a blind carbon copy (BCC)?

Solution: This never used to be a question. Now, with Outlook 2003, it is. Why? Because it went from obvious to hidden.

To use it for a single message, do the following:

1. Open a new message. You will see **To:** and **Cc:** only.
2. Click on either **To:** or **Cc:** to open the **Select Names** window. You will now see **Bcc:**.

To have Bcc: permanently displayed when Word is your e-mail editor:

1. Open a new message.
2. Click on the downward pointing arrow to the immediate right of the **Options** button.
3. Select **Bcc:**.

To have Bcc: permanently displayed when Outlook is your e-mail editor:

1. Open a new message.
2. Click **View**, then **Bcc:**.

Problem: How do I send an e-mail message to a group of people and protect their identities?

Solution: If you want to send out a broadcast e-mail and don't want one recipient to know who the other recipients are, list them all under the BCC as described above.

Problem: How do I change the contact names to display Last Name, First Name instead of First Name Last Name?

Solution: To change the sort order:

1. Start Outlook 2003 and click **Tools, E-mail accounts, View or change existing directories or address books,** and **Next**.
2. Highlight **Outlook Address Book**, then click **Change**.
3. Select **File As (Smith, John)** in **Show Names by**, then click **Finish.**

Problem: I have created a folder with contacts. Yet, when I go to send an e-mail and press the To: button, these names are not available. How do I get access to them?

Solution: Contact folders do not automatically appear when addressing e-mails. Although you may have lots of contact folders, you must explicitly indicate which ones are to be used when addressing e-mails. To do this:

1. Right-click on the desired contact folder, then click **Properties**, and the **Outlook Address Book** tab.
2. Click to select **Show this folder as an e-mail Address Book.**

This also applies to the shared company contacts in the public folders.

Problem: When addressing an e-mail, I used to be able to start typing and Outlook would automatically complete the name. Now it doesn't. What happened?

Solution: You are on a new machine or a new account on your existing machine.

As you work, Outlook builds a list of people you correspond with. These names are stored in the file OutlookProfileName.NK2 in the C:\Documents and Settings\username.domain\Application Data\Microsoft\Outlook folder. If your profile is called "default," the file will be DEFAULT.NK2. What most people do not know is that this file can be moved from user to user or from machine to machine. You can take your AutoComplete names with you.[30]

Simply close Outlook and copy the .NK2 file from one machine to the new one. Install it in the C:\Documents and Settings\username.domain\Application Data\Microsoft\Outlook folder for the new user's name. If the new user uses a profile with a different name, then you must rename the .NK2 to match the new profile name, such as NewProfileName.NK2. That's it.

Should the file ever become corrupt or you just want to start fresh, you can delete the .NK2 file at any time. Outlook will create a new, empty file for you.

You can also delete a single entry. Just highlight it when it is offered to you and press the Delete key.

Legal Issues

"The minute you read something you don't understand you can almost be sure it was drawn up by a lawyer."
–Will Rogers

It used to be simple when all we had to worry about were viruses, spam, database corruption, and a user who was accident-prone. Now we have another item to add to our list: the legal implications of e-mail. This is not a section of answers, but of questions—questions you need to ask yourself, your client, and your client's attorney. Can an employee's e-mail expose you to legal problems? Can you legally open an employee's e-mail message? Can you find an e-mail message you sent to a client who is disputing a bill from 18 months ago?

E-mail Lifecycle

Here is another mnemonic that you are not likely to forget: CRUD. What is CRUD? It is the lifecycle of a document or e-mail message from birth to death. It stands for "Create, Retrieve, Update, and Delete."

Why is this important?

In July 2004, the U.S. District Court for the District of Columbia levied a $2.7 million dollar fine against Philip Morris USA for deleting e-mail more than two months old. This is being called a test case for e-mail retention liability. In 1999, the court ordered Philip Morris to preserve "all documents and other records" that might contain information about a government case pending against the company. In 2002, the routine deletions were discovered. While Philip Morris has protested the ruling, the message is clear—if a company is told to turn over messages pertaining to a specific topic, it had better be able to locate all of them.

More and more business communications are done by e-mail. If you are sued, can you produce your e-mails in a court of law as required under the rules of discovery? Can you produce the e-mails necessary to prove and win your case?

Your company needs to develop a standard operating procedure for e-mail. Which e-mails are kept? Which are deleted? If deleted, when and by whom? If kept, where are they kept? Who can retrieve them? How are they retrieved? And so on. Retrieval is the key.

This has caused a whole new genre of software to be introduced called e-mail archiving. It is being driven by new regulations, such as Sarbanes-Oxley and by companies that need to retain historical access to e-mail messages. Vendors in this area are C2C Systems, IXOS Software, and KVS Inc., which is now owned by Veritas.

Set Company Policy

You must set a company e-mail policy and have a document that advises employees what constitutes acceptable uses of e-mail. You cannot just assume employees will know what is appropriate and what is not. Employees need to know that their actions can drive up network support costs, jeopardize network stability, and open the door to legal problems. Such a policy document may cover the following areas:

- Uses—Is e-mail limited to business communications only or are personal e-mails acceptable? If personal e-mails are acceptable, is there a limit on size, quantity, or type? What types of business correspondence can be sent via e-mail and what must be sent by other means?

- Prohibited content—The policy should state that e-mail should not be used for the creation or dissemination of offensive messages about race, gender, age, religious beliefs, etc. Activities illegal under federal, state, or local laws, such as child pornography, software piracy, and copyright infringement, as well as chain letters and pyramid schemes, are also prohibited.

- Ownership of e-mail—Most companies indicate that all e-mails are the sole property of the business, not the employee.

- Security and confidential information—Employees must take proper security measures. They must not divulge passwords or let outsiders onto the e-mail system. They must not e-mail confidential information to outsiders.

- Etiquette—Employees must display proper etiquette when sending e-mail. E-mail must be checked for spelling and grammar. Employees must be polite and must not respond in all capital letters. Certain industries may need to add a disclaimer to their e-mail.

- Message retention policy—Which e-mails are to be saved and which are to be deleted? If deleted, how long are e-mails to be retained before they are deleted? If saved, where are they to be stored?

- Space and size limitations—Users should be advised about the capacity of their mailbox and what happens if they reach its maximum. They should also agree to keep network traffic to a minimum unless they are conducting business. Many companies that allow for personal use may ask employees to do so outside of normal business hours to conserve network bandwidth.

- Antivirus / Antispam measures—Employees need to be aware of company policy regarding viruses and spam. We have already discussed lots of measures earlier in this chapter. Whatever you decide to implement should be documented here.

- Instant Messages—You want to include language to cover this area as well.

- Risks—Employees need to be aware of the potential harmful effects of their actions.

- Consequences of Violations—Describe what will happen if the company policy is violated.

- Monitoring / Privacy—Most companies indicate that employees have no presumption of privacy. E-mail usage may be monitored. Messages may be reviewed by the company.

With a policy like this, you can help to:

- Limit your legal liability

- Improve network security and stability

- Improve employee productivity

- Protect confidential information

- Improve network bandwidth

Monitoring

In September 1999, Small Business Computing and Communications ran an article entitled "5 Signs you are Headed for a Lawsuit." One of the warning signs was neglecting to monitor company e-mail. Setting policy alone isn't enough; it must be monitored and enforced.

Consider driving on the highway as an example. The policy is the posted speed limit, say 55 miles per hour. The detection is a cop with a radar gun. The enforcement is the court with its fines and points on your license. If there was no chance of ever being detected, how many people would drive 55 mph? I rest my case.

As long as employees are notified in writing and in advance, monitoring normally is not a problem. We previously spoke about using the SBS biweekly usage reports to look at users' e-mail volume. It will also indicate both internal and external volume.

One way to monitor exactly what is happening is to grant a user, such as Administrator, access to all the mailboxes in Exchange. This will let you see all mailboxes in the company from one Outlook screen. It is also helpful when providing technical support, but given the obvious security ramifications, do not do this until you have spoken and received approval from the business owner. Then see Microsoft Knowledge Base Article 821897 for the procedures to grant access to all mailboxes. If the situation arises, companies like SpectorSoft make software that installs on a workstation and records every detail of a user's PC and Internet activity.

Privacy

If two employees are in adjoining rooms and e-mail each other, is this communication private? Well, if the company uses an outside mail service, the answer is no. If you want interoffice mail to be private, you need to use your in-house Exchange Server. In fact, in June 2004, the federal appeals court in Boston ruled that federal wiretap laws do not apply to e-mail messages if they are stored, even for a millisecond, on the computers of the ISP that processed them.[31] A significant portion of my client base are lawyers. They are all concerned about attorney-client privilege, which is why they will not consider outsourcing their e-mail.

When sending e-mail to clients, remember you are using a public conduit, the Internet. Messages are open and sent in clear text. If the message is truly confidential, you will need to encrypt the message or send it by some means other than e-mail.

Disclaimer

The goal of this section is to make you aware of the legal questions and issues that arise concerning e-mail. Since laws vary from region to region and needs vary from industry to industry, it is critical that you seek an attorney in your area who can advise you on your specific situation.

Summary

"The next best thing to knowing something is knowing where to find it."
-Samuel Johnson

We have covered a lot of ground together. You have seen:

- How to install and configure Exchange

- How to connect your mail server to the Internet

- How to avoid potential problems

- Techniques to troubleshoot and repair an Exchange database

- Techniques for managing space and information

But e-mail is at a critical point in history. It is under attack, the victim of its own success. Viruses, spam, phishing, thorny legal issues, and an exponentially increasing volume threaten the very usefulness of e-mail. The trick is to keep our "Killer App" from killing us.

As you have seen, there are so many aspects to Exchange that it is impossible to cover everything in just one chapter. It is a very large topic and a rapidly changing one. A few months ago my clients didn't have blocked ports. Now it is commonplace.

I would like to leave you with a few good resources to help you stay on top of information about Exchange. One nice thing is that you have two different camps to draw from: Exchange sites and SBS sites. Between the two, there is a wealth of knowledge and information.

Exchange sites:

Microsoft General Exchange Information

www.microsoft.com/exchange

Microsoft Exchange Updates and Tools

www.microsoft.com/exchange/downloads

Microsoft Exchange Tips and Tricks Library

www.microsoft.com/exchange/techinfo/tips/previous.asp

Newsgroups

www.microsoft.com/exchange/community/newsgroups.mspx

Blogs

MS Exchange Team Blog—You had me at EHLO

Blogs.msdn.com/exchange

KC Lemson on Exchange and Outlook

Blogs.msdn.com/kclemson

There are over 20 blogs on Exchange. For a list see:

http://www.microsoft.com/exchange/community/default.mspx

Web sites

www.msexchange.org

www.slipstick.com

Notes:

SBS sites:

Microsoft General SBS Information

http://www.microsoft.com/windowsserver2003/sbs/
default.mspx

Microsoft Software Updates and tools

http://www.microsoft.com/windowsserver2003/sbs/downloads/
default.mspx

Microsoft Security Center for Small Businesses

http://www.microsoft.com/smallbusiness/gtm/
securityguidance/hub.mspx

http://www.microsoft.com/security/it

Newsgroups

http://www.microsoft.com/windowsserver2003/sbs/
newsgroup.mspx

Blogs

User SBS links for a list of SBS MVP blogs

www.sbslinks.com

Web sites

www.sbslinks.com

www.smallbizserver.net

www.sbsfaq.com

www.sbs-rocks.com

Other sites:

Antispam

postmaster.info.aol.com

www.sarc.com

www.spamlaws.com

www.abuse.net

E-mail policy

www.email-policy.com

Internet Message Headers

www.stopspam.org/email/headers.html

Also see Appendix A: for more SBS-related resources.

CHAPTER 7
Windows Sharepoint Services: Advanced Topics
BY Jonathan Hassell (Charlotte, NC)

Windows Sharepoint Services (WSS) is one of the best features of both editions of SBS 2003. In Harry Brelsford's introductory Windows Small Business Server 2003 Best Practices book, he gave you an introduction to the power and capabilities of WSS. In this chapter, however, I would like to dig down to the meat of WSS and show you some ways in which you can personalize, customize, and extend WSS on your SBS server machine to enhance your marketability, improve your productivity, and increase your access to company resources both in the office and on the road.

Let's get started with an awesome Microsoft Access 2003 trick!

Using WSS with Microsoft Access 2003

One of the coolest features with WSS is its ability to link with the latest version of Microsoft Access. A lot of small business software runs in Access, whether it's off-the-shelf software or a homegrown application, and it is wonderful to be able to link that data with a WSS site on your SBS server machine. Figure 7-1 shows what this integration looks like at a very basic level.

Notes:

Figure 7-1

Access tables integrated with WSS

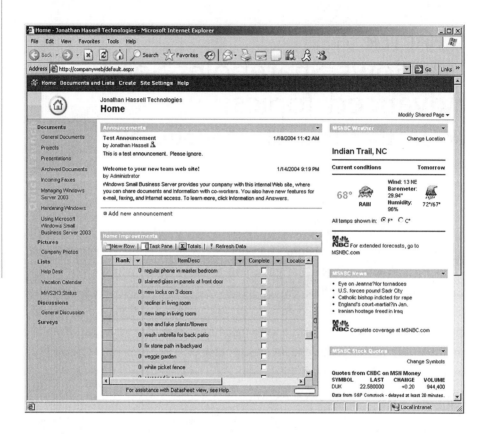

I use this solution to track attendees of my Windows management and security seminars. When customers register for one of my seminars, I keep track of the date of registration, contact information, payment details, and attendee details within Access. Then, at the conference, I can use any PC at the check-in and registration desk to verify registration information via tables linked from Access to WSS. It takes a lot less overhead to check people in over the Web than to carry a laptop loaded with Access. In a pinch, I can even use a PC provided by the hotel if something "undesirable" happens to my equipment and still get necessary information, thanks to the integration of WSS with Access. Using and linking data to and from Access happens in three different phases: exporting data, importing data, and linking data. Let's look at each.

Exporting Data

If you have some really basic data that doesn't change often, you can use the export feature within Access to dump a particular table to a WSS site for easy reference. For example, if you have pricing information for products or services, your representatives and employees don't have to load Access each time they're on the phone with a customer—a definite timesaver.

To export a table from Access to WSS:

1. Launch **Microsoft Access 2003** from the **Start**, **All Programs** bar of a workstation connected to the SBS 2003 network.
2. Click **File**, **Open** to load your database.
3. Right-click on a table in the database window and select **Export**.
4. In the **Save As Type** combo box, select **Windows Sharepoint Services**.
5. The **Export to Windows Sharepoint Services Wizard** will begin. Enter the URL of the WSS site where the exported data should reside. In SBS 2003, this would typically start with http://companyweb. You can also enter a different name for the data, which will take the form of a WSS list and a friendly description if you don't like the defaults. You see this in Figure 7-2.

Figure 7-2

Exporting to WSS

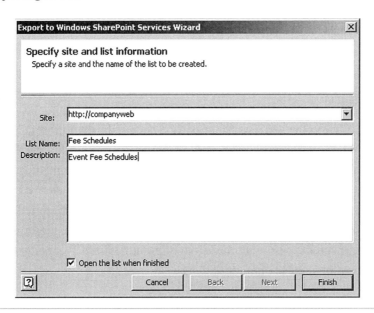

6. Click **Finish** to complete the process.

The exported list looks like that shown in Figure 7-3.

Figure 7-3

Viewing the exported data in WSS

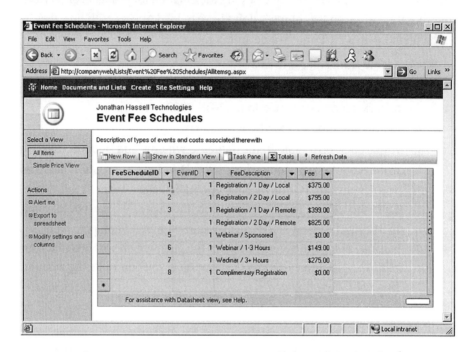

BEST PRACTICE: Export some static data to WSS for easy access to list data for all of your employees, both in the office and on the road.

Importing Data

Taking this a step further, let's try importing some information from WSS into Access. When you import WSS data to Access, Access attempts to import columns and correlatetheir function and format (for instance, formatting currency columns with dollars and cents, etc.). Since Access and WSS use a very similar database engine, it's fairly easy for Access to "inherit" the Required, Default Value, Format, and Decimal Places settings from the WSS columns being imported. If you have set maximum and minimum values, Access will build a routine to enforce those upon import.

Let's begin the import of WSS items into Access:

1. In Microsoft Access 2003, select **File**, **Get External Data**, **Import**.
2. In the **Files of Type** combo box, select **Windows Sharepoint Services** to launch the **Import From Windows Sharepoint Services Wizard**.
3. Enter the URL of the WSS site containing the data to import and click **Next**.

   In SBS 2003, this would typically start with http://companyweb.
4. On the next panel of the wizard, you can choose whether to import lists or views.

A view represents a subset of a list, much like a Top 10 list is a subset of a larger list of rankings. You can select multiple lists to import by holding down the **Ctrl** key and clicking on each item. You can see this screen in Figure 7-4.

Figure 7-4

Selecting lists to import

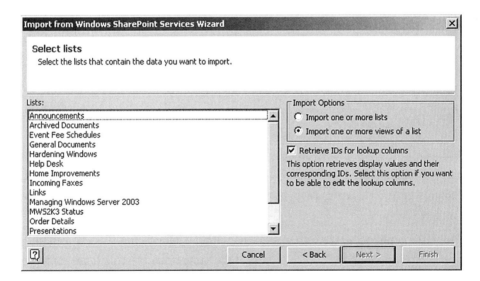

5. Select the action you'd like to take for lookup columns.

   Lookup columns use numbers to identify the contents of other lists. For example, if you had two tables, one with product numbers and names and the other with product numbers and available inventory quantities, you could create a lookup column to the second table to identify the product names. Those lookup columns can be a bit confusing in this dialog, but the bottom line is this: if you uncheck this box, then the imported Access table will contain the actual names, rather than the numeric IDs. If you check the box, the numeric IDs will be imported.

6. The final pane of the wizard will confirm your choices. Click **Finish** to import the table or tables that you chose.

A sample of an imported table is provided in Figure 7-5.

Figure 7-5

Data imported from WSS to Access

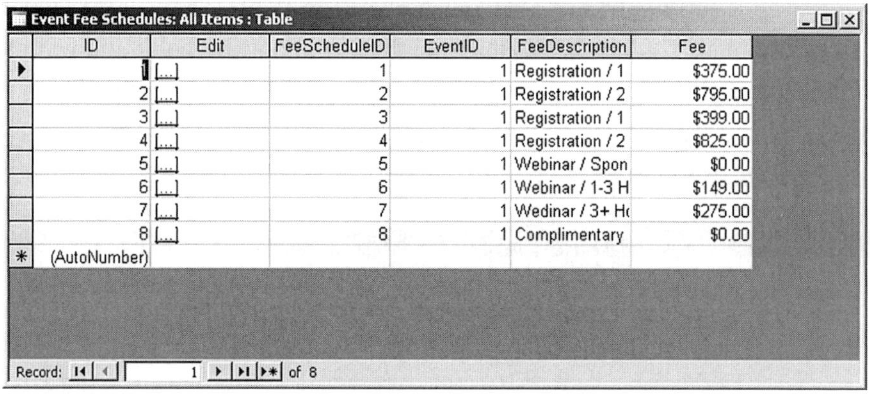

ID	Edit	FeeScheduleID	EventID	FeeDescription	Fee
1 [...]		1	1	Registration / 1	$375.00
2 [...]		2	1	Registration / 2	$795.00
3 [...]		3	1	Registration / 1	$399.00
4 [...]		4	1	Registration / 2	$825.00
5 [...]		5	1	Webinar / Spon	$0.00
6 [...]		6	1	Webinar / 1-3 H	$149.00
7 [...]		7	1	Wedinar / 3+ H	$275.00
8 [...]		8	1	Complimentary	$0.00
(AutoNumber)					

Record: 1 of 8

Linking Data

You can link WSS data to Access, which is the most useful feature since you can keep data stored in WSS but manipulate it using the advanced tools and features of Access. Access uses a stylized calendar icon to represent a list linked from WSS.

Problems could occur if a user is working with the data within WSS and another user is working with the data in Access at the same time. Microsoft has foreseen this event and has implemented a "locking" procedure so if two users change the same record from within both Access and WSS, Windows will send an error message the second time a change is made. Within WSS, the error is actually a Web page and gives the user an opportunity to overwrite the changes made by the first user. If the second user is working inside Access, the user gets a Write Conflict dialog box.

The main benefit of this arrangement is the ability to work with database data once it is stored in Access without the need to have Access running on a local machine. My earlier example of using a PC at a registration and check-in desk is a prime candidate to reap the benefits of linked data. Another example that might apply to you is a field sales representative who works on a simple PC without licenses for Microsoft Office. Sometimes small businesses with limited technology budgets might opt for cheaper laptop computers for mobile users and equip it with just Microsoft Word or other, open-source office software alternatives. You might be in this situation. Rather than hiring an expensive consultant to write a custom interface between your Access database and a Web page for your mobile users, you can just use linked data and tables from Access and WSS.

To link tables:

1. In Microsoft Access 2003, select **File**, **Get External Data**, **Link Tables**.

2. **In the Files of Type** combo box, select **Windows Sharepoint Services**. This will launch the **Link to Windows Sharepoint Services Wizard**.

3. Enter the URL of the WSS site containing the data to import and click **Next**.

In SBS 2003, this would typically start with http://companyweb.

4. On the next panel of the wizard, choose to import lists or views. You can use **Ctrl+Click** to select multiple lists to import, as shown in Figure 7-6.

Notes:

Figure 7-6

Linking data to and from Access and WSS

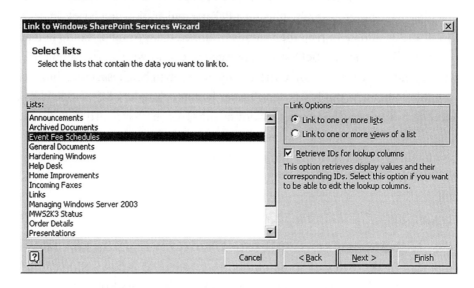

5. Select what to do about lookup columns.

    Remember: if you uncheck this box, the imported Access table will
    contain actual names rather than associated numeric ID numbers. If
    you check the box, the numeric IDs will be imported.

6. The final pane of the wizard will confirm your choices. Click **Finish**
    to import the table or tables that you chose.

BEST PRACTICE: Link data between Access and WSS to provide a
better editing environment for junior employees, give remote users
access to changing data, and manipulate WSS-based data in a richer
database environment.

Views within WSS

Views are simply subsets of lists. They're just a "picture" of a list, displayed
according to a certain set of criteria and preferences that you specify. Adjusting
views can be beneficial for several reasons. For one, you can create a simple
view of complex data for junior employees. You can also see trends and other
important details from data by displaying it in other ways—we all have been

there, done that after looking at the same set of numbers for hours. You can then chart those numbers, see what you were missing before, and figure out what data you need to complete the picture. To continue along our earlier event management example, let's say I want my list view within WSS to only contain the type of event and its associated price. There's no need for my salespeople to see the event ID, the fee type ID, or any of the other data provided by the ancillary columns. To eliminate these columns from the list display, we need to create a custom view.

To create a custom view:

1. Logon to a workstation attached to an SBS 2003 network, launch Internet Explorer, and go to the list within your Company Web WSS site.
2. In the left pane, click **Modify Settings and Columns**.
3. Scroll down to the bottom of the page and locate the section called **Views**.
4. Click the **Create a New View** link.

   The **Create View** page loads. From here, you can choose a standard view, which is simply a few columns with the data located in the correct places; a datasheet view, which more resembles a spreadsheet; and a calendar view, which is appropriate for date-driven data.
5. On the **Create View** page, select **Standard View** since we only need a simple view for our price list.
6. In the **Name** section, give the new view a descriptive name.

   I've chosen **Simple Price View**. You can choose to make it the default.
7. In the **Audience** section, choose between a personal view or a public view.

   Personal views are intended for your own personal use, but anyone with the correct URL can view it—there's no authentication involved. Public views are advertised for everyone's use on the site.

Notes:

8. In the **Columns** section, select the columns you would like to see in this view. I have selected the **FeeDescription** and **Fee** fields for our simple view, which is shown in Figure 7-7.

Figure 7-7

Creating a new view

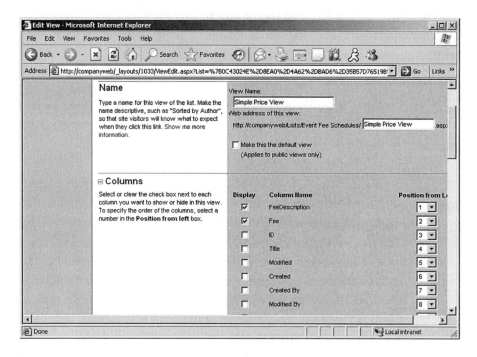

9. In the **Sort** section, choose whether to sort by specific columns and the order in which those columns should be sorted. If you have no preference for this view, leave the default settings intact.

10. The **Filter** section allows you to actually filter the data in the view that is shown so only data that meet specific criteria are used.

    For example, if you have a view that only shows items with prices less than $50, you could create a filter here that restricts the view to only items whose Price fields contain a number less than or equal to 50. If you have no preference for this view, leave the default settings intact.

11. Click **OK** to publish the view when finished.

When I go back to the original view, on the left pane I see the Select a View section. The generic All Items view is listed, but the new view I just created shows up there under Simple Price View. Clicking that results in a much simpler view that's easier to refer to at a glance. Mission accomplished. See for yourself in Figure 7-8.

Figure 7-8
The new view within WSS

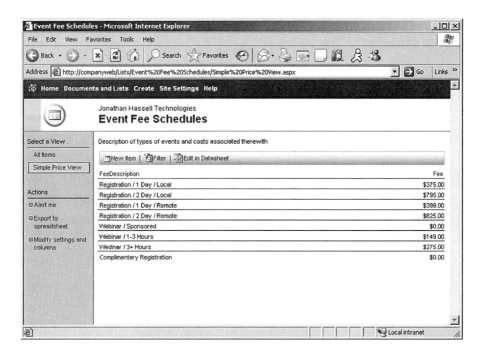

> BEST PRACTICE: Create views in WSS to display complex data in a simpler manner, or to clean up messy data for viewing over the Web.

Advanced View Creation

A few other options are helpful if you are using a large listto glean statistics about the overall corpus of data contained within your list. To access these advanced features, create a new view as explained above, but scroll down. Above the **OK** and **Cancel** buttons you will see several sections that are collapsed by default. Expand them by clicking the plus sign beside each, and then look at the options offered to you.

- **Group By:** this setting allows you to group items that have the same value together in the list. For example, if your list has a column indicating a type of item, and you want all the items with a type of "Portable" to be grouped together on the list, you can select it here and determine the order in which those items are grouped.

- **Totals:** in this section, you can choose to display totals for each column and indicate how those totals will be calculated (either as addition or as a count of the items).

- **Style:** this option lets you select how the list will be presented. You can choose from a basic table, a box with no labels, a box with labels, a newsletter, a newsletter without border lines, a shaded list, or the default view.

- **Item Limit:** you can use this feature to limit the number of items displayed, which is an especially useful option if you have a particularly large list. You can choose a hard limit or allow each user to specify the number of items displayed per screen.

You can see these advanced switches in Figure 7-9.

Notes:

Figure 7-9

Toggling advanced view options within WSS

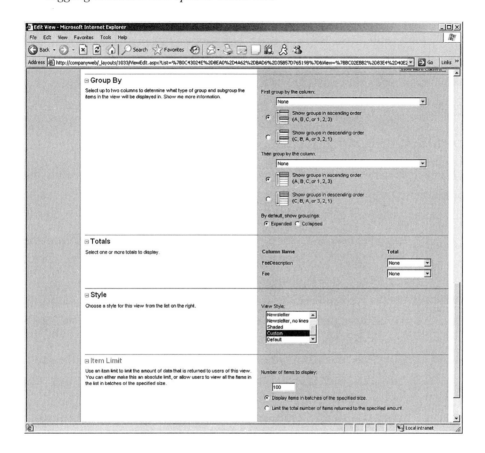

Customizing Themes in WSS

You may want to customize the colors, fonts, and icons used within your SBS server machine's WSS sites to further reflect the look of your company. Or, if you have several WSS sites, you may want to color code them to make it easier for your employees to distinguish between the different sites and their purposes.

To customize themes within WSS, use Microsoft Office FrontPage 2003. FrontPage contains a collection of themes that include design elements like buttons, hover buttons, bullets, backgrounds, horizontal lines, page banners, and font and formatting options. Because of the integration between Office and WSS, it's very easy to change themes on WSS-based sites with FrontPage.

The process of applying a theme changes all design elements contained within the theme simultaneously—you can't just pick one change and apply it, and then pick another, and so on. It also changes all the elements on all pages of the site, too, so you don't have to waste your time reformatting each page within the site.

Basic Customization

The easiest way to customize your WSS site is to start with an existing preformatted theme from FrontPage. You can then make changes to that theme and create your own custom look. To get started:

1. Logon to a workstation connected to the SBS 2003 network. From the **File** menu, select **Open Site** to open your WSS site in FrontPage 2003.
2. From the **Format** menu, choose **Theme**.
   On the right side of the screen, the **Theme** task pane appears.
3. Scroll through the list and select the theme you would like to customize. Click it and select **Apply as default theme**.
4. Click **Yes** to confirm you want the changes applied across the site.
   Now that your selected theme is applied to the site, you can start making changes to the theme.
5. At the bottom of the **Theme** task pane, click the **Create new theme** link. The **Customize Theme** screen appears.
6. Click **Save as** and then type a name for the theme you're creating.
7. Click **OK** to save your custom theme. Now you can get started making real changes.

In this section, I'll focus on changing three elements of the theme: colors, graphics, and text. Let's get started.

Notes:

Changing Colors

On the **Customize Theme** dialog box, click **Colors**. The **Colors** screen appears, which is shown in Figure 7-10.

Figure 7-10
Changing colors on a WSS site

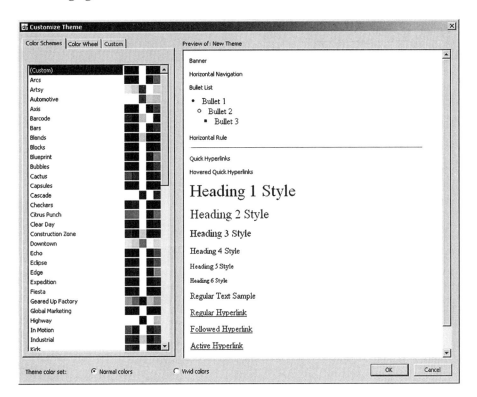

From here, you can change the colors of hyperlinks, horizontal rules, headings, body color, banner text, button text, and background colors. Just select an element, change the color, and then click **OK**.

Notes:

Changing Graphics

In the **Customize Theme** dialog box, click **Graphics**. The **Graphics** screen appears, which is shown in Figure 7-11.

Figure 7-11

Changing graphics on a WSS site

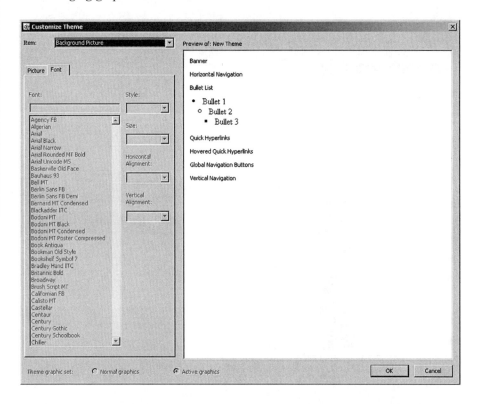

To change any element here, just click the element you want to change—this could be the picture on the background of the page, a banner image on your pages, or navigation buttons—and specify where the new graphics for your site are stored. Click **OK** when you have completed your changes.

Changing Text

In the **Customize Theme** dialog box, click **Text**. The **Text** screen appears. From here, you can change the font used in body text and headings on your pages. Just click the element to change, select the new font and size, and then click **OK**.

You might also want to specify multiple fonts for users who are using systems that don't have many custom fonts installed. To do this, select the preferred font, and then type in a comma, a space, and the alternative "safe" font in the dialog box. For example, if I want Georgia but would like to default to Arial if Georgia is not available, I would type **Georgia, Arial** in the box. Click **OK**.

> BEST PRACTICE: Customize your WSS site to make it uniquely your own. You can also use it as a marketing tool to show off to clients.

Advanced Customization: Using Cascading Style Sheets

Don your Web designer hats! The themes in FrontPage 2003 use Web standards called Cascading Style Sheets (CSS), to apply font and formatting rules across your entire SBS WSS site. FrontPage hides a lot of the complexity behind CSS from you, so in most cases you won't need to worry about it. However, if you want to really dig deep and change just about every element of your WSS pages, you'll need to identify what CSS elements define the styles used on the pages and then learn how to change those elements to meet your personal specifications.

The central point where you can change the formatting specifications used in FrontPage is the **Styles** dialog box, which is found within the **Customize Theme** dialog box with which you're already familiar. From the **Customize Theme** dialog box, click **Text**, and then on the resulting screen click **More Text Styles**. The **Style** dialog box opens, which is shown in Figure 7-12.

Notes:

Figure 7-12

Changing CSS-defined text styles

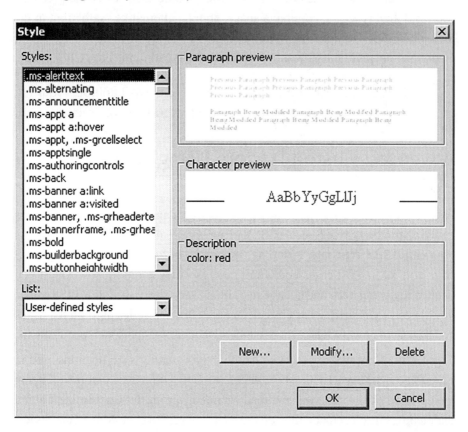

Scroll through the styles to select the element you'd like to change. The formatting that corresponds with each style is previewed to the right, so you don't have to close the box, check the change, and then go back and tweak the change—a frustrating process! Once you have selected the style you want, click **Modify**, which opens the **Modify Style** dialog box, as shown in Figure 7-13.

Notes:

Figure 7-13
*The **Modify Style** dialog box*

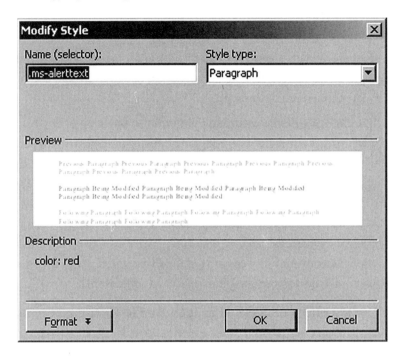

Click **Format** to change the font, paragraph, border, numbering, and position for this style. Once you've made your changes, click **OK** to back out of all the open dialog boxes, and then click **Yes** to confirm your change.

> BEST PRACTICE: Learning how to use CSS to modify and personalize WSS sites is a marketable skill that can be used to create custom solutions—particularly those outlined later in the chapter!

Backup and Restore Options for WSS

Disaster recovery is always a tenuous topic to cover, and my colleague Jeff Middleton has covered it adeptly in his chapter in this book. However, I want to discuss WSS-specific backup methodologies because WSS itself is such a complex beast, with a lot of moving parts that can break. Because of this, you need a complete backup solution—but it shouldn't be difficult, either. My law of the universe, Hassell's Law, holds that with the increasing difficulty of a task and the increasing importance of a task, the less often that task is actually carried out. Don't agree with me? When do you file your tax return? And when was the last time you made a full backup?

Of course, since WSS is a complex beast, there are lots of strategies—and lots of advantages and disadvantages to consider—in backing up data contained in your site. The three main options are:

- **Use the stsadm.exe command-line tool to back up individual sites.** You can get a full-fidelity, complete backup or restore of an entire site by using the stsadm.exe command-line tool with the backup and restore operations. The good news here is that you don't have to have SQL Server 2000. However, you must still be an administrator on the local server computer that is running WSS in order to perform this method of backing up and restoring, which might be a bit much for client sites or junior users in your small business. After all, you don't give the keys to your kingdom to just anyone, right?

- **Use the Microsoft WSS Migration Tool (smigrate.exe) to back up and restore individual sites and subsites.** The bad news here is that you may lose some customizations or settings in the process. For example, security settings for the site, such as user membership in site groups, are lost in the restoration. The good news, though, is that you don't need to be an administrator on the local server computer.

- **Use the Microsoft SQL Server 2000 tools to back up the databases.** You can use the backup tools included with SQL Server 2000 to get a full-fidelity, complete backup of the databases used by WSS on your SBS server machine. When you use this method, you back up and restore the entire configuration database and each content database on your server. From that point, you can then restore any or all of these databases. The good news is that this is the best way to get a complete backup. The bad news is two-fold: you must be running SQL Server 2000 to be able to use this backup method, and you must be an administrator on the local server computer that is running SQL Server. It also takes a heck of a long time if you have a large database.

Each of these options is discussed in detail below.

Using stsadm.exe for WSS Backup and Restoration

Site backup and restore is intended to help you reconnect sites that have become corrupted or need to be restored to a previous state. This process is not intended for moving a site to a new server.

When using site backup and restore, keep the following items in mind:

- You can automate this process using the Scheduled Tasks feature within Windows Server 2003 and through a batch file or a script.

- When you are performing a backup or restore, memory usage and CPU performance are affected, so be sure to schedule these procedures for a time when the WSS site usage is the lightest. This will prevent disruption of users.

- If you are trying to restore a site that uses a different language pack than the one that is installed on the target computer, you will need to install that language pack on the target computer for the restore to be successful.

The stsadm.exe utility uses several parameters within the program to perform operations. We're interested in the backup operation, but first, we need to see which sites are available to back up. You'll find the stsadm.exe program in the C:\Program Files\Common Files\Microsoft Shared\web server extensions\ 60\BIN directory. Running the following command from the command line will tell us that.

```
stsadm.exe -o enumsites -url <url>
```

In the above command, replace <url> with the name of the Web server on which your WSS sites reside.

Once you know the names of sites, enter a command like the following to perform a simple backup of a site:

```
stsadm.exe -o backup -url http://
server_name/site -filename backup.dat
```

For example, to backup my local WSS site, I would issue the following command:

```
stsadm.exe -o backup -url http://companyweb
-filename backup.dat
```

This command will back up the entire contents of the http://companyweb url to a file named backup.dat, which will be located in whatever directory I'm currently in on the command line. If you'd like to overwrite a backup file with the same name (for instance, if you always name the latest backup current.dat and you run this command each night), use the following command:

```
stsadm.exe -o backup -url http://companyweb
-filename backup.dat -overwrite
```

When you want to restore a site, you have three options. You can:

- Restore a site and overwrite the contents of an existing site,

- Restore the backed up site to a new site on the same server, or

- Restore the backed up site to another server that uses a copy of the original server's configuration database.

If you overwrite a site, you completely eliminate whatever was in the site before you began the restore operation. The latter two methods are useful when you're trying to restore data to a corrupted site.

To restore a site from a backup file, either to a new site or a separate server, use syntax similar to the following:

```
stsadm.exe -o restore -url http://backup-
server/companyweb -filename backup.dat
```

That command would restore my backup.dat file to a separate server, called BACKUP-SERVER, and the WSS site called "Companyweb" on that server.

Alternatively, if you want to overwrite your site with the backup data, you can use a command similar to the following:

```
stsadm.exe -o restore -url http://
companyweb -backup.dat -overwrite
```

Using the WSS Migration Tool for Backup

When you use the WSS Migration Tool, you must actually perform two separate operations. First, back up the site to a file. Second, restore the site to the new location. During the backup process, specify the URL for the Web site and the backup file to create. You can also specify the scope of the site migration (migrate just the top-level Web site or the top-level Web site along with any subsites). During the restore process, you specify the new URL and the backup file to restore from.

If you use the WSS Migration Tool to migrate a site based on WSS to another server running WSS, security settings, WSS Central Administration settings, personalizations, and Web page customizations are not migrated.

To back up a site to a file, use a command like the following:

```
Smigrate -w http://companyweb -f backup.dat
```

To restore a file to a site, use a command like the following:

```
Smigrate -r -w http://companyweb -f backup.dat
```

With this tool, you can choose subsites to back up. For example, if you have a subsite on your SBS server machine named "partners," you can choose to back up only that subsite—something you cannot do with the stsadm.exe tool described above. To back up a subsite, issue a command like the following:

```
Smigrate -w http://sbs-server/partners -f
partners-backup.dat
```

To restore it, use a command similar to this:

```
Smigrate -r -w http://sbs-server/partners -
f partners-backup.dat
```

Using the SQL Server 2000 Tools for Backup

If you are lucky enough to have purchased the SBS 2003 Premium Edition and have migrated your databases to SQL Server 2000, then using SQL Server's built-in tools is the most complete way to back up your WSS configuration and content. However, it's also the most costly: such an operation is both time- and computing power-intensive, so it's best to use this method sparingly.

The first step of this method is to distinguish which databases you need to back up. The most common choices are outlined below.

- The configuration database is named sts_config.mdf by default. (Note that this is only the default name. When you created the configuration database, you had the option to specify a different name.)

- The content databases are created with names based on the server name by default (for example, STS_server_name_1.mdf, STS_server_name_12.mdf, and so on). The database names are not sequential. Again, you may have chosen a different naming scheme for the content databases when you created them.

Once you have identified the appropriate database, you can use SQL Server's tools to back up the database.

A practical and effective backup strategy for your WSS installation is to use both of these tools. At longer intervals, such as monthly, back up your entire set of databases using the Microsoft SQL Server tools. At shorter intervals, such as weekly, run stsadm.exe to back up just those site collections that have changed. This will facilitate quick recovery of lost items with a minimum of space usage, while the Microsoft SQL Server tools backups are available for large-scale disaster recovery.

> BEST PRACTICE: Run the SQL Server Tools backup method at longer intervals—monthly or bimonthly—and use the stsadm.exe tools at more regular, shorter intervals to keep your WSS installation completely backed up at the least cost of time and resources to your small business.

Helpful WSS Customizations

To this point I've covered a few ways in which you can use WSS as a foundation and build upon its functionality to create custom Web-based collaboration solutions for your small business. In this section, I'll highlight some of the most efficient and productive customizations of WSS on SBS that have been brought to my attention.

Contract and Service Management

Chad Gross, a small business consultant and SBS MVP, has customized the Help Desk feature of his SBS server machine's internal Web site to use as a service contract management tool. According to Chad, this homegrown WSS customization has actually replaced the venerable Goldmine® software in their small business.

Chad has linked custom customer lists and created custom views, among other things. Chad says, "We use the Help Desk for scheduling. We added various fields that made sense with the way we work, including fields for technician, customer, service call notes, arrival time, finish time, total time on site, and a billed flag, just to name a few. We then created a new view that shows us the schedule in a calendar view. We also created a few other views to help with our workflow. For example, "My Active Tasks" shows the user their calls that have not been completed in a list view, which helps us keep up on our paperwork. I open that view, and see immediately which calls I need to complete."

In true team spirit, the Help Desk customizations that Chad has created work around the company to everyone's advantage. Chad again: "Another view we created is 'Ready to Bill.' This is a list view of our calls that are marked Completed but not flagged as Billed. This gives [our billing manager] a one-stop spot for calls that need to be billed. Plus, with all the call details on there, she can copy/paste into the invoice right from WSS." Obviously this process saves the billing manager quite a bit of time.

Action Points

Here are the main changes that Chad has implemented to create his contract and service management tool within WSS:

- Customize the Help Desk feature (which is unique to SBS) to include a few extra columns. The most useful are technical, total time on site, and a flag indicating whether the customer has been billed or not. You can, of course, add others as needed.

- Create a couple of extra views: one, as a calendar view of the company's current service call schedule, and another that shows each employee's active tasks to help him or her stay on track.

- Create workspaces within WSS for each customer site to store contract information, templates, past invoices, notes from previous service calls, and other tools.

- Link the Customer field within the Help Desk to the appropriate customer workspace for easy navigation between each part.

- Save the custom Customer Workspace as a template so you can use it over and over again with each new client you retain.

Figure 7-14 shows a sample of Chad's customized solution for WSS.

Figure 7-14

Contract and service management with WSS

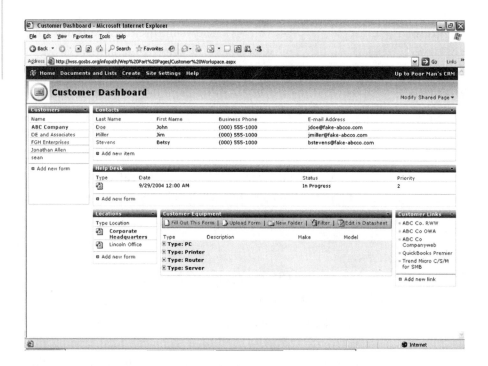

BEST PRACTICE: Keep track of your customers and their associated schedules with a custom WSS solution.

Human Resources Management

Human Resources Management continues to be a big focus in corporate America. Virtually all companies, large and small alike, are examining ways in which they can save money on managing and maintaining their employees. Digitizing human resources with WSS helps you interface with employees, provide them with the tools and forms they need at ready disposal, and take the heat off your HR staff, all in an up-to-the-minute, seamlessly integrated format.

Take a look at the following WSS-based HR portal, shown in Figure 7-15.

Figure 7-15

Human resources management with WSS

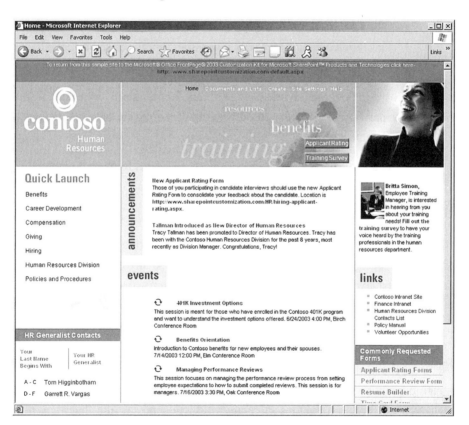

You can see the quick launch menu has been modified to provide easy access to benefits information, compensation, matching programs, hiring and acquisitions, and policies and procedures. The Events area in the middle can include noteworthy dates, such as insurance open enrollment or 401(k) mass vesting dates. The Announcements area can be used to provide links and timely information to Web surfers.

Action Points

Here are the main items to consider when creating a custom HR portal within WSS:

- Create custom quick launch links to different sections or workspaces for each HR item (benefits, policies, and so on).

- Make a quick contacts area with key names, numbers, and e-mail aliases for your HR team so employees can get in touch with the right person.

- Provide a document workspace or library for commonly requested forms like performance reviews, resume templates, time cards, travel requests, and expense reports.

- Offer a survey section to get feedback on programs from your employees.

Sales and Marketing Portals

"Generate leads!" "Drop your new collateral off by Friday" "We have a big customer meeting in two weeks—are you ready?" Do any of these lines sound familiar? Perhaps you—or your customer—have teams of sales and marketing people that need to get together. Or maybe your teams are separated geographically, and everyone needs a place to come together and drop documents, ideas, calendar events, and other items.

WSS was made precisely for situations such as these, when teams need a virtual meeting place to share ideas and pass on information. With a bit of time and skill, you can create a custom sales and marketing portal like that shown in Figure 7-16.

Figure 7-16

Sales and marketing resources with WSS

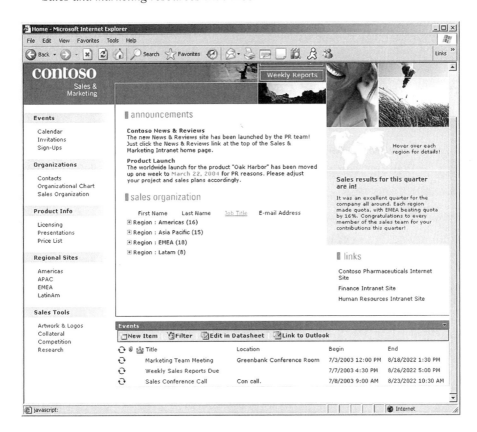

The quick launch menu has been customized into categories to show events, organizations, product information, regional sites, and sales tools. The Announcements pane lists upcoming press events and product launches, and the Sales Organization area lists key contacts on the sales and marketing team. The Events pane is a list view of meetings, due dates for important deliverables, and conference calls so everyone can stay on task.

Action Points

Here are the main items to consider when creating a custom sales and marketing portal within WSS:

- Customize the quick launch bar and categorize it into different sections and different types of resources.

- On the front page, include a contact list for critical contacts on the sales and marketing team, including names, phone numbers, and e-mail addresses.

- Make document libraries to store drafts of collateral materials, contact lists for partners and printers, and other sales information.

- Provide a links page to point to product information on the corporate Web site, competitor's Web sites, and interesting marketing and sales strategy pages.

- Create libraries for presentations, price lists, competitive analyses, weekly sales and marketing reports, news and reviews, etc.

- Include a discussion board as a central place for team members to exchange ideas.

BEST PRACTICE: You can create a sales and marketing portal for your own small business or for your clients to help track events, product information, news and reviews, and other important marketing materials.

About WSS Service Pack 1

To deploy or not to deploy? In mid-September 2004, Microsoft released a batch of fixes for rather smallish bugs found in the original release version of WSS , and true to their common form, they called the updates a "service pack." A list of the bugs the service pack squashes, direct from Microsoft, is as follows:

- When you type http://localhost in the Address box of Internet Explorer on your Web server, you receive the following error message: HTTP 400 - Bad Request Internet Explorer. This is a frustrating bug because it sometimes means you can't test changes you make to your WSS site from the server itself—an important ability if you are using Remote Desktop Connection to administer your server.

- When you try to add a Web part to your online Web Part gallery, the Web part is not added. This issue may occur if the file name of the Web part contains international characters or language-specific characters. For those of us outside the United States, this removes some important functionality from WSS.

- When you restore your Microsoft SQL database to your WSS Web site, the links that are at the root of your Web site are broken. Broken links are the perennial pain in the rear of a webmaster.

- When you relink a form in your WSS Web site that contains the Rich Text format, all Rich Text formatted text is moved from its original position, and it appears after the text that is in plain text format. This one can leave you scratching your head for hours—I sure was at a dentist's office that uses forms to keep track of insurance claim details!

- When you try to sort items in the Threaded view in a discussion board, the oldest item is always listed first. An inconvenient way to return to monitor conversations that you've already visited once, to say the least.

- When you try to back up your WSS Web site to a network location, you receive a "Write error" error message, and the backup is not completed successfully. Combine this frustrating error with the fact that backups simply aren't straightforward with WSS, and you can see where most administrators would choose to ignore backups entirely—not a good solution.

- When you try to create a new WSS Web site on a Microsoft Windows Server 2003-based computer, you receive the following error message: HTTP Error 403.1 - Forbidden: Execute access is denied. Internet Information Services (IIS). You probably won't see this error too much unless you've added another, separate Web server to your SBS network.

- After you install a language-specific WSS template pack, the language of the pack does not appear in the Select Language list on the Sites and Workplaces page. It's a case of "do-and-disappear."

- When you try to upload a large file to your WSS Web site, you may receive the following error message: Form Validation Error. Please correct the information you provided by following these steps, then submit the information again. The URL 'Unified Lab Library/docname.doc is invalid. It may refer to a nonexistent file or folder or refer to a valid file or folder that is not in the current Web. Since many of my clients deal with Word and Excel documents that are significantly larger than typical files, this was a maddening error that really caused some user frustration at the continued use of WSS.

- When you try to search for events in your WSS Web site, you cannot find past or future events. The search results return only the next event. This definitely limits the calendar functionality.

- When you install an update to a WSS server that contains a non-provisioned Web site, the Web site is provisioned by the update. If you have private web sites that shouldn't be made public, you might be surprised at what Internet surfers can discover! This was a pretty big hole that's now fixed.

- When you install an update to a WSS server that has some IIS services stopped, those services may restart automatically after you install the update. This isn't a terribly big problem, but if you have some of these services stopped for security reasons, your machine will have an increased attack surface after the update.

- FrontPage may quit unexpectedly when you try to open a WSS Web page that contains a URL to an image that starts with certain characters and that contains more spaces in the URL than the length of the file name of the image. This is another frustrating bug that makes you wonder what you're doing wrong—luckily it's now repaired!

- When you publish a disk-based Web site in FrontPage that contain pages that have a theme applied and that have a page banner, FrontPage may quit unexpectedly, and you receive an error message. This happened to me in the course of writing this chapter, in fact, and I was pleasantly surprised to see this issue mitigated in this service pack release.

- When you install an update that contains the Mso.dll file, an incorrect service pack level may appear in the About dialog box of a Microsoft Office program such as FrontPage. This service pack corrects this issue by using the earliest date of the Mso.dll file that is installed on your computer. This bug really is just a cosmetic problem that doesn't affect much.

- After you install an update to WSS , some files, such as the Sqmsto.dll and the Sqmstoup.dll files, may have an earlier certificate expiration date than you expect.

- When you locate a home page for a user who was added to WSS by using a Microsoft Windows group, the UserInfo field for that user appears to be corrupted. (You probably wouldn't have come across this one, either.)

- When multiple threads access the same document at the same time in a WSS Web site, you receive an access violation error message. This issue may occur if the following functions access the same document at the same time: Put, Get, Copy, Rename, PropFind, and Unlock. Now this one is frustrating, particularly if a lot of your users embrace WSS: multiple users accessing a documents breaks WSS! It's a good thing this is fixed.

- When you locate a WSS Web site by typing //localhost in the Address box of Internet Explorer on a Windows Server 2003-based computer, you receive the following error message: You are not authorized to view this page. Again, another problematic issue if you're editing your WSS site from the SBS server itself.

- When you try to paste text in the body of a new announcement in a WSS Web site, text that contains extended characters is not pasted. This might not be a big issue for you.

- When you type a non-breaking space in the properties of a file in a WSS Web site and then save the changes to the XML file, the file is corrupted and Microsoft Word, Internet Explorer, or any XML reader cannot read the file. You won't run up against this bug unless you're doing a lot of advanced WSS customization.

This list of problems may seem long, but fortunately the download is easy and the installation is even easier. Point a web browser to the following long URL: http://www.microsoft.com/downloads/details.aspx?FamilyId=875DA47E-89D5-4621-A319-A1F5BFEDF497

Once the file has downloaded, double-click on it and run through the installation process. As always, make a backup.

> **BEST PRACTICE:** Make a backup of your WSS installation, and then download and install WSS Service Pack 1.

Summary

There is a lot of room for extending the functionality of WSS. In this chapter, I've shown you how to:

- Import and export data to and from Access.

- Link data within an Access database and a WSS list.

- Customize views within WSS pages.

- Back up and restore your WSS site and its contents using three different methods.

- Customize WSS for contact and service management, human resource management, and sales and marketing portal creation.

- Assess the scope of WSS Service Pack 1 and download and deploy it

A lot of material was covered in this chapter, but all of it is worth your attention. Enhance the marketability and productivity of your firm by personalizing WSS for your small business. Good luck, and happy customizing! Please feel free to share your customized WSS installs with me—I'm always interested. Send e-mail to jon@jonathanhassell.com.

CHAPTER 8
Remote Web Workplace: Advanced Topics
BY Wayne Small (Sydney, New South Wales, Australia)

Imagine sitting on a sunny beach, waves lapping at your feet, piña colada in hand, relaxing. Now imagine that you can run your business from here as well. Does this sound too good to be true? Not really—you can do all this with Windows Small Business Server 2003 (SBS 2003), if you know how. What's more, SBS 2003 has features that not even the enterprise level operating systems do not have, and that makes SBS 2003 unique.

The ability to have users work remotely from a head office is one of the biggest solutions that I've been implementing here in Australia. That is due in part to the vast expanse of Australia, where offices can be separated by thousands of kilometers. The power and features of SBS give the small business owner unique abilities that often surpass those of larger businesses, including the ability to be more flexible, react quicker, provide greater customer service and, therefore, enhance their business.

What I will show you in this chapter are some of the tips, tricks, and techniques that I have used to solve real problems and meet the business needs of my customers. But before we dive into the technical details of building good solutions, we first need to understand the requirements of different types of small business users.

Requirements of Remote Workers and Mobile Workers

If you ask people what mobility means to them, you will get a very wide range of responses. For some it means simply getting access to their email while out of the office, for others it involves accessing their desktop from anywhere, and yet others determine it to mean having unfettered access to information stored at the home office while they work from remote locations most of the time. The requirements of workers in each of these categories are different, so different solutions are required for each.

The first step in providing a solution for the customer is to understand their specific requirements. So below I've described each of these workers in more detail and presented solutions that address the needs of:

- Occasional remote workers,

- Mobile workers,

- Remote office workers, and

- Business partners.

Occasional Remote Workers

Occasional remote workers are typically those who do most of their work in the office on a daily basis, but want occasional access to office resources from home. They most likely have a desktop computer in the office and a personal computer at home. These workers need access to basic facilities like email and maybe their desktop computer. SBS's Remote Web Workplace (RWW) does a fantastic job for them in this area and provides the portal in which they can access these basic resources quickly and efficiently. These facilities are all accessed via a one-on-one connection between a single user and a single account and/or desktop.

Notes:

Mobile Workers

Mobile workers are also individuals (as opposed to a group of people in a remote location) who need remote access to office resources. Mobile workers, however, tend to be out of the office far more than they are in the office. In some cases, as with one of my clients, remote workers are in the office once every 3 or 4 months and out of the office at all other times. Therefore, the solutions and resources they need are slightly different from occasional remote workers. Mobile workers tend to have laptop computers and Personal Digital Assistants (PDAs) or PDA/phone combinations that are their primary business tools. They require solid solutions that are easy and reliable to use. They may be dialing in from a hotel room one night over a 56k modem connection and the next day they may be accessing your office from one of their customer's sites using a high speed DSL connection. The roaming nature of these workers requires that the amount of actual data they get be kept to a minimum so their computer system still functions well using the different connection types that they may encounter. However, that said, mobile workers still require full online functionality from anywhere in the world.

Remote Office Workers

Remote offices are where you may have several people in a remote site who all have the same requirements to access data from the head office. The business systems are located in head offices. To keep the data traffic between offices to a minimum, remote offices invariably utilize a "thin client environment" such as Web-style interfaces between business systems and terminal server environments. Remote office workers often need to print larger volumes of information than mobile workers or occasional remote workers, so these additional considerations need to be well planned to maximize the use of the system.

The remote office is connected to head office via a Virtual Private Network (VPN) over the internet, direct connection via ISDN or dialup modem, or a private VPN solution over broadband technology.

Notes:

Business Partners

The last type of worker type is becoming a hot topic. Business partners can be customers, suppliers, or companies associated with your customers that need access to information that is pertinent to the efficient running of their operations. Providing information to our business partners is the ultimate goal here, but we must always ensure that security is not overlooked in our attempts to meet their information needs. SBS 2003 features such as the RWW and Windows Sharepoint Services (WSS) can provide such information to business partners in a secure manner.

The table below highlights some of the options that are available to meet the needs of these different types of workers. By no means does one solution fit all clients; each company needs different solutions from their business systems.

Table 8-1

Comparing Types of Remote Workers

Worker Type	Remote Worker	Mobile Worker	Remote Office	Business Partners
# of users	1	1	1+	1+
Outlook Web Access	X	X		
Remote XP	X	X		
Terminal Services client		X	X	X
Virtual Private Network		X	X	
Outlook Mobile Access/Activesync		X		
CompanyWeb (default WSS page)		X	X	X

At this point we have a better idea of the scope of requirements of each type of worker. A number of other factors affect which style of technology solution that we should implement for our clients. We'll now look at some of those factors, including the types of mobile devices and type of internet connection the customer is using so we fully understand how SBS 2003 can be put to work for the customer.

Devices Used in the Field

The types of devices used to meet the needs of mobile and remote workers can vary based on many factors such as portability needs, battery life, function, and physical size. For a remote office scenario, normal desktop computers are likely used. In a mobile scenario, a variety of other tools may be used, including notebooks and mobile devices such as PDAs plus separate phones, Smartphones, and Pocket PCs. You can even link devices together via Bluetooth technology to enhance the overall functionality of a solution. I won't go into detail about desktops as they are fairly commonplace.

Notebooks

Notebook computers range in size and function, including Tablet PCs that can weigh as little as 1kg/2.2 lbs or desktop replacement systems that are a hefty 4-5kg/9 or 10 lbs. Notebooks typically have inbuilt wireless capabilities—either 802.11b or g, but some have 802.11a. Bluetooth is becoming a standard feature. Analogue modems are also standard features; although they are slower than wireless technologies, they do provide for access anywhere/anytime. Battery life ranges from 2 to 5 hours on a single charge depending on the features and speed of the CPU.

Mobile Devices

Mobile devices today are becoming more than just pocket organizers. These business tools allow users to become more efficient in their day-to-day transactions by providing enhanced communications and, if implemented correctly, giving the user a competitive advantage in the marketplace.

Mobile devices provide varying degrees of functionality that suit differing business and personal requirements. Mobile devices can be separated into three categories: the PDA plus separate phone, the Smartphone, and the Pocket PC phone. Each device (or combination of devices) has its own unique characteristics. I've attempted to summarize the key features and benefits of these three different styles of mobile device below.

PDA plus Separate Phone

Essentially two separate devices, the combination of a standalone, fully functional PDA and a normal mobile phone gives the most flexibility. You can interchange the PDA and the mobile phone as each of the technologies improve, which is a good thing if you like to have the latest gadgets. These styles of devices are more suitable for people who don't really want to carry both devices with them all the time (such as the executive who on weekends really only wants his mobile phone with him but during weekdays wants the full functionality of the PDA/phone combination).

Normally both devices will have Bluetooth; using this link, you will be able to access the internet via GPRS over the mobile phone. Downsides to this combination include the need to charge two separate devices and the more complex setup procedure needed to pair the devices together via Bluetooth.

Smartphone

The Smartphone is a single unit that has both limited PDA functionality and mobile phone technology built into it. The Smartphone is a small unit styled either like a "candy bar" or a flip phone. The actual style varies from vendor to vendor, with more options coming onto the market over the next few months. These units lack the touch screen of the PDA or Pocket PC phone and are totally driven via the keypad entry. Smartphone users can benefit from the integrated phonebook that is provided via synchronization with the user's contacts folder in Microsoft Exchange. Smartphones seem to be designed for the executive user who would prefer to call people about an email she has just received rather than send a reply via the keypad entry.

Pocket PC Phone

The Pocket PC phone device combines the functionality of a fully functional PDA and a mobile phone in a single unit. Personally, I find this to be the best device for technically oriented people who need lots of functionality in a single, easy to hold device. Configuring this unit is easier than configuring the PDA and mobile phone combination because there is no need to set up a link between the two separate devices. Functionality is improved via the use of the integrated contacts to call anyone in your Microsoft Outlook contacts list from the phone without having to transfer phone numbers from device to device. These devices have touch screens and allow input from multiple sources, including onscreen keyboard, handwriting recognition, and a clip-on thumb board. These units are large, which may be inconvenient for some people. Microsoft Office applications such as Word and Excel are installed by the manufacturer and can be integral components of the solution you are designing for your customer.

Table 8-2 summarizes the feature differences between the Smartphone and Pocket PC phone. Over time, the feature sets will become more similar as the use of voice activation technology becomes more popular.

Table 8-2

Smartphone vs. Pocket PC phone

Feature	Smartphone	Pocket PC Phone
Inbox	X	X
Calendar	X	X
Contacts	X	X
MSN IM	X	X
Internet Explorer	X	X
Tasks		X
Notes		X
Word		X
Excel		X
Remote Desktop Protocol (RDP) Client		X

Notes:

Figure 8-1 provides illustrations of these three types of mobile devices.

Figure 8-1

Mobile devices

We now have a better understanding of the types of requirements that the customer has and the mobile devices available to help address those needs. The next step is to look at the type of internet access that are available.

Types of Access

The mobile/remote worker can use different methods to connect to the head office, including:

- Dialup modem,

- ISDN/DSL,

- GPRS,

- iBurst technology,

- Wireless hotspots, and

- Customer's LAN.

Each method offers various advantages and disadvantages, and some are more suitable for different solutions than others as discussed below. Many new technologies are emerging onto the market, and I can not hope to cover them all here. I hope that the key points provided here will help you evaluate the new technologies as they become available.

Dialup Modem

Most notebooks have dialup modems built in, which is a good fallback to use when no other access methods are available. Speeds are limited to 56k download at best, but the beauty of dialup modems is that they work just about anywhere in the world over a normal analog phone system.

ISDN/DSL

ISDN/DSL is available in fixed locations only, so it is not a good component for a solution that requires mobility. It is good, however, for the satellite office or the user who works a fair bit from home. Depending on your location globally, charges may vary. Here in Australia, ISDN technology is charged at a premium vs. DSL technology; however, in other locations around the globe, the trend is just the opposite.

GPRS

Short for General Packet Radio Service, this connection is designed to run over the GSM phone network. GPRS speeds vary based on the carrier and signal quality, and can range from 10kbps up to 170kbps. The bandwidth spectrum is shared by multiple users and, as such, performance can not be guaranteed. GPRS is ideal for applications such as email transfer and Instant Messaging traffic. It is not suited for situations that require streaming-style content. In my experience, I've seen average throughput in the range of 30 to 50kbps.

In addition, most telecommunication companies charge quite excessively for bandwidth—the typical charge here in Australia is around 2$^{¢}$ per KB if you are not on a data plan with your carrier.

I've successfully used GPRS for most of my mobile application work around Australia and even internationally in Europe and the USA. Interoperability of the GRPS service between carriers in foreign countries can be limited, though, based upon the agreements your home carrier has with the foreign carrier (for example, Optus in Australia has agreements for GSM phone coverage with many carriers in Europe, but only some of those carriers will also support GPRS over their network).

iBurst Technology

iBurst is a wireless technology that has been rolled out here in Australia only over the last 12 months. I was fortunate to be involved in the trials of it and I think it has some promising features. iBurst utilizes the wireless spectrum and a special array of aerials at the base station to attempt to focus the energy of its signal toward specific users. This gives the users a better signal strength than the normal style of broadcast (everywhere all of the time) that most other wireless technologies use. Speed for the iBurst networks are asymmetrical and can be up to 1Mbps download and 384kbps upload. This can vary based on the plan and carrier you are with.

From my trials of iBurst, I found that it was ideal for a mobile worker who was stationary for a period of time rather than always mobile. For example, I found that if I was parked in a fixed location in between client appointments, the iBurst connection was good and solid. However, if I then started driving, the connection would vary and often drop out. I figure that this is due to the focused transmission approach that they use as a foundation for the carrier. Also, at the time of writing, iBurst was only available for notebooks or desktops. Smaller form factor cards are coming out to suit Compact Flash and SDIO slots and this will allow the PocketPC and Smartphone devices to make use of this technology. To find out more about iBurst, check out http://www.iburst.com.au/. This technology is rapidly spreading worldwide.

Wireless Hotspots

The proverbial wireless hotspot remains an excellent method to connect to the office, with Starbucks providing some of the most well-known locations of

wireless hotspots worldwide. Locally, McDonalds restaurants have started to rollout wireless hotspots as well. Typically these hotspots are based on the 802.11b technology with speed limited to 11Mb/s. You need to bear in mind that behind the wireless device they will often have a DSL connection, which may be the limiting factor in any solution you design. You cannot rely on bandwidth availability because multiple people may share this facility at the same time.

> BEST PRACTICE: While wireless hotspots are great for convenience, remember that in order for them to be easy for the general public to use, they have no security features at all. The responsibility for security rests on your shoulders as the IT consultant. Think of things like ensuring that your Windows XP Professional Firewall is always turned on (ideally you will run XP Service Pack 2 on these mobile systems).

Customer's Local Area Network

Using the network of a customer is also a potential access mechanism for the mobile worker. However, you need to be acutely aware of the security risks inherent in this—not only for you the user, but also for the customer whose local area network (LAN) you are using. You want to ensure that your notebook is fully patched with the latest operating system patches and its anti-virus software is up to date and effective. In addition, you want to ensure that you have the Windows XP Professional Firewall enabled so you don't get hit by viruses running loose on the customer's LAN. Using a customer's LAN also requires the co-operation of the customer, which may or may not be possible. In short, I've added this as an option only to ensure that I can highlight the risks involved in doing so—not only the risks to you, but those that the customer faces as well.

The table below provides a snapshot of the features and restrictions of the connection mediums that can be used by the mobile worker.

Notes:

Table 8-3

Comparing access methods

Method	Cost	Speed	Reliability	Availability
Dialup Modem	$	56kb/s D/L 33kb/s U/L	Good	Almost everywhere there is a phone socket
DSL/ISDN/Cable	$$	Varies—up to 6MB/s download in some places	Good	Fixed installation point
GPRS	$$$$	Up to 170kbps— typically 30-50kbps	Good	Mobile— must have phone coverage
iBurst	$$	Up to 1Mbps D/L and 384kbps U/L	Good	for stationary Main Business Districts only
Wireless Hotspots	$$	Up to 11Mbps	Good	CBD/Local hotspots
Customer's LAN	$	Depends on customer's internet connection	Good	Customer site only

Security, Security, Security

The variety of methods by which users can access data means that we need to be constantly vigilant of how the information is being accessed, by whom and, if possible, what they do with it. While providing access to data for the remote/ mobile user is the prime focus of this chapter, it would be remiss of me not to address the huge security concerns that arise from this. Basic security policies such as strong password policies and daily review of the SBS 2003 performance reports are just the start. I have included some additional tips at the end of each of the key sections that I've covered. You should also read Susan Bradley's' chapter in this book (Chapter 11) on security, which includes some excellent tips for overall security. The chapter by Dr. Thomas Shinder in this book (Chapter 12) focuses on ISA Server 2004-specific security.

We've now got an idea of the various needs of mobile users, the devices they can use, and the connection technologies that are available. Let's now focus on the features that SBS 2003 can provide to the customer and see how I've implemented a number of solutions for actual clients.

Remote Web Workplace 101

RWW allows portal users to access a host of company resources securely via a Web browser connected to the internet from just about anywhere in the world. RWW provides access to:

- Email via Outlook Web Access,

- Window XP Pro desktop computer,

- Windows Terminal Server,

- VPN connectivity to the office and

- Company intranet site (CompanyWeb).

It ensures that all traffic between the client and the server is encrypted using either Secure Socket Layer (SSL) encryption or Remote Desktop Protocol (RDP) encryption. It also ensures that the user is authenticated prior to access being given to any of these resources. Let's take a look at how RWW works so we can understand how it may suit our customers' needs.

RWW—Remote Desktop—How it really works…

By this time you will have a really good understanding of what the customer's requirements are and the limitations of the utility outside of the SBS environment. Now let's delve into the inner workings of the RWW interface to see how truly genius this design is. I tip my hat to the people in the SBS 2003 development team who came up with this brilliant idea. I was fortunate enough to spend some time with one of the programmers who wrote the code behind the RWW interface, Aaron Nonis, who gave me a few more tips and a really good understanding of how it all hangs together.

Users access the RWW via a URL they type into their Web browser. This URL is actually the external domain name that they entered when they originally ran the Configure E-mail Internet Connection Wizard (CEICW)(something like https://mail.correct.com.au/remote). This will take them straight to the RWW login page via an SSL connection over port 443. However, most users don't remember to type the https portion of the URL, so the SBS 2003 development team configured an ISAPI filter called sbsflt.dll that intercepts requests to http (port 80) and redirects them automatically to the https location. This ensures that the user's credentials and passwords are always entered over a secure connection. This also means that if you can train your users to type in the https portion of the URL, you don't need to open port 80 at all on your SBS 2003 server. Given that port 80 is one of the highest scanned ports for the various worms on the internet, closing it down will give users a more secure configuration

> BEST PRACTICE: Give the users a business card with the RWW login instructions printed on it—laminate it so it's harder for them to write their password on it! Also include your support phone number so they can call for help when they need it.

The user will be prompted to accept the SSL certificate that SBS setup has generated. If they have purchased a third-party certified, they will not be prompted to accept the certificate because the certificate source will already be trusted. The reason the user is prompted here for certificate acceptance is that the SBS Connect to Internet wizard can create one for you or, alternately, you can purchase one from the larger trusted SSL certificate providers such as Verisign, Thwarte etc. Regardless of which way you go, everything from this point forward takes place over an encrypted channel between the client and the SBS 2003 server. At this point, the RWW logon screen will display, as seen in Figure 8-2.

Notes:

Figure 8-2
RWW logon. Note the https prefix in the URL address line.

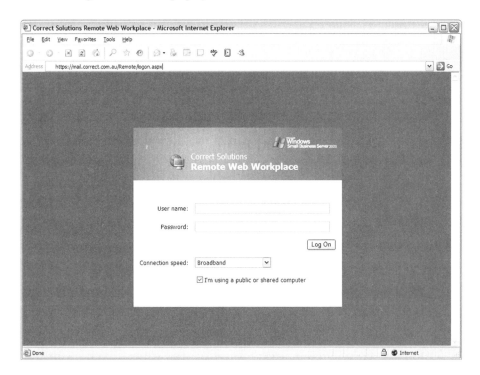

The login options here are user name, password, connection speed, and public/ private computer. Something that few users of SBS know is that this RWW logon page disables Internet Explorer's auto complete feature so user credentials cannot accidentally be saved in a computer they can't control, such as a public computer. The user can select the connection speed setting, which controls the level of graphic detail that the user will see in the RWW sections such as Outlook Web Access and the RDP connection to the internal computers.

In addition, a check box for public computer is enabled by default. This check box sets a session timeout variable on the RWW interface to further enhance security. The default public session timeout is 20 minutes. If you remove the check, then RWW assumes you are connecting from a private computer and, as such, enables a session timeout of 120 minutes. This timeout is for inactivity, not total session time; after this time period expires, RWW will disconnect you from your Windows XP computer and force you to re-authenticate if you wish to access the resources again. This value is stored in the registry and can be changed, as described in detail in the RWW Registry Guide at the end of this chapter.

> BEST PRACTICE: I feel that 20 minutes is far too long for the inactivity timer for a public computer; I normally change this to 5 minutes to increase security on the RWW interface.

By default in a normal SBS 2003 installation, all users can access the RWW because they are all members of the RWW security group. This is a group membership that is given to them as part of the Normal User template. Other base templates in SBS 2003 are available, such as the Mobile User template. The Mobile User template gives people the ability to also access the server via a VPN connection. Users only need to be members of the RWW security group to get to RWW.

Two types of users can access the RWW, so users will see one of two different types of screen once they authenticate.

- The basic user is a member of the Remote Web Workplace security group only. We call this type of user the Knowledge worker (or Kworker).

- The other type of user that is permitted to login is the Administrators group of users—for this they only need to be members of the Administrators or Domain Admins group. You can make a person a member of this group simply by applying the Administrator template to their account. Domain Admins do not need to be members of the Remote Web Workplace group at all to use the RWW interface.

> BEST PRACTICE: In most business environments, not everyone needs access to the RWW. Seldom does a receptionist need to check email from home in the evenings. To that end, I normally create a new default template that I apply to all users which does not include the RWW in its group membership. This gives me more control over which users can access the system remotely. You can easily create new templates via the Add Template Wizard under the Users section in the server management console.

The page you have been presented with has been dynamically built based upon your group membership and some registry settings in the SBS 2003 server. You will have one of either two screens as shown below. Figure 8-3 is what the normal Kworker would see. Figure 8-4 is what the Administrator level user would see. Note the differences between the two screens. The Administrator level screen is designed more with Administration tasks in mind, while the Kworker screen is designed to allow the normal user fast access to things such as email and CompanyWeb

Figure 8-3

The normal user or Knowledge Worker screen

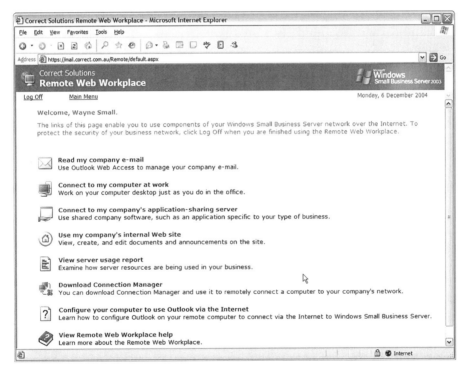

Notes:

Figure 8-4

The Administrator level screen

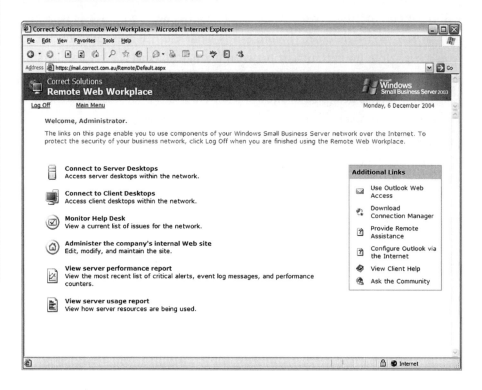

The items that appear on the two screens shown above will depend on how you've configured the CEICW in SBS 2003 and the types of servers in your network. For example, if you do not have any Windows 2000 or 2003 servers configured as Terminal Servers in application sharing mode, then the option for "Connect to my application server" will not be present on the user's screen. The RWW interface makes these options available based on an Active Directory query. You can also add additional items to the user or administrator pages by modifying the code directly. I figure that only the most advanced programmers will delve into the code though as you would not want to break this fabulous interface in error.

One area that the SBS 2003 development team overlooked involves the integration of ISA Server into the Premium product; the CompanyWeb options do not appear on the RWW menus in SBS 2003 Premium. To add these options, you need to go through a number of steps that are documented in Adding CompanyWeb to RWW on SBS 2003 Premium, below. I understand that the soon-to-be-released SBS 2003 Service Pack 1 will resolve this problem so that the manual procedure mentioned here will no longer need to be used.

One of the biggest modifications that I've used to customize RWW to meet my customers' specific requirements is to simply hide sections of the RWW that they do not require. Doing this is a simple matter of altering registry settings in the respective section of the RWW registry. At the end of this chapter I've included all the settings for the RWW portion of the registry along with an explanation of what each key does.

> BEST PRACTICE: Always use Internet Explorer 6.0 Service Pack 1 or higher to access the RWW. Older browsers that are not equipped with the necessary features will not allow your computer to display some features of RWW. Microsoft intentionally does this to increase the security of the solution for you.

Most of the options on the RWW interface are redirections to other internal Web-based resources. Selecting them will redirect you to those resources. Some of the resources include the CompanyWeb intranet site or the internal helpdesk. I mentioned earlier how the information from the RWW interface is sent over encrypted channels; the CompanyWeb is also published via SSL but over port 444 instead of the normal port 443 and the sbsflt.dll has a hand in redirecting the encrypted data stream to the internal CompanyWeb site.

One feature of the RWW interface that is very different from all the others is the "Connect to my desktop computer" or "Connect to my application server" feature. This feature allows you to connect to a Windows XP Pro computer or Windows 2000 or 2003 Terminal Server running in Application Sharing Mode (not Remote Administration Mode) that's located behind an SBS server from anywhere in the world via a simple Web browser.

When you click on the "Connect to my desktop computer" or the "Connect to my application server" link, Internet Explorer downloads the ActiveX control that allows the local computer to connect to the remote computer over the internet. This ActiveX control, called msrdp.cab, is downloaded from the SBS 2003 server's remote directory (c:\inetpub\remote) to the local computer's c:\windows\Downloaded Program Files directory. If you have Windows XP Service Pack 2 installed, you will get a warning message that an ActiveX control has attempted to be downloaded. You MUST allow this to be installed to get past this screen. The RWW then takes you to a selection screen.

This selection screen is populated based on an Active Directory lookup and will contain all the Windows XP Professional computers that have been added to the domain. If you have computers running with older versions of the operating system, they will not appear here. Similarly, if you select the "Connect to my application server" from the RWW, it shows all the Windows 2000 and 2003 servers configured as Terminal Servers in application sharing mode. If you have no Windows 2000 or 2003 Terminal Servers in your domain, this selection will not be present on the menu.

Figure 8-5

Default list of all Windows XP Pro computers available for remote connections

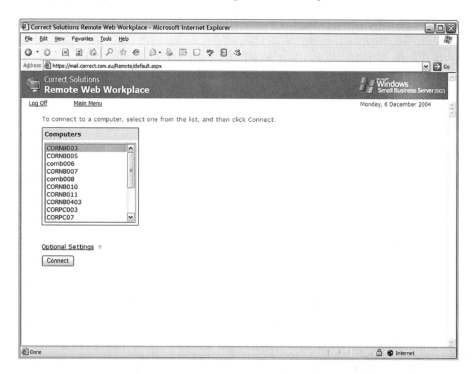

As you can see, the list of computers available for remote connections can be quite extensive and includes any Windows XP Professional computer that has been added to the domain. It's important to note that this list is based on a simple Active Directory query. It does not differentiate between computers that are currently turned on or off; therefore, even computers that are no longer in use can be in this list.

> BEST PRACTICE: Use the Client Computers tools in the Server Management console to delete computers that have been removed from the domain to reduce the clutter of computers in this selection screen. As always, before deleting the client computer, make sure that it will never be used within the domain again because you can't simply restore a deleted computer's account to the Active Directory.

> BEST PRACTICE: You can hide computers from this view to reduce the clutter and also increase security. For example, you may not want the payroll computer to be accessible from outside of your office. To hide computers from the list, see the section titled Stopping certain PCs from appearing in the RWW interface at the end of this chapter.

The Optional Settings section allows you to specify extended RWW functionality to connect the office computer's drives to your local computer, redirect printers from the office computer to the local computer, and select a different screen resolution for the RWW screen. The default settings limit functionality in some ways because they are designed with security in mind. Figure 8-6 shows the extended options expanded. The "Enable files or folders to be transferred between the remote computer and this computer" option allows you to connect the hard drives on the local computer to the remote computer. This does a pretty cool redirection of the local hard drive (for example, redirecting the C drive to a drive accessible from the remote computer). It shows as "C on NOTEBOOK," where C is the local drive on your local computer notebook. The user will receive a security warning about this because it really could be an issue if users are not careful about leaving documents on the local computer (which could be a public system). You should educate your users about this to minimize the potential issues that could arise.

The "Enable documents on the remote computer to be printed on a local printer" does a similar function, allowing you to print from the remote computer to the local computer's printer (described more fully below).

The "Hear sounds from the remote computer on this computer" is disabled by default. This option allows the full, rich set of sounds to be delivered to the local computer as if they were played on the remote computer. You need to be aware that this can be bandwidth intensive, which I suspect is why it's disabled by default.

The last option here is the dropdown list to select the screen size—it defaults to Full Screen, which I encourage most users to use. This ensures that they minimize the confusion between the remote and the local computers.

Figure 8-6

Optional Settings for RWW connections

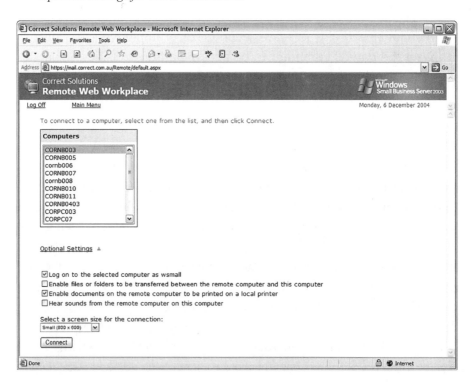

BEST PRACTICE: If you don't want the RWW remote control session to take over the entire screen and you can suitably educate your users, select a lower screen resolution via the Options dropdown list on the selection screen. This will put the remote computer's screen as a window inside the Internet Explorer window.

At this point you select your computer and press **Connect**. If all is going well, the ActiveX control will open a connection between you and the SBS 2003server and you will be presented with your Windows XP or 2000/2003 Terminal Server logon screen where it has automagically typed in your UserID. But what's really going on here? It sounds like a lot of smoke and mirrors, but under the covers it's really ingenious. When you press **Connect**, Internet Explorer tells the SBS 2003 server that you are going to attempt to connect to the selected computer (we'll call it WINXPPC for this example). This message goes from the local computer to the SBS 2003 server over port 443 so it's fully encrypted. The SBS 2003 server checks a registry setting under HKEY_LOCAL_MACHINE\Software\Microsoft\SmallBusinessServer\RemoteUserPortal\Port key, which by default is set to 4125. You can change this, as discussed later in the chapter. For the moment assume the default of port 4125. The SBS 2003 server then starts up a process on the server and dynamically opens port 4125 ready to accept inbound connections. It passes back a URL to Internet Explorer, which tells it which port to connect on. The URL it passes back looks something like this:

https://mail.correct.com.au/Remotetsweb.aspx?Server=CORSYDTSV1&Port =4125&iFS=1&User=wsmall&Domain=CORRECT&redirectPrinters=1 &redirectAudio=2

You can see the port number embedded in the URL as well as other information that is taken from the Optional Settings section we talked about earlier. The Internet Explorer passes this to the ActiveX control installed earlier, and the ActiveX control then initiates the connection to the SBS 2003 server over port 4125. When the SBS 2003 server receives the connection on port 4125, it compares the source IP address (the user with Internet Explorer) that it accepted the connection from port 443 on; if they are not identical, it drops the connection on port 4125. The dynamic opening of port 4125 and then the comparison of the source IP give RWW additional security over any solution I have seen to date. Assuming the source IP is identical, the process running on the SBS 2003 server then handles the inbound connection from the remote user on port 4125 and then proxies it through to the Windows XP Pro desktop or 2000/2003 Terminal server over port 3389.

Now this is the bit that many people get confused with. You DO NOT need to have port 3389 open on your external router or ISA server in order for this to work. All you need is port 443 and 4125 at a minimum. Once the connection is complete, the process on the SBS 2003 server then continues to monitor port traffic and passes it on to the selected client. If the user disconnects their session, the process is closed down and port 4125 is also closed to prevent potential intrusion. Whew—that was a lot to take in very quickly wasn't it. Hopefully Figure 8-7 will enhance your understanding of what we've just gone over.

Figure 8-7
  RWW Under the covers.

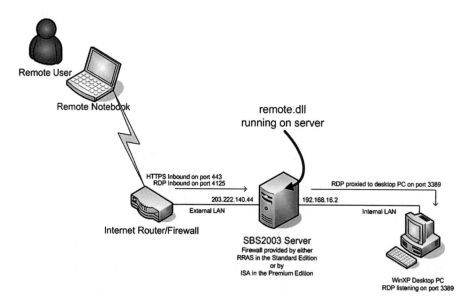

So now you have a better understanding of what transpires in getting the connection between the remote and local computers so you can gain control over the desktop back in the office. Simple huh? But what do you do if you have problems? In the next section, I've attempted to address a few of the more common issues I have seen in the wild that have stopped RWW from working.

Troubleshooting the RWW

Some advanced SBS users in the Yahoo! and Microsoft SBS support groups feel an advanced chapter should only be about troubleshooting. For those select few and the rest of the world who want to join them, this section is for you. Here I present and explain common RWW error messages and their solutions.

By far the most common issue with using RWW to gain control over a remote desktop or server is the ports not being open correctly. To recap—you only need to have port 443 and 4125 open to enable RWW to work. Make sure you pass these ports through your hardware router to the SBS 2003 server.

Figure 8-8 shows the common message you get when port 4125 is blocked, either by the hardware firewall you have running with the SBS 2003 server or some other firewall between you and the SBS 2003 server.

Figure 8-8

The common RWW error message.

If you're using third-party firewall software on the remote computer, check to make sure that it's not blocking outbound requests to port 4125. How do you confirm that outbound requests on port 4125 are working? When we had this problem, we created a basic Web page that can be displayed over port 4125. On the remote computer (the one NOT in the office), type in the following url: http://rdptest.sbsfaq.com:4125. If the remote computer allows outbound requests to port 4125, you should see the Web page as illustrated in Figure 8-9. This test is basic, but in my experience it has helped define the problems as either being client or server related.

Notes:

Figure 8-9

A visible way to see that outbound requests to port 4125 are working from the remote client

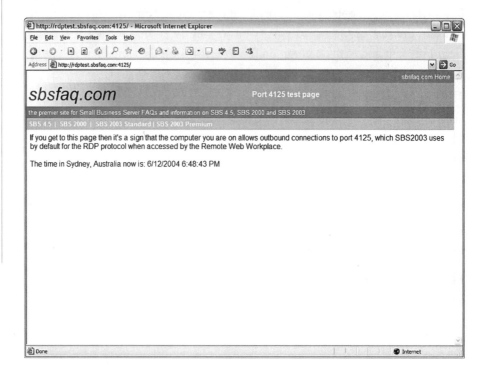

Similarly, additional software firewalls and some AV programs that include a firewall in your SBS network may block port 3389 from getting to the XP Professional desktop computer in your office from the SBS 2003 server. Make sure that this port is open. You can test this for sure by sitting at the SBS 2003 server and trying to connect to the XP Professional desktop computer using the Remote Desktop Connection icon located under Program > Accessories > Communications. If you can connect from the SBS 2003 server to the desktop computer, then you are sure that port 3389 is open and functioning correctly on that desktop computer.

If you still have problems after ensuring you have opened the ports on the hardware router, try testing from the SBS 2003 server itself. On the SBS 2003 server, type in http://localhost/remote, which will take you to the RWW login screen. Login and then attempt to access the Windows XP or 2000/2003 Terminal

Server computer. If this works, then it is almost surely a port issue between the SBS 2003 server and the remote computer (notebook).

If you're connected and suddenly get dropped for no apparent reason, check out Microsoft Knowledge Base at http://support.microsoft.com/?id=821438, which details a situation where your AV scanning may actually terminate the underlying Web application that runs RWW, causing your connection to drop out.

Many more potential issues can exist—I can't hope to cover them all here for each particular environment. These are just the top few issues; these combined with the troubleshooting tips will hopefully arm you with enough to get the basics covered.

RWW for all? Maybe not!

Many people believe that RWW is one of the killer applications on SBS 2003, convincing themselves that they will not need any other technological magic to address all of their customers' needs. In some cases they may be right. However, it is important to understand the features and limitations of RWW before deciding that it is the correct solution for the customers' pains.

Who could ask for more, I hear you ask? Many people need more than RWW to do their work, primarily driven by the applications they need to run. Take for instance the remote desktop capability within the RWW. This cool function allows you to take control of your Windows XP Professional computer. On face value, this is excellent—it gives you access to a Windows XP Professional computer, connects your local printers from your remote site, and optionally can link your local disk drives to your Windows XP Professional desktop in the office. But there are issues with this approach. The printer names you see on the Windows XP Professional system that link back to your remote desktop, for instance, are dynamically created. If you look closely, you will see that the printer name contains the name of the remote computer. Figure 8.10 provides the list of printers that has been automatically created on my system.

Notes:

Figure 8-10

Printer use via RWW\RDP session

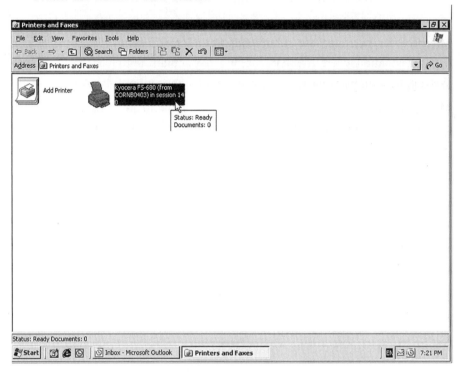

These printer names will change depending on the name of the workstation you logon from remotely and the session number it is assigned. So today it's called "Kyocera FS-680 (from CORNB0403) in session 14" and tomorrow it may be called "Kyocera FS-680 (from CORNB0403) in session 20." For most applications this is not a big issue at all. However, a large number of business applications such as accounting systems store the name of the printer inside the application. In order for the application to function correctly, the printer names need to stay the same. In these instances, using RWW to get access to a Terminal Server or Windows XP Professional desktop is not going to be successful because the application will be unable to print correctly. Knowing this limitation is one of the big deciding factors in whether the RWW access to your Windows XP Professional computer or Terminal Server is the right way to go.

So if RWW/RDP is not the way to go, how do you solve this problem? The only way to ensure that the printer names are consistent is to allow the head office to print directly to the printer. The easiest way to do this is via a VPN between the remote user and the head office. We won't go into configuring a VPN here because all you really need to do is follow the VPN wizards in SBS 2003 and most of the hard work is done for you. The default VPN wizards in SBS 2003 configure a Point to Point Tunneling Protocol (PPTP) VPN server on the SBS 2003 server and also a remote package for deployment to the remote users to ensure seamless configuration of the entire tunnel. You can go more advanced and configure L2TP/IPSec VPNs, but these are not supported by the SBS 2003 wizards and require a fair amount of effort for very little additional return. Once the VPN is configured, you will need to configure the remote computer for printer sharing and share the printer. Figure 8.11 shows how a normal shared printer looks from the application's perspective.

Figure 8-11

Shared Printer that is across a VPN connection

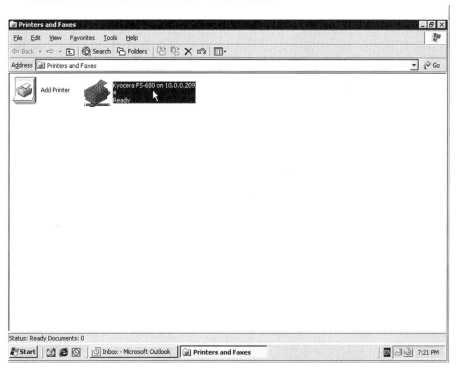

As time progresses, I am hopeful that application vendors will be able to work better with the technologies such as RDP connected printers so we won't need

VPNs as we do now. This, however, has given you an insight into some of the issues and constraints that are present and why you may want to use one method of printing over another.

Customizing RWW

In one of our installations, we needed to provide a customized RWW interface to the client. The scenario was that a number of the customer's clients would need access to their system to use a specific Windows application and to view pictures of motor vehicles that they were about to purchase. The customer was quoted over $60,000 to develop a Web version of their application, which was seriously over the top. The solution I came up with was in two parts, both using features unique to SBS 2003. Part one was a dedicated Terminal Server that their clients could access via the RWW. Part two was to use the built-in picture viewer functionality of Windows 2003 Terminal Server to allow customers to preview their pictures. Tie that all together with a customized RWW interface to limit what they can see and some judicious use of Group Policy on the Terminal Server to limit them further. They also needed to be able to print various reports from the business application to the local printers at the customers' sites.

So how did we do this customization of RWW? We could have done a lot of reprogramming, but this could have led to a large development bill. Instead we spoke with the client and had them accept that the only purpose for RWW in their business was to allow their clients access to the terminal server. All that was required from here was to turn off all sections of the RWW Web page that were not required. We did this using registry settings that are actually part of the design of the RWW. Figure 8-12 shows the resulting screen that was left after we disabled all sections but the "Connect to my application server" option. Details on how to disable sections are included at the end of this chapter.

Notes:

Figure 8-12

Simple customized RWW screen

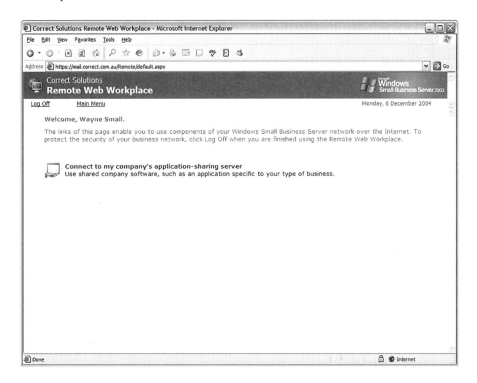

Frequently Asked Questions about RWW

The explanations below address a few of the more common issues related to RWW and reveal a few obscure tidbits of information.

What is Remote.dll?

Remote.dll is the actual backend of the RWW system. It was created by the SBS 2003 development team to pass data through from the external port 4125 to the internal port of 3389 for the RDP sessions, among other things. It's basically the engine of RWW, located in the c:\inetpub\wwwroot\remote directory. It's not the type of thing you should be messing with at all, but I figured it was cool enough to mention. Oh – thanks to Aaron Nonis for the lowdown on how it works. Aaron is the genius who actually wrote this section of the RWW.

Disabling Specific Users from Using RWW

Complete the following procedure to disable specific users from using RWW:

1. Logon as the Administrator on the SBS 2003 server machine.
2. From **Start**, and select **Server Management** and select **Users** in the console tree.
3. In the **Details** pane, click the user name that you want to disable (e.g. Norm Hasborn).
4. Select **Change User Properties**.
5. In the **User Properties** dialog box, click the **Member Of** tab.
6. Click **Remote Web Workplace Users**, and then click **Remove**.
7. Click **OK** to close the **User Properties** dialog box.

Stopping Certain PCs from Appearing in the RWW Interface

By default, SBS 2003 shows all Windows XP Professional and Windows 2000/2003 Application Terminal Servers available for users to connect to in the RWW interface. You can stop specific PCs from appearing. This is a popular feature of SBS 2003 that is actually already available, just hidden under the covers. To implement it you will need to add a Registry key to the SBS server:

1. Run **Regedit**.
2. Navigate down the tree to the following key: **HKLM\Software\Microsoft\SmallBusinessServer\RemoteUserPortal**.
3. From the **Edit** menu, select **New** and then **String Value**.
4. Give the **String Value** a name of ExcludeList (with no space between the two words).
5. Press **Enter**.
6. Right click in the newly created entry and select **Modify**.
7. Add the names of the machines you wish to hide separated by a comma.

Changing the Port for RWW to Something Other than 4125

In some circumstances we have changed the port that the RDP session runs over the internet to the SBS 2003 server from 4125 to something else to get around specific limitations of a firewall or other device. Altering the port number is quite simple:

1. Run **Regedit**.
2. Navigate down the tree to the following key: **HKLM\Software\ Microsoft\SmallBusinessServer\RemoteUserPortal**
3. Right click the entry called **Port** and select **Modify**.
4. Select the new port number you wish to use.

A word of caution: altering the port number here will also require you to open the corresponding port on your external hardware firewall. In addition, if you are running SBS 2003 Premium, you will need to create an additional packet filter to allow the inbound traffic to be able to reach the SBS 2003 server.

Modifying the Public Timeout Values for RWW

I mentioned earlier that the default of 20 minutes on a public computer is way too long. Therefore, I recommend that you change this value to 5 or 10 minutes to provide increased protection for your system in case a user walks away from a public kiosk without logging off.

1. Run **Regedit**.
2. Navigate down the tree to the following key: **HKLM\Software\ Microsoft \SmallBusinessServer\RemoteUserPortal**
3. Right click the entry called **PublicTimeOut** and select **Modify**.
4. Enter the new timeout value you want to have and press **OK**.

Changing the Company Name in the RWW Display Screen

I have used this modification on our demonstration SBS 2003 server. Prior to going out to demo SBS to a new customer, I alter the displayed name to be that of the customer I am going to see. This gives the customer a degree of "ownership" even before they get the quote for the new system.

1. Run **Regedit**.
2. Navigate down the tree to the following key: **HKLM\Software\ Microsoft\Windows NT\CurrentVersion**
3. Right click the entry called **RegisteredOrganization** and select **Modify**.

4. Enter the new Company name you want to see and press enter.

Adding CompanyWeb to RWW on SBS 2003 Premium

When SBS 2003 was released, there was an error involving how the CEICW configured itself with respect to ISA 2000. In particular, it failed to publish the CompanyWeb via the RWW portal. This was noticeable as the links to access the company's internal Web site were missing from the RWW interface. You can easily fix this with a few additional tweaks to the configuration. At the time of writing, I understand that this problem will be resolved in SBS 2003 Service Pack 1 so this tweak should no longer be required.

First, you need to do some work in ISA Servers management console to get the right protocols configured:

1. Run **ISA Management Console**.
2. Expand **Servers and Arrays**.
3. Expand the **SERVERNAME** (yours will be the name of your server).
4. Expand **Policy Elements**.
5. Select **Protocol Definitions**.
6. Right click on **Protocol Definitions** and select **New** then **Definition**.
7. Give the protocol a name—we'll call it **"SBS CompanyWeb 444"**, and click **Next**.
8. Enter **444** in the **Port** number box, **TCP** for Protocol and **Inbound** for Direction.
9. Click **Next**, **Next**, and then **Finish**.

The protocol is now defined. Next you need to create the publishing rule to allow the CompanyWeb to be accessible from the outside world.

While still in the ISA Management Console, do the following:

1. Expand **Servers and Arrays**.
2. Expand the **SERVERNAME** (yours will be the name of your server).
3. Expand **Publishing**.
4. Expand **Server Publishing Rules**.
5. Right click on **Server publishing rules** and select **New** then **Rule**.
6. Give the Server publishing rule a name – we'll call it "**SBS Companyweb Publishing**" and click "**Next**".
7. Enter the **IP address** of the internal server (192.168.16.2 by default).

8. Enter the **External IP address** of the ISA server (this will be different on each system).

9. Click **Next**.

10. Select the **Protocol Definition** you created above from the drop down list **(SBS Companyweb 444)**.

11. Click **Next**, then **Next** and **Finish**.

12. Manually restart the **ISA Firewall Service**.

Now you need to install an SSL certificate on the CompanyWeb site itself:

1. Start **IIS Manager** from the Administrative Tools group.

2. Expand **SERVERNAME**.

3. Expand **Web Sites**.

4. Expand **CompanyWeb**.

5. Right click **CompanyWeb** and select **Properties**.

6. Go to the **Directory Security** tab.

7. Click **Server Certificate** and then click **Next**.

8. Select "**Assign an existing certificate**" and then click **Next**.

9. Select the certificate that is the same as the external domain name ("mail.correct.com.au").

   Do not select the certificate called "publishing.domain.local" as this is used internally by ISA.

10. Click **Next**.

11. Confirm that it will use port **444**.

12. Click **Next**.

13. Click **Next**.

14. Click **Finish**.

15. Press **OK** to acknowledge the final screen.

Almost done now; we just need to modify some of the registry values in the RWW section to enable the sections to appear in the RWW screens.

1. Run **Regedit**.

2. Navigate down the tree to the following key: **HKLM\Software\ Microsoft\SmallBusinessServer\RemoteUserPortal\KWLinks**

3. Right click the entry called **STS** and select **Modify**.

4. Enter the value of **1** and press **OK**.

5. Navigate down the tree to the following key: **HKLM\Software\ Microsoft\SmallBusinessServer\RemoteUserPortal\AdminLinks**
6. Right click the entry called **STS** and select **Modify**.
7. Enter the value of **1** and press **OK**.
8. Right click the entry called **HelpDesk** and select **Modify**.
9. Enter the value of **1** and press **OK**.
10. Exit Regedit

A few additional notes to remember:

- If you ever re-run the Connect to Internet wizard, this procedure will need to be redone because the wizard will set things back to factory defaults

- You need to ensure that you open up port 444 on any external hardware router/firewall that you may have.

RWW Registry Guide

In this section, we delve deeper into the RWW registry settings and get down to the hexadecimal level. I'll provide explanatory context for each setting. Let's get started.

Ok, so now's the bit where I get to show of some of the cool stuff I've done for my clients. We went over how RWW works earlier in the chapter, and I mentioned that there are two different types of RWW screens that users see – the Admin User and the Knowledge Worker. All the registry keys that relate to how these screens are built are stored here. The root of these keys is under HKEY_LOCAL_ MACHINE\SOFTWARE\Microsoft\SmallBusinessServer\RemoteUserPortal.

I won't go into detail on modifying each individual key, but will provide a brief reference for the major entries so you have a better idea about what each entry does.

Notes:

This first section controls overall RWW properties for the RWW interface.

HKEY_LOCAL_MACHINE\SOFTWARE\Microsoft\SmallBusinessServer\ RemoteUserPortal

"URL"=https://mail.sbsfaq.com/remote
> This URL is used to access the RWW interface. It is set by the Connect to the Internet wizard and should not be changed manually.

"State"=dword:00000001
> Shows that the RWW has been correctly published by the Connect to the Internet wizard.

"OWA_SSL"=dword:00000001
> Legacy key from early development. It serves no function in the released product.

"STS_SSL"=dword:00000000
> Legacy key from early development. It serves no function in the released product.

"Monitoring_SSL"=dword:00000000
> Legacy key from early development. It serves no function in the released product.

"SendMail"=dword:00000001
> Ensures that new users (and migrated users) get the introductory email about RWW. It depends on the State registration key above being set to one.

"AllowTrusted"=dword:00000001
> This key when enabled (set to 1) will show the "I am using a public or shared computer" check box on the front page of the RWW login screen.

"Port"=dword:0000101d
> Default (4125) - This is the port number that is used for inbound communication from the external client to the SBS server. RDP traffic is passed over this port to the internal Windows XP Professional or Windows 2000/2003 Terminal Server to allow you to control the internal system from outside on the internet. See below for information on how to modify it and other considerations to be taken into account.

"TrustedTimeOut"=dword:00000078
> Default (120) – This is the timeout value that defaults to 120 minutes used to automatically log off the RWW interface when accessed from a trusted network (one that you have removed the

check on the login screen to confirm you are logging in from a trusted network). See below for information on how to modify it.

"PublicTimeOut"=dword:00000014
Default (20) – This is the timeout value that defaults to 20 minutes used to automatically log off the RWW interface when accessed from a public network. A public network is the default setting whenever you access the RWW from a new computer. For security reasons I do not recommend increasing it. See below for information on how to modify it.

"ISA"=dword:00000000
This setting basically signifies if ISA Server is installed on the SBS 2003 server. Valid options are 0 if it's SBS 2003 Standard Edition or 1 if it's SBS 2003 Premium Edition. It is modified by the Connect to the Internet wizard when you run the wizard. There should be no need to modify it directly and I am aware of no advantage in doing so.

This section deals with the layout of the screens you see when logging into the RWW interface as an Administration level user.

HKEY_LOCAL_MACHINE\SOFTWARE\Microsoft\SmallBusinessServer\ RemoteUserPortal\AdminLinks

"ServerTS"=dword:00000001
Shows the "Connect to Server Desktops" option.

"ClientTS"=dword:00000001
Shows the "Connect to Client Desktops" option.

"Help"=dword:00000001
Shows Help screen.

"Community"=dword:00000001
Shows Community options.

"RA"=dword:00000001
Shows the Remote Assistance Menu option.

"HelpDesk"=dword:00000001
Shows the "Monitor Help Desk" option which is actually located on the CompanyWeb.

"STS"=dword:00000001
Shows the Admin of CompanyWeb.

"PerfReport"=dword:00000001
Shows the Performance Reports.

"UsageReport"=dword:00000001
Shows the Usage Reports.

"OWA"=dword:00000001
Shows Access to OWA.

"CM"=dword:00000001
Shows the link to download the connection manager

"RPC"=dword:00000001
Shows information about Outlook over HTTP

This section deals with the layout of the screens you see when logging into the RWW interface as a Knowledge Worker user.

HKEY_LOCAL_MACHINE\SOFTWARE\Microsoft\SmallBusinessServer\ RemoteUserPortal\KWLinks

"AppTS"=dword:00000001
Shows TS in App Mode – not present if no TS in App mode in the domain.

"TS"=dword:00000001
Shows the "Connect to my work computer" option.

"Help"=dword:00000001
Shows the "View Remote Web Workplace Help" option.

"OWA"=dword:00000001
Shows the "Read my company e-mail" option.

"STS"=dword:00000001
Shows the "Use my company's internal website" option.

"CM"=dword:00000001
Shows the "Download Connection Manager" option.

"UsageReport"=dword:00000001
Shows the "Usage Report" option if the user is also a member of the Usage Report Users Security group on SBS 2003 domain.

"RPC"=dword:00000001
Shows the "Configure your computer to use Outlook via the Internet" option.

True Story...

A colleague of mine, Jeff Middleton, was taking a well-deserved break on a cruise ship off the coast of Panama. (Jeff is also the author of chapters 14 and 15 of this book.) During this time, he had internet access onboard the ship via a ship-bound satellite link, but it was limited in functionality. He found that he could not create a VPN connection at all, and was limited to Web browsing. Unfortunately, one of his customers experienced some major issue and he needed to access their site to resolve the problem. Jeff operates some secure sites and the only way to get into them remotely is via a VPN and then an RDP connection to a W2000 Terminal Server. Jeff was stuck for a way to resolve this issue for his customer until we hit upon the idea of using RWW in a demo network in our office here in Australia. So if you can imagine, Jeff from his cruise ship connecting via RWW to a Windows XP Pro computer located here in Sydney, Australia, and then using that computer to create a VPN connection to the troubled network back home in New Orleans. He then ran the RDP client from the Windows XP Pro computer to access the server in question and resolve the problem.

Now for me, that's got to be a unique way of using RWW to get out of a sticky situation!

Summary

Hopefully you will leave this chapter with a better understanding not only of the requirements of mobile and remote users, but also the features of SBS 2003 that you can customize to improve the functions available to the remote user. I've given a detailed explanation of how the RWW interface works as well as taken a deep dive into the registry to unlock all those secrets that will allow you to fully customize the RWW interface to more closely suit your customer's business requirements.

My thanks to two people in the SBS Development team that helped with a lot of the inner workings of this chapter – Alan Billharz and Aaron Nonis; without their help, a lot of the finer details would have remained shrouded in mystery.

So next time you're on the sandy beach, make sure you use your RWW interface to drop me a line, send me a picture, or even grab me on Instant messenger. You can always get me using any of the above on wayne@correct.com.au.

Safe travels…

CHAPTER 9

Using Microsoft SQL Server 2000 with Small Business Server 2003

BY Alan Shrater (Denver, CO)

Data, data, data. Who has it, where is it, how do we get it into the system and back out again in a meaningful and useful format: the challenges with organizing and using data go on and on! This chapter addresses those challenges by describing how to manage your data using Microsoft's SQL Server 2000 (MSSQL) in conjunction with Small Business Server 2003 (SBS 2003).

Why Do We Need to Organize Our Data?

This may seem like an elementary point, but some of your customers may need to be reminded. Data in a jumbled mass is useless. Let's throw some raw, ungrouped data into the fray to illustrate how chaos reigns unless data is organized:

Sam	Sue	Charles	Rogers	Turner	123 Anywhere Street
Denver	Seattle	Washington	Mississippi	Colorado	456 Some Place

Try to take that for a drive! Put some structure onto it and you begin to transform this raw data into useful information (e.g., Sue Turner, 123 Anywhere Street, Seattle, Washington).

Storing data bits into a structure is the function of a database. But storing data in a structured arrangement is only half the challenge. Being able to retrieve that set of data when you want it, in a manner that is in a meaningful and easily understood format is the other half of the challenge. "When you really think about it, the whole reason any of us technology professionals are here is because the underlying data drives business computing'' (excerpted from page 15-1, **_Windows Small Business Server 2000 Best Practices_** by Harry Brelsford). This fundamental truth drives the need for SBS 2003.

What this Chapter is (and isn't) About

This chapter will *not* prepare you for certification as a Microsoft Certified Database Administrator. It won't even get you prepared for the SQL Server Administration or Design exams. I'm not even going to discuss the mathematics of relational database design and normalization theory. So what is this chapter about?

My purpose in this chapter is to introduce ways to use MSSQL in conjunction with the toolsets that you and your clients are already using with SBS 2003. This is important because, in my experience, MSSQL has not been the driving force behind most SBS implementations.

Most of our clients and many of you SBSers may think you have little or no use for MSSQL. If the business is not using a Line of Business (LOB) application that lives on MSSQL, then what can you do with MSSQL? Microsoft hasn't made that answer clear. (My personal wish is for Microsoft to provide licenses for InfoPath with SBS 2003 Premium that will give an SBS site the out-of-the-box tools to build useful front ends to their SQL Server data stores.)

In this chapter, I hope to spark your interest in some of the ways you can use a relational database and how, using these tools, you might upsell your client to SBS 2003 Premium Edition. Along that vein, I'll compare Microsoft SQL Server Desktop Engine (MSDE) included with the Standard Edition of MSSQL to one of my favorite programs, Microsoft Access 2003, focusing on how Access fits with MSSQL and how to move an Access database to MSSQL.

From there I'll review some other ways to communicate with MSSQL and then use some of these tools to expand on the now-infamous Springer Spaniel Limited (Springer Ltd.) database (SSLDOG) example introduced in **_Windows Small Business Server 2003 Best Practices_** by Harry Brelsford. Using SSLDOG as our base, I'll:

- Extend the table structure using different table creation tools.

- Stuff in some data and look at ways to get the data out.

- Walk you through some reporting alternatives. Sometimes, presenting the results as a simple table is sufficient and sometimes a more elaborate presentation is preferred.

Within the limitations of this chapter, I cannot possibly even begin to present a tutorial on MSSQL. For that, you might consider reading:

- *Microsoft's SQL Server Books Online*—Access these by opening Server Management, expanding Advanced Management, Computer Management, Services and Applications, then right-clicking **Microsoft SQL Server** and selecting **Help**.

- *Teach Yourself Microsoft SQL Server 2000 in 21 Days* by Richard Waymire (ISBN 0-672-31969-1). Richard works at Microsoft in Redmond, Washington and should be considered a friend of the SBS community!

- *MSDE Bible* by David C. Walls and Denise M. Gosnell (ISBN 0-7645-4681-3) for a Microsoft SQL Server 2000 Desktop Engine (MSDE 2000)-centric point of view.

My Path to Pairing SBS with MSSQL

In 1967, shortly before completing my sophomore year at the University of Miami, I was approached by one of my accounting professors, Dr. Jess Brandon. He had the exceptional foresight to understand that business majors needed to know about computing, so he created the first Introduction to Computers class to be taught at the University of Miami School of Business. (Previously, all computer-related courses were taught through the School of Engineering.) Dr. Brandon taught the course based upon programming in FORTAN IV on an IBM 360/40. That computer had its own building and air filtration system, and boasted 64KB of Random Access Memory. It was a giant! Technical support staff used punch cards to load programs and data to tape.

I was his student assistant. It was my responsibility to assist his students and help them debug their programs. And that was my introduction to computing!

As an auditor at a national accounting firm in 1969, I wrote a Report Program Generator (RPG) program to calendar tax filing dates, which include income tax due dates as well as federal and state unemployment, FICA, the depository requirement, and myriad other data. Previously, everything was done with pencil and columnar paper.

Years later, I became involved with microcomputer-based accounting systems, relational databases, and DOS-based programming and reporting tools like MagicPC. Then came Windows and, in early 1992, the beta version of MS Access. Access programming led to MSSQL database management. Now, we can use MSSQL in conjunction with SBS for small business clients.

So that's how I got into SBS; your path is probably somewhat different, but how we get here is not as important as what can we do with this marvelous tool now that we have it.

In 1989, I co-founded Solutions Unlimited, Inc. We originally focused on accounting system sales, support, and integration; we have now evolved into providing full IT services for small and growing companies. We know small business because we live small business. We use SBS 2003 Premium Edition, Microsoft Office 2003 Premium and Developer, and other tools as the base platform to complete the many essential tasks with limited financial and personnel resources we have available. You might say we're a lot like you and your clients.

Why Use a Database?

The first reason to use a database is because you have to. No really, if you or your client is using a LOB application like Microsoft Business Solution, Great Plains for Financial Management, CRM for Customer Relationship Management, or the Microsoft Retail Management System, you are already using a database. What is typically ignored is the fact that these systems allow you to access the data stored within them that you can use in very individualized ways.

You might have some totally unique information that you need to store. Or maybe the information itself is not so unique, but the way you access or manipulate it is. These are generally good reasons to build your own database. Tools available for building your database include:

- Excel

- MSDE 2000

- SQL Server Enterprise Manager

- JET and Access

Each of these has inherent limitations, as discussed below. None can match the abilities of MSSQL! Detailed discussions of MSSQL functionality follow this section of the chapter.

Excel

Given that a database is a way to store structured data, what is the most popular database in use today? The answer is, surprisingly,…(drum roll, please): Microsoft Excel! Well, think about it. If your data needs are simple and the data can be represented in a simple column and row format, then Excel could be the answer to your database needs. There are a gazillion Excel "databases" in use out there. Limitations of using Excel to build your database include:

- Flat file structure, and

- Data integrity.

Flat File Structure

The simple column and row structure employed by Excel is commonly referred to as a "flat file." Over the years, Microsoft has enhanced Excel to provide more basic database functionality (like sorting on a column without creating a jumbled mess of then unrelated data), but, at its heart, Excel is still a flat file. Other programs are better suited for building complex databases.

Notes:

Database Integrity

Another limitation of using Excel to build a database involves data integrity. For example, say you have a table of Dogs, and one of the columns represents the name of father of the dog (FatherName). It becomes increasingly difficult to create a list of all the dogs sired by, say, Pepper, if Pepper is variously listed as Pepper, The Pep, and as "Sammy. You get the point; if the data isn't consistent, you will get inconsistent results. So, in a common flat file representation, the table would look like this:

DogName	FatherName
Brisker	Pepper
Jeager	The Pep
Maria	Sammy

But what if you could point data to another table and use that as a reference source? We could have two tables, one for the dog and another for the dogs' fathers, which might look something like this:

Dog Table		Father Table		
DogID	DogName	FatherDNo	FatherDNo	FatherName
1	Brisker	1	1	Pepper
2	Jeager	1	6	No Data Available
3	Pepper	6		

So, by using a column to reference the data in the other table, we can maintain consistency. (This, in database terms, is referred to as a one-to-many relationship. Here we refer to the father, Pepper, when referencing his offspring Brisker and Jaeger.)

Notes:

But because a dog is a dog is a dog, we can use a single table and point the data back to itself, called a self-join. So using the previous example, the Dog Table becomes…

Dog Table		
DogNo	DogName	FatherDNo
1	Brisker	4
2	Jeager	4
3	Donner	4
4	Pepper	6
5	Maria	6
6	Not Available	6

… and the integrity of the data is assured, Pepper is always DogNo 4, no matter how many pups he sires!

MSDE 2000

"Microsoft SQL Server 2000 Desktop Engine (MSDE 2000) is the free, redistributable version of SQL Server that's ideal for client applications that require an embedded database, new developers learning how to build data-driven applications, and Web sites serving up to 25 concurrent users." Hey, I didn't make this up! I grabbed it straight off of Microsoft's SQL Server's MSDE Home Page at: www.microsoft.com/sql/msde/default.asp

MSDE 2000 is a throttled down version of SQL Server 2000. It has all the functionality of its big brother but with some limitations and without some useful components. Here's the scoop about MSDE:

- MSDE is included with SBS 2003 Standard Edition.

- MSDE has been "optimized" for five concurrent users. That's fine for smaller organizations, but the network will get sluggish as you approach and exceed 10 concurrent users.

- MSDE will support databases up to 2 GB for *each* database in the system. That's a lot of data for a small business. And different and unrelated databases could each use 2 GBs of storage. In our practice, we have supported many Access databases, some with JET backends and some with SQL, and have never come close to exceeding this 2 GB ceiling, but keep it in the back of your mind.

MSDE 2000 vs. Microsoft SQL Server 2000

The table below, excerpted from *SQL Server Books Online*, presents a comparison of the features supported by MSDE 2000 vs. MSSQL 2000 Standard Edition.

Table 9-1

Features Supported by MSDE 2000 and Microsoft SQL Server 2000

Feature	MSDE 2000 Standard Edition	MSSQL 2000
Database Engine		
Multiple Instance Support	Supported	Supported
Graphical DBA and Developer Utilities and Wizards	N/A	Supported
Full-Text Search	N/A	Supported
SQL Mail	N/A	Supported
Replication Publisher		
Snapshot Replication	Supported	Supported
Transactional Replication	Subscriber Only	Supported
Merge Replication	Supported	Supported
Immediate Updating Subscriptions	Supported	Supported
Queued Updating Subscriptions	Supported	Supported
Analysis Services		
Analysis Services	N/A	Supported
Custom Rollups	N/A	Supported
Actions	N/A	Supported
Data Mining	N/A	Supported

The full comparison with these and other editions of SQL Server 2000 can be found at *SQL Server Books Online* (open SQL Server Architecture, Implementation Details, Editions of SQL Server 2000, and select Features Supported by the Editions of SQL Server 2000).

One other thing you need to know about MSSQL or its little brother, MSDE: there's no friendly user interface. Sure, you can open the table, see the nice rows and columns, and enter your data, but where's the user-friendly data entry form? Or how about generating a report, maybe with pictures or charts? Not here! For that you need a front-end like VisualBasic or Access.

SQL Server Enterprise Manager

SQL Server Enterprise Manager is a graphical tool for administering MSSQL databases. Use Enterprise Manager to manage the SQL servers, databases, users, and more. In *Windows Small Business Server 2003: Best Practices*, Harry used Enterprise Manager to create the SSLDOG database and the Tracking table. Without Enterprise Manager, Harry would have had to create the database and table with Access 2003, or programmatically with any language that speaks SQL or Microsoft's COM specification (e.g., Visual Basic, VBA, VBScript, etc.). There's even an object model called Distributed Management Objects, or DMO, that provides methods for creating, modifying, and deleting objects in the database. Access 2003 communicates with SQL Server and MSDE using ADO (ActiveX Data Objects). And for you lovers of the command line, you can run the SQL utility that provides an Open Database Connectivity (ODBC)-based query interface.

SQL Profiler

SQL Profiler is a graphical tool within SQL Server Enterprise Manager. Profiler is used to monitor events in an instance of SQL Server or MSDE. You can use Profiler to debug Transact-SQL statements, test SQL statements and stored procedures, and troubleshoot SQL database issues.

Query Analyzer

Query Analyzer is another great tool, accessed from SQL Server Enterprise Manager, with a graphical interface that allows you to, among other things, run SQL queries, views, and stored procedures; copy existing database objects; debug query performance problems by showing the query's execution plan; and more. Query Analyzer is a meal unto itself. It comes with SBS Standard Edition.

SQL Server Books Online

Also accessed via SQL Server Enterprise Manager, SQL Server Books Online is another feature not found with SBS Standard, but fear not mighty SBSer, you can still get this fabulous reference library by going to the MSDE Home Page and selecting Technical Resources found on the left side of the page (until Microsoft updates things again so we can't find things where we left them ;-) Once on the Technical Resources page, you can elect to "Download SQL Server 2000 Books Online" or "View SQL Server Books 2000 Online on MSDN."

JET and Access

Microsoft released its first desktop database product, Microsoft Access 1.0, in November 1992. Due to the close integration of the user interface with the underlying JET database engine, users were generally unaware that these were actually two separate components. They referred to the product simply as the Access database. The real muscle behind Access's pretty face was Microsoft's JET database engine and its related data storage container. So we really need to think of Access in terms of its two separate components: the Access user interface and the storage container.

Access developers generally use two database containers (MDBs) when they build an Access solution. They use one MDB to store the working side of the application, which contains the code (queries, macros, forms, reports, and modules). The other MDB is used to store data. This split design allows the code MDB to be easily replaced or updated without affecting the data side of the application. So, in very simplistic terms, Access (the front end uses the JET database engine to manage and manipulate the data stored in the back end MDB.

Using Access with MSSQL as the Back End

Using this same general concept, Access can also connect to MSSQL using other database providers such as an ODBC Driver, OLE DB Provider, or SQL Server OLE DB Provider (for Access Data Projects).

Why should you use Access with a MSSQL back-end? I can think of three reasons:

- Reliability,
- Inherit reduction in network traffic, and
- Availability of triggers.

Reliability

Access MDBs are prone to corruption if they suffer an abnormal shutdown from a power failure or shortage, rebooting of any locked up client machine that happens to have the MDB open, or a network problem.

MSSQL, on the other hand, being a transaction based database engine is less prone to corruption. Being transaction based, every change to the database (that's every time data is added, deleted, modified and any change to the database structure) is first written to a log file. The database engine individually processes each log entry to record the change to the database itself. When a potentially disastrous event occurs, the only potential loss that could not be recovered would be the loss of an unwritten log entry.

Inherit reduction in network traffic

Access being a file –server-based application requires that all the heavy work be done on the client machine. When Access needs a bit of data to work on (such as from a query), it has to pull all the data across the network before it gets filtered at the client side. MSSQL, a client-server database, processes the query on the server and sends only the results back to the client. This can substantially reduce network traffic.

Availability of triggers

Access doesn't have triggers, so developers have to implement them at the form level. What is a trigger and why would I want one anyway? Here's an example. A client of mine has an Access application. When the price of an inventory item changed, he wanted the system to record the previous value, the current value, who made the change, and when the change was made. He also wanted this history preserved in a table. In Access, every form that could change the price of an item had to include code that would accomplish this archive function. And what happened if someone opened the inventory item table directly and tried to change the price? Absolutely NOTHING, NADA, ZILTCH! There's nothing in Access at the table level that gets this job done. The change would HAVE to be made from the form and then archived. MSSQL could accomplish this feat easily with a server-side trigger. Simply put, whenever the price of an inventory item is updated, it triggers a stored procedure that adds a record in the archive table. It wouldn't make a bit of difference where the change was made. Not from Access, not from VB, not from Excel. The database doesn't care. When a price is changed, the update event is triggered, and the stored procedure is executed. Done deal!

MSSQL Security from a Mile High

When you use Access as a desktop database development environment, the underlying assumption is that if you log on to the machine, you can build your own database. MSSQL has a different mind set. Having a Windows login and password doesn't mean a thing to MSSQL. Since MSSQL is a server-side database, a user has to have permission to access and use the MSSQL database engine to create a new database. MSSQL controls security with logins, roles, and user accounts.

To access MSSQL, you'll need to pass through three gates:

- First, you must pass through (be validated by) Windows Network Security.

- Second, you must pass through SQL Server's own login step.

- Third, you must be authenticated as a valid User of the specific SQL Server Database.

Now that you've passed through all three gates and you've logged onto your SQL Server and switched to your working database, you still need explicit permission to access the database objects that you may want to view or modify.

MSSQL allows you to use one of two authentication systems: Windows Authentication or SQL Server 2000 Authentication. The difference between these two modes of authentication is the simple determination of whether Windows alone or Windows with SQL Server (Mixed Mode) are responsible for validating access requests.

- Windows Authentication relies on Windows alone to identify and validate a user and pass the related security credentials on to SQL Server.

- Mixed Mode security provides connectivity to non-Windows networked computers and backward compatibility. In this mode, you, the administrator, would be required to manage both Windows and SQL Server passwords.

Way back in ***Windows Small Business Server 2000 Best Practices***, Harry led us through the creation of a simple database, SSLDOG. But Harry created this database on the server as the Administrator user. Here's the gotcha: even though NormH is an Authenticated SBS Power User, he does not have permission to access SQL Server or the SQL Server databases. So, the next thing we need to do is to provide a login for Norm, create a security group and place Norm into it, and assign permissions. Although all that can be accomplished using command line commands, we'll do it the easy way and use Server Management and SQL Server Enterprise Manager. So here we go, fellow SBSers! Let's get connected!

We could just add Norm to SQL Server logons, but Best Practices dictate the use of groups to simplify management. To build a group I'll call SSLDOGuser, follow these steps:

1. Log on to the SBS server machine as **Administrator** with the password **Husky9999!**

2. Click **Start, Server Management**.

Figure 9-1

Add a Security Group—Start Wizard

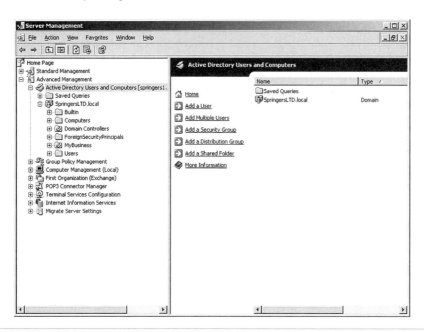

3. In the left pane, expand the **Advanced Management** object, then select **Active Directory Users and Computers**.

4. In the right pane, select **Add a Security Group** to start the wizard. The **Security Group Information** screen appears.

5. In the **Name of the security group: field**, type **SSLDOGuser**.

6. In the **Description: field**, type a description for the group such as, Users of the SSLDOG database.

Your screen should look similar to Figure 9-2.

Figure 9-2

Add a Security Group—Security Group Information

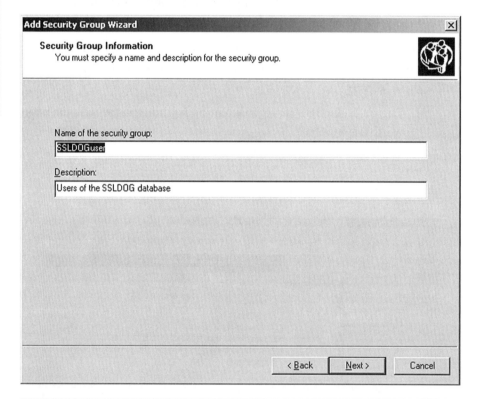

Notes:

7. Click **Next**.

The Group Membership screen appears.

Figure 9-3

Add a Security Group—Group Membership

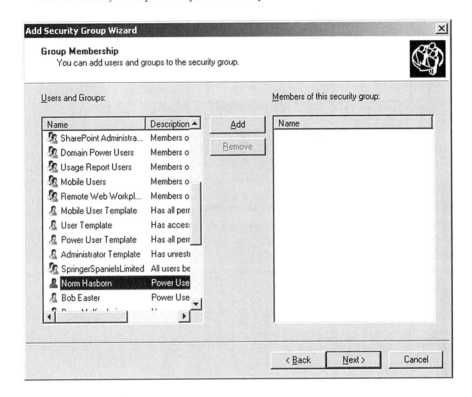

8. Select Norm Hasborn from the list on the left and click **Add, Next**.

9. On the **Completing the Add Security Group Wizard** screen, click **Finish**.

Although Norm is now a member of the new SSLDOGuser security group, he still can't log in to the SQL Server database. For that he has to have a SQL Server login. That will be accomplished as soon as the SSLDOGuser group has a valid login, as described here:

1. If you're not still logged on the SBS server machine, log on to the SBS server machine as **Administrator** with the password **Husky9999!**

2. Click **Start, All Programs, Microsoft SQL Server, Enterprise Manager**.

3. Expand the following objects in the left pane: **Microsoft SQL Servers, SQL Server Group, (local)(Window NT), Security**.

4. Highlight **Logins**, then right-click and select **New Login…**.

    The New Login Properties screen appears.

Figure 9-4

Start Logins

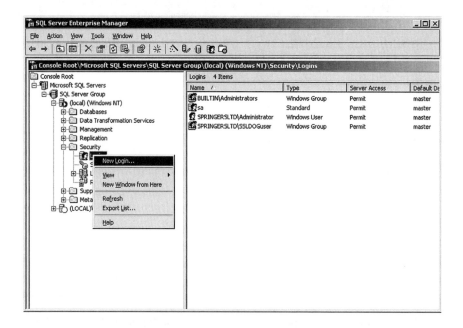

5. On the **General** tab, select the "**…**" button to the right of the **Name: field**.

6. Scroll down the list and select SSLDOGuser when it appears. Click **Add**, then **OK**.

    You're returned to the **SQL Server Login Properties—New Login** window.

Notes:

Figure 9-5

Security—New Login—Add Group

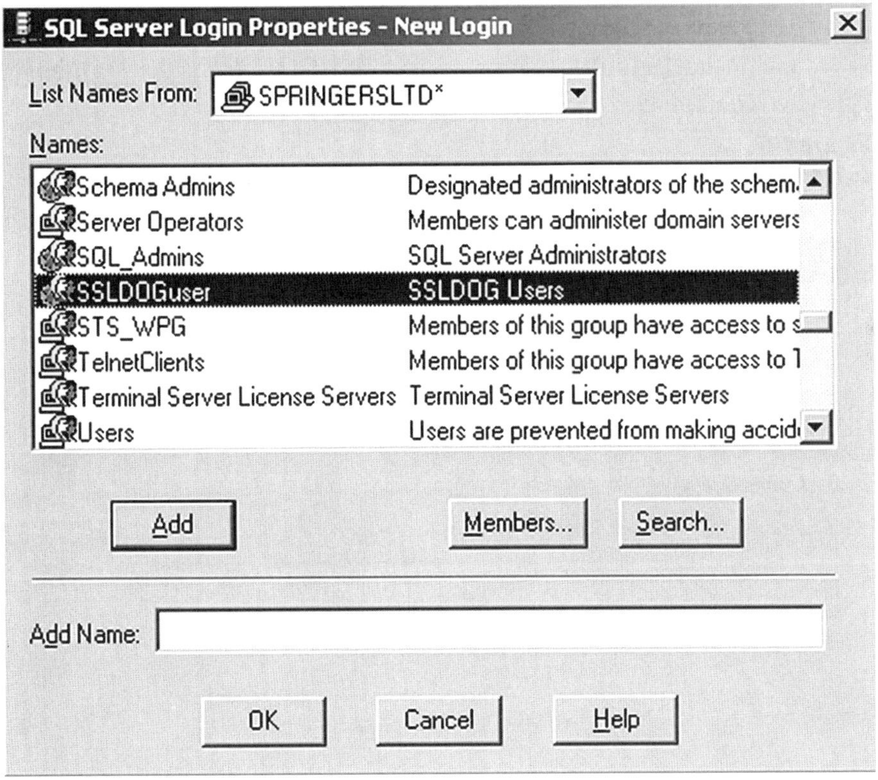

SQL Server Login Properties - New Login   ☒

List Names From: 🖳 SPRINGERSLTD*   ▼

Names:

Schema Admins	Designated administrators of the schem. ▲
Server Operators	Members can administer domain servers
SQL_Admins	SQL Server Administrators
SSLDOGuser	**SSLDOG Users**
STS_WPG	Members of this group have access to s
TelnetClients	Members of this group have access to T
Terminal Server License Servers	Terminal Server License Servers
Users	Users are prevented from making accid ▼

[Add]   [Members...] [Search...]

Add Name: [   ]

[OK]   [Cancel]   [Help]

Notes:

---

7. While still on the **General** tab, verify that in the **Authentication** section that **Windows Authentication** is selected, that **SPRINGERSLTD** appears in the **Domain: field**, and that **Grant access** is selected.

8. In the **Defaults** section, select **SSLDOG** from the **Database: combobox**.

Figure 9-6

Add a Security Group – General

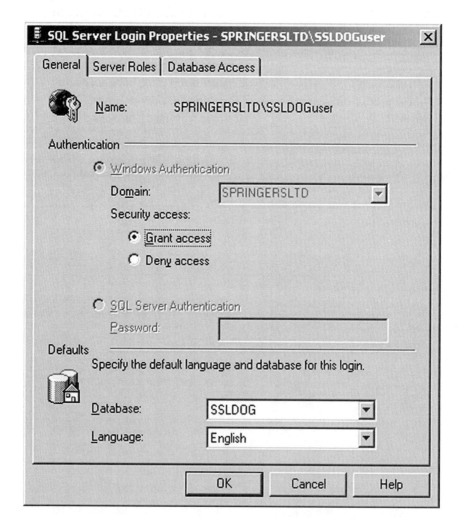

9. Select the **Server Roles** tab. Check the box to the left of the description to add the role of Systems Administrators to this security group. Remember that SQL System Administrators can perform any activity in the SQL Server installation.

Figure 9-7

Add a Security Group—Server Roles

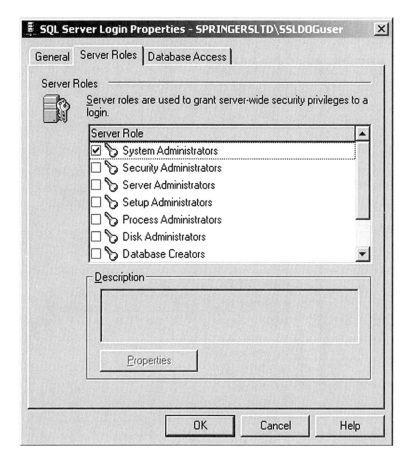

10. Select the **Database Access** tab. Select **SSLDOG** from the list of databases by checking the box to the left of the database name,

    A list of **Database roles for 'SSLDOG':** appears in the lower listbox. Scroll down and review the different roles that could be used to fine tune secured access permissions. Again, since we're keeping things simple for this example, make sure that only **public** is checked.

Figure 9-8

Add a Security Group—Database Access

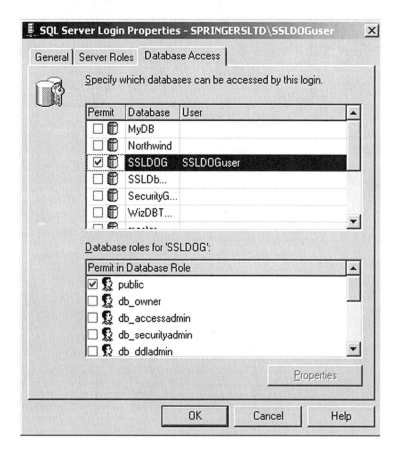

11. Click **OK**.

    SPRINGERSLTD\SSLDOGuser is added to logins.

And that's all there is to it! Norm and any other user in the SSLDOGuser Security Group can now access the SSLDOG database. Next step—let's try it!

Using the Data in a MSSQL Database

MSSQL is a powerful database engine with great tools for designing and administering the database. What MSSQL lacks is a user-friendly interface for data entry or for using the data that is stored in that database. For that, you could resort to writing your own application with VB or VB.NET or C++ or C#, or you could do it the SBSer way and use the tools that are included with the various editions of MS Office 2003. I'll walk you through two them, Excel and Access (my personal favorite!).

Excel is probably the most commonly used product for managing and manipulating databases. For basic index-card type lists, it's an easy-to-use tool for sorting, grouping, searching, and summarizing your clients' data. (Remember what I said about flat file databases.) However, Access excels over Excel when you need to combine data from multiple tables or create a custom data entry form. But both tools can use the data stored in a MSSQL database. Here's how....

Excel

1. Log on to the **President** machine as **NormH** with his password, **Purple3300**.
2. Click **Start, All Programs, Microsoft Office, Microsoft Office Excel 2003**.

   An Excel workbook opens.

Notes:

3.From the **Data** menu, navigate to **Import External Data, Import Data**. The **Select Data Source** window opens and **My Data Sources** should appear in the **Look in: combobox**.

Figure 9-9

Excel Data Connection Wizard—Select Data Source

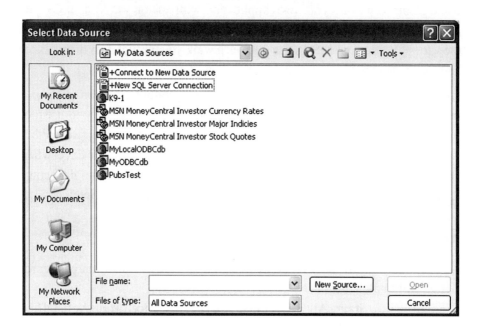

4. Double-click **+New SQL Server Connection** to start the **Data Connection Wizard**.

5. In the **Server name: field**, type **SPRINGERS1**, and accept the default **Use Windows Authentication** for the **Log on credentials**. (That's what we set up in the last series of steps.)

Notes:

Figure 9-10

Excel Data Connection Wizard—Connect to Database Server

Data Connection Wizard ☒

Connect to Database Server
Enter the information required to connect to the database server.

1. Server name: `SPRINGERS1`

2. Log on credentials
   ⦿ Use Windows Authentication
   ◯ Use the following User Name and Password

   User Name: `_____`
   Password: `_____`

   [Cancel]   [< Back]   [Next >]   [Finish]

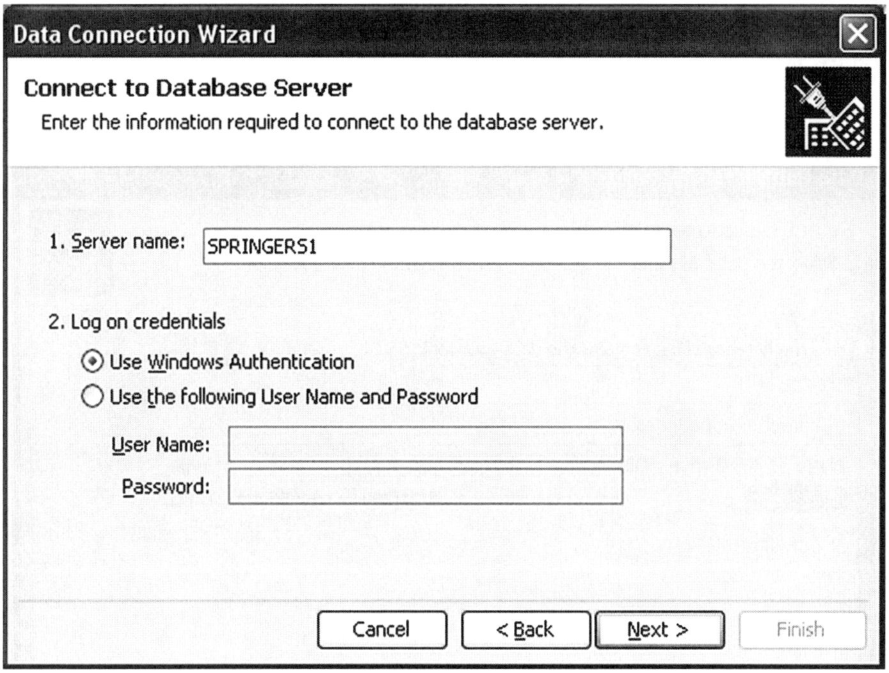

6. Click **Next**.

    The **Select Database and Table** screen appears.

> # Notes:

7. In the **Select the database that contains the data you want: list box**, use the drop-down and select **SSLDOG**, verify that the **Connect to a specific table: check box** is checked, and select the **Tracking table from the list**.

Figure 9-11

Excel Data Connection Wizard—Select Database and Table

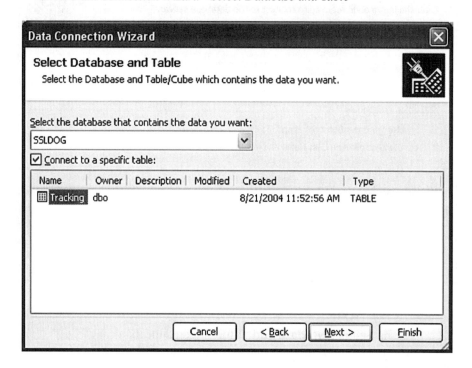

8. Click **Next**.

   The final screen of the wizard appears prompting to **Save Data Connection File and Finish**. Here you can rename the connection, add a description, and search keywords.

9. Accept the defaults and click **Finish**.

   A Data Source Connection has now been created.

10. The **Import Data** screen appears prompting for the location to put the data. Notice the **Edit Query ... button**. Clicking this button will launch another wizard that would allow you to refine your selection of data that will be imported into the worksheet. You can investigate that path on your own.

11. Click **OK** to complete the wizard.

The data has now been imported into the worksheet.

Figure 9-12
Excel Data Connection Wizard—Import Data

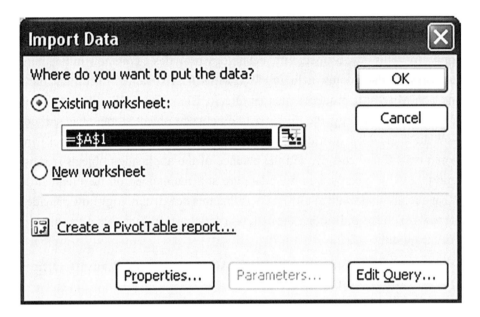

The key word here is *Imported*. You now have a separate and distinct copy of the data that is not connected to the data in the SQL SSLDOG database. It's a snapshot of the data at the time of the import, not a link. This type of import is good for, say, analyzing the month-end or year-end data that you might grab from an accounting system. Just remember that this data is static.

Access

MS Access provides us with two ways to implement a solution using MSSQL as your data storage engine. In earlier versions of Access, you used the traditional JET-based Access database container, the MDB, and linked your data to the application using ODBC. Although you could access the data using ODBC, you couldn't modify the data structures. In addition to the ODBC data links (a typical Access application), the Access MDB would also include all the queries, forms, reports, data access pages (DAPs), macros, and modules. Notice the division between the application's data, which is stored on the server-side, and all the other objects used in the application, which are stored on the client side.

Beginning with Access 2000, Microsoft introduced the Access Database Project (ADP). An ADP doesn't use JET or ODBC to link to your SQL Server database; instead, it links exclusively to your SQL Server database using OLE DB as the connector. This new connectivity technology provides a common architecture for access to data stores including JET, MSSQL, Exchange, Excel, flat files, and non-Microsoft products such as Oracle. Since the ADP inherently uses server-side technology, the dividing line between object storage has shifted. Now the data tables, queries, and data diagrams (the new kid on the block) are stored on the service-side, and the balance of the application objects (forms, reports, DAPs, macros, and modules) are still maintained on the client side. What's really important to us SBSers is that this new technology now provides the tools to create and modify the database structures from within Access itself. Let's try it out.

1. Fire up Access form **Start, All Programs, Microsoft Office, Microsoft Office Access 2003**.

    If you don't have a copy of Access, it's included in Microsoft Office Professional 2003 that's available in a trial version that you can get at http://www.microsoft.com/office/editions/prodinfo/trial.mspx.

2. From the **Menu bar**, select **File, New**.

    The **New file Task Pane** opens.

Figure 9-13

Access Project using new data

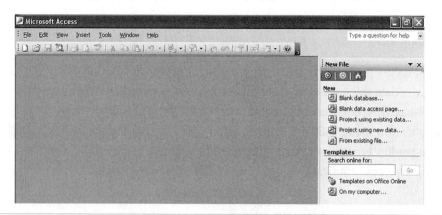

3. Select **Project using existing data....**

   The **File New Database** dialog box opens and defaults to the **My Documents** folder.

4. From the List box, open the **My Databases** folder.

   If the **My Databases** folder doesn't exist, you may create it or store the new ADP in a folder of your own choosing.

5. In the **File name: combobox**, enter **SSLDOGCS**. Verify that the **Save as type:** is **Microsoft Office Access Project**, and click **Create**.

   The **Data Link Properties** window opens. Note that if you selected Blank database…, a JET-based MDB would have been created.

6. With the **Connection** tab active, use the **dropdown** to select **SPRING-ERS1** from the **Select or enter a server name: combobox**,

7. In the **Enter information to log on to the server:** select the **User Windows NT Integrated security radio button**.

8. In the **Select the database on the server: combobox**, use the dropdown to select the **SSLDOG** database.

Figure 9-14

   Access New ADP – Data Link Properties

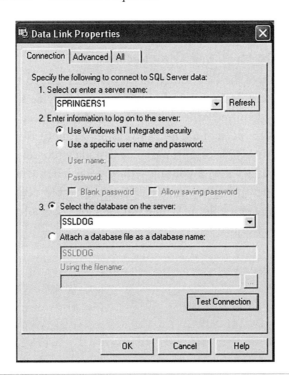

9. Click the **Test Connection** button.

   A Pop-up Windows dialog box appears, informing you that the **Test connection succeeded**.

10. Click **OK** to close this dialog.

11. Click **OK** in the Data Link Properties Window to create the OLE DB data link between this Access application and the SQL Server database.

    The Access project file is created and the Tables, Queries, and Database Diagrams of the SQL Server database are now available. The Access Project opens.

From this Access Project database window, you can build an application complete with a user interface. But before we do, let me show you an anomaly that exists between MS SQL Enterprise Manager and ADPs. In Chapter 14 of *Windows Small Business Server 2003 Best Practices*, Harry had you build the Tracking table and, while still in Enterprise Manager, add two rows of data. Watch what happens when we attempt to add some data to the Tracking table from the ADP.

1. With the **SSLDOGSCS.ADP** still open, select **Tables** from the **left Objects pane**, then, in the **right pane**, double-click the **Tracking** table.

   The Tracking table opens in Datasheet View.

2. From the **Menu Bar**, select **Records**.

   Notice that the Data Entry menu option is grayed and unselectable. Also note that the Tracking table does **not** provide a New Record line (a line identified with an "*"). The problem we've encountered is a basic difference in the inner working of Enterprise Manager and an ADP. An ADP uses a primary key to update records in a table. In lieu of a primary key, a column with unique index (Indexed = Yes (no duplicates)) will be used. The Tracking Table does not have a primary key or a column with a unique index. Let's fix that.

Notes:

Figure 9-15

Access ADP Tracking table not updatable

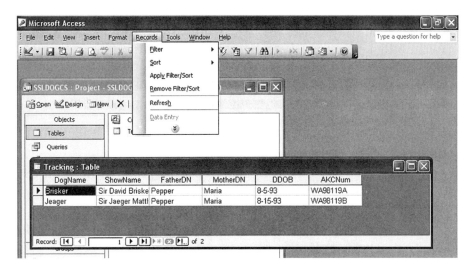

3. From the **Menu Bar**, select **View**, **Design View**.

   The display changes to one with a view of the structure of the table similar to that of the Enterprise Manager's Table Design.

   We need to create a uniqueness to identify a record so that the table is updatable. Since Springer Spaniels Ltd. is involved in breeding, raising, and showing prize Springer Spaniels, we could assume that all dogs have an AKC registration number. The problem here is that the AKC Registration number is only provided after the dog is registered, which could occur many months after the dog is whelped. For simplicity, let's just create a new column called DogID and set it up as the table's primary key.

4. With the row **DogName** selected, from the **Menu Bar** select **Insert**, **Rows**.

   A new row is created above **DogName**.

5. In the **Column Name**, enter **DogID**, and in **Data Type**, enter **int**. In the **lower pane**, select **Identity** and enter **YES**.

   The **Identity Seed** and the **Identity Increment** are automatically defaulted to 1. Now as dogs are added to the table, an automatically incremented unique DogID will be generated.

Figure 9-16

AccessADP Tracking table

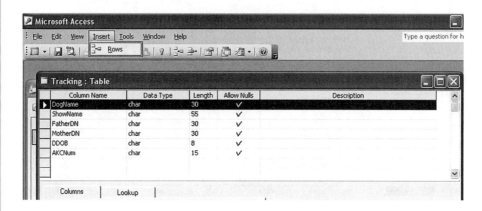

6. Still with the **DogID** row selected, from the **Menu Bar**, select **Edit**, then **Primary Key**.

   A **KEY** appears next to the **DogID** row.

Figure 9-17

AccessADP Tracking table—Identity & PK added

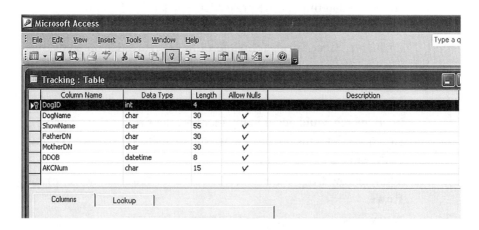

7. Enter **CTRL+S** to save these changes.
8. To return to Datasheet view, from the **Menu Bar**, select **View**, **Datasheet View**.

Note that the first column is **DogID** and the existing rows have been automatically numbered. Also, the last row is marked with an "*" indicating that it is a new record and the **DogID** is **(AutoNumber)**. The (AutoNumber) will be incremented as the new record is saved. You can try it by entering the following values:

Field Name	Value
DogID	This value will be automatically incremented
DogName	Donner
ShowName	Sir Pepper's Pride
FatherDN	Pepper
MotherDN	Maria
DDOB	8-15-93
AKCNum	WA98119C

As you can see, the table is now updatable just as it was from Enterprise Manager. So why use Access if you can add data to the tables from Enterprise Manager? The answer lies at the heart of Enterprise Manager: you don't want your users to have the power to access the structure of your databases. Just give them a tool they can use to do their jobs. Give them a friendly user interface and, with Access, you're only a few clicks away. Here we go!

1. From the Tool Bar, select **AutoForm**.

    Access has generated a simple, yet workable, data entry form complete with VCR type Record Navigation controls.

Figure 9-18

AccessADP Tracking table—AutoForm

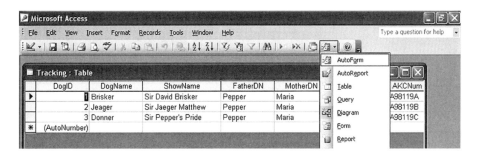

Figure 9-19

AccessADP Tracking table—New AutoForm

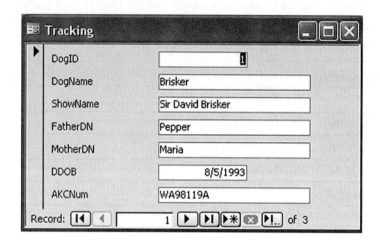

2. From the **Menu Bar**, select **File**, **Save**.

    The Save As dialog box opens.

3. Enter **frm_Tracking** as the Form Name and click **OK**.

Figure 9-20

AccessADP Tracking table—Save frm_Tracking

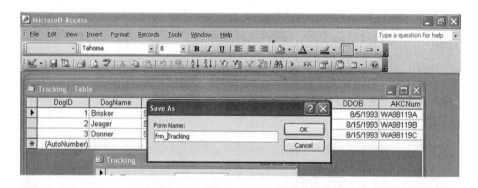

Well folks, that's all there is to the basics and many Access end users never go beyond this basic functionality. But there is a whole application development environment here that you can use to extend your practice and your clients' appreciation of how databases can let them do more and do it better. Among the many great books on Access development; here are a few that I keep in my toolkit.

- *Access 2002 Developer's Handbook Set*, by Paul Litwin, Ken Getz, and Mike Gunderloy, Sybex Press (ISBN: 0782140114).

- *Programming Microsoft Office 2003*, by Rick Dobson, Microsoft Press (ISBN: 0735619425)

- *Access 2002 Power Programming*, by F. Scott Barker, Sams, (ISBN: 0672321025)

Moving from MS Access to MSSQL

Before you introduced SBS to your customers, you've likely found that many had already built one or more Access JET databases for their own or small workgroup use. Now that you have provided them with a full-scale database engine, should they stay with their Access MDB or move (upsize!) it to MSSQL? And if your customers choose to move their databases to MSSQL, what steps do you need to perform to complete the job?

Reasons to Upsize

There are four primary reasons to upgrade: scalability, data integrity, performance, and security. I discuss each in turn below.

Scalability

Scalability is the ability of the database to store more data and/or to support more users. Each Access database is limited to 2 GB. This is generally sufficient for most small business clients, so, in most cases, headroom is not the issue unless the database includes images (such as pictures of inventory products).

The other scalability issue is the number of users. According to Microsoft, Access will support 255 maximum users. In actuality, a properly designed Access database can easily support 15 to 20 concurrent users (although a poorly designed database may have difficulty supporting even two concurrent users). However, you might find that performance becomes an issue. SQL Server, on the other hand, scales to terabytes of data and thousands of users, far exceeding the limits of SBS.

Data integrity

As a file-based system, Access has each user running the JET database engine locally on their machine. That locally running copy can corrupt the shared database if there's a network problem, if the local machine locks up while the database is open, or even if there's a power surge or brownout. Access can be corrupted if different users are using different versions of Access or different DLLs. In contrast, SQL Server, being a true client-server database, rarely corrupts and its transaction-based logging provides recovery of most records in the rare event of failure.

Performance

As a file-based system, Access performs all its work at the local workstation. Access can be set up in two different ways:

- The database can be set up with all the data, queries, forms, reports, and modules in one database, which is then saved on the server.

- The database can be split so the data alone is stored in one database on the server (the back-end database) and the application (the front-end) is stored on each workstation.

In either case, when the user runs the application, the actual work is performed at the local workstation. Here's how it works. The user starts a query to obtain all the dogs "Sir" in their ShowName. Well, Springer Spaniels Ltd. has been around a while and has amassed breeding data on over 100,000 dogs. That query has to bring all 100,000 records from the server to the local machine before they can be processed and filtered. Consider the amount of network traffic consumed by this request.

In a client-server environment, the client passes the request to SQL Server, then the database engine processes the request on the server, gets those records that match the criteria, and returns only those records back to the client. This represents a significant reduction in network traffic.

Security

Finally, ask yourself or your client, "What's the data worth?" MSSQL integrates with Windows Security (demonstrated earlier in this chapter), so there are fewer administrative hassles than with Access. In addition, MSSQL's security model is more robust than Access and provides individualized permissions (for example column by column permissions).

So consider your client's needs and weigh them against the potential costs of data loss and upsizing. Ultimately, it's not a black or white decision, but one complicated by various shades of gray.

Upsize Me: Using the Access Upsizing Wizard

You can move your Access MDB to MSSQL manually or you can use the Access Upsizing Wizard. In either scenario, you must:

- First prepare the database for upsizing. Make a copy of your database and safely store it away (this is known as the ultimate undo!).

- Second, examine the database and identify and fix any issues that might cause conversion problems.

Three common issues that might cause conversion problems are:

- Access allows spaces with the field names (Dog Name) although that has been frowned upon ☹ since version 1.1. MSSQL will not allow spaces unless the field name (or in SQL terms, column name) is enclosed in square brackets ([ ]) or in single quotes (' '). It is better to remove the spaces and use capitalization to enhance readability (DogName) or replace the space with an underscore (Dog_Name).

- The wizard requires a unique index on any table that requires updating. (This is a real gotcha that we'll get back to in a minute.)

- VBA UDFs (User Defined Functions) cannot be upsized, nor can MSSQL handle queries where the parameter contains a reference to a value in a form. For example, if you have a form that supplies the zip code for a parametized query, Access would obtain the value before running the query, no problem! MSSQL, on the other hand, runs the query on the server-side and has no way of obtaining the value that resides on the client-side form. Consequently, the query will not run.

The moral of this story is that you have to do some redesign before things will work properly in this environment.

The test case is a basic Access JET database, an MDB, SSLDOG2.mdb. This database contains a single table (tbl_Tracking), two queries, a data entry form, and a report. The one query (qry_DogList) is used to populate a combobox. The second query (qry_Tracking) relies on a self-join to obtain the names of a dog's sire and dam (father and mother) from the DogID. (This database (SSLDOG2.mdb) is available from the download area of SMB Nation.) So let's run a simple upsizing.

1. Open the **SSLDOG2.mdb** database. From the **Object pane** on the left select **Tables**, on the right-pane select **tbl_Tracking**, then on the **Database Menu** click **Design**.

   The table opens in Design View.

Figure 9-21
Open tbl_Tracking in Design Mode

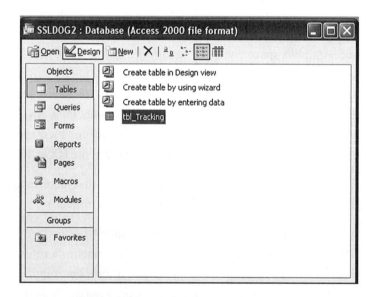

Note that the **DogID** field is an AutoNumber that has been set as the **Primary Key**. This is critical because the Upsizing Wizard cannot create a SQL Server index, and without a unique index, the wizard can't update a table. (And that's the gotcha I pointed out just a moment before.)

Figure 9-22

tbl_Tracking Primary Key

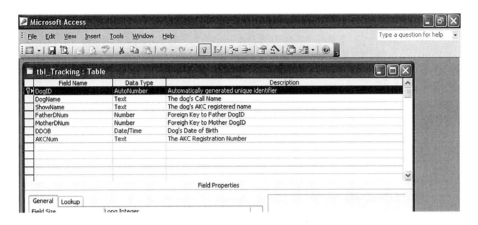

2. Close the tbl_Tracking design form and return to the Database window.

3. From the **Menu Bar**, select **Tools**, **Database Utilities**, **Upsizing Wizard**.

    The wizard opens. We'll create a new database for this project.

Figure 9-23

Start the Upsizing Wizard

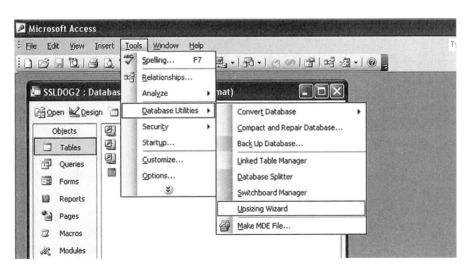

4. Select the **Create new database button** then click **Next**.

Figure 9-24

Create new database

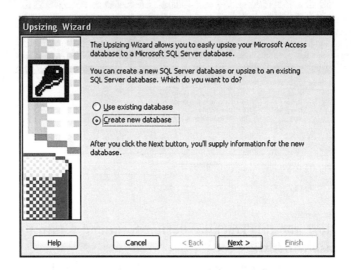

5. Use the dropdown to select **SPRINGERS1** from the **What SQL Server would you like to use for this database?: combobox,**

6. Check **Use Trusted Connection** and accept the default **SSLDOG2SQL** as the **name of the new SQL Server database**.

Figure 9-25

Name the New SQL Server database

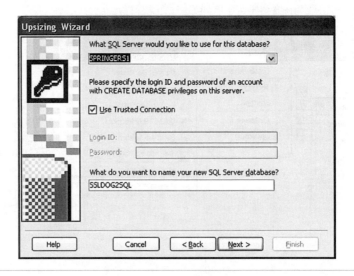

7. Click **Next**. From the **Tables to Export to SQL Server** screen, double-click the **tbl_Tracking** table from the **Available Tables.**

   The table you selected is moved to the **Export to SQL Server: listbox**.

8. Click **Next**.

Figure 9-26

Tables to Export

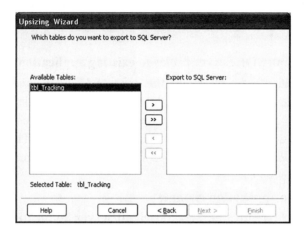

The next screen of the wizard informs us that "The Upsizing Wizard can export table attributes in addition to data" and asks "What data options do you want to include?"

9. Accept the defaults and click **Next**.

Figure 9-27

Export Table Attributes

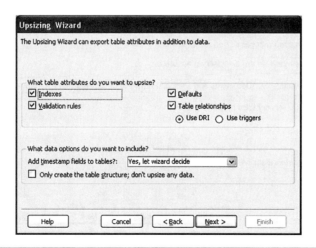

10. The wizard now asks us to decide whether we want to:

- **Create a new Access client/server application**

  This option creates a new ADP, creates the tables, views, and stored procedure in the SQL Server database from the tables and queries in the Access MDB, creates the connection between the ADP and the SQL Server back-end, and attempts to upsize the forms, reports and modules to the new ADP. If you select this option, you must also supply the path to where the new ADP will be created.

- **Link SQL Server tables to existing application**

  This option maintains the existing MDB. It creates the tables, views, and stored procedure in the SQL Server database from the tables and queries in the Access MDB, and creates the connection between the ADP and the SQL Server back-end. This option, however, does nothing to the forms, reports, and modules in the existing MDB.

- **No application changes**

Select **Create a new Access client/server application** and provide the **path** to your new project.

Figure 9-28

Modify or Create New Application

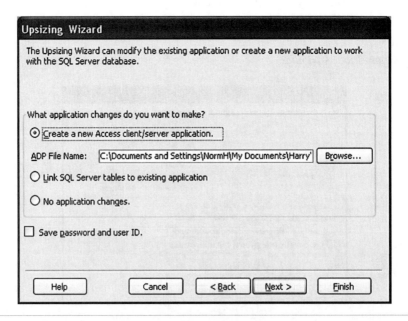

11. Click **Next**.

The last screen of the wizard asks if you want to either Open the new ADP file, or Keep the MDB file open.

Figure 9-29
Finish

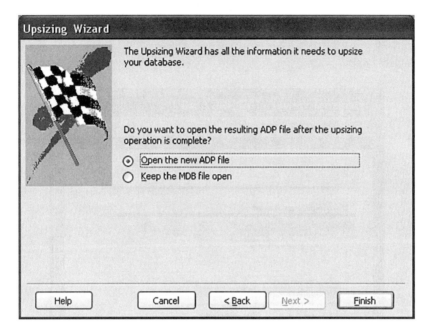

12. Select **Open the new ADP file**, and **Click Finish** to complete the wizard.

Notes:

The wizard creates the new database and opens the **Upsizing Wizard Report**.

The Upsizing Wizard Report is stored in the folder you specified in Step 10 above. The report provides results of the conversion and documents your choices, what succeeded, and what failed. Reviewing this report will help you resolve some of the issues you may encounter from the conversion.

Figure 9-30

Report Page 1

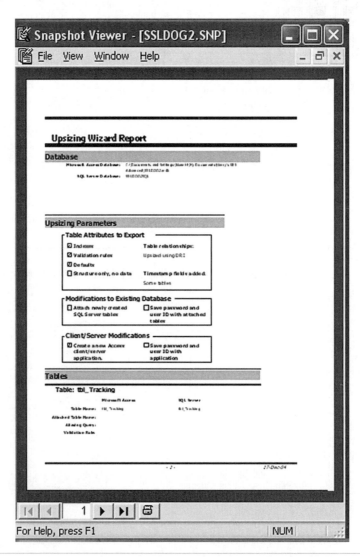

Let's take a look at the new ADP that the wizard created.

1. Take the name of the source database (**SSLDOG2**), append **CS** (for Client-Server), and provide the file type as **ADP** (resulting in file name **AALDOG2CS.ADP**).

   As you review the newly created project, it appears at first that conversion was successful. (The report didn't report any failures.)

2. Open tbl_Tracking in Datasheet view.

   The data looks fine.

3. Do the same with the tow queries (qry_DogList and qry_Tracking).

   Again, the results look fine.

4. Now open the Report rpt_Tracking.

   A dialog box opens informing us that we have an Invalid column name "DogName."

5. Click **OK** to close this dialog.

6. Open the form, frm_Tracking.

   Notice that the control for the Dog Name displays **#Name?** Something's obviously wrong.

Figure 9-31

Tracking Form Problem

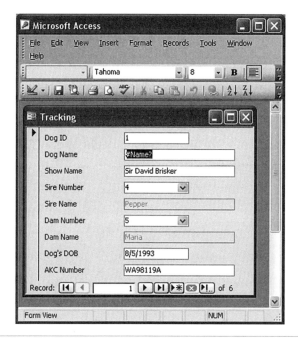

Follow these steps to display the problem.

1. Switch to design mode.
2. From the Menu Bar, select **View**, **Design View**.
3. Enter **ALT+Enter** to open the Form Properties.

Figure 9-32

Tracking From in Design Mode

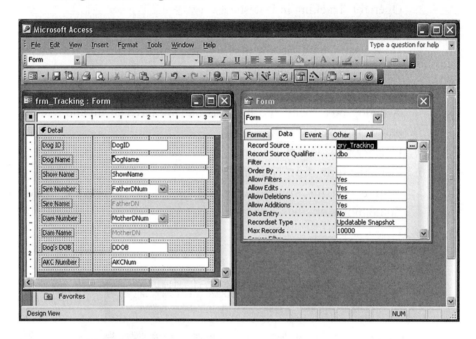

4. On the Properties Form, use the dropdown box to select **Form**, the **Data Tab**, then **Record Source Property**.

   It should now display qry_Tracking.
5. Click the box with three dots to the right of qry_Tracking.

   The query opens in Design View.

Notes:

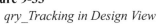

Figure 9-33

qry_Tracking in Design View

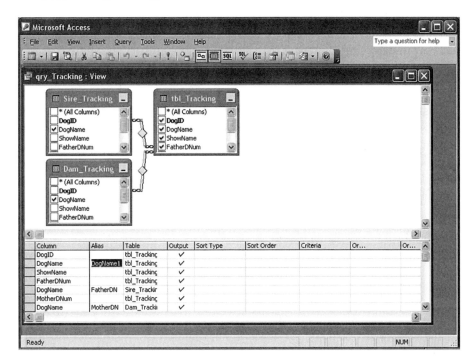

Do you see the problem? The wizard provided an Alias **DogName1**
for the Column **DogName**. The form, on the other hand, was looking
for the column **DogName** from the query. Not finding **DogName**, it
displayed the control error #**Name?**

Follow these steps to fix the problem:

1. Delete the Alias **DogName1** for the Column **DogName**.
2. Close the Query (**Menu Bar, File, Close**).
3. When the dialog **Do you want to save the changes made to the
   query and update the property?** appears, click **YES**.

   We return to the Tracking Form.

4. **Save** the Tracking Form (**Menu Bar, File, Save**) and **Switch** to Form
   View (**Menu Bar, View, Form View.**)

   The Dog Name is properly displayed.

5. Close the Tracking Form and open the Tracking Report.

The report runs fine now since the report relied upon the same query as its record source.

As you can see from this example, the Upsizing Wizard works well. but not perfectly. Expect to roll up your sleeves and do some cleanup. Check out the Access programming references presented earlier in this chapter for more details to help you troubleshoot the conversion, or team up with an Access Developer.Here's some late-breaking news: a Microsoft Project Guide focuses on upsizing Access databases. I found it from the Partners site map, way down at the bottom labeled Project Guides. From there I went to Office System Project Guides (https://partner.microsoft.com/40011742) and about halfway down the page I found the section titled "Upsizing Access Databases to Microsoft SQL Server 2000." There are five sections and lots of good info on why and how to upsize. Each section is tuned for a specific team member:

- Business Decision Maker

- Sales and Marketing Staff

- Technical Staff

- Customer Training Staff

- Project Management Staff

There's even a Project Plan you can use to map out you migration.

Summary

Well, fellow SBSers, that pretty well wraps things up. In this chapter, I've presented:

- Reasons why you should use a database and how a relational database differs from a flat file table

- A comparison between MSDE 2000 and Microsoft SQL Server 2000.

- An introduction to JET, the desktop database engine that Microsoft Access is built upon.

- An overview of SQL Server Security.

- A discussion of how you can use Microsoft Excel to analyze data stored in a SQL Server database.

- An introduction to the Microsoft Access Database Project.

- A discussion of how to move your Microsoft Access JET databases to SQL Server using the Upsizing Wizard.

I hope you've picked up some key insights into database management. From my perspective, this is the thing that business decisions are made of. But most of all, I hope you've found some reasons to recommend the Premium Edition of Small Business Server to the business owners you work with. It's a small price to pay for big dividends.

Thanks, and see you at SMB Nation!

CHAPTER 10
Fax Server: Advanced Topics
BY Kevin D. Royalty (Cincinnati, OH)

Welcome to the advanced chapter on Small Business Server 2003 (SBS 2003) faxing! As a consultant, I have many customers who utilize the SBS faxing capabilities to service their customers more efficiently and cost effectively. In this chapter, I will describe how they are doing this in detail. At the end of this chapter, I will provide information from other consultants who also work heavily with SBS faxing and have uncovered several issues that you might encounter.

Kindly note the following caveat. There is one thing I hope you have done, and that is read the faxing chapter (Chapter 9) from the introductory book in this series, *Windows Small Business Server 2003 Best Practices*. That introductory faxing chapter, in my opinion, does an excellent job of covering faxing in SBS. I reference sections of that book but do not repeat that same chapter information here.

The Appropriate Hardware

This section focuses on how to select the best hardware to support the faxing function in SBS 2003.

Bad Choices

One lesson I learned early in my SBS career is how important it is to use the right fax/modem equipment. However, many of my customers are small businesses that have tight budgets; when these customers can order a server machine preinstalled with a cheapo internal fax/modem for $50 instead of spending a bit more for an "industrial strength" fax/modem, it is hard to get some of them to spend that extra money for more appropriate hardware. But, believe me, after you end up spending valuable billable time working with these cheapo units, both you and the customer will quickly see the mistake. As I write this, my customers who originally bought the cheaper internal fax/modem units have now removed or disabled them, and replaced them with more professional fax/modems. Live and learn!

> BEST PRACTICE: Keep that old fax machine around by hooking the line from the fax machine to the phone connection on the fax/modem of your SBS box. If your fax/modem doesn't have this connection, a simple phone splitter will suffice. This will allow you to slowly transition the customer from paper faxing to electronic faxing. Having the old fax machine around will also allow the occasional non-electronic fax to be sent without scanning it into the server.

Something else has come to light recently that you should know about. Some server hardware vendors will guarantee support for only a limited number of fax/modem units connected to the SBS server machine. This shouldn't be a problem if you are using a multi-port fax card, but if you are planning on using two off-the-shelf internal fax/modems, you might want to reconsider the brand of server you will utilize for SBS 2003.

Best Bets

I'm sure you are asking yourself, "What hardware should I recommend, then?". Ok, I hear ya! Here's my answer.

Single-line Fax/Modems

I recommend *only* the Multitech MT2834ZDX or MT56000ZDX external serial fax/modem for single-line solutions. This hardware will make you look great to your customers when the SBS Share Fax Service performs flawlessly. I'm starting to hear good things about the Multitech external USB modems, too, but haven't tried them yet. Be advised, however, that many SBSers shy away from USB-based modems based on previous bad experiences.

Other SBSers like to use the old 28.8 and 33.6 Suprafax external modems, which you can still purchase from eBay, but I've not used them. Other professional peers in the SBS newsgroups on Yahoo can add to this admittedly short list of best bets for external fax/modems. Harry Brelsford, series editor for this book, favors the v.Everything external fax/modem and is smitten with the 3Com Sportser modem family.

Multiple-line Fax/Modems

If you have a customer who does a lot of high-volume faxing, you will want to read up on what you can do with more than one fax line using SBS. The best multifax devices I've had the pleasure of working with are made by Brooktrout.

Full disclosure time. Laura Often (loften@brooktrout.com) at Brooktrout was kind enough to provide a 2-port unit for the purposes of researching and writing this chapter. Brooktrout makes a 4-port unit, and you can put multiple units in the same computer as well. Installation details come with the card, but I doubt you'll need them. Installation for me was as simple as just putting the card in a powered-off server where SBS 2003 is already installed. Once I powered up, I went into Device Manager and saw the screen that is provided here as Figure 10-1. Cool! No drivers were included with the card, and thanks to the relationship between Brooktrout and Microsoft, installation is effortless. Translation: SBS 2003 natively supports Brooktrout devices.

Notes:

Figure 10-1
Device Manager showing Brooktrout Trufax board installed

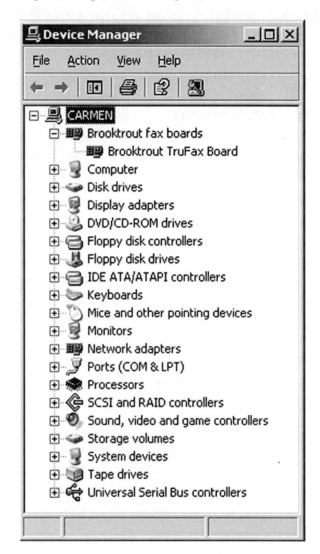

BEST PRACTICE: As any good consultant/tech knows, you should always download the latest driver and firmware for any new piece of hardware. In the Brooktrout multiple fax modem example presented here, you would check www.brooktrout.com.

Fax Routing Destinations

The fax routing destinations are currently limited to four options, but you can use multiple routes at the same time. Table 10-1 describes these fax routing options.

Table 10-1

Fax routing options

Routing Option	Pros	Cons
Print	Works similar to a traditional fax machine.	Once printed, no record exists that the fax came in.
Route through e-mail	Quick, easy delivery of faxes.Can also create a distribution group (of fax recipients) to receive faxes (eg: multiple administrative assistants)	· Limitation of the Exchange Information Store on public and private computers. · If the fax is e-mailed to an individual who is not available, no one can access the fax.
Store in a folder	Can put faxes in folders anywhere on the computer.	· Limited search capabilities. · Need to be aware of permissions of the storage location. · Storage is limited to available disk space.
Store in a Document Library/ Windows Sharepoint Services (WSS)	Only limited to disk space and MSDE/SQL database limitations. Adding full SQL Server adds greater search capability.	Limited search capabilities without SQL.

Let's discuss each of these fax routing options in more detail. I'll also provide examples from working with actual clients.

Print

Printing is usually the first way I set things up if a customer has a traditional fax machine, but I usually also set up an additional method of storing the fax, just in case they need to reprint it or send it out via fax again. Some clients need to store all communications sent or received (check your HIPAA, Sarbanes-Oxley, or other industry-specific laws first!), so I might store these in Document Library/ Windows Sharepoint Services (WSS) or a folder.

> BEST PRACTICE: At a minimum, if you start out printing, choose another storage method for faxes as well. The moment the client needs to reprint or refax a document, you'll have saved the day.

Route Through E-mail

Routing faxes through e-mail was a popular method in the SBS 2000 time frame. But with SBS 2003, you have to be aware of the Exchange Information Store limitations of 16GB for public and private machines (also discussed in Chapter 6). You can store incoming faxes in a public folder, but keep in mind that high volume and large faxes come in .tif format; these files are large and can fill the information store quickly.

The same goes for the private information store, but you do have an "out" if the folder is located in someone's mailbox. You set up auto-archive to archive the mailbox to an archive PST file, but that takes it out of Exchange so no one but the people who have access to that PST file can see the faxes once archived. I have not yet found a way to auto-archive a public folder, but that doesn't mean one doesn't exist.

> BEST PRACTICE: If you are routing faxes via e-mail and have high-volume incoming faxes, consider making an Exchange mailbox for incoming faxes rather than routing them to a specific person. You can set up a rule to notify the customer when the fax comes in, and give the customer access to the mailbox you created to view/forward/ delete the faxes. Also, each week or month you can run auto-archive against the mailbox to get the information out of Exchange so the information store remains manageable.

If you are using an online backup service to back up your server (and specifically the Exchange Information Store), I recommend you do not store faxes in Exchange. Your information store can get very large, again due to the .tif file sizes, and you might be in for a surprise come billing cycle time.

Route to a Folder

With this fax routing option, you only have to worry about disk space limitations and can give your customer permission to maintain the folder and it's contents as they see fit. With the advent of WSS, I see this option being used only until people get used to using WSS.

With SBS 2000, this was my preferred method for storing faxes. If there are regulatory requirements for storing faxes (HIPAA, Sarbanes-Oxley, etc), this is a good method, although WSS would be better due to its version-control features.

Route to a Document Library/WSS

This is my preferred method of storing faxes for my customers who utilize WSS. I do need to point out something that I hope the SBS development team at Microsoft will address: when SBS is installed by the original equipment manufacturer (OEM), you have no control over where the WSS databases are placed. They are always installed on the C: drive, which can fill up quickly. I recommend that you follow the instructions in the article "Moving Data Folders for Windows Small Business Server 2003" (located at http://www.microsoft.com/technet/prodtechnol/sbs/2003/maintain/movedata.mspx) and move these WSS databases to another location on the system. Also, as mentioned above, due to some regulatory requirements, you can turn on version control on a Document Library, such as Incoming Faxes

Multifax Scenarios

In this section, I explore four multifax scenarios that illustrate how to best implement the SBS 2003 Shared Fax service.

Multifax Scenario 1

In this scenario, the customer has two fax lines and they don't want a busy signal when they try to send a fax. Your challenge is to set up a "ring-down" or "hunt group." The customer publishes the main fax number, and the phone company handles rolling the call to the second line if the primary line is busy. Outgoing calls should only be sent on the second line so the primary line is almost always available. This scenario can be expanded for more lines as well.

To configure the SBS 2003 Shared Fax service to address this challenge, follow this procedure:

1. Logon to the SBS server machine as the Administrator.
2. From the **Start** menu, launch the Server Management console.
3. Click the **To Do List**.
4. In the To Do List, under Management Tasks, click the **Start** button next to Configure Fax.
5. Click **Next** on the first couple of screens until you see the Outbound Fax Device screen, as shown in Figure 10-2. .

Figure 10-2

Fax Configuration Wizard – Outbound Fax Device Configuration – Default

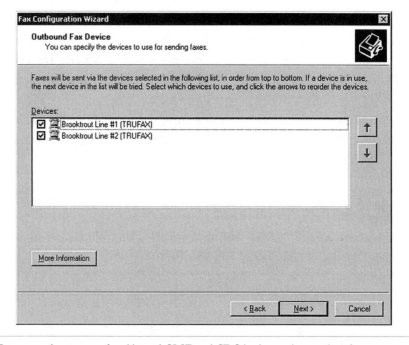

6.   Since we want to allow outgoing faxes on the second line but not the
     first, uncheck the first device, as shown in Figure 10-3.

Figure 10-3
   Fax Configuration Wizard – Outbound Fax Device Configuration – After

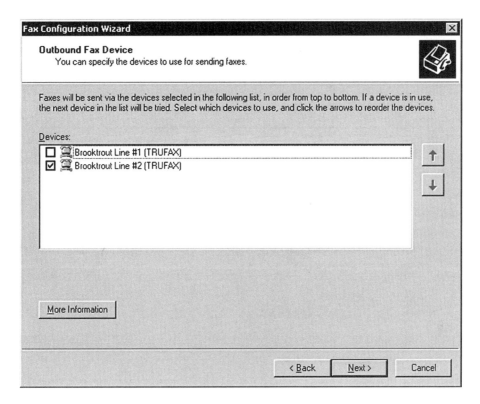

7.   Click **Next** to open the Inbound Fax Device window.

Notes:

8. Check both boxes so both lines can be used for incoming faxes. This is shown in Figure 10-4.

Figure 10-4

Fax Configuration Wizard – Inbound Fax Device Configuration – Default

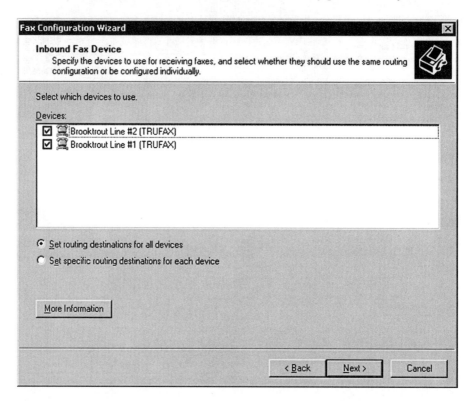

9. Click **Next** to open the Inbound Fax Routing window.

Notes:

10. Under All incoming faxes will be routed to the following location, select Store in a document library.

This will put all incoming faxes in WSS's document library called Incoming Faxes, as illustrated in Figure 10-5.

Figure 10-5

Fax Configuration Wizard – Inbound Fax Routing Showing WSS as the Destination

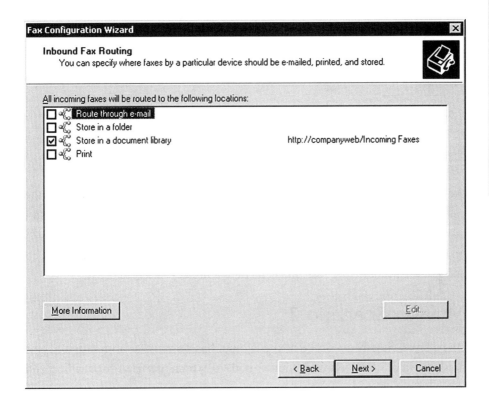

11. Click **Next** to complete the wizard.

We're now ready to do some documentation!

What's that? You hate documentation? Well, I don't know anyone who really likes documentation, but I do appreciate seeing some documentation when I visit an SBS install and need to know quickly what is going on, or what is supposed to be going on. In Figure 10-6 from Server Manager, I've documented the configuration in the description field.

Figure 10-6

Server Management Showing Documentation of Configuration

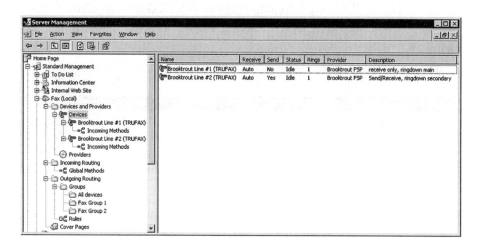

We now have a working environment that fits the requirements set forth by the customer. As you can see, setting up SBS faxing for a scenario like this doesn't take very long. Not counting the lead time needed for the phone company to set up the hunt group/ring down feature, it should take less than an hour to set up and test the scenario we just finished. Take a break - you deserve it!

Multifax Scenario 2

Okay, break time is over. The next customer has a simple configuration of two fax lines in a hunt group/ring down, both of which are used for sending and receiving faxes.

To configure the SBS 2003 Shared Fax service to meet these requirements, follow this procedure:

1. Logon to the SBS server machine as the Administrator.
2. From the **Start** menu, launch the Server Management console.
3. Click the **To Do List**.
4. In the To Do List, under Management Tasks, click the **Start** button next to Configure Fax.
5. Click **Next** on the first three screens until the Inbound Fax Device window opens.

6. Under Select which device to use, check both boxes as shown in Figure 10-7.

Figure 10-7

Fax Configuration Wizard – Inbound Fax Device Configuration with Specific Routing Selected

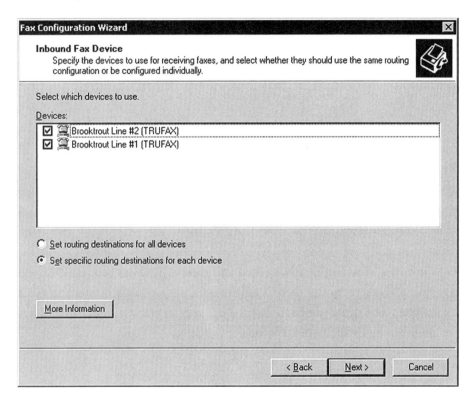

7. Click **Next** to complete the wizard.

Notes:

8. Go into the Server Manager, drill down to the fax configuration, and start your documentation again.

   Your documentation screen should look like the sample shown in Figure 10-8.

Figure 10-8

Server Management Showing Documentation of Configuration

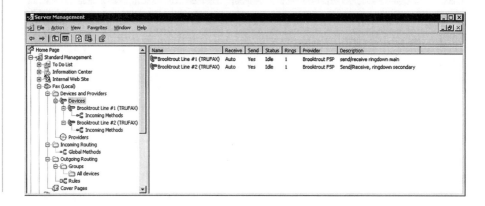

Both lines are now configured to send and receive faxes as requested by the customer. You might notice there is only one fax device in the printer and faxes folder – this is by design since the users don't need to know how many fax lines the client has and which one to chose.

Multifax Scenario 3

Let's get a bit more complicated with this next scenario. Our next customer wants to have the same setup as Scenario 2, but with some restrictions on what lines can send faxes to certain areas. The customer wants to have the main number available for faxing to United States locations only, and the second line for Australian locations, due to a large customer base in that country.

To configure the SBS 2003 Shared Fax service to meet these requirements, follow this procedure:

1. Logon to the SBS server machine as the Administrator.
2. From the **Start** menu, launch the Server Management console.
3. Click the **To Do List**.

4. In the To Do List, under Management Tasks, click the **Start** button next to Configure Fax.

5. Click **Next** on the first three screens until the Inbound Fax Device window opens.

6. Under Select which device to use, check both boxes (as shown previously in Figure 10-7).

7. Click **Next** to complete the wizard.

8. Go back into Server Manager and drill down to the fax configuration, Outgoing Routing, and then Groups.

9. In the detail screen on the right window, right-click to create two new fax groups called Fax Group 1 and Fax Group 2.

10. Go into Fax Group 1 and right-click to create a device that links to the first fax line.

11. Do the same in Fax Group 2 for the second fax line.

12. Under Outgoing Routing and Groups, click on the Rules section.

13. Right-click and select New Rule to create a new rule.
    The Add New Rule window opens.

14. Under Dialed number, , Country/region code, enter 1 for North America.

15. Under Target device, select the Routing group radio button and pick Fax Group 1.

16. Click **OK** to set this rule so only calls to the North America country code of 1 can go out on this line.

Notes:

Your rule should look like the example provided in Figure 10-9.

Figure 10-9

Add New Rule Showing Routing Group Example

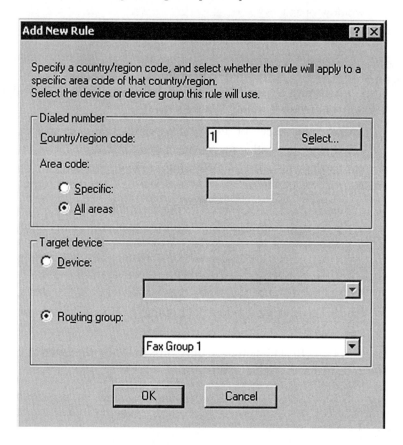

Tip: If we had more than one fax line, we could assign more than one line to Fax Group 1, which would allow any fax line in that group to obey the rule we set up.

To set up the second rule, return to the Add New Rule window in Step 13 and then:

1. Under Dialed number, Country/region code, enter 61 for Australia.

2. Under Target device, select the Routing group radio button and select the device for fax line 2, rather than Fax Group 2.

I suggest this so you can see that both groups and devices can be used when needed. See Figure 10-10 for a combined example.

Figure 10-10
Server Management Showing Multiple Configuration Example

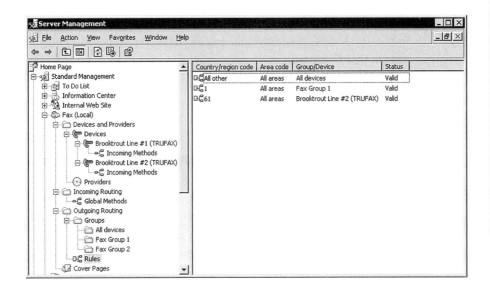

The customer is now set up to send and receive faxes to the U.S. and Australia on specified devices. Excellent work – you deserve another break! If a user on the customer network sends a fax to Australia, it will automatically go to Fax Group 2. Likewise for faxes sent to North America; Fax Group 1 will be selected.

Multifax Scenario 4

This scenario is quite common in many companies. An executive has her own fax line and wants the faxes routed differently than through the company's main fax line. The Incoming Faxes folder in WSS is used to store faxes coming in on the main fax line, but a different folder in WSS (with restricted access) is used to store faxes coming in on the executive's line. This scenario won't go into specifics for WSS, but you will need to create another Document Library just like Incoming Faxes, but restrict the employee access to the executive staff and executive assistants.

To configure the SBS 2003 Shared Fax service to meet these requirements, follow this procedure:

1. Logon to the SBS server machine as the Administrator.
2. From the **Start** menu, launch the Server Management console.
3. Click the **To Do List**.
4. In the To Do List, under Management Tasks, click the **Start** button next to Configure Fax.
5. Click **Next** on the first three screens until the Inbound Fax Device window opens.
6. Under Select which device to use, check both boxes (as shown previously in Figure 10-7).
7. Select the **Set specific routing destinations for each device** radio button then click **Next**.

   The Inbound Fax Routing window opens, like that shown in Figure 10-11. Depending on where the customer wants the main fax line faxes stored, you can set that on this screen. For the executive's line, you can set the destination here as well. As shown in Figure 10-11, all you have to do to change the destination location for the second line fax from wherever it is to the new Document Library you created above.

Notes:

Figure 10-11

Inbound Fax Routing—Separating Destinations for Incoming Faxes

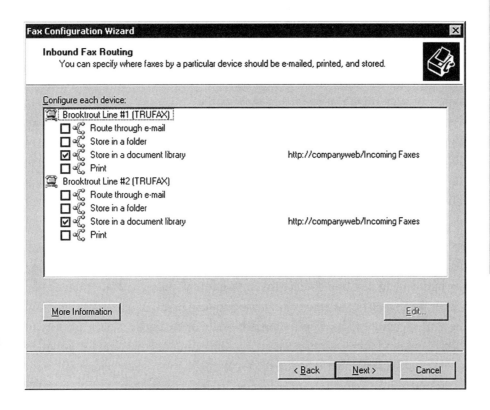

Figure 10-11illustrates that you can change the second routing to go
to a printer, store in a folder, or route via email. Our scenario doesn't
call for that, but you can certainly change the destination to be a
completely different method than using WSS. See the earlier discussion in this chapter on pros and cons of each method of routing faxes.

8. Click **Next** to complete the wizard.

Congratulations! This completes the requirements as requested by the customer.

Notes:

Example of High-Volume Fax Server Usage with SBS

Most of my customers experience what I consider light fax server usage. One exception, described below, is provided to give you ideas on what you can do to position SBS 2003 as a solution for a customer.

My customer with the largest fax usage uses the fax service to blast out two- to four-page faxes to thousands of churches around the country at least three or four times a year. Before the SBS Shared Fax Service was available, a couple of people worked in shifts, manually dialing each and every number and putting the same document back in the machine every time. As you can imagine, it took them quite a while to send these faxes, the long distance bill was large, and they had to pay people to work in shifts to send out these faxes. This ended up being a large money sink for the customer.

Once I installed SBS 2003 for them, we put the entire list of contacts, including fax numbers, in a public contact folder. We set the public contact folder to be visible, so anyone on the network can use it to send faxes (or emails). I suggested the staff separate the faxes into groups by state or area code, set the priority to "low," and send them at non-peak hours. They could then review the e-mailed status messages the next day and retry the failed ones. Their phone bill went down dramatically, and they no longer need people to come in shifts to feed the fax machine. Also, since the priorities are set to low, normal faxes go out when requested, and the occasional incoming faxes come in just fine during the day.

Possible Issues with SBS Fax Services

In speaking to other consultants, some issues were brought to my attention that you should be aware of in case you encounter them in your client sites (or your own site). The discussions below have been edited from e-mails, documents sent to me, and Yahoo SBS2k newsgroup postings, and include references to Microsoft Knowledge Base (KB) articles. I don't include the text of the KB articles here, but reference them by number; feel free to look them up for yourself and see if they apply to any situation you encounter. Also, by the time you read this section, these issues might have been resolved by patches or service packs.

I leave it up to you to verify for yourself if these issues still exist. Note that some of the references below are for SBS 2000 and older versions of Outlook. Some of the issues still applied to SBS 2003 at the time of this writing.

Sending faxes from a program

Have you a need to send faxes automatically from a program? If so, check out Microsoft Knowledge Base article KB 301109 – How to Programatically Send a Fax in SBS.

Problems Adding SBS Shared Fax later

Didn't install fax originally, and now you are having trouble adding it? Check KB 842207.

Errors when faxing to the SBS Shared Fax service

Do you have a computer that is not a member of your SBS Domain in your office that wants to send out a fax through your SBS 2003 server? You might have to change the permissions on the shared fax to give the "Everyone" security group the ability to use the fax. By default, only domain member computers can fax using the SBS Shared Fax.

SBS Shared Fax Dialing Conflicts

It is sometimes difficult to configure SBS Shared Fax Service so that it can do all of the following tasks in one configuration:

- Dial 7-digit fax from Outlook Contact

- Dial 10-digit fax from Outlook Contact

- Dial 1+ 10-digit fax from Outlook Contact

These problems occur because Outlook doesn't export the contact number to SBS Fax using Dialing Rules, and SBS Fax doesn't use dialing rules itself. Additionally, the way SBS Fax stores the previous contact complicates these problems by interfering with the repeat dialing function. That is, if you count on forcing 1+ to solve your problem on first dial attempts, it then breaks the operations for a second fax to the same recipient. In addition, the results are flipped for 7-digit vs. 10-digit success on the first vs. second send attempt. This means that you can't have both 7-digit and 10-digit working on the first dial attempt.

Depending on the approach you choose, you only get 1+ support on the first or second call, and that's also involved with whether you need 7-digit or 10-digit dialing as your priority to work on the first attempt, or only on repeat attempts.

There doesn't appear to be a method by which you can manually edit the dial strings in all cases.

In addition to being extremely confusing in the different behavior for 7-digit vs. 10-digit dialing, there's yet another complexity when trying to compare 10-digit vs. 11-digit (International dialing prefix with 1+ included) because the first dial doesn't work for both at the same time, and the second dial looks identical in the interface, but only works for one or the other.

Here are some fax-related KB articles where you can learn more about dialing issues.

- KB 271382 - Dialing Rules Are Not Followed When the Fax Wizard Is Used. Using the feature of Outlook to force International Dial Code to be attached in the export of each contact dialing record is explained here, but you have to alter the phone number entries to get it to work, and it doesn't solve the entire problem.

- KB 247192 - You Must Enter Telephone Numbers in Canonical Form in Order to Use Dialing Rules

- KB 310786 - Fax Client Dialing Rules Not Being Applied When Small Business Server 2000 Dials

- KB 197637 - Dialing 10-digit Local Calls. If you use neither, you can dial 10-digit numbers with SBS Fax regardless of what KB 197637 indicates. The problem is that some phone companies require area code in the number even if it is local phone number. In our service, country and area code will be dropped if it is local phone number.

In addition, try the online Help for SBS Fax.

Shared Fax Server Gets a Busy Signal

Occasionally, users send faxes to phone numbers that seem to be working correctly when you test them on a phone, but then get a busy signal when dialed by the Shared Fax server.

This seems to be caused by a mistake in the outgoing routing rule that controls the transmission of faxes to those numbers. To correct this problem, follow this procedure:

1. In the console tree of Shared Fax Service Manager, click **Rules**.
2. In the details pane, right-click the rule, and then click **Properties**.
3. Correct any mistakes in the configuration.

This problem also occurs when the user has added a zero before a local area code that would normally be used for non-computer-assisted telephone dialing. In addition, the user might have deviated from the canonical (that is, strictly adhered to) format. To correct this problem, retype the fax number in the following format:

[fax:+country/region_code space (area_code) space fax_number].

You must start and end with brackets and leave empty spaces only where shown. Include all other items exactly as in the following example:

[fax:+1 (818) 5551111]

The word "fax" must be followed by a colon, a plus sign (+), the country or region code, a space, the local area code in parenthesis, a space, and the phone number.

SBS Print as Fax doesn't support dialing rules

KB 310786 - SBS Fax Print as Fax doesn't itself support Dialing Rules

Notes:

Summary

In this chapter, I've covered several scenarios for advanced faxing techniques with SBS 2003, and shown some of the limitations of the SBS Shared Fax Service. I've also mentioned various ways you can route a fax, with pros and cons for each method. I hope you have learned how powerful the multiple line faxing capabilities inside SBS are, and that you can use them to "Wow!" your customers and win new business. When researching the features to write this chapter, I was surprised at the number of possible combinations and scenarios that I could have detailed, and had to choose from what I hope is a common subset that most of you would use for your customers. Definitely continue to explore what SBS 2003 can do for your customers—they will love you for it.

Section THREE
SBS 2003 SECURITY

CHAPTER 11
Advanced Security:
Part 1: General
BY Susan Bradley (Fresno, CA)

Before We Begin Our Journey....

"You must unlearn what you have learned. Already know you that which you need."

In the classic movie in the *Star Wars* series, *The Empire Strikes Back*[1], Yoda instructs Luke Skywalker on the power of the "Force" and tells him that it is used for "knowledge and defense, never for attack." Learning about security in a Small Business Server network is similar. You have to "unlearn what you have learned" and understand it yourself. You have to react in a calm knowledgeable manner. You have to learn to defend, to prevent, not to react. As my good friend Jeff Middleton put it so aptly, "You don't get security from a *Reader's Digest* version of a security manual; it's about administration and control."

My goal is not necessarily to give you the exact steps to secure a network, as there are no such things. There are no black-and-white answers I can give you as to how to properly secure your clients' network. When I joined the Center for Internet Security[2], an organization that through a consensus of government, private, and public entities sets benchmarks for computer settings, I was looking for these black-and-white answers. I soon realized that, given the differences in applications that we all run, there was no single template I could install, nor a checklist I could follow. I had to understand and make a decision about balancing the risks with what I needed my network to do. This chapter, therefore, is not a "how to" in the traditional sense. Rather, the goal here is to guide you to begin strategically looking at the entire network, examining potential threats, balancing the business needs with the security requirements of the firm, finding guidance along the way, and making sure you are proactive without being reactive. It is your job to navigate these threats, determine the best action for protection, examine and prioritize the options. I'm not going to "give you a fish," I'm going to "teach you to fish" to find the information and resources you need to keep ahead of the issues in security.

Our Roadmap

We'll review specific threats to the server and discuss specific remedies for these issues available at the present time. We'll look at the real weakness in the network: the vulnerabilities and lack of control of the desktops. We will develop techniques to allow you to review what you've set up and resources to utilize to keep you properly informed of security issues.

The Times, They Are A-Changin'

Before beginning the discussions related to security guidance, there is one fact that should be made perfectly clear. By the time you complete this chapter, the security issues facing your network or your clients' networks will have changed from what they are today. Security is a moving target and the spammers, virus, and malware writers will have moved the bar from what it is as I write this to what it is when you read this. Welcome to life on the Internet as we know it. What we consider to be relatively secure practices now, will not be tomorrow. Once upon a time, Windows NT was an operating system "good enough" and "secure enough" for businesses. In the years since its release, changes have been made to the NT code base to lower the threat exposure in the Windows 2003 server system, and even more changes are proposed in Windows XP sp2. In the future, more changes will need to be made and what is currently considered "best practices" will not be in the future. Be prepared for how you protect networks to change drastically in the coming years.

The next foundation I believe needs to be established is the idea of the Small Business Server as a platform that can indeed provide a certain level of security for small business clients. Go into the world of security gurus and researchers and if you announce that you run a Small Business Server network, they would probably look at you in horror. We break all of the traditional security rules. We cannot design our security by server role because our server does it all. We place our firewall on our domain controller and put our IIS Web server on our domain controller, our Exchange Server on our domain controller, and now with the 2003 version, our Sharepoint Services on our domain controller. "There are no complex systems that are secure. Complexity is the worst enemy of security, and it almost always comes in the form of features or options."[3] In other words, we do nothing to provide the "traditional and normal" method of defending our domain controller from the outside. Yet, in my years of tracking security events empirically in the Microsoft Communities[4], when we are "attacked" out on the Internet, it is because we are "roadkill." We stepped in the middle of the Information Superhighway straight in the path of a truck full of malware and worms and we got flattened. It is my opinion that we do not get specifically targeted by a "hacker"[5]; that is, we don't get "attacked," we get "stupid." When our servers get compromised in the Small Business Server world, it's because we haven't followed some pretty basic security guidelines.

It's a Compromise

When you install the Microsoft Small Business Server 2003 product into a firm, the word that should be utmost in your mind is "COMPROMISE." As Jim Harrison, Microsoft Software Test Engineer for ISA Server, once said, *"It, more than any product I know, embodies the common conundrum facing any IT manager: that of balancing cost/requirements/security."*

The Microsoft Small Business Server platform flies in the face of supposed "logical and sensible" security practices of separation of duties, yet as long as we follow certain best practices in the industry, we are typically in a better position than are larger-firm "brothers." This is because we are already fully installed into an active directory environment and thus have many more "control" tools at our disposal. But before we get into the tools we can use, let's discuss a bit of risk analysis as applied to the Small Business Server world.

While the Small Business Server platform CAN host a Web site, process e-mail, and provide file and printer sharing and remote connectivity, it's your job as the consultant to guide the client in accepting the risks, mitigating that risk, reducing the risk, or transferring the risk each one of these features and functions provide in a firm. The SBS consultant makes the same choices that larger firms must make when providing features and functionality bonded with Security. As in your own life choices, just because you "can" do something, doesn't mean you have to make the choice to do it. You can blend security and functionality and find a proper balance between the two.

Risk Analysis in a Small Business World

So let's begin the discussion with a bit of risk analysis and a pizza party. In the book, *Writing Secure Code*, by Howard and LeBlanc[6], they discuss the concept of "Threat Modeling." Before you begin to install and implement the SBS platform in your client's environment, you too should sit down and perform this analysis. As Howard and LeBlanc describe the process, it begins with ordering pizza and gathering together the people in the firm to discuss risk factors affecting an application. In the case of a small business, take the owner *and* another person — whom I would describe the "go-to" guy or gal — out for lunch. The go-to guy is the person in the office people "go to" to figure out their current issues with computers. In the process, this person has probably identified all of the current weaknesses in your current system. The go-to guy can help you identify where the true threats to the business lie, ranging from the sticky notes, the weak passwords, and the open back door that is propped open at the firm, to name just a few. Use this process to help identify and prioritize where your security dollars should be spent. Next, make a physical inspection of the computers at the firm, noting location, general handling of documents, media, and physical security. Discuss with staff the typical "security incidents" that they have had in the past. This can be as minor as misplacing floppy disks, not swapping tape drives, and not checking the backups to virus infections, improper set up of firewalls, and application rights. This risk-analysis process will help you understand that more of their risks are caused by our lack of understanding of the firm network and not properly protecting it from automatic attacks than it is from directly targeted attacks.

BEST PRACTICE: Use this process to get to know your client better and build a stronger relationship. You are building a "trusted advisor relationship" here.

Use the concepts that follow to begin your analysis of what is "best" for the firm. Identify the firm's "Security Evangelist." If the firm is too small to have such a role, you in your role as consultant must provide this proactive information.

BEST PRACTICE: Use newsletters (preferably e-mail) or RSS to push tips and notifications to your clients. Use your technical background to filter out the information into understandable data to your clients. Point out resources for e-mail hoaxes (snopes.com) and trusted Web sites for security information (like you). In your role as trusted advisor, be the "filter" for the barrage of daily security-related information.

LeBlanc and Howard use a concept called "STRIDE"[7] to identify threats to applications. Let's adjust it a bit to better fit the small business environment:

- Spoofing identity

- Tampering with data (also called integrity threats)

- Repudiation

- Information disclosure

- Denial of service

- Elevation of privilege

Use these concepts when designing a system for your SBS clientele:

- *Spoofing Identity*—This deals with the threat of someone illegally accessing and using a user's username and password—a real and true threat to the Small Business Server platform. A procedure called "SMTP auth attacks" is being used by mail spammers to authenticate on a system and then, as an "authenticated user," to relay mail from a server. This is a real and true threat to a SBS system and password security, which will be discussed later in this chapter. This concern should be stressed to the small business owner.

- ***Tampering with Data—Malicious Modification of Data.*** Typically in a small firm environment, not a great deal of attention is spent worrying about the security of data "inside the moat" until something occurs to make the owner concerned about inside threats. Discuss with your client any issues she may have had with this in the past, and suggest she may need to be more aware of this in the future. I would also add to this category the issue of modification of data without malicious intent by the party who downloaded or who was affected by the injection of spybot programs. Small firms typically do not take the time to be concerned about permissions and limiting access. While you may be able to trust your employees, you need to be aware that their computers may not be so trustworthy.

- ***Repudiation***—While repudiation in the computer world can mean issues and risks of proper authorization, in the small business world we can expand on that to mean anything from ensuring that file attachments are actually from the sender they purport to be from to the risks of adjusting permissions in a network to ensure that a device or service that the firm needs to operate is fully functional.

- ***Information Disclosure***—In firms bound by regulations such as HIPAA, GBL, contracts with governmental agencies, EU regulations, or in my personal situation, state laws, additional requirements may exist to ensure information retained inside our networks is not improperly disclosed. Discussing these requirements with your client is key is assisting them in setting up the proper balance of use versus security. Given the complexity in this area, I will provide resources for more information, but this chapter will not go into the detail necessary to determine your client's compliance with external security regulations. I expect more exposure in this area in the future and more industries will begin to regulate compliance.

- ***Denial of Service***—Protecting against denial of service threats in an SBS environment is best done by identifying the level of true "uptime" that your client needs. In a small business environment, he may not need, nor be able to afford, a true 99.999999 uptime. Thus many small businesses only have one ISP as their provider backbone. Looking at the risks and threats of loss of uptime from an internal standpoint will be discussed in Chapter 14 which addresses backup and restore plus disaster recovery.

- *Elevation of Privilege*—This is the classic buffer overflow issue that is best protected first and foremost by having a patch management system in place, and secondly, to a lesser degree, limiting the rights and permissions that a user has.

You've identified the potential risks — now what? In no business can you stamp out all risks. Life is filled with risks, but just like we manage the risk of driving a car by using a seat belt and ensuring the automobile is in good working condition, so too do we assign value to the risks we face in our small business networks. In the Microsoft literature they use an acronym called DREAD[8] to prioritize these risks which is summarized as follows:

Type of Risk	Highest	Lowest	Medium
Damage Potential	[3] The attacker or the "bad" code can get full system access and upload content— Example in the SBS space was unpatched servers being infected with "Code Red"	[2] Confidential information is leaked	[1] Minor information loss
Reproducibility	[3] Guaranteed to recur on a predictable basis	[2] Attack vector can be reproduced but only during a certain window of time	[1] Attack extremely hard to reproduce

Type of Risk	Highest	Lowest	Medium
Exploitability	[3] "Script kiddie" or novice computer coder would make the attack	[2] Skilled coder would need to "craft" the attack	[1] Extremely knowledgeable attacker would need in-depth knowledge to exploit
Affected Users	[3] Any user, any time	[2] Only affects some users	[1] Does not effect many users, very unusual
Discoverability	[3] Published vulnerability on the Web, port is open, feature is commonly used	[2] Feature is seldom used, port is not always open	[1] Flaw or bug is very unusual

After you ask the above questions, you need to total up the values (1–3) for a given threat. The result can fall in the range of 5 to 15. Then you can treat threats with overall ratings of 12–15 as high risk, 8–11 as medium risk, and 5–7 as low risk. Use this process to identify those areas in your Small Business Server client's network that need the most immediate security resources, and budget and those items that can be addressed at a later time.

In the small business world, we tend to use analogies to automobiles to best explain computer security. We ask, "Which would you rather be driving, a nice Honda or two Hyundais?" when referring to buying a good-quality server or having a duplicate, redundant server. Remember, just like buying a car, you can pay a little bit extra and get side impact airbags, or you can just live with what comes standard on the automobile. It's your choice of "layers of protection" and "defense in depth."

I will be the first to admit to you that it's not easy. The security information in the marketplace tends to be geared towards large corporations and not small networks. News reports tend to overstate the threats and do not discuss the mitigation that you may already have in place. This is why I'm a strong advocate of community resources like listserves and newsgroups[9]. They can assist you greatly in helping you cut through the "FUD" (fear, uncertainty, doubt) the news media will provide.

- *Action item*–*Perform a formal or informal risk analysis of your clients.*

Industry Pressures

You should then look to the type of data gathered and the industries that influence your clientele. In the United States, there are currently three major industry "pushes" to regulate security:

The health care industry. The Health Insurance Portability and Accountability Act of 1996 was enacted to protect personal health information (E-PHI). This data is required to be protected, logged, and secured. April 21, 2006, is the deadline for small health care plans.

The financial transactions industry. The Gramm-Leach-Bliley Act controls regulations that mandate the proper handling of financial transactions. While typically not affecting a small business firm, the Security and Exchange Commission has new audit guidelines that include analysis of Internal Control as it relates to Technology used in the firm. Called SOX 404 (for Sarbanes Oxley), these regulations may affect you if your small firm is a subsidiary of a larger company. In general all of these regulations require that "best practices" be put in place and certain items documented.

Government agencies. Does your small firm engage in business with a government agency? You may be required to follow governmental guidelines when working as a vendor with the agency.

You should also look to your local jurisdictional requirements for the handling of private confidential data. In the State of California where I live, Senate Bill 1386[10] requires that should unauthorized access occur to data containing two parts that could be deemed "identity" (i.e., names and social security numbers, names, and credit card numbers), and that data is not encrypted, the affected business would have to inform each and every affected customer. This could be a public relations disaster. Thus, setting up your network with security in mind is just good business. A new law, California Assembly Bill 1950[11], requires that we take *"reasonable precautions* (the law provides no definition of this term) *to protect personal information from modification, deletion, disclosure, and misuse."*

Some sample documentation and guidance I recommend in my role as small business consultant is to begin reviewing the following regulatory requirements:

HIPAA

- http://cms.hhs.gov/hipaa/hipaa2/readinesschklst.pdf

Gramm-Leach-Bliley

- Security Check: Reducing Risks to your Computer Systems: http://www.ftc.gov/bcp/conline/pubs/buspubs/security.htm

- Financial Institutions and Customer Data: Complying with the Safeguards Rule: http://www.ftc.gov/bcp/conline/pubs/buspubs/safeguards.htm

ISO 17799

- http://csrc.nist.gov/publications/secpubs/otherpubs/reviso-faq.pdf

Governmental engagements

- http://csrc.nist.gov/pcig/cig.html

SOX 404 (for small companies that are subsidiaries of publically traded companies)

- http://www.pcps.org/pdf/article_mike_ramos_01.pdf

- http://www.isaca.org/Template.cfm?Section=home&Template=/ContentManagement/ContentDisplay.cfm&ContentID=12406

Cross Border Privacy Issues

- http://www.itgi.org/Template_ITGI.cfm?Section=Security,_Control_and_Assurance&CONTENTID=5556&TEMPLATE=/ContentManagement/ContentDisplay.cfm

- EUROPA - Internal Market - Data protection - Data Protection Guide: http://europa.eu.int/comm/internal_market/privacy/guide_en.htm

This is certainly not a definitive listing of guidance for these areas and the documentation is typically not geared toward the small business marketplace. I would urge you to work closely with your clients if they are in one of these industries or are having these issues. In addition, either obtain the resources you need or find appropriate security consulting firms to help you be better informed.

> BEST PRACTICE: You may want to consider this area as a niche marketplace. If you find that you are gaining a reputation in a certain industry and are a consultant for an industry application, take the time to ensure you are informed about the issues affecting that industry. Look for electronic communities and list serves that may be sprouting up online to help you better serve your customers.

Remember that security is about saying "no," not saying "yes." One last issue you may need to keep in mind with your clientele is their comfort level with you. Firms must feel comfortable with your role as the outsourced network administrator who may have more rights and responsibilitites than they do. Security in a small firm is all about balance and choices.

Security Documentation

The security documentation for large firms—and even some for small firms—says to prepare a written security plan, to document that plan, and to plan for resources. With the exception of a few folks who work in accounting firms, most small businesses I know do not write up a security plan. Many times they don't recognize when they have a security problem, when, in fact, they do. Have they got a virus? That's not just a nasty e-mail, that's a security event in their network. Has their home page been hijacked by a nefarious Web search engine? That's also a security event. So when you sit down with your clients to discuss their needs for a secure system, remind them that anytime their computers are not doing what they want them to do and it's as a result of malicious software, they have a security event.

I'm going to assume that you've taken an inventory of the network and know the types of systems you need to support and protect. But if you haven't, that is your very first step. Use a form that you have developed, scripting, or some other means of finding out this information. Microsoft has some basic client information forms at http://download.microsoft.com/download/4/9/5/495fc532-421d-499e-9439-a68c871964b5/OTHER/CustomerProfile.pdf.

BEST PRACTICE: Take some time to review the power of Windows Scripting. For example, if you would like to identify the name and version number of the operating system currently in use on a computer, take the information below, type it into notepad (or a VBS script editor program), save the file as filename.vbs, and then click on that file. You will get back a Windows Script host response of the information from that computer. I would strongly recommend that you spend some time on the http://www.microsoft.com/technet/community/scriptcenter/default.mspx site or purchase the Windows 2000 Scripting Guide "Automating System Administration" by the Microsoft Windows Resource Kit Scripting team (Microsoft Press). More information can be found at the Web site http://msdn.microsoft.com/library/en-us/dnclinic/html/scripting06112002.asp.

```
strComputer = "."
Set objWMIService = GetObject("winmgmts:" _
 & "{impersonationLevel=impersonate}!\\" & strComputer & "\root\cimv2")
Set colOperatingSystems = objWMIService.ExecQuery _
 ("SELECT * FROM Win32_OperatingSystem")
For Each objOperatingSystem in colOperatingSystems
 Wscript.Echo objOperatingSystem.Caption, objOperatingSystem.Version
Next
```

Or consider tools like Bellarc's inventory advisor https://www.beitsmart.com/index.asp or Microsoft Software Asset Management: Microsoft Software Inventory Analyzer: http://www.microsoft.com/resources/sam/msia.mspx.

- *Action item*–*Prepare an inventory of your client's network and keep it up to date.*

Policy First, Technology Second

In taking an unscientific survey of accounting firms, I was surprised to find how many did not have an "Acceptable Employee Use" policy in place. If your client does not have an acceptable use policy that clearly defines what employees can and cannot do in a firm, you are in for trouble. Discuss with your client what he would deem to be acceptable use of that network. In my firm our policies specifically state that no peer-to-peer software is to be installed in the network—without exception—for two reasons: 1) recent reports show that up to 60% of the files on the peer-to-peer networks are malware, and 2) it introduces liability to the firm. Next discuss having policies regarding downloading of software and other practices. Assist your client is preparing a workable policy for his environment. Sample policies can be found at http://www.sans.org/resources/policies/ and should be tailored for your client and his specific needs.

Review e-mail retention policies with your client. The default setting for the Small Business Server 2003 is a 30-day deleted-item retention. Ensure your client understands that e-mail communication is "discoverable" by attorneys, and that he can help prevent getting caught off guard, by handling all e-mail in a timely and consistent manner. If the client has a policy that states all e-mail is to be deleted after 90 days, discuss adjusting the e-mail quotas or recipient mail policies to assist in enforcing this. If the regulatory environment requires retention of all e-mail, set up journaling and archiving to handle this process.

Make sure employees understand their e-mail and Internet can be monitored and reviewed by your client if that is his wish. Conversely, ensure that your client is complying with notification regulations in this area. Depending on the size of the firm, you may wish to confer with its human resource department or outside counsel to best craft this document.

- *Action item* – *Ensure your client has an acceptable use policy in place.*

123 Protect Your Network—The Basics Start Here

So let's begin reviewing how to make a more secure network: First, I'm going to assume that you would already have in place the absolute basics: *firewall, antivirus, and a patch management solution*. If your client does not have these in place, put this book down right now and go install those three basic protections.

Firewall

Your firewall device is already in place either through the use of the RRAS firewall provided by the Small Business Server standard version or the ISA server through the use of the Small Business Server Premium version. The choice of standard or premium versions should be your first decision as a consultant for the needs and requirements of your clients' systems. The ISA server provides additional granularity for reviewing more details of which Web sites were blocked and provides the owner of the firm the ability to restrict the use of the Internet by users on a more detailed level. While the RRAS firewall can block access, it is not on a "user" level and instead can only be controlled on a machine basis. In addition, the "community" that surrounds the ISA Server (www.isatools.org, www.isaserver.org) is very active in providing guidance, information, and, more important, tools to help you administer this powerful firewall.

With ISA server you can block and limit Internet access no matter where the employee may log on as the ISA server controls access by user name. You can also block access by "type" of content. More on ISA Server and the RRAS firewall will be covered in Chapter 12, but in general the guidelines for ISA can be found on the ISA community resources at ISAServer.org (which is ironically maintained by Dr. Thomas Shinder, the author of Chapter 12 in this book).

Additional guidance for blocking and limiting access can be found on ISA community resources such as:

- Controlling Outbound Access for Web Proxy Clients with Site and Content Rules: http://www.isaserver.org/articles/sitecontentssl.html

- Understanding and Configuring ISA content groups: http://www.isaserver.org/tutorials/Understanding_and_Configuring_ISA_content_groups.html

Many in the Small Business Server communities recommend a small hardware firewall on the outside, only opening up those ports you want to have open and forwarded on to the network card of the server. This mainly serves the purpose to "thin" the traffic in the log files and makes it a bit easier to see unusual activity.

But a firewall is, as Security Program Manager Michael Howard says, only a "speedbump." Because we do open up holes in the firewall to do what is necessary, we lower its effectiveness and need to ensure we have other mitigation in place.

Antivirus

Just as you would never drive a car without a seatbelt, never run a computer without an antivirus program. I also look to my antivirus program to add additional social engineering protection features, which include stripping off attachments that are, more often than not, viruses or software clients and users do not need to run. Whether Exchange or your antivirus program pulls off the attachments, determine your paranoia level and strip them off accordingly.

> BEST PRACTICE: Discuss with your client those files they MUST have via e-mail for business purposes. In my opinion, there is usually no need for employees to open up .exe, .pif. or .com files. If your client must send .zip files (zip files have been and still are file extensions used in infections) and wishes to block them at the server, either set up a Sharepoint portal for customers to use or train the computer users to do a simple trick: change the file extension to something like file.renamemetozip. Remind employees to only open up those attachments they are expecting. These days viruses are "spoofing" the senders. When in doubt, instruct the employees to call the sender.

> A little bit of paranoia goes a long way to help protect your client's network. Adjust the antivirus engine to check as often as every hour on the hour for updates. Do not rely on a "once a week" update, nor an antivirus software that requires the computer user to install the update. Ensure that the antivirus update is always done and always in the background.

I will also assume you will purchase an antivirus that covers the server, the workstations, and the e-mail. There are several vendors that support the Small Business Server platform and provide reasonable pricing for it. With the addition of Sharepoint, and in particular if you provide external access, you may want to provide increased protection for the entry point and obtain auxiliary antivirus that protects the Sharepoint database. However, if only authenticated users are allowed access to Sharepoint and you know the virus protection on those authenticated users, I would consider the virus protection adequate for Sharepoint and not obtain any additional software at this point.

Last But Not least—Patch Management

At the time of this writing, the latest version of the Software Update Service that will patch "all of the parts" of the systems and applications on the Small Business server is not yet completed. Thus the current SUS 1.0 version will patch only the Window operating system components in your network. In order to determine the patch needs for any other application in your network you next need the Microsoft Baseline Security Analyzer 1.2 or above to scan your network for patches. The bad news is you are still not able to have a "one tool scans all" for your network. MBSA at the present time misses DirectX and ISA Server and will not notify you of the needed patches for those software applications. Thus, until the next version of SUS (called in the press "Windows Update Service" or "Microsoft Update Service") comes out, you need to keep track of what is and is not covered on your own and either manually push out patches to affected machines or investigate other third-party patch solutions. Microsoft maintains a web site that provides links to the additional patches needed at http://www.microsoft.com/windowsserver2003/sbs/downloads/default.mspx. Discussions of other patch tools can be found at http://www.patchmanagement .org/comparisons.asp.

At the time of this publication, Windows Update does not properly protect your server and is not enough to keep you up to date on patches.[12] Windows Update does not patch ISA Server, SQL Server, Exchange Server, Office, etc. It only covers the Windows components. Thus, if all you have done is visit Windows Update, you are not protecting your client's servers and workstations properly.

As a consultant, I recommend all my clients be on top of security patches as they come out. Microsoft releases security bulletins on the second Tuesday of each month, unless there is an "out of band" security bulletin release. Sign up for security bulletins from Microsoft at http://www.microsoft.com/security/

bulletins/alerts.mspx or utilize a newsreader or RSS feed reader to receive them via RSS feed[13] http://www.microsoft.com/technet/security/bulletin/secrssinfo.mspx.

Once you have a tool, you must identify the process of protecting your client base. First, you must create a test environment to ensure a certain minimum of functionality is maintained after the patch has been applied. I have a copy of Small Business Server 2003 on my home system to replicate patch installation. I then use a process that I call "watching the communities." In the Small Business Server community, in the security communities via listserves, network administrators and Microsoft representatives will report on issues they have seen concerning patches. If you are supporting a mixed network of Macintosh, Linux distributions, and Microsoft, you may need to investigate additional resources of knowledgeable administrators who can share this type of "experience information."

> BEST PRACTICE: Set up a test network to which you can apply the patches before you apply them to your clients' networks. Attempt as best as you can to have those applications you are supporting also installed on your test network. If you are a reseller for a certain application, many times vendors allow you to install a copy of this software in your network, or they may have a low-cost NFR version of the software you can purchase. Microsoft provides this ability to its partners through the "Action pack" subscription available to Microsoft registered partners.

I purchased Shavlik.com's HfnetchkPro package several years back to assist me in pushing patches to both the network and the workstations, given that it includes scanning for all server applications I have installed. I first allow two machines in my office to obtain the patches automatically as they come out. These are my "canary" workstations; they let me know if the patches are safe to push out to the rest of the network. For the server testing, I perform the patch on a separate test server. At my workstation, on the day that I deem "patch day" in my office (after suitable testing phase as discussed below), I scan the network and push patches to all of the computers.

When I apply the patches to my server and my workstations, I begin to use a process of risk analysis to determine the timing of the patches. I don't believe in not applying a patch even if the underlying application is disabled in my network. For me, it's more a matter of timing. All patches will eventually get installed in my network.

I first read the bulletin I receive either via e-mail or RSS feed. I look at the application involved. If the bulletin contains the words "***run code of attacker's choice***" and is rated "***critical***," I'll take notice and keep reading. If it's rated only moderate or low, I can read that bulletin later on in the day. Next, if the bulletin indicates that there is a moderating factor in the operating system I am using, I won't put that security patch on the fast track.

For example, if the bulletin is patching Outlook Express in Windows 2003, I don't read e-mail at the server and thus will not place that bulletin in a "must do immediately" status. Conversely, if it affects Internet Explorer on the server and the mitigation is that the enhanced lockdown mode of IE means the issue is unlikely to occur on the server, again I can safely delay the rollout of that patch. But, conversely, those two programs may warrant that bulletin to be critical to me if I am looking at the threats to the desktop. Even though many Outlook, Outlook Express, and Internet Explorer vulnerabilities may need user interaction, I agree with the Microsoft Security Response Center's analysis that these types of issues warrant a higher threat potential, because my end users use these programs and depend on them.

Next, I look to see what the analysis of the possible threat is and what port may be used in an attack. If it is a port I have open, I will then test that patch on a test server—in my case a small network at home—or it can be a virtual server using VMWare or Microsoft's Virtual PC or Server product, able to be put in place pretty quickly. If I don't have the port open, then I can patch at a later time. I do not feel comfortable advocating a policy I call "patch only the absolute minimum." As we go forward with new methodologies of patching, including hot patches, delta patches, etc., there may be instances where I will go back to the old method of waiting for a service pack to patch my system and only do the bare minimum of patching.

Some vendors in the security industry recommend a method of mitigation, rather than of patching, but I do not think this is wise. In fact, there have been times when, based on my reading of the bulletins, I have pushed out patches to the server and workstations extremely quickly. It doesn't happen too often, but again, in the SBS community space where I "hang around," we will notify others regarding our "read" on an issue, and if we see that a security patch needs to be on a fast track, we will try to get the word out. Otherwise, you as a consultant can set the best time frame for patching with your client. Since the bulletins come out monthly, either a monthly or quarterly process might be the proper arrangement and provide you with the ability to connect with your client on a regular basis.

A sample bulletin is included in Figure 11-1.

Figure 11-1

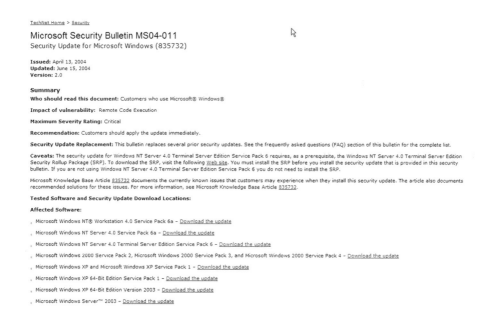

As you can see the information in the bulletin indicates this is a critical patch and needs pretty quick action. Reading the bulletin and clicking and expanding the section titled "Security update information" in Figure 11-2 makes it clear that this bulletin requires a reboot of the server. Thus you need to schedule the installation of this patch during offtime.

Figure 11-2

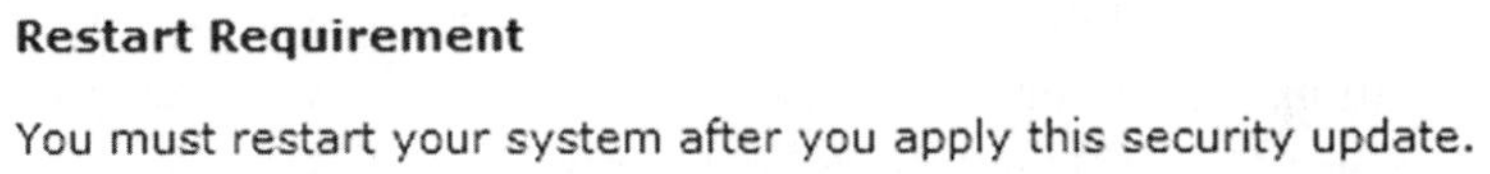

Restart Requirement

You must restart your system after you apply this security update.

Some consultants patch the "high risk" patches monthly, and then wait until the quarter to patch for "lower risk" patches. Several years ago the computer management community would wait until a service pack came out to apply these lower risk patches. These days, service packs are taking a long time between initial announcement and release (the length of time between XP sp1 and sp2 was approximately two years). My personal advice? Don't wait for service packs. Apply those security hotfixes when appropriate for your clients.

In general, my best results when patching have been when:

1. I am assured I have a backup. Consider an image of the drive before patching for any major patch.
2. I reboot the server prior to beginning the process of applying the patch. This assures me that the server is rebooting and functioning normally "before" the application of the patch.
3. I temporarily stop any services that might be getting a patch. So when applying an Exchange patch, I will manually shut off any service with the words "Microsoft Exchange" in it.
4. I assign a risk factor to that patch. Even with small networks, "zone" out the network and follow the practices of the large networks. I install and test them on my computers at home. I install and test them on a couple of computers inside the network at the office. I gather feedback and if everything appears to be running properly, I then apply the patches to the rest of the network within a day or two. Larger enterprises may "zone" a little more, patching perimeter machines first, then interior domain controllers. Since our "perimeter" in the Small Business Server world is pretty thin, once you have approved the patch, you may want to push the patch to all machines.

Remember that an issue caused by a security patch earns a free support call. Bottom line—determine the process that works the best for you and your clients.

- *Action item—Build in your own testing procedures for patches. Ensure that you are patching the server for ALL patches, and if you don't install Software Update Services, ensure that automatic updates are enabled on all workstations.*

But What If There Is No Patch?

Recently a security incident highlighted the problem of vulnerabilities for which there are no patches. In these cases, look to guidance on alternative actions. Blocking files and content, running desktops with lesser privileges are all ways to mitigate and protect if there is no patch. As we move forward, I predict we will need to perform more of these actions to stay one step ahead of the risks and threats out there.

Additional Patches Unique to the Small Business Server 2003 Platform

In addition to security patches, there are additional patches unique to the SBS platform. All critical but not security related patches are located at http://www.microsoft.com/windowsserver2003/sbs/downloads/default.mspx and can be downloaded from that site. Currently the site includes fixes for Sharepoint, Exchange 2003, Pop Connector, and tape backup issues. The page also includes a link for "Top Troubleshooting" issues. Bookmark these pages and review them on a regular basis for updates. Also, consider adding RSS feeds to either a feedreader or inside your sharepoint. Recent RSS feeds include "Top Small Business Server Downloads" and can be found at http://www.microsoft.com/windowsserver2003/sbs/community/default.mspx.

Back up, back up, back up

I will also assume that you have in place a backup mechanism. Whether tape backup or USB harddrive, everyone needs a cost-effective backup to ensure their data can be restored should something "bad" happen. I will assume that for your clients you have this base "minimum" already in place. As part of the risk analysis process, you may want to identify those core databases or documents that contain highly sensitive data and prepare a "checksum" on that data. Using a freely available tool, http://support.microsoft.com/default.aspx?scid=kb;en-us;841290, you can prepare a table of these checksums of critical data and then compare them to the data that you are restoring. A checksum is a unique mathematical number based on the data in the file. Change a bit or byte in that file and the checksum figure is changed. Thus, if you need a method to ensure data has not changed, for any reason, consider adding this process of "checksum" on your critical data.

In your position as the trusted advisor to your client, use this role to proactively recommend appropriate changes to their current infrastructure. Security of data is also subject to internal threats as well as external ones. Thus, don't "just" put uninterruptible power supplies on servers; identify those systems in your office that may need power protection as well. In my office, each workstation, each server has a UPS protecting that computer from immediate data loss due to power failure. Each workstation has its desktop productivity software set to make automatic backups on a regular basis.

Consider recommending "hot spares" or duplicates of other identified "mission critical hardware" such as hard drives, network cards, fax modems, controller cards, or any other devices. If your clients have purchased software assurance with their Small Business Server 2003 platform, they have the ability to load a server as a "cold server" and keep it onsite but offline until the need arises.

Realistic Security for a Small Firm

First off, the enemy of data and information contained in the computer system of a small firm is not the stereotypical body-pierced hacker with spiked hair that attends DefCon, the annual convention for hackers in Las Vegas every August. Your biggest threat to the data and information in that small firm is the owner of the company or the receptionist. Both are just trying to do their jobs and don't have the time to keep up with "best practices" nor the threats and risks on the Internet. It's up to you to begin the process of education and awareness.

BEST PRACTICE: Have a security awareness newsletter or include a "Security tip of the month" in your communication to your clients.

Passwords—The First Line of Defense

First and foremost, the most basic, security-strengthening starts with "passwords" or "passphrases." Ensure the passphrase is long, has both upper and lower case characters, and includes blank spaces, numbers, and Unicode characters (the upper level characters above the number keys). A passphrase such as "My favorite color is Purple!" would be difficult to crack.

While the password policy for Small Business Server 2003 is powerful, you may want to manually adjust the group policy settings the wizard performs. T o do so, open up the Group Policy console, prepare a new organizational unit, and adjust the settings to your and your client's liking. Information on creating a strong password policy can be found at http://www.microsoft.com/technet/ treeview/default.asp?url=/technet/prodtechnol/windowsserver2003/proddocs/ deployguide/dsscc_aut_xbby.asp.

The more the network has "open" to the outside, the stronger I make those settings. The less open to the outside the network is, the less restrictive I make those settings. This is very much a balance function, as passwords affect the end user more than anything else. Additional procedures to protect the password hashes on your network will be discussed later in this chapter.

> BEST PRACTICE: Discuss the timing for changing a password with your clients. In my office I try to do it in a fashion that works with our firm's work cycle. Remember the longer and more complex you make the password, the less often you need to make people change that password.

There are great tools I really favor for testing network passwords. I guess it's the fact I live in the agricultural region of California (the breadbasket of America) that I've come to appreciate the use of tools. Why? Because of the agircultural business didn't modernize with tools of production, the plow would still be pulled by a horse. You get the point. There are great tools in our profession. Use them! And now for those two tools to test network passwords:

- http://www.openwall.com/john

- http://www.atstake.com/products/lc/

Next, Look at the Network from an Overall Standpoint

Where is your Achilles heel or weak link? If your client still has to support Windows 98 as a platform in the firm, this severely restricts the ability for you to "tighten" the screws. Because Small Business Server 2003 and Windows 2003 is still having to support Windows 98 as a client, a couple of key "tweaks" to the server, which are currently not being done, could help it be a bit more "bullet proof." So your first item on the agenda is to migrate all the workstations to Windows 2000 and PREFERABLY Windows XP sp2 as soon as you can. Work closely with your client and help him work with vendors to ensure applications will work on Windows 2000 or XP. I still hear of applications that must be run on Windows 98 because the application is written poorly.

> BEST PRACTICE: I will discuss the practice of penetration testing and reviewing the external open ports of the server in a later section. However, I feel we put too much emphasis on the external issues and not enough on the internal ones. Be a consultant who doesn't use "FUD"—fear, uncertainty, and doubt"—to sell to your client. Remember, your goal is to become the "trusted advisor" to your client.

Changing the Administrator Account

One of the best practices is to change Administrator account on workstations and ensure that laptop computers do not match up their local Administrator account passwords with the domain. Should your laptop get stolen, as is unfortunately an all-too-common circumstance, that laptop contains quite a bit of information that could be used to gain access to and compromise your network. Once someone has obtained unauthorized physical custody of your laptop, make sure you change passwords in the office, as it would be extremely easy for someone to obtain passwords from that laptop. Thus consider laptops to be a security risk and assign them additional protection features. While you can and should change the Administrator password to something long, strong, and hard to break (think of passphrases), renaming the account itself is generally not recommended by the product support teams for the Small Business Server platform.

To change the local Administrator password for a machine in the network, you can use the following script or the group policy (this will be discussed later in this chapter as well):[14]

```
strComputer = "MyComputer"
Set objUser = GetObject("WinNT://" & strComputer & "/Administrator, user")
objUser.SetPassword "testpassword"
objUser.SetInfo
```

- *Action item*—*Change the Administrator password on the server.*

- *Action item*—*Change the entire account on laptops and highly sensitive machines (editing out even the description).*

LAN Manager and NTLM

LM authentication is an older challenge/response for network logons. NTLM version 2 has been available since Windows 2000 SP4 and improves the authentication and security mechanisms.

If you are not supporting Unix or Macintosh clients, you can use NTLMv2 which will increase the security surrounding the password hashes. Passwords are not stored on the server, but hashes are. It is the protection of these hashes that can be increased by the use of NTLMv2 and passphrases longer than 14 characters. Keep in mind that greater than 14 character passphrases will cause issues in a mixed environment of NT, 2000, and 2003 machines.

For reference, the full range of values for the LMCompatibilityLevel value supported by Windows NT 4.0 and Windows 2000 include:[15]

- Level 0—Send LM and NTLM response; never use NTLM 2 session security. Clients use LM and NTLM authentication, and never use NTLM 2 session security; domain controllers accept LM, NTLM, and NTLM 2 authentication.

- Level 1—Use NTLM 2 session security if negotiated. Clients use LM and NTLM authentication, and use NTLM 2 session security if the server supports it; domain controllers accept LM, NTLM, and NTLM 2 authentication.

- Level 2—Send NTLM response only. Clients use only NTLM authentication, and use NTLM 2 session security if the server supports it; domain controllers accept LM, NTLM, and NTLM 2 authentication.

- Level 3—Send NTLM 2 response only. Clients use NTLM 2 authentication, and use NTLM 2 session security if the server supports it; domain controllers accept LM, NTLM, and NTLM 2 authentication.

- Level 4—Domain controllers refuse LM responses. Clients use NTLM authentication, and use NTLM 2 session security if the server supports it; domain controllers refuse LM authentication (that is, they accept NTLM and NTLM 2).

- Level 5—Domain controllers refuse LM and NTLM responses (accept only NTLM 2). Clients use NTLM 2 authentication, use NTLM 2 session security if the server supports it; domain controllers refuse NTLM and LM authentication (they accept only NTLM 2).

Currently the Small Business Server 2003 is set to Level 2—Send NTLM authentication only. However, with full Windows 2000 SP4 and XP machines, or if you obtain the Windows 98 active directory client, you can tighten up the security by changing the Group Policy setting (see Figure 11-3) to Level 3 and you might even test if you can go as high as Level 4.

Notes:

Figure 11-3

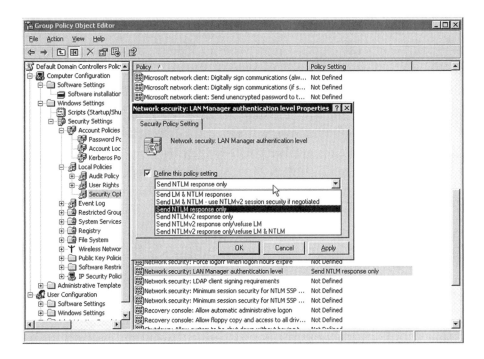

Then obtain the following free hotfix from Microsoft: http://support
.microsoft.com/default.aspx?scid=fh;[LN];CNTACTMS 323466—Availability
of the Active Directory client extension update for Windows 98: http://support
.microsoft.com/default.aspx?scid=kb;en-us;323466 and then add the following
registry key on the Windows 98 clients to force them to use NTLMv2:

HKEY_LOCAL_MACHINE\System\CurrentControlSet\Control\Lsa (you may
need to create the Lsa key)

Value Name: LMCompatibility

Data Type: REG_DWORD

Value: 3

To ensure that upon the "next" password change no LAN Manager hashes (the
older, backwards-compatible, easier-to-break password hashes) are saved on
your network, change the group policy setting as follows:

Method 1: Implement the NoLMHash Policy by Using Group Policy[16]

To disable the storage of LM hashes of a user's passwords in the local computer's SAM database by using Local Group Policy (Windows XP or Windows Server 2003) or in a Windows Server 2003 Active Directory environment by using Group Policy in Active Directory (Windows Server 2003), follow these steps:

1. In Group Policy, (see Figure 11-4) expand **Computer Configuration**, expand **Windows Settings**, expand **Security Settings**, expand **Local Policies**, and then click **Security Options**.

2. In the list of available policies, double-click **Network security: Do not store Manager hash value on next password change**.

3. Click **Enabled**, and then click **OK**.

Figure 11-4

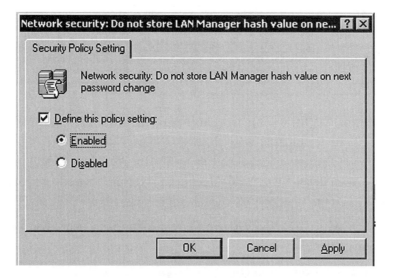

Method 2: Implement the NoLMHash by Merely Using Long Passphrases

But the simple way to stop the storing of LANMan hashes is to just use a password that is 15 characters or longer. Going over the 14 character limit immediately stops LANMan hashes from being stored on the server.

You may need to check compatibility with printers or other third-party devices when attaching to the Small Business Server 2003 network after "tightening up" security settings. In my office with a Konica copier/scanner I was able to put in place all these security settings and leave SMB signing enabled. Before making changes in the group policy, be sure you understand what you are doing and know the proper document the setting.

- *Action item*—*Enable NoLMHash*

Biometric and Smart Cards

Depending on the organization, you may want to investigate the addition of biometric and smart cards. In high-security environments, a smart card is typically added as the log in authentication device on the domain controller. In small firms, the cost of these devices should be compared to the risks that are considered being mitigated. Additional physical protection of the computer room may be enough protection for the typical small business client. RSA Security recently began offering secure tokens in bundles of 10 keyfobs for the small business marketplace.

Guidance for Additional "Hardening" Techniques

As stated before, the Small Business Server 2003 platform is an exercise in compromise. As a member of the Center for Internet Security, I assist in a benchmark-setting process that sets recommendations for "legacy, enterprise, and high-security" levels of guidance for operating systems. SBS 2003 "out of the box" already shuts off many services that it does not use or need for its base functions[17]. Thus IMAP and POP (for external pop connections) are turned off by default. The Windows 2003 domain controller guidance can be used as a guideline, but remember, for any adjustment from the "default," you must test first. Applications are notorious for not documenting which services they rely upon to function properly. Thus test, test, test, back up, and document what settings you are changing before you begin the process of adjustment. Keep in mind that the templates put out by the security industry are not "built" for Small Business Server, you must be sure that when you read these documents, you understand them fully before you begin to make changes and/or apply security templates. With the SBS 2003 platform, I would adjust the server to NTLMv2, as was discussed earlier, and move Exchange to native mode. But I would probably not make too many further adjustments to the security templates on the server without a clear need or compliance reason. Too many adjustments are needed on the workstations first before even beginning to touch the server. The group policy security settings for high security are for military situations only and are too extreme for most businesses. It's not even recommended to run the new Windows 2003 sp1 Security Configuration Wizard on SBS as it has not be designed for the platform.

The documents you can review for more information include the Microsoft Windows Server 2003 Security guide http://www.microsoft.com/downloads/details.aspx?FamilyID=8a2643c1-0685-4d89-b655-521ea6c7b4db&displaylang=en and the Microsoft Threats and Countermeasures guide http://www.microsoft.com/downloads/details.aspx?FamilyId=1B6ACF93-147A-4481-9346-F93A4081EEA8&displaylang=en

To change Exchange 2003 to native mode, follow Microsoft Knowledge base article 829577—Mixed mode vs. native mode in Exchange Server 2003: http://support.microsoft.com/default.aspx?kbid=829577. Since we are typically only supporting one Exchange 2003 server, after any migration is complete, there is no clear reason to stay with "mixed" mode. However, it is a one-way conversion, so as with any change to a system, ensure you have a tested backup or image in place.

> BEST PRACTICE: Do not use your client as a guinea pig. Test this "tweaking" as best you can before making changes to your client's system and always ensure you have a backup or image and you document EXACTLY what you are changing before you change the settings. You can get into extreme difficulties if you begin to make changes to a system and don't understand the consequences.

The rule of the security industry is simplicity, not complexity, and yet, with our "all eggs in one basket" design, the platform flies in the face of that. Michael Howard, in his discussion of Windows 2003, talks about the changes made to the platform to reduce the threat level[18]. Because we place Exchange, ISA server, and Sharepoint on our networks, we do raise this threat level. Yet I would argue that in my network, the main place where my security vulnerabilities lie is on my workstations. More on this later on in the chapter.

- *Action item—Change Exchange to Native Mode*

Identify Procedures for the Openings in the Wall

As you ran the "Configure e-mail and Internet connection wizard" in the to do list of the small business server, you specified certain services you wanted to have operational from the "outside." Figure 11-5 is the first view of your choices in the firewall selections and Figure 11-6 shows the second set of selections.

Figure 11-5

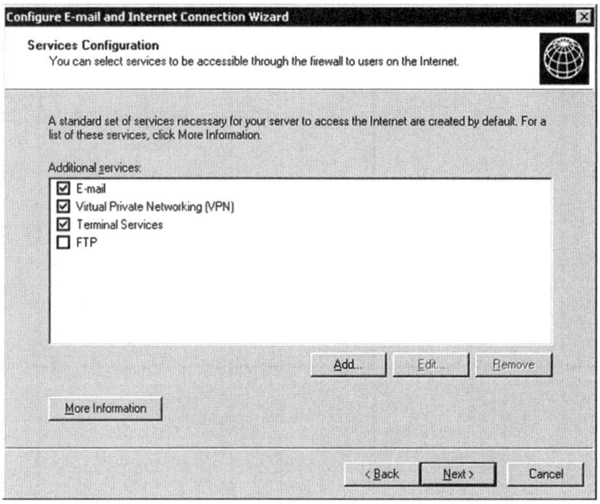

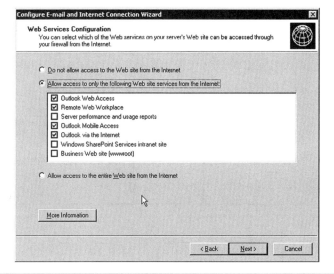

Figure 11-6

Depending on those items you chose, you opened up openings in your firewall (these will be discussed in more detail below):

Services checked in CEICW	Port opened	Web page published	Threat potential	Issues seen in SBS Land
E-mail	25 – Exchange Server internal and external e-mail transfer	n.a	SMTP auth attacks, reverse NDR attacks	Yes, remedies discussed below
Virtual Private Networking [VPN]	1723 – using PPtP	n.a	Same threat level as password, thus don't forget complex passwords here as well	No. Only one vulnerability has specifically been designed to do a denial of service on this port (CAN-2002-1214) and the vulnerability was patched in 2002.
Terminal Services	3389 – remote connection to the server	n.a	TSGrinder can be used to crack passwords	No, as Terminal Server in application mode on SBS2003 is not allowed
FTP	21 – Internal/ External file transfer	n.a	If set up without a password, server used as music and peer to peer host	Yes. Ensure that anonymous FTP access is never set up on your server
Outlook Web Access	80 – nonsecure browser access to IIS webs443 – secure browser access to IIS Webs	Yes	If server is unpatched, worms can infect Web server	Historical issues in the past, however IIS 6.0 has been rewritten, can choose to block port 80 and train users to use https:// to access

Services checked in CEICW	Port opened	Web page published	Threat potential	Issues seen in SBS Land
Outlook via the Internet (RDP)	80—nonsecure browser access to IIS webs443—secure browser access to IIS Webs	n.a.	If server is unpatched, worms can infect Web server	Sasser worm affected 443 port but Windows 2003 was unaffected
Remote Web Workplace	4125—access to client Web site and enables external OWA access to Exchange	Yes	Unauthorized access if password is guessed, but the reality is you will see user lockouts before this occurs	No
Server Performance and Usage Reports	80—nonsecure browser access to IIS webs443 - secure browser access to IIS Webs	Yes	Disclosure of Information if username/password is guessed	No
Outlook Mobile Access	80—nonsecure browser access to IIS Webs443—secure browser access to IIS Webs	Yes	If server is unpatched, worms can infect Web server	See notes regarding port 80 and 443
Windows Sharepoint Services Intranet site	444 - Internal and external access to Sharepoint	Yes	Disclosure of information if permissions are not set properly	No
Business Web Site	80—nonsecure browser access to IIS Webs	Yes	If server is unpatched, worms can infect Web server	Historical issues on port 80 in the past; however, IIS 6.0 has been rewritten

While the above table reflects the standard ports opened up in the Small Business Server platform, there are additional ports that you can open for access and services as listed below:

Additional manual port openings you may make	Port opened	Web page published	Threat potential	Issues seen in SBS Land
External Pop Connection	` `	n.a.	Username and password travel in clear text	No—would normally take someone sniffing wired or wireless connections
Time Synchronization	123 UDP	n.a.	n.a.	W32 time service may be disabled due to "broadband option" chosen during CEICW
IMAP 4	143 Allows for inbound connections to IMAP 4 clients	n.a.	Username and password travel in clear text	No – would normally take someone sniffing wired or wireless connections
IMAP 3	220 Allows for inbound connections to IMAP3 clients	n.a.	Username and password travel in clear text	No—would normally take someone sniffing wired or wireless connections
IPSec	500—external VPN connections using IPSec	n.a.	Increasing scans on this port	No

Additional manual port openings you may make	Port opened	Web page published	Threat potential	Issues seen in SBS Land
L2TP VPN Connection	1701 – L2TP VPN connections	n.a.	Low port scans	No
IPSec	4500 – IPSec Internet Key Exchange {IKE} Network Address NAT transversal	n.a.	Low port scans	No
SQL	1433 /1434	n.a.	SBSers don't open up their SQL server for direct connections	Threat on the Internet, not a threat to SBSers due to our licensing

Securing Our Servers

Here are some additional steps you can take over and above what the wizard does to provide a little bit more security:

Steps for Securing SMTP

Recently the Small Business Server network has been most affected by SMTP attacks by spammers. As a result, your first line of defense should be to ensure that your passwords are complex and alphanumeric. If you are still seeing excess connections to your virtual SMTP connectors, you may find yourself being attacked by spammers using a Reverse NDR attack method. An excellent resource for choosing passwords is the Dr. Jesper Johansson's series on passwords found on the Microsoft TechNet site.[19]

While the Exchange and Outlook chapter will go over this in more detail, in general you want to shut off all unnecessary external connections from your server. Don't send out antivirus notifications, nondelivery reports, or any other unneeded transmissions. The steps outlined below basically shut off all unnecessary outbound e-mail transmissions from your e-mail server. Disallow all "out of office" responses that not only are unnecessary, but also disclose vital information about your firm. These could be used in "social engineering attacks." I personally have been amazed at the amount of detailed contract information that I can obtain in posting e-mails to listserves. The out of office messages that come back to me often have phone numbers, names of people to contact, and other vital information that someone doing a "social" attack could use to pretend to already have confidential information about your firm and thus be a trusted vendor.

In article 324958, check out the section entitled "Clean Up the Exchange Server's SMTP Queues" for the steps you can use to clean up the queue(s).

324958.KB.EN-US HOW TO: Block Open SMTP Relaying and Clean Up Exchange Server SMTP http://support.microsoft.com/default.aspx?scid =KB;EN-US;324958

In general to disable unnecessary outbound e-mail traffic, follow these steps: In Exchange System Manager, expand the **global settings,** double-click on **Internet Message Format**, then on default and click on the **Advanced Tab**.

- ***Action Item**—Disallow all outbound unnecessary e-mail such as:*
  - *Out of office responses*
  - *Automatic replies*
  - *Automatic forward*
  - *Delivery reports*
  - *Nondelivery reports*
  - *Continue to Allow:*
    - *Preserve sender's display name on message.*
    - *See Figure 11-7 for details*

Notes:

Figure 11-7

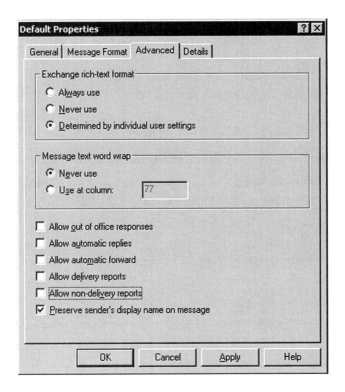

Notes:

*In the next section for Message Delivery, right-click on **Properties**, and on the tabs to ensure the following are selected:*

> *Sender Filtering Tab*
> > *Filter messages with blank sender*
> > *Drop connection if address matches filter*
> > *See Figure 11-8 for details*

Figure 11-8

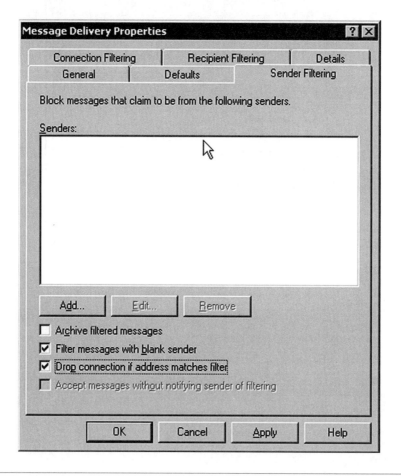

Recipient Filtering Tab
  Filter recipients who are not in the directory
  See Figure11-9 for details

Figure 11-9

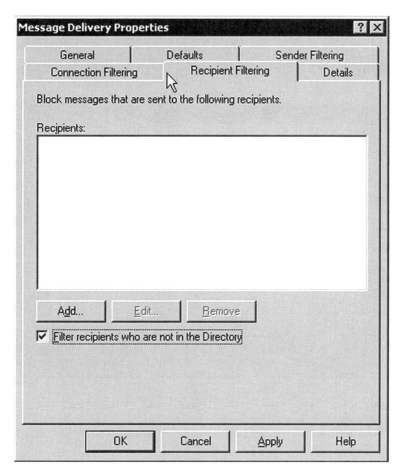

Now click on **Server**, *expand your server name, and click under* **Protocols**. *Find* **Default SMTP server**, *right-click on* **Properties** *and under the* **General** *tab, select* **Advanced**, *and then* **Edit** *(all unassigned):*

Apply Sender Filter
Apply Recipient Filter
Apply Connection Filter
See Figure 11-10 for details

Figure 11-10

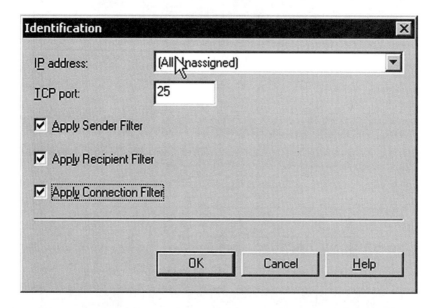

Notes:

Messages Tab
    Send copy of NDR reports is blank
    See Figure 11-11 for details

Figure 11-11

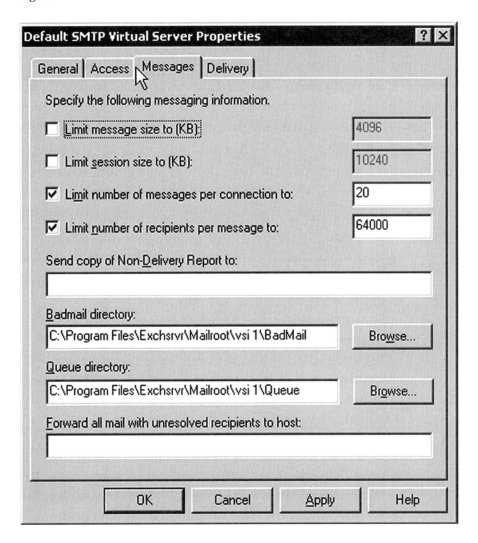

Ensuring that all unnecessary outbound traffic is disabled will help a great deal in securing your mail server.

- **Action item** – *Secure your mail server.*

Terminal Server

While we can no longer do Terminal Server in Application mode on our domain controller, we still have the ability to have remote control over port 3389. A tool called TSgrinder [20] has been used in the past to brute-force break the password on the Administrator account. It's a relatively minor task to rename the password. If you like a bit more "security via obscurity," you can even set up a duplicate account that appears to be the Administrator account (including the detailed description); but only assign this account the lowest level of user rights on that domain. However, it's recommended to ensure all functionality of third-party programs and wizards to rename only Administrator accounts on workstations and especially on laptops.

To rename the Administrator accounts on all the computers in the domain via Group Policy, follow the "how-to" inside the help file on the server:

To complete this procedure, you must be logged on as a member of the Domain Admins security group.

1. Begin by opening **Server Management**.
2. Click **Advanced Management**, right-click **Group Policy Management Console** (GPMC), then click **Add forest**.
3. In the **Add forest** dialog box, enter the domain name. When prompted **Do you want to add this forest with this domain?**, click **Yes**.
4. In the **GPMC** tree, click **Forest:*/ForestName/***, click **Domains**, right-click **/DomainName/,** then click **Create and Link a GPO Here**.
5. In the **New GPO** dialog box, in the **New** box, type the name that you want to use for this policy (for example, Rename Administrator account), then click **OK**.
6. In the **GPMC** tree, click **Group Policy Objects** located under the **Windows Small Business Server** domain name, right-click the **Rename Administrator account Group Policy object** you created, then click **Edit**.
7. In **Group Policy Object Editor**, click **Computer Configuration**, click **Windows Settings**, click **Security Settings**, click **Local Policies**, then click **Security Options**.
8. In the details pane, double-click *Accounts: Rename Administrator account*.

9. Select the **Define this policy setting** check box, then type the new name for the Administrator account.

10. Click **OK**, and then close **Group Policy Object Editor**.

11. Close the **Group Policy Management Console**.

12. After changing the Administrator account name, you must log off, then use the new name to log back on as an Administrator on the server.

To open **Server Management**, click **Start**, then click **Server Management**. To change the name back to Administrator for the account, repeat the preceding procedure. To revert to the Administrator account, do not disable the **Rename Administrator Account Group Policy**; instead, change the name back to "Administrator" using the GPMC tool, and then clear the **Accounts: Rename Administrator Account** check box. After the system updates the information, disable the **Rename Administrator Account Group Policy**.

One more piece of advice you might follow on the server is to make sure the description for the Administrator account is also changed. As Dr. Jesper Johannson, a Security Program Manager at Microsoft reminded in a Webcast[21], just because you changed the name of the account, if the description still reads "Built-in account for administering the computer/domain," it's still an indicator that you renamed the account. When setting up the "bogus" Administrator password account, be sure to add this same description to that field. Again, be sure to test this in a lab setting before making such changes to production systems.

File Transfer Protocol

Small Business Server administrators who opened up their servers to anonymous FTP access will soon find themselves hosting the latest JLo or Britney dance tune. Many times the only way to remove the file is to boot into safe mode. Even with authenticated FTP, the username and password travel in clear text. You may wish to investigate the use of ISA, VPN, and Sharepoint or using WebDav to provide you more secure options in large file transfers to your site. Additional guidance can be found at http://support.microsoft.com/default.aspx?scid=kb;en-us;310110 and at http://support.microsoft.com/default.aspx?scid=kb;en-us;Q323470.

Outlook Web Access, Outlook over HTTP, and Any Other Application that Transfers over the Nonsecure Browser

Historically, as long as you patched for software vulnerabilities with the vendor-recommended patch within a reasonable period of time, you were protected and stayed safe. Remember how I called us in SBS land "roadkill"? A lot of that "roadkill" was due to our stupidity of not performing regular maintenance on our boxes. In recent times, the number of days between release of security bulletins and the release of exploit, which in turn morphed into a worm, has gotten shorter and shorter. If you control and secure a number of computer networks, you might not have enough time to get to a network before the worm hits. Therefore, you must develop some sort of battle plan. Triage your clients and shut unneeded down ports. You can honestly still have nearly full functionality in a Small Business Server 2003 network and not have the www port (port 80) open from the outside. By either adjusting the ISA or RRAS firewalls to block port 80, you then merely inform your clients to type in **https:/ /** rather than **http://** for their remote connectivity. Historically, the www port has been a popular port to target, whereas port 443 has not. Again, discuss the strategy with your client and proceed accordingly.

Web Site and Remote Web Workplace

Google has been said to be the hacker's best friend. Perform a search for c:\inetpub and you are looking at Microsoft Web servers that a hacker can target. In the Small Business Server world, we have our own "brand identifier." Enter the phrase "Remote Web Workplace" in a Google search (or any other search engine) and you will locate businesses that have left their remote portal open for search engines to find. While security by obscurity should not be your only defense, there is a way to exclude your site from being "Googled" if you accidentally chose to "open up your entire Web site" when running the wizard. More information and tips and tricks into securing or limiting the use of Remote Web Workplace by users in the office can be found in Chapter 8 written by Wayne Small from Australia.

Alan Billarz of the Small Business Server development team offered the following files to help "hide" your Small Business Server from Google's robots.

1. robots.txt — Allows a search of your business Web site, but hides SBS-specific sites from search robots.

2. robots2.txt — (Must be renamed to robots.txt) Denies search of your entire Web site.

For more information, check out these sources:

http://www.robotstxt.org/wc/robots.html

http://www.searchtools.com/robots/robots-txt.html

http://www.searchengineworld.com/robots/robots_tutorial.htm

Many Web sites implement this functionality. For example, you can check out http://www.cnn.com/robots.txt.

1. robots.txt

```
# Place this file at the root of the Default Web Site (%system drive%\inetpub\wwwroot)
# to allow search engines to catalog your Business Web site, but not catalog the other
# SBS-specific Web sites.
#
# Note that you must choose to publish the root of your Web site to allow the search
# engine robot to read this file. In the Configure E-mail and Internet Connection Wizard
# choose to publish Business Web site (wwwroot)

User-agent: *
Disallow: /_vti_bin/
Disallow: /clienthelp/
Disallow: /exchweb/
Disallow: /remote/
Disallow: /tsweb/
Disallow: /aspnet_client/
Disallow: /images/
Disallow: /_private/
Disallow: /_vti_cnf/
Disallow: /_vti_log/
Disallow: /_vti_pvt/
Disallow: /_vti_script/
Disallow: /_vti_txt/
```

2. robots2.txt

```
# Place this file at the root of the Default Web Site (%system drive%\inetpub\wwwroot)
# to prevent all search engines from cataloging your Web site.
#
# Note that you must choose to publish the root of your Web site to allow the search
# engine robot to read this file. In the Configure E-mail and Internet Connection Wizard
# choose to publish Business Web site (wwwroot)

User-agent: *
Disallow: /
```

- *Action item—Block robots from searching your Web site.*

- *Action Item—Don't open up your entire Web site in the first place.*

Sharepoint, the New Kid on the Block

Port 444 is being "borrowed" by Sharepoint because Outlook Web Access wouldn't share space on 443. It is currently identified on www.incidents.org on their database of ports as being the home of simple network-paging protocol and currently is not a source of major traffic. Sharepoint depends on the choice of either IIS Security and WMSDE (a special version of MSDE which is discussed in Chapter 7 on Windows Sharepoint Services and is not limited to the 2 gig limit that MSDE is) or IIS and SQL server, depending on the implementation of Small Business Server you choose, standard or premium.

When you use the SQL server implementation of Windows Sharepoint Services, you use the Windows Authentication method that utilizes the Windows NT Integrated authentication method. You connect to SQL server using the IIS application pool. The alternative authentication method for SQL server (which is not the default) is using the SQL server authentication (SA Auth). Using this method, the password for the Administrator account is sent over the network and can be (and HAS been) detected to be a method of vulnerability.

To allow for anonymous authentication for externally available public sites, you will have to turn on anonymous authentication within IIS as well. In Small Business Server Standard, this is performed by running the Configure e-mail and Internet connection wizard and following the documentation in the Whitepaper at http://download.microsoft.com/download/1/7/6/176c5f1e-a0a1-4d10-81f6-42283327617e/PublishWSS.doc. Be sure you have followed the steps to disallow local logon access in part 6d of the document.

In the premium version, the addition of ISA server adds more steps to allow for external access for authenticated users: How to publish http://Companyweb to the Internet by using ISA Server 2000 on a server that is running Windows Small Business Server 2003, Premium Edition: http://support.microsoft.com/?kbid=838304.

- *Action item—Be sure that you have blocked local log on for anonymous access of Sharepoint users.*

POP Protocol

If you manually adjust the server to allow for external POP connection from the outside understand that the username and password are being transmitted in clear text. Load up a copy of "Snort"[22] and sniff the traffic on your system. You will be amazed and the information transmitted. There have been various vulnerabilities in some POP programs, but no security issues of any note have surfaced on the Small Business Server platform.

Time Service

The w32time service uses port 123 via UDP (a connectionless protocol that does not wait for a syn/ack like tcp) to synchronize with an external source. At this time, no threats have been seen on this port.

IMAP

The ports used in IMAP 3 and 4 (port 143 and 220) have not been a major threat vector in the past, but nevertheless, because the service is tied to the use of e-mail and requires username and password authentication, you should always ensure that the passwords chosen per network are strong.

IPSec Stuff

Let's face it, typically in a small business network, we tend not to use the higher-priced security protocols like IPSec. Usually we are on a budget, we tend to have older, mixed systems and thus cannot support the newer/newest protocols. In the past there have been some vulnerabilities in the CISCO implementation of their IPSec (CAN-2002-1103), but as of this writing it is not seen as a real target in a SBS network. I am seeing more consultants begin to implement IPSec in VPN connections.

L2TP

Like the IPSec port vulnerabilities, port 1701 used for L2TP hasn't been one the Small Business Server world typically has opened up and utilized. Again, this too is not seen as a real target in a SBS network.

IPSec

Typically, port 4500 has not been a used port in the past, again due to the budgetary and mixed network issues mentioned. This port is not seen as a real target at this time.

SQL Server

Last but not least we have ports 1433/1434. These ports are used by SQL slammer for data control and transfer. Historically these have not been a huge security risk in the Small Business Server world for one major reason: We weren't licensed to host databases that opened up like this. Thus, this is the best example of the argument: "If you don't use it, don't open it up and you won't get nailed." When SQL Slammer or Sapphire made me unable to complete my eBay purchase on a Friday night in January at about 9:30 Pacific Standard Time (yes, I know exactly what I was doing when that worm hit the Internet), it really didn't cause too much of a fuss in the Small Business Community.

Staying Informed

So that's all you need to know how to secure your server, right? Wrong. We've just looked at some steps to take on only part of your network. Furthermore, these are our current issues, right now, this very moment as I'm writing this chapter. Tomorrow, our threats will be completely different. So how can you stay aware of the potential issues facing your Small Business Server networks? By staying informed. The CERT Web site tracks known vulnerabilities by the port that the exploit attacks: Ports Associated with Known Vulnerabilities and Exploits: http://www.us-cert.gov/current/services_ports.html. Another excellent site for staying informed of security issues is the Web site http://www.incidents.org. Their daily diary of Web events keeps me informed of the latest issues I am facing. I advise you to sign up for their RSS—which stands for "really simple syndicate"[23]—feed of their daily reports. RSS is a relatively new technology based on a standard XML format and can be pulled into your Outlook by using readers from Newsgator[24] or IntraVnews[25]. It can even be pulled into Sharepoint using a number of Web part readers, including SmilingGoats Feed reader[26]. I'd also recommend reading additional security books such as the one by Ben Smith,

David LeBlanc, and Kevin Lam, *Assessing Network Security (Pro-One-Offs)*, Microsoft Press, and an upcoming book by Dr. Jesper Johansson and Steve Riley, *Protecting your Windows Network*, published by Addison Wesley.

- **Action item** – *Stay informed with security bulletins.*

In Conclusion

When you are looking for an easy answer on the ways to best secure and protect your server, follow this advice: If you don't use it, don't open it. It's that easy. But if it's open, patch it. Monitor it.

The Rest of the Network–Where the Real Security Threats Are

So, we're done right? All we need to worry about is the security of the server, right? Hardly, we've barely begun our examination of the risks to the network.

We've barely begun the process of locking down our networks. As I am writing this chapter in Summer of 2004, we are currently fighting off as many attacks attempting to intrude on our computer workstations as we are defending our servers.

User Mode

Where small businesses need the most help and guidance, in my opinion, is in the area that provides the most "bang for the buck" in securing a network. We need to make computer users in our networks truly computer "users." In any computer, there are three levels of rights: "user or restricted user," "power user," and "administrator." If your users can load software on your Windows 2000 or XP computer at any time, your systems are running with administrator rights. Running as a user means that your system is better protected, especially in situations where a vulnerability is "live" on the Internet and there is yet no patch for the issue and where user installation or interaction contribute to the vulnerability.

As Aaron Margolis so aptly stated in his blog on running as User[27]

"The #1 reason for running as non-admin is to limit your exposure. When you are an admin, every program you run has unlimited access to your computer. If malicious or other "undesirable" code finds its way to one of those programs, it also gains unlimited access. A corporate firewall is only partial protection against the hostility of the Internet: you still browse Web sites, receive e-mail, or run one or more instant messaging clients or Internet-connected games. Even if you keep up to date on patches and virus signatures, enable strong security settings, and are extremely careful with attachments, things happen. Let's say you're using your favorite search engine and click on a link that looks promising, but which turns out to be a malicious site hosting a zero-day exploit of a vulnerability in the browser you happen to be using, resulting in execution of arbitrary code. When an exploit runs with admin privileges, its ability to compromise your system is much greater, its ability to do so without detection is much greater, and its ability to attack others on your network is greater than it would be with only User privs. If the exploit happens to be written so that it requires admin privileges (as many do), just running as User stops it dead. But if you're running as admin, an exploit can:

- *install kernel-mode rootkits and/or keyloggers (which can be close to impossible to detect)*

- *install and start services*

- *install ActiveX controls, including IE and shell add-ins (common with spyware and adware)*

- *access data belonging to other users*

- *cause code to run whenever anybody else logs on (including capturing passwords entered into the Ctrl-Alt-Del logon dialog)*

- *replace OS and other program files with Trojan horses*

- *access LSA Secrets, including other sensitive account information, possibly including account info for domain accounts*

- *disable/uninstall anti-virus*

- *cover its tracks in the event log*

- *render your machine unbootable*

- *allow malware to gain admin control over those computers on the network where your account is an administrator*

...and lots more

When the Small Business Server 2003 "connectcomputer" routine is run, it assumes that you have administrator rights as you attach it to the network, and it leaves you in administrator rights upon completion. Remember that when you give someone administrator rights, "The default permissions allotted to this group allow complete control over the entire system. As a result, only trusted personnel should be members of this group". [28] The "Users group is the most secure, because the default permissions allotted to this group do not allow members to modify operating system settings or other users' data."[29]

You, as the trusted advisor, need to take the network and your client to the next step.

> BEST PRACTICE: This next series of steps and recommendations is not for all environments. You need to discuss with your client how much trust he has and how much guidance he will take from you. But begin to plant the seeds. If he is not comfortable in locking down the workstations because he suspects employees will feel like they are not trusted, remind your client of the number of social engineering attacks, phishing attacks, etc., and how your employees are truly the weak link in the computer system.

The first step is the easy step. Log on to the computer as the **Administrator**, click on **Control Panel**, then on **User**, and ensure that the user on that domain is logging in as a "user" or restricted user. This will ensure that the workstation stays protected while in operation. Even a power user is deemed to be "admin lite." A knowledge base article refers to power users as insecure as they can be converted to have administrator rights: http://support.microsoft.com/default.aspx?scid=kb;en-us;825069.

Now comes the fun part. Identifying those programs that refuse to run without local administrator or power user rights and then force them to behave. Some are quite notorious in their requirements for local administrator or power user rights. The tricky part is determining what registry keys to open up for the proper permissions. In general, if you open up the permissions to the location of the program where it resides, this normally is enough to get the program to be operational without additional rights. However, if merely opening up the permissions in this manner does not work, you may have to do a bit more detective work. This is where a couple of programs from Sysinternals.com come in handy, Filemon and Regmon as well as a PC magazine tool called InCtrl5.[30] Using these programs can assist you in determining the registry keys where the program is getting "stuck."

While this process may be workable for a small network, "sneakernetting" or the act of having to manually "touch" each machine is probably a bit restrictive for larger networks. For this we can call on our group policy power, and upon determining which registry keys need additional "permissioning," we can then apply these at the server level.[31]

First begin by either setting up a new organizational unit (OU) or using one that you have previously built. After identifying the file or registry that needs to have the permissions adjusted, utilize the power of group policy to push out this permission across the organizational unit. Jeff Middleton, SBS-MVP from Computer Focus, Ltd., provides the exact guidance for using the power of group policy:

Managing Non-Security Compliant Software Applications in a Secure Way (contributed by Jeff Middleton)

• **Secure Everything Else, Expose the Non-Compliant Application**

You are faced with securing a workstation, but an application on that desktop states in its vendor documentation that it requires administrator access or power user access on that local desktop. Even faced with vendor demands, you can make non-compliant applications like QuickBooks available in a securely configured workstation or Terminal Server environment. You must give the users some extra privileges on the specific folder and registry keys as they do not inherit maximum permission to access or control by default. When you consult the documentation from manufacturers like Intuit, they require that the entire computer operate by global means, elevating the user's rights by making the user a Local Administrator. In fact, this designation provides the end user the entire computer's local file system and entire registry as places this user has Full Control. In layman's terms, this is the equivalent unlocking the door to your house and leaving the front door open. Rather than managing the security access for the couple of items that Intuit itself installs from its own product CD, Intuit is suggesting that all folders and all registry locations must have all the security blocks removed.

What we want to do instead is to manually do ourselves what Intuit itself should do when it installs. We will accomplish what Intuit wants by doing the reverse of what Intuit suggests. Rather than elevating a user or group in permissions to do anything at all anywhere on the computer, rather we will instead designate a security group with which we will strip away the default security on the explicit folders and registry locations that concern this one product: Quickbooks. There is no difference in the result, the program will operate exactly as it needs to do, except that you need to have the specific information about the product in order to know what couple of places need this attention.

To be clear on this point, Intuit ultimately is concerned that the user of Quickbooks have unlimited control over specific folders and registry locations which by default provide that level of access only to Administrators. Rather than make our users Administrators who have far more power than needed to access these locations, we instead remove the security on the locations themselves.

After a normal installation of QuickBooks, do the following:

1. *Create a new Security Group:*

   AppSec RegFldr Quickbooks 2004

2. *Add your users as members to this group.*

3. *Give this group **Full Control** permission to the following registry locations:*

   HKEY_LOCAL_MACHINE\Software\Intuit\QuickBooksRegistration

   HKEY_CLASSES_ROOT\.QPG

4. *Give the group also Full Control rights to the folder locations where the application is installed:*

   C:\Program Files\Intuit\Quickbooks Pro

There you have it. The entire problem solved by providing access for our Quickbooks users to control just one folder tree, and two registry locations!

- ***Understanding Application Specific Security as a Process***

You probably want to know how we know to go to those specific places, and why we know those were the only places involved? We accomplish our task by adjusting permissions in the most obvious places, and for this you need just the slightest bit of information in understanding how software applications work when they are installed.

We will look at some rare exceptions to our starting point later, but let's start with what addresses 95% of the situations. The most common situation you will find with a new Windows-based software application is that it will modify information about four things:

1. **Data Files**—*Data files are going to be either located in the Program's Folder or in a location that you choose, perhaps on a network-shared location.*

2. **Program Files**—*Creates a new program installation folder and places all of the files it needs in that location or in a folder tree below it. Most often, these applications install beneath the location:*

C:\Program Files\[Application or Maker's Name]

3. HKLM\Software Registry Entries—The application prepares some settings to be stored or updated in the registry itself, but the main location of interest is in this location:

HKEY_LOCAL_MACHINE\Software\[Application or Maker's Name]

4. HK_Classes Root Registry Entries—This registry location is less familiar to most people because it is generally used only as a reference table by the Operating System, Application programs, and Hardware Drivers. The design of Windows calls for this registry location not to be modified by users; rather, it's supposed to be essentially "read-only" for users in normal use. This is because it's supposed to be a definitions location, not a data and settings update location. In programming terms, this area is supposed to house "constants," not "variables." Only the Local System is supposed to write to this area during normal use, and the Administrator has rights to modify this location mostly to perform installations and repairs.

If you review the list of the four locations above, you will notice something pretty obvious. Two of the areas clearly are "stamped" or identified by the product or manufacturer's name as part of the location identity. The data file location can be considered to be a familiar identification we are accustomed to managing, so that leaves on the Classes Root (abbreviated: HKCR) location as a real challenge to figure out. After the first time you look in the HKCR, you will realize you need help dealing with that area, this despite the fact that the other locations are pretty easy to manage.

The good news is that perhaps 60-70% of all software stating that it requires users to be Administrators will actually run fine if you do nothing more than grant the User Group to have full control over the *program's main folder tree, and the registry tree location for that program indicated in HKLM\Software.*

Another 25-30% of the programs may require you to identify a location in the HKCR registry as well. It may require the program to be installed by that user with Administrator rights, and subsequently normal user rights function correctly. In both cases, one of two things is usually going on. Some products are saving information about each specific user's activity in the HKCR location, even if it's nothing more than a reference to your password, or your initials, or perhaps naming a preferred printer or the CD drive you installed from for each user. This is not to suggest it's not wrong that the application does this; rather the point is that it's not only wrong, it's being done for typically trivial reasons!

- ***Easy Stuff You Usually Can Ignore***

If you know your Windows applications and registry technical details well enough, you realize that we didn't cover one other place that most applications will create new entries when you install the application or run it as a user:

HKEY_USER\Software\[Application or Maker's Name]

There's a really simple reason why I skipped this in the explanation above: each user owns his own user registry. Every user automatically has FULL CONTROL of his own HKEY_USER registry location, therefore there's rarely a reason to be interested in this from a security standpoint. By design, this is where the application designers like Intuit should be placing their "user specific" information that the user requires unrestricted rights to modify things within. In addition, this location is always available to that user, it's saved between sessions, and each user has his own separate location unique from all others.

If the manufacturer wanted to have a location, common to all users, but handled properly, the application should place that information inside the HKLM\Software and should specifically set different security access when it installs; otherwise, they should handle it as a data file consideration.

Periodically we run into an application which still manages to confound the plan to handle HKEY_USER properly. This type of application fails our expectations because it performs a setup process during installation which creates configuration only in the location known as HKEY_CURRENT_USER instead of HKEY_DEFAULT_USER. The difference may seem subtle if you are not familiar with this.

HKEY_DEFAULT_USER is a location that is the "template" for any new users who log on to this workstation. They inherit whatever is defined there, just like profile location of **C:\Documents and Settings\Default User**. However, the point that confuses many people is the registry location of HKEY_CURRENT_USER, a location which is a dynamic pointer to whichever HKEY_USER location that applies at any time. HKEY_CURRENT_USER isn't a location; rather it's an alias for the current user's actual HKEY_USER registry location. The reason for this is that, internally, software can operate without knowing who the current user is, just by addressing "the current user."

If an application installs information that every future user will need, writing that only to HKEY_CURRENT_USER updates the user running the system only at that time. If the update were provided to HKEY_DEFAULT_USER, future new users would obtain these new settings, but this still leaves out previously existing users already defined on the system, but now needing to have their HKEY_USER information updated with this new application's default settings. Doesn't that sound confusing? This is why some product manufacturers tell you that you "must run the installation again" for every new user; therefore, every new user needs to be an Administrator, because installing the entire application means writing to everywhere all over again, just to update *this one user's registry. In this one point, you begin to see why product makers ignore the Windows rules and put common information in a common location where it doesn't belong, but goes nonetheless.*

For the products that handle this correctly, in case you are curious, you now know why there is a registry location for the "RunOnce" entry. That key can be used to validate if the user requires a "user setup." Other applications handle this with a more elegant solution: They place default information in the HKLM\Software keys they create which are defaults for any user, and when the program fires up for a user, it first verifies that the HK_CURRENT_USER contains the defaults, and if not, they are added at that time. This is really the best solution possible.

- *Application Security Management PowerTools*

You can probably surmise from the information presented in the previous paragraphs that it is fairly easy to do most programs without much homework or investigation. But what about those situations that, unfortunately, require technical investigation? Now it is required that we move into a somewhat more complicated area. Below are some of the tools you will want to consider using:

     o *Google!*

        Absolutely, "google"[32] the product with the key word of Permissions or Administrator and you will be surprised how often someone else has already uncovered and documented the registry keys and folders that need to be "unlocked."

     o *Regmon[33]*

        This tool is frequently used to watch for a specific registry activity, but what it does is provide a view of all registry activity. However, it can be a bit overwhelming with information that is returned.

     o *InCtrl5[34]*

This is a tool which you can use to view the actions taken on that system while a program installs, or runs, to see all the files, folders, and registry locations that are attempted or successfully accessed. You can run the tool once as the Administrator to see it all processes and commands as they succeed, then run it again as a regular user to see what subsequently still succeeds. Mostly, it will allow you will to figure out quickly where the trouble spots are — the places that are discussed in this documentation about HKCR and %windir% locations. The nice thing about InCtrl5 is that it produces reports that are, while still very detailed, at least organized pretty closely to the process you are actually performing. You can even cut and paste information from the reports directly to your Group Policies or use the output to analyze within an Excel spreadsheet.

- *Understanding the Exceptions to Our Security Management Process*

There are still are a couple of ways that application makers can spoil our plan to lockdown the workstations to the normal User permissions level and cause the application to not run normally. Below is a list of the most common issues that remain out there and are becoming increasingly more difficult to resolve:

1. *Application "requires" files to be installed in or below the %windir% location, that is the C:\Windows folder, and yet "requires" users to be able to write to that file periodically. (This location is read-only to users by default.)*

2. *Application has a similar consideration to the previous point, but instead attempts to write temporary files, or even permanent files to a location like %windir% or even beneath C:\Program*

Files\[folder name]. (This location is read-only to users by default users.)

3. *Application remembers locations used by the last user (i.e., a different user on the same machine) and attempts to reuse files stored in a user-specific location. Examples are the My Documents folder or a Profile folder.*

4. *Application uses the old standards of Windows 3.x or 16-bit applications which refer to homefolders or require drive letter paths for profile information. (These can usually be handled with NT/9x style user profile folders set with the domain account profile settings.)*

5. *Application expects to use a hardwired location for legacy-based folder locations — for instance, writing temporary files to %windir%\TEMP and ignoring the %TEMP% environment variable, or writing to the registry-based profile information on the same point. (By default, this location is read-only for users now, and while this might be solved by granting permissions on this one folder, opening permissions on TEMP folders that are common to System use should be avoided if ever possible).*

The really nasty exceptions above will also cause problems with Terminal Server Application Mode environments where you have multiple users on the same computer concurrently. Similar problems can arise in XP Home Edition use where the User Switching operations can leave an application open for one user, then switch a different user to the foreground.

- **Documenting and Managing Application-Specific Security Domain-Wide**

In the sections above, we have outlined some issues and solutions for managing the security restrictions on a single computer, or even a way to address doing it computer by computer. Yet, this is not only tediously time-consuming, it's hard to keep track of over time. It's even difficult to remember how to "fix an application" again months later on a different computer, if not just for another user. And what do you do about upgrading from QuickBooks 2003 to version 2004 if you can't remember how you solved it last year?

What we need here is a plan to simplify the process and document it at the same time. Fortunately, you now will learn one of the most effective uses of Active Directory Group Policy for handling all of this for you. This is a surprisingly low-profile tip on how to handle registry and folder management permissions, so don't be surprised if you have trouble finding more documentation on it. It's rather hard to locate, but it's very easy to implement.

It turns out that the process we use to figure out how to "fix" one machine will give us all the information we need to make that fix apply to all the machines we want at once. To accomplish this, you probably test out your registry and folder permission changes at a single workstation. Once you know you have the problems solved, you take the notes on the registry/folder information in the form of a Notepad file, and you move to your SBS Server now. Better yet, do this next step via a Remote Desktop control of the SBS from the workstation where you tested it! You will see why that's the best idea in just a moment.

What we will cover next is how to use Group Policy to set Registry and Folder Permissions that we can apply to more than one computer. By creating a Group Policy, we can manage it at the SBS (or any Domain Controller or even remotely controlling a Domain Controller). But the best part of this is that you can do it once, and this method actually documents the change in a way you will always be able to locate and modify it in the future. Therefore, part of what we will do next is intended to "make the permission changes," but there's also a bit of strategy in how we do this that helps as documentation for later review.

The key point to observe is that we want to create a unique Group Policy which has the sole purpose of managing this permissions issue, nothing more. It's a good idea to avoid putting this into an existing policy or mixing it with other policy settings simply because you want to make it easy to understand years later.

- ***Group Policy for Application Security Management***

Let's start by revisiting the information we determined at the local machine, which you will recall looked something like this for QuickBooks:

1. Create a new Security Group:

AppSec RegFldr Quickbooks 2004

2. Add your users as members to this group.

*3. Give this group **Full Control** permission to the following registry locations:*

HKEY_LOCAL_MACHINE\Software\Intuit\Quick BooksRegistration

HKEY_CLASSES_ROOT\.QPG

*4. Give the group also **Full Control** rights to the folder locations where the application is installed:*

C:\Program Files\Intuit\Quickbooks Pro

Here are the elements we will use explained in more detail:

- ***Create and Name the Security Group***

 *If you actually implemented on one or more computers from the earlier explanation, you realize that you already have Steps 1 and 2 done, assuming that you created a Domain Global Group rather than a workstation Local Group. However, now I want to make a point about the name of the group that was recommended. You might assume that the name **AppSec RegFldr Quickbooks***

2004 *was unduly complicated for your needs. It's true this works if you created the name even with something like QB Users, but that's not helping as much with documenting what we are doing and why.*

The group name suggested is intended to be a flag for us. This group wasn't just created to give permission to various users to run the program like any other program or to enforce security on the data folder location like you do with most accounting software anyway. No, the name was suggested to make the point that this is all of the following:

1. *AppSec = Application Security*

2. *RegFldr = Registry- and Folder-related*

3. *Quickbooks = the familiar name of the application*

4. *2004 = the version of the product involved*

Once you gain some experience with this, you come to realize that each of these things are important clues you will regret not having later if they aren't there to begin with! Here's that list again with further explanation of each point.

1. *AppSec = By indicating it's AppSec, we know that if we remove it, we probably not only remove the access to the program, we probably cause the program to stop working.*

2. *RegFldr = This group points out that we are managing Registry- and Folder-related issues, not just user groups or e-mail distribution groups*

3. *Quickbooks = The familiar name of the application enforces how we related it to our business needs.*

4. *2004 = The version of the product involved tells us that if we upgrade and remove the program, everything related to this is no longer needed, and we can clean it up! Otherwise, if we replace this version with the next, you actually must modify or create a new set of registry and*

folder permission-management settings, because the old paths will no longer apply in most cases.

- ### Create and Name Your Group Policy

Now that we have a Security Group to manage this process with, we next need to look at the Group Policy we want to create. It needs to have a name too, right?

Here's your next opportunity to inform yourself with documentation. You could name it something like this:

Allow Users AppSec RegFldr Quickbooks 2004

You probably already see the logic there. This policy is to "allow users" of that group to do what that group accomplishes, as described above. If you have already started using Group Policy for other things, you realize that it can be confusing, as the number of policies grows for which you must remember what the point of the policy was, the scope, and in particular, whether it manages computers or users. This tells us not only that we are controlling users (not computers), but that we are granting access with this policy. Keep in mind, you might just as well have another situation where you want to deny users access to a folder, or registry location, or even an application. This makes it clear at a glance just what we are doing. The only step left is to actually implement the policy, and now we will see how that is done.

Open the SBS Administrators Console, or the Group Policy Management Console, and you begin by creating a new Group Policy. For the sake of discussion, let's just assume that we want this policy to apply to every computer in the network. In fact, here's a convenient part of the way this works. You actually can apply the type of policy we are creating to every computer, even if the computers don't have this application installed! The way this group policy works is it only affects folders and registry locations if they exist, and it doesn't create them, just sets the security if they exist.

In most cases, in practice, you probably have your workstations in a single Organizational Unit and you would apply this policy at that location.

- *Open up the **Server Management**, expand **Advanced Managment**, and click on **Active Directory Users and Computer**, click on **Add a Security Group**, click **Action** and then **New**. In the window that pops up, type in **AppSec RegFldr Quickbooks 2004** and enter a description. See Figure 11-12.*

Figure 11-12

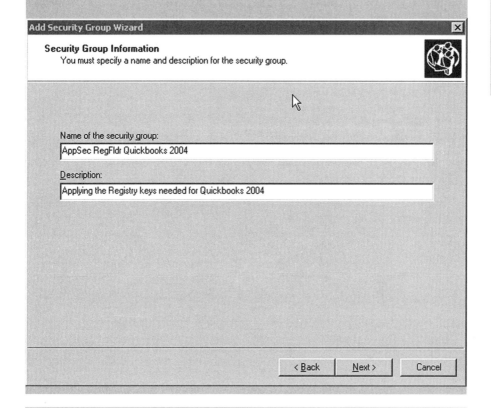

Add Security Group Wizard

Security Group Information
You must specify a name and description for the security group.

Name of the security group:

AppSec RegFldr Quickbooks 2004

Description:

Applying the Registry keys needed for Quickbooks 2004

< Back   Next >   Cancel

Notes:

- *Highlight those users that need to be added to this group. See Figure 11-13.*

Figure 11-13

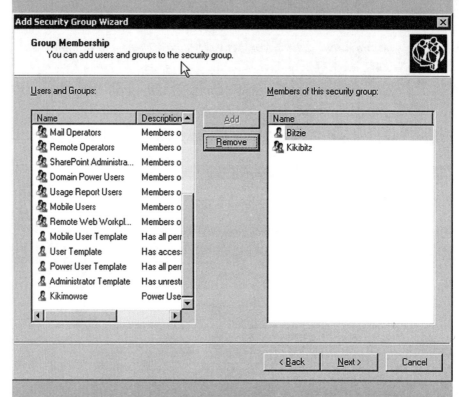

- ***Create the Policy Elements for Folder and Registry Settings***

  Refer to the Group Policy Editor view to the section at the top.

Notes:

- Expand **Group Policy Management**, expand **Group Policy Objects**, right-click on the **Group Policy Object** section, and click **New** (Figure 11-14)

- Click on the name of the GPO you just created, right-click, and edit. See Figure 11-15.

Figure 11-14

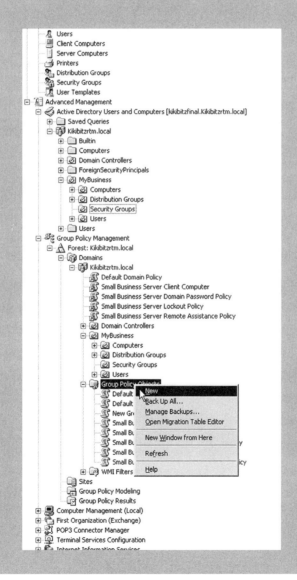

Figure 11-15

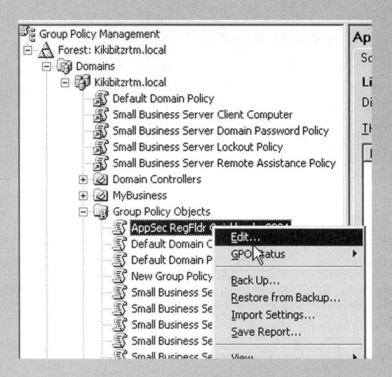

You are now going to drill down on the items beneath Computer Configuration | Windows Settings | Security Settings. At that level, among the next tabs beneath are Registry, plus the File System tab. We will start with the File System because it's a bit more familiar to most people. Remember, this is the point at which you will wish that you either are working in an RDP Session controlling the SBS from your test workstation, or you want to have pasted into a Notepad file a copy of each of the required registry and folder change paths:

Notes:

1. *Right-click on* **File System** *and choose* **Add File**. *See Figure 11-16.*

Figure 11-16

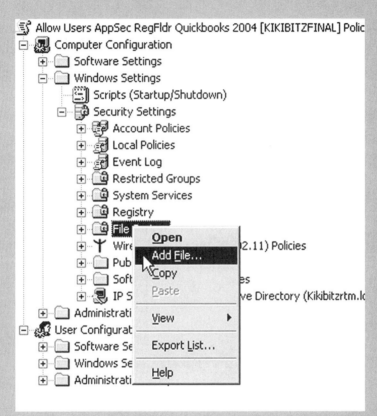

2. *A Browse Files dialog box opens. Now, you may realize here that you can't browse to the local drive of a different computer, but there is an open blank at the top where you can paste in the path you copied from the test computer.*

Notes:

3. *You accept the change and you now have a permissions selection box displayed. By default, it indicates "Administrators, Creators, System and Users" as the entries. See Figure 11-17.*

Figure 11-17

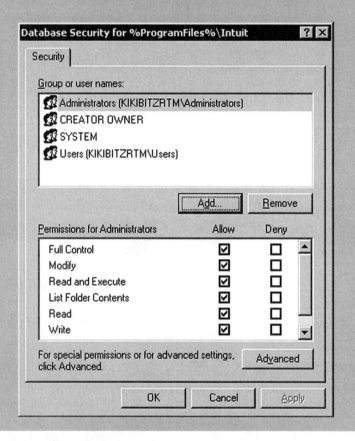

Notes:

4. *Click on **Find** and drill down to choose your **AppSec RegFldr Quickbooks 2004 Security Group**. See Figure 11-18.*

Figure 11-18

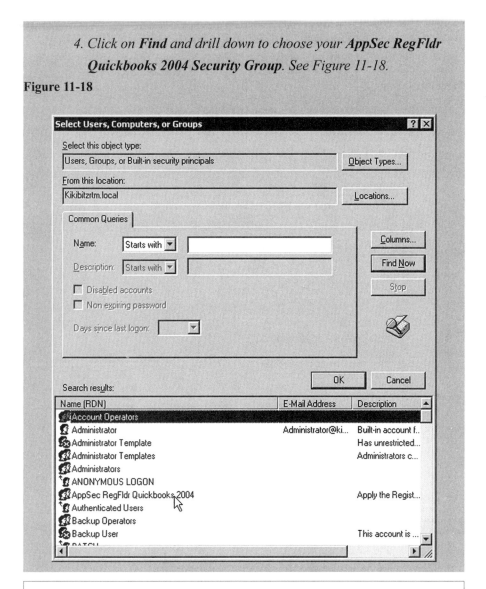

5. Choose *Allow Users AppSec RegFldr Quickbooks 2004: Full Control*. *Close this selection panel. See Figure 11-19.*

Figure 11-19

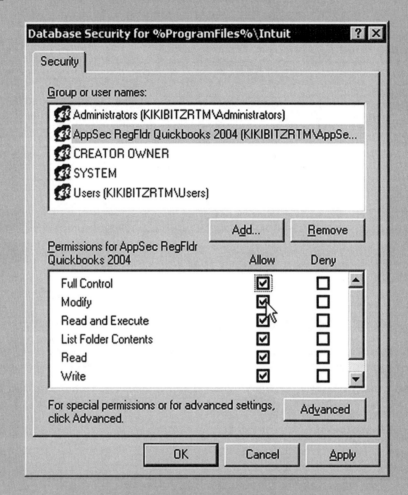

6. *The last panel prompts you to approve propagating the permissions to the tree below the folder selection. This is what you want to do—it's the default option:* "**Configure this file or folder then...Propagate inheritable permissions to all subfolders and files.**" *That means that the local permissions will be supplemented with the new permissions. Caution: If you*

cause the permissions to be replaced and you don't include System and Administrator, you can have some very seriously odd behavior, even worse. If you replace permissions, be aware that you are doing something much more complicated and less safe. See Figure 11-20.

Figure 11-20

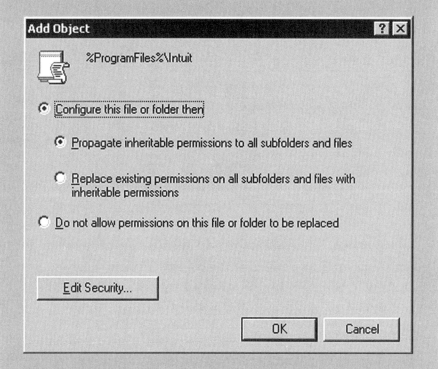

7. *Now you see the results: the new policy element shown in the right-side panel. Note that if you pasted in something like "**C:\Program Files\Intuit**" when you finish saving this, it's automatically converted to something like "**%SystemDrive%\Program Files\Intuit**" to make it a valid, generic path at all computers.*

That was the entire edit process for one folder. Now we do the same steps for the Registry keys, and the steps are the same, with one small difference. If you used Regedit at the workstation with the "Copy Key" method to get the key path, you will see that the full registry path in that key isn't what is expected in the Group Policy setting for Registry. You need to "trim" the front part off to make it read as you need it. What you capture as "Copy Keyname" in Regedit shows like this, but this is **incorrect** syntax for Group Policy items.

HKEY_CLASSES_ROOT\.QPG

To enter it in the Group Policy section, you trim off the "HKEY_" portion. If you attempt to add the full key text above, you can't click the button to accept that as an entry. It has to read as follows, using the **correct** syntax:

CLASSES_ROOT\.QPG

Once you have save the policy element, you may notice that you can later revise the Security settings, but not the path item. This curious limitation isn't explained anywhere, but your only option for revising it is to delete the key and recreate it. This should give you another hint about the recommendation above to make your Group Policy identifications not only specific to the product, but also for the version of the product.

Your last step is to force the new policy to apply to the intended workstations. Generally, these policies are going to apply if you use GPUPDATE and force an update of the policies for that machine.

For Windows XP or 2003, the command is GPUPDATE /FORCE.

- **Verification in Managing Application Security with Group Policy**

In many cases where similar methods have recommended how to "remove" security from registry or folder permissions, a common *suggestion is to simply add Everyone: FULL CONTROL in the registry and be done with it. Please don't do that! I suggest this for your own sake.*

One of the advantages of the method outlined here is that there's one more place where we have left a trail of "documented" changes, and it's probably the most important one in the final review. Once you have deployed a secured application with this method, you will want to confirm that what you think you were changing is actually now changed. Therefore, you can go back to the test machine and inspect the ACLs on the folders, and the registry keys you modified. You should now see the new Security Group listed with the correct permissions. Once again, you can understand the power of using a specific, descriptively named Security Group, because you can tell not only that the permission change occurred, you know what it is and you see where it is actually being applied. If you had only added Everyone: Full Control, do you think that would stand out as an edit, much less explain why it was done, by whom, or in what manner?

Unfortunately, Microsoft didn't provide any means to add notes within the Group Policy settings to explain or document the keys being managed. Other than the name of the policy and the name of the Security Group you assign, there's really no way to document this in a way that remains attached to the policy itself. As a result, you can see why the recommendation is made to be very explicit in the naming of the Security Group and the Group Policy. These are all you have to go by in the future to understand why you made these changes, and if you can eliminate them at some point in the future.

For more basic information about the application of group policy in networks, please refer to Chapter 4

- *Action item*—*Limit the privileges on your network.*

Get Your ACLs in a Row

When setting up a user with the wizard, ensure that you do not give the user more rights than they need. The user templates have been specifically created to ensure users of the computer only get to do on the server what they are supposed to do. If the application you are installing specifically demands "Local administrator" rights, this does not mean you choose the "Domain administrator" template when setting up the user. In a typical Small Business server, there is no more than two Domain Administrator accounts on that server. The rest of the users all log in with a user template or remote user template. Don't confuse terminology and end up giving a person in the office full rights to the server in the process.

Review the permissions on a folder. If you grant rights to the root of that folder and someone maliciously gains access, that person has a great deal of power at his fingertips. In my own network, I suffer from something I call the "fatal finger syndrome." In a common shared file area of the network, employees will click on a folder and accidentally slide their hand at the same time. Suddenly the entire contents of the folder are slid under the neighboring folder. Long ago I put into place two actions to ensure that I would always be able to get a file back. First I invested in a program that sets up a recycle bin on the server. Any accidental deletion is maintained for the preset number of days that I have enabled. The next process I have put in place is a procedure using a tool called "robocopy." Robocopy is a robust file copying program first released for Windows NT and now in the Windows 2003 resource kit. At lunchtime, this routine is set up as an automated task to copy over data files. Thus in addition to the RAID drives, the tape backup, and the recycle bin feature, I have one last additional way to ensure that data is not irretrievable. With Windows 2003, they have built much of this functionality into their Shadow File Copy process. When your workstations share files up to those drives that have the Shadow File copy routine in place, you can retrieve specific files. However, I would recommend that the instructions on retrieving files is known only by key personnel. This process to restore one file may not be reasonable for all of your clients to handle properly.

When setting up the server to be accessed by employees, customers, or vendors, review very carefully those permissions you grant. Set up additional organizational units, and ensure that users working remotely are restricted in their access. Review the shares and permissions by running a script to make sure you have set this up properly. This can be done with the following script:

```
strComputer = "."
Set objWMIService = GetObject("winmgmts:" _
 & "{impersonationLevel=impersonate}!\\" & strComputer & "\root\cimv2")
Set colShares = objWMIService.ExecQuery("Select * from Win32_Share")
For each objShare in colShares
 Wscript.Echo "AllowMaximum: " & vbTab & objShare.AllowMaximum
 Wscript.Echo "Caption: " & vbTab & objShare.Caption
 Wscript.Echo "MaximumAllowed: " & vbTab & objShare.MaximumAllowed
 Wscript.Echo "Name: " & vbTab & objShare.Name
 Wscript.Echo "Path: " & vbTab & objShare.Path
 Wscript.Echo "Type: " & vbTab & objShare.Type
Next
```

Copy the contents to Notepad, save it as a vbs file, and run the program to audit the folder shares you have on a system. It will enumerate the shares that you have on that system.

- *Action item—Review the permissions you have given to users on folders.*

Physical Access

In my office we have placed cable locks on all computers, have an alarm on the building, and have taken steps to ensure that access to and from the building is monitored. We restrict the personal use of company computers and the use of personal machines on the company network. In fact my personal laptop, which I affectionately refer to as "the prostitute" as it has attached itself to any number of hotel and wireless networks, has never been a member of the network at the office. I keep an "air barrier" between it and more corporate networks as an additional layer of protection. Obviously, this may not work for you, but just remember that while we have a "hard layer on the outside," before the advent of using internal firewalls as in the use of XP sp2, we have an extremely "gooey" inner part.

If you have physical access to any computer, your security is gone. It's well known in the industry that a Linux boot disk http://home.eunet.no/~pnordahl/ntpasswd/bootdisk.html can be used to easily reset the Administrator password of workstations. For servers, it's a bit more cumbersome with the addition of the active directory, but still not impossible. Sysinternals.com in fact sells a product with just this task in mind, but it can also be accomplished in other ways.

Physical security, even in small firms, is extremely important.

- *Action item—Add appropriate physical locks and alarms.*

Sharepoint Rights

When setting up users in the Sharepoint system, also be aware that the rights granted here may provide more access than you want. Be miserly in your granting of Administrator rights, no matter what the application.

When you install Windows Sharepoint services, the site for content is separated from the site for administration. Thus when setting up the site, understand what "Administrator" rights allow you to do in Sharepoint and assign it sparingly. However, remember that Administrators to the Sharepoint site are not Administrators of the server. Top-level administrators can create subsites and and delegate permissions by using site groups. Web-parts (such as the Smiling Goat RSS feed reader, for example) that contain applications are subject to security and code access security. Thus if you find that in order for a Web part to function properly it needs access to additional folders, examine the rights you are applying and the folders you are allowing it to access. Determine whether you are allowing anonymous access and assess the risks accordingly.

Securing the Sharepoint Content

It goes without saying that you should back up the Sharepoint, using either the ntbackup that ensures it is backed up by using the volume shadow copy process or by using the stadmin process that does a "flat file" backup.

If you have enabled the recovery of SharePoint files, you can recover a file or list item by restoring the entire site from a backup to a subsite of http://companyweb, selecting the file or list item you want to restore, extracting it, and uploading it to its original location. To enable the recovery of individual SharePoint files, please use the following procedure:

1. Click **Start**, click **Control Panel**, click **Scheduled Tasks**, then click **Add Scheduled Task**.

2. Click **Next** on the first page of the **Scheduled Task Wizard**.

3. Click **Browse**, go to **%SystemDrive%\Program Files\Common Files\Microsoft Shared\Web server extensions\60\Bin**, then double-click **Stsadm.exe**.

4. Select how often you want this task to run, then click **Next**.

5. Select the time you want to run the schedule, then click **Next**.

6. Enter administrator credentials, then click **Next**.

7. Select the **Open Advanced Properties**, click **Finish** check box, then click **Finish**.

8. On the **Task** tab in the dialog box that appears, in the **Run** box, type **"%SystemDrive%\Program files\Common files\Microsoft shared\Web server extensions\60\Bin\Stsadm.exe" -o backup -url http://Companyweb -filename target path -overwrite**. The target path is where you save the backup of your internal Web site. Click **OK**. You must type the quotation marks.

If you have enabled this before, you can follow the steps below to restore the missing files:

1. Click **Start**, click **Command Prompt**, then type **"%SystemDrive%\Program files\Common files\Microsoft shared\ Web server extensions\60\Bin\Stsadm.exe" -o createsiteinnewdb -url http://companyweb/sites/RestoredSite -ownerlogin DOMAIN\administrator -owneremail administrator @DOMAIN.local -databasename STS_RESTORE**, where DOMAIN is your server domain and administrator@DOMAIN.local is your administrator's e-mail address. Include the quotation marks as part of the path. Press **ENTER**.

2. Type **"%SystemDrive%\Program files\Common files\Microsoft shared\Web server extensions\60\Bin\Stsadm.exe" -o restore –url http://Companyweb/Sites/Restoredsite -filename target path - overwrite**, where target path is the location you chose to save your SharePoint backup. Include the quotation marks as part of the path. Press **ENTER**.

3. Open **Internet Explorer**, and in the address bar, type **http://Companyweb/Sites/Restoredsite**. The site that appears is the same as your company Web site.

4. In the restored site, navigate to the missing file.

5. Right-click the file, select **Save Target As**, and then select a location to which you want to save the file.

6. Repeat steps 4 and 5 for all missing files.

7. Open your company Web site, navigate to the location where the missing files should be, and then on the **SharePoint** toolbar, click **Upload Document**.

 NOTE: The second method is provided in the SBS Server help. You can find it by following the steps below:

1. Open **Server Management**.

2. Click **Standard Management->Backup**.

3. Click **Restore Sharepoint files** in the right pane.

In addition to ensuring that you can easily restore the site, there are some additional steps to "lockdown" content such as Web sites and Lists that can be performed. Each of the two have Access Control List (ACL) which contains Access Control Entries (ACE) that list user names, domain group names, and cross-site group names. To override the site-wide permissions that the WSS automatically grants at the Web site level, you can set permissions specifically to lists within in site. Remember, that when you are setting up Sharepoint you can inherit the site security from the parent site or set up unique permissions to restrict rights to the site accordingly.

The Sharepoint Res kit shows the following types of Site Groups you can set up in your Web site: http://www.microsoft.com/technet/prodtechnol/sppt/reskit/c0661881x.mspx.

Notes:

Site Group Name	User Rights Included
Guest	None
Reader	Use Self-Service Site Creation View Pages View Items
Contributor	Use Self-Service Site Creation View Pages View Items Add Items Add/Remove Private Web Parts Browse Directories Create Cross-Site Groups Delete Items Edit Items Manage Personal Views Update Personal Web Parts
Web Designer	Use Self-Service Site Creation View Pages View Items Add Items Add/Remove Private Web Parts Browse Directories Create Cross-Site Groups Delete Items Edit Items Manage Personal Views Update Personal Web Parts Add and Customize Pages Apply Themes and Borders Apply Style Sheets Cancel Check-Out Manage Lists
Administrator (this is where your users will default to in SBS 2003)	Use Self-Service Site Creation View Pages View Items Add Items Add/Remove Private Web Parts Browse Directories Create Cross-Site Groups Delete ItemsEdit Items Manage Personal Views Update Personal Web Parts Add and Customize Pages Apply Themes and Borders Apply Style Sheets Cancel Check-Out Manage Lists Create Subsites Manage List Permissions Manage Site Groups View Usage Data

Remember that while these are the default selections, you can adjust the rights to your own needs. Only Guest and Administrator, for obvious reasons, cannot be customized., but keep in mind the dependencies of some items. If you delete View Items, the Add Items, Edit Items, and Delete Items are also removed. Only place a user in the type of group you want her to be in. The default right that a Sharepoint user in Small Business Server is set up as is **Administrator**. You may wish to adjust that depending on the needs and wishes of your organization. Site permissions allow the Sharepoint Administrator to control the user's ability to read content and modify content within a site. Some rights are dependent on one another and will be automatically added. The following is a list of these rights. Remember that for each group named above, you can edit and remove the rights you wish.[35]

Right	Permission	Groups Included	Dependency Rights
Add and customize pages	Can create ASP.NET, ASP, HTML Web pages for a site	Web Designer Administrator	Browse directories View Pages
Add items	Add documents to documents libraries or items to lists	Contributor Web Designer Administrator	View Items View Pages
Add and remove private Web parts (Web modules)	Add and/or remove Web parts to pages	Contributor Web Designer Administrator	Update Web Parts View Items View Pages
Apply style sheets	Apply a style to the entire site	Web Designer Administrator	View Pages
Apply themes and borders	Apply a theme and/or border to a site	Web Designer Administrator	View Pages
Browse directories	Browse a Web site's directory structure	Contributor Web Designer Administrator	View Pages
Cancel check-out	Can cancel the check-out performed by a user	Designer Administrator	View Pages

Right	Permission	Groups Included	Dependency Rights
Create cross-site groups	Delete and create cross-site groups, change membership	Contributor Web Designer Administrator	View pages
Create subsites	Create subsite	Reader Contributor Web Designer Administrator	View pages
Delete items	Delete items and documents	Contributor Web Designer Administrator	View items View pages
Edit items	Edit existing list items and document in the Web site	Contributor Web Designer Administrator	View items View pages
Manage Lists	Delete, create, edit lists and change settings	Web Designer Administrator	View items View pages Manage personal views
Manage list permissions	Change permissions for a list	Administrator	Manage lists View items View pages Manage personal views
	Create, delete, and edit personal views	Contributor Web Designer Administrator	View items View pages
Manage site groups	Edit, create, and delete site groups, change the rights assigned to the site group	Administrator	View pages
Manage Web site	Perform tasks for the site or subsite	Administrator	View pages
Update personal Web parts	Update Web parts	Contributor Web Designer Administrator	View items View pages

Right	Permission	Groups Included	Dependency Rights
Use self-service site creation	Use to create top-level Web site	Reader Contributor Web Designer Administrator	View pages
View items	View items in lists, documents	Reader Contributor Web Designer Administrator	View pages
View pages	Browse pages	Reader Contributor Web Designer Administrator	None
View usage data	View reports on Web site use	Administrator	View pages

For Sharepoint lists, the rights set on a unique list will override the site-wide rights. Thus you can set a list, such as an announcement list for a certain user to have no rights to view the list even though that user has the right to have read-access to a Web site.

As you can tell, the Security adjustments you can make in Sharepoint can be a bit overwhelming. I'd advise you to start with the basics, use the defaults, and begin to make some sample sites at your own office. Start making adjustments and determine the proper balance of rights/users accordingly.

- *Action item—Review the Sharepoint users and adjust their rights to users or Web designers where appropriate.*

XP Service Pack 2

Small Business Server 2003 was released prior to the shipment of XP sp2, and thus in anticipation, the Server shipped with a group policy setting in place to limit the use of the firewall coming out in XP sp2. After the shipment and finalization of XP sp2, it has been announced that the group policy settings will be revisited upon the final release of XP sp2 and adjusted accordingly. By the time you read this, XP sp2 and the group policy will have been released for SBS. In the meantime, I would strongly recommend you review the following documents and, in your test, networks install the inf file to add the group policy settings for the sp2 firewall. The addition of firewalls internal to the network allows for better protection of internal clients. Currently with our practice of using too high of user privileges, workstations are truly our weakest link in our networks.

More information on XPsp2 will be finalized as XP sp2 is released in the meantime resources can be found at:

- http://www.microsoft.com/technet/prodtechnol/winxppro/maintain/winxpsp2.mspx

- http://www.microsoft.com/windowsxp/default.mspx

- http://download.microsoft.com/download/4/2/c/42c9b5d4-25d7-414c-a149-648ca4149596/WFINF_Guide.doc

- http://download.microsoft.com/download/6/8/a/68a81446-cd73-4a61-8665-8a67781ac4e8/WF_XPSP2.doc

Without the special Small Business Server 2003 group policy settings patch, you can manually update the group policy settings:[36]

1. Install Windows XP sp2 on a computer that is a member of the domain containing the computer accounts of the other computers running Windows XP on which you plan to install Windows XP sp2.

2. Restart the computer and log on to the Windows XP sp2 computer as a member of the **Domain Administrators security group**, the **Enterprise Administrators security group**, or the **Group Policy Creator Owners security group**.

3. From the **Windows XP desktop**, click **Start**, click **Run**, type **mmc**, then click **OK**.

4. On the **File** menu, click **Add/Remove Snap-in**.

5. On the **Standalone** tab, click **Add**.

6. In the **Available Standalone Snap-ins** list, click **Group Policy Object Editor**, then click **Add**.

7. In the **Select Group Policy Object** dialog box, click **Browse**.

8. In the Browse for a Group Policy Object, click the Group Policy object you want to update with the new Windows Firewall settings.

9. Click **OK**.

10. Click **Finish** to complete the Group Policy Wizard.

11. In the **Add Standalone Snap-in** dialog box, click **Close**.

12. In the **Add/Remove Snap-in** dialog box, click **OK**.

13. In the console tree, open **Computer Configuration**, **Administrative Templates**, **Network**, **Network Connections**, and then **Windows Firewall**.

Repeat this procedure for every Group Policy object that is being used to apply Group Policy to computers that will have Windows XP SP2 installed.

However, it is ***much*** easier to merely add the specific Small Business Server 2003 Update for Windows XP sp2 Knowledge base article 872769 that specially adjusts the group policy setting for network connections, allows local program exceptions, allows remote desktop to go through the firewall, allows file and printer sharing in a preconfigured manner as well as other adjustments. In general, connectivity for ActiveSync and Help and Support Center are preconfigured with the Small Business Server template. The major port connection statically adjusted is port 135 to allow for remote assistance to the client.

- The SBS 2003 update can be found at: http://www.microsoft.com/downloads/details.aspx?familyid=d70097c2-4317-40e0-b7da-feb52c6b6386&displaylang=en but it also is applied if you visit the Windows Update site.

- The white paper can be found at: http://go.microsoft.com/fwlink/?linkid=33331

- After applying this update you will also need this: 842933 - "The following entry in the [strings] section is too long and has been truncated" error message when you try to modify or to view GPOs in Windows Server 2003, Windows XP, or Windows 2000: http://support.microsoft.com/?kbid=842933. It is expected that this will be on the Microsoft download site.

- SBS 2003 now supports the application of sp2 via the connect computer wizard. Download details: Update for Windows Small Business Server 2003: KB 884032: http://www.microsoft.com/downloads/details.aspx?familyid=a8f72fdd-6d82-4c2b-8078-114460826a40&displaylang=en and 884032 -. Update is available for the Windows Small Business Server 2003 Client Setup feature to deploy

> Windows XP Service Pack 2 to Windows XP Professional-based clients: http://support.microsoft.com/?kbid=884032.

As your end users use the new features of XP sp2, you will not that the firewall will prompt the end user when it needs to utilize additional connections. Thus it may build connections for using the integration of Word 2003 and Sharepoint or other connections.

As of this writing, the Shavlik.com HfnetchkPro program uses NetBios connections (port 137-139) to perform its scans. Thus you will either need to turn off the personal firewall (which can be scripted) and try again or create a filter to allow outbound NetBios connections and inbound return responses. You may wish to look into their "Agent" based HfnetchPro to assist in this process as well. More information about the necessary changes or adjustments are provided by Shavlik.com on their Web site and in their newsforums.

Visit the Microsoft Web site for the latest information.

- *Action item—Apply XP sp2 (or any new SP or update) after an appropriate testing period.*

- *Action item—Apply KB 872769 to the server to adjust the group policy to enable the firewall inside your office.*

- *Action item—Apply KB 842933 to allow you to edit the group policy.*

Internet Explorer

At the time I am writing this, Internet Explorer was perceived in the security tech industry as being due for an overhaul. At the same time, Web sites began to practically overrun browsers with popups, spysoftware and another malware that was and is about as much of a threat to our networks as viruses and external attacks can be. In fact Russian hackers exploited unpatched Windows 2000 servers and an unpatched Internet Explorer vulnerability to steal passwords and other sensitive information. The practice of using your computer with limited user rights is still not widely embraced by many firms in the small business space.

If you are in a small firm that does not have a "culture" of having computers run in user mode, or have a great deal of "road warriors" using laptops that are extremely difficult to run with restricted rights, an alternative approach for mitigation of risks and threats is recommended. First and foremost, keep yourself as patched as possible. Next change your Internet Explorer settings as follows:

1. First change your IE to run with Internet zones in "High Security."
2. Change your "trusted sites " to run at all times in "Medium" zone.

This serves several purposes. First it blocks all sites from running Active X and other potential malicious scripting. Next it protects you once you place "business sites" into the trusted zone as well ensuring you are "prompted."

I add to workstations an Internet Explorer tool bar that makes it easier to add sites to the trusted sites section.

http://www.microsoft.com/windows/ie/previous/webaccess/pwrtwks.mspx

This toolbar still works on Windows XP (sp1 and sp2) and Internet Explorer 6 and allows the information worker to easily add Web sites to her trusted sites zone setting.

Another mitigation technique widely recommended is to disable Active Scripting and Java. "Disabling Active Scripting and ActiveX controls in the Internet Zone (or any zone used by an attacker) appears to prevent exploitation of this vulnerability. Disabling Active scripting and ActiveX controls in the Local Machine Zone will prevent widely used payload delivery techniques from functioning."[37]

The guidance in Knowledge base article 833633 also describes the process by which you can strengthen the settings: http://support.microsoft.com/default.aspx?scid=833633. At the time of this writing, Security bulletin 04-025 was released as an "out of band" patch to remedy this issue. But it pointed out an interesting security issue. A threat was in place, a vulnerability identified, and there was no patch available. Thus in order to best protect the computers in a network, you, the consultant, are being called upon to take remedial action to minimize the risks. Again the notifications and security bulletins identified actions to take in place of patching, since there was no patch at that time. Balance the threat in the network to the firm you are analyzing. In my firm of IT workers, we do perform a great deal of Internet research and thus are at higher risk for potential browser and desktop issues. Given the inherent stronger protection of XP sp2, I cannot stress enough how important it is to deploy this as soon as you can and to urge your clients to permanently retire their Windows 9X clients.

Another very good resource on the settings recommended for browsers is the NIST guidelines for Windows XP: http://csrc.nist.gov/itsec/download_ WinXP.html[38]. For any web browser you choose, ensure that you take the time to adjust the settings and disable potentially malicious activity. You can use the IEAK (Internet Explorer Administration Kit) to customize the Internet Explorer for your desktops.

Malware, Malware Everywhere

Before applying XP sp2, you might be wise to scan those XP computers for the latest security issues of malware and spybots. Because we ask our Web browsers to act as more than just Web site "rendering," all of them are susceptible to vulnerabilities over the Internet from malicious Web sites, e-mail, or other issues. If your Internet browser visits a site that intends to inject code into your registry, and you are not running your browser with high security, you don't stay up to date on patches, and you do not have a tool to ensure that your registry is not adjusted, you can get your system infected with trojans, spyware and other "scumware" that is near impossible to clean out.

While XP sp2 definitely raises the bar and ensures the registry is much better protected, if your clients do general online research, I would still advise that they be trained to use any browser in a "high security" setting to better protect themselves.

Using an alternative browser is not the answer, since all of the Web browsers in the marketplace have been targeted with security issues and need to be patched and maintained. I still recommend Internet Explorer be your browser of choice due to the fact that with Software Update services (and later with Microsoft update services), you, the consultant, can patch all of the Web browsers in your client's networks in a controlled fashion. The symptoms of "scumware" are excessive pop-ups on a Web site and general slowdown of the machine. One of my fellow SBS MVPs, Michael Jenkin, shared this list of his favorite Malware clean tools:

Moosoft	http://www.moosoft.com/	Registry cleaner tool
Hijack This	http://www.spychecker.com/program/hijackthis.html	Use this to review your registry. It's recommended to review this CAREFULLY as you could accidentally remove a registry item that is needed
AdAware	http://www.lavasoftusa.com/default.shtml.en	Ad-Watch is a good tool to ensure that your registry is proactively protected.
Process Explorer	http://www.sysinternals.com/ntw2k/freeware/procexp.shtml	Helpful in investigating programs operating on your system
Spybot S&D	http://www.safer-networking.org/en/index.html	Use this and AdAware
CWShredder	http://www.spywareinfo.com/~merijn/downloads.html	Removes the Cool Web search tool. At the time of this writing, the CWShredder author no longer maintains the tool but it still may be of help.
SpySweeper	http://www.webroot.com/	Also has an Enterprise version of Spysweeper. A last minute add on to the list is the brand new Microsoft Anti-Spyware beta tool that was released in January of 2005.

You may also want to review your antivirus programs to see if they are beginning to include spyware protection.

In the **Trend CMS Suite**, you enable the Spyware protection enabling it as follows:

1. Load the main console for the Trend CSM Suite
2. Click on **Scan Now**
3. Click on **Scan Now Settings**
4. Check the box for **Scan for spyware**
5. Change the setting for Spyware from **Pass** to **Clean**

Be prepared to use several tools to clean out a machine and you may even need to manually review the registry using regedit. If the system still gives evidence of "scumware," I would strongly advise you to "flatten that system" and reinstall from scratch. The most virulent of these pests can dig deep into the registry and leave behind trojans and rootkits. A rootkit is a backdoor program that is extremely hard to detect and hides from detection. An excellent ongoing resource for security information are the Security Management columns by Jesper M. Johansson, Ph.D., CISSP, MCSE, MCP+I located at http://www.microsoft.com/technet/community/columns/secmgmt/smarch.mspx.

When you begin to clean a system, my fellow SBS MVPs recommend the following steps:

- Run **Disk Cleanup** from clicking on **My Computer**, then on the **C: Drive**, then on **Properties**, then on **Disk Cleanup**.

- Next review the profiles and files:

   o Begin first by resetting the file view:

   - Open up **Explorer**, click on **Tools** > **Folder Options** > **View**
   - Click on the option to **Show hidden files and folders** and close

   o Go to **C:\Document and Settings** and then for each logged on user profile folder that appears, drill down **..\{user}\Local Settings\Temp** and delete all temp files. In some infected systems, SBS MVP Kevin Weilbacher has found literally from 5,000 to over 20,000 files and folders in these temp files.

   o Then reboot the computer and run the spyware utilities again

- Run **Regedit (Start > Run > Regedit)** and manually review **HKLM\Software\Microsoft\Windows\CurrentVersion\RunOnce** and **..\Run listings** for any suspicious settings.

- Run **Regedit (Start > Run > Regedit)** and manually review **HKCU\Software\Microsoft\Windows\CurrentVersion\RunOnce** and **..\Run listings** for any suspicious settings.

Keep in mind one thing that fellow SBS MVP Jeff Middleton points out. This is truly intrusion detection analysis. You may want to document the programs that have wormed their way into your systems and determined what their "payload" was and what information or data they were retrieving. Some of the "scumware" is merely tracking your surfing habits on the Internet. The worse case scenario is that you have a backdoor trojan. You may want to drive image the computer for later analysis. Robert Hensing[39], a member of the Microsoft Security Incident Response team, has discussed how Administrators surfing at the servers on pornographic sites had inadvertently downloaded back door trojans on their systems.

I cannot stress enough the value of security education in an organization. Business computers should be used for business and you as the consultant need to impress upon the small business owner that his "bad" Internet habits of file swapping, opening unusual attachments from e-mail, and surfing on questionable sites can lead to a compromise of his system.

- *Action item—Always have a CD-ROM or USB pen drive with the latest "scumware" cleaning tools to assist you in this process. Discuss backup strategies with your clients to ensure that if you do need to reinstall a system from scratch their data will have been backed up.*

If Patching Isn't Available, What Then?

Typically we have relied upon patching as the means to defend our systems from attack. But in 2004 we saw that patching was not enough. Remediation techniques for Internet Explorer, such as disabling Java and Active X scripting, are just some of the issues to consider for your clients. The Secunia.com Web site is just one source among others I will list later on in this chapter that gives guidance for alternative ways to protect your systems. In general, you should attempt to restrict your server and your workstations to do only what you have authorized them to do. You should refer to the earlier discussion of user rights as the best methodology for protecting your workstations. Bottom line: Restrict what external programs can do to your systems.

- ***Action item**—Find resources for alternative measures to protect your server and network while a patch is in the works. Look for community Web sites and resources.*

Content Filtering

In combination with ISA server, you may want to investigate and leverage the power of gateway-based content filtering to scan all incoming Java, ActiveX, JavaScript, scripts, plug-ins, and cookies. More add-ons and discussions can be found at www.isatools.org and www.isaserver.org.

Patching the Third-Party Programs

Just because Microsoft programs need patches does not mean that the rest of the world is immune. Real Player, Macromedia Flash, Adobe Acrobat, Apple Quicktime are just a few of the programs you probably have in your client's network that may need updating. The Secunia Web site (www.secunia.com) is an excellent Web site that tracks vulnerabilities by vendor and provides an RSS feed of all known public vulnerabilities. For a fee you can obtain a service that just tracks the applications you need to track. For Line of Business applications, you may need to search out an e-mail notification service directly from the vendor for version and security upgrades. At the present time, I know of no patch vendors with the ability to scan and push patches to applications. However, keep a eye out for this as it appear some vendors are looking into performing this much needed service.

Where You Least Expect It

Security, as we said earlier, is always dependent on your weakest link. The laptop that was stolen at the airport, the wireless access point that didn't have WPA enabled, the password written on a sticky note, the office that doesn't have an alarm system are all examples of weak links to consider. A laptop containing sensitive information should either have EFS enabled or have a virtual PGP drive installed on it. (At the present time, I am not including EFS as a discussion point, as few line-of-business applications I am aware of will go on record supporting EFS. For more information, please see http://www.microsoft.com/technet/prodtechnol/winxppro/deploy/cryptfs.mspx. This may be a very viable add-on in the future. but at this time I cannot go on record as recommending it without vendor support. I do, however, recommend it as a means to protect sensitive data on laptops, and suggest you also investigate the solutions offered at www.pgp.com.)

Protect Data Transfers

E-mail is one of the easiest ways we transfer information, and we spend the least amount of time protecting it. Many a time I have received confidential income tax information sent to me in a mere e-mail. When working with your clients, advise them that whenever they send mail unencrypted, it is able to be opened and intercepted by anyone along the way. Just recently, a court ruled that an Internet service provider had not violated the United States wiretap laws when it intercepted a mail transmission to Amazon.com and directed a bookstore with which they were affliated to offer the books to the customer. Thus when sending EPHI (electronic patients health information) in the HIPAA world, or Adobe pdf versions of tax returns in the business world, protect the data with encryption. You can either set up individual digital certificates at each Outlook mailbox location, or you can set up a digital certificate at your server. For sending encrypted e-mail, which is required for transactions and correspondence with governmental agencies, there is a package to follow located at the Web site https://dodeca.verisign.com/digitalidCenter.htm. The process of sending an encrypted e-mail can be a bit cumbersome to the uninitiated. The sender and receiver of the encrypted e-mails have to first swap public certificates by digitally signing the e-mail. Then and only then do they have the ability to send encrypted e-mail. An alternative to use is a service like www.hypersend.com that allows you to encrypt the sending and storing of the e-mail via transit.

- *Action item* – Add digital certificates for encrypted e-mail where needed.

But What About Those Security Templates?

If you've noticed, I've been quiet on those built-in security templates that can be pushed out via the Windows group policy settings and can be found here: http://www.microsoft.com/resources/documentation/Windows/XP/all/reskit/en-us/Default.asp?url=/resources/documentation/Windows/XP/all/reskit/en-us/prdd_sec_umgs.asp. The reason I haven't brought them to your attention is that to follow them you must understand what might occur if you should apply them. I would argue that in your typical Small Business Server network, you will never ever apply the high-security template to your workstations, might apply the secure template, and might be stuck down there in the compatible template. Never apply these templates on a firm-wide basis unless you have fully tested these settings on one workstation, have tested all applications, and, more important, have tested with all network devices. They are effective, but review the impact before applying them.

Just Because They Are Part of Your Network Doesn't Mean You Should Trust Them

Typically, the issues in networks occur from remote connections. I can control everything inside my office to a certain degree; I have a hard time doing the same to external connections. I make sure any laptops that are part of my network and not in the possession of one particular employee of the firm are kept in a locked location in the office. When they are "checked out" by an employee, they are inspected to confirm all parts are in place, the unit is functional, and it is "ready" for connection to an external hostile network—that is, the laptop is up to date on patches, the firewall is in place, and the antivirus is current.

> BEST PRACTICE: Have a training session with laptop owners on the proper security handling of machines. Train them on how to make sure the firewall, antivirus, and patches are up to date. Consider ensuring that all laptops are on Windows XP sp2, as it contains this feature in its security center and will automatically notify the laptop owner when any of the three are disabled or need updating.

Remote Access to the Network

Your biggest threat to your network—besides the local administrator rights to each machine—is remote access to the network. Workstations at home that VPN back into the office have historically been an entry point for worms and viruses to a protected network. The fact that "Junior" at home downloads Kazaa and plays online group gaming is indeed a threat to your network. In my office I make it a firm policy that all employees' computers have antivirus and firewalls, and the firm purchases the annual subscription for them as a company policy. Again your first line of defense in VPN security is strong passwords[40] to ensure that only those authorized persons gain access. There are some additional features that you may wish to discuss with your client, but be aware that they do add complexity and overhead and your security budget may be better served in other areas.

The first is a technology available for Windows 2003 called network quarantine where through the use of group policy, your VPN clients are "vetted" before they enter the network. Later releases of Windows 2003 called Longhorn is expected to include network protection features which will "vet" the connection on even network clients.

- http://download.microsoft.com/download/0/7/e/07ed1953-0ab5-41ea-b5da-41cf8bb9cdae/Quarantine.doc

- http://download.microsoft.com/download/a/e/2/ae25c0a2-f11f-4bb2-bf83-52ace5b46a26/StepByStep_QuarTestlab.doc

Hardware firewalls are beginning to add a similar feature of scanning the VPN traffic for viruses as it enters the network. The addition of the layer of "what you have" authentication with RSA's Secure ID for Windows[41] adds an additional authentication protection for VPN connections by requiring an additional password only available via an external keyfob that the user has with him.

But again, remember, if you aren't even doing the basics, you are missing the real threats you have. Don't overspend your security dollars where there isn't a security issue. I personally have yet to see an authentication threat on a VPN connection to warrant the cost and expense of an additional authentication factor for a small business. You may need to add this as part of compliance with regulations, however, so be aware of the industry and the requirements for your client.

- *Action item—Identify additional procedures for laptops and remote computers.*

Wireless

Wireless access can be a security nightmare or a security advantage. The traditional stories of how "best" to secure wireless by using WEP encryption and removing the SSID broadcasting to better lock it down are old wives' tales. Setting up wireless properly is covered in Chapter 4 but to confirm that it's set up as it should be takes a laptop, or PDA, a wireless card (I use an Orinoco B Gold card), and a program called "Netstumbler"[42] for the laptop and "Ministumber" for the PDA. These programs give you the beginning tools to "find" wireless access points. In the book *War Driving: Drive, Detect, Defend; a Guide to Wireless Security*, the authors state that during their review of the statistics from the third World Wide War Drive, approximately "one of every four access points currently deployed is in a default configuration."[43] There are Web sites on the Internet that list default passwords for routers (http://www.phenoelit.de/dpl/dpl.html). Your first step in ensuring that your wireless is set up securely is to at LEAST change the default Administrator password of the WAP.

The next myth of wireless is to put in place MAC filtering. As the authors point out in *War Driving*, "Most commercial- and consumer-grade wireless networking equipment sends the MAC address [in] clear text even if WEP is enabled." Thus, using a program called "Airsnort" (http://airsnort.shmoo.com/) and given a bit of time, a person can "sniff" the wireless traffic, determine what the allowed MAC addresses are, change the MAC address on her computer to one that is allowed on the network, and then get on that network.

WEP was and still is an implementation of RC4 encryption standard that is flawed. The weaknesses of WEP are detailed at http://www.drizzle.com/~aboba/IEEE/rc4_ksaproc.pdf. WPA is vulnerable to an offline dictionary attack (http://wifinetnews.com/archives/002452.html), but at the present time there is no automated cracking tool. Bottom line: Review the information in Chapter 4 to set up 802.1x to ensure you are set up securely.

- ***Action item*** *– Review wireless connectivity.*

Let's Review What We Have Set Up, Shall We?

Unless your firm is in a regulated industry, you will probably not need to perform a "formal" security audit. However, I would recommend that AT LEAST on an annual basis, if not more often, you take the time to perform a visual and verbal security audit with your clients and discuss with them security issues they have had in the past. I would include virus infections in this category, as well. I consider patch management to be part of a normal network process and should be included in a mandatory maintenance package you should offer to your client.

Discuss with your clients unusual activities in their networks. If they are suddenly seeing incidents affecting them via a certain threat vector, you may need to adjust your network protection to better assist in protection of the network. I find that many times employees don't mention that they've had issues with pop-ups or that Internet Explorer is having scripting errors indicating issues with spyware. Instead, they just accept the behavior as normal. Empower your clients and their employees to discuss any unusual happenings with the systems.

Some documents that you may like to review to assist you in discussing issues with your client include:

- Common Sense Guide to Cyber Security for Small Businesses http://www.isalliance.org/resources/papers/Common_Sense_sm_bus.pdf

- eSecurity Guide for Small Business (page 11 includes a document that you can use to begin the discussions with your client http://download.microsoft.com/download/2/5/1/2518982c-228b-40a8-a7bf-f683b37a0f38/eSecurityGuideforSmallBusiness.pdf

The Center for Internet Security has a benchmarking tool that can be used to "score" a server and ensure that the server is maintaining that benchmark. You use the tool to compare your server's security settings with the settings as defined by a consensus team of security experts and Microsoft. Since there is no specific template for the Small Business Server 2003 platform, you must be aware that comparing the platform to the domain controller policy does mean that the score will be lower and different than a server that is running just Windows 2003. However, I still find this tool of interest for the documentation as well as for setting your own benchmark and rescanning the server on a regular basis to make certain you are still within the original base number you received. At the time of this writing, the Windows 2003 benchmarks should be released. (http://www.cisecurity.org/)

Remember that there are three types of assessments: First is a patch audit. This type of test I would argue should be done at least on a monthly basis, since security patches typically come out on the second Tuesday of the month. The tools usually used for this are Hfnetchk, or MBSA[44], but more patch tools can be found at http://www.patchmanagement.org/comparisons.asp. At this time Software Update Service doesn't report enough in this area to be a proper patch analyzer, but the next version of SUS or WUS due out next year is expected to perform this process.

Next is a vulnerability audit. This is the process where you apply a bit of "proof of concept code" or vulnerability assessment tools to your network to see if you are truly vulnerable. Many of them are listed at http://www.insecure.org/tools.html, but again one of the easiest to use for the Small Business Server environment is MBSA. It also tends to be the least intrusive in not causing issues on a Small Business Network. It also tends to be the most SBS "friendly" and has guidance specific to SBS. Be aware that other vulnerability scanners may not understand you are running all the things we are running on the SBS platform and thus may recommend settings that are not wise to use in our networks.

Last is a full security audit that examines policies and procedures as well as the "human element."

To perform a "basic" security audit of your client, ensure the basics are in place:

1. People

    - Ensure that skills and knowledge are in place to make the end users, the employees, aware of the issues.

    - Ensure an acceptable use policy is in place at the firm; if there isn't one, guide the firm into writing this documentation.

2. Technology

- Identify assets that need physical protection.

- Review the workstations' patch status, antivirus protection, firewall status.

- If portable devices are in place in the firm, review the procedures in place for removing the laptop and reattaching it to the network.

- Identify external services that introduce additional threats (e-mail, remote access) and review the protection on these additional threats.

3. Data

- Review legislative environment in which you or your client must work, and any additional procedures that may need to be in place to protect the data. Review the types of information that need protecting and where the data is located. Identify additional procedures of protection if data is on a device that is at higher risk.

Use the STRIDE model discussed at the beginning of this chapter to predict the threats to that network. Remember the basic rule in risk management is to assign it to someone else, remove the risk, mitigate the risk, or accept the risk. Determine the "price" for these risks and remember our DREAD formula to assign priorities to issues that you find during your review. Additional guidance for security assessments can be found at http://members.microsoft.com/partner/projectguides/system_security/default.aspx.

To perform a more in-depth audit needed for regulatory purposes (HIPAA, GBL, etc.), you normally want go beyond a technological review and ensure that you also review policies. The AICPA through Systrust[45], the ISACA through their COBIT[46], and the ISO through the 17799 documentation[47] all provide guidance to perform these procedural-type audits. If your client requires this level of audit for regulatory purposes, I would advise you to obtain guidance from a CPA, CISA, or CISSP who specializes in this kind of audit process.

- *Action—Perform an audit to ensure the business's policies are being followed.*

Casing the Joint

If you truly wanted to break into a network, you would begin by throwing some packets at ports, examining the traffic coming from that network. and looking for the banners that would advertise what version of the operating system you were running to best determine where the system is the weakest. From these banner scans you can discover what operating system version, patch status, and other information would guide the attacker. Obviously, if we are going to perform an external examination of the network we just installed, we already know it's a Windows 2003 platform.

Understand What You Are Doing Your Testing On and Test from the Right Place

Not too long ago a security vendor sent out a press release that the Small Business Server 2003 platform was shipped with 25 vulnerabilities and had major weaknesses (http://www.predatorwatch.com/vulnerability_alerts.html). There was just one problem with their analysis. Based on my "read" of their investigation, they were scanning the security of the server from the "inside" of the server. Needless to say, we have a gooey inner core that is indeed a bit "squishy" in the middle, which is actually how it should be for maximum efficiency. How "insecure" you are from the outside will depend on what ports you have open and what services you are running ("listening").

Thus always perform your examination of mail relay, of open ports, and of wireless openings from a device that is not on your domain and is, in fact, on a totally different public IP address. Ensure that you have the full approval of the client—a "get out jail free card" as they say in the industry. Sniffing out open wireless access points and walking up to the potential client announcing what you found wouldn't exactly paint you as a trustworthy consultant.

So let's jump over to a port scan. My personal favorite is a GUI based scanner called Foundstone's Superscan (http://www.foundstone.com/?subnav=resources/navigation.htm&subcontent=/resources/proddesc/superscan.htm). The methods to scan the outside of your network can be done with Nmap[48] or merely by going to www.grc.com. The Shields-up test site examines the ports it reports what it sees "open." Please note that on the GRC Web site, a difference between "stealth" and "closed," in my personal opinion, is not a goal to strive for. What you are looking for is to ensure that only those ports you want open from the outside are truly open. Check to make sure that the ports you intended to be open from the outside are the only ones truly open from the outside. I consider this to be a mandatory step for any network system set up by a consultant and should be redone on a regular basis.

•   ***Action item***—*Always review what ports are open from the outside.*

Yes, Virginia, This Is Why We Audit

One of the biggest changes you will notice on the Small Business Server 2003 platform (and the Windows 2003 platform) is the amount of auditing and audit logs that get pushed out on a regular basis. Ensure that you, as the consultant, set up the monitoring e-mail to be sent to you and review them on a regular basis. This is your first line of defense. One of the typical issues we have historically seen in the Small Business Server platform is something called a SMTP auth attack whereby spammers attempt to authenticate on a system using an easy-to-crack username and password. (Remember this is why we rename the Administrator account and use strong passwords.) When an event like an SMTP auth attack occurs, you will find a trail left behind in the security logs where they are trying to get in. If you don't enable the audit logs, you will be blind to what is occurring and will not have any documentation should a legal action be required.

Ensuring that your passwords are longer than 14 characters and complex means that any dictionary attack program is going to start showing up as security failures in your audit logs. Security audit logs will show a failure like this when a SMTP attack is occurring, which shows a failure of a network logon (type 3)[49]:

Security 529 7/1/2004 2:17 AM 5 *

Logon Failure:

  Reason: Unknown user name or bad password

  User Name: asdf

  Domain:

  Logon Type: 3

Logon Process: Advapi

Authentication Package: MICROSOFT_AUTHENTICATION_PACKAGE_V1_0

Workstation Name: *SERVERNAME*

Caller User Name: *SERVERNAME$*

Caller Domain: RRR

Caller Logon ID: (0x0,0x3E7)

Caller Process ID: 1720

Transited Services: -

Source Network Address: -

Source Port: -

Again, if you see anything unusual that you are unsure of, my advice would be to check with the community resources for guidance.

IIS/ISA Logs

Depending on the ports you have open, you may need to review these more or less based on what each client has open. If you have port 80 open from the outside, you can get quite entertained by the traffic that attempts to break in. Most of it is "harmless" packets of data from infected PCs just looking for another "roadkill" on the Internet. If you need to perform any detailed analysis I would advise you to download the Logparser tool from http://www.microsoft.com/downloads/details.aspx?FamilyID=56fc92ee-a71a-4c73-b628-ade629c89499&displaylang=en. But you can also open up a log file from the quick-and-dirty tool called Excel (yes even a spreadsheet can be used to review the logs). IIS Logs are found at %SystemRoot%\system32\Logfiles\<server_name> and the types of fields captured are shown below[50].

Field	Description
Client's IP address	The IP address of the client machine that made the request.
User name	The name of the authenticated user who accessed your server. This does not include anonymous users, who are represented by a hyphen (-).
Date	The date the activity occurred
Time	The time the activity occurred.

Field	Description
Service and Instance	A Web site instance is displayed as W3SVC# and an FTP site instance is displayed as MSFTPSVC#, where # is the instance of the site.
Computer name	The server's network basic input/output system (NetBIOS) name.
IP address of server	The IP address of the server that the request was serviced through.
Time taken	The duration of time, in milliseconds, that the action consumed.
Bytes sent	The number of bytes sent from the client to the server.
Bytes received	The number of bytes received by the client from the server.
Service status code	The HTTP or FTP status code.
Windows status code	The status of the action, in terms used by Windows.
Request type	The type of request received by the server (for example, **GET** and **PASS**).
Target of the operation	The URL that was the target of the operation.
Parameters	The parameters that are passed to a script.

For forensic and criminal investigative purposes, or merely just to make your life easier, matching up the happenings in your IIS logs with that of the ISA (or other firewall) logs just makes sense. For example, you can observe whether all the devices that logon are in time sync with one another.[51]

In general when you see a "200" code in the Service Status section, that means that the request has been processed. A "400" code means that it has been denied.[52] When a new event in the Internet is occurring and you see unusual "tracks" in your log files, watch the newsgroups and communities for guidance. Many times I have found that by placing enough of the unique string of a log file into Google, I could diagnose an unsuccessful attempt of Code Red or Nimda infection or other attacks. Use your own server as a "baseline" for normal activity and again use the community resources to guide you when you see anything unusual.

- *Action item*—Review the audit logs on a regular basis. Investigate anything unusual and compare notes with others.

NetStat—More Powerful Than You Realize

The command netstat–ano is a little utility that tells you what connection is being made from your server. The knowledge-base article http://support. microsoft.com/default.aspx?scid=kb;EN-US;281336 discusses the use of this command combined with task manager to determine the process of attempting to travel outbound from a server. If you suspect a Trojan has compromised a system, this is a quick and dirty way to examine what is making outbound connections from your server.

MBSA—You Can't Knock the Price

While I am personally annoyed at times by the results it gives, the free Microsoft Baseline Security Analyzer[53] does provide us with a walk through our systems and a top-level overview well suited for our "roadkill" status. What annoys me is when it can't quite read a patch and while it truly is installed and I truly am just fine, it tells me that the file "checksum" is "equal to or higher than what was expected." Then when I eyeball the expected file and the actual file side by side, I find the same patched version. It also provides you with basic vulnerability scanning on your system and gives you a good "roadkill" view of your system. Currently MBSA does not scan for DirectX or for ISA server, but it is anticipated to include these in the future.

> •· *Action item*—*Perform a patch audit on a regular basis.*

Don't Forget the Basics

Remember our basics of firewall, patching and antivirus? We've reviewed the firewall and we've reviewed our patch level. Now let's ensure our antivirus signatures are up to date. In my networks, I have an antivirus package that gives me a console view I can review and make sure all of my systems are up to date on the dat file. I also stay aware of the latest viruses and the method of infection to ensure I have covered that threat vector. If need be, I will block file extensions if a new threat occurs.

Let's Not Get Stupid

In addition to possibly opening up a business for lawsuit, peer-to-peer file sharing software puts a network at risk. Never allow any sort of gaming, peer-file sharing, or nonbusiness-type application in the firm. Warn your clients of the risks of letting unauthorized downloading from and surfing on the Internet. Allowing "Junior" to entertain himself on an office computer while the owner works during the weekend may cost that owner more than she realizes. If vendors need outside Internet access, my advice would be to set up an open wireless access point completely separated from the firm network and on a separate IP address from the ISP. Being a little bit paranoid goes a long way to keeping a network safe.

Reviewing the SANS Top 20

On an annual basis, the SANS Institute publishes the Top 20 Internet Security Vulnerability listing[54] and how to get rid of the issues that cause the biggest problems on the Internet.

The listing reflects the top ten Windows and top ten Unix-based vulnerabilities and is a good guideline for Small Business Server Consultants to follow, as it identifies the typical "Roadkill" targets on the Internet. For 2003, the top ten Windows issues were as follows:

1. **Internet Information Services**—This primarily relates to IIS 5.0 installations. Default installs of IIS were subject to denial of service attacks, exposure, or compromise of sensitive files or data, execution of arbitrary commands, and complete compromise of the server. Anyone who has been in the SBS community knows that we, too, were affected by Code Red and Nimda. At this time there are no listed vulnerabilities in the version of IIS [IIS 6.0] contained in Small Business Server 2003 that would lead to complete compromise of the server. It is always advisable to be aware of any issues, given SBS's historical risk levels and the fact that port 80 is always in the top ten scanned ports on the Internet. Secunia's Web site tracks IIS 6.0 at http://secunia.com/product/1438/.

- *Action item—Keep an eye on advisories listing IIS 6.0 and keep up to date on patches. This issue is corrected by patching with Windows Update.*

  2. **Microsoft SQL Server**—Both SQL server and MSDE have been the target of several serious attacks in the past. Hackers (both of the professional and script kiddie variety) understand that databases are where the gold mine of information lies and thus have targeted these applications. Traditonally, ports 1433 and 1434 are in the top ten scanned ports on the Internet. Ensure that you use MBSA to scan your network AND attached workstations for hidden versions of SQL/MSDE. The SQL Security Web site maintains a list of applications that include SQL server versions http://www.sqlsecurity.com/DesktopDefault.aspx?tabid=31. While the Small Business Server 2003 WMSDE and SQL server is installed in a manner to make certain you are patched, and the system is set up in a manner that ports 1433 and 1434 are normally not open to the outside world, being aware of the issues with this application is wise. SQL server is not patched with Windows Update or SUS[55] and instead patches must be identified with MBSA or a third party patch tool. Secunia tracks the advisories at http://secunia.com/product/7/.

- *Action item—Keep an eye on advisories listing SQL Server, and keep up to date on patches. This issue is currently **not** patched with Windows Update.*

  3. **Windows Authentication Issues**—It cannot be stressed enough how important passwords are, and here they arc at number three in the SANS top 20. In addition the advice to disable the storing of LM hashes on the server can be done in an SBS 2003 environment.

- *Action item—Stress to your client how important passwords are. Enable the password policy when you are prompted by the wizard to do so. Consider auditing the strength of the passwords with LC4/5 or John the Ripper tools.*

  4. **Internet Explorer**—As was previously discussed, ensuring that ActiveX and other scripting is properly controlled is vital to your network. While historically one could say that keeping up to date with patches was enough, the security news in the month of June of

2004 clearly showed us that alternative actions needed to be evaluated. Tracking the issues and recommended alternatives can be found at http://secunia.com/product/11/.

- *Action item—Safe surfing should be stressed to your clients. The discussions and ideas about protecting Internet Explorer, XP sp2, and the limitations of the use of local admin should be discussed with your client.*

5. **Windows Remote Access Services**—Misconfiguration of file and printer sharing, Anonymous Logon null sessions, and other misconfigurations of remote access are unlikely in the Small Business Server 2003 platform if you keep one rule in mind: Follow the wizards. The additional protection in Windows 2003 prevented it from being affected with recent Blaster[56] and Sasser[57] worms. This protection is built into Windows XP sp2 as well.

- *Action item—Keep up to date on patches and recommend updating to XP sp2 as soon as possible. Keep sharing of folders to the minimum necessary.*

6. **Microsoft Data Access Components** (MDAC)—These are database technologies found in many versions of Windows including Small Business Server 2003. MDAC is updated with Windows Update. Secunia currently is tracking the issues for MDAC 2.X on their site at http://secunia.com/product/1807/.

- *Action item—Keep up to date on patches.*

7. **Windows Scripting Host**—This allows servers to be more easily managed by introducing JavaScript and Visual Basic Script. I would not recommend any actions to disable it on our networks, as it is my opinion the less we can automatically control, the worse off we are.

- *Action item—Keep up to date on patches.*

8. **Outlook and Outlook Express**—It is not recommended that you install Outlook on a server, but Outlook Express is installed on a base Windows 2003 system. The easy mitigation technique is to not read e-mail from the server, ensure you are up to date on patches throughout the rest of the office. and balance this with antivirus software. At the present time Software Update service does not patch Office applications. Secunia tracks Office vulnerabilities at http://

secunia.com/product/24/ and at http://secunia.com/product/2276/. You can use the Office update site to search for updates (http://office.microsoft.com/officeupdate/) and the Office Update Inventory tool to scan computers for their patch status (http://www.microsoft.com/office/ork/2003/journ/offutoolv2.htm). But third-party tools that combine server, desktop, and office scanning provide a much more efficient way to protect the network.

- *Action item—Keep up to date on patches.*

9. **Windows Peer-to-Peer File Sharing**—As was discussed previously, this is a classic "don't do that" or DDT issue. Consider disengaging or requiring a extra retainer fee to continue your business relationship with the client if they continue to operate in this manner. Make sure the company manual includes an acceptable use policy that forbids this activity. Block ports commonly used by peer-to peer-applications if necessary.

- *Action item—Just don't let your client do this. Period. Guide your client in preparing an AUP document that forbids this.*

10. **Simple Network Management Protocol (SNMP)**—In my own network, I have found many devices that have SNMP with a common key phrase or community string value. Since small networks typically do not have open those SNMP ports used by these devices, this final top ten item has traditionally not been a concern for me. While I have made sure I changed the default SNMP or that a device did not have a blank name, I have not seen this as an issue in our SBS community.

- *Action item—While you are setting up printer devices, review the SNMP settings. At this time, this is not a major security issue in our small networks.*

Tools to scan for the SANS Top 20 are located at http://www.sans.org/top20/tools04.pdf.

Penetration Testing

I'm including "Pen Testing" as a topic of IT auditing, even though the typical script kiddie/DefCon hacker/true expert wouldn't earn too many brownie points in the hacker world boasting about "taking down an SBS box." Typically it's just easier to lift up the keyboard of the server and find the post-it note with the passwords on it, or call up the office manager and just ask for the password than it is to use a John the Ripper[58], employ LC4 or LC5[59] password cracker program, throw TSgrinder[60] attacks at us, use Netcat[61], or run a Nmap[62] scan of our external ports, use DumpSec[63] or LSAdump[64], try SQL Server injections[65], or rely on any number of targeting penetration testing techniques. The chance that any one of the top 75 tools found on http://www.insecure.org/tools.html are being specifically and deliberately used to crack into a small business network by an outsider is, in my opinion, probably rare. The chances that the office manager will accidentally misconfigure something in the network if she decides to install an application without your guidance are probably vastly more likely. In fact, I personally know of clients who have enabled the guest account on a server thinking that this would allow temporary access to a vendor when instead it just opened up the server to be used as a mail relay and ended up getting their server blacklisted. If you've ever had a server blacklisted, you know how long it takes to remove that distinction. Needless to say ensuring that your clients are either technical enough to understand what they are doing or comfortable enough in letting you handing the network entirely is the balancing act all consultants in the small business world face.

If you are interested in finding out more about penetration testing techniques, Chapter 8 and 9, and Appendix A of the book, *Accessing Network Security*, by Kevin Lam, David LeBlanc, and Ben Smith (ISBN 0-7356-2033-4) is an excellent primer for the kinds of procedures one would use to investigate a firm and the computer equipment.

It's my opinion that this level of penetration testing is not needed in the Small Business Server world. We're not specifically targeted. But we need to be aware that some of these targeting techniques are just "borrowed" by the spammers and automated attackers. For example, dictionary attacks combined with SMTP authentication attacks are now a pretty regular event on our systems. So while you don't need to be worried about the "specific targeter," you do need to be concerned about the automated ones. Your network will indeed be "roadkill" without these precautions.

Take One Last Look Around

Whenever I travel and stay in hotels, I always take one last look around the room to be certain I haven't forgotten something or left something behind. In the last few pages we've talked a lot about the issues "out there" and we haven't spent too much time about the issues "in here." Your clients' trusted employees can do a lot of damage to a firm either intentionally or unintentionally. When an employee leaves, ensure that building alarm codes are changed, keys and locks are retooled (if deemed necessary), and that the employee has a brief "exit" interview to determine all company-owned technology property has been returned. I disable the account of employees after they depart, but I leave the mailbox behind and intact for a time after in case information needs to be retrieved. Also consider performing a ghosting of a hard drive in a computer of an employee who has left under extreme circumstances.

If someone in your client's office also performs administration duties, request that she keeps a computer log file next to the server to describe what she did. As an outsourced consultant, you may not always have good documentation of what has occurred to that server or various workstations. Impress on your clients how important it is to know the sequence of events and when they should call you in.

Ensure you keep regular backups and take copies offsite. Malicious damage that cannot be quickly recovered from can be very economically damaging to a firm.

Don't forget to review on a periodic basis the security policies and settings for the firms you administer. Ask what other software or services they might be using in the firm. New technologies arrive each day that advertise great benefits but may hide hidden costs. As an example, the free VOIP product Skype was developed by the same folks that developed Kazaa. In the Skype privacy policies, it states:

"From time-to-time your computer may become a Supernode. A Supernode is a computer running Skype Software that has been automatically elevated to act as a hub. Supernodes may assist in helping other users to communicate or use the Skype software efficiently. This may include the ability for your computer to help anonymously and securely facilitate communications between other users

of the Skype Software who, due to network and firewall constraints, cannot establish direct connections. The system has been designed so that being a Supernode will not interfere with the normal operations of your computer."[66]

Many companies[67] put specific wording in their acceptable use policy to make it clear that employees are restricted from utilizing any such P2P software, external instant messaging or any other applications in violation of security policies. Regularly review your clients' policies and update them as needed.

When You Shouldn't Be Touching That System

There might be a time, even in the Small Business Server client base that you service, when you become aware something has occurred that is either beyond your capabilities or should be handled by authorities. Any action on your part to investigate the system without making a proper forensic image of the drive could end up damaging the chain of evidence. Ensuring that you do not damage log file evidence that can be used to examine the incident is extremely important. The Secret Service has a document online to assist in gathering information (http://www.ustreas.gov/usss/net_intrusion_forms.shtml) to give you some ideas of the forensic evidence they need to keep.

In the United States, typically the U.S. Secret Service, the branch of the U.S. Treasury in charge of computer crimes, will not prosecute unless the computer crime dollar amount exceeds $75,000 or above. The Secret Service[68] works with the local district attorney's office to prosecute these cases. If your client and you believe that a targeted network intrusion of this magnitude has occurred on your client's network, contact your local authorities and specifically ask for their computer crimes division. You may find that you need to contact a division in a large city for this type of organization.

I do not consider incidents such as our "stupidity" of nonpatching or the misconfiguration of a system where we are "hacked" along with everyone else who handled their network systems insecurely enough to warrant notification to computer crimes divisions—unless, you are in jurisdictions like California, where additional requirements such as notification of affected client data are in place for such intrusions. Consider making a call to your local authority that covers computer crimes to determine the requirements for your area. Determine when you need to notify the authorities and where they are located before you truly need this information. Many law enforcement organizations provide public service seminars to keep you informed.

We're All on the Same Highway

I hope I have provided you with some thoughts and ideas for ways to better deploy the Small Business Server securely in this chapter. I know I haven't given you the answers, and in fact have probably just filled your head with more questions and concerns. It's up to you to consider the needs and requirements for your clients. I cannot give you a template or a checklist. Small businesses are too unique to fit into a cookie-cutter template. It's up to you, the trusted advisor, to discuss what is needed by your clients to make sure their business can function, their network works, their livelihood thrives and stays safely protected while doing it.

SD Cubed Plus C

Microsoft's security push is called "SD cubed +C." That's Secure by Design, Secure by Default, Security by Deployment + Communication. Microsoft handled the Design of the Small Business Server 2003, they adjusted the settings by Default, but it's up to you and me for the final steps of Deployment and Communication.

For the last part of the puzzle, Communication, I will leave you with my lists of online community resources. We all share the same information superhighway out here and we have the ability to see the patterns and follow up with the solutions. In closing, the following are my favorite resources. Enjoy them, and I hope to see you soon in the community where I hang out, the Small Business Server newsgroups. Say "Hi" when you see me on the Information Superhighway and don't forget to be careful out here!

- **Last Action item**—*Stay informed!*

Small Business Server Specific

Type of Resource	Name Link
Newsgroup	Microsoft Small Business Server 2003 Community Newsgroup http://www.microsoft.com/windowsserver2003/sbs/community/default.mspx
Listserve	Small Business Server Listserve, covers all versions of SBS Send an e-mail to Sbs2k-subscribe@yahoogroups.com
User/Reseller Groups	Peer group of SBS consultants http://www.microsoft.com/windowsserver2003/sbs/community/usergroups.mspx
Monthly Web Chat	*MCP Magazine* SBS help desk chat http://mcpmag.com/chats/
Web Sites	SBS Web sites http://www.smallbizserver.net http://www.sbsfaq.comhttp://www.sbs-rocks.com http://www.sbs-links.com
Conferences	SMBNation annual and regional conferences http://www.smbnation.com
Web Blog	RSS feed of Charles Anthe (Release Manager) http://blogs.msdn.com/canthe/
Online newsletter	Harry Brelsford online newsletter Sign up at http://www.smbnation.com
Web Blog	Susan Bradley's Web Blog http://www.msmvps.com/bradley
Web Blog	Taz Network's Blog http://www.taznetworks.com/rss/webblog.html
Web Blog	Chad Gross (SBS-MVP) http://msmvps.com/cgross/
Web Blog	Kevin Weilbacher's SBS Blog http://msmvps.com/kwsupport/
Web Blog	Stevereno.Net http://www.stevereno.net/sbs/sbs.php
Web Blog	Gavin's Fragments http://interprom.blogspot.com/
Web Blog	Dean Calvert's http://msmvps.com/calvert/
Web Blog	Eriq Neale's SBS/MAC http://simultaneouspancakes.com/Int/
Web Blog	Javier Gomez's SBS blog http://msmvps.com/javier/

Type of Resource	Name Link
Web Blog	Jeff Louck's blog http://www.msmvps.com/sbs/
Web Blog	Wayne Small's blog http://www.msmvps.com/sbsfaq/
Web Blog	SBS Documentation Blog http://blogs.msdn.com/sbsdocsteam/
Web Blog	SeanDaniel.com's blog http://seanda.blogspot.com/
Web Blog	Scott Colson's CRM world http://msmvps.com/crm/

Security

Type of Resource	Name Link
Web Site	Early warning Web site of happenings http://www.incidents.org
Listserve	Patch Management Listserve sponsored by Shavlik http://www.patchmanagement.org
Web Site	Training and resources for security http://www.sans.org
Web Site	Secunia tracks vulnabilities by application http://www.secunia.com
Web Site	2600Mag the Hacker Quarterly http://www.2600mag.com/
Webcasts	TechNet Webcasts http://www.microsoft.com/technet/community/ webcasts/default.mspx
Web Site	NIST guidelines http://www.nsa.gov/snac/ index.cfm?MenuID=scg10.3.1
Web Site	Windows 2003 Resource Kit Tools http://www.microsoft.com/downloads/details.aspx? FamilyID=9d467a69-57ff-4ae7-96ee-b18c4790cffd &displaylang=en
Web Site	Blackhat briefing online Webcasts http://www.blackhat.com/html/bh-multimedia- archives-index.html
Web Site	DefCon online conference information http://www.defcon.org/html/links/defcon-media- archives.html

Type of Resource	Name Link
Books	Hacking Exposed Windows 2000, Windows 2003 http://www.hackingexposed.com/home.html
Tools Site	HackingExposed http://www.hackingexposed.com/tools/tools.html
Book	Microsoft Command-Line Microsoft® Windows® Command-Line Administrator's Pocket Consultant ISBN 0-7356-2038-5
Book	Microsoft Scripting Guide Microsoft ® Windows® Windows 2000 Scripting Guide 0-ISBN 7356-1867-4
Book	Writing Secure Code Writing Secure Code Second Edition Howard and LeBlanc – ISBM 0-7356-1722-8
Book	Threat Modeling Threat Modeling ISBN 0-7356-1991-3
Book	Accessing Network Security ISBN 0-7356-2033-4 Smith, LeBlanc, MSPress
Book/Web Site	Always use protection http://www.alwaysuseprotection.com/
Book	Protecting your Windows Network Dr. Jesper Johansson and Steve Riley, Addison Wesley
Other Resources	Links for more Information http://www.defcon.org/html/links/links-o-rama.html

Web Blogs/RSS Feeds of Interest

Security

Type of Resource	Name Link
RSS Feeds	US CERT technical warnings http://www.us-cert.gov/channels/
RSS Feed	Microsoft Security Bulletins http://www.microsoft.com/technet/security/ bulletin/secrssinfo.mspx
RSS Feed	Security Focus Vulns and News http://www.securityfocus.com/rss/index.shtml
RSS Feed	Security Pipeline http://www.securitypipeline.com/rss/all.jhtml

Type of Resource	Name Link
RSS Feed	Microsoft Download Site (the Thundermain Feed) http://www.thundermain.com/rss
RSS Feed	Secunia's tracking of Vulns/Viruses via RSS http://secunia.com/information_partner/ anonymous/http://secunia.com/ rss_latest_virus_alerts/
RSS Feed	SANS/Incidents.org Daily Diary http://isc.sans.org/rssfeed.xml
RSS Feed	RISKS digest http://catless.ncl.ac.uk/rdigest.rdf
RSS Feed	Michael Howard (author of Writing Secure Code) Blog http://blogs.msdn.com/michael_howard/
RSS Feed	F-Secure Web Blog – the folks at F-secure have an excellent blog that tracks Virus actions http://www.f-secure.com/weblog/weblog.rdf
RSS Feed	Dana Epps' excellent security-focused blog http://silverstr.ufies.org/blog/
RSS Feed	Aaron Margosis blog on running as limited user http://blogs.msdn.com/aaron_margosis
RSS Feed	PacketStorm feed of new tools http://www.packetstormsecurity.org/ whatsnew100.xml
RSS Feed	Spyware Blog http://www.netrn.net/spywareblog/
RSS Feed	Robert Hensing Blog http://blogs.msdn.com/robert_hensing/

Other Content

RSS Feed	The EHLO Blog – The Exchange Team Blog http://blogs.msdn.com/exchange
RSS Feed	MSDN Bloggers (full RSS feed of all bloggers) http://blogs.msdn.com
RSS Feed	Microsoft Watch RSS Feed – feed of an IT journalist who reports on Microsoft http://www.microsoft-watch.com/article2/ 0,1995,1097192,00.asp
RSS Feed	Microsoft Monitor RSS –feed of industry analyst Joe Wilcox http://www.microsoftmonitor.com/index.xml

Type of Resource	Name
	Link
RSS Feed	Anne Stanton
	http://thenorwichgroup.blogs.com/

Just for Fun (okay, it's what *I* consider fun)

Book	*The Cuckoo's Egg*
	The Cuckoo's Egg: Tracking a Spy Through the Maze of Computer Espionage, Cliff Stoll ISBM 0743411463
Movie	*War Games*
	The classic movie about breaking into computers that started it all.
Movie	*The Net*
	Sandra Bullock stars in Hollywood's version of viruses and computers
Movie	*Hackers*
	Angelina Jolie and company in a Macintosh view of the Windows World
Movie	*Sneakers*
	Robert Redford and company in a movie about cryptography. Trivia—the gentlemen who is the "A" in RSA actually designed the equations that are projected onscreen during the Presentation.
Movie	*Antitrust*
	Hollywood's version of a Computer monopoly
Movie	*Swordfish*
	You can't crack a password that fast
Movie	*Enemy of the State*
	They are indeed watching you

Summary

So there you have it—more security topics surrounding the SBS experience then you might have initially imagined. The important takeaway from this chapter is to appreciate that security is both technical and non-technical in nature. There is both the command-line level and the business thinking level. Hopefully I've successfully presented both sides while remaining your loyal SBSer. Now its time to move onwards to Chapter 12 with a focus on ISA Server 2004!

CHAPTER 12
Advanced SBS 2003 Security: Part 2: ISA Server 2004

BY Beatrice Mulzer (Cocoa, FL)

WITH Dr. Thomas Shinder (Dallas, TX)

Introduction

This chapter has been produced for SBS consultants who want to know more about Microsoft's Internet Security and Acceleration Server (ISA Server 2004), besides what the SBS wizards configure. At this time, it is still unclear what parts of ISA Server 2004 are going to be integrated into the SBS Server management console and how deep their integration will be. The SBS development team has done a great job on SBS 2003 and I look forward to seeing what cool things they came up with for Service Pack 1 (SP1). Assuming that ISA configuration for Outlook Web Access (OWA), Outlook Mobile Access (OMA) and Remote Procedure Call (RPC) over HTTP will still be wizardized, I concentrated on some additional rule settings and configurations that will be a huge value-add for you and your client.

For the longest time I've had a love/hate relationship with ISA 2000, even though I've known that it is an awesome tool working in my favor. Its monitoring and reporting functions have been especially helpful in demonstrating to business owners that the things I told them were not a bunch of baloney (such as proving that a certain user was running her own business on e-bay from the workplace).

In this chapter, you will learn how you can control a network with the power of ISA by understanding how the giant ISA wheels click. This chapter does not cover every intricate detail; if you need more in-depth information on

ISA itself, I highly recommend Tom Shinder's book, *Configuring ISA Server 2004* (Syngress).

If you want the one-hour overview, you've come to the right place. Due to the nature of our business, uncertainties and other uncontrollable influential factors that are not yet foreseeable (like very rare software bugs), we will have a site posted at http://www.smbnation.com/isaupdates.htm that will include information on ISA SBS Server configuration scenarios of interest for our SBS community.

In the meantime, grab a cup of java and enjoy.

> BEST PRACTICE: Do not configure notifications for detected ISA attacks to send you alert notices by email for every intrusion attack like IP spoofing, Ping of death, WinNukes, and UDP bombs, or your inbox shall be filled with 200 ISA emails a day, minimum!

Attention: This is Not a Commercial

Business owners should be able to trust their technological devices to work and be dependable without even having to think about their security implications.

Over the last decade, we have come to take technology advances, such as the Internet Technology infrastructure, for granted. Why do I talk about this? As an SBS consultant, how many small businesses do you walk into where you find them hooked up directly to a cable or DSL modem? Most small businesses jump onto the Information Highway like a bunch of sheep without a herder, and then they wonder why they get creamed by all the hungry bugs running loose on the net. BAA!

As an SBS consultant, you have the role of herding little groups of sheep. You must provide a reliable and safe computing environment as an integral part of your services so your sheep can frolic about without getting eaten alive by marauding viruses and other junk.

With ISA Server 2004, you can provide this level of protection and comfort. No doubt about it, ISA Server 2004, which is included in the Premium Edition of SBS 2003, is an enterprise-level firewall (depending on who you talk to).

The real question is, why would you want to install an advanced enterprise-level application layer firewall, Virtual Private Networks (VPN), and Web caching solution on an "entry level" server? The answer: because you can! And with the new graphical interface and intelligent wizards in ISA, it is easy to drill down to specific settings for customized configurations. With multilayer firewall services and application layer filtering combined, it makes its predecessor ISA 2000 look like the little Garden Gnome in your front yard.

ISA Server 2004 was designed to protect Microsoft-specific applications like OWA, Windows SharePoint Services (WSS), Routing and Remote Access Service (RRAS), and Active Directory services integration. This product, being an enterprise-level firewall, is more than sufficient to protect your small business network once it is installed and configured properly (see, there is a catch). As I write this chapter, the only information the SBS development team shared with me was that the ISA Server 2004 setup and configuration with SBS is such "…that the users need to go through a couple of setup pages followed by running our CEICW wizard to configure ISA Server 2004 on SBS." Thanks guys! Microsoft's "simplicity goal" is a great concept, and once you get used to the SBS wizards (especially in the 2003 release), it is easy to get…ahem, lazy (or should I call it "more efficient?").

In case you decide to implement more customized configurations after running the SBS wizards, I offer you a condensed ISA crash course that will be just enough to get you stuck in the quicksand.

Why Should I Install ISA Server 2004 on SBS 2003?

First I queried the beloved SBS-MVPs and a few others in my quest to seek peer contributions and second medical opinions on why you and I should get excited about ISA Server 2004 in the SBS 2003 time frame. Here's what was said:

1. **Support for three network adapter cards.** This allows you to create a wicked demilitarized zone (DMZ) that is waaayyy cool and very sophisticated. To be honest, this is probably beyond the scope of most SBS 2003 customer sites.

2. **Better support for VoIP traffic.** With VoIP making inroads into the small business community running SBS 2003 using applications such

as Vonexus (www.vonexus.com), the firewall must be up to the challenge. There are many improvements in ISA Server 2004 over its predecessor version. Note Vonexus will be featured in the *"Extending Windows Small Business Server 2003"* book that SMB Nation Press intends to publish in 2005. This topic will also be further explored on the updated version of the chapter to be posted at SMB Nation's Web site (this will be discussed later).

3. **Perception.** Les Connor, SBS-MVP reports: *"I have a couple of independent financial services offices that have SBS, they are affiliated with international orgs. They have compliance requirements pushed from HO. HO has been leery of allowing all of the functionality of SBS into the independent offices, as it takes away from their ability to control and restrict and force compliance. They *always* ask about the firewall. Say 'linksys', and you don't stand a chance of getting their approval. Say ISA, and they say "Cool" (no, they don't ask about the ISA configuration) ;-)."*

4. **Overall Functionality Improvements.** Jeff Middleton, SBS-MVP, shared this buffet of ISA Server 2004 benefits with me: *For me, ISA means: I have had business owners who have used the ISA logs to document employment contract violations including use of company equipment to surf and distribute porn, illegal music, and spending 3hrs in the afternoon shopping instead of...uh...working. ISA reveals this in a trailing audit log. If the owner is concerned, they can look at it if they need to. As an IT Pro, I have used it to identify same subnet attacks from ISP connected interface. I use it to determine if poor performance on the web is due to DoS attacks. For customers with secure data needs, ISA has been useful to provide staff to credit checking websites, and absolutely nowhere else on the web allowed. I anticipate using ISA 2004 to filter VPN tunnels used in site to site links. I've also used it to identify how illegal software or viruses entered the network when a user went to Yahoo mail and downloaded the objects from personal emails."* Note the VPN capabilities of ISA Server 2004 are discussed near the end of the chapter.

5. **Legal Eagles and Inside Jobs.** Amy Babinchak, a popular "poster child" of the SBS Yahoo! Group (see Appendix A for more information on how to join this newsgroup), shared the following: *"ISA 2004 is in the unique position of having a legal reason to entice all to*

upgrade. ISA 2004 doesn't trust the internal network anymore. With ISA 2000 the computers on the inside were completely trusted to do whatever they pleased on your internal network. ISA 2004 doesn't trust the internal network anymore than it trusts computers on the Internet. Worms, Trojans, mlaware, hacker tools are going to have a much more difficult time doing their nasty work on your LAN if an infected laptop shows up from the field if you have an ISA 2004 Server in place. If you have an infected computer on your LAN with ISA 2004 in place it is a whole lot less likely that that the infection on that computer could cause damage to another companies computers in California and subject your company to a lawsuit."

6. **Hey Good Looking!** ISA Server 2004 has an improved user interface and simply looks better. Sometimes good looks work wonders. Seriously—it's clear that ISA Server 2004 is easier to use then prior releases.

But there is another side to this ISA Server 2004 discussion. To quote Dr. Thomas Shinder, ISA Guru extraordinaire,

"You should NEVER put the ISA firewall on an SBS box, as this violates all the core tenets of network security. Put the ISA firewall in front of the SBS box."

So, there you have it. Tom recommends putting the ISA firewall on an appliance or another server so that it can shield the SBS server. But that of course isn't the SBS way and doesn't reflect the consensus of the SBS community (Microsoft SBS development and marketing teams and real world SBSers).

In the ideal secure small business environment with no budget limitations, I agree 200 percent with Tom. Now, if we could just get our customers to see it that way, too. Especially if you or your client already purchased SBS Premium for SQL only (for argument's sake) and now they ask why they shouldn't use the ISA firewall product that came with it.

The question is, how sophisticated of an attack is a small business going to be under? The bulk of attacks will most likely come from script kiddies passing by on the Internet, trying their latest downloaded tools from sites like http://www.astalavista.com. After failing to engage the server, script kiddies will move on to easier targets (your neighbor on the Windows 95 machine), unless you incorrectly configured ISA or you really pissed someone off. Oops.

Just kidding, folks! I am not going into that discussion.

So, therefore, I have two options for you. If you have money to boot, the **ideal** combination would be to implement a dual firewall scenario.

- Place a hardware firewall in front of the server. A basic CISCO PIX will run around $500. You can also use any other appliance that manages Layer 2/3 filtering.

- Use ISA Server 2004 on the SBS server for Layer 4-7 filtering.

Most small businesses are not able to afford (or don't want to expense) additional hardware so, as one of my friends puts it: "The poor man's firewall-does all filtering (all layers) on the server. It's a step up from not having any firewall!" While that's a bit harsh on ISA Server 2004, this is the **next best** solution if you don't have money to boot.

At times, your client will fit the poor man's category and not dish out the additional $$$ because it is more important to go on a cruise or buy a boat, but that is their business decision. Make sure to spell out your recommendations in **writing** and have them sign off on their choice. I call it CYA and prefer to leave the MBA explanation to Harry.

When Should I Install ISA Server 2004 on SBS 2003?

Should you even go there? Well…I leave that up to you, but recommend waiting at least until SBS 2003 SP1 has become available. The point I'm making is that, as of this writing, the SBS 2003 SP1 is just about to enter beta testing (January 2005). Regrettably, the SBS product team at Microsoft has been unable to provide me an advance peek of SBS 2003 SP1 to see how ISA Server 2004 will be integrated efficiently and effectively in the SBS 2003 product. While I'm sure that the Internet Connection Wizard (ICW) will be updated to accommodate ISA Server 2004, I can't speak authoritatively as to how that will happen. Read on as I'll provide a link back to SMB Nation's Web site where you can download an updated version of the chapter after SBS 2003 SP1 is released that will make this specific discussion more current. Yeah!

If you can't hold your horses and decide to install prior to SBS 2003 SP1, be warned: most SBS 2003 networking wizards (CEICW, Remote Access Wizard, etc.) will be broken. Once you install ISA Server 2004 on the SBS server, you will have to configure any network settings manually thereafter. That is not the end of the world, but since ISA Server 2004 blocks all communication until you configure required Access Rules, Web Publishing Rules, SMTP Rules, add Computer sets, Connections settings, OWA, OMA, ouch and STUFF…. you get the picture. Try this on your friend's network first!

SBS 2003 SP1 will be available shortly after the Windows Server 2003 SP1 release (due out in the first half of 2005). It will include all of the service packs for the SBS components including Exchange, Outlook, SharePoint , and ISA Server 2004 (for premium edition only).

In the meantime, individual service packs for SBS 2003 components (Exchange, Outlook, SharePoint, and Windows XP) are available as a separate download and can be installed directly on SBS 2003 without waiting for the release of SP 1.

So if you're the experimental type and like to have lots of fun (like spending the entire weekend and lots of sleepless nights reading log files, experimenting, and scratching your head while drinking coffee enhanced with hydrocarbon hydroxyl derivatives), I'll give you some configuration steps throughout this chapter that will get you started.

For starters, let's warm up the old Single or Dual NIC (network interface card) discussion.

Single NIC or Dual NIC?

So you've decided to install ISA. After evaluating the financial situation, required security level, Internet usage, and other factors, you get to make the next decision: should you have a single or dual NIC installation?

Uni-Homed (Single NIC) Installation

This one is easy. If you have a server with a single NIC and you want ISA firewall functionality, you will need to either get an ISA-appliance (or other hardware appliance) or a second NIC. End of story. Installing ISA on a single NIC server will accomplish nothing other than allowing you to use the server for Web-caching.

If you install ISA Server 2004 on a uni-homed machine, you will lose most of the firewall features like application layer filtering (which is a new feature in ISA Server 2004), as well as support for the SecureNAT and firewall clients. On top of that, you will need to deploy a fully functional firewall.

To avoid any misunderstanding, the firewall on the server will remain fully functional, protecting itself. But it will not act as a network firewall, so client machines on the SBS network would not be protected. ISA will still secure Web-proxied connections made through the single NIC firewall, allowing connections explicitly configured by the firewall's system policy. The only allowed connections will be to local client machines via Web Publishing Rules. The only outbound connections through the single NIC ISA firewall will be truncated HTTP/HTTPS and FTP—only Access Rules. At least you still have a high level of protection for forward and reverse proxy connections with a single NIC.

A Quick Word About ISA Server 2004-based Hardware Firewalls

It wouldn't be right to ignore ISA Server 2004-based hardware firewalls and, in reality, all firewalls run some type of software, either embedded or on a custom operating system. Microsoft has decided to move ISA Server 2004 into the appliance market, so let's see why you would opt to install an ISA-based hardware firewall appliance, or any other application filtering firewall appliance.

•   Ease of deployment. One nice thing about an ISA Server 2004-based hardware firewall is its out-of-the-box setup wizards and templates that greatly simplify the process of setting network security policies and procedures.

•   ISA is preinstalled, preconfigured, and turnkey ready. This also diminishes the possibility of mis-configuration, which accounts for a large number of security breaches.

•   Extensibility of third-party add-ons like anti-virus software. Besides getting up and running in a short period of time, you also avoid putting additional stress on server performance.

Now you have the perfect scenario, with one drawback: in case of hardware failure, you would have to return the entire device to the hardware vendor. In contrast, you can easily replace a component failure like hard disk, NIC, or memory on a server.

And the biggest reason for small businesses to re-evaluate this option: initial suppliers of ISA Server 2004-based firewalls are currently retailing the appliances using not necessarily all ISA features, and look at the price! At last check, Celestix was selling the MSA2000 for $3,500. HP is offering the HP ProLiant DL320 Firewall/VPN/Cache Server appliance for $3,500. Pyramid, a German-based company, is retailing the ValueServer Security appliance for roughly $2,500 (after conversion from the Euro), which is a firewall appliance only.

Tim Leow, a rep from Network Engines, provided insights about their NS6300, which retails at $3,995. Tim feels that the benefits of purchasing an already hardened firewall appliance with a built-in patch agent far outweigh the price. You get all the ISA Server 2004 features and automatic updates on the operating system, ISA, and NEWS (Network Engines Web server updates) and never have to even think about it after initial setup.

So you can give your clients these arguments and let them decide which product to install on the cost/benefit equation.

If your client already purchased SBS Premium, deciding to add a second NIC (for about $100) and installing ISA Server 2004 is easy. Paying the consultant for a couple of hours to implement this configuration just became a deal.

Dual-Homed (Dual NIC) Installations

Congratulations! By using the preferred dual NIC method, you will be able to benefit from the cool features and functionalities in ISA Server 2004. The dual NICaroo enables you to use the following ISA Server features:

- Firewall clients
- VPN server
- IP Packet filtering
- Multi-network firewall policy
- Server Publishing Rules
- Application Level Filtering

Not to mention the excellent logging capabilities and ability to create non-"Web" protocol Access Rules, by golly, you just bought the kitchen sink! To have ISA and not use two NIC's is like never taking the Ferrari out of second gear. You get the point: use two NICs with ISA. Period.

Using Common Sense to Enhance Security

The first line of defense is to physically **lock** the server and attached appliances in a closet. "Really," your client is going to say, "There's no need for that." Until the day comes when the eager service guy visits the office for a repair call and inadvertently knocks the server out of commission. In my case, a very meticulous repairman decided to vacuum up after finishing a messy repair job. I would usually be pleasantly surprised that a repairman took his work ethics so seriously, determined to leave a job site looking as good as originally found. (Honestly, how many repairman do you know who do that?) Anyhow, the repairman got the kudos for a job well done while I got a server down call.

Matter of fact, the server did not respond to a remote call, nor was it responding to any local boot-up attempts. The server, as I was told over the phone, was "dead in the water." Upon arrival, inspecting the obvious hardware failure, I found that a server power supply cable had been unplugged from the UPS to make room for the vacuum cleaner cable.

So the moral of the story is, even a state-of-the-art firewall will not save you from an attack by an overly zealous HVAC-technician if the server and attached peripherals are physically accessible.

What's New in ISA Server 2004?

The new features of ISA Server 2004 described in the section are:

- Application-Layer Filtering (ALF)

- Links Translator

- Secure Remote Procedure Call (RPC) over HTTP

- Firewall User Groups

- FTP policy

ISA Server 2004 includes numerous new features as well as enhanced existing features that I have not described here. For additional information on ISA Server 2004, go to http://www.microsoft.com/isaserver.htm. Do I sound like a sales person...hey Microsoft, where is my commission?

Application-Layer Filtering (ALF)

ALF—no, it is not that fuzzy TV character thing from outer space. ALF is a new advanced protection feature in ISA Server 2004. To understand how ALF works, we first have to take a look at the Open System Interconnection (OSI) model and the difference in packet filtering methodology, where these filters are applied.

Figure 12-1

OSI Model and TCP/IP Model

OSI Model						
Application Layers			Data Flow Layers			
Application 7	Presentation 6	Session 5	Transport 4	Network 3	Data Link 2	Physical 1
E-mail	POP/SMTP	POP/25		IP	RIP	
Newsgroups	Usenet	532		ICMP	IGRP	Cables
Web-Apps	HTTP	80	TCP	ARP	ATM	
File Transfer	FTP	20/21	UDP	IPSec	OSPF	Frozen
Host Session	Telnet	23	SChannel	IKE	PPP	Yellow
Directory Sv	DNS	53	SPX	IPX	L2TP	Garden
Network Mg	SNMP	161/162			ATM	Hose
Application Layer Filters		Circuit Filters		Packet Filters		
TCP/IP Model						
Application			Transport	Internet	Network Access	
Protocols				Networks		

The discussion about filtering provided below focuses on:

- Packet filtering,

- Circuit layer filtering, and

- Smart application filtering.

Packet Filtering

Most (inexpensive) hardware-based firewalls operate at Layer 3, the network layer. A **Static packet filter** parses specific fields within the packet's IP and protocol headers of the packet traversing the network and compares the result with a set of predefined rules, dictating which packets are passed or dropped based on the source/destination IP, source/destination port and application or protocol information contained in the packet. It does not know the difference between a real or a forged address. A more advanced version, **dynamic (stateful) packet filter** monitors the state of active connections and uses that information to determine which packets can traverse the firewall. In simple terms, the dynamic packet filter is aware of the difference between a new and an established connection keeping this information in a kernel-based rule table. Therefore, a dynamic packet filter has a much tighter security bearing than a static packet filter.

If someone were to substitute the actual source address on a malicious packet with a source address of a trusted host, a packet filter, static or dynamic, would not be able to recognize a malicious code that uses a common port number for an authorized application like port 3389 for Remote Desktop Protocol (RDP). The packet filter would let the code pass through without knowing if this is a valid request or response.

Circuit Layer Filtering

For access to Windows Media technologies using Telnet, RealAudio, Internet Relay Chat (IRC), and other Internet protocols, ISA uses **circuit layer filtering**, which works in union with dynamic packet filtering. Circuit filters operate at Layer 4, the transport layer, inspecting TCP and UDP sessions, not packets. The difference is that they can restrict access by source and destination address and port number (by host machines, not users) and can, therefore, prohibit access by specific protocol to a specific host machine.

Application Layer Filtering

The **application layer filtering** being performed by ISA Server 2004 inspects traffic crossing the firewall based on the application layer protocol and connection state, deciding which packets are allowed to pass through to the application-layer proxy services and secured network circuit. The application layer filter runs proxies that examine and filter individual packets, verifying the contents of each packet up to Layer 7 of the OSI model. For example, if running an HTTP proxy, only packets generated by this service can pass through the firewall. ISA not only looks at the packet header information, but at the complete packet.

Smart Application Filtering

In addition to application layer and circuit layer filtering, ISA uses **smart application filtering** to control application-specific traffic with application specific, data-aware, and command filters. Therefore, ISA can reject, accept, redirect, and modify VPN, HTTP, FTP, SMTP, POP3, DNS, H. 323, RPC, streaming media, and conferencing traffic based on its contents.

Links Translator

ISA Server 2004 contains a link translation feature implemented through the ISA firewall Web filter to allow internal links like a SharePoint site to be translated into a publicly accessible site. At times, Web sites may include references to internal name spaces, which will appear as broken links. The link translation feature can be used to create a definition dictionary for the internal computer names and map to a publicly known name, enabling access to the internal site.

Secure RPC over HTTP

All non-encrypted Outlook MAPI client connections can be blocked with the ISA RPC policy. Exchange Server Publishing Rules allow remote clients to connect with the Outlook MAPI client over the Internet. In order to encrypt the connection, the client must be configured to use secure RPC.

Firewall User Groups

As a firewall administrator, you can create security groups based on pre-existing Active Directory groups. This increases control and allows for flexibility when determining access based on user or group membership.

FTP Policy

FTP upload and download can be limited by the ISA Server 2004 FTP policy. This way you can set a rule that a certain user or group can upload to the company FTP site, but cannot download from public Internet sites.

> BEST PRACTICE: Change port numbers of common applications. If you are currently using a firewall, you can play a game on script kiddies by changing the port numbers of common services. Microsoft Article Q187623 details how to change the Terminal Server listening port. By changing the TS port number to, say, 5631, when being port scanned, the attacker will think this a PCanywhere port and not even think about trying to access using RDP.

Meet the New Interface

You can't miss the new interface in ISA Server 2004. It is much more user friendly and task oriented than its predecessor. Someone with no prior ISA experience will be able to click through most of the functions, as shown in Figure 12-2.

Notes:

Figure 12-2

Getting started with ISA Server 2004

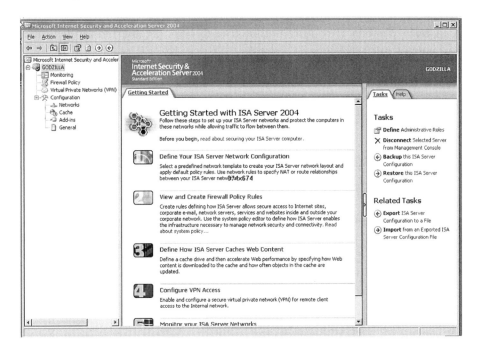

The console is laid out in three sections. The left pane contains tree nodes for easy navigation to management settings of the Monitoring, Firewall, VPN, and Configuration nodes. The middle pane (details pane) houses the dashboard, policies, and help links, depending on what node you are currently navigating in. The right pane houses the Task and Help tabs.

Notes:

The Monitoring node opens to the dashboard and gives an immediate status of monitored items. Alerts, Sessions, Services, Reports, and Connectivity are instantly presented. You are instantly alerted of any issues. In this case, the red X in the Alerts box would prompt the user to click the Alert tab to get more in-depth information, as seen in Figure 12-3.

Figure 12-3

Dashboard Monitoring—cool!

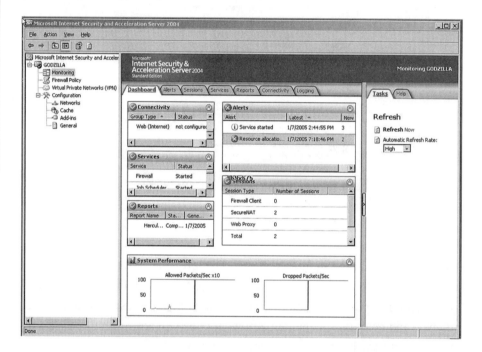

Figure 12-4 shows the Alerts window under the Monitoring sub-node. In the right pane, you can acknowledge selected alerts and configure alert definitions. (Monitoring will be covered later in this chapter.)

Notes:

Figure 12-4

Viewing Alert details

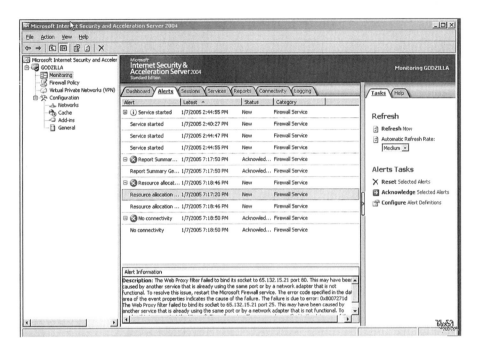

The Firewall Policy node, as shown in Figure 12-5, lets you create access rules, publish Web-, Secure-, and Mail Publishing rules, and create New Server Publishing rules. It is easy to edit system policy, import and export system policy, and view policy rules. Under the Toolbox tab, you can manage protocols, users, content types, schedules, and network objects. Everything is easily accessible at your fingertips. This easy GUI will also help shorten the training curve for SBS consultants and technicians, now aspiring ISA Server 2004 administrators.

(Access and Network rules will be covered later in this chapter.)

Notes:

Figure 12-5

Managing Firewall and System Policy Window

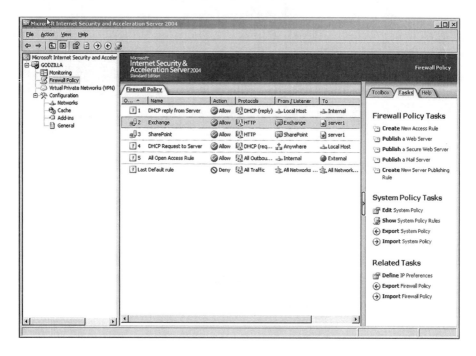

With the improvements in the VPN node, an administrator can enable, configure, and manage the VPN server directly from the ISA Server 2004 firewall management console instead of going into Routing and Remote Access Service (RRAS) or the ISA management console. Since VPN connectivity has been wizardized on SBS 2003, I would expect to see continuous integration of this function after the release of SP1. As you can see in Figure 12-6, there are easy links for getting started in the detail pane, as well as Client and Configuration tasks on the right pane, offering a simplified VPN client access configuration.

Notes:

Figure 12-6

  Configuring VPN Client Access Page

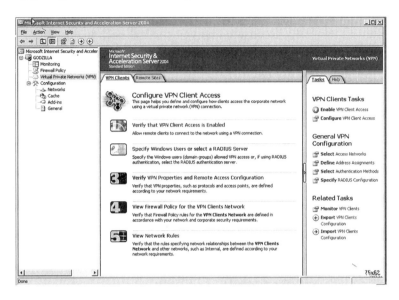

The Configuration node contains four sub-nodes: Network, Cache, Add-ins, and General. The details pane explains each of these sub-nodes, as shown in Figure 12-7.

Figure 12-7

  Configuration Overview

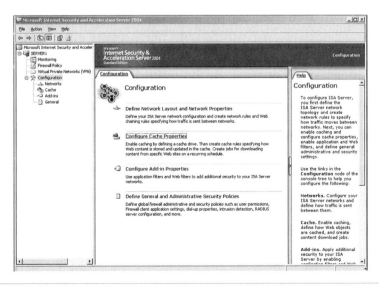

Visit www.microsoft.com/technet for the latest updates for any Microsoft product.

                                                                                              .1

Most likely an SBSer would skip the Network sub-node, which manages configuring multiple networks. In case the VPN wizard will not be integrated with SP1 or you are just a do-it-yourselfer, you could choose to configure an Edge Firewall template. To ensure that you can roll back to previous settings, when configuring a template, export current configuration and user settings to an .xml file, as shown in Figure 12-8.

Figure 12-8
Exporting firewall configuration to .xml

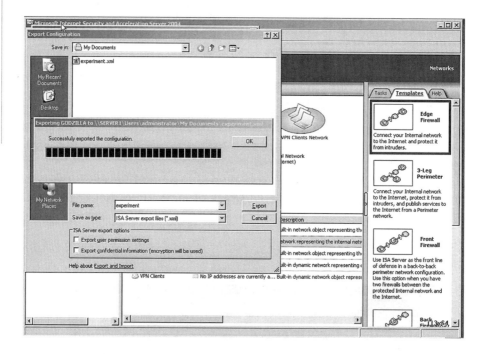

By default, the cache in ISA Server 2004 Server is set to 0. If you decide to use the caching option, you must first enable the cache by editing the "Define Cache Drives" rule. ISA Server 2004 no longer supports active caching. If you want to reduce external bandwidth usage and increase performance for network users, configure forward caching. Forward caching stores frequently accessed Web objects (everyone hitting MSN or CNN at 8 a.m.), increasing the request response time for internal users. The request will be answered by the caching server without needing to access the Internet to retrieve content again.

Reverse caching would rarely be used by SBSers unless a Web site is hosted by a separate internal server. In this case, reverse caching will speed response times for external users requesting internally hosted objects, since they are cached by the ISA Server 2004 Server and will not have to be retrieved from the internal server, which will also take a load of internal traffic as well.

The Application Filters tab, as depicted in Figure 12-9, is where application and Web filters are manipulated in the Add-ins sub-node. By default, several filters are already installed and enabled; these can be viewed, modified, or disabled here. This is the console where you configure the Message Screener to thwart unwanted e-mails as well as the SMTP filter to protect your published SMTP server from buffer overflow attacks (this will be covered later in this chapter).

Figure 12-9

Application Filters located under the Add-ins sub-node

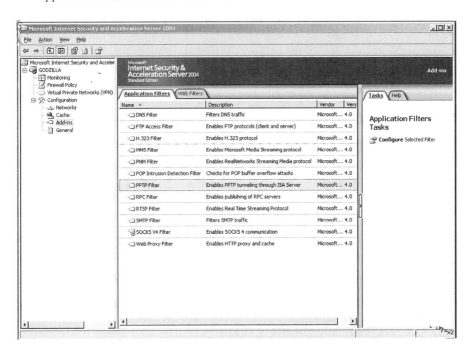

Last but not least, the Configuration sub-node, meant for general housekeeping like firewall chaining (just kidding, that would be for a very large SBS installation…), is used to configure Link Translation and Intrusion Detection and define firewall client settings.

Figure 12-10

General Administration and Security Policy options

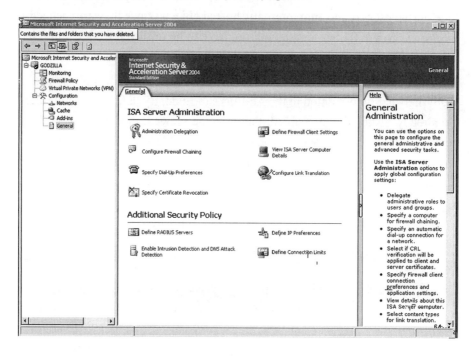

Okay, now that we got a look at the tip of the iceberg, let see how clients interact below the surface. But first—join me in a study break for a drink! See the BEST PRACTICE below.

> BEST PRACTICE: To create the perfect Cosmopolitan Martini, mix ½ oz of Cointreau, 2 oz. of Grey Goose Orange Vodka, juice of 1/4 lime and a splash of Cranberry juice. Ice down the Martini glass, dip the rim in sugar and add a couple of Blueberries. Yumm!

ISA Client Protection

To protect the network, data is controlled on the external NIC by ISA Server 2004. Data packets can only pass after the firewall service processes the rules and determines if the request is serviceable.

ISA protects three types of clients:

- Firewall clients,

- SecureNAT clients, and

- Web Proxy clients.

This section also takes you through the process of enabling automatic browser configuration and blocking unwanted applications. Before installing and configuring all client types (all three clients can be configured on a single machine), determine which applications and services are required by your internal clients.

Firewall Client

First of all, **never** install the firewall client software on the SBS server itself. The client installation files are usually located in \\server\msmpclnt\setup after the ISA Server 2004 Server install and can be pushed out by Group Policy or script. Once a client machine has the ISA firewall client software installed, outbound TCP and UDP connections established by Winsock applications are directed to the Firewall service. The firewall client also sends user credentials, which are logged showing the user name in the log file. You now have the option to encrypt the communication channel between the firewall client and ISA Server 2004. The ISA Server determines whether access is allowed or denied and, consequently, communications may be filtered by application filters and other add-ins.

Note: The Firewall only works with the Windows operating systems.

Follow these steps to install the ISA Firewall Client by Group Policy.

1. In the SBS server management console, expand **Advanced Management, Group Policy Management, Forest:yourdomain, Domains** and right-click your Domain Name.
2. Click **Create and Link GPO Here**.
3. Enter a descriptive name like **Firewall Client** for the GPO and hit **Enter**.
   The policy will now show last on the GPO Link Order.
4. Right click the **Firewall Client** GPO.
5. Expand **Computer Configuration**, expand **Software Settings**, right-click **Software installation**, point to **New**, and then click **Package**.

6. Navigate a path to **Server\mspclnt\ms_fwc.msi**, and then click **Open.**

7. Click **Assigned, OK.**

8. Close the GPO Editor.

If you do not want to deploy the firewall client software to a specific group of clients:

1. Right-click the Installer Package in the GPO.

2. Go to the Security tab and add the specific group.

3. In the **Allow** column, clear **Read** and **Apply Group Policy**.

You can install the ISA firewall client software on Server 2000, 2003, and all versions of Microsoft Windows (XP, ME, NT and 98), except for Windows 95 (and the ISA Server).

SecureNAT Client

As the simplest client, the SecureNAT client requires no client-side software installation or configuration. The SecureNAT client does not have the ability to use complex protocols, so no complex protocol support is required by application filters. The Dynamic Host Configuration Protocol (DHCP) service on the SBS server serves up the IP address of the internal NIC as the default gateway. SecureNAT client requests are then directed to the NAT driver, which substitutes the local client IP address for a global IP address for valid Internet access.

The biggest benefit of SecureNAT is its support for non-Windows client operating systems and non-TCP/UDP protocols. The Windows firewall client does not intercept non-TCP/UDP communications, which are not evaluated by the firewall client. After the firewall client determines that access is allowed, SecureNAT client requests are filtered by application filters.

Web Proxy Client

A Web proxy client is a client computer that has a Web browser application that is CERN compliant and can be configured to use a proxy and the ISA Server. The Web proxy client is configured through its own user interface. No additional software installation or configuration is required. Web browser settings can be configured manually or by the firewall client software.

Configuring the Browser

The ISA Server can be configured so that the firewall client's browser is configured during setup. The browser will then use the specified automatic configuration script, which is based on the options set in Web Browser Configuration (shown in Figure 12-11). Configuration options are set in the ISA server management console through the Configuration/Networks tab.

Automatic Browser Configuration

Follow these steps to automatically configure the browser.

1. In the **ISA Server Management Console**, **Server**, **Configuration**, **Network**, **Tasks** tab, click **Edit selected Network**.
2. Click the **Firewall Client** tab. Under Web browser configuration on the Firewall client computer, select **automatically detect settings** so the client automatically attempts to find the ISA server.
3. Select **Use automatic configuration script** and the **use default URL** radio button, then click **OK**.

This is illustrated in Figure 12-11.

Figure 12-11

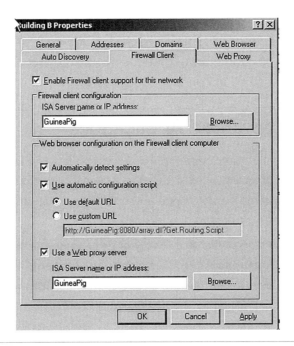

Manual Browser Configuration

If the firewall client software is not installed, the browser application can be manually configured using the default URL configuration: http://server/array.dll?Get.Routing.Script and configuring the ISA server as the proxy.

The Web proxy client can also send user credentials to the ISA Server 2004 server for logging. This allows you to control access to sites and content based on a per user/group basis. The Web proxy only handles HTTP, HTTPS (SSL), HTTP-tunnel, and FTP downloads. If you want to FTP upload, the client machine must be configured as a SecureNAT client.

Regardless of client type, when ISA Server receives an HTTP request, the client is treated as if it is a Web proxy client. Even when a firewall client or a SecureNAT client makes an HTTP request, the client is considered a Web proxy client. This has specific implications for how the client is authenticated.

Both firewall client computers and SecureNAT client computers may also be Web proxy clients. If the Web application on the computer is configured explicitly to use ISA Server, all Web requests are sent directly to the firewall service, including HTTP, FTP, and Secure HTTP (HTTPS).

> BEST PRACTICE: To use a Web browser on the ISA server, it must be configured using the internal NIC IP address. If the server computer name or DNS name is used, it will be resolved to the external NIC IP address and, consequently, the browser on the server must be configured to connect through ISA Server.

Blocking Unwanted Applications

Even though you may have configured an access policy denying downloads of executables and other extensions (discussed later in this chapter), users may still have unwanted applications pop up on their workstations. (Not that they would bring in a CD with apps downloaded at home!)

One way to put a stop to that and save you from having to uninstall endless, useless, brainless, worthless #@&* mystery "I don't know where that came from," applications is to configure application blocking. You wouldn't block a "mission-critical" application, like Kazaa, would you?

1. In the **ISA Server Management Console, Server, Configuration, General**, click **Define Firewall Client Settings**.
2. In the Firewall Client Settings, click the **Application Settings** tab.
3. Click **New** and enter the application executable name without the file extension.
4. On the dropdown, select the **key** to **Disable** and select a **value** of **1**.
5. Click **OK** and then click **Apply.**
6. Click **Apply** again above the middle pane, as shown in Figure 12-12.

Figure 12-12
Don't forget to click Apply here

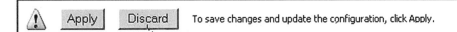

Tom Shinder explains:

The default setting for Outlook is set to 1 (disabled) because we don't want users to access external SMTP and POP3 servers. They should only be using POP3 and SMTP servers under corporate control. In addition, there can be some issues with new mail notifications if you set it to 0 (enable). By setting the value to 0, and then creating access rules that require authentication, the Outlook client can't access the Internet servers because they can't authenticate as SecureNAT clients (if they are configured as SecureNAT clients).

Same goes for Kazaa. Since we create access policy that requires authentications, if we disable the Kazaa application in the firewall client settings, it will never be able to reach the Internet since authentication is required and it can't use the firewall client to authenticate.

That's the power of the ISA firewall and the firewall client!

Notes:

Figure 12-13

Block that unwanted application!

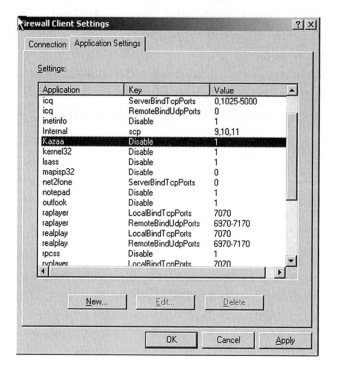

Network Rules and Access Policy

ISA Server 2004 no longer uses the LAT (Local Address Table) to define inbound and outbound connections. To establish a route relationship, ISA now uses network sets and network rules.

Not having seen the beta of SP1, I am left to guess that a simple SBS network set will automatically be configured by a wizard, and a default firewall policy will be configured to allow all inbound and outbound connections between the SBS network and the external network.

Once a network set is created, relationships to External, Internal, VPN clients, and the Local Host will be managed by network rules. But, network rules only define the route relation between the network sets, so an access policy will have to be applied in order to define what IP traffic is allowed within that route relation.

Are you still with me? Hang in there.

Network Rules

To ISA, a network is a rule element that contains one or more ranges of IP addresses, including one or more computers, corresponding to a physical network. ISA comes preconfigured with the following networks:

- **Local Host**—This is the ISA Server; as the local host, it cannot be modified or deleted.

- **Default External**—These are all computers or IP addresses that are not included in any other network. External networks can be modified or deleted.

- **VPN Clients**—These are currently connected clients in an address range that was configured by VPN properties and cannot be deleted.

- **Quarantined VPN Clients**—These are like VPN clients, but are quarantined because they did not pass a specific quarantine restriction (i.e., having specific anti-virus software or specific patches installed on the system).

BEST PRACTICE: Do not enable VPN quarantine

If you don't configure the complex requirements for VPN Quarantine, all VPN objects will be quarantined and never leave the quarantined network. You should have developer knowledge and must install the CMAK (Connection Manager Administration Kit) = Hands Off

Note: You can also create your own internal, external, and perameter networks by specifying IP addresses, but each IP address can only be included in one network.

Network Sets

After creating networks, you can group them together into network sets. These sets can include one or more networks or explicitly exclude one or more networks. ISA comes with two default network sets:

- **All Networks**—Includes all networks defined for ISA Server and automatically includes all new networks.

- **All Protected Networks**—Includes all networks automatically, including all new networks except the default external network.

Network rules can be applied to individual networks as well as network sets.

Network Rules

When creating network rules, you **cannot** define a network rule between a network and itself. Traffic between hosts on the same network is routed and network address translation (NAT) is not supported.

ISA comes with three default rules:

- **Local Host Access**—Defines a route relationship between all other networks and the local host, defining connectivity to the ISA server.

- **VPN Clients to Internal Network**—This rule defines the route relationship between the VPN client network and the internal network.

- **Internet Access**—Defines the NAT relationship between the internal network and external network.

Network rules are processed in order. ISA Server determines the address relationship between two addresses according to priority order as shown in Figure 12-14. The first rule that ISA finds that matches defines the address relationship. So a network rule with a route relationship between two networks can subsequently be overridden by a higher-order network rule for a particular address. Oh, did I forget to mention Network Relationships?...read on.

Notes:

Figure 12-14

Network Rules and their Relationships

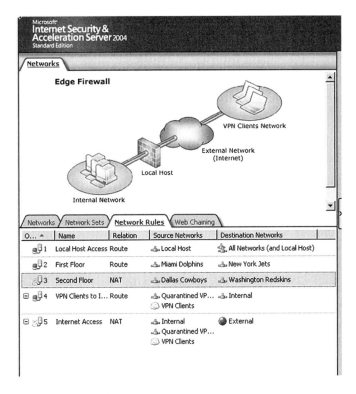

Network Relationships

The two types of network relationships are:

*   **Route**—This will relay the client request directly from the source network to the destination network without requiring address translation. This is a **bidirectional** relationship, defining not only the route from the source network to the destination network, but also vice versa.

*   **NAT**—With network address translation, ISA Server replaces the client IP on the source network with its own IP. This is a **unidirectional** relationship.

    BEST PRACTICE: Make sure you've configured the proper relationships between networks or ISA will drop all traffic between those networks.

Follow these steps to create a network and add network rules:

1. In the **ISA Server Management Console, Server, Configuration, Network**, click **Create a New Network** in the right pane.
2. Give the network a descriptive name like Building B then click **Next**.
3. Leave the default **Internal Network** and click **Next**.
4. In the Network Addresses Window, click **Add** and enter the internal network address range for the set of computers you want to include in this range, then click **Next**.
5. Click **Finish.**

Now you are ready to create the Network Rules and define the network relationship:

1. In the Networks window, click the **Network Rules** tab.
2. In the right pane, click **Create a New Network Rule**.
3. Give the network rule a name like Building B Internet Access, then click **Next**.
4. In Network Traffic Sources, click **Add**.
5. In the Add Network Entities Box, expand **Networks**, click **Building B**, and then click **Close**.

   This is shown in Figure 12-15.

Figure 12-15

   Adding a newly created Network as a Traffic Source

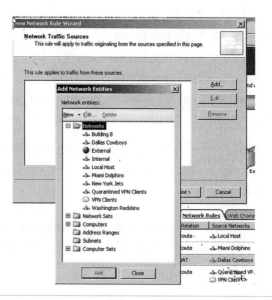

6. Click **Next**.
7. In the Network Traffic Destinations screen, click **Add** and expand **Networks**.
8. Click **External**, click **Add** and **Close**, and click **Next**.
9. Decide if this is a NAT or Route relationship. In our case, since the clients will be accessing the Internet, choose **Network Address Translation** then click **Next**.
10. Click **Finish**.

Voila, you've just created your first network rule. Now that we have opened a communication channel to the external network (Internet), we need to configure access rules.

Access Rules

Access rules can be applied to all IP traffic or a specific set of protocol definitions. These rules determine **how** clients from the source network can access resources on the destination network.

Internet access primarily depends on the design and order of access rules that ISA checks when a client requests an object.

In order for access rules to function, they are made up of the following five policy elements:

- Protocols
- User Sets
- Content Types
- Schedules
- Network Objects

Protocols

Protocols are defined by their type (TCP, UDP, ICMP, or IP-level), direction, port range, and protocol number. The ISA firewall has a wide variety of preconfigured protocols, which you can use to create Access, Web Publishing, and Server

Publishing Rules. With the Protocol wizard, you can create your own protocols, which can be modified and deleted. The built-in protocols can not.

Protocols are categorized into functional groups in the Toolbox, as shown in Figure 12-16. These categories were created to assist in selecting the appropriate protocol for a specific scenario. Some protocols are listed in more than one category and all protocols are listed under the All Protocols category. The User-defined category contains protocols you defined.

Figure 12-16

Protocols categorized into functional groups

1. To create a New Protocol, go to the **ISA Management Console**, **Firewall Policy** and in the right pane, click **Toolbox**.
2. Double click **Protocols**. On the toolbar beneath Protocols, click **New** and then click **Protocol**.
3. Give the Protocol a descriptive name.
4. In the Primary Connection window, click **New** and select **Protocol type**, **direction** and **port range**.
5. Click **OK** and **Next**.
6. Set a port range for a secondary connection if that is required. If not, leave the default as No and click **Next** and **Finish**.

User Sets

In ISA Server 2004, firewall policy rules can be applied to IP addresses or users that are grouped together in sets. The following preconfigured user sets are:

- **All Authenticated Users**—A predefined user set representing all authenticated users except SecureNAT clients (unless they are also VPN clients using VPN credentials).

- **All Users**—A predefined set representing all users, both authenticated and unauthenticated.

- **System and Network Service**—A predefined user set representing the Local System and Network Service. This user set is used in some system policy rules.

Users will have to authenticate using the appropriate authentication protocols. The Firewall client sends the users' credentials transparently and uses integrated authentication. The Web Proxy client can use different authentication methods.

Follow these steps to create a new user set.

1. In the ISA Management console, open the Firewall Policy. On the new **Toolbox** tab in the right pane, click **Users**.
2. On the toolbar beneath Users, click **New**.
3. Add a name for the **New User set** and click **Next**.
4. In the Users window, click **Add** and **Windows users and groups**. Now you can select Users or Groups from Active Directory (AD).
5. Choose your users or groups, then click **Next**, **Finish**.

Content Types

When you create an HTTP protocol access rule, you can specify Multipurpose Internet Mail Extensions (MIME) types and file extensions that the access rule applies to. This gives the administrator very granular control when configuring the access policy, controlling access not only on a protocol and destination basis, but also by specific content.

Content types can only be applied to HTTP and tunneled FTP traffic that passes through ISA Server. It does not apply to any other protocol like HTTPS.

When a client requests outbound HTTP content, the ISA firewall will send the request to the Web server. Depending on the header information returned by the Web server, ISA will check the object's MIME type or its file name extension when returning the object. At this point, the ISA firewall determines if a rule applies to a content type that includes the requested file name extension, and processes the rule accordingly.

When an FTP request is made, the ISA firewall checks the file name extension of the requested object. If a rule applies, process the rule accordingly based on the content type that includes the requested file name extension.

Even though ISA comes with a list of content types, you can create your own. When creating content types, specify the content's MIME type and file name extension. For example, to include all director files in a content type, select the following file name extensions and MIME types:

- .dir

- .dxr

- .dcr

- application/x-director

When configuring a MIME type, you can use an asterisk (*) as a wildcard character, but only with MIME types, *not* with file extensions. The wildcard can only be used once, at the end of the MIME type after the slash mark (/). To include all application types, enter **application/***.

The following content types are preconfigured in ISA:

- Application

- Application data files

- Audio

- Compressed files

- Documents

- HTML documents

- Images

- Macro documents

- Text

- Video

- VRML

Because Web site administrators have complete control over the MIME type associated with the content that is returned by the Web server to the users, it can be difficult to control. At times you will see content you thought you had blocked, only to learn that the content had been associated with a different MIME type then generally used. See the Internet Information Server on-line documentation for the default association MIME types (too darn lengthy to reproduce here!).

More information on HTTP filtering is included in the Access Rules and Application Filters section of this chapter.

Follow this procedure to create new Content Types in the ISA Management console.

1. Go to Firewall Policy. In the right pane, click **Toolbox** and expand **Content Types**.

2. On the toolbar right below Content Types, click **New** and enter the Name for the content type.
   In **Available Types**, you can select an existing content type. Click the file name extension or MIME type, or you can add a new content type by entering a new file name extension or MIME type.

3. Click **Add** and **OK**.

Schedules

Schedules can be applied to access rules to define when they are in effect. The schedules included in ISA Server 2004 are:

- **Weekends**–Permits access on Saturday and Sunday only.

- **Work Hours**–Permits access from 9 a.m. to 5 p.m. Monday through Friday.

- **Always**

Schedules only affect new connections. If you are using the Work Hours schedule and Sally logged on at 4:40 p.m., she will remain logged on after 5 p.m. and will have to be manually disconnected. If another user tries to log on at 5:10 p.m., access will be denied.

Follow these steps to create a schedule.

1. Go to ISA Server Management, Firewall Policy. In the right pane, click the **Toolbox** tab and expand **Schedules**.
2. On the toolbar below, click **New** and type a name for the schedule.
3. Select the days and times in the schedule and use the radio buttons to set Active/Inactive time.
4. Click **OK**.

Network Objects

Network objects are the last element required for configuring access rules.

When you create a rule, you must specify the source and destination for which the rule is applied. Source and destination are considered network objects. Computers can be categorized into different types of network objects:

- Computer—A computer represents a single IP address.

- Network—A network consists of a range of IP addresses.

- Network sets—Network sets include one or more networks.

- Address ranges, subnets, and computer sets—Address ranges and subnets consist of a range of IP addresses.

- Web listeners—Web listeners determine which IP addresses and ports on the specified networks will listen for Web requests. When creating a Web publishing rule, you select a Web listener to be used to apply to the rule. A Web listener can be used by more than one Web publishing rule.

Follow these steps to create a new network object.

1. Open the ISA server management console.
2. Expand ISA server, Firewall Policy and click **Toolbox** in the right pane.
3. Expand Network Objects. On the toolbar right below Network Objects, click **New**.

You can choose from several items as depicted in Figure 12-17, then follow the on-screen instructions.

Figure 12-17
Creating New Network Objects

Finally, the Fun Part...

Now that we have met the five essential ISA Firewall Access Rule elements, we can go on to configuring access rules for outbound access through the ISA firewall.

Access rules differ from Web publishing and server publishing rules in that they apply to outbound connections only, whereas Web publishing and server publishing rules apply to inbound or receive directions.

To block unwanted Internet sites (yes, that is an access rule), first we need to create a URL set of sites to be blocked.

1. In the ISA Server Management Console, Server, Firewall Policy, click **Toolbox** in the right pane.
2. Expand the **Network Objects** and right click **URL Sets**.
3. In the dropdown, click **New URL Set**.

This is illustrated in Figure 12-18.

Figure 12-18

Creating a URL Set

4. Add a descriptive name for the URL set (e.g., **Consulting sites**).

5. Click **New**, add a site name (e.g., http://www.smbnation.com) and click **OK.** You can add as many Web sites as you like.

   Now we can continue with creating the access rule. You will be using an HTTP filter, which is discussed in more detail later in this chapter.

6. In the ISA Server Management Console, Server, Firewall Policy, click **Create New Access Rule** in the right pane under Tasks**.**

7. Give the access rule a descriptive name like Denied Sites and click **Next**.

8. Click **Deny** in the Rule Action window and click **Next**.

9. Choose **Selected Protocols** from the dropdown, click **Add,** expand **Common Protocols**.

10. Click **HTTP**, **Add** then close the window and click **Next**.
11. In the Access Rule Sources, click **Add** and expand **Networks**.
12. Click **Building B**, **Add** then close the window and click **Next**.
13. In the Access Rule Destinations window, click **Add** and expand **URL Sets**. Click **Consulting Sites**, **Add**, and **Close**, then click **Next**.
14. In the **User Sets**, leave the default **All Users** and click **Next**, **Finish**.

Congratulations! You successfully blocked your client machines located in Building B from accessing consulting sites that may give them too many ideas, as shown in Figure 12-19. The third rule down shows all denied URL sets.

Figure 12-19
Denied sites Firewall Policy

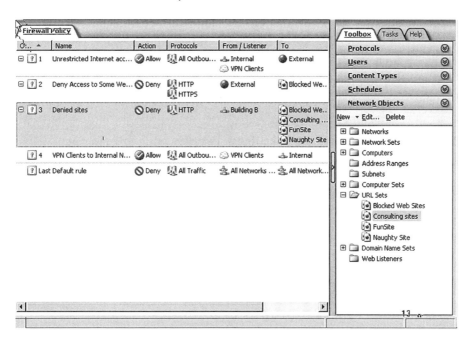

Automating the Tedious Task

Now you are thinking hey, there are way too many Web sites that need to be blocked. To truly block all unwanted sites, you would literally spend the entire week entering Web sites manually. There has to be a list you can download. You can get some of those URLs at http://isastuff/mine.nu under "Destination Sets" ISA Server 2004. This site contains URLs of banned ads, sex and warez sites.

So how are you going to import them into the ISA URL set? There is a script called AddRuleAndUrlSet.vbs located on the ISA CDROM\sdk\samples\Admin that will add the URLs to the ISA URL set.

Russ Fustino, a Microsoft Developer Champion, creator of Russ' Tool Shed-Tinkering with Visual Studio.NET and an avid fisherman to boot, shows how to transfer the contents of the .xml file in a breeze, without needing to write a lengthy script:

Open the XML file in Internet Explorer, and then:

1. Copy all the lines with the URLs.
2. Paste these into Notepad (not Word) or another text editor as plain text.
3. Use the Replace function to change all occurrences of <fpc4:Str dt:dt="**string**"> **to: urlset.Add " (after Add, a space and then an inch mark)**
4. Change all occurrences of: </fpc4:Str> to: "(just an inch mark)
5. Select all and copy/paste into the vbs file after the line with urlset. "Add http://www.widgets.com"

The finished product will read like this at insertion point in the script:

WScript.Echo "Creating a new URL set containing sites to be blocked ..."

Set urlset = urlsets.Add ("Blocked Web Sites")

urlset.Add "http://www.northwindtraders.com"

urlset.Add "http://www.widgets.com"

urlset.Add "*1st-fuss.com"

urlset.Add "*123adult.com"

urlset.Add "*123banners.com"

urlset.Add "*123go.com"

urlset.Add "*1-2-free.com"

urlset.Add "*247media.com" and so on until you get to the end which then looks like this:

urlset.Add "*netsaits.com"

urlset.Add "*netseller1.com"

urlset.Save

WScript.Echo "Creating a new access rule ..."

Set newrule = policyrules.AddAccessRule("Deny Access to Some Web Sites")… and the rest of the script.

NOTE: be sure to use " inch marks and not " quotation marks.

Figure 12-20

Script executing adding URLs to ISA blocked URL Set

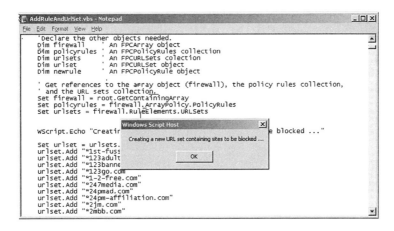

Figure 12-21

Blocked Web Sites Properties after populating the ISA URL set

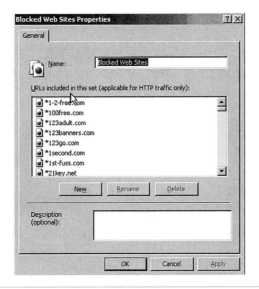

Blocking Unwanted Instant Messaging Protocols

Another access rule that may come in handy is restricting instant messaging protocols.

1. Open the ISA server management console, Firewall Policy and click **Create New Access Rule**.

   The New Access Rule wizard opens, as shown in Figure 12-22.

Figure 12-22

Entering a New Access Rule

2. Enter a descriptive name for the new access rule, such as **No IM allowed in this office** and click **Next**.

Notes:

3. Leave the radio button on **Deny** and click **Next**, as shown in Figure 12-23.

Figure 12-23

Default choices for Rule Action

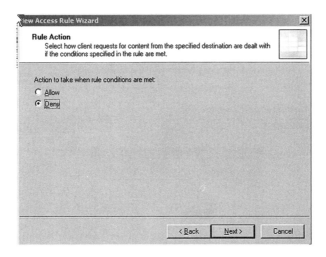

4. Choose **Selected Protocols** and click **Add**, as shown in Figure 12-24.

Figure 12-24

Adding selected Protocols

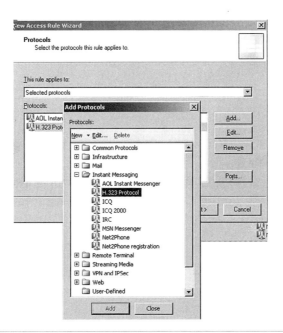

5. Expand the **Instant Messaging** folder, select your protocols, and click **Close**, **Next**.

6. In the **Access Rule Sources** window, click **Add**, as shown in Figure 12-25.

Figure 12-25

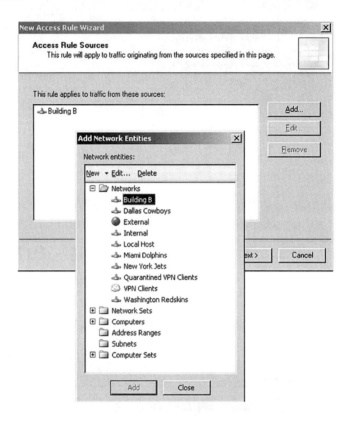

7. Expand the **Networks** folder, choose **Building B**, click **Add**, **Close**, **Next**.

8. In the **Access Rule Destinations** window, click **Add**.

Notes:

Figure 12-26

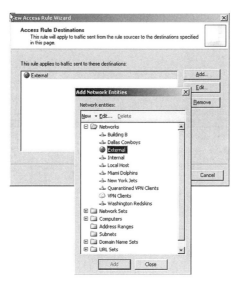

9. Expand the Networks Folder and choose **External**, click **Add**, **Close**, **Next**.

10. Accept the **All Users** default. I

    If you want to apply this to a specific user or group, you have the choice here to add a new **User Set**, as shown in Figure 12-27, or add a User set you already created.

Figure 12-27

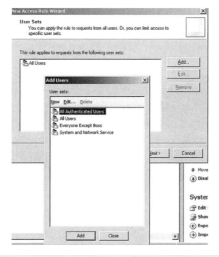

11.   Click **Next** and **Finish**.

Figure 12-28 illustrates the finished access rule denying all Instant Messaging protocols for everyone except the Boss! Note: Even though this appears at the bottom of the list, under Order, it is #1.

Figure 12-28

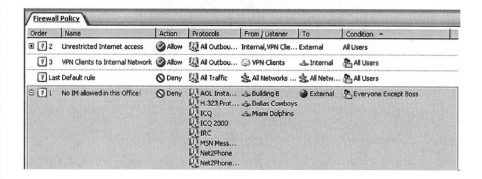

Interestingly, you are not able to configure a schedule when you are in the Create New Access Rule wizard. To add a specific schedule to an access rule, right click the rule in the Firewall Policy window. A dropdown opens, offering several choices as depicted in Figure 12-29.

Figure 12-29
Right clicking on the Access Rule

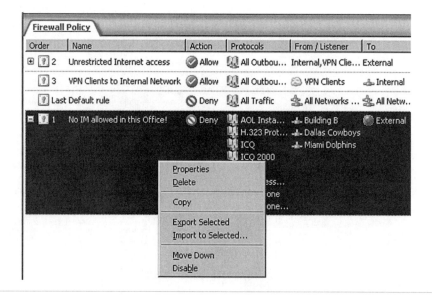

If you would like to quickly modify this access rule, choose Properties. The Properties window opens and you now have access to the Schedule tab as well as other choices, as shown in Figure 12-30.

Figure 12-30

Access Rule Properties

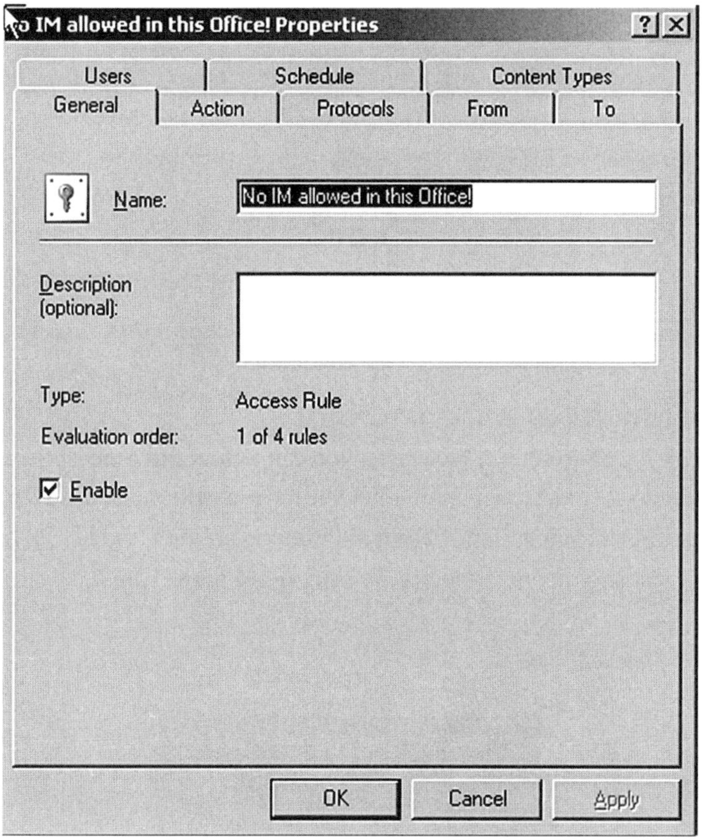

Notes:

You can select either the preset schedules that come in ISA server or create a new schedule by clicking **New** on the Schedule tab, as shown in Figure 12-31.

Figure 12-31
 Schedule

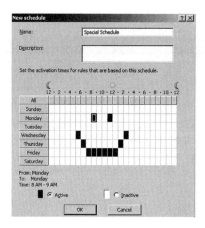

Redirecting from a Denied Site

If you block access to certain Web sites, you can redirect all requests to a specific site. In order to set redirection, right click the **access rule** and choose **Properties.** On the Action tab, select that if **Deny** conditions are met, the HTTP request is redirected to a site that you specify, as shown in Figure 12-32.

Figure 12-32
 Denied Sites redirection

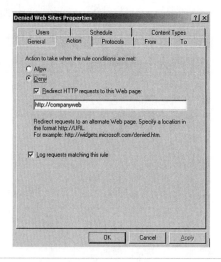

Application Filters

Application filters are registered with the firewall service and perform protocol-specific or system-specific tasks like authentication and virus checking. They can access a data stream and datagrams that are associated with a session within the firewall service at the application level.

Application filters included with ISA server are:

- FTP access filter
- H.323 filter
- Intrusion detection filters
- RPC filter
- SMTP filter and Message Screener
- SOCKS filter
- Streaming media application filters
- Web Proxy filter

FTP Access Filter

SecureNAT clients require the FTP access filter for secondary connections. The FTP filter forwards FTP requests from SecureNAT clients to the firewall service. Secondary ports are dynamically opened and closed as required by FTP. The FPT filter also performs address translation for the SecureNAT clients. During installation of the FTP access filter, the following protocol definitions are installed:

- FTP client read-only
- FTP client
- FTP server

The FTP access filter supports passive and standard mode FTP connections.

1. To apply FTP access filters to specific firewall policy rules: Open the ISA management console, Firewall Policy and click a specific policy.
2. In the task pane, click **Edit selected Rule**.

3. In the Unrestricted Internet Access Properties window, click the **Protocols** tab then click the **Filtering** tab on the right bottom.

4. Click **Configure FTP** to select or deselect **Read Only**.

   This is illustrated in Figure 12-33. You could also right click the access rule and choose Configure FTP from the dropdown menu (but why do it the easy way if there is a hard way?).

Figure 12-33
Configuring FTP protocol policy

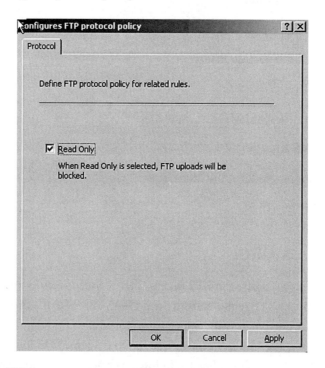

H.323 Filter

The H.323 filter enables rich multimedia, conferencing, and real-time collaboration capabilities while defining how components (terminals, gateways) engage in audio, video and multipoint conference communications. H.323 enables communications over packet-switched networks and accommodates varying uses where there is no guarantee of Quality of Service (QoS), such as IP-based networks and the Internet.

H.323 is used for peer-to-peer, two-way delivery of audio and video phone data, and was designed to interact well with PSTN (public switched telephone network) or Internet phone gateways. H.323 is an emerging standard, eliminating the problem of incompatibilities between different multimedia conferencing solutions. One of the benefits of H.323 is that it has provisions for bandwidth management since video and audio traffic are bandwidth hogs and could clog an entire network.

You could create access rules that limit H.323 protocol access. If you want to deny a client's H.323 access to video, outbound calls, or applications like NetMeeting, you could create a rule that allows only access to the inbound calls protocol. Since ISA only allows explicitly specified access, only this protocol would be allowed. To create a rule that allows only access to the inbound calls protocol:

1. In the ISA server management console, go to **Server**, **Configuration**, **Add-ins** and click the **H.323 filter**.
2. In the right task pane, select **Configure Selected Filter**.
3. Click the **Call Control** tab and select the **Media Control**. This is illustrated in Figure 12-34.

Figure 12-34
H.323 Call Control tab

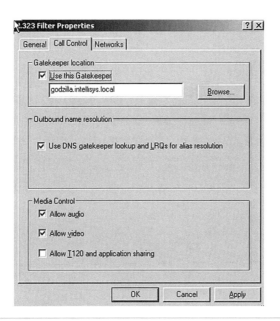

4. Click the **Networks** tab and select the networks you want to accept connection requests.

BEST PRACTICE: Note that H.323 is a major actor in the VoIP play now running in small businesses around the world. The point is that when you hear VoIP, think H.323 in ISA Server 2004!

Intrusion Detection Filters

ISA comes with two intrusion detection filters:

*   DNS intrusion detection filter

*   POP3 application filter

DNS Intrusion Detection Filter

The DNS intrusion detection filter works with DNS server publishing rules to intercept and analyze all inbound DNS traffic.

You can select which DNS attacks trigger alerts. The DNS application filter will check for DNS host name overflow attacks, ensuring that a response for a host name does not exceed 255 bytes. The DNS length overflow filter checks the DNS response for an IP address length field that should be 4 bytes. You can also select an alert to be triggered when a zone transfer is requested (see Figure 12-35).

Figure 12-35
DNS filter intrusion settings

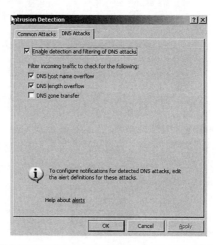

You can also configure common alerts on the Common Attacks tab:

1. Go to ISA server management, Configuration, General and click the **Enable Intrusion detection and DNS Attack Detection** link.
2. There you are offered the choices, as shown in Figure 12-35.

Figure 12-36

Common Attacks Intrusion detection

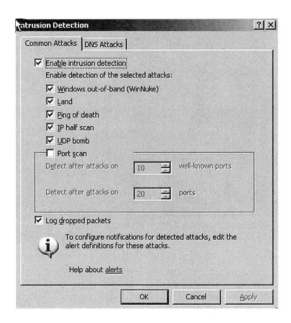

POP3 Application Filter

The POP3 filter checks for buffer overflow attacks by intercepting and analyzing inbound traffic on servers that are published via ISA server publishing rules. You can only enable or disable POP3 intrusion detection; there is no configuration choice available, as shown in Figure 12-36.

Notes:

Figure 12-37

POP3 intrusion detection properties

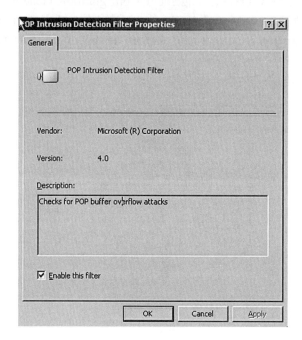

RPC Filter

Users like to use their Outlook MAPI client remotely to access Exchange just as well as when they are directly connected to their local network. Accessing RPC services remotely can require a large number of ports to be opened statically (UDP/TCP 53 DNS, UDP/TCP 88 Kerberos, TCP 123 NTP, TCP 135 DEC endpoint resolution also known as RPC endpoint mapper, UDP/TCP 389 LDAP Access, TCP 445 Microsoft Directory Service, TCP 3268 LDAP to GC's). The potential for viruses and worms designed to attack RPC and DCOM services is significant.

A conventional firewall that is not RPC application layer aware will be vulnerable to this type of attack, infecting not only the clients but the Exchange server as well. By using the ISA server RPC filter, Outlook MAPI client connections are forced to establish a secure connection with the Exchange server. Outbound worm connections are blocked by the RPC filter, which prevents RPC worms from leaving the network so local hosts cannot infect other computers on the Internet.

With the RPC filter, you can enforce secure Outlook MAPI connections from the client. By enabling this feature, ISA will drop the request if it is not initiated through a secure encrypted channel.

You cannot configure RPC settings, only enable or disable them, as shown in Figure 12-38.

Figure 12-38
  Strict RPC compliance is enforced by default

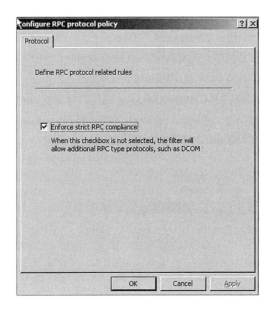

BEST PRACTICE: Never disable the ENFORCE STRICT RPC COMPLIANCE option because the DCOM traffic and other RPC-type protocols will be allowed. Strict compliance for RPC protocols is enforced by default.

SMTP Filter and Message Screener

ISA uses two components to filter SMTP:

- **SMTP Filter**

- **SMTP Message Screener**

All traffic arriving on port 25 will be intercepted by the ISA SMTP filter and inspected; if the rule permits the traffic, it is passed on. The filter checks if SMTP commands are larger then the set limit; if so, the commands are considered an attack. Each SMTP command has a maximum length attached with it, which represents the permissible number of bytes for each command.

To configure the SMTP filter:

1. Go to ISA management, Server, Configuration, Add-ins.
2. Click the **Applications Filters** tab then click **SMTP Filter**.
3. Click **Configure Selected Filter**.
   The SMTP Filter properties window opens.
4. Click the **SMTP Commands** tab, then
5. Click on **SMTP Command**,(e.g. AUTH) and click **Edit**.
   Now you can enable or disable the SMTP command or change the maximum length, as shown in Figure 12-39.

Figure 12-39

Configuring SMTP Commands

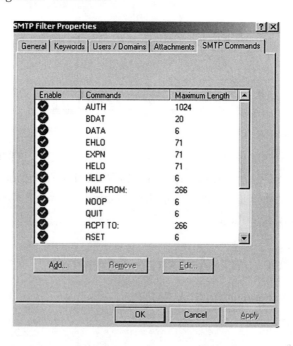

Do not be fooled by the **Keywords, User/Domain/Attachment** tabs; these features will not work unless you install the SMTP Message Screener.

Blocked Email Logging

You can log blocked SMTP commands by enabling the SMTP Filter event alert. The alert is disabled by default. To enable the alert:

1. Go to the ISA Management/Server, Monitoring, Alerts tab.
2. Click **Configure Alerts Definitions** in the task pane.
3. Select the **SMTP Filter Event**.

BEST PRACTICE: When configuring the SMTP filter buffer overflow, the AUTH command is considered part of the MAIL FROM command. The command will only be blocked if they exceed the MAIL FROM and AUTH command issued. So, if the maximum length in the AUTH is 1024 bytes and in the MAIL FROM is 266 bytes, a message will only be blocked if it exceeds 1290 bytes.

SMTP Message Screener

The Message Screener is an optional component that does not need to be installed with ISA server. It is designed to filter spam; intercepting all traffic arriving on port 25; and filtering keywords, attachments, and e-mail messages from unwanted senders, domains, and whatever else you specify.

Beware: Make sure to enable and configure the Message Screener after installation or it will drop all messages.

Incoming mail can be filtered by:

- Keyword

- File attachment

- Sender and Domain

Message Screener will only be applied to the rules that you enable and specify. If you do not specify these, all e-mail messages will be dropped.

By default, SMTP Message Screener logs are located at C:\Program Files\Microsoft ISA Server\ISAlogs.

Installing Message Screener

1. Insert the ISA CD and launch the ISA setup.

2. Let it run through the initial installation steps and, when prompted, choose **Modify**.

3. When prompted by the ISA Installation wizard to choose which feature to install, highlight **Message Screener** and choose to install the feature to the local drive.

4. Follow the on-screen instructions and click **Finish**.

Figure 12-40

Selecting the Message Screener Feature

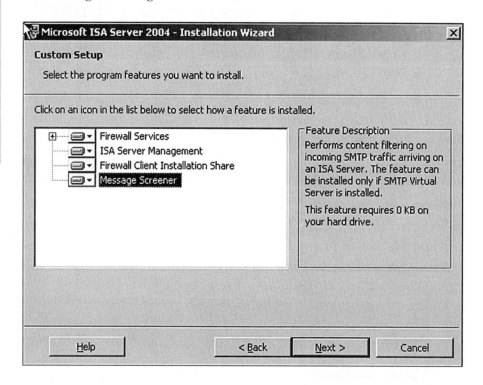

Message Screener can be installed on another server as long as IIS 6.0 or IIS 5.0 is running. In this case, you will also have to configure server publishing rules so the Message Screener and Exchange Server can communicate with each other.

Installing the SMTPCred Tool

Once installed, you have to set up a connection between the Message Screener and the ISA firewall.

1. Locate the SMTPCred.exe tool at C:\Program Files\Microsoft ISA Server.

2. Double click the **SMTPCred.exe** file.

3. **Enter** the proper credential.

4. Click **Test, OK** as shown in Figure 12-41.

Figure 12-41

   SMTPCred.exe tool

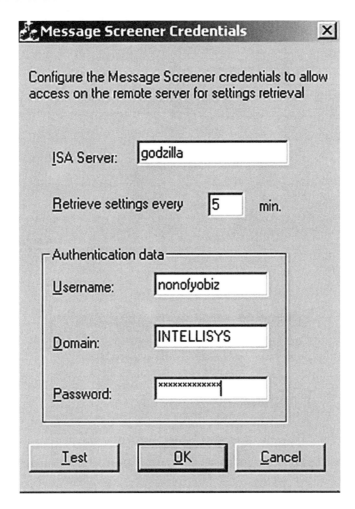

Now that the Message Screener is installed, you are ready to configure the final filter settings on the SMTP application filter rule.

1. Go to ISA Server, Configuration, Add-ins.

2. Right click the **SMTP Filter** rule and click **Properties**.

3. Click the **Keywords**, **Users/Domain** or **Attachments** tabs to config-
    ure specific settings, as shown in Figures 12-42, 12-43, and 12-44.

Figures 12-42, 12-43, and 12-44

Configuration options after installing the Message Screener

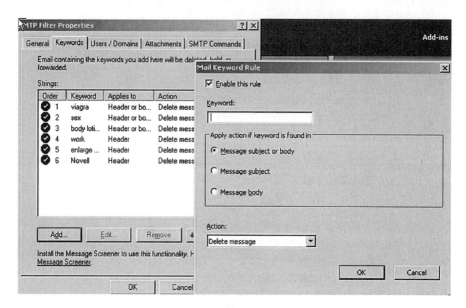

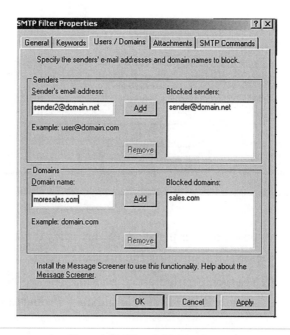

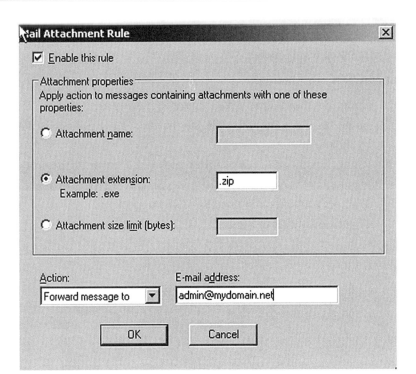

SOCKS Filter

The rule is, if socks have several holes, or one really, really large one, use them in the garage. Most of the time, I can't even find their counterpart. Matter of fact, all of my left socks seem to disappear in the washer/dryer. Did you know that there is a place on another planet where all left socks end up? It's true; I've seen it on a Ren & Stimpy episode.

Now, all speculation aside, the primary responsibility of the SOCKSv4 filter that comes with ISA is to support local hosts like Linux and Mac clients, which cannot be configured as firewall clients. SOCKS applications have their requests forwarded to the firewall service where ISA checks the access policy rules. You will have to configure the ISA as the proxy server for each SOCKS application individually.

The SOCKS filter is disabled by default, but ISA can be configured to listen for SOCKS requests on any port. The default SOCKS port is 1080, but this can be modified. Windows clients should never use the SOCKS filter because they can be configured as firewall clients.

To configure SOCKS filtering:

1. Go to ISA management, Configuration, Add-ins.

   In the details pane, you will see that the SOCKS filter is disabled by default.

2. Right click the **SOCKSv4 Filter** and click **Enable** on the dropdown.

3. Right click the **SOCKSv4 Filter** again and click the **Properties** tab to select networks that need SOCKS support.

   This is illustrated in Figure 12-45.

Figure 12-45

SOCKSv4 support configuration

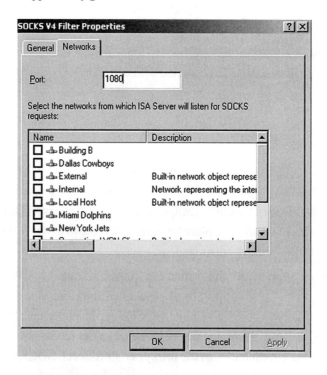

BEST PRACTICE: Use your old socks to check the oil in the car. Stuff them under the hood, and next time when you are in a suit on your way to a client site and the only gas station in 20 miles does not have a paper towel..., use the stinking SOCKS!

Streaming Media Application Filters

You guessed it; this application filter allows firewall and SecureNAT clients to use streaming media protocols (if you specify an access rule). Three application filters manage access to common protocols:

- MMS filter—This is the Microsoft Windows Media (MMS) filter, which is the default client in Windows XP. MMS can be configured under access and server publishing rules.

- PNM filter—This is the Progressive Networks protocol (PNM) used by Real Player. PNM can be configured under access and server publishing rules.

- RTSP filter—This is the Real Time Streaming Protocol (RTSP) and can be used by Windows Media Player 9 and later, Quick Time 4 and Real Player G2. RTSP can be configured through access and server publishing rules.

The only way to allow for streaming media is by creating a protocol access rule, as discussed earlier in this section.

Web Proxy Filter

The Web proxy filter works at the application level to allow connections from clients requesting Web-based traffic that are not configured as Web proxy clients to be forwarded to the firewall. Even though the Web proxy filter cannot be disabled, it can be configured to apply to specific protocols. The Web proxy filter is applied to HTTP by default and configured as follows:

- TCP Protocol

- Port 80

- Outbound direction

Once the Web proxy filter is enabled for a protocol, it can use authentication and HTTP filtering features if applicable.

You can configure different authentication methods for Web requests. Access policies can be configured to allow or deny users, groups, or a set of computers.

If the rule applies to a specific user, ISA checks the Web request properties and determines how the user will be authenticated. Authentication methods supported by ISA are Basic Authentication, Digest Authentication, Integrated Windows Authentication, and client and server certificates. All methods can be used simultaneously on a Web listener.

ATTENTION: The Web proxy filter can be unbound; ISA will not intercept requests from clients if the Web proxy filter is disabled for a specific protocol. If you unbind an HTTP filter as shown in Figure 12-46 for the SOCKS protocol, this will affect all rules that use the HTTP filter globally.

Figure 12-46
Changing HTTP properties globally

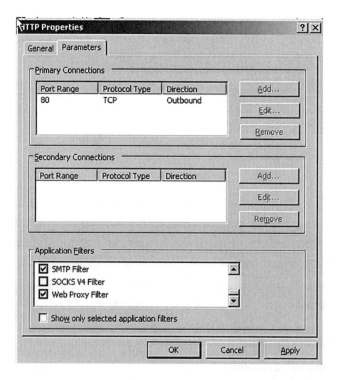

The HTTP filter is tightly connected with the Web proxy filter. All communications through the ISA firewall are subjected to application layer inspection when the Web proxy client is bound to the HTTP protocol.

Since the HTTP filter is the most prominent feature in the application layer filtering arena, you may now take a break, make yourself a pot of coffee, and return to this book in no more than five minutes so we can delve deeper into HTTP filtering.

HTTP Filtering

If you like to have granular control over your network, take a closer look at the HTTP security filtering capability in ISA Server 2004. All right, all right, it's THE paramount cool tool, and we should have some cannon shots or fireworks here….so just imagine that and read on.

The HTTP application layer filter examines HTTP commands and data passing through ISA Server. HTTP filters can be applied to access rules and Web server publishing rules.

The power of HTTP filtering is that HTTP policy can be configured on a per rule basis, enabling settings for some rules but not for others, including the option to configure what is available from specific sites at specific times to specific users! For example, if you want to block access to banking Web sites or e-bay during business hours (except for lunch and before/after hours), you now have the capability to enforce this easily, as discussed earlier in "Finally, the fun part."

HTTP Security Filter Overview

To configure policy rules after creating an access or Web publishing rule:

1. Open Microsoft ISA Server Management, Server, Firewall Policy.
2. In the details pane, right click a rule and click **Configure HTTP** on the dropdown menu.

   The **Configure HTTP policy for rule** window opens, as shown in Figure 12-47 with the General tab

Notes:

Figure 12-47

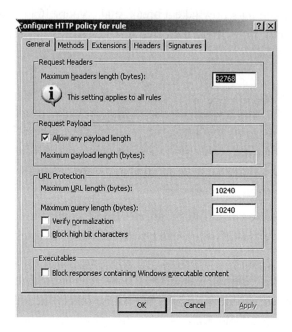

Default settings in the General tabDefault Settings

Described below are the default settings for each tab:

- General tab

- Methods

- Extensions

- Headers

- Signatures

General Tab

The available options on this tab are:

- **Maximum headers length (bytes)**—In the **Request Headers, Maximum headers length (bytes),** you can specify the maximum number of bytes that can be included in an HTTP request. This setting applies to Web servers and Web sites, and is generally meant to help protect against buffer overflow attacks by excessively long headers.

- **Request Payload**—If you want to block requests exceeding a specified length, clear the **Allow any payload length** box and enter the maximum size you want to allow. In a Web Publishing situation, estimate the maximum file size you want a user to be able to POST and use it as the payload length. Any larger POST is considered a potential attack.

- **Maximum URL length**—Under **URL Protection, Maximum URL length** is 10240 by default. Exploits send excessively long URL's in order to invoke a buffer overflow against a Web server. URL requests exceeding this value will be blocked.

- **Maximum query length**—The **Maximum query length** is part of the URL query appearing after the question (?) mark. Internet worms use long GET requests using the URL to embed the payload. Any queries exceeding this value will be blocked.

- **Verify Normalization**—To block URL requests that contain escaped characters after normalization, select **Verify Normalization.** That would not be the guys from "O Brother, Where Art Thou?" but URL-encoded requests with characters that were replaced with a percent (%) sign followed by a number, where the percent sign represents a space. A request for http://smbnation/new%20info/default.htm is the same request as http://smbnation/new info/default.htm. Common practice by attackers is to use the percent sign creating a "double-encoded" URL request that could be accepted by Internet Information Services (IIS). By selecting **Verify Normalization**, the request will be twice normalized (decoded) and the request will be rejected if the first normalization does not match the second normalization. Enabling this feature may also block legitimate requests from poorly written Web sites.

- **Block high bit characters**—Selecting **Block high bit characters** will block exactly what it says it blocks. Therefore, requests and responses from languages using extended character sets will be blocked. This feature will also block certain attacks on servers running IIS.

- **Block responses containing Windows executable content**—To block responses that contain Windows executable content beginning with two ASCII characters **MZ** (okay, did you know that stands for Mark

Zbikowski, who was an early Microsoft programmer? Check out your DOS, Windows and NT .exe programs.), select **Block responses containing Windows executable content**.

Methods Tab

On the Methods tab you can specify to block HTTP requests based on a method like POST, HEAD, GET, or SEARCH. HTTP methods are a set of instructions sent in the HTTP request notifying a server to perform specific actions on a resource. The available options are:

- **Allow all Methods**—If you set **Allow all Methods**, no blocking will be done based on method.

- **Allow only specified methods**—Select **Allow only specified methods** (as shown in Figure 12-48)to effectively block all methods except those specified. This would be the most secure way to configure Web and Outlook Web Access Publishing Rules.

- **Block specified methods**—Select **Block specified methods** where all others are allowed except for the specified methods.

Figure 12-48
Adding HTTP Methods

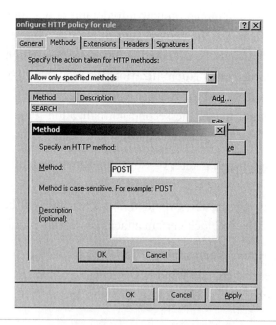

Extensions Tab

Here you can control which extensions are allowed through the firewall by clicking **Add** and adding your extensions like .exe, .zip, .asp etc. The available options are:

- **Allow all extensions**— If you select **Allow all extensions**, all file types will be allowed through the ISA firewall.

- **Allow selected extensions**—If you allow selected extensions, you will only allow the specified file types, which is the most secure option.

- **Block specified extension**—Select **Block specified extension** to allow all requests except for specific extensions, as shown in Figure 12-49.

Figure 12-49
Blocking Extensions

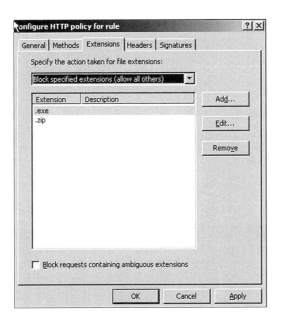

Headers Tab

In the **Headers** tab, you can add the headers to be blocked. The Server Header is a response header where you can specify which information a server header can return to a client request. This can contain information like the server name and software version. You can edit the server header response to:

- **Send original header** and leave it unchanged,

- **Strip header from response** and return no header at all, or

- **Modify header in response** to bamboozle a possible attacker, as shown in Figure 12-50.

In addition, when the proxy server is located between a client and a Web server, the Via Headers option provides a way for the proxy server to ensure that they are also included in the response path. By choosing **Send default,** the default header will be used or you can replace the Via Header with a modified header.

Figure 12-50

Headers

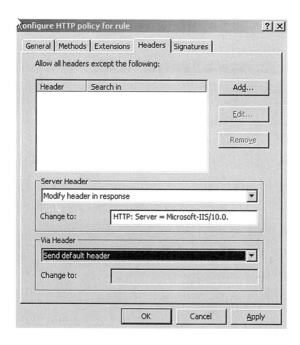

Signatures Tab

In the Signature tab, as shown in Figure 12-51, you can block HTTP requests or responses based on the presence of a specific signature. A signature can either be in the header or body. Make sure to be specific when adding signatures; if you were to add only a letter (e.g., "e" as a signature), any request or response containing the letter "e" would be blocked.

Figure 12-51

Blocking by Signature

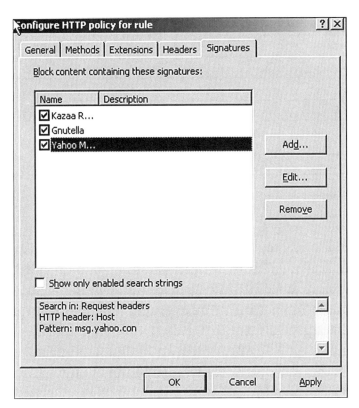

Signatures can also be determined using Network Monitor, which is beyond the scope of this chapter. I provide the following table (Table 12-1) with common applications and their HTTP headers for your viewing and implementation pleasure.

Notes:

Table 12-1

Common Applications and their HTTP Headers

Application	Location Response headers	HTTP header	Signature
MSN Messenger	Request headers	User-Agent:	MSN Messenger
Windows Messenger	Request headers	User-Agent:	MSMSGS
Netscape 7	Request headers	User-Agent:	Netscape/7
Netscape 6	Request headers	User-Agent:	Netscape/6
AOL Messenger (and all Gecko browsers)	Request headers	User-Agent:	Gecko/
Yahoo Messenger	Request headers	Host	msg.yahoo.com
Kazaa	Request headers	P2P-Agent	KazaaKazaaclient:
Kazaa	Request headers	User-Agent:	KazaaClient
Kazaa	Request headers	X-Kazaa-Network:	KaZaA
Gnutella	Request headers	User-Agent:	GnutellaGnucleus
Edonkey	Request headers	User-Agent:	e2dk
Internet Explorer 6.0	Request headers	User-Agent:	MSIE 6.0
Morpheus	Response header	Server	Morpheus
Bearshare	Response header	Server	Bearshare
BitTorrent	Request headers	User-Agent:	BitTorrent
SOAP over HTTP	Request headers	User-Agent:	SOAPAction

BEST PRACTICE: To block access to Web sites containing malicious code, create a signature by using <iframe src="?"/> in the response code and limit the search to 100 bytes. This code above is an example that would have Internet Explorer use endless CPU resources.

System Policy and Remote Access

The system policy is actually a set of firewall policy rules that are installed by default when you install ISA Server. System policy controls how the ISA Server enables the infrastructure needed to manage network security and connectivity.

Not to spend too much time on system policy, I encourage you to take a look at it and get familiar with the **Edit System Policy** interface. This policy manages access to and from the local host system; do not use it to configure network access to and from another host.

Even though the EICW post SP1 will most likely cover the configuration of system policy, I wanted to show you how to set up the system for remote management.

1. Go the ISA Server and click the **Firewall Policy** node in the left management pane.

2. Under **System Policy Tasks** in the right pane, click **Edit System Policy**.

   The System Policy Editor window opens (see Figure 12-52).

3. Under the Configuration Groups, Remote Management, click **Terminal Server** and then click the **From** tab on the right.

4. Click **Add** and then expand the **Networks** folder and click **External** or **Internal** or both (depending on where you will access the server).

5. Close the window, click **OK** to close the System Policy Editor, and then click **Apply**, which appears over the top of the middle pane.

Voila! Now you are able to access via RDP by typing "mstsc" on run command from your Windows XP client.

Figure 12-52

System Policy Editor

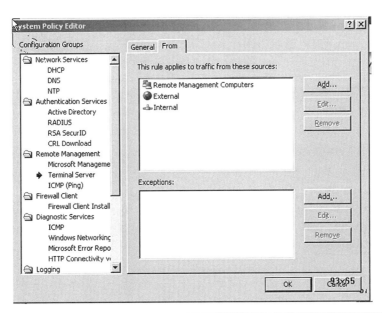

ISA fact: ISA processes system policy rules first. A system policy rule that allows the Local Host access to the External network overrides any access policy rules you may have configured to specifically deny such access.

A Word about Multi-Networking

Another new feature in ISA Server 2004 is its ability to configure multiple network access policies, which will protect your network against internal and external threats. There are 30 access rules by default, controlling inbound and outbound access on the ISA Firewall. You can even limit communication between clients in your own organization.

In ISA 2000, all hosts in the LAT table were considered internal and, therefore, not subjected to filtering or being firewalled. ISA Server 2004 now contains several built-in network definitions, differentiating between the:

- Internal network (primary network addresses),

- External network (any other network address),

- VPN clients network (assigned addresses to VPN clients), and

- Local host network (ISA server addresses).

You can configure individual relationships among different networks. ISA Server 2004 applies firewall and security features to traffic between all networks and objects compared to ISA 2000 Server, where traffic was inspected solely based on the LAT.

SBSers may need to connect several networks to the ISA Server and control Internet access of any of these networks. This is beyond the scope of this chapter, but please email Harry and he may post a walk-through on http://www.smb nation.com/isaupdates.html.

Monitoring, Logging and Reporting

New or refined features of ISA Server 2004 discussed in detail below are:

- Monitoring

- Logging

- Reporting

Monitoring

ISA Server 2004 contains a built-in log query facility for querying information contained in the ISA logs. Logs can be saved to the MSDE to speed up queries. By default, the MSDE has a 2GB limit and, once reached, a new log will be created automatically. Query results will show in the ISA Server console and can be copied into other applications for further analysis.

ISA Server 2004 provides a range of monitoring tools to help you track network status and server traffic, making it easier to verify that your network is running as expected and help troubleshoot when needed. With the dashboard, you quickly get a summary of connectivity, services, reports, alert, session, and system performance, as shown in Figure 12-53.

Figure 12-53

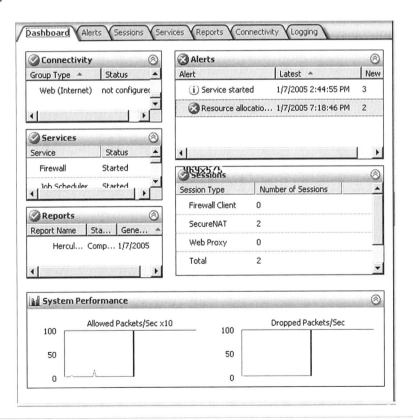

Dashboard monitoring overview. You can quickly see which ISA Server services are running on the server by clicking on the **Services** tab. Stop or start services by right clicking on the service. A bit misleading is the "Service Uptime" option, which does not give a real-time uptime until you click **Refresh Now** in the right pane.

Figure 12-54

ISA Services at a quick glance

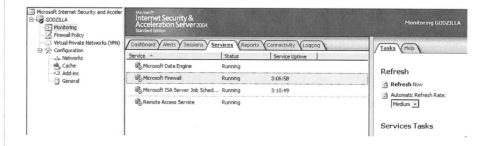

ISA Performance Monitor

The Microsoft ISA Server 2004 team took all ISA Performance counters and placed them in a preconfigured Perfmon console, which you can access through Start, All Programs, Microsoft ISA Server and clicking ISA Server Performance Monitor. This will give you a real-time display of Dropped Packets, TCP Connections, Session, etc. You can add performance counters by right clicking in the graph area and selecting **Add Counters.** Figure 12-55 illustrates the ISA Performance Monitor in Action.

Notes:

Figure 12-55
ISA Server Performance Monitor Display

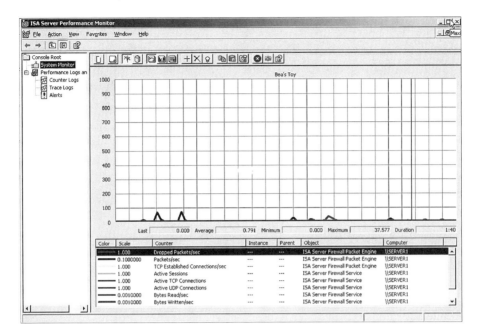

My all-time favorite is viewing ISA server performance in a Web format. You have been able to do this for a long time with the Performance Monitor in NT, which allows you to view real-time performance in IE within the network and publish it to the outside. All you have to do is set up a Web site in IIS and then save the ISA Performance Session as an html file to the source folder in IIS. (Setting up IIS sets is beyond the scope of this chapter.) Once you pull up the Web page, the frozen graph will appear. Click **Ctrl+F** (or the red x) and it will warn that all data will be erased. Click **Yes** to unfreeze the display. ISA Performance Monitor will start feeding real-time data into your IE session, as shown in Figure 12-56.

Notes:

Figure 12-56

Displaying ISA Performance Monitor in html format

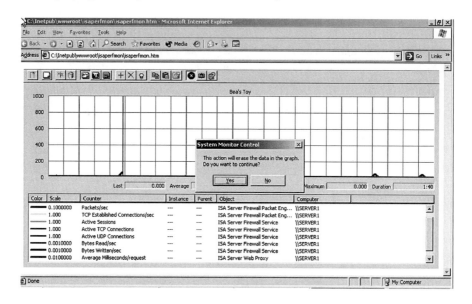

Logging

What struck me immediately was the real-time logging feature as shown in Figure 12-57. This screenshot also shows denied connections for DHCP and DNS requests from a network client 192.168.16.11 to our default 192.168.16.2 SBS server. No access rules had been configured at that time and the ISA/SBS hybrid server (192.168.16.2) will deny its own children! That is because the **Last Default Rule** denies traffic from all networks, including its own. Remember the ISA motto: Trust no one!

Figure 12-57

Denied Connections

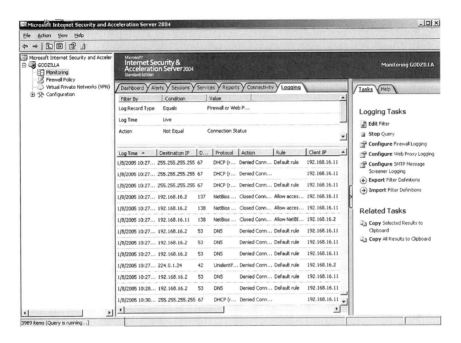

Just to prove the point, Figure 12-58 shows that despite DNS and DHCP requests still being denied, a connection on port 3389 passed through by the same client. Remote access was enabled in system policy and, voila!

Notes:

Figure 12-58

Access by RDP—created through system policy

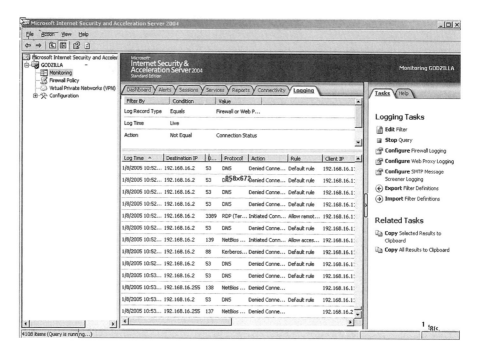

You can view all active connections by clicking on the sessions tab in the monitoring node. From the session view, you can sort and disconnect individual groups or sessions. If you have several clients to monitor, you can focus on specific objects by using the session filter as shown in Figure 12-59.

Notes:

Figure 12-59

Session Filtering

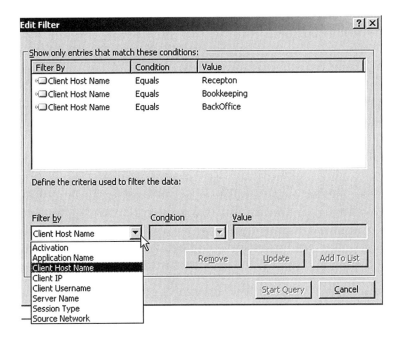

The **Edit Filter** link is located in the task pane, from where you can enable filtering. If you click the **Logging** tab in the dashboard, you'll see that you can filter the real- time logging as well. (Isn't ISA cool?) The filter is similar to the session filter, and you can configure it to view only the values you requested. If you logon to MSDE, you can also filter by log time. You can log either to the MSDE or to SQL server. Logging MSDE format is by default located in the ISALogs folder in your ISA installation folder. You can run queries and export the results to a text file.

If you decide to log to SQL, you will be able to query the database with the SQL standard tools. In this case, you have to create a system policy rule allowing NetBios transport to the local host SQL database. I recommend that you use Windows authentication over SQL authentication. You also need to configure the SQL server to accept ODBC connections from the ISA server. There are two SQL scripts on the ISA CD, w3proxy.sql and fwsrv.sql, which will create the Web proxy and firewall recording tables. Don't forget to configure the proper permissions on the SQL server for ISA to query and insert data.

Personally, as an SBS consultant, I like the KISS (keep it simple, silly) method and let the MSDE do the logging for me. If you decide to use SQL, we will post the steps on http://www.smbnation.com/isaupdates.html for your viewing pleasure (eventually).

Reports

Another one of my favorite functions in ISA is the reporting feature. As you can see in Figure 12-60, the graph and table type display are the same as in ISA 2000. Links on the left pane take you quickly to points of interest, and it is easy to track bandwidth usage and access, and to analyze trends.

I have always employed the performance monitor and report functionality when meeting with my clients. First of all, they are very impressed with how smart I am (perception is everything!) and second, if you have to make an argument for a processor or memory upgrade or just plain need to get a new server or prove Internet abuse (customers never believe that so–and-so in their office would do that!), these are the best tools around. With ISA Server 2004, you can provide hard data that the employee has visited certain sites, done banking chores, e-bayed, and hogged bandwidth.

Figure 12-60

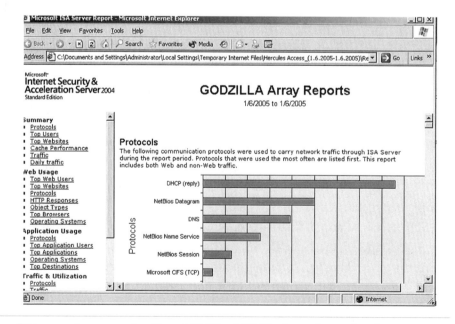

ISA Reporting feature

My experience has been that small business owners are afraid to lock down their office Internet usage so they don't have to deal with disgruntled workers. Politics in a small office can be very beleaguering, especially when the mob gangs up—I know. Make sure to pick your battles, and if the Office Manager runs the show, don't forget to appease the right person (hint, hint).

ISA Server 2004 includes real-time reporting so you can see Web Proxy, firewall, and SMTP Message Screener logs in real time. The log entries are displayed in the monitoring console while simultaneously being recorded into the firewall log file. From a session view, you can see all active firewall connections and disconnect individual or group sessions if necessary.

You can configure reports to save a copy to folder or network share. Using ISA Performance Monitor, you can publish the report to a Web site virtual directory where other users can see it, or you can configure email notification after a report has been created.

To configure a report in ISA Server 2004:

1. Go to ISA Management, Monitoring and click **Create and Configure Report Jobs**.
2. Click **Add** and enter a descriptive report job name, the click **Next**.
3. Select the content to be included in this report and click **Next** (see Figure 12-61).
4. Select when to run this report (daily, weekly, or on specified days), then click **Next**.
5. In the Report Publishing splash screen, you can choose to publish the reports to a share, but you can also leave this blank and click **Next**.
6. Set **Send e-mail notification**, enter your email, and click **Finish.**
7. To further customize reports, click **Customize Reports.**

Notes:

Figure 12-61

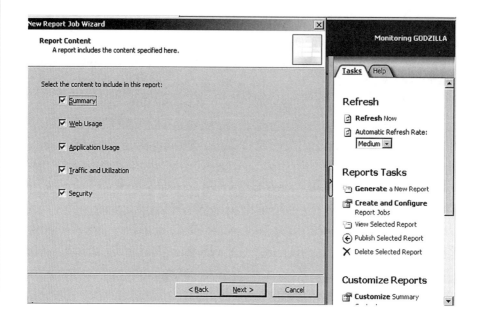

Selecting content for Report JobsAlerts

We can't talk about monitoring and ignore setting alerts. To configure an alert, go to:

1. ISA Server management, Monitoring, Configuring Alert Definitions in the right task pane.

2. Click **Configure Alert Definitions**.

   The Properties window opens; use this window to edit previously defined alerts or to add your own alerts.

Notes:

When configuring alerts, you can choose the event from a predefined list of **Events**, as shown in Figure 12-62.

Figure 12-62

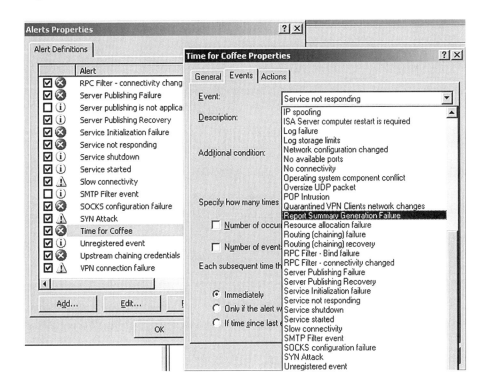

Time for Coffee Alert when Event is Report Summary Generation Failure

3. Use the **Actions** tab to send e-mail or run a program, report to the Windows event log, and start and stop services.

4. Click **OK**.

    To get more information on an alert, expand the + sign next the Alert in the details pane and it will give a description in the **Alert Information** box on the bottom of the screen.

5. Once you have dealt with an alert, right click that Alert in the Details pane and select **Acknowledge**, which will set the status from New to Acknowledged, or **Reset**, which will clear the alert.

VPN Improvements in ISA Server 2004

Here's a question I'm asked quite often when delivering a seminar on SBS: "Who still uses VPNs when you have Remote Web Workplace (RWW)?" Well, I have several clients who do. In situations where the user has a laptop that travels from work to home and hotel, there really is no other choice than VPN for accessing data on the company network.

Once after doing a new install, I received a phone call from a client who was at home trying to use RWW from his laptop and getting very concerned. "I can't connect when I click on my computer name," he said (not realizing he was already working on his machine). At that point, I gently walked him through by clicking on the download connection manager to install the VPN client.

Being on the laptop that he uses at work, all necessary applications were already installed locally, so he really just needed to connect to the data source. Since then, this employee also got a permanent workstation at work but continues to use the VPN (as with all things in life, it is about having a choice).

ISA Server 2004 offers several VPN improvements, namely:

- **Stateful filtering and inspection for VPN**. VPN clients are configured as a separate network and can have distinct policies created for them, such as checking VPN client requests and statefully filtering these requests and opening connections dynamically based on the access policy.

- VPN client support for **SecureNAT clients** to access the Internet without having to install the firewall client software on the client system.

- **VPN monitoring and logging** the VPN client activity just like any other ISA Server client.

Other improvements include site-to-site VPN links and VPN Quarantine, which are outside the scope of an SBS network. A site-to-site link could connect a branch office to the main office network using a third-party firewall appliance like a Sonic Wall, Firebox, PIX, etc. using IPSec tunnel mode which was not possible with ISA Server 2000. Setting up VPN connectivity is integrated into the SBS Server management console at this point in time and should not need any further configuration. It will be interesting to see if the SBS development team will build additional VPN functionality configuration options into a wizard interface that will take advantage of the new ISA Server 2004 VPN capabilities. Any new and additional information on ISA Server 2004 VPN configuration, will be posted at http://www.smbnation.com/isaupdates.htm.

Hardware Configuration

Wonder if your SBS server can manage an additional application? ISA will run on an entry-level server. The system requirements are based on load expectations derived from available bandwidth (Internet usage capacity) and the number of users and their application usage. For fewer than 500 users, a single processor PIII 550mhz, 256mb RAM, and 150mb of disk space would be sufficient as a stand-alone ISA server. (For comparison, the Sonic SOHO3 runs on 133Mhz with 16mb RAM.)

Most servers these days pack a lot more power and are truly underutilized. In case you have to beef up your ISA performance though, you get the most bang for your buck by increasing CPU speed and increasing the processor cache to L2/L3, which improves performance on memory caches. I use Table 12-2 to summarize some of the hardware configuration discussion.

Table 12-2

Microsoft's Hardware Configuration Recommendations

Internet link bandwidth	Up to 5 T1 7.5 megabits per second (Mbps)	Up to 25 Mbps	Up to T3 45 Mbps
Processors	1	1	2
Processor type	PIII 550Mhz	P4 2-3 GHz	Xeon 2-3 GHZ
Memory	256 MB	512 MB	1 GB
Disk space	150 MB	2.5 GB	5 GB
Network adapters	10/100 Mbps	10/100 Mbps	100/1000 Mbps
Concurrent VPN conx	150	700	850

Considering that the average SBS client uses DSL or broadband, has a newer Pentium or Celeron processor (more than 550mhz), and can max out the SBS server to 4GB RAM and the ability for other hardware updates, I am not too concerned about the load ISA is going to add to the server. The more policy rules you apply, the higher the load will be, but you can monitor ISA Server performance with the ISA system monitor, discussed earlier in this chapter under Monitoring.

Improving Performance and Bottlenecks

ISA Server transfers large data loads between the CPU, memory, and network devices; therefore, ISA Server performance is based on the performance of system elements around the CPU. You can improve the overall performance by using a fast memory front side bus (FSB) and I/O buses.

I would recommend adding 512mb of RAM for a single processor server and 1,024mb of RAM for a dual processor machine. Another limiting memory factor could be the size of the non-paged pool. Because ISA Server handles numerous simultaneous connections, it requires non-paged system memory. The table below lists Windows Server 2003 guidelines for minimum and maximum non-paged pool sizes based on physical memory.

Physical Memory (RAM)	128	256	512	1,024	2,048	4,096
Min. non-paged pool size	4	8	16	32	64	128
Max. non-paged pool size	50	100	200	256	256	256

If the SBS server machine runs slower after installing ISA Server 2004, you can check for common bottlenecks by using the Performance Counter (Start>Run>Perfmon).

To check for memory bottlenecks, use the \Memory\Pages/sec performance counter. The hard page fault (memory\pages/sec) should not exceed 10, which indicates that you may need to increase memory.

To check for CPU bottlenecks, use the CPU Processor\%Processor Time performance counter. If the CPU performance counter runs high while the NIC and disk I/O are below capacity, you should either upgrade the CPU or add a second processor. If the ISA server has high response times and low CPU percentage, the bottleneck is elsewhere.

BEST PRACTICE: Analyze performance results and establish a baseline. Sample performance from a remote machine to get true samples and review logged data periodically using the System Monitor Display. This way, you can confirm that resource usage is within acceptable limits and will be able to forecast future trends.

Summary

Wow, that was a mouth full and we didn't even cover all features and capabilities that come with ISA 2004 server. If you like more in depth information on ISA, I recommend Tom Shinder's *Configuring ISA Server 2004*. Make sure to practice lifting weights before you pick up that book.

Making the decision to install ISA 2004 Server on an SBS Server will be one based on individual needs, budget, requirements, your knowledge and involvement, well each individual situation. There is no cookie-cutter answer. Needless to say, not having a firewall at all is purely absurd but most small businesses don't understand the risk they are exposing themselves to by not having one or believing their $99 Linksys or Netgear will do the job. Especially since I've noticed that nobody bothers to change the factory default admin password on every single one I run into.

Having a hard time selling ISA? Just point your client to packetstormsecurity.com or securityfocus.com or even astalavista.com so they can see how easy it is for any Joe Schmoe to gain access to tools for compromising systems. The way I see it, it is time for instant paranoia. If you just run ISA for thirty days on their system so you can show the log files on detected intrusions, scans, spoofs and whatever else hit them without their knowledge, you will find firm believers in security and a client happy to pay the couple of bucks for ISA. Compared to hardware appliances, ISA has better application layer filtering capabilities as firewall appliances in the same price range or higher. Coupled with the ability to control internet usage and reporting features and ISA's primary focus on protecting Microsoft applications and Active Directory integration, as well as the granular control administered through an easily configurable interface you can't get a better bang for your buck.

Now, I didn't say that it would be fingerlicking easy to configure ISA, especially with all the proprietary third party applications out there needing their own special implementation considerations, but if you get involved with ISA and have been looking for a niche, offering penetration testing on top of security configuration would be a huge value-add for your clients. Scenario: Think about a client where you are competing for a contract, you do the penetration testing first and then walk into negotiations already having footprinted their network and exposed all security holes. This will not only establish you as an authority, but will make you a first class contender. Hey, it's called white hat hacking or ethical hacking and you should try it on your friends networks first.

Funny thing is, I never really sell Small Business Server with a single feature like RWW or the promise to efficiently manage desktops and the rest is just an add-on. I can see ISA Server 2004 to be a huge feature that can generate SBS sales, as well as a niche and job security for years to come.

Flex that Firewall Muscle, and you'll be looking good!

Section FOUR
SBS 2003 Advanced Topics

CHAPTER 13
System Monitoring
BY Lawrence A. Rodis (Las Vegas, NV)

This chapter will cover almost every dimension that is important to understand and apply when monitoring a Small Business Server 2003 (SBS 2003) network. After a brief discussion about why we should bother with monitoring, I'll review the standard tools that come with SBS 2003. I'll then focus on performance monitoring and how to integrate third-party server applications, other network equipment, and client desktops and laptops into the monitoring mix.

Toward the end of the chapter, I provide valuable information on patch management so you can fix some of the issues that show up when monitoring systems. Additionally, I'll describe some actual monitoring scenarios for single and multiple networks.

Why Monitor?

As a consultant for small and mid-sized businesses in Las Vegas, I've found that most of my clients run SBS 2003 or SBS 2000 because they like its flexibility and features. These clients need their systems to perform in a reliably—it's essential for business survival and performance efficiency. Systems need to be at current patch and update levels, antivirus (AV) software needs to be running properly, and backups must occur regularly. My clients can't afford to have security breakins or to have malware or spyware impacting their environment.

Clients' specific security requirements determine my overall monitoring approach. For some clients, my firm provides monitoring and maintenance of just the server; for others, it involves monitoring and maintaining their entire network. By monitoring their systems, I can achieve these goals for them and provide the desired reliability and security.

Prior to becoming a small- and medium-size business technology consultant, I worked for Intel Corporation supporting computer systems for manufacturing at the enterprise-level. At Intel my group spent a great deal of time developing and implementing system management products that could be used to reduce the number of administrators required to operate a factories IT systems..

Some dynamic and very capable tools are available for managing enterprises, the best of which are products such as Intel Landesk, Microsoft System Management Server, Computer Associates Unicenter, or Tivoli. Each can provide enormous leverage when managing thousands of systems. However, the cost and effort to deploy a system of that sophistication is not reasonable and appropriate, in most cases, for the small to medium business market. The approach I have fine-tuned for my clients and my own network involves taking the primary concepts of these tools and scaling them down to the SBS arena. Microsoft has helped small to medium businesses by providing some of the required tools either natively inside SBS or in the form of free downloads directly from Microsoft.

The approach I describe in this chapter enables me to run my own firm in a more proactive manner instead of always being reactive to the issues that invariably arise. I also want to be able to do this job remotely and automaticaly without spending an exorbitant amount of money on tools. Fortunately, I'm pretty close to reaching my goal. However, I still have to get on the clients' networks to do some of the monitoring. Many of the tools I rely on for this are either free outright or free if your network is small enough.

One of my additional monitoring objectives is to be able to properly manage as many client networks as possible while keeping personel overhead low. This last goal allows me to maximize my investment and increase company profits.

BEST PRACTICE: In creating this chapter, I have incorperated information from the various SBS Help files as well as the MS Knowledge Base and Technet. I highly recommend you utilize these resources, too.

Standard Tools Included with SBS 2003

The standard tools that come with SBS 2003 include:

- Server Status Report

- Health Monitor 2.1

- System Monitor (Previously called Perfmon)

- Event Logs

The following pages will document the Server Status Report, Health Monitor, and System Monitor. We won't really cover the Event logs as they are already defined for you and other then for minor file settings (I use 2048KB log size and overwrite as needed) you can't configure them.

Server Status Report

Before diving into the thick of system monitoring, it's a good idea to review Chapter 12 of *Small Business Server 2003 Best Practices*, which describes the Server Status Report of SBS. However, as befits an introductory book, the author Harry Brelsford did not go into how a Server Status Report is built from the ground up. Once you understand the basic foundation of the Server Status Report approach, I think you'll understand just how powerful the monitoring tools are that Microsoft has provided with SBS 2003. These tools will allow you to create operational efficiency for the networks you manage.

Let's look at several components in more detail. The basic Server Status Report pulls information from the event logs and from some preset System Monitoring (perfmon) counters. Additionally, it can be configured to attach predefined or custom log files. For the moment, let's focus on the base report, which is the foundation of my initial review. Of course, if there is a notification in the base report that flags my interest, I will examine the relevant log file that is attached to the base report.

The performance section of the Server Status Report provides a pretty good overview of the server's performance, but it is important to note that it can't be customized. So how can you improve the report? Event logs, which are discussed later in this section. If you can create additional critical events, these incidents can be reported in the Server Status Report. If the information is not critical, the best you can currently do is receive it as an attachment.

A frequent question I receive when talking about monitoring with other system administrators is how do I configure the report. First of all, when setting up the Server Status Report, I use the default configuration. I select to receive the performance report daily and the usage report bi-weekly. I also have the report sent to me exclusively at my firm's e-mail address. I normally don't select to show the report to any of the clients via the Web because they usually don't have the knowledge to understand what the report is conveying. And, after all, that's why I get paid the big bucks for my analytical and experiential value.

After making the report selections, the next step is to identify what other files need to be included in the Server Status Report. I normally include the following files with the Server Status Report:

- A customized perfmon report,

- Firewall log files (ISA or other),

- Custom anti-virus log file, and

- Backup log files, either the NTlog file or third-party backup logs such as the Veritas Backup Exec files.

In SBS 2000 I included the event logs, but because the Server Status Report in SBS 2003 accurately summarizes and documents the critical events, I no longer need this event log attachment. Throughout the chapter I'll introduce the methods I use to create the additional log files or to generate the events required to create my Server Status Report.

The other thing I do is change when the Server Status Report is delivered. Contrary to Harry's recommendation in his introductory SBS 2003 book, I have found that 7 a.m. is just not a good time to deliver the Server Status Report for some of the businesses I support. Many of my SBS clients work in construction; these folks are already heavily into their workday by 7 a.m. In addition, some of my health care clients running SBS are already up and running their businesses by this time of the morning. Therefore, I execute and send the Server Status Report at 4 a.m. Of course, I set up my SBS backup routine schedule so the backup job is finished well before the Server Status Report is sent at 4 a.m.

Health Monitor

Health Monitor 2.1, which comes with SBS 2003, can monitor hardware, software (operating systems and applications), and network devices or applications accessible via HTTP, TCP, or ICMP protocols. It performs simple fault detection, performance monitoring, and event notification. Further, it can perform some basic actions in response to the information it gathers.

When it comes to application monitoring, Health Monitor can perform basic running/not running monitoring on all application services; however, for it to perform more sophisticated monitoring, the software needs to publish its performance data using Windows Monitoring Interface (WMI). If you have custom applications that you need to monitor, you can (hopefully) convince the developer to use WMI to instrument their code.

Now that you have an understanding of what Health Monitor does, lets check out how it works with Data Groups and Collectors and Action Creation to generate performance events. Additionally, I will provide you with some alternatives for generating events on the server that originate from other applications or devices.

Data Groups and Collectors

Data collectors are the basic building block for monitoring. This is where you specify what and how you want to monitor, as well as define any trigger limits when you want something to occur. You can group collectors into data groups so they are easier to manage. If you read the Help files regarding Health Monitor, you will learn that collectors can be used to gather data on the following:

- Performance Monitor Counters—Tracks system-level or application-level metrics such as processor utilization, network activity, Active Server Pages (ASP) Queue length, or Microsoft SQL Server metrics.

- Windows Events—Provides information about hardware, software, system, and security events written to the Windows Event Log.

- Windows Services—Tracks whether a system service such as Microsoft SQL Server is running.

- Processes—Tracks whether a specific process is running.

- HTTP Addresses—Tracks responses from specified URLs on Web servers to verify if the site can be accessed and if Web forms are being processed correctly.

- Windows Management Instrumentation Instances, Data Queries, and Event Queries—Tracks any WMI instance, query, or event notification (for example, you can check file versions or monitor network adapters).

- Ping (ICMP) Monitor responses—Tracks results of pinging systems through the Internet Control Message Protocol (ICMP).

- TCP/IP Port Connections—Tracks responses from connecting to TCP/IP ports.

- COM+ Application Statistics—Tracks transaction rates, processor usage, and other metrics from COM+ applications.

For each of the collectors you are interested in monitoring, you will need to define the condition that you want satisfied before some sort of action occurs. You can specify one of the following conditions:

- If the current value is X.

- If the average value is Y.

- If the change from the last sample to the current sample is greater or less then some threshold value (useful for running to not running conditions).

You can select a duration that must exist prior to performing the action. This can be further qualified by setting a schedule for when the condition to be watched is valid.

Action Creation

The default actions that are created for you are:

- Store the alert in the monitoring database with instance name, and

- Store alert in monitoring database without instance name. Use this option when the instance information is not provided so that the log includes "unknown" as a response.

Further, when you create actions, remember to name your action accordingly since you may request the same action multiple times with slight variations. This enables you to perform slightly different actions based on the event that occurs.

Additional actions you can specify are:

- Command Line Action—Executes a file that can be run from the command line. You also define the command-line options.

- E-mail Action—Sends a Simple Mail Transfer Protocol (SMTP) e-mail message to specified recipients. You specify the text of the message.

- Text Log Action—Writes text that you specify to a specified text-based log file.

- Windows Event Action—Generates a specified Windows event that is written to the application event log.

- Script Action—Runs the specified Windows Script Host (WSH) script that you specify.

Each of these options is discussed in detail below.

Command Line Action

Launch Health Monitor before creating a command line action:

1. Go to **Start, All Programs, Administrative Tools, Health Monitor**.
2. Right-click **Actions** and select **New, Command Line Action**.

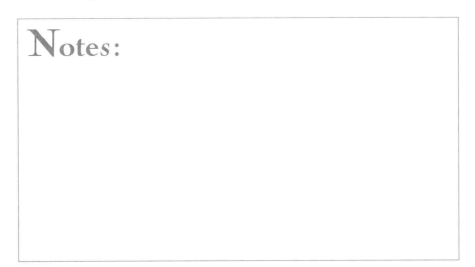

Notes:

As you can see in Figure 13-1, the command-line action is pretty straightforward. The interesting thing is that it will be true for all other actions and will enable you to pass parameters to the script. Additionally, you can select the amount of time (value greater then zero) that the process is allowed to run. If your script needs to use the screen, you can select that option as well. Finally, with the schedule window feature, you can limit when the action is able to run.

Figure 13-1

Notice the command line action settings.

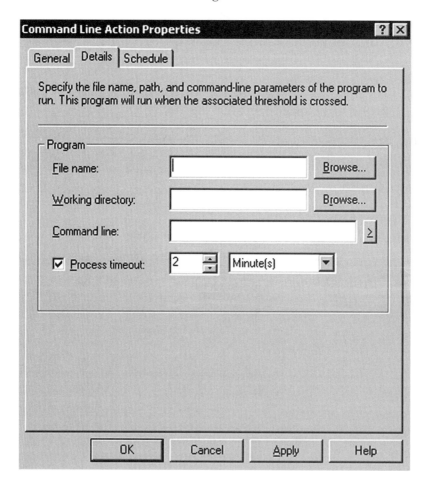

E-Mail Action

To create an e-mail action:

1. Right-click **Actions** and select **New, E-Mail Action**.

    As you can see in Figure 13-2, the e-mail action screen is straightforward. E-mail actions also allow you to pass some key parameters to the message and to specify who will receive the e-mail message.

2. In the SMTP Server location, enter your Server's name to insure that the e-mail is sent.

    Also be sure to enter your e-mail address or another appropriate e-mail address.

Figure 13-2

Notice the e-mail action parameters.

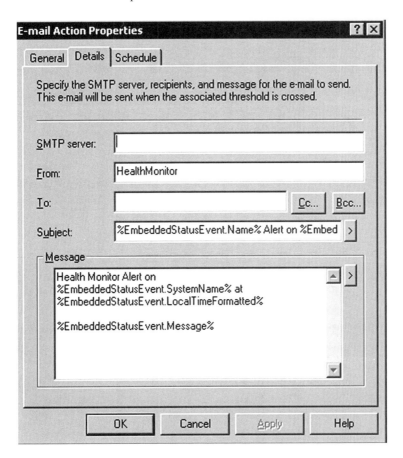

Text Log Action

When you create a text log action, you can establish an easily readable record of the actions you send to the log. While I don't use this feature, it allows you to quickly read what has happened on the system and to do some reasonable diagnositics. You can pass parameters to the log and the schedule when the action is valid.

To create a text log action, right-click **Actions** and select **New, Text Log Action**.

As you can see in Figure 13-3, the text log action screen is pretty simple. You can specify the file name, maximum file size, and whether to use ASCII or Unicode test. Once the file size reaches the maximum, the action will not continue to log until the file is deleted or the size reduced.

Figure 13-3

Notice the text log action properties.

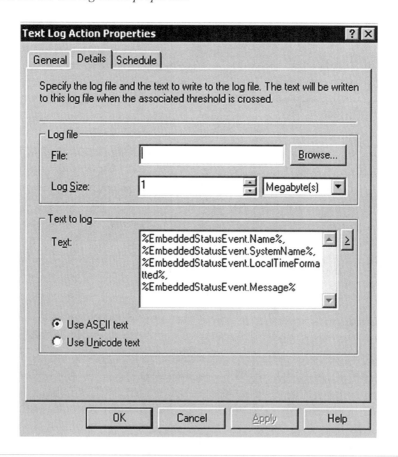

Windows Event Action

The Windows event action allows event log entries to be generated in the application log. You can specify the event type you will receive: Informational, Warning, or Error. You can also assign parameters. This action is the one that I use the most.

To create a windows event action, right-click **Actions** and select **New, Windows Event Action**.

As you can see in Figure 13-4, setting the parameters for this action is the simplest. Other than changing text, the most you can change is the event type. (Hey Microsoft: how about allowing us to specify if the event is a system, application, or security event?)

Figure 13-4

Windows event log action properties.

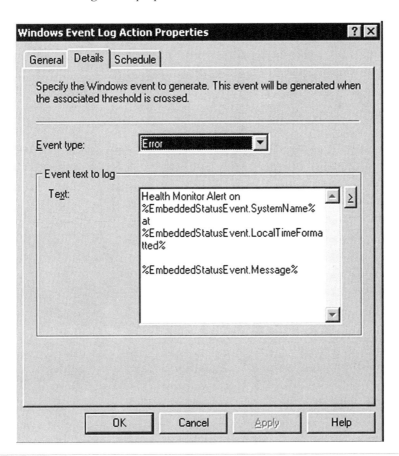

Script Action

Much like the command line action, the script action is used to run scripts that you create. However, instead of running .bat files or executables, you can generate WSH scripts with VBScript or Jscript. Given Microsoft's lack of support for Jscript, I'd recommend VBScript.

To create a windows event action, right-click **Actions** and select **New, Script Action.** Figure 13-5 below shows you the parameters for this action.

Figure 13-5

Windows script action properties.

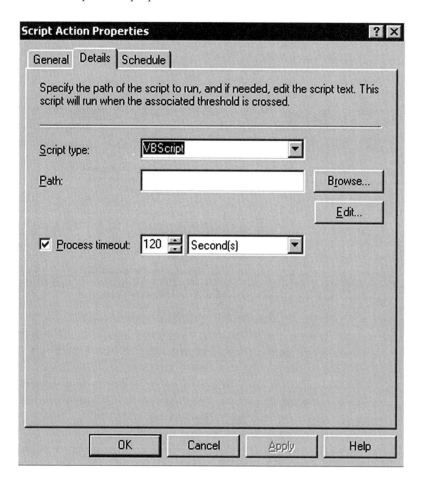

What to Monitor?

Once you have clearly defined what you want to monitor and how you want an event to trigger, it's important to determine what you want to do when the event happens. Remember: e-mail messages may not always be sent depending on the condition of the system when the event occurs. For instance, sending an e-mail to a remote system when the network is down isn't really useful because the e-mail won't be received until the problem is fixed. It's important, therefore, to consider how notifications will be processed

The rest of this section describes the various components that need to be monitored:

- SBS Core monitoring,

- Exchange Server 2003,

- ISA Server 2000,

- SQL Server 2000,

- Windows Sharepoint Services (WSS),
  - Third-party applications and,
  - Other systems.

SBS Core Monitoring

Microsoft was generous in that they defined some data collectors and actions to be performed when an issue is identified during monitoring. However, if you look at the *Windows 2000 Resource Kit* (Microsoft Press) and *"Mastering Windows 2003 Server"* by Mark Minasi (Sybex), you realize that other performance statistics should be collected. Specifically, several queue length and utilization counters were not included. Furthermore, a few additional processes and events need to be watched as part of the core system.

Table 13-1 presents a list of all data collectors that should have actions generated if a certain limit is exceeded. In the performance monitoring section, I'll provide additional values that need to be tracked but do not have automated actions performed. Also, since the Shared Fax Service is part of the base SBS system, I've included it here even though Microsoft has categorized it under a separate monitoring group not explicitly identified with SBS.

For any of this to make sense, make sure the time recorded on all systems is synchronized. Please ensure that you impliment network time protocol (NTP) before using Health Monitor on multiple systems.

Table 13-1

Important Data Collectors

Name	Type	What is being monitored	Action
Allocated Memory	PM	Avg value > Physical memory for at least 10 min.	Log to DB
Disk Activity	PM	If disk activity >95% for 4 hours.	Log to DB
Low Disk Space	PM	If disk space on any partition is less then 500MB.	Log to DB
Low Disk Space percentage	PM	If % of free space on any critical drive is <25%.	Log to DB, Log Event
Memory Available	PM	If available memory is less then 4MB for >10 min.	Log to DB
Printing Errors	PM	If printing job errors are greater then 0.	Log to DB
Process (inetinfo)	PM	If private memory utilization is >1GB for over 10 min.	Log to DB
Process (lsass)	PM	If private memory utilization is >1GB for over 10 min.	Log to DB
Processor Activity	PM	If idle time is less then 5% for at least 10 minutes.	Log to DB
Received Fax Failures	PM	If received fax failures is greater then 0.	Log to DB
Received Fax Failures	PM	If received fax failures is greater then 0.	Log to DB
System Up Time	PM	If system up time is less then 600 (system just rebooted).	Log to DB, E-mail

Name	Type	What is being monitored	Action
Paging File %Usage	PM	Percent of pagefile being used. Set limit to 80% of pagefile.	Log to DB, Log Event, E-Mail
Physical Disk %Disk Time	PM	Disk usage above 60%.	Log to DB, Log Event
Server Bytes Total/Sec	PM	Amount of traffic server is processing. Set to 30% of bandwidth.	Log to DB, Log Event
DHCP Server	SM	If process is not running.	Log to DB, Log Event
DNS Server	SM	If process is not running.	Log to DB, Log Event, E-Mail
Fax Service	SM	If process is not running.	Log to DB, Log Event, E-Mail
Error Reporting Service	SM	If process is not running.	Log to DB, Log Event, E-Mail
Event Log	SM	If process is not running.	Log to DB, Log Event, E-Mail
IPSEC Services	SM	If process is not running.	Log to DB, Log Event, E-Mail
Kerberos Key Distribution Center	SM	If process is not running.	Log to DB, Log Event, E-Mail
License Logging	SM	If process is not running.	Log to DB, Log Event
MSQQL$SBS Monitoring	SM	If process is not running.	Log to DB, Log Event, E-Mail
MSSQL$Sharepoint	SM	If process is not running.	Log to DB, Log Event, E-Mail

Name	Type	What is being monitored	Action
Print Spooler	SM	If process is not running.	Log to DB, Log Event, E-Mail
Routing and Remote Access	SM	If process is not running.	Log to DB, Log Event, E-Mail
SB Core Service	SM	If process is not running.	Log to DB, Log Event, E-Mail
Security Account Manager	SM	If process is not running.	Log to DB, Log Event, E-Mail
Server	SM	If process is not running.	Log to DB, Log Event, E-Mail
Terminal Services	SM	If process is not running.	Log to DB, Log Event, E-Mail
Uninterruptible Power Supply	SM	If process is not running.	Log to DB, Log Event, E-Mail
WINS	SM	If process is not running.	Log to DB, Log Event, E-Mail
WWW Publishing	SM	If process is not running.	Log to DB, Log Event, E-Mail
Fax Server	SM	If process is not running	Log to DB, Log Event, E-Mail
Logical Disk Manager	SM	If process is not running	Log to DB, Log Event, E-Mail
Account Lockout (Event ID:539)	EM	If event log gets an event 539.	Log to DB, E-mail
SBS Backup failed event (event ID 5634)	EM	If event log gets an event 5634.	Log to DB, E-mail

Name	Type	What is being monitored	Action
Logon/Logoff Failure	EM	If event log gets more then four event 529s in five minutes.	Log to DB, E-mail
RAID Controller Disk Error (Controller Specific)	EM	If event log gets an event from the RAID card.	Log to DB, E-mail
Disk (Event ID 7) bad block	EM	If event log gets an event 7.	Log to DB, E-mail
UPS (all events until you can filter better)	EM	If event log gets an event from the UPS.	Log to DB, E-mail
Security Log 512	EM	Windows is starting up.	Log to DB, Log Event, E-Mail
Security Log 513	EM	Windows is shutting down.	Log to DB, Log Event, E-Mail
Security Log 514	EM	An authentication package was loaded by the Local Security Authority.	Log to DB, Log Event, E-Mail
Security Log 516	EM	Internal resources allocated for the queuing of security event messages have been exhausted, leading to the loss of some security event messages.	Log to DB, Log Event, E-Mail
Security Log 517	EM	The security log was cleared.	Log to DB, Log Event, E-Mail
Security Log 518	EM	A notification package was loaded by the Security Accounts Manager.	Log to DB, Log Event, E-Mail
Security Log 608	EM	A user right was assigned.	Log to DB, Log Event, E-Mail
Security Log 609	EM	A user right was removed.	Log to DB, Log Event, E-Mail

Name	Type	What is being monitored	Action
Security Log 610	EM	A trust relationship with another domain was created.	Log to DB, Log Event, E-Mail
Security Log 611	EM	A trust relationship with another domain was removed.	Log to DB, Log Event, E-Mail
Security Log 612	EM	An audit policy was changed.	Log to DB, Log Event, E-Mail
Security Log 768	EM	A collision was detected between a namespace element in one forest and a namespace element in another forest. (Occurs when a namespace element in one forest overlaps a namespace element in another forest.)	Log to DB, Log Event, E-Mail
System Log 6006	EM	Event Log was shutdown.	Log to DB, Log Event, E-Mail
System Log 6008	EM	Unexpected shutdown.	Log to DB, Log Event, E-Mail
System Log 6009	EM	System restarted.	Log to DB, Log Event, E-Mail
System Log 1001	EM	System crash.	Log to DB, Log Event, E-Mail

After looking through that table, you're probably thinking "Okay, much of that makes sense, but where did he come up with all those security events to monitor?" Well, I was crusing around technet one day and found Chapter 9 - Auditing and Intrusion Detection in the book *Microsoft Solution for Securing Windows 2000 Server*, located at http://www.microsoft.com/technet/security/prodtech/win2000/ secwin2k/09detect.mspx. The other items are defaults from the SBS setup except for a few extra services, performance metrics, and events I came up with. One I'm particulaly proud of is the generation of the extra action for four logon/logoff failures within a five-minute time frame. My thought on this was to try and outsmart the hacker who is aware of account lockout policies and develop a new policy that takes this into account.

Once you've implemented these monitors, if you start getting too many triggers during backups or other maintenance activities, you can exclude those objects from running during those time frames. This will ensure that you are not inundated with messages that are not real errors.

Exchange Server 2003

Because Exchange Server 2003 is deployed by default with SBS 2003, some additional Exchange-related objects that warrant monitoring are listed in Table 13-2.

Table 13-2
  Exchange Server 2003 objects to monitor

Name	Type	What is being monitored	Action
MSExchangeIS Mailbox	PM	Send Queue Size < 40 (you may need to play with this number).	Log to DB, Log Event, E-Mail
MSExchangeIS Mailbox	PM	Send Queue Size < 10 (you may need to play with this number).	Log to DB, Log Event, E-Mail
MSExchangeIS Mailbox	PM	Messages Sent/Min > 40 (you may need to play with this number or ignore the event when e-mail blasts occur).	Log to DB, Log Event, E-Mail
Simple Mail Transfer Protocol	SM	If process is not running.	Log to DB, Log Event, E-Mail
Microsoft Exchange Information Store	SM	If process is not running.	Log to DB, Log Event, E-Mail
Microsoft Exchange Management	SM	If process is not running.	Log to DB, Log Event, E-Mail

Name	Type	What is being monitored	Action
Microsoft Exchange MTA Stacks	SM	If process is not running.	Log to DB, Log Event, E-Mail
Microsoft Exchange Routing Engine	SM	If process is not running.	Log to DB, Log Event, E-Mail
Microsoft Exchange	SM	If process is not running.	Log to DB, Log Event, E-Mail

ISA Server 2000

If you've installed SBS 2003 premium edition, you've likely implemented ISA Server 2000 (this is the typical scenario). You would then want to concentrate on monitoring these ISA Server 2000 objects listed in Table 13-3.

Table 13-3

ISA Server 2000 objects to monitor

Name	Type	What is being monitored	Action
Application Log 15001	EM	ISA Server detected windows out of band attack.	Log to DB, E-mail
Application Log 15002	EM	ISA Server detected IP half scan attack.	Log to DB, E-mail
Application Log 15003	EM	ISA Server detected land attack.	Log to DB, E-mail
Application Log 15004	EM	ISA Server detected enumerated port scan attack.	Log to DB, E-mail
Application Log 15001	EM	ISA Server detected generic port scan attack.	Log to DB, E-mail
Application Log 15005	EM	ISA Server detected UDP bomb attack.	Log to DB, E-mail
Application Log 15006	EM	ISA Server detected ping of death attack.	Log to DB, E-mail

Name	Type	What is being monitored	Action
Application Log 15007	EM	ISA Server detected windows out of band attack on IP address %1.	Log to DB, E-mail
Application Log 15101	EM	ISA Server detected IP half scan attack on IP address %1.	Log to DB, E-mail
Application Log 15102	EM	ISA Server detected IP half scan attack on IP address %1.	Log to DB, E-mail
Application Log 15104	EM	ISA Server detected land attack on IP address %1.	Log to DB, E-mail
Application Log 15104	EM	ISA Server detected enumerated port scan attack on IP address %1.	Log to DB, E-mail
Application Log 15105	EM	ISA Server detected generic port scan attack on IP address %1.	Log to DB, E-mail
Application Log 15106	EM	ISA Server detected UDP bomb attack on IP address %1.	Log to DB, E-mail
Application Log 15107	EM	ISA Server detected ping of death attack on IP address %1.	Log to DB, E-mail
Microsoft Firewall	SM	If process is not running.	Log to DB, Log Event, E-Mail
Microsoft H.323 Gatekeeper	SM	If process is not running.	Log to DB, Log Event, E-Mail
Microsoft ISA Server Control	SM	If process is not running.	Log to DB, Log Event, E-Mail
Microsoft Routing and Remote Access	SM	If process is not running.	Log to DB, Log Event, E-Mail
World Wide Web Publishing Service	SM	If process is not running.	Log to DB, Log Event, E-Mail

SQL Server 2000

If you've implimented ISA, it's also important to monitor the SQL server process to make certain it is running. Additionally, you will want to understand the application you are working with and the transaction rates. This will help in monitoring transactions that might indicate improper usage.

Third-Party Applications

If you are running third-party applications (and who isn't?), you'll want to monitor the services they provide. It is also valuable to trigger some action on some of the events they log, and you may want to create some triggers for any performance counters they utilize. I always monitor the AV service I'm using to ensure that I know when/if it starts to misbehave in a client's environment.

Other Systems

In a small business environment, it is essential that you monitor the following systems:

- Firewall
- Routers
- External Web servers
- Print servers
- Video security servers

As you recall, Health Monitor can monitor external machines and applications by using HTTP, Ping, and TCP/IP responses. But what if you need more information and the device doesn't support logging events to the server's event log?

If the device supports the syslog feature, you can use a third-party tool that runs on the SBS server to create a syslog to include in your daily monitoring reports. In addition, other resources will review the syslog and generate Windows events that enable you to create actions based on those events. The tool I use is SL4NT, which is available at http://www.netal.com/download.htm. The 0.3 version is freeware and does what I need; however the 3.1 version is much slicker and has more valuable applications. Follow this procedure to install and configure the 0.3 version:

1. Copy **SL4NT.CPL** to the **SYSTEM32** subdirectory of the Windows 20003 installation directory.
2. Copy **SL4NT.EXE** to a directory of your choice and execute the command line **SL4NT -i**.

The service will be registered with the Control Manager and started afterwards. After installation, you will find the service listed with the name "SysLog" in Control Panel, Services.

After installing SL4NT, your syslog-enabled devices that send messages to the SBS server will have the messages logged into the event log. The big distinction I've found between the free version and the paid version(besides the price), is that the paid version lets you filter entries, which helps you decide what log is needed and what level you want to have them entered in. You can also have it perform additional actions based on a particular event. Because this feature is available in Health Monitor, I don't find it necessary to pay extra for it. Since I use the freeware version, I need to create actions in Health Monitor for any syslog entries I want to relog as warnings or errors.

Performance Monitoring

The purpose of performance monitoring is to understand trends in usage so that you're not caught off guard with a system that can't keep up with usage. You can also use it to understand current performance issues when they arise.

I remember back at one company when this great new application came out that would download to your system all the news you always went to the Web to retrieve. Guess what happened to the server and the network when everyone started using the application? It crawled to a standstill. If performance monitoring had been in place, the administrator would have observed an unexpected increase in network utilization that continued for a few weeks. That would have been the alarm for him or her to start looking for the cause.

Windows Server 2003, the underlying operating system in SBS 2003, provides us with several tools. The one I use the most and the one we will spend some time discussing here is System Monitor. (As of Windows 2000, System Monitor is the new name for Performance Monitor.) In fact, when you set up the performance-based data collectors in Health Monitor, you were really using System Monitor in the background.

The key steps we need to perform are:

- Determine what performance counters are needed to watch and over what time period (business hours would be good). .)

- Capture the data into a log file.

- Review the log files in a meaningful manner.

What to Monitor

How do we capture the log files? We could use the Windows Interface and open System Monitor (under Administrative Tools) and go to the Performance Logs and Alerts section. But unless we're going to collect data 24/7, that approach won't work well. I don't habitually examine performance data for a 24/7 period because non-work hours for businesses tend to be pretty uneventful and averages get skewed for the slow periods. So, I generally monitor systems during work hours and sometimes during normal maintenance hours (backups and report generation.) Hint to Microsoft: let us use the schedule tab to actually define a schedule.

You may want to call on System Monitor to help you determine what counters you want to monitor. Table 13-4 lists the performance counters I routinely use in my SBS consulting practice.

$$\boxed{\text{Notes:}}$$

Table 13-4

Common objects to monitor

OBJECTS	COUNTERS	REASON
Logical Disk (each disk)	% Free Space	Need to track disk space usage.
Memory	Available Bytes	Records memory available on the server. Low or lower values indicate a potential problem.
	Pages/Sec	Record the current rate of paging. Average value of >20 pages a second indicates that you could benefit from more memory.
MSExchangeIS Mailbox (total)	Receive Queue Size	Number of incoming messages waiting to be delivered. Growing counts are bad.
	Send Queue Size	Number of outgoing messages waiting to be delivered. Growing counts are bad.
	Messages Sent/Min	Number of messages sent a minute. If this number is high, you may be a mail relay and not know it.
MSSQL$ SHAREPOINT: General Statistics	User Connections	Number of connected users. Should not exceed your total user count.
Network Interface (each interface except the loopback)	Bytes Total/Sec	Rate of throughput on a single card. Watch for changes.

Notes:

OBJECTS	COUNTERS	REASON
Paging File	% Usage	Percentage of the paging file in use. While windows will grow the paging system, you don't want this to happen as it will most likely result in a fragmented page file.
	% Usage peak	Peak size of the paging file. This is the key measurement but you want to track %usage so you determine when it happens.
Physical Disk (each physical disk)	%Disk Time	Percentage of time the disk is spending servicing read or write requests
	Average Disk Queue Length	Records the number of waiting disk read/write requests. If the number is over 2 for long, consider adding additional disk subsystems.
Processor (per processor and total)	% Processor Time	Need faster CPU if your average time is over 60%.
Terminal Services	Inactive sessions Active sessions	Track inactive sessions. Track total terminal server sessions.
Web Service (total and individual sites)	Current Anonymous Users	Number of current anonymous Web connections.
	Current Total Users	Total number of current Web connections.
	Current Non-anonymous Users	Number of current non-anonymous Web connections.

Now we need to understand how to configure performance monitoring logs. The tool for doing this is called logman and we can use it to collect data for specific intervals. We will run logman twice, once to tell the system what counters we are interested in, and once in the scheduler to tell it when to run and what to do when we are done. The basic syntax used to tell logman what to collect is:

```
logman create counter collection_name -cf
filename_of_counters -o logfile for example

logman create counter normal_counters -cf
d:\perfmon\normal_counter_list.txt -o d:\logs
```

This creates a counter set "normal counters" with the list of counters being in d:\perfmon\normal_counter_list. The log file will be created in d:\logs. To schedule the log file, I use the following command inside the task scheduler:

```
logman    start    collection_name    -si
collection_interval15:00 -rf time_ to_collect -
rc batch_file. (For example, logman start
normal_counters -si 15:00 -rf 10:00:00 -rc
d:\rename_log.bat).
```

This will start the collection of counters defined in normal_counters, perform data collection every 15 minutes, run for 10 hours and, when the schedule is over, run the batch files rename_log.bat.

Wonder why 15 minutes are needed for a collection interval? It's a Microsoft best practice so that you keep the overhead of data collection low. I use the rename_log batch file feature to save the data original log file from being overwritten and to allow a new file to be created the next time it is run.

The last piece of the puzzle you may ask is where do I schedule the execution of the logman start procedure? I use the Scheduled Task Wizard in the Control panel and set the task to run right before the client's workday begins. I also select the task to run only on workdays.

The last bit of insight I need to give you is the format of the counter definition file: "filename_of_counters" The format is *computer*]*object*[*instance*]*counter.*

You can determine the exact counters to use by going into system administrator tools and selecting performance logs and alerts, counter logs and creating a set of counters to monitor. When this is done, look at the properties and you will get the format you need to use. In fact, if you save the file into html format (the only supported format), you can edit the list from there.

How to Review the Data

Now that we have the logfile, we can attach it to our Server Status Report so it shows up in the daily mail. Now we need a method for reading the data. I normally keep the data in binary format, so the only way to view the data is to:

1. Open System Monitor, then click **Start**, **Administrative Tools**, and **Performance**.
2. Right-click the System Monitor details pane, click **Properties**, and select the **Source** tab.
3. Under Data Source, click **Log files** and then add one or more files that you want to use as a datasource.
4. To add files to the list, click **Add** to open the Select Log File dialog box.
5. Double-click the names of the files you want to open.
   The default settings will include all of the data counters in your data set; however, you can remove some of them if you need to get a better look at a few counters.
6. When you need to explore certain timeframes more carefully, reduce the timeframe by clicking the **Time Range** slider.

Another valuable feature of System Monitor is that you can re-save the data you just looked at into .cse or .tsv format so you can view multiple days-worth of data or create more sophisticated charts in Excel.

Now that you know how to collect and view data, what do you do next? It's important to review the current data and make certain you're happy with the performance and save it as a baseline. Then on a monthly or quarterly basis, go back and review the data against the baseline to look at trends. I'll normally examine a full week's worth of data so I can capture anything unique that may happen on a particular day. I'll also look at the data whenever somebody complains about sluggish performance. Additionally, I may start capturing more data, perhaps even process-specific data, to determine the specific causes of system performance issues.

Hardware and Software Inventory Monitoring

Do you know everything about every device on your network? Are you certain? How? If you rely on Active Directory-registered (AD) computers, you'll only get the systems that are AD aware and joined to your network. If you look at the network neighborhood, you still only see the machines that have Lanman compatibility. This leaves a whole class of devices that won't show up with the standard Microsoft operating system tools.

Fortunately, tools from Microsoft and other companies have freeware versions that you can use to help you understand what is on your network. The Microsoft tool is Microsoft Baseline Security Analyzer (MBSA). Other options include HFNetChkPro from Shavlik (www.shavlik.com), LogInventory from Schmidts(http://www.loginter.net), and Network Security Scanner from GFI (www.gfi.com). I provide brief descriptions of each of these tools here.

Microsoft Baseline Security Analyzer

MBSA is an effective tool that will scan your network for Microsoft systems and some of its deployed software applications and versions. MBSA will report on missing security updates for installations of the following:

- Microsoft Internet Information Server 4.0

- Microsoft Internet Information Services 5.0 and 6.0

- Microsoft SQL Server 7.0 and SQL Server 2000, including Microsoft SQL Server Desktop Engine (MSDE) 1.0 and MSDE 2000

- Microsoft Exchange Server 5.5 and later (including Exchange administration tools)

- Microsoft Internet Explorer 5.01 and later

- Microsoft Windows Media® Player 6.4 and later

MBSA will also identify misconfigured settings for the following applications:

- Internet Information Server 4.0

- Internet Information Services 5.0 and 6.0

- Internet Explorer 5.01 and later

- SQL Server 7.0 and SQL Server 2000 (including MSDE 1.0 and MSDE 2000)

- Office 2000 and later

MBSA won't identify other systems on the network or missing ISA patches. Additionally, it's difficult to move around in the report to find the issues for each machine. If you use MBSA and request a SCAN of your network, you'll get a summary report that looks like Figure 13-6.

To launch MBSA:

1. Double-click the desktop icon for MBSA.

2. Once the application is launched, select **Scan more than one computer,** enter the Domain name you want to scan, and then select **Start Scan**.

   You'll eventually get a screen that looks like Figure 13-6. If you click on one of the machines listed in the summary, you'll get the screen that looks like Figure 13-7. By clicking on the results detail, you will receive more detailed information on the problem and pointers to a fix. These fixes can be configuration changes or software patches or updates.

Figure 13-6

MBSA Sample Summary Display.

Computer Name	IP Address	Assessment	Scan Date
SRCG\GILLIAN01	10.255.255.69	Severe Risk	8/14/2004 1:37 PM
SRCG\LARRY	10.255.255.68	Severe Risk	8/14/2004 1:37 PM
SRCG\SRCG01	10.255.255.2	Severe Risk	8/14/2004 1:36 PM

Notes:

Figure 13-7

MBSA Sample Detailed Security Display.

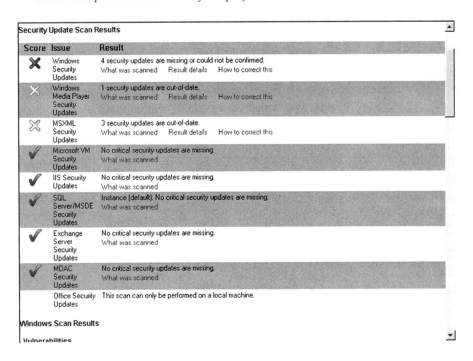

HFNetChkPro

The nice folks at Shavlik helped to developed MBSA for Microsoft, so you can thank them for helping support the cause. The folks at Shavlick have their own product beyond MBSA that understands ISA and can also do patch management. HFNetChkPro is free for small networks (10 or fewer Windows boxes). Much like MBSA, HFNetChkPro does not enumerate non-Windows systems, so you might not get a full understanding of all the devices on your network.

One issue with HFNetChkPro is that, unlike MBSA, it will not identify any misconfigured items that are potential security holes. Another issue I have with HFNetChkPro is that it tries to identify all of the computers listed in Active Directory (AD) but does not attempt to identify devices that are not in AD.

To launch HFNetChkPro after installation:

    1.   Double-click the HFNetChkPro desktop icon.

2. Select **Scan My Domain**.

    Figure 13-8 is a sample high-level screen from HFNetChkPro after a scan of a small domain has been run. It provides a summary of issues it has encountered. If you drill down to a suspect computer, you will see that, unlike MBSA, HFNetChkPro does not look at configuration issues (illustrated in Figure 13-9). Figure 13-9 also provides more detailed information about the scan results for a particular computer. Drilling down on particular issues will reveal the reason for the issue as well as how to resolve the problem.

Figure 13-8

HFNetChkPro high-level scan summary.

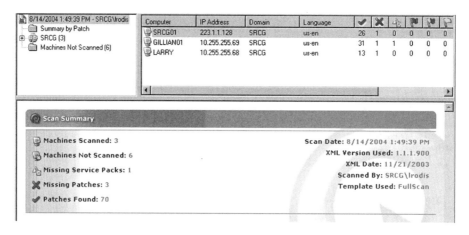

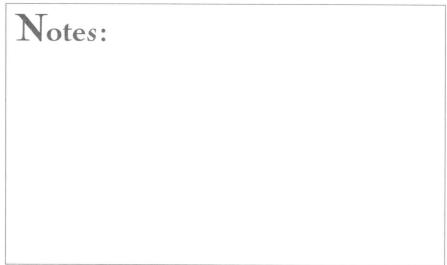

Notes:

Figure 13-9

HFNetChkPro detail scan summary for a particular computer.

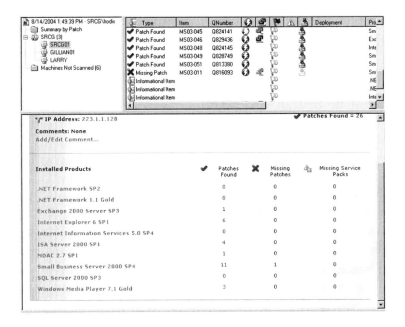

LogInventory

If you need to get a full and detailed inventory of your systems without patch management or vulnerability, Schmidt's LogInventory is a nice product. The freeware version that supports 20 IPs is available at: http://www.loginter.net/ en/loginventory_downloads.php.

LogInventory provides a detailed list of the hardware and software located on each machine. After installing LogInventory, you query the network, generate a report, and then view the results. As you can see from Figure 13-10, the left-hand side of the report provides an expanded presentation of all the scanned network hardware (although they call it PCs), the software installed, the hardware detected on each machine, and all of the users logged in at the time of the scan.

Notes:

Figure 13-10

LogInventory high-level scan summary.

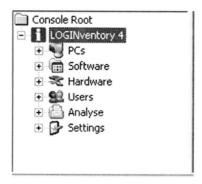

If you expand the PCs out and select an individual PC, you'll see a screen similar to Figure 13-11, which shows information about the hardware and software on the system. It even includes the Keycode used for the operating system installation. (Don't worry – I conveniently erased it here so you can't copy my code. J) If you drill down on drives, you will get information on the types of drives that are installed. If you then move to the software heading, you can get a list of software packages that have been installed. I use LoginInventory to track the hardware and software installed on specific units. It's like Belarc advisor in functionality but it will run in a network environment for a reasonable price. Keep in mind, though, that while you can save reports to HTML, you can't use LogInventory in an automated fashion.

Notes:

Figure 13-11

LogInventory sample individual machine summary.

Property	Value
Drives	(Double-click for details)
Partitions	(Double-click for details)
Memory	(Double-click for details)
Network	(Double-click for details)
SCSI/IDE	(Double-click for details)
Sound	(Double-click for details)
Video	(Double-click for details)
Monitor	(Double-click for details)
Printer	(Double-click for details)
Software	(Double-click for details)
User History	(Double-click for details)
Journal	(Double-click for details)
Manual Properties	(Double-click for details)
Name	LARRY
Unique Identifier	LARRY
System Manufacturer	VIA Technologies, Inc.
System Product Name	P4X266-8233
BIOS Vendor	Award Software International, Inc.
BIOS Version	6.00 PG
BIOS Date	20011109
CPU Name	Intel(R) Pentium(R) 4 CPU 1.60GHz
CPU Type	GenuineIntel
CPU Subtype	x86 Family 15 Model 2 Stepping 4
CPU Speed	1600
Processors	1
Memory Size	512
Operating System	Microsoft Windows XP Professional
OS Version	5.1.2600
OS Language	English (United States)
Windows Product Key	
Machine SID	S-1-5-21-823518204-492894223-854245398
Service Pack	Service Pack 1
Windows Directory	C:\WINDOWS
OS Creation Date	11/28/2003 9:18:47 AM
User Account	lrodis
User Name	Lawrence A. Rodis
PC Domain	SRCG
Logon Domain	SRCG
Logon Server	\\SRCG01
LogInfo Version	4.00.0.11 (local)
Scan Timestamp	8/8/2004 12:05:10 PM
Scan Result	OK

Network Security Scanner

GFI Network Security Scanner (NSS) is a full-blown security scanner with a variety of useful features. The free version is quite valuable and it may be just what you need to do what you desire (especially during the free full-functionality period). For many of my clients I use the paid version because I like the increased functionality and the price is reasonable. With the paid version, I can schedule scans and patch deployments (more about that in the next section), as well as compare/save scans. One more thing; my firm is a GFI reseller, so if you need a product, contact me.

I use NSS to inventory my network. It will tell me all about the different devices on my network as well as some of the possible security issues with them. These issues go beyond the missing service packs and hot fixes, which we will discuss in a bit. If you run a full network scan and look at the report, the summary will look similar to Figure 13-12. Each of the icons presented under "details" corresponds to an issue. The leftmost listing indicates a potential major vulnerability (which is normally a good thing to know). In the case of 10.255.255.1, it is telling me that the box is potentially vulnerable to a *ypasswd* issue. Even though this did not turn out to be a problem, it was useful to know that it was a potential issue. You can ignore the vulnerability warnings that don't apply or filter them out if you need to show the report to someone who is a worry wort. Filtering the non-vulnerabilities is not difficult because one of the other features is a difference report, which provides a comparison between a baseline report and the current report.

Figure 13-12

NSS sample high- level scan summary.

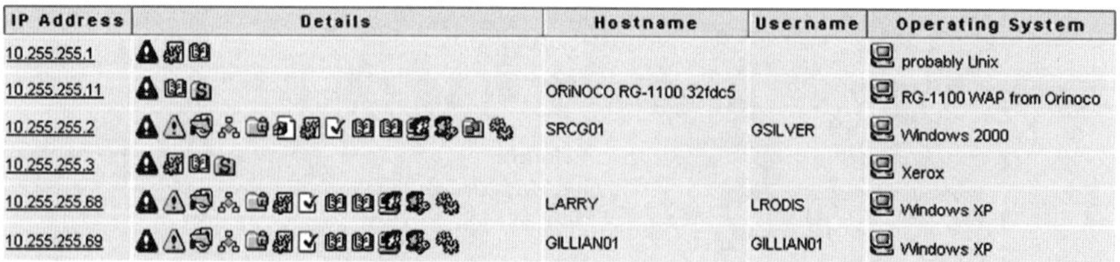

IP Address	Details	Hostname	Username	Operating System
10.255.255.1				probably Unix
10.255.255.11		ORiNOCO RG-1100 32fdc5		RG-1100 WAP from Orinoco
10.255.255.2		SRCG01	GSILVER	Windows 2000
10.255.255.3				Xerox
10.255.255.68		LARRY	LRODIS	Windows XP
10.255.255.69		GILLIAN01	GILLIAN01	Windows XP

The NSS report provides information on:

- Vulnerabilities,

- Potential vulnerabilities (undetected patches),

- Shares,

- Network devices,

- Password policy,

- Security audit policy (even lets you set it network wide),

- Basic motherboard information,

- Software started from the registry,

- Installed patches,

- NetBIOS Names on the PC,

- Users and groups,

- Current sessions, and

- Services.

By doing a comparison scan, you can clearly determine what changes have ocurred. Remember: when you are monitoring a system, managing change and determining the results of the change are essential to resolving any potential issues.

Patch Management

Everyone should be aware of the need for keeping systems patched. In fact, just to prove how serious Microsoft is about system maintenance, they offer three and a half tools for doing this:

- Windows Update—this is not an automated tool and I do not describe it in detail here.

- Office Update—this is not an automated tool and I do not describe it in detail here.

- Software Update Service (SUS)—described in detail below.

- Microsoft Baseline Security Analyzer—I consider this to be half a tool because it lets you manually deploy updates on the server, but it will not help with workstations and it is not automated.

Microsoft is working on a new super patch management product called Windows Update Service (WUS). WUS promises to be a better tool than all of the other Microsoft Tools. However, until I can evaluate the true capabilities of this new tool, I use either the free version of HFNetChkPro or GFI Network Security Scanner, as described below.

Software Update Service

Software Update Service will deploy system and office patches to all Windows-based 2000 and newer systems. SUS can be scheduled to download and push all updates, which I find to be very useful. It won't patch SQL, Exchange, or ISA, so you'll be stuck using another tool for that. Additionally, you'll need to use another tool to get reports to determine what systems have which updates. We won't talk about SUS anymore in this chapter, but a detailed manual on SUS is available at: http://www.microsoft.com/downloads/details.aspx?Family Id=38D7E99B-E780-43E5-AA84-CDF6450D8F99&displaylang=en.

HFNetChkPro

Earlier I spoke about how to use HFNetChkPro to scan your network. It's possible, as part of the scanning process, to have it install the missing patches and updates immediately or at a specific time. I've occasionally had issues with the scheduled scans doing everything the product is supposed to do and sometimes I've needed to manually reboot the updated machine. Another issue with HFNetchkPro is its inability to obtain a remote report, so you will need to logon to the server and perform a scan to make certain everything went according to plan.

Figure 13-13 demonstrates that you can elect to deploy patches and updates. In addition, you can schedule the deployment or elect for them to happen

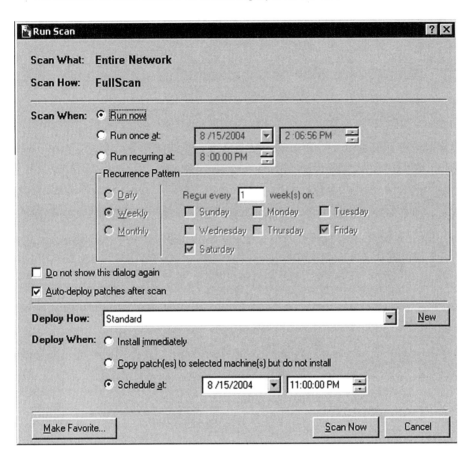

immediately. Figure 13-14 is the status screen that lets you see the deployment status of the patches and updates.

Figure 13-13
HFNetChkPro scan window with auto deployment selected.

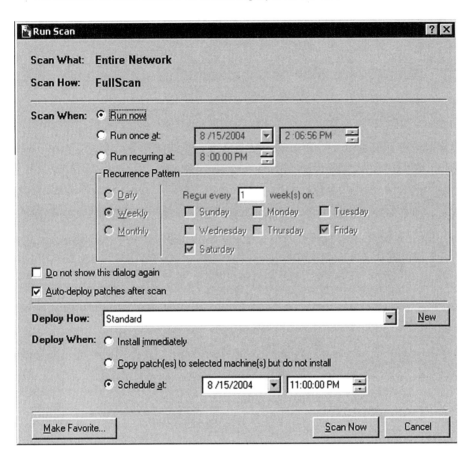

Notes:

Figure 13-14

HFNetChkPro deployment status screen.

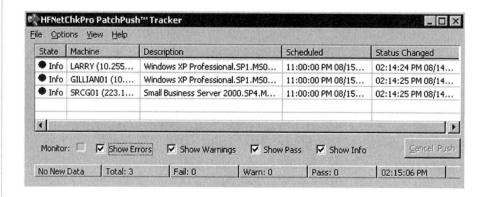

Network Security Scanner

With GFI Network Security Scanner, the patch management process is a bit more detailed. In particular, you need to perform the following steps:

* Perform a scan of your network.

* Select on which machines to deploy the patches.

* Select which patches to deploy.

* Download the patch and service pack files (this is normally a partially automated task).

* Set patch file deployment parameters.

* Deploy the updates.

Deploy patches, services packs, and custom software. The patch deployment agent consists of a service that will run the installation at a scheduled time depending on the deployment parameters indicated. Additionally, NSS can be used to do custom deployments; this is good for third-party applications or for optional windows components.

When the NSS scan is complete, right click on a machine and select **deploy Microsoft updates**. Next, select services packs or updates. Your final selection is all machines or selected machines. You can then manually or automatically download the service packs or updates. When the patches are downloaded, you can schedule the deployment or have the patches pushed immediately to all affected systems. Figure 13-15 shows the deployment screen for NSS.

Figure 13-15

GFI's NSS deployment status screen.

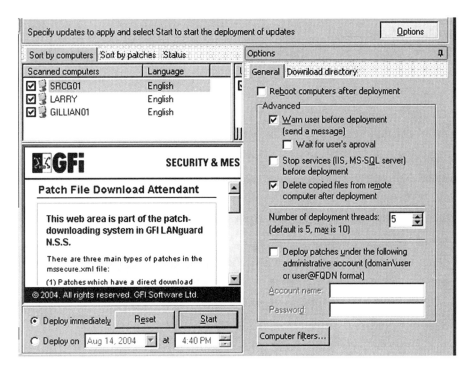

A Day in the Life

As I start to wrap up this chapter, I thought I'd tell you about how system monitoring goes on a typical day in my business. The first scenario is how I maintain a single network and how I used to handle multiple networks. The second scenario is a new method that provides a single starting point for all the networks that I monitor.

Single Networks or a Small Collection of Sites

The first thing I do in the morning is review the e-mails from the night before or earlier that morning to make certain I have received a Server Status Report from all of the networks that are being monitored. A missing report signals that a problem has arisen. If this is the case, I then determine the cause of the missing report before contacting the client and informing them of the issue and implementing the appropriate solution.

Next, I make sure the backups for all of the SBS servers were completed successfully. I do this by checking the Server Status Report or by having an e-mail sent on successful and failed backups. If any sites haven't sent a backup message, it means the backup is hung and we need to figure out why. If any backups failed or are still running, I know I need to look at the logs, find out why the backups have not been completed, and send an e-mail to the client indicating the issue. I'd rather be proactive about informing the client of the challenge than wait for the client to find out on his or her own that the backup failed.

The next step is to review the main server status page for each of the monitored networks. If nothing extraordinary is found, sit back and take a break. Next, check with the AV vendors to determine the current pattern level and then check to make certain that all networks and desktops have the correct patterns loaded.

Next it's time to review any messages from Microsoft to see if there are any updates or security fixes. If there are, I'll then schedule out which clients need to be updated and when. Remember - not all clients are monitored in the same way, so their update schedules will differ. At this point, review the security scan files from the sites to determine if any new information is being issued on them and, if so, figure out the changes and if any actions need to be performed.

For my healthcare clients, I'll regularly write up a HIPPA security audit and note any abnormal events as well as any changes that may have occurred. Also, I'll routinely review performance logs against baselines to determine what is changing and if we are approaching any thresholds.

At this point I turn my attention to other tasks like answering e-mails, planning or implementing deployments, researching new areas, or handling other customer requests.

Monitoring Multiple Networks.

I've graduated from just monitoring a few customers' sites and now remotely manage many sites. In this transition I've found that the method outlined above, while useful, lacked the scalability I wanted. In my previous life I spent some time with products like LanDesk, Tivoli, and CA Unicenter, which are great for managing large enterprises but aren't cost effective for smaller customers. I got really excited at first when Microsoft launched Microsoft Operations Manager (MOM). Unfortunately, MOM doesn't work across active directory domains. Until it does, I need to rely on another product for help. Luckily, the folks at Level Platforms (www.levelplatforms.com) have a product called Managed WorkPlace that does all of this and a lot more.

Managed WorkPlace is subscription-based product that integrates remote monitoring, real-time alerting, inventory management, Web-based reporting, and trouble ticketing. The product is made up of two components: Onsite Manager on the client side and Service Manager on the consultant site.

Managed WorkPlace consists of a Service Center installed at your central site, which communicates with Onsite Manager installed at each of your customers' sites, communicating with the Service Center through a secure connection (SOAP/XML through HTTP/HTTPS). Figure 13-16 shows the overall architecture for Managed Workplace.

Figure 13-16
Level Platform's Managed WorkPlace Overall Architecture.

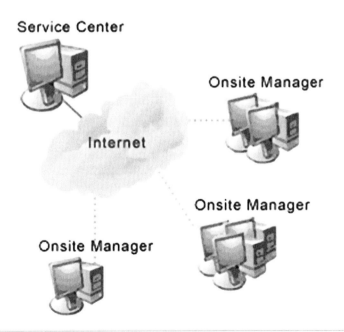

Onsite Manager, which is installed at the customer site and perhaps even on the customer's SBS server, is a simple, lightweight application that provides:

- Continuous monitoring of all devices and applications on the network for existing or potential problems,

- Analytical measurements,

- Filtering,

- Prioritizing of events and exceptions, and

- Automatically repairing problems and escalating issues to Service Center as required.

Figure 13-17 shows the All Devices inventory screen from Service Center. Figure 13-18 shows a summary of Windows Site Events.

Figure 13-17

Onsite Manager top-level inventory view.

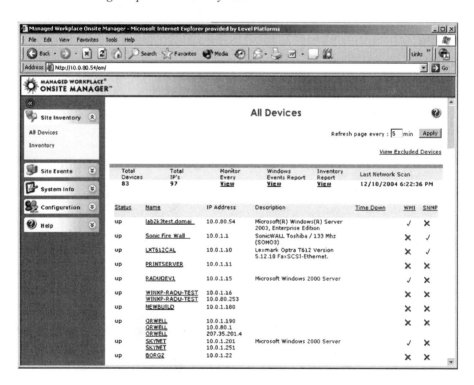

Figure 13-18

Onsite Manager top-level site event view.

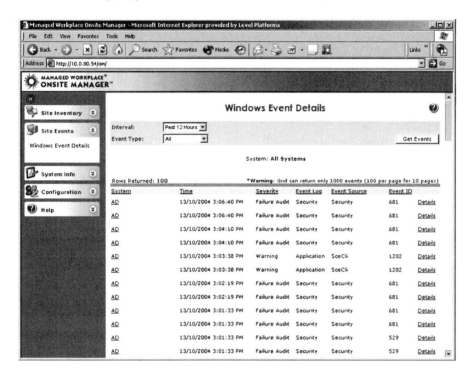

Service Center is the real key for me because it aggregates all of my client sites into a single view for me to review. Now instead of needing to verify that each site sent me a status report and then reviewing the report, I can pull up Service Center and start reviewing issues immediately. While I still need to review some log files and use some other tools for site audits and patch management, Service Center allows me to quickly determine what the status is at each site. Figure 13-19 shows the high-level view within Service Center from which you can see the status of multiple sites.

Notes:

Figure 13-19

Service Center top-level view of multiple sites.

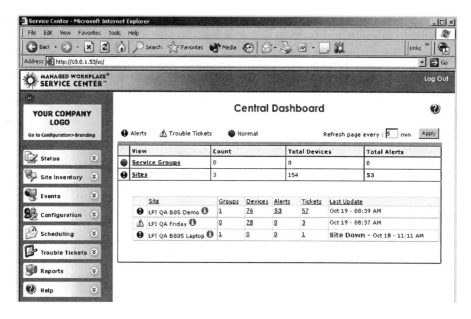

If you're having a problem at a particular site, you just start to drill down on that site to get more detailed information. You can then click on groups or devices until you get to the level of detail you need to understand the issue. You can also view alerts by site, group, or individual device at a site. Additionally, you can create a group of like devices across customer sites and then monitor those devices from that view. Service Center will also create simple trouble tickets that you can then modify. The trouble tickets system can even be used to kick off events in Microsoft Customer Relationship Management. With some minor customization, it can also be used with other applications.

By integrating Service Manager into my arsenal, I've been able to save some time everyday by reducing the number of reports I need to review due to it's ability to show me problems quickly.

Notes:

Summary

This chapter includes the why, what, and how of system monitoring. We covered the tools that Microsoft includes in SBS 2003 for network monitoring (Server Status Report, Server Performance Report, Health Monitor, and Event Logs) as well as other tools you can download from Microsoft and from third-party vendors. Hopefully, with the information that I've presented in this chapter, you can go out and start monitoring the systems you manage in a more proactive and consistent manner.

CHAPTER 14
SBS Disaster Recovery

BY Jeff Middleton (New Orleans, LA)

© Copyright by Jeff Middleton and SBSmigration.com. Reprinted by permission.

Introduction

You need either a roadmap or a lot of experience to know where you are going with SBS repair or disaster recovery. If you arrived here with a lot of experience, this chapter will act as a reference. If you need a roadmap, then here is where you learn the bare essentials of why an SBS server starts up and does what it should. With a detailed understanding of a normal boot sequence, you have something to compare against in diagnosis of a server which fails to reach the optimal results you expected on a boot or in operations. But what exactly happens during the boot sequence and leading into stable operations? This chapter provides insight to the anatomy of SBS 2003, what happens when the system starts from a cold boot, and why that brings your server to life, as long as it's healthy. When it isn't healthy, that's when you are approaching, or maybe already into the trauma of a disaster recovery.

SBS Anatomy Course: Disaster Recovery Clues

I must say that as I wrote this section, I found anatomy to be a relevant metaphor, helping create a picture that illustrated the independence and codependence of these concepts. In the next few sections, I fill in the concepts on what "binds" the core processes of an SBS Server together—to maintain health and ensure survival. I want you to get a picture of an SBS Server's structure and understand what lifts up a server from a cold state (powered off) to the point where all the core server functions are operational. Table 14-1 provides a summary of the sections we will cover next.

Table 14-1

The Anatomy of SBS Server

The Anatomy of SBS Server	
Normal Boot Process: • Hardware Boot • Master Boot Record • OS Loader • Kernel Phase • GUI Logon • Infrastructure Completion	Muscles and Coordination
Windows Self-Repair and Restore:	The Immune System
Services and Drivers:	The Vital Organs
File System:	Skeleton
Registry:	Spinal Cord of Windows and SBS
Integrated DNS and Active Directory:	Cerebral Control Left Lobe
The Exchange:	Cerebral Storage Right Lobe
Applications:	The Skilled Appendages

Notes:

Our SBS Anatomy Course Begins with Boot Startup

Microsoft Windows Server Resource Kit defines four phases of Windows Startup, however, an SBS server is just a tad more complicated than the typical workstation when it comes to diagnosing repair points. You need a more detailed breakdown in defining the disaster recovery phases in the process. With this in mind, I've redefined Microsoft's original four phases, paying more attention to the control or milestones involved. As Table 14-2 shows, I want to break down disaster recovery for SBS into to six phases.

Table 14-2
The six phases of SBS server boot progress.

Operating System Progress Phase	Disaster Recovery Viewpoint	Recovery Resources
Initial Phase	1. Hardware Boot	·Hardware-Based
	2. Master Boot Record	·Pre-GUI Tools ·Recovery Console ·Parallel Boot ·Non-Windows Restore
Boot Loader Phase	3. OS Loader	
Kernel Phase	4. Kernel Phase	
Logon Phase	5. GUI Logon	·Windows GUI-Based Tools
	6. Infrastructure Completion	·Technical Skill Resource

In the table above, you can see how a disaster recovery approach varies depending upon how far along in the boot process you are. The column on the left indicates what Microsoft considers to be the Operating System startup stage. The middle column subdivides into the six phases I want to identify for disaster recovery concerns. The last column reveals what intervention is required to be successful during startup before you ever even reach the GUI logon into Windows itself. And yet, most of the powerful resources to repair Windows are found after the GUI logon phase.

Notes:

Typically, other tools become available to help narrow this process and identify points of failure if you can get into the Windows GUI. You can review event logs there, but only if your boot process makes it far enough to record that data. Unfortunately, Windows needs to get pretty far along before that information is updated.

The Normal Boot Process: Muscles and Coordination

The OS boot process, as I've previously seen defined by Microsoft, involves four principal stages. From these I've elected to expand the definition here for SBS with two additional incremental milestones of related OS boot and operations:

1. **Hardware Boot:** Initially under BIOS control, hardware boot is not specific to the OS that will be booted; it's independent. The process is looking for the location where the OS Boot files will be found. That could be any bootable device media, such as floppy, hard disk, or PXE-driven network boot. All of these have either a Master Boot Record or something that emulates that. It's actually the starting point of the OS specific boot file locations.

2. **Master Boot Record:** A boot sector entry leads to discovery of the NTLDR bootstrap loader for Windows. In the next phase, NTLDR searches the same partition where that boot sector entry for NTLDR was found, looking further (at a minimum) for the files boot.ini and Ntdetect.exe. In addition, in some cases, two additional files are required by Windows to support additional boot functionality. Ntbootdd.sys provides support of certain SCSI-type controller media, and Bootsect.sys is a file that contains a copy of an alternate OS boot sector file, used to launch an alternate Operating System. The %systemroot% location need not be on the same partition, or even the same device media at the OS Loader. That means you can use a boot floppy to start up Windows in a different configuration, or in a different location than normal with an alternate installation.

3. **OS Loader:** NTLDR uses the reference from Boot.ini to locate the Windows System Folder location to continue the boot sequence. NTLDR then initiates a series of steps to bring the OS up. The first visual sign for the operator is the screen change followed by the Boot Loader Menu defined within the boot.ini file. From that selection, NTLDR continues, with support of the option for the operator to request alternate boot conditions such as Safe Mode or DSRM mode. Hardware Profile options will be offered if they are defined beyond the default. The information for the Hardware Profiles comes from within the System registry. When the location in the %systemroot% folder was specified in the boot.ini selection, NTLDR proceeded to load the registry hives and critical boot drivers. In addition, NTLDR launches Ntdetect to identify the basic hardware present to begin initial transition to the Operating System initialization in Kernel Mode. If no errors prevent the loading of the device drivers, hardware detection, or registry initialization, NTLDR passes control to the Ntoskrnl.exe.

4. **Kernel Phase**: NTLDR initializes the Kernel Phase of OS boot, an action which begins well before the logon to Windows is presented. It will be using the same %systemroot% location as indicated by the boot.ini reference. The kernel initializes all the drivers and begins the final phase of startup.

5. **GUI Logon:** At the point the OS has prepared the core services sufficient to accept a User Session, the Secure Logon is presented at the console. In virtually the same timeframe, a remote session via Terminal Services logon is also accessible. However, neither of these is required from the standpoint of "operational readiness" of the system. As a general rule, and this applies to SBS itself, no local logon is required for the system to be fully functional in all respects, ready to do the business of what SBS itself is designed to accomplish. Some third-party applications may require a local logon, but this is not only rare, it's also a very bad practice in server application design. There's

only one element of the local logon of interest regarding disaster recovery issues. Windows itself considers the GUI logon to be the trigger of a successful boot in storing the settings for "Last Known Good Configuration." This is probably a trivial point in the grand scheme of disaster recovery, because you normally must log on in order to shutdown a Domain Controller (the default with SBS is the way), so at some point you will log on to trigger this milestone. In addition, "Last Known Good Configuration" is really protection against changes that normally would occur only by administrative reconfiguration.

6. **Infrastructure Completion:** Microsoft doesn't designate this "boot milestone" in its official documents, so I'm creating the designation here because it just makes sense to define how an SBS "finishes booting." There isn't a breakpoint or transition between Kernel Phase and what happens next; rather what happens is a continuation of Kernel Phase launching all the services, device initialization, and application loading caused by services starting. The GUI Logon milestone is reached at the point that it first "becomes possible" to support the user environment. Meanwhile all the other triggered services still queued for startup continue to launch and stabilize at an operational level. Therefore, I'm defining this transition period as the Infrastructure Completion period. As you probably know, an SBS server continues to show disk activity even after the logon prompt is offered, and it can continue for a several more minutes under normal circumstances.

Notes:

Yet I think we have one more summary topic we should take a quick look first. Windows provides a number of features that might be your last option to try before you must roll up your sleeves for specific technical repairs, or global restore from backup. The next section presents built-in repair and recovery features in Windows, as well as a few found in the Exchange Server component of SBS.

Windows Self-Repair and Recovery Options— The Immune System

Microsoft has included many features in the design of Windows to provide options and alternatives to work in the GUI, or to get back into the GUI to perform a repair. Some are more effective than others, and some are really quite useless for all but the rarest type of recovery conditions.

A round-up of common recovery and repair techniques, which you find in Table 14-3, could be useful information starting from this point. From there, we dig into the details of what we could be repairing.

Table 14-3

A Review of Windows Repair and Resolution Options Featured in SBS.

Repair and Resolution Options	
Boot-Time Alternatives	
Boot to Safe Mode	Provide boot recovery with a limited number of drivers and services started.
Boot to Alternate Hardware Configuration	Typically not a disaster recovery feature, rather this allows for using different hardware configurations for different situations to be stored for use on demand.
DSRM Safe Mode	For the purpose of restoring a System State, including the Active Directory, this is the only boot option which allows that.
Last Known Good Boot	In the event of corruption of the registry itself, or recovery from the installation of fatally flawed drivers, this option uses a different Controlset, but the same registry hive file.

Virtual Rollback Protection Options	
Recycle Bin	Like in any other Windows computer, the Recycle Bin provides an undelete for locally deleted files provided they were deleted using the Windows interface or applications in Windows.
Volume Shadow Storage	The virtual storage and access provided by VSS allows recovery of files deleted from remote computers, provided that the administrator has granted this option to be used. Another feature of this service is the ability to enable backup for open files while in use, something that certain utilities for backup and recovery benefit from.
Automated System Recovery Disk	An ASR disk is an option to use in addition to the normal bare metal recovery requirements. You still require the original Windows Media and a full backup, including System State, but the ASR disk improves on the speed to restore.
Device Driver Roll-back	1. Open the Device Manager. 2. Right-click the device for which you want to reinstall the previous version of the driver, then click **Properties**. 3. Click the **Drivers** tab. 4. Click **Roll Back Driver**.
Intervention Access Methods	
Recovery Console	Solving a historically common problem, the Recovery Console provides the means to boot a Windows machine to edit or replace files on an NTFS partition, but without requiring the launch of Windows. It has some limited use as compared to other third-party tools, but it's a valuable option.
NTFSBoot-Enabled Browsing Disks	A number of third-party manufacturers make available tools to access NTFS partitions for many purposes related to recovery and repair, typically more robust than the Recovery Console.
Drive Relocation	Perhaps the simplest way to do maintenance on a disk drive is to move it to another computer that is functional. This solves many access and permission problems, particularly if you have the means to run the computer from a previously built drive image of the same drive.

Parallel Install to Common Partition/Drive	Parallel Install represents the greater effort method to accomplish access to a drive or partition if moving the drive is too complicated or not an option.
Invasive Repairs	
Alternate Registry Files	Either by intervention manually or using an ASR disk, you can replace the registry files with those from a backup on the machine in the Repair folder or those restored from backup.
Repair: Fast or Full	Running Windows Setup provides for two immediate options for Repair. The difference between the two is that fast repair doesn't examine the same level of detail.
Repair: In-Place Upgrade on a DC	In-place repair is the process to repeat the steps of setup installation, but to reuse as much of the configuration already present as possible. Essentially this will validate the registry and drivers, supplying whatever entries are in error, or missing.
Remote Intervention Accessibility	
Manage Computer – Remote Machine	Remote Management of a Windows computer can make it possible to access services and event logs on a remote machine where you are unable or it is inconvenient to log on locally.
Remote Registry	The very same Regedit tools you use on a local computer can be used to manage registry settings on a remote computer for repair, analysis, or management.
Administrative Shares (i.e., C$)	By default, Windows allows Administrators to gain access to each drive volume from a remote machine via the "root" shares on each partition. This can provide access to modify files and folders on a machine were local logon is not possible.
WMI and Scripting	Windows Management and Instrumentation is a core feature in allowing uniform access to a wide variety of features and function that control everything from hardware to API calls. This makes it possible to automate auditing and repairs in custom tools.

Group Policy	Member computers in a domain can be controlled for settings and preferences via Group Policy, including many security-related features.
Fault Tolerance Above the Operating System Level	
Exchange	
· Maintenance	Exchange performs a great deal of maintenance and repairs automatically, daily, and on restarts. When maintenance is combined with auditing features reported to the Event Logs, you may find you don't need much intervention to keep the Information Stores healthy.
· Deleted Items Retention	Exchange automatically sets a period of time to keep things which users or Administrators have chosen to delete. Rather than totally disposing of them, the retention feature holds them outside their previous container, but in a way they can be recovered by the Exchange Administrator.
· Recovery Store	Though the SBS version of Exchange allows only a single Information Store and Storage Group, the Recovery Store provides the technical means to extract mailbox contents without shutting down the primary stores.
Active Directory DC Replication	Having multiple Domain Controllers means that you can recover from the loss of a Domain Controller by replicating the Active Directory back to it once it returns to service.

Services and Drivers: Cardiac and Pulmonary System

In an emergency triage of an injured person, you know the medic is going to be checking for signs of a heartbeat, reading the pulse rate, and looking for clear indications of breathing. And so it is with a Windows computer, including our SBS server. No doubt, some of us think of the periodic flicker of disk drive lights as being very much like a sign of life. When disk drives show constant bright or all dark, that's not a good sign. We know that if we can get into the Task Manager, we will study that processor graph like a heart monitor, and recognize the cycle of fluctuations as the periodic surging by some Service taking a breath. No question, we use the Task Manager as the cardio-pulmonary monitor for the system.

The earlier section, "The Normal Boot Process," revealed that a significant aspect of the startup sequence is to handle loading and initialization of the core services and drivers. We saw that the boot sequence includes a process of identifying the "boot-critical" services and drivers. NTLDR loads them to memory, and then NTOSKRNL initializes them. The boot drivers are fired first, and then as the GUI Logon phase begins, the remaining drivers are loaded and initialized. The remaining services launch depending upon their startup priority and dependence upon other services.

What we will do next is to examine a little bit about how you can approach working with services and drivers as part of a boot time failure, as well as for auditing.

Services Startup

Table 14-4: Service Startup Analysis that follows shows an interesting way to look at the Services, comparing their characteristic for launching from the boot options selecting a Normal boot, Safe Mode boot, Safe Mode with Networking, or Directory Services Recovery Mode.

This table presents a lot of valuable information. You can review it as a comparison between the various startup modes. In addition, each column reflect a known working condition on a single machine I can use for reference later. I say this because I captured the related information from a server in my office, however, on your server, you might see different conditions as "default." The reason is that, depending upon what you have configured on your server as options, your server may have some services that show as disabled or manual in my table that actually are enabled in yours.

I know this sounds confusing, so let me give an example. If you choose to use Sharepoint for report monitoring, you will see related services set by the To Do List wizard that show as inactive on my server. Therefore, you might want to review your own server without considering this table to be authoritatively "right" or meaning that your server is "wrong" if it disagrees on a few items. However, your SBS 2003 server certainly should look pretty close to this.

With this table, my goal is to illustrate the significant number of services that don't start in various modes other than Normal. You may also notice that I also included anti-virus services installed by Trend Micro CSM Suite V2.0, simply to illustrate the behavior of a third-party application follows the same logic.

Table 14-4

Services Startup Analysis from different boot menu options.

Service Name	Startup	Normal	DSRM	Safe Network	Safe
Alerter	Disabled				
Application Layer Gateway Service	Manual	X	X		
Application Management	Manual				
ASP.NET State Service	Manual				
Automatic Updates	Auto	X	X		
Background Intelligent Transfer Service	Manual				
ClipBook	Disabled				
COM+ Event System	Manual	X	X		
COM+ System Application	Manual		X		
Computer Browser	Auto	X	X	X	
Cryptographic Services	Auto	X	X	X	X
DHCP Client	Auto	X	X	X	
DHCP Server	Auto	X	X	X	
Distributed File System	Auto	X	X		
Distributed Link Tracking Client	Manual				
Distributed Link Tracking Server	Disabled				
Distributed Transaction Coordinator	Auto	X	X		
DNS Client	Auto	X	X		
DNS Server	Auto	X	X		
Error Reporting Service	Auto	X	X		

Service Name	Startup	Normal	DSRM	Safe Network	Safe
Event Log	Auto	X	X	X	X
Fax	Auto	X			
File Replication Service	Auto	X	X		
Help and Support	Auto	X	X	X	X
HTTP SSL	Manual	X	X		
Human Interface Device Access	Disabled				
IIS Admin Service	Auto	X	X		
IMAPI CD-Burning COM Service	Disabled				
Indexing Service	Disabled				
Intersite Messaging	Disabled				
IPSEC Services	Auto	X	X		
Kerberos Key Distribution Center	Auto	X			
License Logging	Auto	X	X		
Logical Disk Manager	Auto	X	X	X	X
Logical Disk Manager Administrative Service	Manual				
Messenger	Auto	X	X	X	
Microsoft Connector for POP3 Mailboxes	Disabled				
Microsoft Exchange Event	Manual				
Microsoft Exchange IMAP4	Disabled				
Microsoft Exchange Information Store	Auto	X			
Microsoft Exchange Management	Auto	X	X		
Microsoft Exchange MTA Stacks	Disabled				
Microsoft Exchange POP3	Disabled				

Service Name	Startup	Normal	DSRM	Safe Network	Safe
Microsoft Exchange Routing Engine	Auto	X	X		
Microsoft Exchange Site Replication Service	Disabled				
Microsoft Exchange System Attendant	Auto	X			
Microsoft Search	Auto	X	X		
Microsoft Software Shadow Copy Provider	Manual				
MSSQL$SBSMONITORING	Auto	X	X		
MSSQL$SHAREPOINT	Auto	X	X		
MSSQLServerADHelper	Manual	X	X		
Net Logon	Auto	X		X	
NetMeeting Remote Desktop Sharing	Disabled				
Network Connections	Manual	X	X	X	
Network DDE	Disabled				
Network DDE DSDM	Disabled				
Network Location Awareness (NLA)	Manual	X			
Network News Transfer Protocol (NNTP)	Disabled				
NT LM Security Support Provider	Manual	X	X	X	
OfficeScan Master Service	Auto	X	X		
OfficeScanNT Listener	Auto	X	X		
OfficeScanNT RealTime Scan	Auto	X	X		
Performance Logs and Alerts	Manual				
Plug and Play	Auto	X	X	X	X

Service Name	Startup	Normal	DSRM	Safe Network	Safe
Portable Media Serial Number Service	Disabled				
Print Spooler	Auto	X	X		
Protected Storage	Auto	X	X		
Remote Access Auto Connection Manager	Disabled				
Remote Access Connection Manager	Manual	X	X		
Remote Desktop Help Session Manager	Manual				
Remote Procedure Call (RPC)	Auto	X	X	X	X
Remote Procedure Call (RPC) Locator	Manual				
Remote Registry	Auto	X	X		
Removable Storage	Manual				
Resultant Set of Policy Provider	Manual				
Routing and Remote Access	Auto	X	X		
SBCore Service	Auto	X	X	X	X
ScanMail_MailAction	Auto	X	X		
ScanMail_Monitor	Auto	X	X		
ScanMail_RealTimeScan	Auto	X	X		
ScanMail_Web	Auto	X	X		
Secondary Logon	Auto	X	X		
Security Accounts Manager	Auto	X	X		
Server	Auto	X	X		
SharePoint Timer Service	Auto	X	X		

Service Name	Startup	Normal	DSRM	Safe Network	Safe
Shell Hardware Detection	Auto	X	X		
Simple Mail Transfer Protocol (SMTP)	Auto	X	X		
Smart Card	Manual				
Special Administration Console Helper	Manual				
SQLAgent$SBSMONITORING	Auto	X	X		
SQLAgent$SHAREPOINT	Manual				
System Event Notification	Auto	X	X		
Task Scheduler	Auto	X	X		
TCP/IP NetBIOS Helper	Auto	X	X	X	
Telephony	Manual	X	X		
Telnet	Disabled				
Terminal Services	Manual	X	X	X	
Terminal Services Session Directory	Disabled				
Themes	Disabled				
Uninterruptible Power Supply	Manual				
Upload Manager	Disabled				
Virtual Disk Service	Manual				
Volume Shadow Copy	Manual				
Web Usage Logging Service	Auto	X	X		
WebClient	Auto	X	X		
Windows Audio	Manual				
Windows Image Acquisition (WIA)	Disabled				
Windows Installer	Manual				
Windows Internet Name Service (WINS)	Auto	X	X		

Service Name	Startup	Normal	DSRM	Safe Network	Safe
Windows Management Instrumentation	Auto	X	X	X	X
Windows Management Instrumentation Driver Extensions	Manual				
Windows Time	Auto	X	X		
WinHTTP Web Proxy Auto-Discovery Service	Manual				
Wireless Configuration	Manual				
WMI Performance Adapter	Manual				
Workstation	Auto	X	X	X	
World Wide Web Publishing Service	Auto	X	X		

[Trend Micro Services shown in **Bold-Italic** in the table are not part of the SBS default product.]

Repairing Services Configuration Manually

Most services are installed by the application installer provided by the manufacturer who supplied that service to do something of value. It's a sad reality that with viruses, Trojans, and spyware, we now find frequent circumstances where a bogus or even dangerous service has been created that has no valuable or desirable use. The worst condition might be when these bogus services cause the server to crash without booting completely. On the other hand, maybe the worst condition is a backdoor Trojan that was installed as a service and has made your entire network a security vacuum.

Admittedly, the majority of occasions that I've seen corrupt services cause a machine to fail to boot were not "evil services"; rather they were broken services no longer working correctly. You can deal with them the same way. It's possible to edit the registry to keep them from running at startup or running at all; or, you can manually delete them if that's the worst case option you have left. I'm going to talk about three ways to accomplish halting a service from running.

- Disable Service From Within Windows GUI in MMC Console

I'm starting with this option because it's pretty obvious, and I want you to become oriented to what we are doing here. You can open the Manage Computer console on your machine, drill down to the Services and Applications sub-tree, and from there locate the Services sub-tree. For our illustration, let's use the Messenger service. Look at the properties on that service and you see a tab panel like the one seen in Figure 14-1.

Figure 14-1

As an example, a review of the Messenger Service general properties panel.

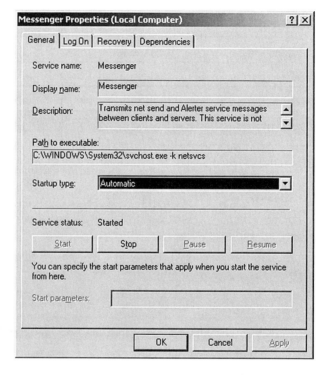

You can see the "Startup type" drop-down selector indicates that this service is set to start "Automatic." To prevent this service from starting at all, you could reset the selector to "Disabled." Setting it to "Manual" might also prevent it from starting, but that's not assured because if another service or startup key calls this service, it may launch at that time in response to the request. Hopefully, these are familiar concepts to most folks reading this.

In Figure 14-2, having switched to the Dependencies tab, you see that this service will fail to start up if one of the four other specified dependence services fails to start. With this thought in mind, look back again at Table 14-4: Service Startup Analysis. When you start the computer in Safe Mode, the reason that practically none of the services are initialized is that the core services they depend upon have been "blocked" from starting. The cascade of impact down through the dependency tree prevents starting each of the other services that require the un-started core services.

Figure 14-2

Messenger Service Properties Screenshot—Dependencies

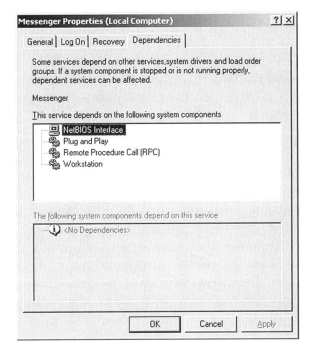

One of the points to take away from this is that if you block services from starting up by overriding the default "Startup type," you may have some surprisingly unexpected results. So be careful! What would you do if the computer didn't start normally because disabling a service caused more trouble than you expected? I'm glad you asked. Please move on to the next point below.

- Disable Service From Within Windows GUI in Regedit

In an earlier section of our anatomy of SBS, we took a look at the Registry. You might want to compare a view of the Messenger Service inside the registry itself, versus the normal Management Console view of the same information. We see the Messenger Service Registry View in Figure 14-3, while in Figure 14-1 showing the General tab in Messenger Service Properties as viewed in the Management Console.

You can see the registry is storing the information presented in that management console from the Properties pages shown in the previous two figures. The registry path location is listed in the bottom of the captured screen, in the status line of Figure 14-3.

Take particular note that among the registry keys in which you can recognize the content, it's not hard to deduce that the REG_DWORD key labeled "Start" is probably the key that controls the "Startup type" for that service.

Figure 14-3

The Messenger Service as viewed from a Regedit screenshot of the service details in the registry.

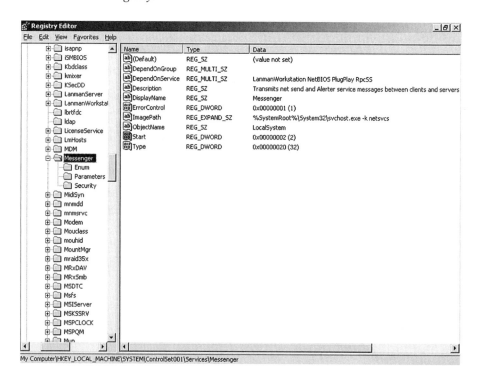

We have just figured out where to look in the Registry to find the control of this service. Now we just need to know how to set the "Startup type" to affect what happens during the boot phase of the computer. Note that the value stored here is a number, not the text label you see in the management console.

Table 14-5

Service Registry Start Values (shows a table of values to use in the Start regkey)

Value	Start Type	Value Descriptions for Start Entries
0	Boot	Specifies a driver that is loaded (but not started) by firmware calls made by the x86-based Ntldr or Itanium-based IA64ldr boot loader. If no errors occur, the kernel starts the driver.
1	System	Specifies a driver that loads at kernel initialization during the startup sequence by calling Windows XP Professional boot drivers.
2	Auto load	Specifies a driver or service that is initialized at system startup by Session Manager (Smss.exe) or Service Controller (Services.exe).
3	Load on demand	Specifies a driver or service that is manually started by a user, a process, or another service.
4	Disabled	Specifies a disabled (not started) driver or service.

With the information provided to us by examining the Regedit view of the services, we now know how to change the startup of a service, even if we can't get into the Manage Computer, and then drill down to the Services console to reset it. But you might be asking yourself, "Why would I be able to access Regedit and yet not be able to get into the Manage Console view?" I'm glad you asked. You will see where this is going in the next point below!

- Disable Service From Within Windows GUI in Regedit and Remote or Detached Registry

Now that we know how to use the Registry Editors like Regedit or Regedt32 as a tool to manipulate the startup type of a service, let's put that information to more powerful use. Did you know that you can edit the registry of a remote computer across the network? Did you know you can edit the registry for a computer by moving a copy of the file to another computer? You can see that this could be useful information if what we are trying to do is prevent a service from locking up or crashing our SBS server during startup.

Take a look at Figure 14-4: Registry Import Features. It indicates the option to access external registry files either with "Connect Network Registry," the "Import..." option, or the "Load Hive..." feature.

Figure 14-4

Registry Import Features

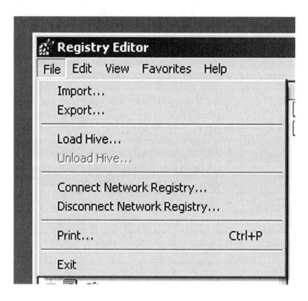

Connecting to a remote computer is a fairly familiar idea; we do this all the time via remote shared folder access point. Within Regedit, you have a very similar computer selection box option to choose a remote computer to connect to, review, and edit. The registry of a remote computer may be accessible in your network—that is, unless you have enabled security features to prevent that sort of access. Among security gurus, there's a lot of debate about the idea of exposing remote registry management. On the one hand, since it requires Administrative rights to accomplish it, some folks say that it's a reasonable thing for Administrators to do. On the other hand, some folks say there are not enough occasions where you would want to do this, much less need to do it. You can imagine the latter group hold the opinion that this should be blocked as part of a security practice within the network. I'm not taking sides in the debate here. I'm identifying this as a feature that offers a choice.

We have two ways to handle Registry Import as a detached object, and it's an option that is a little bit more confusing. "Import…" allows you to paste a piece of a registry into the current registry, generally under the assumption that you exported it from somewhere. You can actually paste the registry into a place inside your current registry tree. It doesn't even have to be "the correct" place, but you do have to be careful. This is temporary, of course, but it's still a little bit odd to use the registry of ComputerA as a chopping block for chunks of registry from ComputerB. However, this is a unique way to browse and edit a registry export file from another computer or even your own computer.

The second way to handle a detached registry is to load an entire registry hive. For instance, you could load the System hive from another computer. Now do you see? You can actually copy the System registry (the entire file) from a computer you can't start, then modify the values of a service or device driver that is causing the startup to fail. After making the changes you want, you move the registry file back to the original computer.

Repairing Driver Configurations Manually

Once you grasp the basic concepts explained in the previous section on Manually Configuring Services, you can apply those same skills and techniques to manipulating Devices and their driver configuration. The entries in the registry are stored in a different location, of course, but the basic concepts are the same. Rather than retracing basically the same thing again for Devices, I'm going to touch on some details that apply to both Services and Devices that I haven't covered yet.

In both cases, Services and Device drivers have a configuration component stored in the registry, but they also have the "program" part which is launched or loaded with respect to that item. This is the executable, or driver itself. Figure 14-1 showing the Messenger Service console panel indicated the "executable path" as one of the features you can see. You can also see that information directly in the registry entry view in Figure 14-3.

Those same concepts apply for Devices and their drivers, though it can be a little more complicated with a driver because of unique characteristics of hardware or virtual devices that bind to a cascade of related things. Device drivers are notorious as the weakest and most vulnerable aspects contributing to system instability with a Windows-based configuration. In some respects, that tradeoff seems unavoidable if Windows is to remain an open hardware supporting platform. Microsoft has taken great pains to pursue improvements in Driver compatibility, compliance, and recovery in the case of a failure in either the operations or installation of a driver. Yet, the problem lingers on. And now we have spyware that attempts to install any manner of object possible, including device drivers and services.

I want to look next at going beyond the need to repair or disable a Service or Device driver via access to a registry entry. Let's consider the possibility that you actually may need to replace the related files. It's certainly not impossible to attempt, but it can be a challenge to do successfully. First of all, you have to figure out what the driver is, and where you go to get a "trusted" version of it. You also can't assume that just replacing a single file will fix a problem; many devices come with entire applications that might need to be refreshed. I'm offering this caution in advance simply to suggest that replacing driver files is not a trivial thing, and you could make your boot problems worse—not better—in the process. But if you want to explore it, the underlying concepts are pretty basic.

If you need to remove files or replace the files running under Services and Devices, you are going to need a way to get the related Service or Device to release the file by shutting it down. Fortunately, we talked a little about that in the previous section. That assumes you are going to do this from the local machine while it's running. But what about the idea of replacing the files without starting the system into Windows first? There are options.

You can use the Recovery Console feature included with Windows XP and Server 2003. Another option would be to move the hard drive to another machine, or to boot the system with a parallel installation, or even use a third-party application that allows you to edit the System Partition contents independently. In fact, there are so many ways possible to pursue this, I'm just going to make a point about one of the simpler ways.

What follows in is an excerpt from a Microsoft Knowledgebase article on using the Recovery Console to replace a device driver. The Recovery Console provides a variety of basic command line tools to perform tasks you will need if you can't get your system to boot, and you don't have any better way to gain access to the file system.

Extract the Driver Files from the Windows Server 2003 Installation CD-ROM

Installation files are stored on the Windows Server 2003 installation CD-ROM in compressed folders known as cabinet (.cab) files. Driver files are stored in the Driver.cab file. To use original driver files included on the Windows Server 2003 installation CD-ROM to replace damaged driver files:

1. Insert the Windows Server 2003 installation CD-ROM in the CD-ROM drive.

2. At the command prompt in Recovery Console, type **expand d:\i386\driver.cab /f:*filename* [*path*]**, and then press ENTER, where:
   - *d:* is the CD-ROM drive letter
   - *filename* is the name of the file you want to expand
   - *path* is the folder where to copy the driver file

   Typically, driver files (.sys) are stored in the %SystemRoot%\System32\Drivers folder. For example, to replace the Atimpab.sys driver file, you might use the **expand d:\i386\driver.cab / f:atimpab.sys %systemroot%\System32\Drivers** command.

   Note: In this command, you must use the **/f** switch because the Driver.cab CAB file contains more than one file.

Replace the Driver Files by Using the COPY Command

If the driver files you want are not located in a cabinet (.cab) file, you can use the Recovery Console copy command to overwrite the damaged files:

1. At the command prompt, type **copy [*source_path*] *source_filename* [*destination_path*] *destination_filename***, and then press ENTER, where:
   - *source_path* is the path for the source replacement file
   - *source_filename* is the name of the replacement file
   - *destination_path* is the path for the driver file you want to replace
   - *destination_filename* is the name of the driver file you want to replace

For example, to replace the Atimpab.sys file with a known good copy from a floppy disk, you might use the **copy a:\atimpab.sys c:\winnt\system32\drivers\atimpab.sys** command.

Note: The copy command in Recovery Console does not support wildcard characters. Because of this, you can copy only one file at a time. If you must replace more than one file, use multiple copy commands.

2.   When you are prompted to confirm that you want to overwrite the existing file, press Y, and then press ENTER.

Before I conclude the review Services and Devices, I wanted to point out that you can find information about devices and the drivers they use in the Windows Management Console under Device Manager. If you expand the tree of objects listed, you can see the typical Windows Devices. But there's one more tip I want to pass along. Open the console to the same view as shown in the next figure, Figure 14-5 Device Manager, and a view of hidden Device details, and click to highlight **Device Manger** in the right-hand pane. Now pick from the top menu item View. When you enable the option for **Show Hidden Devices**, this reveals almost as many more devices than you saw previously. Many of these are virtual devices, software devices. Others could be legacy devices. If you look at the property panel on any of the devices in the hidden section, or at the normal objects, you should see you have a GUI view of basically the same parameters you had available for Services in the previous section.

Notes:

Figure 14-5

Device Manager and a view of hidden Device details

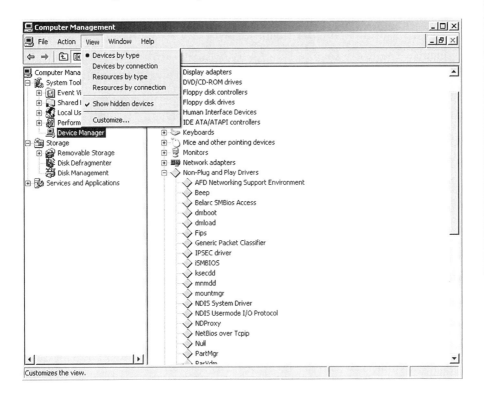

File System: Skeleton

This section discusses the file system skeleton.

It's Just Files on the Drive Until SBS is Powered On

This is a really basic concept. Everything you need to know about disaster recovery starts with the understanding that the hard drive holds all the files in a cold condition after a power down. Therefore, the key to getting the entire system running in a normal condition, or a disaster condition, is probably held in your hand, provided you are holding the disk drive!

What seems too often to evade understanding is that with the right manipulation of the files, an installation will work on a different computer—actually boot from it. On other occasions, just inspecting it from another machine is a help, although you probably don't need to be able to boot from it just to repair file issues. Mounting it in another computer gives you the means for inspection and making changes. Performing remote registry and device driver modifications may reach a point where the complexity of the working through that process overrules the logic that it is actually feasible with sufficient time and investigation. But too often, this course of repair is pursued only on a totally dead server or in a badly crippled condition. I think file and registry level repair of services and drivers is something everyone should practice in a lab to develop as a skill, and to become comfortable with a more frequent attempt to use this option.

To practice this sort of technique, you need a lab cadaver. (Okay, sorry. That just slipped out.) That would be a "test bench machine" in the computer technology parlance.

Caveat: Ignore security issues to focus only upon folder locations

Let's take the idea of the file system in cold storage and explore it. As part of our autopsy process, we will assume we can go anywhere we want, with no security, no open files to worry about. We can just go look at anything at all. Obviously, it's a lot easier to discuss the file system without talking about permissions, but we can't go through the whole concept that way. Therefore, to make this flow a little faster, I'm going to look at the file system in this section only in a "spatial" way, not in a "security access" way.

I want to focus upon where things are, not so much on "who can access it and why," which seems a more familiar way to approach things. Besides, if you are acting as the Administrator, you can gain control of any file, so security isn't the first thing you look at in the file structure for disaster recovery. Chances are more likely your pursuit of file level access will progress in this order:

- Which file do I need to address?

- Where is that file?

- How do I get access to its location or to modify it?

- What security context is going to complicate that?

Viewing the Registry as Files

I cover the Registry in much more detail later, but I want to make the point here that the majority of the Registry is stored as files when the machine shuts down. If the Registry is corrupted by something, there's another copy in a different file. If you run a System State backup, you have yet another copy of the Registry stored in yet another file.

For all the times the people become confused about what the registry is, and how it works, the fact that it's a file, and it's also accessed in memory, can tend to be confusing. Most people think of the Registry in terms of how Regedit or Regedit32 present it; yet it is a database file regardless. So if you look into the table of information below and find you don't get as much detail on the registry as you wanted, I devote an entire section below to the registry in which I examine it with more detail than I will apply to the entire file system itself. The registry is that important, and that's why I pulled that information aside for later. If you simply can't wait, I guess you could turn forward a bunch of pages to look at Table 14-8: Registry File Locations. But don't forget to come back!

Viewing the SBS System and Application Files

Okay, let's look at the key Operating System files on an SBS Server, shown in Table 14-6: Key OS File Locations. By that I mean, let's assume that you can look at this drive because it's mounted as a data drive in another server, and you can explore it without concern about damage. If you want to do this, simply make a drive image of your own server, then take the imaged drive over to your workstation and fire it up.

Notes:

Table 14-6

Key OS File Locations

System Folders and Files	Explanation
OS boot files	The initial boot of the system can come from either the same partition as the **%systemroot%**, or an alternate. Therefore, the bootstrap files will be located on the media that begins the sequence, such as a floppy or hard disk, or via a boot device emulation such as PXE boot. The files are placed in the root folder of the boot device.
Boot.ini	The typical BOOT.INI for an SBS 2003 Server looks like this: [bootloader] timeout=30 default=multi(0)disk(0)rdisk(0)partition(1)\WINDOWS [operating systems] multi(0)disk(0)rdisk(0)partition(1)\WINDOWS="Windows Server 2003 for Small Business Server" /fastdetect *Note: Only one text line follows [operating systems]. The text wrap shown here is formatted to fit this page size.*
boot log	If you start in Safe Mode, a boot log file is created for you which indicates the drivers and services that did not load. You can also append a Boot.ini switch **/bootlog** to the startup parameters line force this on normal boots. The file location is: **%SystemRoot%\Ntbtlog.txt**
Latest Servicepack package	**%SystemRoot%\$ServicePack**
Hotfix Undo files	Trick question. The short answer is that Microsoft doesn't create undo files, something I think should change. What is done with hotfixes, QFEs, Updates, and Service Packs is to keep copies of the files that are installed in the system folder of your machine. It's a remarkably complicated concept, managing the replacement of critical system files that perform updates now. You may find this interesting reading if, in fact, you can make sense of it: Description of the Contents of a Windows Server 2003 Product Update Package http://support.microsoft.com/default.aspx?scid=kb;en-us;824994&Product=sbserv2003

System Folders and Files	Explanation
Crash dump file	A crash dump file is generally not useful to anyone other than a Microsoft Product Support Engineer with the tools to read and analyze it. Most IT professionals are, outside of a supported incident, just trying to reclaim the disk space it took by deleting it! A complete memory dump records all the contents of system memory when your computer stops unexpectedly. If you select the **Complete memory dump** option, you must have a paging file on the boot volume sufficient to hold all the physical RAM plus 1 megabyte (MB). By default, the complete memory dump file is written to the **%SystemRoot%\Memory.dmp** file.
Pagefile	The pagefile is located in the root folder of a drive partition by default. You have the option to create more than one pagefile for the purpose of improving performance based upon disk activity isolation. However, moving the pagefile to a different partition will not help if you are running on the same drive as the system partition, or in a RAID configuration that includes the system partition on the same volume. If you do not have a pagefile.sys located on the system partition, you will not have the ability to preserve a crashdump file.
Operating System	The Windows Operating System has elements located in several places on the drive(s) of your system. Normally, the answer you might jump for on this question is it's the %windir% folder or %systemroot% location. Both are valid answers. However, over time and evolution with Window's design, it's a fair argument to suggest that the Windows Operating System now manages and requires files and folders located in each of the folders indicated below. Another way to look at this is that your server probably won't run correctly if you alter permissions in a certain way or delete any of these folders: .\Documents and Settings\ .\Program Files .\[root folder] %systemroot%

Notes:

System Folders and Files	Explanation
System State	In the previous item above, we looked at the very same point. System State is a backup of the critical Operating System Folders, and all the folders above are critical. However, I suspect you wanted a more detailed bit of information here. Therefore, here's another answer: check the backup log on your server. (*see NTbackup Job Log in this table*)

The summary answer is that you normally consider a System State backup to be everything you would expect to need to restore the Operating System and Applications. In addition, with a Domain Controller, it includes the essential Active Directory database and related files.

A recommended practice would be to ensure that you enable the NT Backup Job Advanced option to back up all System Files. The **Automatically back up Protected System Files with the System State** option is the default setting. This setting does cause your backup to be substantially larger, but that's because it's not providing the full protection of all those files. |
| Registry | The registry is actually a set of files, not a single file. It's split between at least two locations. The primary location is the "system registry" folder location:

%systemroot%\system32\config

In the location above, you will find the primary registry hives for System, Software, Security, SAM, and Default. You will find related files for each of those described in more detail in the Registry section that comes later.The other location(s) for registry files are where the User Registry Hive(s) are stored. See the next item below. |
| Setup Repair Folder | During the initial setup. a copy of the primary registry hives are placed in a repair folder located at:

%systemroot%\repair

In addition, during the Text Mode of setup, copies of the registry files are stored in the registry folder location **%systemroot%\system32\config** using the same filename, but with the **.SAV** file extension. |

System Folders and Files	Explanation
User Registry Hive	Each user account User hive will be stored by default in the %Userprofile% folder location. The filename is NTUSER.DAT. If the Userprofile has been redirected, that location could be found elsewhere, but by default it is beneath the user specific path beneath: **.\Documents and Settings\[username]**
Backup of the registry	Every time you run a System State Backup of your SBS 2003 Server, a backup of the registry is copied to the location indicated below, with additional System Profile and Event Logs backups: **%systemroot%\repair**
Service Executable Path	Services can be identified during startup with boot.ini command options. Using **/bootlog** creates a log file to record startup conditions. Services are not required to be running from a specific folder location. That means the file executed as a service could be anywhere. You would need to consult the registry information that launches the service or refer to a GUI-based tool or script to get that information. The most common location of Microsoft-supplied services is as you would expect: **%systemroot%\System32** The location above is the most common for Windows OS services, but Microsoft Application-related services are just as likely to be running from the folder associated with that application, located somewhere below: **.\Program Files\[application folder name]**
Device Drivers (includes all currently installed, previously installed, or available by default)	**%systemroot%\System32\devices** You have a boot.ini option /sos which causes the display of the device drivers on screen as the system startup proceeds. This may be familiar to you when you use Safe Mode startup option, but you can add this to a normal startup to troubleshoot the full list of devices, not just the limited set used in Safe Mode

System Folders and Files	Explanation
Event Log files	The Event Logs are stored by default in the same folder as the System Registry: **%systemroot%\system32\config**
Files for the Hardware Abstraction Layer (HAL)	Using the Boot.ini, you can define the actual hardware abstraction layer (HAL) that is loaded at startup. For example, type **/HAL=halmps.dll** to load the Halmps.dll in the System32 folder. This switch is useful to try out a different HAL before you rename the file to Hal.dll. This switch is also useful when you want to try to switch between starting in multiprocessor mode and starting in single processor mode. To do this, use this switch with the **/kernel** switch. This illustrates that the HAL files are located in the %systemroot%\System32 folder. However, this can be misleading if you do not understand how the HAL normally behaves. Whatever the type is for currently assigned HAL, a copy of that original resource HAL file is renamed to a default standard name. Therefore, to determine the HAL being used by a computer, the name of the file itself is no help. If you can't get into the registry or GUI to identify it, your next best option is using the /HAL parameter as a startup option.
"Last Known Good Condition" file set	Trick question. There is no separate copy of the files because "Last Known Good Condition" is an option that refers to a backup sub-tree inside the System registry hive. In other words, you will not find a set of "known good" drivers stashed away other than in default resource locations like Drivers Cache, but these are technically not the same as Known Good," but just a resource folder.
"Safe Mode" file set	Once again, trick question. There isn't a separate set of "Safe Mode" files with respect to drivers and such. However, there is the fact that Safe Mode doesn't attempt to load all startup files, just a subset. About the only file you have involved in a Safe Mode startup that isn't otherwise loaded or accessed normally is the SAM database on a Domain Controller. Normally AD handles security management.

Notes:

System Folders and Files	Explanation
"Repair" resource folder	The Fast Repair option performs all the repairs as the Manual Repair option, but you are not prompted for choices. Additionally the Fast Repair option tries to load each Windows registry file (SAM, SECURITY, SYSTEM, and SOFTWARE). If a registry file is damaged or cannot be loaded, Repair copies the missing or corrupted registry file from the **SystemRoot\Repair** folder to the **SystemRoot\System32\Config** folder. Because the Fast Repair option can replace registry files with those from the **SystemRoot\Repair** folder, it may revert part of your operating system configuration back to the time when Windows was first installed. If this occurs, you need to restore your last "system state" backup or manually copy a more recent version of the registry files from the **SystemRoot\Repair** folder to the **SystemRoot\System32\Config** folder by using Recovery Console. The files located in the Repair folder are from the last time you created a System State Backup with NTBackup in Windows Server 2003, or in the case of Windows 2000, if an Emergency Repair Disk was created while including the option to also back up the registry files to the repair folder.
Domain Replication Folders	The SYSVOL is the location Active Directory uses for replication of AD-related information. You can establish additional folders to replicate unrelated to AD by using the network replication functionality of Distributed File System (DFS). Typical location is **%systemroot%\sysvol.**
Active Directory	Please do not perform a manual or fast repair on a domain controller without specific knowledge of how to restore a backup of the Active directory database. If you choose these options on a Windows 2000 Server domain controller, you run the risk of overwriting the Active directory database at **%systemroot%\\NTDS\ntds.dit**. The **Ntds.dit** file contains your Active Directory, including user accounts.
Group Policies	**%systemroot%\sysvol\domainname\Policies \POLICYGUID**

System Folders and Files	Explanation
Group Policy .ADM Templates	[Q316977] You probably want to recognize that the template files might be stored either in the AD replication folders for each policy or they could be pulled from a location local to each domain controller, one that isn't replicated. In Enterprises, it's a strategic decision to avoid replicating ADM templates to reduce replication traffic volume. The local folder per server is: **%Systemroot%\inf** The replicated location in SYSVOL is: **%systemroot%\sysvol*domainname*\Policies\\POLICYGUID\Adm**
SBS Setup and "To Do List" results Log Files	**C:\Program Files\Microsoft Windows Small Business Server\Support** **C:\Program Files\Microsoft Integration\Windows Small Business Server 2003\Logs**
IIS Metabase (critical to Exchange)	Internet Information Services provides core operations functionality to Exchange Server, and critical information for both IIS and Exchange are stored in the metabase file. The metabase is essentially an alternative for the sort of information that would typically be stored in the Registry. On an SBS, you should probably think of this as "another registry file"—it's that critical. The metabase file stores settings normally held in memory during server operations, and the storage is provided until the next startup. It's not referenced interactively during operations. The location is: **%systemroot%\system32\inetsrv\metabase.bin**
NTbackup Job Log	NTbackup includes the option to save a log of what it processed. Enable detailed logging to see exactly which files are backed up with the system state. To enable detailed logging, in Ntbackup.exe, click **Tools**, click **Options**, and on the **Backup Log** tab, click **Detailed**. These backup logs will be found here: *(the path below wraps due to text formatting)* ***Drive*:\Documents and Settings \Administrator.*Logon_domain*\Local Settings \Application Data\Microsoft\Windows NT \NTBackup\Data folder**

System Folders and Files	Explanation
NTbackup Excluded Files List	NTbackup normally skips specific files intentionally. So how would you know what is excluded? Check this registry location on your SBS server: HKEY_LOCAL_MACHINE\SYSTEM\CurrentControlSet\Control\BackupRestore\FilesNotToBackup Table 14-11 NTbackup Excluded Files List, shown later in this chapter, shows the complete list of default entries in this regkey location.
Additional Key File Locations	The item just above, NTbackup Excluded Files List, includes many other interesting file references which were omitted from this table, because they appear separately in a later table reference, Table 14-11 NTbackup Excluded Files List.

The Registry: Spinal Cord of Windows and SBS

In this section, I dive deep into the Registry. Hang on!

Registry Primer

The Registry is a database of settings and references. It consists of both permanent and dynamic information, and usually it's represented visually as an inverted tree of information, similar to an Explorer view of the file system.

The majority of the Registry is continuously updated when running, but retained between operating sessions (shutdowns) and stored in permanent file sections called hives. Each individual hive is stored as a discrete file. The dynamic information is generated as the system starts up, maintained during the operating session, but discarded when the system is shut down.

In addition to the set of files we call Registry Hives, we are going to review the "family relatives" of cousins and clones of these files, the files with similar names but different file extensions that you will discover sitting right next to each other when you explore where the Registry files are physically stored. We will look at the process Windows uses to update the Registry using these related files, and how we can make use of some of them in disaster recovery.

From there, I'll go in two different directions. First we will explore inside the registry to see where we have both Fault-Tolerance options to use for recovery, as well as configuration options we can use in migration scenarios. Later I go outside the home of the Registry to explore where we can find backup copies or previous conditions of the current Registry. All of this is going to reveal many ways you can return a non-bootable system to life, undo a regrettable change to your system, or perhaps recover or migrate your complete system to another completely different server hardware platform.

I know that many of you reading this section will already be familiar with a lot of these concepts from your previous experience. What I'm trying to do is to pull together the various components you perhaps understand separately, but have never seen the relationships of these components meshing together in this way. My goal is to help you see the Registry not as a single monolithic database, rather as the nexus of all the critical concepts you may not have seized upon. Hopefully, I will help you discover some ideas that can lead you to a totally different level of disaster recovery options. So, even if all these concepts are familiar to, at least skim across this section to take in the specific elements I highlight—making sure you recognize the relationships between these elements.

The Registry: Hives, Files, and Dynamic Content

I expect that you are already somewhat familiar with the screen shown below in Figure 14-6: A view from Regedit of the Registry Hives, which illustrates the root levels of the Registry. Let's start first by looking at the general organization of the registry nodes as shown in the Regedit screenshot and think about how the arrangement shown relates to the descriptive purpose you see in Table 14-7: Registry Nodes and Abbreviation Summary that follows after it.

Notes:

Figure 14-6

A view from Regedit of the Registry Hives

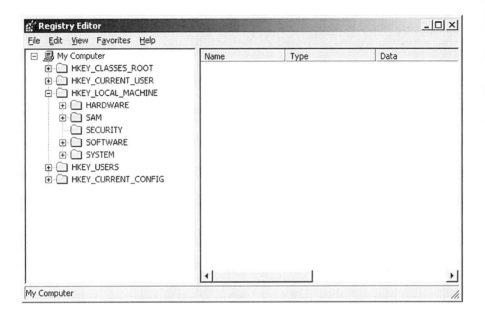

Below the icon representation of My Computer, you can see in the figure the five root level nodes of the Registry, plus the child-nodes of HKEY_LOCAL_MACHINE, which are equally significant for our investigation. If you aren't familiar with the exact significance of each root level sub-tree, Table 14-7 below provides details of each node shown in the Figure 14-6.

To avoid distracting from the main point in the screenshot, the HKEY_USERS folder was not expanded to reveal several sub-trees below it, though Table 14-7 includes additional comments about those elements as well. I'm just going to acknowledge a point here briefly, and come back to the HKEY_USERS node for details later. Specifically, HKEY_USERS contains the child folders HKEY_CURRENT_USER and ".DEFAULT," plus a listing of sub-trees indicated by symbolic links that are a numerical string associated with specific User account SIDs (Security Identifiers).

For the moment we want to focus upon the distinct roles of each of the other hives, in particular those located in the HKEY_LOCAL_MACHINE section of the Registry. Please notice that Table 14-7 presents common abbreviations for the longer names of certain nodes: for instance, HKLM is frequently used as a shorthand abbreviation for HKEY_LOCAL_MACHINE. I know how much we all hate acronym overkill when reading manuals, so I try to use the abbreviation only when referring to a deeper-level key string or in a section of text devoted entirely to just one Registry hive. Otherwise, I find using the full name helps keep the references more clearly in mind as we bounce between locations in the discussion.

Table 14-7
Registry Nodes and Abbreviation Summary

Registry Nodes and Abbreviation		Description
HKEY_LOCAL_MACHINE	HKLM	Contains configuration information particular to the computer (for any user).
HKLM\ Hardware		The HARDWARE key stores data about the computer hardware the system detects. **It is not a hive, therefore it's not stored to a file at shutdown.** This key is re-created each time the system starts. It includes information about devices, the software drivers, and other resources associated with devices.
HKLM\ SAM		The SAM key contains information used by the Security Accounts Manager. **Servers running Windows Server 2003 and acting as domain controllers use this key to store user and group information pertaining to the directory service restore mode. Domain controllers maintain domain user and group information in Active Directory to manage user security.** However, Windows NT 4.0 and earlier, as well as Windows Server 2003s that are not part of a Windows Server 2003 domain, use SAM. All the data in this key is in binary form.

Registry Nodes and Abbreviation		Description
HKLM\ Security		The SECURITY key contains security information used by the system and network.
HKLM\ Software		The SOFTWARE key stores program variables that apply to all users of the computer. The system stores some of its variables in the subkeys in SOFTWARE. In addition, the SOFTWARE subkey contains subkeys representing the vendors, including Microsoft, who produce the software running on the system.
HKLM\ System		The subkeys in the HKLM\SYSTEM key store entries for the current control set and for other control sets control sets that can be used, or have been used, to run Windows Server 2003. Windows Server 2003 maintains at least two control sets to ensure that the system always starts.
HKEY_CURRENT_CONFIG	HKCC	This acts as a pointer to the currently running Hardware Profile subkey content showing hardware-related configuration data.
HKEY_CLASSES_ROOT	HKCR	In Windows 2000/XP/2003, this information is stored under both the HKEY_LOCAL_MACHINE and HKEY_CURRENT_USER keys. It represents a merged result of the SOFTWARE\Classes subkeys in Current User and Local Machine. It consists of configuration data for COM objects, Visual Basic programs, or other automation.

Notes:

Registry Nodes and Abbreviation		Description
HKEY_USERS	HKU	This contains the root of all user profiles on the computer.
HKU\ .DEFAULT		If no profile is available (prior to user logon), or if a new user with no existing profile has just logged on, then the sub-tree is built from the user profile settings established for a default user, as indicated here.
HKEY_CURRENT_USER	HKCU	This sub-tree contains the user profile for the user who is currently logged on to the computer. The user profile includes environment variables, personal program groups, desktop settings, network connections, printers, and application preferences. The data in the user profile is similar to the data stored in the Win.ini file in Windows 3.x. Actually, this sub-tree is just a pointer reference to the User hive.

The Registry: A Vocabulary Review

Let's take a moment to establish some vocabulary with a few terms and relationships that are important to understand.

Figure 14-6 revealed the three logical elements of structure and information you see represented by Regedit as your view into the Registry.

- **Hives**—These are the parts of the Registry stored in files. Each of the nodes represented just below HKEY_LOCAL_MACHINE are in fact hives, except HARDWARE. The other two hives appear below HKEY_USERS, as we will explore a bit later.

- **Dynamic Content Nodes**—This is information not stored in files when the system is shut down; rather it is created dynamically at the time the computer is started and maintained only for that session, then discarded at shutdown. This is the case for the HARDWARE sub-tree.

- **Symbolic Links**—You know the concept—think of it as a "shortcut." It's a way to show something here, but the content is "over there." Several root level nodes shown in the Regedit view are represented as being in that location physically, but they are not there structurally in the database. HKEY_CURRENT_CONFIG is an example, because the information is actually held deeper inside the HKLM\System hive. A Symbolic Link is used because the System hive location reserves the option of having more than one Hardware Profile. Therefore, presenting HKEY_CURRENT_CONFIG as a Symbolic Link provides a way for programming to find the current Hardware Profile without having to hard code an actual path. It just makes sense. It's a symbolic path relative to whichever profile is "the current configuration."

Now, I've just revealed another element of the Registry structure to explore by mentioning Hardware Profiles. We have some terms here to get comfortable with. More important, I want to ensure you don't confuse these specific concepts with each other.

- **Hardware Profiles**—*This is a user-oriented startup preference, a feature option.* Most Windows users don't use this option, but it's quite simple to understand. To explain this, I'll use the example of a laptop-type computer. Many laptop users have a set of equipment and configuration settings they use at the office that are not convenient when working outside the office, disconnected as the laptop is. A Hardware Profile is a feature you can use to save different configurations you want to switch between without having to "un-configure" the previous settings. This provides the option to redefine video, network, and drive connections, all without losing the old settings. In this way, you can define functionally different hardware setups you can use without having to set up a process each time you switch. It's very much like defining your computer for two or more different hardware platforms you use, all based upon a scenario you find convenient to preserve for use again. You'll discover that Windows is remarkably more portable between hardware platforms than most people think. You just have to know a few tricks to make it work to your advantage.

- **ControlSets—*This is a nearly transparent recovery option for a specific corruption possibility with the system hive.*** When you work on an important document, you probably make a habit of saving periodically. If you are cautious and organized, perhaps you are even incrementing the name of the document to keep a revision history. That's the same concept represented with ControlSets, with only a subtle difference. Referring to Figure 14-7: Registry Controlsets Select Key, the numerical value of ControlSet000x doesn't indicate a history rank or repair preference; it just distinguishes it from the others as a unique name. Up to four ControlSets might be listed in the Registry below HKLM\System. In normal circumstances, these represent configurations that were previously successful in starting the computer and bringing Windows to an operating condition. Windows uses these to produce fault-tolerance internally within the System hive itself. Choosing "Last Known Good Configuration" as a safe boot recovery option (F8 at boot screen menu) is a way of trying a different but previously successful ControlSet. This functionality of preserving multiple ControlSets is transparently managed by Windows each time you boot the system. If you examine the sub-trees below any of the ControlSets, you will discover that Hardware Profiles are actually a sub-set node below the ControlSets. This reveals that Hardware Profiles are a user configuration option that appears in each "backup" copy of the Registry's fault-tolerant technique of keeping ControlSet history versions.

Notes:

Figure 14-7
Registry Controlsets Select Key

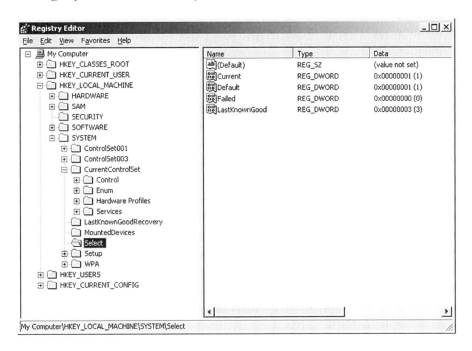

If you have closely examined the Registry with Regedit, you probably will have discovered some sections seem to repeat information shown elsewhere within the overall Registry. There are three reasons this occurs:

- **Symbolic Link Aliases—Showing the same sub-tree in more than one location.**

    o   To simplify developer's issues, several sections of the Registry appear "aliased" as a "root" level path, when they are in fact actually populated with contents at a lower level branch in a hive. HKEY_CLASSES_ROOT and HKEY_CURRENT_CONFIG are examples of this. HKEY_CURRENT_CONFIG actually resides in a deeper location in the System Hives. In Windows 2000 and later versions, HKEY_CLASSES_ROOT represents a "merged" result of similar information found in the Software Hive and the HKEY_CURRENT_USER Hive.

o   Conversely HKEY_CURRENT_USER is a hive that is then mapped in beneath the HKEY_USERS section, indexed with the Security Identifier (SID) of that user. The logic of this isn't critical to understand, but it's significant to understand that the relationship is there. It's the same registry hive when it's saved.

•   **Fault-Tolerance—To recover from a partially damaged registry or configuration fault, previous revisions of certain critical sections are maintained.**

o   The CurrentConfiguration is what is currently being used at that time, but it's mapped from one of the numbered ControlSets. The additional ControlSets listed represent a fail-safe history revision. If a system startup should fail, you have the option to try a previously successful variation. This is at the heart of what you controlwhen you boot in "Last known good condition." It's one of the other sets. These configurations still share substantial common information.

o   Hardware Profiles are useful for booting the system with support of different hardware configurations already defined. Again, the sections are representative of different configurations, but still based upon common information elsewhere in the same hive.

•   **Default Templates and Settings – Sometimes a section of registry as either a default template or supplemental default for a User configuration registry area.**

o   This metaphor should be familiar to how the user profiles folders below "Documents and Settings" establish the file/folder conditions. Just as there is an All Users and Default User configuration in the folder profile, the Registry emulates that concept in just a slightly different manner. Where you see effectively identical sections of Registry for both HKLM\Software and CurrentUser\Software, the HKLM\Software section is the equivalent of "All Users," but the CurrentUser setting will override it if they differ. Of course, Group Policies can also reverse that priority.

o   The Default User section of Registry has two purposes, one is obvious, the other is not. You would expect this serves as a template for creating the profile for a new user to receive. (Again, Group Policies or Roaming Profiles might override that as well.) Yet, the less obvious role for the Default User profile is to provide the desktop settings for the system when no user is even logged on. In the status when the Ctrl-Alt-Del prompt is presented at the console, the active User profile is the Default profile itself.

The Registry: Hives Are Non-Volatile Permanent Files

The active registry hives are stored in two distinct locations:

%SYSTEMROOT%\System32\Config

%USERPROFILE%\Username

The Registry hives used by the system and common for all users are placed as a set in the unique Windows system folder, in the path location indicated above, with only a specific user's own User registry hive stored in his or her respective profile folder.

The location for %SYSTEMROOT% is, of course, a fixed and permanent location determined when the Windows installation itself was created. The User Profile path location is typically unique to each local user, and it can be redirected or relocated as an administrative option. This means that the majority of the system Registry hives will stay in one place in below %SYSTEMROOT%\System32\Config, but from session to session the User hive could be loaded from a place that changes from user to user, even from session to session for the same user.

Notes:

It should be no surprise that the location of all the registry hive files are actually stored—where else?—in the registry! See Figure 14-15: Registry Hives List Key.

Figure 14-8
Registry Hives List Key

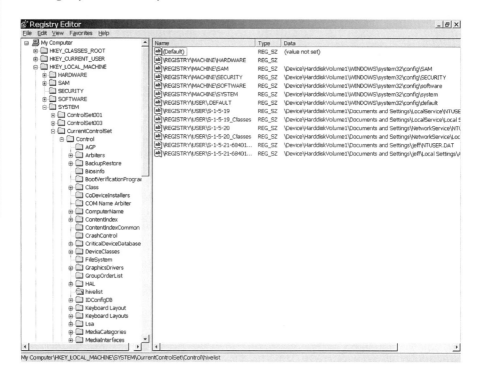

Now that I've explained the relationships of repetition and the "tree view," take a look at Table 14-8: Registry File Locations. Here you see a breakdown of which sections of the Registry are hives, where they are saved to disk, and which files are associated with each hive.

Notes:

Table 14-8

Registry File Locations

Filename and Folder Locations: Where the Registry Files are Saved		
HKEY_LOCAL_MACHINE		
\Hardware		[Created Dynamically]
\SAM	Sam, Sam.log, Sam.sav	%Systemroot%\System32\Config
\Security	Security, Security.log, Security.sav	%Systemroot%\System32\Config
\Software	Software, Software.log, Software.sav	%Systemroot%\System32\Config
\System	System, System.alt, System.log, System.sav	%Systemroot%\System32\Config
HKEY_CURRENT_CONFIG		Alias to HKEY_LOCAL_MACHINE \System \CurrentControlSet \Hardware Profiles\Current
HKEY_CLASSES_ROOT		Alias to HKEY_LOCAL_MACHINE \Software\Classes
HKEY_USERS.DEFAULT	Default, Default.log, Default.sav	%Systemroot%\System32\Config
HKEY_CURRENT_USER	Ntuser.dat, Ntuser.dat.log	%USERPROFILE%\Username

The first thing to notice is that the sets of filenames typically include the same base filename plus an extension that is either "blank," .SAV, .LOG, or .ALT. There's a logic here: The registry hive itself in every case is the one without any file extension.

The other two files typical to every hive serve roles in ensuring "fail-safe" backup information. The .SAV files are created by Setup when Windows was first installed and normally will just remain as they are from that point forward. The .LOG files have a continuing purpose to protect changes being written to the Registry Hive files as needed. The SYSTEM.ALT file is a variant approach unique to the SYSTEM hive. Here's how that works.

- .SAV Registry Files

During the original installation of Windows while running Setup, you probably realize there is a transition from Text Mode to GUI Mode Setup (Graphics User Interface) where you get a more Windows-like screen appearance on screen for the first time. Just before Setup makes that transition from Text to GUI Mode, the registry files that have been created at that point are preserved with the .SAV file extension. What this provides is a copy of these files just in case the next phase of Setup goes badly. If the balance of Setup doesn't complete to the end, Setup can use the .SAV file as a reference point to return to and start over from without starting from the very beginning of detection in Text Mode.

- .LOG Registry Files

During the course of operations with your Windows system, changes to the Registry are routine and ongoing for many reasons. Windows uses a mechanism for this which provides protection against losing "uncommitted" changes in case something like a power failure occurs before the changes are written and saved properly. A simplified explanation of this is that when an update action is called for, the changes are first written to the .LOG file. From that point, the actual Registry hive file is first flagged for update pending, the update is next committed, and finally the commitment flag is written to the hive. In the event of a power failure in the middle of the hive update, the .LOG file can be detected at startup and the change completion will be performed. This method of update applies to each of the Registry hives, except the System Hive. That's where the SYSTEM.ALT comes into play.

- .ALT System Registry File

The logic of protecting against power failures and Registry Hive corruption applies to the System hive as well, but the challenge here is even more complicated. The System hive is extremely critical to the operation of the computer, and it loads so early in the startup of Windows that it can't be "fixed" during startup like a .LOG file provides support to do. The update process for the SYSTEM and SYSTEM.ALT files is to commit the changes to the SYSTEM hive file first (using the same manner of steps), and only after that completes successfully then perform the same update to the SYSTEM.ALT file. This way, both files get the same update in sequence, but in the event of a failure, one of the files will not be in a corrupted condition. In normal conditions, these two files will have the very same content status, other than in the nearly instantaneous transition period of an update. That means, in general, both files are suitable to be the SYSTEM hive on any system boot cycle.

Registry Recovery Tips: Repair Folder, .ALT File, and SAV Files

When running, NTbackup saves copies of the current registry files in the Repair folder, providing you with another copy of the valuable files in a different location on the same drive. You can either restore your last "system state" backup or manually copy a more recent version of the registry files from the *SystemRoot***Repair****Regback** folder to the *SystemRoot***System32****Config** folder by using Recovery Console.

In the case of the SYSTEM.ALT file, you could rename the original SYSTEM file and try that one, or you can perform a repair which attempts the same thing.

The .SAV files are your last-chance effort to boot the machine to attempt a follow up restore. That would actually roll back the installation to the original first boot condition. Technically, that's faster than a repair or in-place upgrade, so you have to really want to get there to try that on a production machine.

You may well find that you have as many as four different copies of some of the registry hives on your hard drive at any time. Not all are equal, and going after them manually is an advanced concept, but it's useful information in a pinch.

Integrated DNS and Active Directory: The Left Lobe

In the previous sections, I have taken an approach of expanding the amount of information you have to consider, making you look at more details. Most of you probably haven't given much thought to that granular detail on the boot process, how the file system dissects, or what the individual registry entries for services. I know the registry details probably started to get a little scary if you stayed in that section too long.

From this point forward, I will back away from that approach for two reasons:

- Active Directory is a very complex topic

- You don't need detailed understanding of Active Directory to do disaster recovery.

This latter point exposes a curious characteristic of Active Directory. It's a lot like flying on a plane. You don't need to know how the planes fly or why the schedule is set as it is. Because you really don't have a lot of choice in the matter, you just respond to what your options are in dealing with it.

The more I have learned about Active Directory, the more I have enjoyed playing with it, because there is a lot of tinkering you can do! I love doing scripting to explore it, parse it, move things around, and generally try to see more ways to use AD effectively. But most of that has very little to do with being an SBS Administrator.

For the SBS Administrator, Active Directory is a foundation of how a network domain can be managed, and most of us learn as little as possible about it to get by. The need to know drives us further into other areas of Windows and SBS, but in AD we tend to prefer it to be a black box we don't look inside. And as it turns out, that generally works out fine. So rather than talk about how it works, I'm going to stay on track for what it does for us, and what we have to be concerned about with regard to disaster recovery with AD.

Overview of Active Directory Functionality

I want to make a quick summary of what Active Directory provides us functionally on an SBS so that when I move forward, you have a sense of the scale and value of our investment in AD.

Active Directory manages the following primary roles in our SBS network:

- Account Identification for Users, Security Groups, Computers, Contacts as objects

- Sites and Services, the shared infrastructure of a distributed operation

- Domain Controller identification and coordination of policies and operations data

- Domain-based resource publications, such as printers, shares, and resource servers

- Granular Authentication and Access Security

- Group Policy for centralized and flexible distribution for Users and Computers

- Multi-Level Administrative Control and Access Filtering

- Workstation management and deployment tools

- Logon and Session Management, Access Control

That's an incomplete list, but you get the idea of this being complex. Now, out of that entire list of things, it's no surprise to me that when somebody blows up an SBS server or intentionally reinstalls it from scratch, inevitably the loudest complaint in the Microsoft Newsgroups comes down to: All of the User Profiles at the workstations changed! *What!?!*

It's ironic, isn't it? The entire infrastructure of the SBS server was unilaterally replaced, and yet the big complaint is that everyone on staff lost their favorite desktop wallpaper or screen saver, the icons on the desktop and start menu have changed, and in many cases the My Documents information is not the same. Don't forget the Internet Explorer Favorites! Does anyone but me every wonder what else has gone missing in that process? Okay, now you get the idea of what I want to talk about in this section on Active Directory.

The Concept of a Windows Domain Preceded Active Directory

Active Directory represents the evolution of the NT Domain Directory Management. Let's start with the idea that with a Domain you can establish a central point of managing user accounts and computers. Unlike a workgroup where every workstation has a local User Account list, in a domain you have a central one. Using Domain Accounts means you no longer have to manage passwords and permissions at every workstation because the workstations all recognize the central authority, a Domain Controller.

In Windows NT 4.0 and earlier, the concept of a domain was managed by Domain Controllers in a way that appears on the surface to be very similar. For backward compatibility, many things still work the same way. The deeper you dig into it, however, the more you realize that Active Directory isn't the same at all; rather, it's impersonating a lot of the processes of the old Windows Directory Service, as well as now handling the Exchange Directory too. That means, in many cases, the objects stored in Active Directory must have all of the identifying tags for backward compatibility, current needs, and cross-purpose attributes for converging features like the combined directory service for Windows and Exchange.

Unique Identity, Unique Domains

An unfortunate misconception is that the identity of Users and Computers is based upon the common name of the object alone. The fact is that every object stored in the directory is represented by a unique identifier called a "Globally Unique Identifier" (GUID) or a "Security Identifier" (SID), or sometimes both concurrently. To make management of all the aspects Active Directory deals with more scalable and flexible, just about every object in the directory has more than one "unique" identifier. There may be more than one way to identify that object "uniquely," depending upon the circumstance.

To use a simple analogy, if someone says "Jeff" at the dinner table, I'm pretty sure they are talking to me. But if I were at a sports arena, there could be more than a couple people named "Jeff" within earshot and that would be confusing even if it's simple. Your Active Directory information will quite often allow you to use a simple reference as long as it doesn't create confusion, but you should understand that at a much deeper level in the storage management there is a more complex identifier being used. When you add a user or a computer to your domain, Active Directory will let you refer to it by a nickname or alias that is simple; but it stores and indexes that object in a technical way that ensures it can tell the difference between this object, and any new object that might try to claim the same nickname or alias. Even if you delete an object from Active Directory and then re-create it again with the same information, it won't mistake it as the original object.

What this reveals about disaster recovery concerns is huge. Since every aspect of security and policy is based upon unique identification, you can't re-create a User or Computer from scratch and convince the Active Directory that it's the same User or Computer previously removed. The only way to have an object remain as a "unique identifier object" is to not delete it from Active Directory, or restore the entire Active Directory to a time when the object still existed.

This issue just scratches the surface on what a problem it is to consider protecting Active Directory and all the objects it is responsible for managing. The place where most people see this break the surface is when the new User accounts with the same names don't log on to the workstations using the old profiles, and visually this appears as the desktops being refreshed.

The second symptom is that the workstations don't log on to the domain until you remove them from the domain and rejoin them. But what is happening is that the computers are not rejoining the original domain; they have joined a new domain with the same name as the original.

Lost Identity and Reconstruction

The last paragraph above makes the point that if you reinstall your SBS server from scratch without doing a restore from backup, you can name it all the same if you like, but that won't make it the same domain. The identification handshake goes both ways.

If you have a network with 20 Windows XP workstations, 20 users, and a single SBS server, when you reinstall that SBS server from scratch, you will be orphaning all those computers, all those users, and everything that they are tied to by their identification. Neither the workstations or the users will accept the new SBS as their Domain Controller until you force them to do so. But that doesn't eliminate a lot of other things that are more difficult to force or convert. You will need to reconstruct all the user and computer relationships. You won't necessarily need to reinstall the workstations, but you will have to address the entire configuration of the domain at each, plus clean up things at the server as well. It's a significant hurdle.

Many things in your business use of Windows and Windows-based applications are tied to the unique identity of the user or domain, and you may not even realize it. The security identifications form paths of access for Users, Group Memberships, Policies, Shared Folders, Public Folders, Mailboxes, and Outlook Rules. When you change the domain, it's actually worse than if you deleted all the workstations and users from the current domain. Re-creating the entire thing means not only re-creating the installation of the server, it means also re-creating the security template that touches everything in the entire network organization.

As a general rule, what will happen is that even if you change the things you recognize have been affected, you will still be plagued by nagging issues for some time to come—some things you might not even recognize as related.

Domain Authority and Security with Shared Central Organization

One of the things about SBS Server that makes it a challenge is we typically deploy it where it's the only Domain Controller in the network. That means the problems described just above can occur if you have a crash of your SBS Server and reconstruct it from scratch. A restore from backup of the same server would preserve the Active Directory as well as the configuration of the machine. However, very often it is this desire to get a "clean and new" installation that tempts us to abandon a recovery from a backup. Certainly there are times when a restore from backup is not possible if you have failed to do routine System State and full data backups. In this case, your loss can be tragic—far beyond the Active Directory concerns. Microsoft hasn't given us simple ways to restore the Active Directory to an SBS server without restoring the entire system and application configuration to the server at the same time.

This is where the idea of multi-master Domain management emerges as a solution. If you have another Domain Controller in your network, that DC can maintain a copy of the Active Directory at the same time as your SBS is managing it. Each Domain Controller in Active Directory shares a common AD database in which changes can be initiated at any Domain Controller. Authoritative roles of replication and Flexible Single Master Operations (FSMO) Role determine how to ensure all changes are resolved and replicated correctly as a unified result over time. In addition, the way Active Directory treats the multi-master management means the domain can survive as long as one domain controller is still in operation, even if it doesn't hold all the FSMO roles.

It's certainly possible that changes could be lost if a Domain Controller goes offline permanently before replicating its changes to the rest of the DCs, or if the synchronization process in replication is not successful. Still, the goal of AD multi-master Domain Controllers is to ensure all machines can do virtually everything any other Domain Controller can handle. The five unique FSMO roles are primarily designated to be the authority if collisions in requests occur or if a higher level process is periodically distributed out. The FSMO roles ensure there is a final authority to determine an outcome on things or to initiate unique management processes.

For instance, the RID Master role in allocating additional RID pools to other Domain controllers allows each Domain Controller to work from an allocated pool of account RIDs and only periodically request a new pool. The account requests for individual RIDs are not distributed by the RID Master itself unless it is either the only DC available or happens by coincidence to be responding to the account request. Take a look at the other FSMO Role designations in the following table.

Table 14-9

FSMO Role Descriptions

FSMO Roles for Domain Controllers	
Schema Master	**One master role holder per forest.** The schema master FSMO role holder is the domain controller responsible for performing updates to the directory schema.
Domain Naming Master	**One master role holder per forest.** The domain naming master FSMO role holder is the DC responsible for making changes to the forest-wide domain name space of the directory.
Infrastructure Master	**One master role holder per domain.** The infrastructure FSMO role holder is the DC responsible for updating an object's SID and distinguished name in a cross domain object reference.
RID Master	**One master role holder per domain.** The RID master FSMO role holder is the single DC responsible for processing RID Pool requests from all DCs within a given domain.
PDC Emulator	**One master role holder per domain.** The PDC emulator FSMO role holder is a Windows 2000 DC that advertises itself as the primary domain controller (PDC) to earlier version workstations, member servers, and domain controllers. It is also the Domain Master Browser and handles password discrepancies.

The orderly transfer of FSMO roles is called, logically enough, a "Transfer." The alternative used when the previous role holder has gone away for good or can't be contacted is referred to as a "Role Seizure." The latter gives us a way to take control of the Active Directory management in case one of the primary FSMO role holders fails. So the revelation is that any surviving Domain Controller is suitable and capable for either preserving the domain or for repopulating a new or returning Domain Controller with historical data from the Active Directory replica it is holding.

Meanwhile, it deserves mention that all the Domain Controllers in the domain are replicating any changes to the shared Active Directory. I'm not going to get too deep into the replication process because it's a rather complicated topic, but I want to leave you with the understanding that Active Directory is designed to preserve information, and populate it to all Domain Controllers. The FSMO role holder assignments ensure one server is authoritative on redefining unique settings in Active Directory or that FSMO role holder preserves uniqueness through unique delegation , as in the example of the RID Master given above.

Recovery by Restore or Replication

Now that we have the groundwork to understand that the FSMO roles in a domain can actually be moved around in an emergency or in a planned deployment process, we can feel pretty comfortable that Active Directory gives us survivability as long as we have a Domain Controller operating or the ability to restore one from a full System State backup.

So now we should return to the example for SBS Server and see what makes sense to us. We have the option to run another server to maintain a backup copy of Active Directory, or we need a way to quickly recover the Active Directory and the SBS Server operations if needed. In the overall scheme of things, the SBS Server is usually critical to the operations of the business because of all the responsibilities it has as an Exchange Server, file server, Internet gateway, and for any applications it hosts. This suggests that the business needs are down as long as the SBS server is down. If you choose to recover your domain by using another Domain Controller, you have one set of options. However, if your plan is to bring the SBS Server back online from a backup, you have a different set of options.

Either way, if the Active Directory is all that you care about, you could easily declare the second DC as the winning idea, but that wouldn't bring the other services back immediately. Recovery of the SBS Server remains a unique challenge because it has so much responsibility to the organization, and the Active Directory is not the entire picture. Given that Active Directory can only be restored to a Domain Controller by restoring the System State, this implies that the path to restore the Domain Controller is either parallel or identical to what is needed to restore the entire operations. And there you have the argument for why recovery of the SBS Server is not only important, it's probably going to be a higher priority than a second Domain Controller would be.

Even if you can recover the SBS role as a Domain Controller by bringing it up to date via replication from another Domain Controller, it's only the process or reinstallation or restore or recovery that will put the application server role of the SBS back in order.

Active Directory and DNS

This section starts by declaring the relationship of Active Directory and DNS as being so close it's almost the same thing. The fact is that Active Directory is a database, and DNS provides the means to locate things within it. If your DNS Server configuration is wrong, you might well experience problems that look like a failure of Active Directory. This concurrent relationship is easily misunderstood if you think of DNS as being "the tool that finds addresses on the Internet."

If you configure your SBS server the way Microsoft recommends, the DNS Server will be responding to all DNS queries of any kind, including internal searches of the Active Directory. When an Internet-based address is needed, DNS looks to see if that information is already in the cache, and if not, DNS forwards the query to an Internet-based DNS server for a resolution.

The DNS Server running on your SBS contains zones for the local domain that include information relevant to the Active Directory. Therefore, your process of managing Active Directory needs to include consideration for what details the DNS Server is caching internally, as well as the references stored in the Active Directory database.

One of the reasons I wanted to emphasize the tight relationship between DNS and Active Directory is that you really can confuse yourself about Active Directory being "messed up" if you don't realize how very important it is to keep DNS properly configured. If you allow your server to request information from Internet-based DNS servers directly (via DNS configuration on the Network Adapters), you can get bizarre behavior from an SBS acting as a Domain Controller and Exchange Server. It can be as if you are asking the Internet DNS servers to give your internal information what they can't possibly know!

Accounts, Policies, Rights, and Security

Many SBS Administrators never even venture into the realm of customizing the group memberships, group policies, rights, or security templates on their domain. I understand this, but I'm not sure I agree with it. On the one hand, if you never customize anything on your server or in your domain, you have nothing in particular to reconstruct if you do a clean install! I guess this is part of the reason that I'm so focused on disaster recovery, because I invest a lot of time in managing my customer sites and the domains that run them.

Be a Groupie!

Group Policy is a feature I really love to use because it lets me help simplify the management and use of the workstations for me and for the staff. I also have the option to control the range of functionality on workstations. For certain features I would rather not have available, my preference is enforced. I can remove the feature if I feel it doesn't serve a valid function, but it does expose some risk. For instance, I block many of the options to reconfigure hardware or to modify the registry. These are user rights just not needed by the typical users in my customer sites.

As an extension of that logic, it is possible to use the customization of both Local Policies and workgroup-oriented policies to go beyond enforcing a setting. You have the ability to protect specific user data or details from exposure to misconduct, accidental loss, or worse, unauthorized inspection by other staff members. What I'm driving at is security doesn't necessarily refer to secrecy or criminal security exposure. Sometimes we simply need a way to provide a sense of order to the operations.

For me, trying to provide an orderly environment just makes sense. So I invest time in determining from the owner or the staff what would help them, and I then deliver those things if possible using the features of Active Directory. As a result, the Active Directory represents to me a depository of invested knowledge and goal-oriented customization I don't want to lose in a disaster. And yet, it's rather easy to protect it. What is required is the commitment to preserve the contents of Active Directory and preserve a way to recover them via backup or a restore with replication from another Domain Controller.

The Exchange: The Right Lobe

I'll now present the right lobe: Exchange Server 2003.

Why Is Exchange the Right Lobe?

If you know your human brain anatomy, you know that the right lobe of the brain is the creative and artistic hemisphere, with the left lobe as the hemisphere takes on the analytical and fact-processing jobs.

When I chose to identify this section on Exchange as "The Right Lobe," I was definitely tipping my hat to acknowledge that Active Directory was introduced to join the Windows Directory Services with the Exchange Directory Services. Active Directory is the converged directory to manage the security, accounts, authentication, and policy roles of Windows Directory with the document management, communications, and collaborations possible from Exchange. Very few SBS sites would say "Wow! Active Directory has really created power for my business!" Right? But with Exchange, I have seen many businesses running SBS dramatically transformed, reinvented, and energized with the ability to create solutions and communicate.

When both directory services were converged, we ended up with the majority of Active Directory looking like a powerhouse of Windows Directory service features, no question. But when you add an Exchange Organization to the business organization, you have many required updates to Active Directory—what's called a "Schema Update." The Domainprep process makes it possible for Active Directory to store the bits and pieces of mail- and collaboration-related information for user and group objects, but it also enables the Domain organization to locate and communicate from server to server within an Organization and beyond to other Organizations, other domains, and other managed boundaries.

What you will learn from study of Exchange installation, and perhaps even more from Exchange removal or disaster recovery processes, is that Exchange is threaded throughout an SBS Server because an SBS Server runs all the things you normally see scattered across many "role servers."

Bumping into Exchange Everywhere

One of the reasons that Exchange brings hesitant embrace from SBS Administrators is because it's complex and invested in many aspects of the SBS Server. Exchange isn't just an application as much as it is an extension of Active Directory and networking and database management all threaded into an application interface. You can enjoy the use of Exchange without completely understanding it, and this is a credit to how it operates. Yet, you will be hard pressed to troubleshoot Exchange Server issues if you are shy about learning what exactly Exchange does, and how. My goal here is to reveal an outline of this, even if I don't have room to explain things in detail.

Part of the trick to troubleshooting Exchange is to learn what other services it relies upon for support and conduit and then determine how to confirm whether your problem is actually with Exchange or with the other resource it's trying to work with. Sometimes that other source is your networking or firewall. Other times it's a Web server interface. Still other times it's the DNS and Active Directory that is the partner to the success or failure you are experiencing.

SBS installs monolithically from setup and we sometimes have trouble determining how the pieces fit together. I think of Exchange as being as subtle and yet as vital as the mortar between the bricks in a wall and covering just as much real estate in your server, touching on many other component services and resources.

Exchange is all of the following things:

- Group of interdependent services

- Communications engine

- Documentation management database

- Transaction record and scheduling engine

- An extension of information specific to Users, Groups, and Distribution List

- An alternative to the file system format for storing objects

- Business-critical information manager

- Unique collaboration space

- Frontline portal to your business organization

- A flexible data engine

With all that territory covered, you could throw your hands up and declare that it's not possible to troubleshoot or do disaster recovery of something that complex, right? That's certainly the conclusion some people arrive at, but it's not the only answer. Exchange can be treated as a "segmented cluster" of recovery environments. By that I mean, you can recover parts of Exchange without even dealing with other parts of it. It's really possible to segment the product and recovery that way.

Is It a Server, Organization, Information Store, or Group of Services?

The answer is "all of the above." When you install the first Exchange Server to your organization, something very transparent occurs during the setup when you are running SBS. Four distinct blobs of creation happen in such a way that on an SBS, you really don't realize it's not all one thing. This is compounded in subtlety because your SBS Server is already a DNS Server and a Domain Controller. Let's look a little closer at what is happening under the hood.

- **Active Directory Schema**—To add the first Exchange Server, your Active Directory Schema is updated. That's programmer and Directory Services speak for "the database has some new fields added to include e-mail-related stuff for users, groups, and contacts." Exchange also requires a series of specific organization references and services details added inside AD. DNS is already present; it now has an extended database to review and some additional references to support in Active Directory. The Exchange Organization is established, and this first server is registered as a host for that Organization. All this is happening at the Active Directory level.

- **Exchange Server Application**—The server itself is meanwhile installing all the Exchange operations services in the local registry and creating folder space locations for doing its processing. The default for Exchange 2003 is to place this in the C:\Program Files\Exchsrvr folder tree. Beneath that tree, several database folders are created, including the MDBdata and Mailroot folders. The balance of how Exchange runs on this box is all part of the application design, but that is really unique to the machine specific installation. Preference settings for this machine determine how the application behaves on this machine locally and are kept in the local Registry or perhaps in reference files locally. Organizational changes and preferences would be stored at higher levels up in Active Directory itself.

- **The Storage Group Container**—Once this Exchange Server has the entire operational configuration present, it's able to now establish a Storage Group as a designated reference to house Information Stores. In an SBS, this appears as a series of hierarchical clicks you have to drill down through in Exchange System Manager. However, what is revealed is that this cascade in SBS has only "one of each" because it's an SBS Server, and that's the limitation of the product. With SBS 2003, the option to mount a Recovery Store made it possible to have another Information Store, but its unique purpose really makes it yet another unique "one of each" item in the grand scheme of things. What's important to get from this part of the description is that the Storage Group is part of the reference unique for this server, but it's still a management reference only. It's the parking space location—you will park the database in it.

- **The Database Objects**—The final part of our breakout are the Information Stores themselves—the Private Store and the Public Store. These are actual databases, and they include not only the database files them-selves (EDB and STM files), but also included are the transaction logs that refer to updated information affecting objects moving through the database stores. One of the most commonly asked questions about migration or recovery of an SBS Server with regard to Exchange is "What do I have to save to keep all my data?" Turns out that the Private and Public Stores retain what you are looking for, which actually includes some server side rules for processing mailbox-specific prefer-ences for the owner, the user.

If all this happens on a single box like an SBS, you might think it's all a single update, single reinstall, but it's not. An important part of this is that you can remove or rebuild these pieces separately in many respects.

- The Private and Public stores can be dismounted, mounted, or replaced separately.

- An Information Store can be saved and restored as a whole, even relo-cated to another server with certain conditions met. It's a standalone object, but you have to make sure the namespace connections are handled properly if you move it.

- Storage Groups provide options you don't get to use in SBS Exchange.

- The Exchange Server Application can be removed or reinstalled with-out requiring you to forfeit either the Information Stores, or the Active Directory-based information about the Organization itself. That means you can maintain consistent association of e-mail attributes on your users and groups without having the same Exchange Server involved. It becomes possible to replace or reinstall Exchange Server as an appli-cation without starting over with everything else above or below the Server Application level.

- The Exchange Organization defines the binding to Active Directory, as well as the point from which multiple servers and sites converge for iden-tification and addressing. Removing an Exchange Organization effec-tively kills everything below it in the hierarchy. For this reason, you can't easily remove an Exchange Organization from Active Directory without first clearing out the referenced Exchange Servers, as well as the site references to those servers. But you can remove and reinstall a server back into the same organization if needed. At the organizational level, it looks like a substitution of the same server, though some unique references do have to be refreshed. In the case of SBS, if you are removing the one and only Exchange Server from the Organization, there's very little practical difference caused by removing the entire Organization. The normal assumption is that when you remove the last Exchange Server, the Organization ceases to exist. However, if you are only repairing the server without changing the Active Directory references, the change isn't noticed. If needed, you can re-create an Exchange Organization within your Active Directory if you have reason to remove it. The main requirement would be to match the naming of the Organization exactly.

That provides us a quick overview of the hierarchy of an SBS, a single server with a single Storage Group containing a single Information Store. That Information Store contains the single Private database, a single Public database. The option for a Recovery Store would sit in parallel to the Information Store as a means to extract objects from the store, but it lacks the operations functionality of that original Information Store. With each of these "one of each" objects defined as a container within a container, in our SBS-based domain it's all stored on the single server and becomes the one Exchange Site for the entire Exchange Organization.

As a closing thought on this explanation, it's no wonder that managing an SBS becomes confusing when you look at Enterprise documentation on Exchange. Much of the isolation, fault-tolerance, and options for recovery based upon multiple Information Stores, multiple Storage Groups, and even multiple servers mean nothing to us. The only thing we have in a disaster recovery for SBS server is that inevitably it's the same server that will be be repaired, restored, or reinstalled. This builds a lot of value in knowing what we can save to bring back again or to protect ourselves from losses.

Now we move on to look at some dependencies you will find Exchange threading into on your SBS server, as well as some client station considerations.

Inroads to Exchange

Exchange Server represents a particular complication with an SBS server when it comes to disaster recovery. Exchange Server installs with interaction at many different levels, including:

- Exchange Information Store databases

- Active Directory database schema

- DNS-integrated attributes and records

- Network connectivity and secure access control

- User object attributes and security access

- Internet Information Server (IIS)

- Outlook integration at every profile for every workstation

In the section above, we looked at the first two items, the Information Store Databases as well as the relationship to the Active Directory Database Schema. I made some references to the User objects, but let's look at that and the remaining items more closely now.

- **DNS-Integrated attributes and records**—Exchange relies upon DNS for many reasons. Exchange depends upon Active Directory, and DNS is required to access Active Directory information, and that's where Exchange details are stored for the mail-enabled objects. In addition, Exchange needs DNS support to resolve normal SMTP mail transactions to locate remote servers on the Internet. For internal Exchange processing between multiple Exchange Servers, the integration of AD and DNS would again establish another dependency.

- **Network connectivity and secure access control**—It is probably a very obvious point that network connectivity is critical for using an Exchange Server to reach both the client workstations as well as remote servers and DNS servers when that is involved. That means not only is network transport required, but the firewalls between the opposite end of the connection must allow for the open ports to pass the required traffic. We would think of Port 25 as the primary mail server port for communication with other SMTP servers, but additional ports are required for reaching MAPI or POP3 clients, not to mention the traffic that passes with OWA when using RPC tunneling. Having the ports blocked at a firewall for any one of these would produce a symptom one might mistake for an Exchange Server error, when that's actually not the case.

- **User Object Attributes and Security Access**—Each object which is mail-enabled has this information stored somewhere in Active Directory; it's just another attribute field for that object. That means that even if your Exchange Server is offline, the attributes are actually still accessible in the Active Directory. In addition, most every aspect of Exchange involves some level of security protection to prevent unauthorized access, or to allow selective interactions. These two concepts illustrate the blended overlap of how Active Directory stores Exchange-related information, and yet Exchange depends upon Active Directory security and authentication services. That's the result of the two directory services converging, after previously operating stand-alone under Windows NT 4.0.

Among the changes introduced with Exchange 2003, Microsoft decided to enforce the most strict default settings to prevent Exchange Administrators from being able to view mailbox contents. This reflects the concerns of privacy laws, but it also reflects a greater concern for employee-to-employee privacy protection specifically. In a typical Enterprise, the need for an Administrator to casually review the contents of any particular user's mailbox is far less than with the many small businesses. By contrast, in small business it is quite common that the System Administrator is also the Exchange Administrator, and yet also the first-line technical support of the end-users on staff. Removing the blocks from access to the mailbox is a common step that is available, reversing the default, which allows the ability to provide more personal support in many cases. And, of course, many small business owners consider it a right and in their own best interests to inspect the employee's mail and schedule information. This illustrates one interesting aspect of interpreting security in different contexts, but it also reveals how tightly bound SBS Server administrators are in granting significant access to the company they support.

- **Internet Information Server (IIS)**—I confess I was confused when I found out my interpretation of IIS as a Web server implied that it had nothing to do with Exchange Server. In fact, Exchange is rather dependent upon IIS for significant functionality. One of my revelations I tell a story about later in the chapter is how I found out that a corruption of the IIS Metabase without a backup meant I would be reinstalling Exchange Server!

I'm including an excerpt from Microsoft Knowledgebase KB 843093, and I recommend you look at that KB if you find yourself in dire straits with metabase corruption. The excerpt below does as good a job to summarize the role of IIS with Exchange as I could possibly do, so take a look:

Overview of the IIS Metabase (Excerpt from KB 843093)

IIS was introduced as a separate product when Microsoft Windows NT 3.51 was released. Exchange 2000 Server runs on IIS version 5.0. The core IIS service is named "IIS Admin." The core executable file for IIS is Inetinfo.exe. IIS provides the following functionalities for Exchange Server:

- It provides core protocol and connection management services.

- It provides core security and authentication mechanisms.

- It provides core file access and caching.

- It provides the separation of memory spaces and other functionalities to help increase the stability of Exchange.

- It controls speed and bandwidth throttling.

- It is the host for the Simple Mail Transfer Protocol (SMTP) service and for the Network News Transport Protocol (NNTP). These services are included in the host operating system.

- It is the host for Exchange 2000 Server protocol additions, such as the Microsoft Exchange POP3 service and the Microsoft Exchange IMAP4 service.

The IIS 5.0 metabase is a database that is used to store configuration and property information about IIS. This database is located in the following location:

%systemroot%\system32\inetsrv\metabase.bin

Most IIS settings and IIS-related service settings are stored in the metabase. The metabase replaced the registry for the storage of IIS-related information because the metabase is faster than the registry. Additionally, using the metabase for storage of IIS-related information helps keep the registry from growing too big. The metabase also lets you set properties that are inheritable. The metabase is currently based on the X.500 standard. For example, the metabase has a schema.

The actual metabase does not reside on the hard disk. It is held in the computer's memory. When the computer is shut down, the metabase is committed to the hard disk. Additionally, metabase tools such as MetaEdit, Adsutil.vbs, MetaSnap, and MDUTIL extract the metabase information from the computer's memory. These tools do not read the metabase information from the Metabase.bin file.

Note: We recommend that you do not scan the metabase file by using a file-level antivirus program.

- **Outlook Integration at every profile for every workstation**—You might not think much about Outlook as a disaster recovery issue with Exchange, unless you have started using some of the more sophisticated features. There's two ways to look at this. One perspective is to realize that you could configure Outlook with cache mode enabled to keep a copy of the mailbox information locally. I've heard some folks suggest that this "protects the mailbox contents" in case the Exchange is down or worse. That may be true, but establishing another synchronization link this way also means under certain conditions breaking that link becomes a complication following a recovery of the Exchange Server. You might next be visiting every workstation and modifying every user profile on ever workstation to restore or bypass that synchronization link. This probably doesn't thrill the System Administrator. Sometimes the resolution is just to remove and reenter the Exchange Server Mailbox connection, but it's a tedious step to do. These problems are worse if you have a clean install replacement of your SBS server even if you remount the previous store by some means.

Why invest in Exchange Skills?

The broad details of Exchange disaster recovery suggest that you want either the short answer or the long answer, but you need to sit back for the long answers. Exchange is a big topic. Managing Exchange is something people invest a career in for Enterprise, and it certainly could become a major skill set for an SBS Administrator to get comfortable with. We don't have space in this chapter for the long answer to Exchange disaster recovery as a broad topic; however, there is a chapter on Exchange in this book. Therefore, what I'm going to cover will give you a reality check on Exchange crisis scenarios and a bit deeper insight into your last resort recovery options.

There's so much about Exchange that an SBS Administrator isn't likely to need to know how to set up, much less repair. Is Exchange overkill for small business? It's an interesting question. I think Exchange is overkill for sending and receiving mail, but I wouldn't have it any other way for managing communications of an organization!

What I've come to know about Exchange is that I don't need everything required to run a massive enterprise. I don't handle dozens of mail servers, remote site synchronizations, the complexities of shared administrative responsibilities. All of the interconnection features for other kinds of deployments simply don't happen in Exchange in an SBS running on a single box. We have such a small-scale requirement, and yet, in an SBS organization you are still likely to find the full range of "end user" requests and needs. The Administrator of Exchange doesn't need all the features, but the staff really gains a lot from having that bodacious collaboration, document management, and communication transaction server under the hood. I love Exchange, I hate Exchange, and I just can't do without it now. Probably the single biggest point of resistance I have to falling in love with Sharepoint is that I see so much functionality fulfilled in Exchange already, and it's more mature, it's amazingly resilient, and it solves problems for me and the organizations I work with.

I have about six years of experience with Exchange in SBS, I'm very impressed at how durable and valuable the product is. Exchange always has intimidated me and yet it has become one of the features within the SBS package that don't expect to be dead if the server crashes. The automatic recovery and repair functionality that is standard in Exchange just amazes me. I've heard stories about people who have lost information in Exchange, or had horrific cleanup situations from virus injections to Exchange, and I admit, I've not dodged every bad experience. I've lost data, but very little. I've had to do repairs, but generally they were successful. I've had to figure out conditions when Exchange refused to work, but I've never reinstalled an SBS server because of Exchange issues. Never. The recovery tools and documentation always looks a bit confusing and complex to me, and yet it does work.

Let me share a little story with you, this is a bit of a history revelation about the Migration Chapter.

You learn from the worst experiences

Probably the single most important thing that I learned about SBS disaster recovery, and what ultimately built the technical framework of the Migration Chapter in this book, was gained from a series of very nasty crashes I suffered while doing in-place upgrades from SBS 4.5 to SBS 2000. The cause of the crashes turned out to be an odd convergence of issues regarding a particular Adaptec RAID controller driver, Microsoft Windows Performance Monitor, and a section in the finalization of SBS Setup at 99 percent completion. I never found out what exactly was happening, but what resulted was a BSOD crash at the very end of a seven-hour-long upgrade which had only one specific symptom: Exchange would not mount the Information Store. Everything else was fine. However, only after this happened more than once on a sequence of virtually identical servers at different customers where I performed upgrades did I come to know for certain the problem: the IIS metabase was being corrupted.

Because it was happening at the end of setup, I didn't have a backup of the metabase, and therefore the only fix was to gut the server installation. The repair was to completely remove Exchange, completely remove IIS, begin again with domainprep, and then reinstall everything that came in the process. Removing Exchange was a chore in itself because in this situation, the /RemoveOrg option in setup didn't work either. My only option was to go into the local registry on the SBS and start deleting all the Exchange Services and related references. Then I had to delete all the installation folders, except of course I kept the Information Store saved on the side because that was the customer data.

With SBS 2000, that also meant rerunning the SBS Setup when finished and reinstalling service packs. Was I done there? No. In fact, before I could reinstall, I had to manually install Exchange and specify the old SBS 4.5 namespace for the Exchange Organization and Storage Group, because that was also inconsistent from the old version to the new version of Exchange. But I did learn a very valuable bit of information in that process: There wasn't anything special being done to the Exchange Store during SBS Setup or Exchange installation, I could just reattach the old Exchange Database from the SBS 4.5 server.

Heading Towards Fully Functional

Once I had Exchange Server back functional, and IIS was again operational underneath it, I still had to regain the Information Store mount and repair the store from any damage caused in the dirty shutdown in the BSOD. Finally, I would reconnect the users to the mailboxes they originally owned. What a mess! What a huge amount of work! What an amazing, eye-opening experience!

After coming to realize the value of the recovery skills I had learned, the single most amazing part was that I had just totally ripped off the SBS server's head while reconstructing the Exchange Installation, and afterward the server…ran better. After a few crashes of this type occurred, I determined how to avoid the crash proactively and finished some in-place upgrades uneventfully. But I was also able to see a comparison to how much better the clean reinstall servers ran compared to servers at a different customer site that were sluggish. I had incentive now. I went to those other sites and ripped the head off them too! The cleaner install of the related services improved the operation of the servers.

Along the way, I gained the insight and will to separate Exchange and the Directory Service upgrade process. But that wasn't the major point; rather, I learned it was possible to completely reconstruct the Exchange installation, even on an SBS server. It was also possible to remove and reinstall IIS, and I could remount an old Exchange Store to a new server. The rest is just history leading up to Swing Migration. But what it revealed to me at the same time is that I could take confidence in reconstructing Exchange or recovering it from even the most brutal conditions of failure. I know how to do that now.

The Exchange First Aid Kit

In the SBS scale of things, we try to deal with technical problems more often than not by whatever works faster, not what is a more complete resolution. We try to "optimize the compromise" as I outlined in the earlier part of this chapter.

I believe most SBS IT Pros will never have the time or mandate to do Enterprise-class disaster recovery methodologies, at least not based upon a single chapter with the scope of this one! What we usually end up with in Exchange is the need to do one of the following:

- Restore an Information Store database

- Repair a damaged database

- Recover mail deleted from an Information Store

- Repair the functional operations to transact mail send and receive

- Completely reinstall Exchange on an existing server

- Bring forward an Exchange Store or the mailboxes to a new server

- Repair a broken SBS Server without breaking Exchange

Probably the main complaint I have about Exchange with crisis situations is that it has taken me a long time to come to realize that Exchange produces more error events without a concurrent explanation than any other SBS featured product. You end up having to go search on the pop-up error and then look for the Event Viewer error numbers and search for that combination. Unlike many Microsoft products, it won't always tell you what the error is in sufficient detail, so you have to search for it. If you don't know how to search Knowledgebase articles or Google for information, you are at a disadvantage. Turns out, one of the skills with Exchange repair is the ability to find the wealth of information that doesn't show up when an error message appears on screen.

System State and Full Recovery Backup: The Critical Organs

If you manage an SBS server, you had better be familiar with what a System State Backup and Restore represents to you: Everything. Without a System State Backup, you have given up your best chance at restore from backup or restore to the same Active Directory with a rebuild, unless you have other domain controllers.

What you probably don't realize is that even a System State and complete data backup are not actually making a backup of everything in a way you might want it later.

You should pay special attention to three additional database systems with unique backup requirements: Consider doing a separate backup of both the SQL Databases and the Sharepoint Services databases separately from the normal backup. Furthermore, the IIS metabase as well is a candidate for separate an object specific back task if you do a lot of customization on the website. Each of these three system have unique characteristics:

- SQL Databases cannot have a database backup performed by the Operating System while the files are open, unless you use a backup program designed for that with a special agent. NT Backup doesn't provide that as in previous versions; therefore you need to create a "flat file backup" using SQL native tools, such as in Enterprise Manager.

- Sharepoint Server database is actually backed up with a full backup, but there's a catch. The restore process will work just fine if you are restoring to the original server, but it's complicated to recover to another server. Therefore, an "export" of the Sharepoint databases makes this much easier. The backup can be done with the tool for Sharepoint, STSADM.EXE.

- IIS Metabase is the third item I mentioned as an exception, but it's yet a different condition. You can fully back up and restore the IIS Metabase with a normal backup, but the complication is it requires a System State restore. That means if you have a problem with your Web site and want to restore the metabase for that reason, you would need to do a full

System State restore of your Domain Controller! I'm not suggesting that you need to take this precaution unless you are routinely altering the IIS metabase for reasons unrelated to the role of SBS as a Domain Controller and Exchange Server.

Here is a summary of information related to what NTbackup normally provides us protection via backup with regarding the System State, data and Exchange. The three points above are mentioned again for emphasis.

Table 14-10
Full Recovery Backup Definitions

What is a Full Recovery Backup?
To run NTbackup on your server, whether it is via the SBS Backup Wizard or manually, your selections must include: •   All Drive Partitions •   System State •   Information Store (Exchange Server) If you also run SQL Server, you must perform a supplemental backup to disk of the Exchange Databases before running your NTbackup or you must stop the SQL Services before the backup begins.
What is a System State Backup?
As noted above, the System State is a subset of a complete backup. It's actually a specific selection in your backup program. As a general summary statement, the System State should include the contents of: C:*.* *[only boot specific files]* C:\Documents and Settings\All Users\[selected files and folders] C:\Program Files*.* C:\Windows*.* That isn't a complete backup by any stretch, nor is that a universal statement of what is backed up on your computer specifically. The contents of a System State will vary from machine to machine, depending upon the configuration and the applications installed. It

also depends upon options chosen in the NTbackup program or your preferred backup utility.

What is excluded from a Backup?

Even when you select a Full and Complete backup, you will not record quite literally all the files on the local drive. What you will record are all the files essential to recover that computer, but additional files might be omitted for one reason or another. Some files are skipped intentionally because they are automatically created on every restart or if they are missing. This includes the pagefile.sys and the hibernation files.

However, there may be occasions when you want to back up files that NTbackup normally skips. So how would you know what is excluded? Check this registry location on your SBS server:

HKEY_LOCAL_MACHINE\SYSTEM\CurrentControlSet\Control\Backup Restore\FilesNotToBackup

In addition, a similar registry key location on your SBS server determines specific registry keys not restored in a backup, as indicated here:

HKEY_LOCAL_MACHINE\SYSTEM\CurrentControlSet\Control\Backup Restore\KeysNotToRestore

I've included a list of default files and folders excluded from backup in the table the follows this one.

What else should I back up or perform before making a Full Recovery Backup?

- SQLserver databases if you don't have a third-party application that uses agents

- Sharepoint Services flatfile backup

- IIS Metabase Backup (optional, but useful if you customize your Web site a great deal)

Another exceptional issue to know about is that NTbackup uses an exclusions list—things omitted from the backup operation. I've included a table of the default entries from my reference server to illustrate what that includes, or should I say excludes? You can add or remove entries by editing the Exclude Files list, found on the Options tab list in the Backup Utility program. The information is stored in a registry location; I've identified that in the table on file locations.

Table 14-11

NTBackup Excluded Files List

Default Exclusions from NTbackup on SBS 2003	
ASR Log File	%SystemRoot%\repair\asr.log
ASR Error File	%SystemRoot%\repair\asr.err
Client Side Cache	%SystemRoot%\csc* /s
Internet Explorer	%UserProfile%\index.dat /s
Memory Page File	\Pagefile.sys
Microsoft Writer (Bootable State)	%SystemRoot%\Registration*.clb *.crmlog /s
Mount Manager	\System Volume Information\MountPoint ManagerRemoteDatabase
Netlogon	%SystemRoot%\netlogon.chg
Power Management	\hiberfil.sys
VSS Default Provider	\System Volume Information*{3808876B-C176-4e48-B7AE-04046E6CC752} /s
VSS Service DB	\System Volume Information*.{7cc467ef-6865-4831-853f-2a4817fd1bca}DB
VSS Service Alternate DB	\System Volume Information*.{7cc467ef-6865-4831-853f-2a4817fd1bca}ALT
Task Scheduler	%SYSTEMROOT%\Tasks\schedlgu.txt
Temporary Files	%TEMP%* /s
Winlogon debug	%WINDIR%\debug*
Catalog Database	%SystemRoot%\System32\CatRoot2* /s
MS Distributed Transaction Coordinator	C:\WINDOWS\system32\MSDTC\MSDTC.LOG C:\WINDOWS\system32\MSDtc\trace\dtctrace.log
DRM	C:\Documents and Settings\All Users\DRM* /s

DNS Server	%SystemRoot%\system32\dns\backup\dns.log C:\WINDOWS\system32\dns\dns.log
NTDS	C:\WINDOWS\NTDS* C:\WINDOWS\ntds*
NtFrs	C:\windows\ntfrs\jet* /s C:\WINDOWS\debug\NtFrs\NtFrs* C:\windows\sysvol\domain\DO_NOT_REMOVE_ NtFrs_PreInstall_Directory* /s C:\windows\sysvol\domain\NtFrs_ PreExisting___See_EventLog* /s C:\windows\sysvol\staging\domain\NTFRS_*
Registry Writer	%SystemRoot%\system32\NtmsData*

Directory Services Recovery Mode (DSRM)

If you ever need to restore your System State on a Domain Controller, you will need to boot the computer in the Directory Services Recovery Mode (DSRM). This seems to confuse more people than it should.

Regardless whether your Domain Controller is the only DC in the domain or one of many, if you are going to perform a full System State restore, you must also restore a copy of the Active Directory database. In other words, you not only roll back your server configuration, you roll back the domain database as well. Obviously, in some cases you want both rolled back; but in other cases you don't prefer that. This is where you need to understand Authoritative Restore or a Non-Authoritative Restore (aka: Normal Restore).

The effect of an Authoritative Restore is that all other Domain Controllers will be forced to accept the Active Directory database you just restored as the most current data, the authoritative reference. That means all other Domain Controllers will abandon their locally stored database settings and adopt the one you just restored.

A Normal Restore of Active Directory has the effect of not causing other Domain Controllers, if any, to prioritize the database being restored.

As a practical matter, what happens with the restore of the information in Active Directory is that all of the Update Sequence Number (USN) index values determine priority. A Normal Restore performs the restore without revising the USN values; they remain what they were at the time they were backed up. As such, any data with a higher (newer) value would have priority in comparison in the next replication cycle. An Authoritative Restore represents the restored items with a new, higher USN value, effectively declaring it to be the most current.

With an SBS Server and no other Domain Controllers, the difference is subtle. If you have other Domain Controllers, the main idea is to determine whether you want the restored DC to receive current information from the other Domain Controllers, or the reverse, in which you force all Domain Controllers to accept what you just restored to this one DC.

To perform an Authoritative Restore, you complete the process of restoring the System State and then follow-up with the following commands:

1. From a command prompt, run NTDSUTIL.
2. Type **authoritative restore** and press **ENTER**.
3. Type **restore database**, press **ENTER**, click **OK**, and then click **Yes**.

That step informs the replication services to force an update to the USNs.

Bare Metal Restore and the ASR Disk

Automated System Recovery (ASR) is a feature provided in Windows 2003 Server in which your recovery process from a bare metal condition is expedited. This is similar to the concept of "1 disk recovery" offered by third-party manufacturers of commercial backup and recovery products.

If you have no ASR disk, your normal process is to complete the installation of Windows Server itself, including the reloading of all drivers and configuration steps until the point where you can begin to access the Windows Backup Utility. This requires the full process of building the basic Windows installation before the restore begins.

An ASR disk provides the ability to restore a Windows 2003 or SBS 2003 Server using a normal System State backup, but without the requirement to do a baseline installation of Windows first. You still require all of the same tools and media, but the step is more automated. ASR doesn't restore your data files, but it will put you back into a functional condition faster than without it. ASR is a useful tool, and you can create it with the Windows Backup Utility. To perform a recovery with an ASR disk, here are the steps involved:

Table 14-12
Automatic System Recovery ASR

To recover from a system failure using Automated System Recovery

1. Make sure you have the following available before you begin the recovery procedure:
   - Your previously created Automated System Recovery (ASR) floppy disk.
   - Your previously created backup media.
   - The original operating system installation CD.
   - If you have a mass storage controller and you are aware that the manufacturer has supplied a separate driver file for it (different from driver files available on the Setup CD), obtain the file (on a floppy disk) before you begin this procedure.

2. Insert the original operating system installation CD into your CD drive.
3. Restart your computer. If you are prompted to press a key to start the computer from CD, press the appropriate key.
4. If you have a separate driver file as described in Step 1, use the driver as part of Setup by pressing F6 when prompted.
5. Press F2 when prompted at the beginning of the text-only mode section of Setup. You will be prompted to insert the ASR floppy disk you have previously created.
6. Follow the directions on the screen.
7. If you have a separate driver file as described in Step 1, press F6 (a second time) when prompted after the system reboots.
8. Follow the directions on the screen.

Source: Microsoft Windows Server 2003 Resource Kit

Notes:

Complications with Bare Metal Restore

- Short Filenames (SFNs) are not as much of a problem anymore

A few years back I became a bit notorious in a small circle of online discussions, but also within the Small Business Server developer team. It seemed that I had stumbled across a significant flaw in the assumption of how Bare Metal Restore would work with an SBS Server or, actually, any Windows 9x/NT family computer prior to Windows 2003. I was able to prove the statement that "there is no such thing as bare metal restore to a known good condition using file-by-file restore from backup." That wasn't intended to be an overly bold statement, just a simple one because it was true.

Bare Metal Restores using Windows Backup Utility (aka: NTbackup) contained a flawed concept that was present in third-party products as well because the problem was in the API of Windows. The issue is very simply referred to as Short Filename (SFN) mismatch on restore. The cause of it was rather simple: the backup and restore API didn't provide the means to force files to restore both the Long Filename and the Short Filename that was originally assigned to it (prior to making the backup). This seemingly trivial problem caused a total break of most all SBS applications because the majority of SBS 2000 and earlier Microsoft products use SFN-based file paths in the registry to record services and DCOM references.

The SFN logic for the Windows file system is that the names are generated as the files are created, with incremented ~1, ~2 characters replacing a portion of the filename. However, the problem came from restoring files in alphanumerical sequence, when in fact they had almost certainly been created in a different order than that. Apply that logic of breakdown to the folders reference wherever they are stored and you have a lot of broken file paths. Fortunately, Windows 2003 introduced a fix for the most critical situation, bare metal restore. You should find that Windows Backup Utility will attempt to restore both short and long filenames to their original values in a bare metal restore. That means a bare metal restore can put you back into a previous condition without breaking the file paths recorded in the registry or anywhere else.

- Drive Image Restores

In my opinion, a drive image copy of the system partition is the most valuable recovery tool you can have for a Windows computer, even if it's stale. Some folks can debate whether it's actually more valuable than a System State backup. Having both is ideal.

A Drives Image contains an exact copy of the partitions, all files, and all folders. It is essentially a duplicate of the previous condition of the server or workstation, including the entire information that a System State records. What you know about a Drive Image is that it worked the last time the machine shut down, and that same drive condition probably worked on the following boot for the same reason.

In situations where you need to recover an SBS Server, it's exceedingly valuable to have a drives image sitting there so that you can boot the computer from it to see what happens. If the server starts up normally, you have a good hardware condition. Furthermore, you can use that as a parallel install of the server to inspect the production drive contents. You can even compare the contents of the imaged drive to that of the production drive you are having trouble with.

If you have a System State backup, you can recover a server only after you either perform a repair or a reinstall of Windows. Yet if the server won't boot correctly, you end up doing a repair before you can do the restore, and that takes time. If you had a drive image, you could perform the restore of the System State directly to the imaged drive, and if you also have a full backup of the data, you are going to be finished faster than doing a reinstall or repair first. What's more important to me is the parallel boot means I may well be able to avoid doing the System State restore entirely.

Finally, a Drive Image has the reputation of not being useful if you must change drive controllers or the entire server hardware. That's really not entirely true. A current drive image can be used as the basis of an in-place upgrade to repair difference in the configuration of the installed system. Even if the Drive Image won't boot on different hardware, with a follow-up repair you usually can make it work.

I don't prefer to choose between a Drive Image and a System State backup. Like I said, I'd like both.

Applications: The Skilled Appendages

Within SBS you will find many additional applications that allow you to take a bit more detailed view of your options for backup and restore above and beyond the global backup with the System State and a full file backup. Keep in mind, you should always consider your baseline backup strategy includes the complete backup of the System State, plus all files and folders on all partitions.

I won't be talking about applications too much here because of a simple fact: If you can boot the SBS server back into the GUI, most applications restore and repair with the same techniques as normal with any server; there isn't a special condition. I've tried to devote special attention in other sections on the unusual cases.

The good news is that Exchange Server is handled quite elegantly with the internal SBS version of SBS Backup. You have the option to back up the Exchange Server Information Store routinely with the scheduled nightly backup. Simply include the Information Store in the list of checkboxes you want handled.

SQL Server requires a little more invested effort. You will need to either obtain a third-party backup program that supports an agent to backup the SQL without shutting it down or use the tools in SQL to make a backup to a separate file the full backup can record.

The same is true with Sharepoint Services if you want a backup that is portable to recover on a different machine. Another problem with Sharepoint in the current revision is its inability to perform a single file restore from the database backup. You might find that moving to another machine for the recovery is your only option, and that's where the STSADM tool comes in handy for doing portable backups.

With regard to other applications, such as line of business applications are purchased separate from SBS, you should very carefully discuss with the manufacturer your needs for that product. If the product is SQL-based, address it in the same manner mentioned just above.

Notes:

Tools and Skill Requirements

This section discusses appropriate disaster recovery tools and associated skill requirements.

What Is a Qualified Technician Prepared to Do?

In every business, someone—whether it's an in-house technician, the business owner, or the IT Consultant—must be responsible to plan for resolving a diverse array of minor problems, any of which can initiate a domino effect to disaster. Repairing a single Domain Controller and complex applications server like an SBS is not simple, don't take it lightly. This is not the job for the typical business owner to DIY (Do it yourself). A moderately skilled technician can learn all the skills of disaster recovery with SBS over time, but that could take years, and might take many disaster experiences to become well practiced. I strongly recommend getting help from someone experienced if you lack deep skill and experience yourself.

Let's look at a list of issues in Table 14-13 which could start of as a simple problem, and end up as a disaster before the event is over.

Table 14-13
Scenario Thinking!

Scenario-Based Skill Repair/ Recovery Preparations
Server System
• Boot/System GUI Inaccessible
• Controller/Drive Replacement
• Machine/Replacement
• Domain Corruption/Replacement
• System File/Registry Contamination
Data Files
• Data Deletion
• Data Corruption
• Data Contamination
• Data Theft

Complex Data Risk Scenarios
• RAID Crash
• Exchange Store Corruption
• Offline Folder Synchronization
• Encryption
Second Collision Cascade Issues
• Minimize Downtime for Repair
• Transaction Data Synchronization
• Corruption or Virus Leads to Un-trusted Data
• Scavenging Before a Format

I refer to "Second Collision" Cascade Issues in the last section of Table 14-13. This concept is borrowed from the analysis in automobile safety design. In an auto crash, the first collision occurs when the cars impact one another. Before the car comes to complete rest, everything else not bolted onto the car is likely to be dashed about the interior. The second collision is what happens to the occupants of the car when they impact the car interior themselves. If they aren't restrained by seatbelts or air bags, people get hurt. It's not the impact of the vehicles that hurts the occupants; rather it's when the occupants collide with their own vehicle interior. We generally look for better options in computing. We can protect the cargo with more options that just can't be done with people.

In an SBS-based operation, the second collision might be that as the hard drive crashes, it corrupts your Exchange or the System Registry. This leaves you with not only hardware issues to resolve, but also the cleanup of the "second collision." Replacing the hard drive doesn't repair the data. In fact, restoring your backup doesn't recover the data changes that occurred between the time of the last backup and the disk crash. This recovery may require a cascade of skills such as:

- Diagnosing the drive crash, replacing the drive

- Regaining the ability to boot the system to do a restore of the system and data

- Restoring the data to previous condition, addressing the system level changes based in that rollback

- Examining the damaged drive to see if you can pull off useful data not in the backup set because it occurred later

- Synchronizing the backup data with the post-backup/pre-crash data

- Getting the organization back to useful access as soon as possible, perhaps even as the recovery process is being concluded in parallel

Just yesterday, a friend of mine was looking for help in recovering a crashed SBS server he uses in his home. No surprise to me, there was no System State backup because his server is experimental and for casual computer use, and yet we spent a day recovering it! The problem revealed a failure cascade. The disk crash caused a boot failure and an apparent corruption to the Active Directory. The repair process we pursued for this "casual machine" began to look like a drive replacement, then system-state repair, followed by an Exchange recovery/repair. All this destruction—due to a drive crash—reveals how quickly this becomes a complicated mesh of recovery concepts. Remember, this was considered an unimportant server. No preparations, just reaction to the disaster. A predictable failure cascaded into a wide open disaster event. The drive was simple to replace, but the collision cascade was a nightmare. The hard drive was comparatively cheap compared to our time invested in recovery. What a shame he wasn't better prepared.

In most small business scenarios, a similar "second collision" comes when a trivial technical failure collides into the "business operations", causing the loss of production. Think about it: What happens to all those business-critical deadlines that needed to be met that day? Some of the issues are simple; all that's needed to be done is to take the proposal files off the dead drive. How about a copy from yesterday? Wouldn't it be great to have a plan for accessing the data without actually having the server working? It's not that you can't do it. The question is this: How prepared are you to deal with that situation when it happens?

This leads us to several important questions. What do you expect to happen when you have a disaster recovery situation? What do you expect to be on your list of options, response, and turnaround? That's were we go next!

Disaster Resolution—Your Action Plan

The best recovery plan is the one that happens automatically—you get notified that it was handled for you. This is one of the core concepts in Fault-Tolerance for hardware systems or software security systems. You want to know what almost happened, but was prevented. That's why it's best to start building these elements into your plan in advance, so you can celebrate success with proof that, because you were prepared, disaster was avoided.

When you put a new SBS Server into service, find a way to budget the following component features as part of your Disaster Pro-Active Plan for protection by design:

- Redundant power supply chassis

- UPS standby power unit

- Fault-tolerant RAID storage

- Hot-spare drive Installed

- Daily backup of the entire server (optimistically)

- Offsite Storage of recent and complete recovery backup devices

- Real-time anti-virus management for Exchange and all computers

- Effective security patch management deployment tools

- A reliable data and system backup management application

That list includes all the basic stuff you see consistently recommended by IT Professionals everywhere. The opportunity to recover a server, a domain, or an entire business operations infrastructure starts by having a deployed package designed to be *durable and recoverable*.

From there, when facing any Disaster Recovery scenario, the following concepts should be fresh in your mind immediately after your disaster occurs:

- What is your worst-case fall-back solution?

- What is your most optimistic goal?

- What is the cost of time versus recovery of data and system operations, which helps you determine where the breakpoint is to fall back?

- Were your preparations adequate to deal with the situation in front of you, and do you have the skill to attack the problem with the best possible outcome, or do you need help?

It turns out that SBS does not need to be the worst-case scenario for disaster recovery if you have prepared yourself. Yes, it's a complicated server, and a deep and broad challenge if you don't approach it strategically.

In the worst case, repairing SBS needs to be looked at as if it's a long chain of basic recovery concepts. But the disaster doesn't have to extend beyond the box if you have prepared properly. This is fundamental. Think of this next concept as being what a forest fire battle strategist calls a "fire break." The firefighters determine a buffer they will concede to loss in the fire. That point is the fire break, and they make a strategic stand to hold everything beyond in safety.

It's fundamental, it critical, it's strategic. You simply must establish a fall-back strategy you know you can rely upon. You must decide on and accept a calculated loss, with a guaranteed return of service

Disaster Resolution—Your Toolkit

Most IT Pros use a fairly small selection of highly valuable tools to do 95 percent of their work. Some of these tools are basic items that, in the right hands with the right skills, can work miracles.

10 Baseline Tools for the Technician

1. **An NT Boot Floppy.** It never ceases to amaze me. I carry around an NT Boot Floppy for months without needing it. At some point I will find a rational reason to sacrifice that disk for another purpose because I need a blank floppy, and have none spare with me. Even if it's been a year since I last used the NT Boot Floppy, within a week I will invariably run into a server I need to parallel boot for diagnosis, and I don't have a boot floppy! Do as I say, not as I do, keep a boot floppy with you, and don't use it for other things.

2. **Standard Installation CD Disks for the current OS.** I hate "pre-configured recovery CDs". Too often in the search for "easier recovery methods" I find hardware manufacturers now providing us with "recovery CDs" that are actually automated reinstall disks, not your basic installation resource disk like a retail package of Windows includes. You can't easily do a parallel install, or even certain kinds of repairs, without a regular disk. This is why most IT Pros actually carry extra installation CDs in their bag for the most common Operating Systems they see.

3. **Spare and Removable Drives.** You can never have enough disk space or enough hard drives. Or, for that matter, you can never anticipate when you would like to make an image of a server's partitions before attempting a risky or complex repair. For that reason, I have put up with the hassle of carrying a spare EIDE hard disk in my pack for years.

4. **Server Compatible Drive Imaging Software.** Drive Imaging Software has gone from being an exotic concept to being the single most valuable tool I can get that doesn't have any free alternative from Microsoft already built in. The poor man's drive image method is to build a mirror against another hard drive, perhaps that spare drive mentioned just above. But that still doesn't address the flexibility of being able to manipulate server partitions for size or location, or just making a compressed yet complete backup. The ability to do a backup to disk with Windows NT Backup provides some of this opportunity, but it's missing an extremely important functional difference: exact copy. Being able to restore a partition with the same partition table intact is a blessing in disguise for many situations.

5. **NTFS Drive Inspection utility for parallel access techniques.** Under many conditions, your ability to recover or examine a server is expedited by the ability to boot from media that allows you to examine files on an NTFS partition, without having to first launch the Operating System itself, particularly if it has failed. An alternative is to move the drive(s) to another machine that is functional, though that may present some technical challenges.

6. **Disk Repair Tools to recover files on damaged drives.** I don't use these every day, but some tools I have for recovering files have paid for themselves on every occasion I've needed them. It's worth it to

invest in relatively inexpensive file and disk repair tools that work below the Operating System level, similar to what a data recovery service might use on a damaged drive. I'll mention two such product examples, not so much to endorse them, but to clarify what type of repairs I'm suggesting are valuable to attempt with the right tools. You might look at Steve Gibson's SpinRite, or Ontrack Recovery Systems EasyRecovery product suite.

7. **Patch Management and Diagnosis Tools.** By now we all under-stand the relationship between viruses and critical security patches: If we aren't patched, our machines are waiting to be attacked. For an SBS server, cleaning up or just diagnosing what has happened is too painful to consider when compared to just keeping it patched. Re-gardless, the IT Pro needs to have portable tools to validate the patched condition of the machines in the network, and the SBS in particular, to avoid going to the next step: Disaster Recovery. Microsoft Baseline Security Analyzer is a good start, but you may need some other tools for specialty applications and third-party products.

8. **Access to another computer for forensic work.** Some very simple repairs can be accomplished with nothing more than another machine to work from. I've repaired non-bootable servers on many occasions by simply moving the boot drive to another box to complete a CHKDSK file cleanup on the drive. Put it back in the server, and it boots!

9. **If possible, a previously created drive image of that server.** One of the more valuable situations for Drive Imaging is to prepare a "ready to deploy" backup of a server in a previously proven func-tional condition. There are several advantages to having a good drive image from the same image. For one thing, if you know the drive previously ran the server just fine, therefore the drive is good, the Windows installation on it is good. This is an easy way to diagnose whether you have a hardware problem (bad device) or a corrupted Windows installation. You can boot it just to test the process in ques-tion. Another opportunity is to boot from the imaged drive to inspect or compare contents on the production drive. You can get a lot of work done quickly this way. Of course, the best reason of all is that if you had a major crisis, buy putting the imaged drive into the server, you could immediately perform a restore from backup to get your

server back online. You don't require a repair first or even an install first. You just do the restore immediately onto that drive.

10. **Automatic System Recovery (ASR) Disk for that SBS Server.** I talked about the ASR disk a couple of time earlier in the chapter. I know that you probably got the impression that I don't consider "one disk recovery" to be either a panacea for system recovery, or even my best chance tool to recover a server. However, some of my attitude stated in this chapter is influenced by my goals in the chapter. I wanted to explain skill based options that always are valuable, and I find things like an ASR disk distracting because it's too easy to expect an ASR disk is magic, and you don't need to prepare any other options.

The fact is, an ASR disk with a total recovery backup including System State, Exchange Information Store, and all of your data files is an excellent recovery investment. The ASR disk does provide a faster bare metal recovery of that server than rerunning Windows setup, and the ASR disk will simplify your process. However, ASR disks are only valuable for recovery on the identical system. It is intelligent enough to recreate the original partitions on the original drive volumes, and place everything back where it was using NT Backup. However, the ASR disk doesn't solve your problems if your recovery hardware has changed from the hardware you created the backup originally. The key to your success with an ASR is not the ASR disk, rather it's the full recovery backup with the System State, and everything else you need. That backup is the value item. The ASR disk makes it much easier to use. The backup is valuable without the ASR disk, and in fact, that backup will allow you to recovery to different hardware on shich the ASR disk isn't possible to use.

Therefore, I recommend you create an ASR disk to go along with your System State backups of your server. I also encourage you to understand how to do a bare metal recovery without the ASR disk, just in case you need to know how to do it the "skill based" restore steps yourself.

6 Strategic Backup Considerations for the Company Server

1. **Primary Cartridge Media—Backups and Cycle Management**
   - Tape

- Optical

- DVD-R

- Hard drives

In recent years, the cost of hard drives has dropped when compared to the storage capacity of other media such as tape cartridges. An actual hard disk is now the least expensive device for storing more than 80 Gigabytes of backup media, potentially 160 Gigabytes of source files! The history with tape backup is that the tapes were cheaper, which made up for the great expense of the tape drive itself. However, tape is on the way out unless the makers of the tape drives become more responsive about the excess cost involved. Hard drives are much faster, lower cost, and moving into position to replace tape in the near future.

Optical backup, such as DVD Recorders, are a great option for backing up anything that can fit on a 4.7 gigabyte disk, but two problems remain. These devices still lag behind most every other media in terms of transfer speed, and they aren't yet commonly supported as a direct backup device by all major data backup manufacturers, including Microsoft. Another form of optical media is on the way out as well: The magneto-optical drive, like tape drives, is being pushed out by use of low-cost hard drives.

The main challenge with hard drives is being solved quickly, but the drives are still susceptible to damage in transport when being moved offsite. This probably has more to do with the folks handling the drives not understanding that those drives are not shockproof, despite being as heavy as they are.

The alternative problem with disk drive backup is that with so much capacity provided, too often it's tempting to keep doing multiple backups on the very same drive without ever changing out the drive. That can lead to a loss of all the backups in the case of a virus, fire, or other catastrophic event, which would be protected simply by rotating backups offsite using separate drives.

2. **Remote Storage/Backup Transfers (over the wire via Internet)**

High speed Internet access makes possible another new technical attack on the old problem of protecting data for a small business.

Services are available that host your data backups offsite and allow you to transfer the backup contents routinely via an Internet connection. This can be a great value to supplement your main backup plan. While a significant point in favor of this type of backup is that it can offer protection from catastrophic loss, it is rarely the ideal backup for system recovery purposes. First, there's the dependency on remote connectivity. But a second and greater problem is likely to be the slow transfer rater or the delayed delivery of complete backup media for a total restore. Typically the remote storage method of backup only pull modified data on a routine cycle, having created a baseline backup for a benchmark to get started which could take days to record over the wire by this method.

These services can provide an ideal supplemental recovery and protection service, particularly if they are offered with additional services that meet the business needs. Such services could include having the support provided by an accounting service who normally handles the business records.

3. **Limitations of Drive Imaging**

- Cold Imaging. When we talk about drive imaging, most often it's with respect to performing "cold images." That means the server has been shutdown, then booted in a non-operational manner using an alternate Operating System install or perhaps a DOS, Windows PE, or Linux disk to launch the imaging tools. Cold imaging provides the means to create a fully faithful copy of not only the files on a hard drive, but also the entire organization of the files in the partition. Even the contents of the partition table are brought with it, which file-by-file backups normally don't store. You don't need to completely understand the technology to appreciate the benefits: You gain the option to record or restore a drive partition to its exact previous condition, including if want to search for or repair hidden or deleted file contents.

- Hot Imaging. Hot Imaging is a relatively new concept. It works differently from cold imaging by creating a "point in time" image of a server while it is still in operation at the time of the imaging. This is also known as a "snapshot backup," because it's similar to capturing a photo of something in operation, such as an airplane in flight. However, like a photo of an airplane, there are problems related to restoring a "hot image" for a very simple reason: You normally restore an image to a machine in a cold condition. That means the hot image backup includes the files in the status they appear to be in while in use, but the server must startup from the file condition captures "mid-flight", not in a cold start condition. This can lead to the reverse of an "open file" backup; rather it's an "open file" startup. Not all files and data structures can be properly backed up for a cold start if you capture them with a snapshot while open.

For instance, Exchange Server maintains transaction logs and references when it is running, which it cleans out during shutdown. Even worse is the condition in which Exchange simply is not compatible when attempting to give access to a particular file or record in a database "this instant." Exchange, and SQL Server too, are designed to use "agent-based" backups as well as to support connections via the Virtual Storage Services (VSS) of Shadow Copy to grant access to files in use. The degree to which these applications are compatible to snapshot imaging tools will vary. In some circumstances, it's safer and more reliable to actually stop the services for Exchange before launching the snapshot backup. It's far more likely that the snapshot of the cold databases will be reliable, and that the imaging software can safely access those files, even though Exchange is immediately restarted even as the snapshot is still being recorded.

With VSS-based support, the idea is that an area of memory or disk is used to cache contents of a file condition before an overwrite change is made. That means that the condition of the snapshot is tracked by storing everything about to be changed in a dedicated cache area. It works remarkably well.

4. **Segmented Data Backup/Recovery and Migration Concepts**

SBS server provide the means via NT Backup to capture all of the data and applications on your server. However, it may not capture it in the most convenient way for a segmented recovery of just that application, or for maintenance backup and restore processes.

With any of the major applications indicated below, your segmented restore and recovery process is almost always the same process as it would be for a standalone server that isn't as complex as an SBS server. It's not SBS that is the complication, rather it is the potential that these application may require unusual backup and restore processes for anything other than a global recovery.

• SQL

• Exchange

• SharePoint

• Open File/Dynamic Data

• Custom Applications

Exchange, SQL, SharePoint, and many other core applications, such as Internet Information Services (IIS), also provide some level of "native" backup and restore processes above and beyond what you probably use for your nightly backup. Don't be confused; the "full backup" of an SBS Server using the SBS Backup Wizard, or any comparable third-party application will give you the ability to restore everything.

The option to do a segmented recovery of a particular service that may be more efficient for a particular purpose. For instance, a SharePoint database is a bit more difficult to move to a completely different server and domain than it is to restore it back to the same server, unless you do an application level backup and restore. Therefore, if you intend to move database applications to totally different machines, you might want to investigate how that application offers support to "export" and "import" a native backup, rather than relying upon the more global disaster recovery-based solutions for the entire server contents.

5. **Critical Backup and Restore: The System State**

The Windows System State is probably the most critical operational backup you need to make, because everything else depends upon it. It's exceptionally difficult to recover an SBS Server if you need a System State backup, but don't have one. In the next section I discuss some approaches to addressing even this condition, but I don't want to leave the impression that this is a casual point. Every SBS Server should have a System State backup from some point in time saved, even if it's from day one. It's a shame to have no backup of the system at all, but I've heard of this many times.

The .Windows System State on an SBS Server might be described succinctly as the difference between what that server's system partition looks like at the first installed condition of setup—on day one of installation, before anything of SBS is installed—and what it looked like at the last reboot. I'm not talking about the first completed SBS installation; I mean when it's just a plain Windows Server installation with basically nothing on it. The System State condition is what defines all the Operating System conditions, all the applications installed, and all the user logon profiles, plus all the registry contents, the drivers, and the event logs. Believe it or not, even with all this information, we still haven't got a complete list!

One of the points I try to make about Exchange Server backups is that they are very risky if you don't have a concurrent System State backup as well. I generally do both in all cases I'm doing either. I feel that strongly about it.

In addition to the System State backup, create an Automated System Recovery disk to use in a bare metal restore situation.

6. **Exchange Mailbox Level Protection**

The Exchange Information Store backup you perform with the SBS Backup Wizard using NT Backup provides the means to recovery individual mailbox, but you need to use the Recovery Store option to accomplish it. That process is designed for you to mount a previous version of the same Information Store as a Recovery Store. From there, you can access the mailbox to retrieve contents, or export the mailbox as a whole.

Probably the better answer for most mailbox or individual item recovery in a mailbox is to use the automatic "deleted items retention" feature of Exchange. This allows you to comply undo the deletion of a mailbox, or of items that were stored in the mailbox, provided the user didn't force the item into a permanent deletion condition. Neither of these options will recovery an email that was not kept in the Information Store long enough for a normal backup operation to complete, typically that would be the nightly backup.

Five Concepts for *Complete* Platform Shift or Recovery

In this section, I convey the five concepts for a complete platform shift or recovery.

1. **Bare Metal Restore of Same System and Domain from a Valid Backup**

   Bare metal restore refers to installing the complete configuration onto a bare drive, a drive in exactly as raw condition as you purchase with not data or system files on it. For this scenario, let's assume that the server hardware remains constant, you are restoring everything back onto the same hardware used in creating the backup. As an example, suppose your server becomes severely infected by a virus with uncertain damage to the system, or hard drive failure leads to a replacement with an identical hard drive.

   As a technical matter, it's not essential with bare metal restore that the hardware be the same in all cases; rather this is the baseline condition for my explanation. In a later section, you will see how to deal with the added complication of introducing different hardware. Changing hardware really just implies additional steps taken that extend the complications in the first phase of work.

Notes:

Table 14-14

Bare Metal Restore: Three phases of progress
Establish a Bootable Windows System installation
Return the system configuration of applications and data to a functional condition
Reestablish Active Directory to one of the following circumstances
New, clean, and functional AD database, which unfortunately requires reconfiguration of all the domain member computers and re-creating all users and custom groups to reestablish normal domain operations.
Restore a functional recovery point of the same domain database, which includes all configuration details present at that time, but may not include more recent changes to passwords, newer computers additions, or revised preference settings.
Restore and synchronize the AD database from another DC which has remained operational in the meantime.

To accomplish the most basic aspect of that repair or recovery, you have a choice of several methods to get started, depending upon the resources you have on hand and prepared in advance.

Table 14-15

Bare Metal Restore: Four Technical Approaches to Solve It
Windows Setup and Total Restore – Use Window Setup to build a baseline install, then restore from most recent routine backup media, commonly a tape backup.
Integrated Automatic System Restore – Having prepared in advance, use either Windows ASR or third-party method to restore the full system from most recent backup media using a "configuration reference media" like the ASR disk. This is essentially a streamlined version of the previous approach, automated to avoid some manual steps in setup and driver configuration.
Drive Image and Total Restore – Having prepared in advance, restore a disk image to the server from a previous good condition. Now restore from most recent routine backup media. This is typically faster than a rerun of setup, plus in the case of Windows 2000 and earlier, it avoids SFN restore problems. This is a reliable way to recover or test recovery, the drive image process can be absolutely certain to put you back to a known good condition. The restore process therefore is updating a known

good baseline from a previous condition of the same server.

Recover the server by any method above, then Recover AD from another DC via AD Replication – If an additional Domain Controller is existing in the domain, you can use any of the previous methods of restore, but you can use AD replication to bring the SBS server up to current AD configuration. This isn't a server recovery; this is a domain recovery blended on top of the server recovery.

2. **Storage Subsystem Changes: Recover/Transfer SBS intact onto different Devices**

The need to move a complete Windows installation intact to another hard disk drive is something that comes up frequently, but for a variety of reasons. Typically it's part of a planned upgrade, one found among the list suggested below:

• Replace a drive with a similar type drive, just larger capacity

• Replace a single drive with an array of drives (single to RAID5)

• Introduce or upgrade a hardware array controller subsystem

• Change drive type, such as from EIDE to SCSI or SATA devices

• Add additional drives to expand total disk space, while redistributing partition locations

• Redefine a RAID5 partition by shifting partition sizes and allocations

Unfortunately, for each of those planned conditions, there's also the possibility that you might find yourself confronting the very same "plan" but without planning to do it in advance. This, of course, would be for a disaster recovery in which you are forced—or choose—to attack the recovery while addressing one of those storage subsystem replacements or upgrades at the same time. For instance, this could include some of the following scenarios:

• Hard drive failure

• Catastrophic RAID array collapse

• Drive controller failure

• Failure of motherboard with integrated storage controller

Installing a different storage subsystem is frequently a challenge for unexpected reasons. An implication is that either you are changing to a different boot controller built into your existing motherboard or that one or both boot controllers is "slot based," so that you can add it to the system.

For a transition involving two concurrent drive subsystems install in the same server at once, we have the following concerns:

- Can the old subsystem and the new one coexist in the same motherboard, or will this configuration fail due to conflicts between the two drive controllers?

- Can the current server or enclosure address the power requirements to support a direct transfer of the existing files over to the new subsystem?

- When you transfer the system intact to the new subsystem, will the installed drivers and boot configuration really boot properly due to differences in how the Windows configuration is seen in hardware or OS settings?

- Once you resolve each of those concerns, you return to the issue of the previous point on Bare Metal Restore, specifically how to transfer the system?

3. **Replace SBS Server motherboard**

   Aside from the hardware removal and installation issue, replacing a motherboard is, again, a potential challenge for unexpected reasons. I'm assuming this board is being replaced for performance upgrade or replacement after failure, but the balance of the system is remaining in use. We have the following concerns:

Notes:

Table 14-16

Challenges to Motherboard Replacement
Drive Controllers – The single most frustrating situation is that of the hardware subsystem being incompatible with the new motherboard. Physical hardware constraints that block a card or driver incompatibility with secondary compoents are very frustrating because you usually don't know about it until after you obtain the new motherboard. Using an identical motherboard will bring the most predictable results, but is not an essential requirement. The biggest challenge may be having your boot drive controllers built into one or both motherboards.
Network Adapters – Replacing the motherboard may imply replacing one or both of the Network Adapters (NICs) at that same time the motherboard is substituted.
Video Card – Typically, the video card may also be built in on a server board, but generally the differences should be insignificant enough to prevent a successful transfer.
HAL Variations – A change of motherboard often does involve changing the designated Windows HAL, either because you choose to change from single-CPU to multi-processor board or, in some cases, the reverse. Changing the HAL is really the only unique problem here, and there are a variety of options available, depending upon your situation: If your existing server is operational, it's possible to use Windows GUI in Device Manager to redefine the HAL prior to moving a drive image.   If you are not able to "prepare" for the HAL change, or find out after your transition is underway, you can still use a feature of Windows Setup Repair to correct a HAL. The only exception is if between the two HALs involved, one is ACPI-based and the other is not ACPI compliant. This would be rare with any server built in the past four years.

4. **Move an SBS install intact to different Server hardware**

Changing the entire Server System out is just a matter of combining the motherboard swap with a storage subsystem change techniques. You have all the same issues. The complexity problem is defined mostly by why you are making this change. It might have become necessary as a planned upgrade move, or a disaster recovery process that is planned for response, or as the only option in recovery without preparations.

Microsoft documents the process to restore SBS to different hardware using an approach of installing a baseline Windows Server configuration, then perform a complete restore using Directory Services Restore Mode. A variety of complications can be involved in completing this process, but you can refer to KB 263532 for details.

Here's another method that almost always works. It has some advantages because it doesn't require the time to preinstall a copy of Windows. For experienced technicians, there are ways to improve upon this which I will leave to you to imagine with only the basic logic presented to spark your interest. You can work the process with just a bit of cheating, unless you know the drive controllers are identical in both machines (like the same RAID or SBSI controller model) would allow a direct swap of the drives. This all assumes you can't relocate either driver controller from one of the boxes to the other. The whole process can take anywhere from 30 minutes to 2 hrs. By the way, *don't do this with production drives without a full recovery backup without testing it first.*

For this process, you require:

- Removable drive controller, such as a PCI based EIDE, SATA, or SCSI card

- Hard drive, used to transport your installation from one box to the next, matching the interface controller to be used (item above)

- Drive Imaging software, or the ability to do a complete software or hardware mirror of the original drive System Partition to the transfer drive, then later the transfer drive to the target computer's permanent drive subsystem

- Method to move data files, either on the transfer drive, or by restore from backup, or some other approach.

Notes:

Table 14-17

Shifting SBS Intact to different Server
Preparation on the Previous Server
Install a cheap PCI based drive controller, EIDE or SATA would do, plus a matching drive as a transport device for the move.
Get a drive with enough capacity for the System Partition to go with it. - Install the controller in the original box, attach the drive, just as if you were making this a secondary drive installation permanent as a secondary drive.
Boot the machine in the normal manner, install the drivers for this new controller.
Take note of the NIC configuration for the IPCONFIG /ALL output.
Shutdown
Make a drive image from the original System Partition over to the temp drive.
Disable the production drives and confirm that you can now boot from this new drive and controller. Note, if you have applications or Exchange databases on other partitions, they will error out unless you image them over too.
If the boot works, you are ready to move THIS drive and controller to the new box.
Transfer to the New Server (continued from above)
In the new box, install this transfer drive and controller, boot the machine from it in Directory Services Recovery Mode to prevent slow startup of Active Directory until you can repair the NIC bindings.
If you succeed in booting it, you are almost done. Simply install whatever additional drivers are needed to complete the configuration, and reset the NICs as needed. Note, until you get the NICs configured, you will see a

mess of errors. Don't worry about that, if it's booting, you can fix it. Make sure the binding order is correct for the NICs, with the primary NIC at the top of the list.

Once you repair the NIC binding and IP configuration, and after you have installed the drivers for your permanent drive controller. Following a successful shutdown, now image the drive partitions to the new production drives.

Following a successful startup, you can now image or restore from tape any additional partitions you want to move.

The idea proposed in Table 14-17, as I suggested, usually works. There are reasons you might get stopped cold, and these are actually the same reasons you might be stopped by a hardware upgrade of any kind. Table 14-18 provides some basic ideas about how you would approach resolving some of the most common issues.

Table 14-18

Basic Recovery Transition	Technical Repair or Diagnosis Approach
Note: Each of these can be repaired technically or by running an In-Place Upgrade of the same OS version.	
Unusable hardware configuration, defective or incompatible	If this configuration would fail even to install with Windows setup run from scratch or might not even launch setup, you really have no choice but to choose alternate hardware devices, or a supported device configuration.
Controller or Boot Drive initial order not matched to boot.ini ARC parameters	Adjust CMOS-based device priority order, change SCSI ID order, change EIDE master slave configuration, or revise the Boot.ini

Notes:

Failure to boot from Mirror Drive	Software based drive mirroring of disks and partitions can result in a condition where the file system is completely intact on the partition, but the partition isn't market as "Active" for boot. Another scenario can be where the ARC path in the boot.ini file points to the primary drive in the mirror set, but doesn't poing to the mirror mate unless you recable the mate to the controller and ID assigned to the original disk.
Failure to boot from hardware based RAID Volume	RAID controllers typically maintain a priority table for boot order of attached RAID volumes and devices. In the course of replacing RAID members, or adding new devices, it's quite easy to alter the boot preference to a non-bootable device or volume. The RAID boot table is not maintained by Windows, therefore only the RAID controller interface would reveal that change to you
Boot.ini parameters wrong	Drivers properly configured, but boot.ini doesn't correctly call them, you must determine the boot.ini change needed
Supplemental Boot files missing (SCSI drivers)	Boot in Safe Mode to place the drivers in the %systemroot%\system32\devices
Boot Controller Driver not preinstalled	Either perform a very technical manual install from a parallel boot, or find a way to boot normally on an accessible boot device in order to preinstall these drivers in advance
HAL mismatched	Boot.ini provides the means to call the HAL during startup
USB thumbdrive or disk changes drive order assignments	It's possible to cause a shift in the drive assignments seen by the computer at bootup simply by having a USB thumbdrive or external disk attached. Try booting without the device attached.
Video device unsupported	Boot to Safe Mode with VGA, or add a different video card to the system

Oddly enough, most every one of those conditions could be solved by technical diagnosis or, in the worst case, you could perform an in-place upgrade of SBS (boot from CD1) and after 45 minutes, you probably would find your problem had been resolved. A successful repair is not guaranteed, but you have a pretty good shot. If repair still doesn't make the system work, you might go next to Microsoft Product Support Services for assistance. PSS will likely walk you through steps similar to what this middle section of this chapter covers, repairs performed in the file and registry for corrupted devices, services or applications.

5. **Domain Recovery: Save the AD, kill the server**

This is the final frontier in disaster recovery, unless you already had a functioning Domain Controller in your network before you had a crisis with your SBS Server. To completely understand this scenario, I want you to simply imagine the idea of a totally dead SBS Server. Perhaps the hardware isn't useful, and you also believe that the contents of the hard drives are not to be trusted.

The next sequence of issues contains the really nasty situations. These are the scenarios where you think you would rather not have the system repaired, because you still won't trust it. But you might have no choice. In any case, we start with a review of an array of problems that can cause your system to either fail on boot or boot into failure. I recommend you try these ideas out first in a lab test arrangement. I'm offering these ideas less for daily use, more for the what they reveal about how your System State recovery is changing many things on the system when actually only one specific change would do the trick to get you booting again.

Typically a power supply failure, a power damage, a drive failure, or a drive array collapse leads to a condition that causes great uncertainty: You don't know for sure what you are fighting against and therefore can't positive what to do about it. Let's take a look at the sort of problems you might be facing.

IMPORTANT: I am not suggesting that each of these conditions in Table 14-19 requires either a server reinstallation, or that you have no other options. This next table, and the final resolution of "killing the server, saving the AD" is only an illustration of why you might choose a final exit strategy to totally redo your server. You should always contact Microsoft Product Support Services for advice before attempting these "Last Resort Ideas", or abandoning your server configuration entirely.

Table 14-19

Boot Recovery Ideas (Possible temporary repairs to gain recovery)		
Each of these conditions normally call for a System State restore, but that may require restoring a bootable condition. In all cases, you probably need to move the system drive to another computer to attempt the suggested resolution, or perhaps the Recovery Console can be used. ***WARNING: Some of these concepts are totally unsupported by Microsoft, and could cause more damage than they solve. These are last resort options.***		
Corrupted Item	**Safe Repair**	**Last Resort Idea**
System Registry	Boot to Last Known Good Condition, use Safe Mode, or run Windows Setup Repair	Rename the System.ALT registry, or copy the backup copy of System from Repair folder, but only after all other options are eliminated. Restore System State afterward
User Registry	Delete the User Profile	Logon as a different user, move the entire Documents and Settings\[User] folder to another location so that a clean one is created.
Security Registry	Windows Setup Repair	Rename the Security.SAV registry, or copy the backup copy of Security from Repair folder, but only after all other options are eliminated. Restore System State afterward
Software Registry	Windows Setup Repair	Rename the Software.SAV registry, or copy the backup copy of Software from Repair folder, but only after all other options are eliminated. Restore System State afterward
Damaged or missing System 32 Drivers	Windows Setup Repair	Identify the driver involved, then copy it from a redirected restore of a previous System State condition, or expand it from the installation CD

Corrupted Item	Safe Repair	Last Resort Idea
Pagefile	Delete the pagefile	Delete the pagefile
Event Logs	Rename the Event Logs (requires parallel boot)	Rename the Event Logs (requires parallel boot)
File Structure damage	Parallel install to perform CHKDSK	Run CHKDSK on the drive in a different computer
Physical Disk damage	Not supported, reinstall typically recommended	Repair the disk in a different computer, or copy files off for salvage
Damaged TCP/IP configuration or DNS	Windows Setup Repair	Boot to Safe Mode if possible, otherwise a parallel access to the registry could allow for deleting the TCP/IP information
Corrupted Active Directory	Not supported, reinstall typically recommended	"Hard Recovery" repairs of Active Directory are permanent, lossy, and not a useable or supported configuration to go forward, but you might be able to export objects to simplify recovery and recreation of a new domain

Again, even if you can correct these problems, you might not trust the system anymore. That's when you may move to the next option: saving the Active Directory and going to a clean and trusted installation.

For whatever reason, you decide you want to replace the old server with a new one, and you want a clean installation, but still retain the old Active Directory. In essence, this is a scenario for Swing Migration as described in the next chapter.

We can get down and dirty on this challenge even further. To perform a Swing Migration, you need to have a domain controller running. I have accomplished this in the past by a fairly painful, but functional process:

- Build a temporary server from scratch to become, for a brief time, the host for the old SBS Server's identity.

- Perform a bare metal restore from backup to bring the old SBS version of AD onto this box.

- If the restore has hardware compatibility problems, do an in-place upgrade to make the server just minimally operational only as a Domain Controller.

- Once you have the DC role functioning, you replicate off this server over to another temporary server.

- The second temporary server becomes the TempDC described in the Swing Migration chapter, and you are in position to follow that course to eventually bring the final SBS back online.

As complicated as that sounds, this concept can work. I regret to say that I've actually found myself in situations where it became the most obvious course of recovery for a customer in crisis, a customer not keeping routine backups in order. Being able to pull that off was quite a moment of pride for me, because the customer was expecting me to do just that: pull off the Disaster Recovery of his business.

Summary: Thoughts on Disaster Recovery

Some result can be predicted, and you should know how to do that. In an earlier section, I mentioned during my description of the Normal Boot Process the idea that the successful outcome of a Windows boot sequence is determined when it starts, because the critical boot configuration must already be present. You should consider this as an analogy for a disaster recovery scenario. Your success is most likely if you have ensured a successful recovery before the crisis occurs. You need a backup in order to restore. You need a plan in order to respond swiftly. You need practiced skills in order to work effectively, and confidently.

In this chapter I discussed a wide range of business and technical issues. I have tried to focus upon how a business that is unprepared for a disaster is in no better condition than the IT Pro who is unprepared to support them. Part of the preparations the IT Pro needs to master is how to communicate with the customer what is possible, what is practical, but ultimately what can be realistic for expectations, and preparations. This is part of supporting small businesses professionally.

Furthermore, there is no substitute for core skill familiarity on how an SBS server operates if you intend to maintain, or recover one. I concentrated upon understanding critical boot and core services in this chapter simply because these are the skills that I use to approach disaster preventions as well as resolutions. I fix problems before the server is collapsed.

As I mentioned very early in this chapter, of course you should know how to use NT Backup or some global recovery product, that only makes sense. If you know how to reinstall a server, and if you know how to restore it from NT Backup entirely, you have two valuable skills. In this chapter my goal has been to bring forward information that supplements reinstallation and restore with a better appreciation of prevention, repair, and segmented recovery. I don't agree that recovery always means roll-back if the skill is there to fix the one thing that is holding back routine operations. Your best option could be correcting a service, or a device driver, or the need to repair a single application.

Much of what I included in this chapter is from the foundation of skill and knowledge I gained through experience in disaster recovery preparations and response, yet that also made it possible for me to define the Swing Migration method in the next chapter. I knew the idea could work, because I had performed all of the elements separately as disaster recovery steps in segmented application repairs.

Swing Migration is the ultimate approach to segmented backup and recovery as I have tried to explain it here. Swing Migration is a concept that slices a complex SBS server into pieces to be migrated by different paths and reassembled again. If that concept makes sense to you, or more importantly, if you find Swing Migration to be a valuable skill, then you will find the chapter now concluding runs a parallel course to the next one about to start.

I welcome you to get in touch with me via SBSmigration.com for any feedback you might want to offer, or to review my additional resources on migration and disaster recovery in the future. I will be providing corrections and updates to this chapter at my website, as well as a continuing story on what comes next.

CHAPTER 15
Migration

BY Jeff Middleton (New Orleans, LA)

© Copyright by Jeff Middleton and SBSmigration.com. Reprinted by permission.

Part 1: Why Choose a Swing Migration? Migrating Windows/SBS 2000 Domain (or later) to SBS 2003

Introduction: Migration as a Lifecycle Philosophy

Migration and disaster recovery planning are two of my favorite topics to write about because they have such solid value for both the IT specialist as well as the customer/business owner. We deliberately design and manage networks of computers based upon disaster recovery preparations and scenarios. Yet, I find that migrations are treated as an independent unrelated process from disaster management. I don't understand that logic. To me, migration and disaster recovery are the same topic, or at least they should be looked at as a parallel set of skills and technical craftsmanship. Both should have the goal to retain a customer to a familiar condition, with the opportunity to go forward without frustrations. And, of course, we should assume that means the staff isn't losing anything they need or rely upon.

For many System Administrators, it's baffling to realize a staff member has no idea where the document he wrote is stored. He knows only that it's in the Most Recently Used list. Yet, the reality is that providing continuity to how people work is as important as sustaining continuous operations. Disaster recovery is an investment in being able to rapidly return to a reliable operating condition. Migration is about going toward to a reliable condition, moving forward while filtering out the obsolete, corrupted or distrusted tools we call application software and operating system components. What these two "strategic actions" have in common is that they share a common payload; we are just moving in a different direction with it.

I have long treated every upgrade/migration for each customer as an opportunity to fine-tune both talents and techniques I expect to use in a disaster recovery. It just makes sense. If you are about to make radical changes to your investment in hardware, or software, or network design and user experiences, isn't "radical change" very much what you try to avoid in disaster recovery scenarios? Isn't change so often the preamble to disaster? I assume a migration process is going to run into trouble, and I plan to roll back, even if that means abandoning hours of work. Better yet, I like the idea of making measured progress, even if I run out of time for concluding the full conversion, provided I can pick right up from there later that week. I think of that as an "offline migration" where the pace of the migration isn't determined by the hours in a weekend, or a night, but rather by the time needed to do the job well.

So often I hear from the very same IT people who want to do everything possible to get their servers and networks recovered from a disaster back up and running in an condition identical to last operational mode. Yet they want their upgrade/migrations to be "totally clean." Mind you, I don't argue with wanting a clean migration; I just reject the notion that to get a clean installation means that you give up all the invested effort in what is actually familiar and functional in your network, domain, and the user experience you provide the staff. To me, the highest priority is to provide continuity with direction for growth. I specifically don't want to create work.

Long time IT professionals know full well that, over time, any Windows-based computer can become "cluttered," even burdened by the debris left behind by perpetual changes, updates and yes, the occasional semi-disaster that can happen with unstable applications, viruses, and like causes. Yet, we tend to think of the customer "data" as safe to retain, if not outright mandated to preserve, right? I think it's time to view the data of the organization as not just the documents, but also the structure and management organization of the network. We need to think of invested infrastructure we need to migrate, not just documents.

In a very simple statement, Active Directory is intending to shape how an organization works, who can do what, and how we IT professionals help control and embrace the operations plan that the business management and the IT management have established. To throw away the Active Directory during an upgrade just makes no sense to me, and yet this is what is so often done. Yes, it's a challenge to migrate the directory services, mostly because Microsoft has shown little leadership here for small organizations using Small Business Server. Dumping the domain entirely happens because we can't separate out how to get a cleanly installed server without being forced to have an equally clean Active Directory.

In the SBS world, only recently has Microsoft attempted documentation on how to retain domain management, security, and structure while refreshing only the SBS server itself, or upgrading to a new version. That's the ADMT method for migration with SBS 2003 white paper. And yet, it really doesn't preserve the original configuration very well. In fact, the most familiar things are lost: server name and domain name. That breaks the links across the network, including our precious Most Recently Used document links. While that's a minor thing to some people, it is not minor in the big picture.

If all of my UNC paths are broken, and if my end result isn't essentially identical internally to what a clean install or in-place upgrade would provide, I don't have a great solution there. Maintaining a lifecycle shouldn't mean abandoning so much connectivity. What I have is yet more clutter left behind, and I lose a sense of confidence that things are right. The next odd problem I encounter makes me wonder if said newly discovered maladies were caused by a break in the registry, the paths, the names, the configuration.

Following the release of SBS 2003, like many IT Pros, I was at the frustrating crossroad of being very skeptical of all the upgrade paths Microsoft was presenting as a whitepapers. I felt no enthusiasm for any upgrade option among a clean install of the domain, in-place upgrade, or ADMT as a technical domain transition upgrade. It's my nature to redefine problems where I don't like my choices. The answer I devised is what I now call a Swing Migration, the topic presented here in this chapter, and the flagship of my website at SBSmigration.com.

At the time I first solved the technical project steps, I could see the obvious value to publish a formal reference about SBS migration and disaster recovery based upon core elements I had used for years, to bring three things to my outline:

- Explain how to use Migration and Disaster Recovery as common skills and procedures

- Document a migration/upgrade strategy that illustrates a flexible method to maintain the continuity of a domain, while replacing the single SBS Domain Controller as transparently as possible

- Explain in plain language the steps the migration process, so the reader understands why it works rather than just learning the blind keystroke steps involved

My initial offer to give Microsoft a whitepaper on this concept was cordially welcomed, but became tangled in endless complications blocking its release that way. Yet, the technical merits of my approach were not the issue. What marvelous luck, the timing was also perfect for merging the topic into this book! My original whitepaper draft soon extended to become this chapter. Since that time, I've continued to improve the content, include feedback and experiences of many more IT Pros who have used this approach, and I've expanded the documentation for other Windows platform scenarios, including other SBS versions. This chapter remains a valid documentation set, but I have been able to both streamline the approach and build value to IT Pros with tools to automate many tedious steps, and SBSmigration.com provides technical support to customers who purchase the commercial project guide called a ***Swing It!!*** **Technician Kit**.

I have structured this chapter on migration as follows:

- I first propose what I consider should be the benchmark of an ideal upgrade method, explain how I accomplish that, then compare the alternative options.

- I next review the details of handling everything you are migrating.

- Finally, I devote the remainder of the chapter to outlining the preparations and process to swing your SBS-based domain over to a temporary server, and from there, back again onto a new server. I show how you can construct a new SBS server right back into the very same domain with identical namespace preserved.

Here's one thing about my chapter on migration and the methods I describe that I want to be clear about upfront. I am outlining a process based primarily on well-documented steps Microsoft identifies in knowledge base articles on disaster recovery, not upgrades! My point is I've created an outline for upgrading your domain that Microsoft documents separately by individual components as how you recover those components individually. To suggest the method I suggest is unsupported by Microsoft is a open to debate. The processes I've outlined are the very same ones that Microsoft Product Support Services would walk you through in various circumstances to recover a crashed SBS or a crippled domain. What I did was to shorten those steps into a more tightly defined process that defines an upgrade plan!

I feel very confident that, the more skill and experience you already possess in managing Active Directory, Exchange, and DNS environments, the easier it will be for you to recognize the process I present here is really quite nifty and makes a great deal of sense. If you have worked your entire technical life in SBS and small networks, you may have never looked at multi-DC operations and disaster recovery. For those of you who seek to understand this process, you have a great opportunity here. What I explain in the balance of this chapter will reveal a significant view of what defines the difference between a Domain Controller setup, an Active Directory Domain Services setup, and an Exchange Server setup to run from a Domain Controller. As tightly as this relationship is on an SBS server, you are about to learn how to explode these relationships, then reconstitute them as an identical domain running on a clean server, but with a new version of SBS installed in the process. I can't help but think that some of you will find this rather exciting to explore and try on your own!

Notes:

The Ideal Migration Process

What Makes a Clean SBS Domain and Server Migration Process?

While most people can define what constitutes a clean SBS domain and server migration process, they have trouble making it happen! All kidding aside, we all know what we want:

Clean Install Without Giving Up Everything—It may seem like a contradiction, but it's a very real and basic problem: We want to keep all the stuff we don't want to re-create and to preserve all the familiar things about the operations and user experience, but still get a very clean and reliable installation. This actually isn't such an odd idea, and after all, it's not hard to do if you become familiar with what drives the user and network experience to look and feel the same, while creating a clean Operating System and Applications install.

Transparency—I want the server, the domain, the applications, and the data to be just like they were before, but with the new server and OS version, plus added enhancements. Ideally, I want the server name the same, the workstation-based access and shortcuts all working as before, and all the current configurations for Outlook and printers to work just as before with no specific work at the workstations required.

Standard Deployment Tools—In addition, the new features of the server should deploy just as documented by the SBS Product Guide, with no exceptions encountered along the way in the upgrade that are either undocumented or cause support and configuration problems down the road.

Minimized Customer Downtime—If all that's not enough to ask, then in addition, from the customer's perspective, I'd like it to be possible to minimize, even eliminate the downtime for my domain operations and workstations, and preserve the data and e-mail operations throughout the process, without having to "lock everyone out" for an extended period of time.

IT Staff Not Working Weekends and Holidays—From the IT staff's perspective, the ideal upgrade wouldn't require working the entire weekend, racing against a clock to complete the process by Sunday night, or staying up all night to finish by the next morning, or working under intense pressure to meet whatever deadline has been imposed so they can quickly finish a process that takes down the entire network.

Parallel Operations and Offline Upgrade—Better yet, it would be best if the upgrade can take place parallel to the existing operations, without putting the existing server through a lot of preliminary work or at risk of a configuration problem due to the upgrade itself. Ideally, the upgrade should proceed independently of the production environment and provide the option to fall back at anytime and use the existing production environment for a longer period of time and without impact on the operations in the meantime.

Handle a Same Hardware Clean Install or New Hardware Replacement Option—Sometimes we need new server equipment; sometimes we really want the same hardware but just a clean install. Sometimes it's a combination of both, reusing the drive set and replacing the slow server, or maybe it's somewhat the reverse. Regardless, the options to do what is needed for each case present the real challenge of making a living performing server and domain upgrades. No two are alike, and it's just as important each one done right.

So, is all that possible? The answer is a fairly confident "Yes"! In fact, your biggest decision may be to determine whether your situation requires all the steps to make all that possible, or whether just solving 75% of the problem without fuss is your main goal. For instance, some people won't care about migrating DHCP, WINS, and the printers hosted at the server; others will. Let's look at what you can get from the full summary.

An Expert's Level Overview of the Migration Logic

The most skilled System Administrator is probably now anxious for a quick snapshot of the process described in bare-bones language. In Figure 15-1, I've shown an illustration of the overall process. You can see the starting point of the Existing SBS 2000 in the upper-left corner, with two branched paths that arrive at the Completed SBS 2003 in the upper-right corner. The migration of the domain, including all of the Active Directory-related components, follows the lower loop and proceeds independently until your SBS 2003 server is fully configured. Only at that point will you perform the process of migrating the data, including the Exchange databases, as shown as the shorter upper loop. The original SBS server, with all its data and all the network clients still attached, remains in service the entire time the new server is under construction. Therefore, the transition time—when the production domain is actually taken down—lasts only as long as it takes to complete the data transfer, that top loop in the illustration.

Figure 15-1

Migration overview illustration

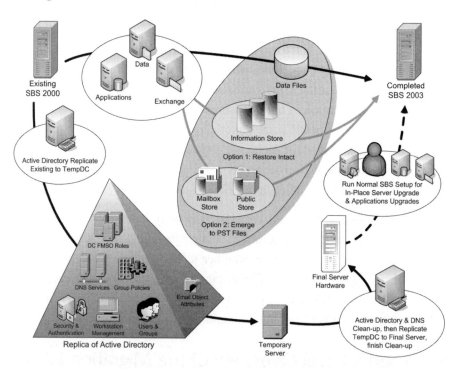

Here's your technical summary below, with just one paragraph of caveat that explains the reason we do an upgrade, introducing a pair of new DCs with one as a temporary DC, not just the one we want at the end in the process. Later in the chapter, the steps are covered again in fuller detail to aid you with planning and to serve as a training education. The actual migration steps are what make up the back half of the chapter.

The following point is not really an SBS restriction, but nonetheless deserves mention because this next point drives the entire migration logic. There's no reliable, documented, and supported way to rename a DC that is also an Exchange Server. So, to build a new server from scratch as Windows 2003-based, add it to an existing domain, yet finish with the same Netbios/AD name for that server as a DC that already exists in the domain, we have to "swing" AD off the previous DC and eliminate the DC we want to replace. We clean up AD and DNS, and once that namespace is clear, we can add a new DC in that place. The steps are as follows:

- [TempDC] Clean install a Windows 2003 Server (using SBS media) as a workgroup server only.

- Manually join it to the existing SBS domain, preparing this server as a Temp DC.

- Install DNS, perform DCpromo, and designate as a Global Catalog Server.

- Replicate DNS and AD, then shut down and disconnect.

- Seize all FSMO roles.

- Purge the AD metabase and DNS of all previous DCs, Exchange, and DNS Server references.

- [NewSBS] Clean install Windows 2003 Server just as before, reuse the original SBS server name and IP. This server will look just like the previous SBS for name, IP, AD, and UNC/URL paths.

- Install DNS, perform DCpromo, designate as Global Catalog Server.

- Replicate DNS and AD.

- Seize all FSMO roles, purge the Temp DC from DNS and AD.

- Finish normal SBS Setup using this server.

- Complete the balance of migration of Exchange, all Data, and shared resources.

- If desired, perform a migration of the intact Exchange Information Store as a direct mount of the previous IS just as if it were an offline restore. Reconnect mailboxes.

- Perform a direct substitution of the new server for the old SBS.

- Deploy Applications as normal for SBS.

There you have it, and if you are familiar with Active Directory and how DNS and Exchange are embedded with it, you have a great start in understanding these steps. If you are accustomed to working with multi-DC, multi-domain, and fault-tolerant DC disaster recovery, you have an advantage in understanding this process is sound.

One point the IT guru might raise about those steps: Why seize DC roles instead of transferring them? It's simple: We are trying to leave the existing domain running. We want the existing production DCs to assume that the new DC disappeared; meanwhile we are convincing the NewDC that the previous domain DCs disappeared even though they are still running our production operations. This way, both operate normally because they each think they remain in charge of managing their own "AD realm." However, once we start modifying the AD, we probably don't want one realm of AD to try to figure out what the other realm of AD has been doing! That would be a mess to sort out.

If you felt very strongly about using transfer rather than seizure of FSMO roles, the solution for you would be to create a drive image of the original SBS server, and then perform DC join and the transfer while running from that image. Once the transfer is complete, you put your original production drives back in operation, and as far as the original SBS is concerned, the new DC membership never even happened. Somebody may now suggest doing it without an image, but instead with an Authoritative Restore to roll back the AD on the production SBS to previous condition before the new DC was joined. To that suggestion…I say you are welcome to pursue whatever you like, but it's a level of complication that doesn't really simplify the migration process as a whole, even if it's technically sound.

What is migrated or documented for transition?

Here's a quick summary bullet list of items we will look at in detail in a later section.

- Active Directory, Group Policies and AD Integrated Objects

- Exchange Server Migration

- Migrating WINS and DNS

- Migrating the DHCP Server

- Website Migration

- Server-Based Shared Printers (some issues here)

- Server-Based Folder Shares

- Server-Based NTFS Permissions, Data Files

- Workstation-Related Issues with Profiles and Offline Folders

What is *not* migrated?

The bullet list of items below is not a summary or all-inclusive list, but it gives you an idea of the types of things you will need to re-create or handle independently. Some of the items listed are either unsupported in SBS 2003, unreliable to transfer, or technically impractical to shift. Another possibility: Independent processes of migration exist, such as SQL Server configurations, which are not SBS-specific and so are not reiterated here for that reason.

- Exchange Server-Specific Application Settings
    - o SMTP Connector Configuration
        - NDR Handling
        - Masquerade domain
        - Trusted IP Relay Partners
    - o Mailbox Store Management
        - Deleted Mailbox Retention Policy
        - Administrative Management Permissions and Delegation

      o POP3 Connector Configuration

- Exchange Organization Recipient Policies

- SQL Server Configuration

- VPN/Dial-up Connections not used in Site Connectors

- ISA Server Rules and Policies

- 3rd Party Applications (Anti-Virus, Backup Programs, Server-based Fax Connectors)

- Unsupported features dropped from SBS (Exchange IM, Modem Sharing)

How often is SBS product restriction the problem here?

If you are technically skilled and also understand the basic rules of SBS product restrictions, then this should all now make sense to you. In particular, from the standpoint of "Why delete all the DCs and Exchange?", the answer is that we have no choice. But you might still be wondering what it is about SBS that causes a complication here. In case the SBS product restrictions are the sole point of confusion for you, here's a quick review of how it drives our process.

- Specifically, SBS can install only on a domain that has no trusted domains; therefore only one Forest and the domain is by definition the root of the forest.

- The SBS as DC must be at the root of the forest, and the SBS by default normally holds all FSMO Roles.

- SBS by default installs to create a new domain from scratch, but the product allows for an in-place upgrade of an existing domain that complies to the product restrictions.

- Though it's widely discussed that SBS cannot be added to an existing domain, that's not entirely the whole picture. SBS doesn't preclude upgrading an existing Windows Domain to an SBS domain, as just mentioned. Therefore, you can simulate this by building your own new

DC in an existing domain, and then nudging it into the baseline condition that will meet all the requirements for an "in-place upgrade of an existing DC."

- A widely incorrect impression is that SBS doesn't allow for additional DCs in the domain. Not true— you can have as many DCs as you want to add until you run out of licenses and CALs! What you can't do is run more than one SBS in the same domain for a period longer than the transition time to shut down one or the other. However, to accomplish that, by definition you must have those machines running with different names, even if they are both apparently SBS servers. That's our trick! We run more than one instance of SBS concurrently, briefly swing off the original SBS, then swing back onto a new DC with the original name reused.

- The majority of the muddy process here is what is done to preserve the original SBS or DC Server name as part of the migration process. That's what forces us to install to a TempDC, then swing back onto our final DC. It's really not an SBS issue, but a complication in the design of AD: You can't rename DCs running Exchange.

Q&A from the Gurus with Even More Ideas

Q: Do I really have to build a DC twice?

A: We do that to solve the problem of re-creating a domain controller with the same name as the existing one. Therefore, the answer here is that you are welcome to build just one new DC in the existing domain and that meets the requirements for adding an SBS to an existing domain. That will be an operational solution. It's certainly an option if you don't care about changing the server name from whatever it was before. Just realize, you will break all references to your original UNC and URL paths to the server regarding batch files, shortcuts, favorites, and recently used links.

I suppose someone will suggest using the new tools Microsoft has discussed about DC renaming, but this is really outside the scope of our process. If it does eventually save some time, I'd welcome not building a DC twice; but since the installation process involved is pretty simple and runs mostly unattended, we don't look at this too closely.

In this scenario, you are accepting a fair amount of change to your network. By continuing with the DC you have just built, which has a different server name than the previous SBS, you will be causing all network shares, shortcuts, printer connections, and perhaps some Group Policies to become voided. The UNC path to places hosted by the old SBS server would have been used in many different places, some rather subtle. About the only circumstance in which this choice is fairly transparent is if you either are replacing all the workstations at the same time as well, or if you had used another server as a file and print server host but later switched it to SBS to reduce the number of servers you operate.

Q: Could I use Virtual PC to do some of this rather than another Server?

A: Yes, this is certainly possible, perhaps even preferable in some situations. A good method would be available if you plan to bring in new SBS server hardware and you want to do everything on that one box. How would you do that?

In advance:

- You would install the baseline of Windows 2003 Server only on the hardware to get started, but would not go past the point of Workgroup Member Server.

- Next, install an instance of VPC hosted from this new Windows 2003 Server.

- With VPC, create an installation of Windows 2003 Server running in a VPC windows.

Note: All of the steps above could be done in advance, particularly if you are a consultant or reseller. You could prepare all of this part in advance, perhaps even use Sysprep to make the primary server installation easy to reuse again.

Ready to migrate:

- From the VPC-based Server instance, you do the TempDC join to the existing domain.

- You complete the process using this virtual server instance to seize all roles and prepare to disconnect from the original SBS production LAN.

- From here, you do the AD cleanup within the VPC environment instance of AD.

- Once you have all AD and DNS preparations complete on the TempDC instance, you follow the process outlined for the final SBS DC-based upon the installed Windows 2003 Server instance you have running in the primary environment on this server.

- Having completed the DCpromo and related transfers of FSMO roles, you are in the position to shut down the VPC instance permanently on this server.

- Complete the final AD cleanup, and you are ready to finish the SBS installation.

As interesting as that process sounds, I don't want to mislead anyone into thinking that it's really any simpler, because it's not. It may offer some portability and repetition of preparation for you, but you have some added constraints.

The biggest constraint to mention is this: You probably should not use SBS media to create either of the Windows 2003 Server baseline installations because SBS product specifically limits how long you can preserve an installation from SBS media without completing the DC promo process. Without bringing the installation past DCpromo, after an initial six-hour grace period, the installation will reboot the computer every 100 minutes. I will discuss in detail later in the documentation, but know that you can't preserve even a virtual image in this condition without accepting this point. As such, you may have problems with completing the required tasks in VPC if the host computer decides to reboot in the middle of your VPC process.

Q: Can I avoid doing an Exmerge with Exchange using LegacyDN, or must I use LegacyDN even if I don't want to?

A: You can avoid Exmerge if you want to go the route of using LegacyDN to solve any namespace issues you might run into. While I discuss in later parts of the documentation, I bring up this topic here to identify that our migration process for all other aspects regarding AD and the server itself really don't require you to use the LegacyDN approach. Rather, LegacyDN is one of the options that has been included in this overall migration discussion.

Q: Is this migration process 100% reliable and safe?

This is an excellent and fair question. This migration process is reliable and consistent if you handle the steps responsibly, and if you ensure that your replication processes are completed at each step. If you chose to use FSMO role transfers rather than seizures, and if you choose to use Exmerge rather than LegacyDN, then you really have nothing exceptional involved here, just a technical process more commonly used in Disaster Recovery scenarios or migration methods used in multi-domain transitions and upgrades.

As with any technical process, you can make an unanticipated mistake that leads to problems, but since most of this process involves working offline, you'll find it fairly safe and reliable overall.

Q: How can I perform this upgrade process with my original SBS server hardware redeployed as the new SBS 2003 server?

A: Performing a swing upgrade back to the original SBS server hardware is achievable, and while it doesn't pose a technical problem, it redefines a few preferences I have in doing migrations. You just need to decide whether you want to maintain the same level of roll-back possible with a separate server for the final target of the upgrade. The short answer is that you lose the open-ended timeline when you take the original SBS offline to install the new platform configuration. Depending upon your skill and resources, you might be able to keep the previous condition on a drive image copy you can go back to.

Three possible approaches come to mind, each one depending upon whether or not you have the additional resources available. The main tool you would want to have, as always, is drive imaging software.

- When you reach the point of doing the second server, you could use a spare hard drive for the construction process. When you finish the upgrade and are satisfied with the complete result, you image that back over to the production drives at a convenient opportunity. This allows you to keep the original SBS production installation intact, though you can't run the SBS server at the same time you are building the new one. Still, this offers the opportunity to do the upgrade progressively over a series of evenings or weekends.

- Another alternative is to image the original production server over to a temporary computer with compatible hardware features. You run the production LAN from this temporary server during the time you take to finish constructing the permanent server. However, this implies a need for a migration of a different type: how to shift a configured server installation to new hardware with minimum effort.

- Of course, there is the obvious approach, but it's not really consistent with the entire spirit of this migration technique: You reformat the production drives and do the upgrade on them. As an alternative, you could make a drive image to a temporary drive to preserve the production system configuration. If needed, you can put the server back online with that drive if the upgrade doesn't go as expected.

If you intend to use the method outlined in this chapter to redeploy on the same server, you must pay attention to a very important point. The specific sequence of the steps in this documentation are presented in an order with the assumption that you want to export some settings and the Exchange Information Store from your current SBS *after* you build the new server. I allowed for this in organizing the steps. Therefore, you will need to do the "export steps" described in the Phase 5 section first before you finish Phase 1—before your current SBS server is actually gone forever!

Q: I have multiple Domain Controllers and I want to continue to run that way after the migration. Can I still use this method?

A: Although a little complicated, this is still manageable. You will reach a transition point in the upgrade where you are ready to substitute the new SBS for the old one. At that time, you must demote your DCs from the "old" domain, then DCpromo them into the "new" domain. This should be transparent in most cases.

A constraint of the SBS product is that all DCs must be online during the SBS setup phase. The method I've described assumes you delete all other DCs from AD before you move to the SBS setup phase. Anything else becomes not only difficult to document for me, but dramatically more complicated to administer. I'm not really comfortable suggesting the seizure of roles rather than transfers if you have additional DCs that could be seeing administrative changes during the process. I also cannot promise the replication process is doing what we think it's doing in the timeframe expected. Therefore, you have two threads of logic you can choose between while still using this method.

1. You could swing the DCs over to the construction domain, but that means you aren't working offline, and your production domain is missing some servers for the duration.

2. Alternatively, you could do the method as described here including the removal of all DCs in the offline AD processing. You would then need to demote the DCs out of the production domain just before you introduce the new SBS, because it's not going to like seeing computers that claim to be DCs from another world, yet have valid SIDs. With the SBS connected, you could immediately DCpromo your additional DCs back to their established role in the "new AD" configuration. As a general rule, this should be fairly safe, but that's not to say this won't cause problems.

Q: I have multiple Exchange Servers. Can I still use this method?

A: The answer is that you can't do the exact method as written here. You will need to bring your existing domain and Exchange profile into a baseline condition of only one Exchange Server, or you will need to swing the Exchange upgrade separately.

The logic I present could work for you, but it's dramatically more complicated. It depends upon whether your additional Exchange Server is also a DC and how the Information Stores are managed across both DCs. I will make some basic statements that I hope will be useful, but I'm not going to get into a detailed discussion on this point here or elsewhere in this chapter.

- If your additional Exchange Server is also a DC, you need to consider what I just described above, and now compound that with Exchange Information Store issues.

- Even if your additional Exchange Server is just a member server, you would be the one who has to figure out whether you prefer to kill the entire Exchange Organization as I described, or to swing all Exchange mailboxes to be preserved on that server and to preserve the Exchange AD information as well. There's a dramatic difference between the alternatives.

- It's not that I can't imagine making this work; rather, I can't imagine Microsoft fielding a support call on your Exchange or AD issues if you go this route in multi-server mailbox realm. Therefore, unless you can condense back down to a single Exchange Server and the "concepts" of an SBS-type configuration, you don't have my encouragement to beat up on Exchange and AD as I've described here. The simplicity of SBS isn't where you are playing anymore, so this upgrade concept isn't really intended for your situation.

Q: I don't think I will be able to upgrade offline (for some reason), so is it okay if I do this Swing Migration on my live domain in real-time, rather than offline as you describe them?

A: I wouldn't want anyone to take disaster recovery techniques, apply them offline, and expect to get it all correct on the first try. These tools are usually used to solve a problem when all other options have been exhausted.

I've outlined an efficient, brute-force migration path with deep tree edits to Active Directory using NTDSutil and ADSIedit that yield a rapid solution to our scenario problem. But there's no "undo" function in the realm in which you are operating. We are rocking the copy of AD very hard with the FSMO shifts, and it's efficient because we don't have a huge domain and lots of DCs to sort out at the same time. Doing this offline isn't just a feature of the process—it's a global safety net as well. You can't lose the production domain if you aren't working on it. In the lingo of golf, I feel comfortable taking a "mulligan," which means starting from scratch a second time and using another offline DC construction process that didn't go right on the first round.

Therefore, I neither offer encouragement nor extend tolerance to people who try things like this in a way they can't do over or undo. To be blunt, if you aren't working offline, you aren't following the documentation steps or the plan I have recommended, which means taking the safe and responsible approach.

The only steps I have outlined for modifying the online AD are to simply update AD to allow a Windows 2003 Server as a DC, and then to create it. At that point, when we detach the new DC, the production domain is really going to be quite safe. The further away from this you drift, the less support there will be to bring you back, including that of Microsoft. Microsoft has documented a way to swing a live domain, and it's called the ADMT Method. That's probably your better option.

Comparing Various Alternatives for SBS 2003 Upgrades

I admit it. I wanted to introduce you to my own migration strategy before we got into the comparison options. My goal was to condition you to expect more from the migration, not less. I don't like the tradeoffs in each of the other methods that will be described, but each has its potential for a valuable place in your options list.

Microsoft has provided documentation for SBS 2003 which provides guidelines for upgrading from previous SBS versions via three methods: Reinstall, In-Place, or using the Active Directory Migration Tool (ADMT). In this Migration Chapter, we review a fourth method, the one that most closely resembles a traditional DC transition within a single domain, what I call a "Swing Migration."

Let's look at an overview of the four main alternatives for upgrading an SBS server machine from SBS 2000 to SBS 2003:

- **Scratch Install (reinstall server/domain from scratch as clean install to new domain)**
  - o Abandons the domain accounts and configurations
  - o Workstation profiles for users are abandoned, require transition at every station
  - o All settings and preferences are re-created from scratch
  - o No specific solution provided for maintaining security preference in data or Exchange configuration, Group Policies, Security Groups, and similar items
  - o Essentially this implies significant work at all workstations, all servers, replacement of any other DCs, in addition to the server

- **In-Place Upgrade (install over the current installation)**
  - o Puts the production server at risk with interactively performed live transfers
  - o Doesn't directly support change of hardware
  - o Requires preliminary clean-up of current server prior to install
  - o Fails to provide a clean server configuration

- **Microsoft ADMT Method**
  - o Requires rename of server, domain, and therefore all namespace paths are broken, including shortcuts, printer connections to the SBS, URLs in the LAN
  - o Extensive interaction required between the production domain and the new SBS under construction, including modifications to the existing SBS configuration
  - o Requires hardware replacement
  - o Requires substantial re-creation of server configuration
  - o Unfamiliar tools required that essentially have no particular value for any other situation other than a migration
  - o Result is not identical to what results in a scratch installation of Active Directory

- **Temporary DC Swing Method**
  - o Resembles familiar tasks in most steps
  - o Flexible regarding hardware changes
  - o Namespace is maintained if preferred
  - o Perhaps as little as one hour of interruption to the production domain
  - o 90% of the process can be completed not only offline, but without the need to work nights and weekends.
  - o Virtually no preparation work performed on the current production SBS
  - o Virtually no changes made to production domain or SBS, and virtually all steps are performed in a controlled, offline construction process with no risk to the production configuration.

Depending upon your situation, coupled with your technical skills and experience, you may find one or more of these options to be frequently preferred and, quite likely, at least one or more of them to be generally unacceptable alternatives. I've performed production upgrades with SBS using all of these methods other than ADMT. Here's a summary opinion on each of these methods:

- **Scratch Install**: I'm told that this term is confusing to some international professionals because the phrase "start over from scratch" apparently is an idiom that often doesn't translate, but I bet the concept does! In English, this refers to a game or race with a starting line scratched in the dirt; another meaning is to begin a game without any points. In the case of an SBS installation, it implies we have nothing preserved, and the installation begins as if no previous server existed. Obviously, the data would be brought forward, but all system files and the domain organization is dumped. Typically, that means starting with a bare drive condition on the server and installing from the CDs without regard to what might have come before. For some people, this seems to make more sense than it usually does for me. I rarely will do this for a customer who already has a domain established, though I would migrate a workgroup or peer-to-peer network this way because this implies creating structure where there previously was none.

I want to make the specific point that reinstalling a domain from scratch by reusing the same "names" for everything, including the server and domain, will not produce an identical replacement of an existing domain. This frequently confuses inexperienced System Administrators. A domain is based not just upon the "text names" used, but also upon a unique numerical sequence that assures every new domain creation is distinct. This is explained as "the SIDS don't match," referring to the Security Identifiers (SIDs) for the domain. In other words, even if you perform literally identical steps to create a domain over and over, you will never convince the workstations that the new Domain Controller is actually the old Domain Controller, because the numerical identifier doesn't match! This one point explains why the other three upgrade methods have merit: They all preserve the SIDs. Basing any upgrade upon an existing Domain Controller or technical Domain Security migration method preserves the interlocking numerical identifiers, and therefore all the related security and management processes that are not name-based are instead SID-based.

- **In-Place Upgrade:** I actually don't mind using In-Place upgrades as a strategy if the current server and domain organization are in good shape. In fact, the process of an In-Place Upgrade is an essential step in the Swing Migration process. For those of us who have done In-Place

Upgrades on an SBS, we all know two things. First, there can be an awful lot of clean-up and preparation to get the server ready to accept the upgrade installation at all without blocks or failures occurring. Second, it's just a fact that not everything goes right, some things require post-setup repairs, and sometimes the overall results are even entirely usable. It just depends how clean and close to "normal" the server is you plan to upgrade on top of. That explains why many people don't trust In-Place Upgrades: They don't trust the existing platform. And there you have reason that the Swing Method uses an In-Place Upgrade on a very clean server after we have flushed the AD and built a clean server from scratch. It's the best of both worlds, far better than what most production SBS servers look like after years in services.

Many people might be surprised to learn that I did a handful of SBS 4.5 to SBS 2000 upgrades with In-Place Upgrades, not clean installs. This method required the least amount of time, which translated to a lower cost to my customers. Of all the methods available, I found the In-Place Upgrade made it easiest for me to envision where the proposed job would start and end, without affecting the client's computers. Like many people at that time, I was not only unfamiliar with Active Directory, I found it intimidating. I performed In-Place Upgrades by working on a drive image of the production server. If the upgrade was clean and successful, I put it into service. If it looked like a mess, I tried a different option. However, it does involve taking the server offline to complete the work.

- **Microsoft ADMT Method:** I find almost nothing attractive about the ADMT method, and very little advantage to it other than in a unique condition where, by direct coincidence, I really *do* want to change all the namespace, yet keep all the security account relationships. This would probably be the case should a company change identity, such as by merging with another organization, but want to keep not only most of the equipment but also the applications. I don't encounter this situation very often.

- **Swing Method:** This is the method explained throughout the balance of the chapter. I didn't invent the concept of a swing upgrade, nor even the individual steps involved. Rather, what I did was to blend together a combination of concepts from Enterprise-type domain fault-tolerance concepts, server replacement concepts, and disaster recovery concepts. The method I've described is based upon the technique of "lifecycle" preservation of the domain and a particular computer identity in it, namely the SBS server. I've identified the technical process of replacing not just a server identity, but the identity established in Active Directory for the individual roles this SBS server holds as a Domain Controller, a DNS Server, and an Exchange Server. These are the three critical identities of the SBS in Active Directory not based entirely upon "namespace"; rather, they involve Globally Unique Identifiers (GUIDs) or SIDs. The swing process I'm describing uses the functionality of Active Directory to preserve AD information even as Domain Controllers are replaced, all by shifting roles to other servers. As that progresses, I clean up behind the steps of removing the old servers so I can reintroduce a new server while reusing the original name. When the cycle of replacement is complete, I reintroduce a clean installation of Exchange in such a way that the namespace is either identical or can be addressed using "namespace" editing tools. What results is the preservation of not only the domain security identifiers, but also the entire namespace I started with. This is the most transparent upgrade possible.

So, there you have a quick opinion on each method. I think most people can feel reasonably familiar with either an In-Place Upgrade or a clean Scratch Install. In the interests of focusing our interests, I won't really be discussing those approaches any further. Instead, I believe the challenge is looking at the technical methods that engage preservation with clean installations as upgrade paths.

To help you with a decision about the two most technical methods, I've put together the following figure to identify the key differences between most sophisticated approaches of the ADMT method Microsoft presents, and the Swing Migration I've outlined in the balance of this chapter.

Comparing Swing Method versus the ADMT Method

The table below shows a comparison of the Swing Method versus the ADMT method, including a view of the flexible options the Swing Method provides.

Table 15-1

Migration Comparisions

Transition Topic	Swing Method	Swing Variation	ADMT/Default Method
SBS server Name / Maintaining UNC Paths	Retained	Revise (Optional)	Rename (Required)
Internal LAN Domain Name	Retained	Rename not Recommended	Rename (Required)
Continuous Operations	Continue to Operate during upgrade for days or even weeks	Extended shutdown period expected during upgrade	
Exchange Data	Forklift intact: Information Store Retained LegacyDN Option: allows namespace		Mailbox transfer breaks Single Instance Storage, modifies both current production server and migration
	Exmerge to PST files then Import (lose compaction of single instance storage)		
Outlook Rules	Retained within Store	Outlook Export (Required)	
Alternate E-Mail Addresses	Retained within Store	Re-create or scripted transfer	
Public Folder Security/Rules	Retained within Store	Export to file loses these settings	
Shift to New Server Hardware	Allows New or Same Hardware (optional)		Different Hardware (Required)
Maintain LAN IP Subnet	Flexible		Not very Flexible
Domain Workstation User Profiles	Retained—No change	Roam plus re-create settings	ADMT Account Migration

The Swing Method provides an extremely transparent result, because most everything you end up with on the finished server related to Active Directory, Exchange, or DNS is virtually the exact original information simply replicated or shifted over. If you want to revise things like the server or the Exchange Organization, you can do that. Clearly, the majority of the information is the same as before, so this ensures the most predictable results when the server goes back online. Furthermore, most all of the preparation work and installation process can be thoroughly tested and evaluated over a flexible amount of time, without the deadline crunch of a weekend or nighttime effort. The upgrade goes into service only when you are ready to do that, and you can know you have a confident upgrade condition.

Choosing a Method and Migration Authority: Microsoft or Jeff?

Okay, I laughed when I typed that, so feel free to join me. Throughout the migration steps I've provided, I've included references to authoritative Microsoft Knowledgebase articles and white papers I found helpful, so this migration approach isn't entirely stacked on my word alone. I've tried to distill the information needed to perform the migration I suggest, so you wouldn't have to search any other references. While my goal was to provide a complete and uniform instruction set, I still felt it valuable cite authoritative references to support those instructions.

I realize many people will reject my method in favor of the ADMT method not on technical merit, but simply because Microsoft published its paper as a supported method and has been somewhat publicly mute on the approach I've outlined. I do not imply that Microsoft does or does not endorse the process I have outlined, simply because no matter how much interaction I have with Microsoft, I'm not granted the option to make or speak for their policy.

However, I did seek and receive collaborative discussions from Microsoft experts while I was preparing this documentation. I want to express my gratitude for their technical consultations. I feel confident that no greater technical complications are introduced by using the Swing Method than are introduced in using ADMT. In fact, the ADMT method probably wouldn't be the preferred choice of the SBS Development team, because it is somewhat disruptive to the namespace. To use a concrete analogy, you can compare the two methods to choosing between home renovation and new house construction preceded by a tear-down of the existing structure: two different approaches, both with technical issues respective to the process, both with issues in the final outcome. You choose which suits your situation best.

The Swing Method is conceptually sound and has already been used by a number of the SBS MVPs in production scenarios with actual customer sites. I'd be willing to wager that the next released version of SBS will include documentation of a method similar to what I describe here—or at least be based upon the same underlying principles. Again, I say this not to speak for Microsoft's plans, but to share my observation that Microsoft would rather see SBS upgrades emulate the flexibility and reliability of Enterprise strategies and upgrade techniques. Essentially, that is what I've outlined here.

Simply put:

- We are reserving an offline DC (for disaster recovery purposes) while migrating the online DC and Active Directory—one of the goals of multi-master DCs in migrations.

- We are providing a reinstallation of an entire Exchange Organization back into the original domain—a supported repair and recovery process.

- We are protecting ourselves with roll-back options as well as maintaining operations in parallel—all sensible migration processes.

These three concepts are based upon the best practices in Enterprise upgrade management. The only thing we are doing differently the reversing of "roles" of the offline DC and the online DC. Enterprise has no choice but to migrate the entire AD in a live upgrade while holding a single DC offline. With SBS, since we typically have only a single DC, we instead keep the production SBS online and upgrade the offline "clone," because we can substitute a single DC into a LAN the scale of most SBS networks.

Now it's time to explore the details of how this is all possible!

Detailed Overview: The Swing Migration Plan Technical Logic

The outline summary presented earlier in this chapter may have been just a bit shy on explaining the detailed steps in a Swing Migration. Let's look at this in more detail now, expanding the description and issues involved.

Migrating an SBS server and domain should be viewed as having four basic migration challenges:

1. Transferring Active Directory and related Integrated DNS Configurations
2. Retaining behavior of Exchange, Outlook operations, mailbox store integrity and security
3. Retain continuity of workstation-based configuration, network namespace paths, user experience
4. Transparency of timeline and continuity in settings when shifting data files, e-mail operations, shared folder and printer settings, security templates

All other considerations relate back to these four concepts. Also, the importance of having a timeline for the process may not stand out in there, but it is a huge factor.

Traditional SBS Upgrade: Shut Down for a Weekend

It's not uncommon for IT professionals to plan a three- to four-day SBS migration plan, possibly holding the server or even the entire network shutdown the whole time. This is strategy is used to "freeze" the entire operation, then bring it back up after the core transition process has been addressed for the migration.

Freezing an entire company's operations, working against a deadline over a weekend or holiday, and knowing that you have a very complex process all contribute to making SBS migrations extremely stressful. And, based on my experience, it doesn't really get less stressful with experience. The only means by which you can significantly reduce your stress level is by either gaining control over a reasonable timeline or implementing a fall-back plan to abort an upgrade that's not going well. That means you might spend as much as one-third of your time during migration either performing disaster recovery preparations or transferring configurations that provide for a roll-back option.

Swing Upgrade: AD Snapshot…Offline Build…Server Swap Deploy

The migration plan outlined in this chapter accomplishes something quite remarkable: the timeline becomes open-ended, the unique disaster recovery preparations are unnecessary, yet the process is relatively low-risk. Perhaps the best aspect of this method is that it retains as much continuity as an in-place install, but has the advantages of providing a clean server installation. We retain the maximum possible consistency from both an administration view as well as the user experience.

The list of four challenges above are all addressed quite elegantly, because we retain the entire AD and we have the potential to bring the Exchange Information Store over intact. Those two points provide the maximum continuity possible. There's one more desirable advantage: The production domain remains viable and operational while the migration is proceeding, and that's what makes the timeline open-ended. You can start when you want, work for a period of hours, days, or weeks, then transition when convenient. It's possible to make this transition with no weekend work at all, or at the most only a trivial consideration of downtime. You don't need to devote substantial amounts of time to disaster recovery preparations of the production server because you barely modify or manipulate it. This means the maximum effort is put toward migration, not recovery preparations.

This migration method takes the approach of temporarily adding a domain controller to the existing domain as a method to capture the entire Active Directory contents as well as the related AD Integrated DNS configuration. Exchange-related Active Directory information is captured in that process as well. With this done, we begin a process that is best-described as simulating a disaster recovery scenario: What if the original SBS server died, and we needed to rebuild the domain from only a surviving DC?

The trick of the process is that the original SBS isn't dead, it's completely functional and running the active production operations. That's one of the great benefits of this method: We can keep using the production LAN, even while constructing the new SBS server "offline." Here's how that works.

Swing Out: Shifting Active Directory Off the SBS and Across Domain Controllers

We are able to add another new DC with a fairly simple process, using the SBS 2003 media, but bypassing the automated installation setup process. The SBS media doesn't prevent these steps, nor is it a license violation to use the media to manually create an SBS-based Domain Controller, or to build a replacement SBS for an existing one. We accomplish this by using SBS 2003 media, but stopping the automatic installation process at the first point the server becomes only a standalone workgroup member server. From there, the manual steps of joining the existing domain, performing adprep, and doing the DCpromo manually allows us to create a new Windows 2003 DC in the existing domain. Once the server and domain have been synchronized by replication, we have our candidate for the next step.

We simulate the loss of the original SBS by detaching the DC we just created from the production LAN, yet running it offline as if the whole domain was now under its control alone, because all other DCs are permanently out of contact. We go through the Microsoft-documented process of removing all "permanently offline DCs" that remain in the directory. In this condition, the new DC is taken through a process by which we force the steps to remove all DCs and the Exchange directory. Unfortunately, like computers that are DCs, Exchange Servers have a unique designation in AD, so we can't introduce a new computer as an Exchange Server if the name is already in use. That means we purge the Exchange Server Organization, because with there being only one Exchange Server and its removal, no Organization remains behind.

When we later reintroduce a new SBS server to the same Active Directory domain using the same name as before, all of this technical information is reconstructed cleanly, but based upon the same AD user and computer accounts, including the SIDs. That's what produces a clean AD without losing the original accounts and related information. We only purge the information the normal SBS will re-create automatically.

Swing Back: Making room for the SBS to Return in AD

By clearing out AD reference to the old SBS server, the Exchange Organization, and all related history of other DCs, we arrive at a clean existing domain hosted by this one temporary DC. We can now add another new DC, one named the same as our original SBS server, having the same IP as the predecessor. We accomplish this by again building a new DC using SBS 2003 media and following the same steps as before. Once this permanent SBS replacement is a DC, we can purge the temporary DC out of the directory. With this condition, we again have exactly what the SBS automated setup would have created: an SBS media-based DC, which is the root of the domain, with no other DCs to contact and no pre-existing Exchange information. In doing the process twice, the steps become quite familiar.

We complete the automated SBS setup and all the configuration is completed for us. The only thing that remains is to migrate our previous Exchange data, data files, and shared resource references, the final steps of any migration or replacement.

What makes this process distinctively different is that we are able to retain our domain SAM—and therefore all the user and computer account SIDs—so we can do all this work offline. We end up with an SBS using the existing domain, and we retain the name of the original SBS server, so we can preserve the UNC path for shared resources.

Along the way, we have enjoyed the opportunity to pull over additional settings and information besides the AD. We can transfer the DNS, WINS, and DHCP information quite easily. Moving the shared folder and printer definitions is a bit more complicated, but I can share some tricks to getting that done.

Managing the Transition Timeline

We can see that building the server in the swing process above quite possibly didn't even require a reboot of the production SBS. We avoided all that if the current Service Packs were previously installed. Admittedly, zero reboots isn't really the goal, and we might find it convenient to do reboots for force replication, but certainly production wouldn't be impacted. This could be done conveniently.

The only decision remaining is how to handle the Exchange mailbox contents and related configuration. We will also need to move the data over. But what this reveals is quite significant. The swap time to change out the servers becomes mostly a function of how fast you can transfer the data and Exchange Information Stores to the new server. From there, since the machine looks identical to the previous one, you are very close to going back online immediately. This means that you are looking for a way to get a predictable shift of the Exchange and a fast transfer of data.

Restocking Exchange—Issues for Completing the Final Configuration

If we can reintroduce the Exchange Information Store by direct restore as an offline backup, we can even retain all the Exchange Rules and references intact. Overall, this makes the most transparent upgrade and migration process because very little is changed. Not only that, but it would mean the Exchange could stay online the entire time other than for the file transfer from server to server.

After completion of the normal SBS Setup, you will have a new Exchange Store with empty mailboxes. You can either use Exmerge to restock (import) that mailbox with the contents exported from the previous Information Store, or perform a more technical but efficient migration of pushing the entire Information Store into the new Server, just like an offline restore. Mounting the original Information Store has the benefit of bringing over all of the interrelated security, mailbox rules, and secondary mailboxes intact. It's a very tempting answer to avoid detailed administrative reconstruction with Exmerge. Let's look at what the options are:

- **Exmerge**—Exmerge has the benefit of being the lowest common denominator: It always works. The problem with Exmerge is that it is not only time-consuming, but you lose the single instance storage of the Information Store. You lose the configuration of shared mailboxes and public folders, as well as the Inbox rules and preferences the users stored previously in the Information Store. Later versions of Exmerge have improved upon the amount of information that can be exported with Exmerge, but in general, Exmerge isn't favored by System Administrators who want the most transparent and simple upgrade process possible. It is a preferred process for cleaning up stale content to purge from the store.

- **Forklift an Identically Named Organization and Server**—An alternate method is to migrate the Information Stores directly by mounting the old Information Store just like an offline backup would be done. This is sometimes referred to a "forklift" migration, because you literally dismount the stores from one server, then mount them on the new server just like a restore from backup. It's a process you may or may not find Microsoft willing to call "a supported upgrade path." Clearly, a forklift upgrade would be a concern in a complex domain organization or with many Exchange Servers and a long history of many different management servers contributing to the process. A multi-server Exchange environment is far more complex. However, in an SBS upgrade, it seems to be a less intimidating thought that an Exchange Store running on one server should have problems running on another server with the same name, in the same domain, right? Doesn't that sound a lot like a disaster recovery plan to you?

- **LegacyDN to Solve Namespace Variations**—Yet another variation on process is to use the same forklift method, but also to include use of LegacyDN to correct for a change in namespace that might be required. LegacyDN is a Microsoft Product Support Services tool originally designed to solve disaster recovery conditions. Specifically, it provides the means to mount an Exchange Information Store on a computer, even a domain different from the original home from which it came. The primary reason to do this is for repair or maintenance on a database without shutting down the original server, or for temporarily bringing an alternate server online while the original is being maintained or upgraded.

As scary as that might sound, take this perspective on the idea: If you are able to mount the Exchange Information Stores intact on the new server with LegacyDN, try it and see if you have issues; you can always Exmerge the database to go to the "supported" method if that becomes needed for some reason. You are simply putting the option at the back end, trying the much simpler process first. LegacyDN first, and if needed, Exmerge later.

The Exmerge utility as well as LegacyDN are available with Exchange Resource Kits, and also on Exchange 2000 Service Pack 2 or later SP distribution media. The details of the Exmerge process are pretty self-contained in the Exmerge documentation—no special issues to concern you surrounding SBS.

That's the complete storyline. Now we move to the actors and scenery.

Detailed Overview: Handling Unique Migration Tasks

Performing Familiar Windows Setup Tasks

The outline of the swing migration involves mostly familiar tasks, with a couple of technical steps in the middle. Most System Administrators are familiar with installing Windows Server from scratch to a new machine, as well as reloading a computer with previously used settings. You make a list of what you need to reenter during setup, and the process isn't too complicated. Frequently these same IT professionals or system managers are familiar to some degree with performing DCpromos, installing DNS, and moving data to another server. When you come down to it, the majority of the steps here are familiar before you start the first time.

In an entire day of perhaps six hours' work, there's probably less than 45 minutes' worth of unfamiliar tasks. Since you go through the same steps twice, the second pass is easier than the first, and next time you use this method…you will have already performed every step twice! This method of migration is easy to learn the first time through and becomes familiar very quickly.

The balance of whatever time it takes you to customize the server, add third-party applications, or migrate the data with both depends upon your situation and your preference on how to handle it. What this migration method does is take care of the hard part with an open timeline and reasonable steps.

Integrated DNS and Active Directory Editing Tasks

The revisions to Active Directory and DNS required in this migration process are listed below. The items to be performed manually, but are in fact part of any method of SBS 2003 installation and migration, are shown in italics:

- **AD Additions (Updates)**
  - o *Schema extended for Windows 2003 Domain Controllers*
  - o *Schema extended for Exchange 2003 Domain Controllers*
  - o *Related modification consistent with operations of Windows 2003 and Exchange 2003*
  - o Registration of the new Domain Controllers (final and migration-related)
  - o Registration of the new DNS Servers (final and migration-related)
- **Edits and Deletions to Active Directory During Migration (Housekeeping)**
  - o Original SBS server roles as DC, DNS, DHCP and Computer Deleted
  - o Temporary DC Roles as DC, DNS, and Computer object-deleted
  - o NTFRS (DC replication objects) and Site location server-specific containers are removed as DCs are removed
  - o Mailbox to User Mapping may require deletions and reconnection
  - o LegacyDN value for Exchange Objects may require revision
- **DNS Configuration Edits (Housekeeping)**
  - o Original SBS server DNS entries are flushed, including DC role record

o *All DC, Exchange, and Web Service records are re-created automatically*

As you can see in the outline above, we manually perform several steps normally automated by the SBS Integrated Setup process, but which prevent us from joining a new DC into an existing domain. From there, we do the steps necessary to take control of the existing domain, and then flush out the old AD and Exchange records. That enables us to meet the requirements to return to the SBS Integrated Setup again.

Exchange Information Store Migration Tasks

We can handle the Exchange migration task with one of three methods:

- **Forklift** is the direct transfer of Information Store to new server as an Offline Restore

- **LegacyDN** method is the same as Forklift, but also extends options for addressing changes in server, domain, or organization namespace.

- **Exmerge** is a universally compatible method of exporting all mailboxes to .PST files, then importing them back to the new server. However, this preserves mailstore contents, but not much more. Since Exmerge doesn't handle the Public Store, we would need to use an Outlook client to export the Public Store to a .PST file, then reverse that as an "import" with the restore process.

Since LegacyDN is just a variation on the Forklift process, we next look at a comparison of the two concepts, Exmerge vs. Offline Restore (Forklift).

➤ **Exmerge Is Not a Completely Graceful Strategy**

If forklifting the Information Store as an Offline Restore looks to scary, look at the disruption and administrative frustrations of using Exmerge as documented by Microsoft KB 327928:

When you use the ExMerge upgrade method, you must:

- Export all your users' mailbox data to .pst files by using the ExMerge utility and then export Public Folder data to .pst files on a Microsoft Outlook (MAPI) client.
- For each profile at each workstation, export Outlook Inbox Rules as well as export Offline Storage files (OSTs), if present
- Document all mailbox "alternate recipient" and "send as" permissions which were established administratively in the past for each mail enabled user
- Document all Public Folder security permissions
- Import your mailbox and public folder data from .pst files.

Some disadvantages to the ExMerge method include:
- You have to create new mailboxes for all users before the import.
- You have to re-create all permissions on Public Folders.
- You cannot reply to old e-mail messages from users on this server.
- You have to reconfigure all connectors.
- You have to re-create distribution lists.
- You have to re-create Custom Recipients.
- Server-side Outlook Rules are not retained
- You have to create new Exchange Client Profiles at each user desktop. If the server name does not change, new Client Profiles may not be required.
- Any users with Offline Storage files (.OSTs) have to export them to .pst files before they connect to the new server.

As you can see, the Exmerge process isn't trivial or transparent, and it also takes quite a while. A critical part of the time-consuming process is the disruption of operations—you must have the Exchange shutdown for an expended period of time to do both the export and then the import sequence. This can take hours, even an entire day.

Besides, at that point you won't be done yet via the Exmerge strategy. You still need to visit every workstation to identify and export all the Outlook Inbox Rules in each user profile, because some of these are "server side" rules that will be lost with the store replacement. And as I bet you've already guessed, this also means you get to do the reverse sequence to import them all back again!

> ### Unsupported Methods? Offline Restore and LegacyDN

In the scope of our concerns, Exchange Server 2000 provides a fairly similar Information Store condition for what we need to run in Exchange Server 2003. In many cases, the previous store can be treated as "transportable," potentially mounted in the new server just like an Offline Restore would be handled. Essentially, if the store is in good condition on the original server, it typically mounts on the replacement server if the namespace matches. Since we go to specific effort to match the namespace, this has a high success rate for "normal" scenarios.

Microsoft realizes "offline restore" of an Information Store to a different server is a valuable option. It's also a concept being considered as a feature request, although not currently "supported" in production. Yet, this is how maintenance and disaster recovery are frequently handled! Microsoft Product Support Services created a tool called LegacyDN, which adjusts the configuration of the Information Store to allow mounting databases to completely different servers or within different organizations. The Microsoft view on an "unsupported method" for production use is simple: If it works, Microsoft is happy for your success. If it doesn't work, Microsoft is not eager to either ensure that it's supposed to work or proactively support troubleshooting the process at no cost to you.

The benefits to us going this route in an SBS migration are huge. It makes it possible to "snap" the Exchange Store from one server to the next, producing the most transparent and immediate migration possible. In fact, the only issues that I have observed as a consistent nuisance in doing this is associated with the Public Folders. Upon investigation, it appears that some of the security attributes in Public Folders are just not that stable when many kinds of changes are performed. Something as simple as a reference to an obsolete (deleted) Security Account entry on a Public Folder causes a break in function. Such issues are not so much migration problems as stability problems in general with Public Folders. Unfortunately, we really have no better options.

The main argument is that a forklift move wasn't planned for in-production design, even if it's quite frequently available and successful. On the other hand, Microsoft focuses a lot of consideration on multi-server Exchange Organizations, as well as far more complex conditions and larger scale than occurs in the SBS world. The LegacyDN utility is designed to work only in a recovery lab, under the condition that only a single Domain Controller is online, and yet that's fine for an SBS scenario. We don't have a great alternative to look at for restoring Exchange Information Stores between different version servers. When you look at all the considerations, everything is a compromise.

When all the considerations are reviewed, I've consistently arrived at the conclusion that I'd rather try this if I can, because it saves all sorts of detailed information, and organizational behavior. Snapping the Information Store onto the existing AD produces an amazing savings in time, while minimizing disruption in the process.

Notes:

Detailed Overview: Migration Logic Handles Most Critical Objects

Figure 15-2
SBS server Roles Illustration

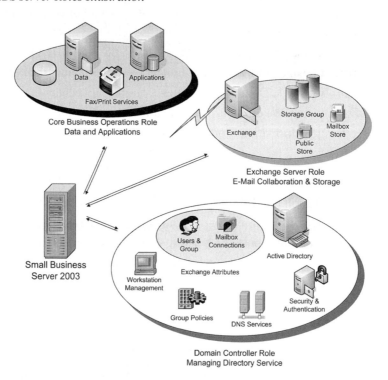

As you can see in the illustration above, I'm trying to present the four roles of an SBS server in such a way to show how we deal with "segmenting" SBS during the migration process. From a migration viewpoint, SBS has these four roles that travel as three "platform" considerations. We are able to segment the migration process to treat each of these platforms distinctly as a migration task managed by a preferred technique for that role.

1. **Domain Controller Role**

    The management of Active Directory presents the challenge best handled by "replicating the AD" across a series of Domain Controllers. Effectively, we "bridge" between the original SBS server over to the new one using a temporary DC as the transport mechanism.

2. **Exchange Server Role**

If we are starting with only one Exchange Server in our domain, and we preserve the domain itself, we gain an option to re-create the Exchange Organization without much effort. We let SBS Setup re-create the Exchange Organization and server installation. Handling the database portion of Exchange becomes a choice of methods, but it's only dealing with the data, not the more complicated process of server installation. Saving the Exchange database move for the transition day means we have an open-ended timeline, because this one application drives the business as a time-critical process more than any other application provided with SBS.

3. **Core Business Role (Data and Applications Server)**

The two server role considerations as Data and Application Server reveal a similar challenge for both roles. We need to keep this information available for the business to use before and after the migration, minimizing the downtime. Therefore, we leave this running on the old server and snap it over as our transition day task. We can allow SBS to install the SBS Applications for us, so there's minimal effort required there.

Active Directory, Group Policies, and AD Integrated Objects

Our migration process brings across all User and Computer accounts by replication between DCs, which means there is no separate configuration. In fact, in a greater detail, here is a list of the significant objects that are brought across, which might be of concern to you as System Administrator.

- User Accounts

- Security Groups

- Distribution Lists

- Mailbox Preferences and Address Lists

- Computers

- Group Policies

ault Domain and Default Domain Controller Policy

- RRAS Connection Agreements

- Sites and Subnet Definitions

In summary, the migration of the Active Directory process is complete in preserving the entire Active Directory contents.

Exchange Server Object Migration

If you go with Exmerge, you will keep your mailbox and public store contents and not much more of the existing server-side configuration or functionality. The details were covered in the task discussion above.

Otherwise, of concern in migration Exchange are the following items, which are possible to migrate intact if you use the method of directly mounting the existing Information Stores to your new server as you would the restore of an Offline Backup:

- Information Store Contents, Rules, and Security

  o Private Mailbox Store (user mailboxes)
  o Public Folder Store
  o Inbox Rules, Security Permissions
  o Public Folder Rules and Security Permissions
  o Single Instance Storage

Each of the following are not preserved and must be manually reconfigured on the new server, or else we rely upon the SBS To-Do List configuration options for "as new" configuration settings.

- Connectors, Routing Agreements, Recipient Policies

  o Authentication, Access Security, Relay Configuration
  o Relay Partners

isit www.smbnation.com for additional SMB and SBS book, newsletter and conference resources.

o Default Recipient Policies (SMTP Address defaults)

o POP3 Connector, Third-Party Fax Connectors

Migrating WINS and DNS Service Configurations

Our migration process provides the means for transferring both the DNS and WINS contents, with replication between partners as we do the DC migration itself. There are no additional steps required to be outlined separately.

Migrating the DHCP Server

In many cases, it isn't necessary to migrate the DHCP Server database, though it might be handy to move the configuration settings. Our migration technique provides the opportunity to do the settings move quite easily, and the database move only requires a Reskit tools.

Website Migration

Any custom Websites hosted by the original production SBS server should be migrated separately using your choice of tools. A default installation of SBS server 2000 has no such sites that need to be transferred; the needs here are customer-specific. One possible approach is to save a copy of the Webroot contents and transfer it to the new server. However, due to security considerations, you may want to consider a location other than the Webroot for republishing it on the new server.

Server-Based Shared Printers

As with the shared folder descriptions above, the automatic relocation of printers from one server to another is not handled transparently for us in this migration process. In a measured comparison, the transfer of the printers is actually even more complicated than the folders are for automated relocation.

The main issue here is that printer definitions include not only the Shared Printer references names and security in the registry, but also the underlying drivers and ports for that machine. Creating ports and re-creating shared names is not difficult to automate if these are all standard ports and the share names are "simple" to generate. But the issues with trying to automate the transfer of drivers and descriptive names are quite a challenge to make foolproof in automation. Unfortunately, this means you may also have some interaction with individual workstations in order to remap the printers, depending upon your manner of management of the printers in your domain.

Some of the complexity can come from whether you allow users to have sufficient privileges to add and remove hardware, ports, and drivers, but even with those rights provided, you may still have confusions. If the new printer is not added in with an identical share name, description, and driver designation, you may end up with multiple instances of the "extinct" printer resource plus the new printer resource.

Re-creating printers is sometimes tedious, but there's really no simple way to transfer printers from one Operating System version to another without making assumptions that might not work in all cases. It's probably best handled as a manual process, or a semi-automated process of your choosing.

Server-Based Folder Shares

- Shared Folder Access Permission

Shared Folders information is stored locally to the computer hosting them, unless the domain has been configured to use Distributed File System (DFS). DFS is not suggested as the solution to this problem, but mentioned here as an explanation outside the scope of this discussion.

Our migration process is not able to handle the migration of the Shared Folders as transparently as, for instance, the DNS Server configurations are moved. However, with some basic information or perhaps even some scripting help, we can transfer the custom shared folder information from the original SBS server to the final one. The answer to this issue is that our migration handles it, and you will need to determine to what level of detail you wish to pursue a technical migration versus and non-technical process of simply re-creating the shared folder information from casual or detailed notes.

Server-Based NTFS File Tree Permissions, Data Files

- NTFS Permissions on Shared Folders

There is generally no impact upon the NTFS Permissions on the server, nor anywhere in the network on other machines. The only exception might be related to any and all folders which rely upon NTFS permissions, which are inherited directly from the volume root of the System Partition on the SBS server. This is true because Windows 2003 applies tighter security upon the System Partition (typically C:\), and if shared folders below that are inheriting permissions, this tighter permission level could affect access to those files. The best practice to address this would be to either move the shared folder location to a different partition, or to disable the inheritance of permissions from above the shared folder location, and then reset to establish the permissions desired to cascade down from there.

- Data Files

The migration of Data Files is obviously a great concern, and your options are generally wide open here. There are no specific issues introduced by the migration process that inhibit how you might choose to transfer or reconnect your data files. Here is a partial list of possible methods to handle the reconnection of your new server with the data files previously stored on the original SBS server:

o Physically connect the old server drives to the new server permanently, re-establish the shared folder locations, and operate from there.

o Physically connect the old server drives to the new server temporarily, and then perform an XCOPY similar tool for transfer from one media volume to another while preserving (or not) the NTFS ownership and permissions tree.

o Use Drive Imaging tools to move volume images off your old server to your new server drives, or with a double transfer using a temporary drive installed first in the source machine, then next in the target machine.

o Using conventional tape backup or other backup storage media, perform a redirected restore of the data from backup media while placing it onto the new server in a comparable or modified location as suits you. This could include preserving the NTFS permissions or not, depending upon your preference and support provided by your storage software.

o Though not as preferred by comparison to the previous illustrations, all of the following concepts represent variations on a solution for either being unable to connect the old drives to the new server or having both servers on the same LAN at the same time.

  • Transfer the entire folder tree from the old server to a workstation, then push back up to the new server.

  • Both install the original server drives in a workstation as "secondary drives" (not to boot from) and then push the folder tree over

  • Build a workstation configuration on a temporary drive that can boot the original server with the production drives as secondary drives, and then accomplish the same results.

SBS Shared Fax Data and Transaction Log History

The activity history database as well as the archive folders of faxes can be directly copied over as data files. After completing the SBS setup on the new server, you can replace the new contents with your historical information if you like.

Our migration strategy does not outline a process for transferring the configuration settings of previous SBS fax operations, so you will need to re-create that by the means of you choice.

A frequent problem with upgrades from existing domains is a failure with installation of the Fax Services. Changes in Windows security permissions policies assigned to the Shared Fax service operation may need to be revised.

Workstation-Related Issues with Profiles and Offline Folders

- Workstation User Profiles

Profiles are no problem at all. If we don't lose the AD and SIDs, the profiles are unaffected. You don't touch them, they work just as before.

The greatest concern is typically related to the preservation of the Logon Profiles for Domain Accounts, as well as local accounts for the workstation. The preservation of the entire Active Directory means there are no changes to the User Account SIDS, and therefore no change in the profiles folder mapping at each workstation. Stated simply, the user is the same user by all respects because the Domain is the same by all respects.

In most cases, either no issues arise at all, or the only issue may involve resetting the Computer's Domain Account members (remove and rejoin) if the migration process causes the computer's domain account password to expire without renewal. Even in the case of the workstation account requiring a refresh, this has no impact upon the local workstation profiles and user-related files.

- Redirected and Roaming Profiles

These are two optional features you may or may not be using to keep a copy of the workstation profiles on your server. These are handled with no problems as well. There's nothing about the migration process that needs to be managed in this area, provided the shared folder location you established is re-created on the new server, with the same permissions structure. This means the same NTFS permissions on the files/folders and there is compatible access available through the share permissions.

- Offline Folders

Offline Folders are slightly more complex situation, but you can manage it. I recommend you take steps to synchronize the Offline Folders before you replace the server, ensure the server has a copy of the current files, and avoid caching new files on the client-side during the server replacement phase. In other words, if you have nothing that needs to be synchronized, then you have the ability to ignore the offline folders no matter how your approach this. The folders should once again sync if the domain is the same and the server UNC path and share permissions are the same.

When you put faith in the client-side cache, you don't know whether you have it perfect until the backend of the project. It's preferable not to have any of the investment in the offline folders, as this could cause a complication you would spend additional time on later.

I'm hesitant to fully endorse trusting offline folders during a migration process because the technology is very specifically tied to server and domain identity with explicit details. Perhaps a better way of putting this is that Offline Folders are a very dynamic and emerging technology from Microsoft. Ergo, perhaps Offline Folders are exposing too many complications to an already complex task. Offline Folders is the only place in this entire data migration where I have concerns data loss could occur. There is no specific SBS-related issue here, so I advise you to consult current information available online from Microsoft if your migration scenario must include unique conditions involving Offline Folders.

All Other Services and Applications Not Listed

I don't cover the balance of the SBS-specific applications and services if they are not discussed in detail in this section of the chapter. It's not that they can't be migrated, rather that the migration process is specific to that product, as well as being a process independent of SBS and the migration technique we use here.

This means that you will need to consult the normal documentation resources for details on migration of the follow items or anything else not already mentioned above:

- **SQL Server (SBS 2003 Premium Edition database services)**

- **ISA Server (SBS 2003 Premium Edition firewall)**

- **SUS Server (patch management)**

The chapter on Disaster Recovery may provide useful information in addressing some of these concerns. But in general, the migration of these applications are not SBS-specific issues.

Now onward to part two of this monster chapter!

Part 2: How to Perform a Swing Migration

Everything we've covered in this chapter so far has been an analysis of options and the orientation to this method. We've looked at why you might want to proceed down this path, and by now you should have a good sense of the concept and an idea of the opportunity it offers. From here I will shift to explaining how it works, showing you the steps you can follow to produce your first Swing Migration, leading you down the technical path of preparations and implementation.

To refresh you memory, let's take another look at the pictorial illustration, shown in Figure 15-3, and compare it to the technical steps that follow just below.

Figure 15-3

migration overview illustration

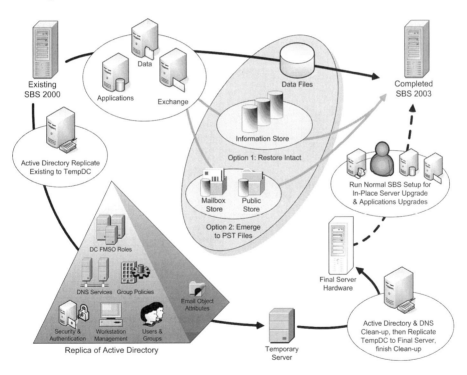

Defining Our Migrations Steps Into Five Phases

The diagrams that follow below outline the upgrade process to illustrate a sequence of steps you will perform. The total process has five main phases.

1. Preparation
2. Constructing a Temporary DC to move the process offline
3. Building your Permanent DC Offline
4. Resuming the SBS Integrated Setup Offline
5. Handling Exchange and Data Migration to Transition Online

You should notice that you perform almost the identical steps first on what is indicated as MigrationDC server as a temporary domain controller, then repeats them again on SBSnameDC, your final server. Figure 15-4 shows a flow-diagram of Phase 1, leading into the similar Phase 2 and Phase 3 steps we use to migrate the Active Directory.

Figure 15-4

Phase 1 – 3 Flow

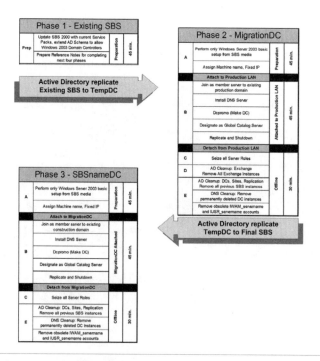

Once Phase 3 is completed, we have a Windows 2003-based server which holds our original Active Directory configuration. From this point, we proceed with doing an In-Place install of SBS 2003 just as if this domain had always been only a Windows 2003 domain. The only unique aspects of the migration method we encounter in Phases 4 and 5 are associated with the option to directly mount the previous Exchange Information Store (Figure 15-5 shows the flow). That is essentially the main content in Phase 5.

Figure 15-5
Phase 4 – 5 Flow

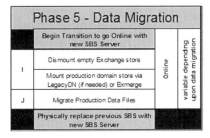

In each of the flow-diagram figures, you will notice four columns of information for each phase:

- **Documentation Section Reference**—The left-side column indicates a "letter," referring to a section of the documentation provided on that phase

- **Summary Actions**—The summary of the step is described by the larger center column.

- **Production LAN Impact**—The inside column on the right indicates whether or not the Production operations are affected during this process. As you may notice, most of the steps are conducted offline.

- **Time Requirements**—The time required for the steps described is estimated in the outside column on the right.

Distinguishing Between the Server Name References Used

Since the summary goal is to create an SBS server using the "same name" as before, I've chosen to call the first temporary DC the "MigrationDC", while referring to the final machine as the "SBSnameDC". Of course, you should feel free to name the servers according to your preferences, and obviously retain the actual SBS name you currently use. There's no impact on the process if you prefer to name the "MigrationDC" something more informative like "TemporaryDC". I simply wanted the documentation to make it clear the first DC is how the AD migration off the "ExistingSBS" is accomplished and the second DC is what achieves the name change back to our original SBS server's name.

From this point in the documentation, the servername refers to the respective servers instances according to the following logic:

- **Existing SBS**—The server your upgrade is starting from, typically an SBS 2000.

- **MigrationDC**—The server used to migrate the AD off the Existing SBS.

- **SBSnameDC**—The server you build with the same name as the Existing SBS, but during the period prior to Phase 4.

- **Final SBS**—The future condition of the SBSnameDC, but after you have completed the SBS Setup in Phase 4.

Summary Timeline Considerations

You may notice I haven't really provided a global timeline in this documentation because, as I've explained, it's pretty much open-ended unless you are redeploying the original server hardware as your new server hardware. There are very few time-sensitive issues, but here's an overview of them:

- Expect that your very first try at this migration process might take 10 to 12 hours, assuming you are not familiar with NTDSutil, ADSIedit, Exmerge, or Offline Restore processes.

- If you have done this migration plan once before so that the concepts are familiar, the time required for completing Phases 1 through 4 might take you six to seven hours if you do them in direct sequence. If you build the member server portion of both servers simultaneously, you can cut your time down by an hour. If you are able to work from prepared server images (assuming you do this migration frequently for different sites), you can eliminate another hour, putting closer to four hours.

- The time you need to transfer data files and Exchange is dependent upon the method you use. Exmerge of larger stores could take a day to cycle through. Performing an Offline Restore might finish in as little as an hour.

- SBS server portion of install must be moved past DCpromo stage within six hours, or within a window of 100 minutes time following the last reboot.

- After taking the snapshot of the AD, you must keep track of any AD changes in the production domain, so the longer the migration process takes you, the more you might have to re-create. Most SBS domains have very few user account changes or even password changes during the course of a month, much less a week.

- The crucial timeline pinch is the impact on productivity (or weekend relaxation!) when you reach Phase 5 and proceed to shutdown the Exchange for transfer. This period determines the "apparent" migration time as seen by a customer. Everything else is fairly transparent to the business operations and staff.

Once you've gained some experience and familiarity with the process, you can to complete a full production migration, including completed third-party apps, in just one day, with interruption to the business operations being as little as one to two hours. Wouldn't you like to do a complete domain upgrade on a Tuesday or Wednesday and still be home for dinner?

Pre-Upgrade Disaster Recovery Precautions

The best practice is to always have prepared your Domain Controllers and Domain as a whole for a bare metal recovery, meaning a clean drive and machine built back from scratch. This is a disaster recovery baseline you should have already in your management strategy.

Well, guess what? Our entire migration is almost exactly a bare metal recovery process—minus the disaster! We are working offline, but rebuilding the same domain and same server, so we don't have to prepare for disaster on the production server if we don't make serious changes to it, right?

The following is a recommended incremental "risk analysis" of the steps we are performing, not a full risk analysis of the business operations overall.

The chapter on disaster recovery (Chapter 14) can provide you more insight as to what you should be doing for a baseline.

- **Prior to Phase 1**—A System State backup prior to starting is sufficient. You might be comfortable just confirming the previous night's routine System State backup was successful. You install Service Packs remove the Exchange Server Instant Messaging if it's present. The balance requires simply preparing notes. If you are very conservative, you may want to make a full system recovery backup in preparing for an Active Directory recovery, assuming you are preparing for the worst-case scenario in the Phase 2 steps as well as the Service Packs.

- **Phase 2 (Steps A & B)**—The production domain is involved only during the initial steps of this phase. During that brief period, you are connected just long enough to add your new Domain Controller to the production domain, replicate AD to it, then disconnect. You never need to reconnect again. This step generally isn't a high-risk process, so a System State backup is usually sufficient for disaster recovery. A full AD rollback is probably not anticipated, but you will be adding DC and DNS changes affecting AD. Technical information on how to back out the changes to the production domain without requiring an Active Directory restore has been included here.

- **Phases 2 (Steps C and later) though Phase 4**—At this point, you have moved to working entirely offline, detached from the production domain. It's not necessary to do any disaster recovery process; since you are working offline with a "clone" of the AD, the worst you can do to yourself is kill your AD or your offline DC and have to start over. The production domain isn't at risk, so this is quite safe and efficient.

- **Phase 5**—This is the transition point where you are ready to migrate the data and remaining configuration. Yet, in many cases, you will still be working with the old server and new server running parallel to each other. While the traditional disaster recovery preparations actually come at Phase 5, they depend upon how you handle the transfer. That's where you look at your process for risk factors.

  Suppose you start your Server transition on a Saturday morning, knowing you got a good complete backup of the production SBS the previous night. If nothing else, you could disable the Internet connection to make a final backup of Exchange before you shift the servers. The backup from the night before would presumably include System State, Online Exchange Stores with logs flushed, and all data files. You might move the backup device over to the new server and do the restore of the data files, but not the Exchange stores (we can't do a restore that way). The Exchange Stores could be migrated to a portable disk drive to transfer a copy over to the new server.

- **Summary Requirements**—Amazingly enough, it's actually possible to make the entire process practically nothing done in the way of disaster recovery preparations. Begin with a System State backup to start Phase 1 and an Exchange Online backup to flush the logs, followed by an offline transfer of the files. *The old server drives may be all you need as your disaster recovery backup!*

BEST PRACTICE: You never see a Microsoft KB that discusses the registry editing tool Regedit without a very scary-looking warning to the effect "You could kill your computer with this tool, so don't blame Microsoft." Okay, it's a little less blunt. Nonetheless, during this migration we don't use Regedit specifically, but we do use two other tools that make Regedit look like a beanbag weapon. NTDSutil and ADSIEdit are two of the most efficient killers of Active Directory you could ask for. Any mistake you make with these tools in a production environment would be potentially lethal disasters. Since we work offline with these tools, we have the safety of starting over, but that's about all. You should be prepared to start over from the beginning if you make a mistake. Better yet, don't make a mistake, and be certain that you read the entire step description I've provided, and understand it fully before you press Delete! There is no Undo command here. Familiarize yourself with the process before you start to use these tools.

Key SBS Product Features Dropped or Set as Defaults by SBS 2003

This section discusses key features from prior SBS releases that are not found or setup by default in SBS 2003.

Earlier Version SBS Server Application and Features not Supported in SBS 2003

The issues listed here are not related exclusively to this migration method; rather these are conditions of SBS 2003 I thought should be mentioned somewhere in case you are not aware of these changes in the SBS product definition with this version.

- Terminal Services in Application Mode (not allowed on SBS server, use a member server)

- Shared modem Service (no longer supported; can't be migrated, either)

- Remote Storage Service (not allowed on the SBS)

Microsoft Connector for POP3 Mailboxes no longer supports Authenticated POP or CRAM-MD5 encryption

- Exchange components no longer supported:
  - Microsoft Exchange Instant Messaging
  - Microsoft Exchange MSMail Connector
  - Microsoft Exchange Connector for Lotus cc:Mail
  - Microsoft Exchange Chat Service

- Windows Internet Connection Sharing not included (SBS provides an alternate solution)

- Client configuration for legacy OS version (NT/9x/ME) requires traditional Windows methods, not SBS-specific wizards

Setup Checklist: Compliance and Blocks to an Upgrade to SBS 2003

The checklist below will help you understand the conditions preventing you from running SBS Setup on the new Domain Controller if setup encounters unsuitable or unlicensed configurations defined for SBS 2003.

Remember, it's not the existing production SBS server configuration we are going to modify for compliance. Rather, we have compliance conditions that apply to the new Domain Controller and revised Active Directory configuration that will be constructed. This is another part of the reason we have cleaned up the Active Directory and DNS information.

Blocks: Microsoft Enforced Blocks to Upgrade an Existing Active Directory Domain:

To simplify your review of preparations, here's an abbreviated list of blocked conditions Microsoft documents for an In-Place upgrade of an existing domain or SBS server. As discussed further below, you might encounter many more blocked conditions with a direct upgrade of an actual previous SBS 2000 server.

Domain and AD Configuration

- No domain trusts to other domains allowed

- All domain controllers defined in AD must be in contact

- NT4.0 level DCs not allowed, SBS 2003 installs only in AD Native Mode

- The domain controller being upgraded to SBS must hold all FSMO Roles

Namespace and Illegal Characters

- Netbios domain name contains non-standard characters

- DNS domain name cannot contain DBCS (Double Byte Character Set) or extended characters

- For both cases above, assume you should investigate this further if you are using anything else besides a-Z (upper or lower case), 0-9, or a hyphen.

Server Hardware Requirements

- Minimum of 256 megabytes of memory installed

- File system for the System Partition must be NTFS

- Maximum of two physical processors supported

Enforced Settings: Specific Configuration Conditions SBS Server Setup Enforces or Defaults

The enforced setup conditions below probably won't surprise anyone since these have been present in prior SBS versions, but a couple of the new default settings caught me by surprise in my first installations.

Enforced Condition

- You must be logged on as the Root Administrator account during Setup, and the account name must be Administrator. (The account name can be changed later.)

- Unique SBS Licensing mode supports User or Device CALS, but enforces connection compliance, unlike standard server, which issues warning only.

- All domain controllers defined in AD must be accessible during SBS Setup. (This partially explains why we delete all other DCs in the migration steps, even if we must re-create them.)

Default (no prompt for defaulted condition in advance; you can change it later)

- Directory Services Restore Mode account password will be synchronized to the Root Administrator account password during setup.

- Password policy enforcement will nag to be enabled (recommended to accept).

- Mailbox quotas are established, and mailboxes over default quotas lose functionality until brought into the quota requirements, or the quota condition is lifted by administrative action.

- Exchange Circular logging installs are enabled until you run the To Do List item configuration for Backup/Restore Wizard.

- Root Administrator account is the only Exchange Administrator established.

- Mailbox Security sets Deny Access to all mailboxes but their own Exchange Administrators.

Expected Conditions: Swing Method Upgrade "Blocks" and Recommended Conditions

To address the Microsoft requirements, as well as to bring the documentation process into a reasonable scope, I've outlined the following guidelines.

Expected Upgrade Considerations

- Typical Expectations—You are typical if this describes your condition:

  o Your current domain is an SBS 2000 or SBS 2003.

o You have no additional DCs in your network before starting the migration.

o You have no additional Exchange Servers other than the SBS you are replacing.

o You desire to replace your existing SBS with a new one using SBS 2003, while retaining the original server's Netbios servername and Domain name and the same internal LAN IP address.

o You desire to retain all user accounts, workstation accounts, and member server accounts.

If all of the above are true, you will be completing Phases 2 and 3 as documented.

• Alternative Expectations—ou are compatible if you plan to intention- ally change your SBS server name, but keep the original Domain name and Forest

o You can complete the steps outlined for Phase 2, then go immediately to Phase 4.

o Phase 3 is not essential other than to regain the original SBS server name on your final server.

o You will need to address the change of server name issues related to Exchange, as well as the UNC namespace changes in your network as a whole which are not discussed in detail here.

Unique Upgrade Considerations

• **Compatible Exchange Server Conditions—Alternatively, these steps can be used as well if all of these are true:**

o *You understand these documentation steps intentionally, unilaterally, and permanently remove all instances of Exchange Organizations, all Exchange Servers, all Exchange Connectors, all Exchange Site replication settings. One that is done, the SBS Setup re-creates only the typical Exchange conditions and supported features found in SBS.*

o Your current domain is based upon Windows Server 2000 or 2003, or SBS 2000 or 2003.

o You currently either have no Exchange Server, or only one Exchange Server, and you plan for the SBS-based Exchange Server to become your only Exchange Server.

o If you have an Exchange Server currently, you will be migrating the Exchange Organization and Information Store entirely to the new SBS server concurrently with the SBS server assuming control of your domain, not attempting for it to coexist for a delayed transition after the SBS upgrade is completed.

o If you have more than one Exchange Server, you will be using Exmerge to move the mailboxes and a similar method for the Public Folders. (You should not attempt to forklift an Information Store that has previously operated in a multi-server Exchange environment.)

• **Compatible Domain Conditions—The following Domain conditions are enforced:**

o SBS product doesn't support Domain Trusts or multi-Forest conditions. All trusts must be eliminated prior to Phase 4.

o *SBS Product Setup doesn't support having any DCs offline. This method addresses this by deleting all other DCs in the domain by the end of Phase 3 other than the one we are upgrading.* Therefore this method embraces four expectations:

  • NT4.0 Servers BDCs are being retired permanently, or "come along for the ride" in the migration steps, always connected to the migration LAN (not the production LAN). You will delete all other Windows 200x Server DCs referenced in AD except these NT 4.0 DCs.

  • Permanent Retirement: Any additional DCs (including NT4.0 or AD level DCs) that exist can be permanently deleted from the domain, will not return.

- Member Server Role: You plan to reintroduce Windows 200x Servers as member servers to the new SBS 2003-based domain after the upgrade, meaning you DCpromo demote them out of the existing production domain before connecting them to the new SBS LAN.
- Future DCpromoOption is Acceptable: Once you have your new SBS 2003-based domain operating, any member servers can be DCpromo updated to be DCs again.

- **Incompatible Domain/Exchange Conditions—Don't use this method for this situation:**

  o You are committed to a live Forest Upgrade, removing and reintroducing the root DC with an SBS (This set of complications is strongly discouraged for many reasons, not the least of which is it's out of scope.) You agree with the following:

    - You are experienced in multi-DC Forest upgrades.
    - You are willing to disconnect these additional DCs and "bring them along in the replication steps" throughout the transition.
    - You understand this migration plan wasn't intended for this scenario.
    - You realize that Microsoft Product Support for SBS strongly recommends and supports alternative methods for that type live migration scenario.
    - You are retaining a multi-server Exchange Operation.

Recommended General Practices: Keep This Migration Method Simple and Compliant

One of my goals in designing this migration method was to streamline the process, making it far more predictable than an In-Place Upgrade approach directly on an existing SBS 2000 server. If you have performed In-Place Upgrades in the past with either SBS 2000 or SBS 2003 moving from a previous SBS version, you know the wide variety of "preexisting conditions" SBS setup actually blocks. This has normally meant you needed to add time and effort, investigating and cleaning out those things not allowed. Not only is this a tedious process I prefer to avoid, we find ourselves editing our production server condition only as a transition process! That always makes me nervous about the next reboot to come, should the server remains online for a while longer. Don't you agree?

Therefore, one of the elegant benefits of this migration method is you have next to nothing in the existing SBS server configuration to modify in advance. Additionally, you have very few blocked conditions even possible when you perform the Swing Migration using the steps outlined in this chapter. For the most part, the previous SBS server condition matters not one bit. We need only to keep three things in mind:

- **Avoid pre-installing Non-Critical Services and Applications**—I don't recommend you install or configure any additional services or applications on your migration candidate Domain Controller prior to completing the SBS Setup if it isn't suggested in the steps in this chapter. You might introduce a blocked condition without realizing it.

- **Swing Migration avoids most Block Conditions**—The blocked conditions we might still encounter if you follow the steps of the Swing Migration are really only related to the contents of Active Directory, DNS, or the Information Store itself. The configuration of the existing production SBS server really doesn't matter at all. You won't need it to meet the upgrade conditions because the existing production SBS server will be nonexistent in the "migration domain" at that point.

- **Upgrades with Non-SBS Domain Conditions**—If you are upgrading from a non-SBS domain, it's possible you could have previously established domain Trusts or Forests, additional Exchange Server definitions, or the expectation to use features in the final configuration that are not allowed on an SBS server.

Exchange Concerns: Technical Concerns with the Exchange Organization and Information Store

- **Bring current Exchange 2000 to Service Pack 3:** If you are certain you are going to simply Exmerge the contents, this is not an absolute requirement, However, if you are considering an attempt to Offline Restore the old Information Store to the new server, you should update the service packs.

- **Make Offline Backup copies of Information Store**—I encourage you not to directly shift your production Information Store in a forklift attempt without making an offline backup copy first. You should be prepared to either roll back the migration process to use Exmerge or even to put the original SBS 2000 (prior version server you are upgrading) back online with the Information Store in a condition unchanged from the last mount on that same server.

- **LegacyDN and Namespace Issues**—You will not be able to shift the Information Store intact if the LegacyDN values on the store are illegal for Exchange 2000/2003. That generally would only be the case if you haven't yet moved past Exchange 5.x, or if you did an In-Place Upgrade of SBS/Exchange previously and used the LegacyDN utility.

- **Uninstall Exchange Instant Messaging (EIM)**—Exchange Instant Messaging should be gracefully uninstalled on your production SBS server before forklifting your Information Store over to the new server. EIM attaches attributes to the User objects, so clearing those can improve the likelihood of your success. You won't have that feature available anyway as soon as the migration is completed.

Notes:

Phase 1: Domain and Migration Notes Preparation

This section outline phase one relating to domain and migration notes preparation.

15-6a and 15-6b

phase 1 tasklist and illustration

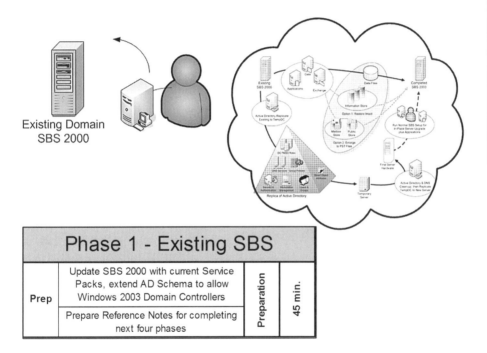

Existing Domain
SBS 2000

Phase 1 - Existing SBS			
Prep	Update SBS 2000 with current Service Packs, extend AD Schema to allow Windows 2003 Domain Controllers	Preparation	45 min.
	Prepare Reference Notes for completing next four phases		

Phase 1 will take you through the minimal preparation of the production domain, outlining the notes you need to prepare from your current domain for reference in the later phases. We also look at a handful of conditions Microsoft built into SBS Setup as blocked conditions we don't want to see.

By the way, your "Best Practices" handbook should probably include making a full System State and server backup before you even go past the next heading. But look at you…there you go anyway! You just can't trust advanced users reading an advanced user topic, huh?

Preparing the Existing SBS Domain and Server Configuration

We start with just a few minimal steps to prepare our existing server. We will not return to pull the balance of the configuration and data from the original server until Phase 5. Therefore, the original server is minimally altered, and it can stay online. We delay so we can still use as it is currently configured and then transfer the data and related settings when we prepare to finally shut it down.

> **Important:** This migration outlines a sequence designed to allow the production server to remain in production. Steps in Phase 5 are presented last in the transition timeline with the expectation that the old SBS and the new SBS are both accessible at the same time and to allow for keeping late changes to related data and settings. Do not proceed from here with Phase 2 until you have reviewed the requirements of Phase 5. Determine how you will prepare for the required steps outlined for ***Finalizing the Migration for Exchange, Data, and Shared Network Resources.***

This raises the point that if the server is being shut down and then redeployed during this upgrade, we can't wait—we have to do the export of configuration indicated in Phase 5 as one of our first steps now.

The minimum steps required here are to:

- Adding Service Packs for Windows and Exchange

- Extend the AD Schema to permit us to add a Windows 2003 Domain Controller

- Remove Exchange Instant Messaging if it was installed

We don't do the same level of detailed clean-up as an in-place upgrade:

- The migration process is designed to flush out all of the AD- and DNS-based Exchange Organization and Server information, and our new server is based upon a clean install.

- SBS Setup takes care of most of the new Server setup on that clean system

Begin Configuration Updates

1. **Redeploy the SBS server hardware: Go to Phase 5 preparations first, then return to continue from here**—The plan to reuse the hardware implies taking the production server offline amid the construction process in Phase 3 requires you to prepare the Exchange, network services, and data migration tasks while the original server is still operational, not as the final phase.

    You likely can make any choice of method, meaning you could use Exmerge, or Forklift, or LegacyDN in modifying the Forklift move, but you need to address that before you shut down the production SBS server. If this is part of your strategic plan, you should review all of Phase 5 first before you begin anything.

2. **Load Current Service Packs**—Your production server specifically needs to be at current Service Packs for Windows Server and Exchange Server. That means that at a minimum, you are required to install:

    1. **Windows Server 2000 SP3 (SP4 is preferred) or Small Business Server 2000 SP1**
    2. **Exchange Server 2000 SP3**

       Note: The minimum requirements for in-place upgrade for SBS 2000 to SBS 2003 are the initial guideline we have, and yet we don't need to meet all conditions enumerated there. Since we aren't upgrading the server, we are really just preparing for two things we need (Active Directory and Exchange-related matters). Active Directory must be updated to allow a Windows 2003 Server to be created. That requires extending the Schema, which requires Windows 2000 Service Pack 3 or later.

When moving the Exchange databases later, we don't need all the steps for an in-place upgrade. The reason is that we are not migrating the Exchange Server within AD; we are, in fact, flushing it, then reinstalling Exchange from scratch. However, we do want our Information Store in best condition to attempt an Offline Restore (forklift) migration if possible. For more information on these details, you can review this Microsoft Document:

Upgrade Requirement Messages for Windows Small Business Server 2003 Setup

http://download.microsoft.com/download/e/f/5/ ef5f82ae-620d-409b-a995-a71a461a3220/SBS_ SetupRequirements.doc

3. **Extend AD Schema**—On your production SBS 2000 DC, the AD schema must be extended to introduce a Windows 2003 server to a Windows 2000-based AD organization.

   Note: You perform this step on the pre-existing DC, in this case the old SBS 2000. You don't need to repeat this step when building the second DC.

   From the **pre-existing SBS DC,** open a command prompt window. Using the Win2003/SBS2003, locate the **CD1\i386 folder**, then execute these two commands from that directory in the order indicated below:

   ADPREP /forestprep

   ADPREP /domainprep

Expert Tip: During the progress of incremental steps executed within each of the two ADPREP commands, a line appears periodically indicating "The command has completed successfully," and yet the system appears to still be busy. This will repeat several times. All steps are completed when you receive a response that returns a command prompt by forestprep, indicating "ADprep successfully updated the forest-wide information" or a similar response after domainprep.

Technical Background

If the existing AD domain has not yet been extended to include a Windows 2003 Server as DC, we must now *go to an existing DC to Extend the AD Schema* using the ADprep tool on the SBS 2003 media. An essential detail of Extending the AD Schema is the requirement to have all DCs in the domain at or above the minimum requirements for the Windows 2003 Level Schema, which includes Windows 2000 SP2 on all DCs. The following reference may be useful for greater detail:325379 How to Upgrade Windows 2000 Domain Controllers to Windows Server 2003   http://support.microsoft.com/?id=325379However, the essential steps are listed below.

4. **(If Applicable) Uninstall Exchange Instant Messaging (EIM)**—I recommend that you remove Exchange Instant Messaging on your production SBS server prior to attempting to forklift your Information Store over to the new server. Doing so can improve the likelihood of your success, and you will lose that EIM feature anyway as soon as the migration is completed.

   Exchange Instant Messaging is a component of Exchange 2000 not supported in SBS 2003 and may have attribute information established in the Information Store itself that affects the compatibility of that store being mounted directly on the new server. If you plan to Exmerge your mailboxes, you could skip this one task on the production server.

   Remove the Domain Name Service (DNS) _rvp record and the Instant Messaging Home server by following these steps (reference: Microsoft KB319758):

   1. Start the DNS snap-in. To do this, click **Start**, point to **Programs**, point to **Administrative Tools**, and then click **DNS**.
   2. Expand the DNS server computer, expand **Forward Lookup Zones**, expand the forward lookup zone that you want, and then click **_tcp**.
   3. In the right pane of the DNS snap-in, right-click **_rvp**, and then click **Delete** on the shortcut menu that appears. Click **OK** to confirm the removal of the record.

4. Right-click the forward lookup zone, and then click **Update Server Data File**.

5. Click **Start**, click **Run**, type **cmd** in the **Open** box, and then click **OK**.

6. At the command prompt, type **ipconfig /flushdns**, and then press **ENTER**.

7. Type **exit**, and then press **ENTER**.

8. Start Exchange System Manager. To do this, click **Start**, point to **Programs**, point to **Microsoft Exchange**, and then click **System Manager**.

9. Expand **Administrative Groups**, expand the administrative group that contains the instant messaging server, expand **Servers**, expand the server that contains the instant messaging server, expand **Protocols**, and then expand **Instant Messaging (RVP)**.

    Note: If Administrative Groups is not displayed, it may not be turned on. To turn on Administrative Groups, right-click the Exchange Organization in Exchange System Manager, and then click **Properties**. Click to select the **Display Administrative Groups** checkbox.

10. Right-click the Instant Messaging server that you want, and then click **Delete**.

11. Click **Delete** to remove the Instant Messaging virtual server.

12. Quit the Exchange System Manager snap-in.

13. Restart the Exchange 2000 Server computer.

5. **Make Server Hardware Replacement Upgrades**—If you are replacing the production server hardware as part of the migration, you have completed the basic reconfiguration of your current production Domain and SBS 2000 Server.

Notes:

Milestone

Production Server Remains Online The remaining migration steps until Phase 5 are performed on either your temp server or the permanent server you build after that. Until you reach the point at which you shift your data files and Exchange Mailbox Stores, you can continue to operate the production domain.From this point forward, the only changes related to the migration process that will occur to your production Domain and SBS server will be the following:

- You will build a new server and then establish it as a Domain Controller and Global Catalog holder. The instance of this Domain Controller in the production domain can remain there in the production Active Directory without concern after you detach the server, as this migration plan calls to be done. However, you may observe a warning in the Directory Services Event Logs indicating the detached DC is failing to replicate with the production SBS server. These can be ignored. Only if your production domain Directory Services appear to operate in an abnormal manner should you pursue this as a concern.

- Similarly, with the new DC described in the previous point, you will likely find it convenient to establish replication configurations for DNS and WINS between the new DC and the production SBS prior to disconnecting. Again, you may see an Application and DNS Event Log warning noting replication errors for WINS and DNS once this server is disconnected. You can ignore these errors if the operation of your domain remains normal.

- Only if you experience production operational problems should you be concerned to "undo" those settings changed on your production domain.

Notes:

Prepare Your Migration Notes and Automated Migration Tools

Hey! You with the short attention span, the "I hate documentation" gurus—I'm talking to you now. You hate making lists of things you need to have later, right? I know, because I'm one of you. Sorry, but you just can't escape this part. Because when the blanks appear on the screen to be filled in, if you don't have the information matching the original SBS server's configuration, you might get a break in your process. This is reasonably important stuff here, okay?

Keeping a list of information you need along the way during the migration is essential. Although each little item you write down make not seem like much in itself, when you get done, you'll find that list looks pretty darn long!

You may need to confirm how you want to handle any changes you make by preference, so a list of original settings is useful. If you plan to build the new SBS side-by-side with the old one, you'll only need to glance at some of this on the other machine as you go.

What do we not need to prepare because it's done automatically?

As full as your list is, you may notice some things curiously are not included. Here's a list of information you not record because the upgrade process is designed to transparently migrate and preserve these things:

- Username and passwords
- User account permissions and settings
- User Security groups
- E-mail Distribution groups
- Computer names
- Group Policies
- Domain SAM or SIDs references
- Workstation profiles or assignments
- Logon Scripts

What Exchange data references might we need to prepare?

Depending upon the method you plan for migrating your Exchange contents, you may need to record a little or a lot of your E-mail and mailbox-related items. I've not produced a table to illustrate what you might need for this; there's just too much to illustrate within a blank table in this book. However, while the following bullets are simply a summary, you should have *at least* this much information prepared:

- Exchange Forklift Method
    - o Public Folder E-mail Addresses and Permissions
    - o User Mailbox alternate E-mail Addresses

- Exchange Exmerge Method
    - o Potentially everything but the mailbox contents might be lost.

Notes:

Table of References: Phase 2 and Phase 3—Migration of AD

When you are building both the first and second new Domain Controller, you will want to refer to configuration information about the production server. The following two tables show the type of information you will want to have on hand, based upon when you will need to have that information.

Baseline OS Installation Phase	
SBS Server Name	
Netbios Domain Name	
DNShostname Domain Name	
Domain Administrator account name and password	
Product Registered Owner and Company Name	
Network Adapter Settings	(per adapter interface)
LAN IP, Mask and Gateway	
WAN IP, Mask and Gateway	
DHCP or static configuration	
DNS and WINS Server references	
Internal vs. Internet Designations for the Interface	
DNS Details	
Critical Static Entries	
Forwarder Settings	
Forward Lookup Zones	
Summary of DC-related records	
Static Routing and Gateway Details	
Drive Volume Details	
Drive Letter assigned per volume	
Drive Letter for CD/DVD devices	
Root Folder permission requirements	(per partition on server)
Total allocated and Free disk space per volume	(per partition on server)

Notes:

4

Table of References: Phase 4—Resuming Setup for SBS 2003

Migration/SBS Integrated Suite Setup Phase	
SBS Organization Profile Contacts Default Entries	
Contact Names	
Contact Address	
Phones and Fax	
Exchange Information	
Organization	
Site	
Storage Group Name	
Information Store names	
Exchange LegacyDN value (the internal reference to the Exchange configuration details)	
E-mail Domains Hosted by Exchange	
POP3 Connector Mailbox Configuration Details	
Alternate e-mail proxy addresses per user/account	(per user/account)
Server Public Host Name (and Masquerade alias if any)	
Any Unique RRAS Device Identifications and Configuration details (modems and VPN ports)	
Shared Folders Resources	(per share)
Sharename	
Share Description	
Share Permissions Template	
Resource Folder Name	

Notes:

Table of References: Phase 5—Post-Setup Configuration Finalization Phase

After the migration has reached the point of completing the SBS Setup steps, you still have more information to configure before the new SBS looks like the old SBS. If you do a technical migration of things like WINS and DHCP, you don't need to have a list of critical items from that.

What remains to be addressed may depend upon the details you did or did not automate in the process above.

Post-Setup Configuration Finalization Phase	
Group Policy Revisions due to Namespace changes (if any)	
DHCP Details	
Scopes	
Exclusions	
Reservations	
Scope Option Preferences	
Shared Printers Resources	(per printer)
Sharename	
Printer Description	
Printer Location	
Share Permissions Template	
Security	
Port Name	
Customized Website Content	
Logon Script Revision Management	
Essential commands to keep or revise on new server	

Notes:

Table of References: To-Do List—Internet Configuration Wizard Details

Some of this information isn't requested in the wizard, but it's helpful to have the information together in one place, not just for the upgrade but for the long-term as a reference.

Internet Services-Related Configuration
ISP Connection—Public Addresses
Public IP (or range)
Subnet Mask
Public Gateway
Primary DNS (used as DNS Forwarder)
Secondary DNS (also used as DNS Forwarder)
ISP reference Username
ISP reference Password
NAT Interface (if router/firewall provides NAT to SBS)
Interface IP
Subnet Mask
Gateway
Router Admin Username
Router Admin Password
ISP Hosted Information
Hosted DNS—Reference MX records
Backup Mailserver IP you allow to relay to your Exchange
Hosted DNS—Reference WWW records
Your Hosted Website IP

Notes:

Phase 2: Transfer AD from Existing SBS to MigrationDC

15-7a and 15-7b

phase 2 tasklist and illustration

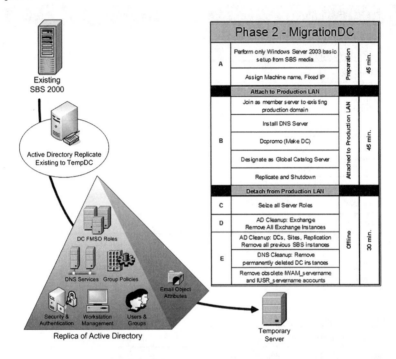

	Phase 2 - MigrationDC			
A	Perform only Windows Server 2003 basic setup from SBS media	Preparation	45 min.	
	Assign Machine name, Fixed IP			
	Attach to Production LAN			
B	Join as member server to existing production domain	Attached to Production LAN	45 min.	
	Install DNS Server			
	Dcpromo (Make DC)			
	Designate as Global Catalog Server			
	Replicate and Shutdown			
	Detach from Production LAN			
C	Seize all Server Roles	Offline	30 min.	
D	AD Cleanup: Exchange Remove All Exchange Instances			
	AD Cleanup: DCs, Sites, Replication Remove all previous SBS instances			
E	DNS Cleanup: Remove permanently deleted DC instances			
	Remove obsolete IWAM_servername and IUSR_servername accounts			

Existing SBS 2000

Active Directory Replicate Existing to TempDC

DC FMSO Roles

DNS Services   Group Policies

Email Object Attributes

Security & Authentication   Workstation Management   Users & Groups

Replica of Active Directory

Temporary Server

Now, before you leap forward, I have the one, most important hint you must have completely blocking out your vision as you proceed. Ready?

Your best practice handbook should sound like an annoying, constantly barking dog during both of Phases 2 and 3 to make you double-check two things:

➢ **You MUST have the DNS references configured correctly at every step**

➢ **You must shift the DNS settings several times as you install DNS and replicate AD and before you modify FSMO roles, because this doesn't work otherwise!**

The steps I've outlined make it clear when you need to adjust the DNS entries, so don't snooze past a change of the DNS setting. It's absolutely the most critical mistake you are most likely to make.

Step A. Install a clean baseline of Server 2003 _only_ (SBS 2003 Media)

The following steps can be conducted with the new machine disconnected from the production LAN for Steps 1 through 5. Therefore, these steps could be done in advance.

The remaining steps from Step 6 forward require communication to the production domain. A reseller consultant might choose to do the first five steps in preparation before going on site, or perhaps using a standard deployment image. In any case, the steps listed below assume the machine is disconnected to start, and that if a DHCP Server is present on the LAN, the server will be set to a static IP in Step 6.

1. **Install new DC from SBS 2003 Media**—Boot from SBS 2003 DVD/CD as normal and run normal installation of Windows Server only. (You will interrupt the SBS portion of setup.)

    There are no special tasks required here. The normal setup steps you proceed through are listed below to help you recognize the point at which you deviate from the scripted setup sequence of a normal SBS install.

Technical Background
For reference, here's a summary of the screens and steps you progress through during a normal Windows 2003 setup by default:

- Complete the text mode setup, including any special configuration and boot device driver setup you require just as you normally would do.

- Continue with GUI mode setup that indicates the left sidebar of five steps as follows:
    - o Collecting Information
    - o Dynamic Update
    - o Preparing Installation

- o Installing Windows
  - Regional Settings
  - Registration Owner Name and Company Product   Key (use the SBS product key if you are using SBS media)
  - Server Name and Password—At this step you must know the name you intend to use for this server, or you may change the machine name at a later step.
  - Date/Time and Time Zone
- o Finalizing installationo
- Following a reboot, you will be given a standard Windows logon screen requiring Ctrl-Alt-Del. This is your cue to interrupt the setup sequence.

2. **Eject media prior to the Secure Logon request to terminate continuation of SBS Setup, or logon and cancel the dialog box that launches**—After the forty-minute period during which the automated five-step sequence above is completed, you will halt the normal SBS install.

Expert Tip: Think of this as only interrupting the normal SBS Setup process, because you will pick up at this point again later, just with your final server having already been joined to an existing domain. This is how we are able to complete SBS Setup with a server created in an existing domain. We are emulating the migration process involved in moving an existing domain over to an SBS domain. We actually pick up again at this very same point in the automated SBS setup when we reach Section F, after we do some cleanup.

At the secure logon prompt, you should have either ejected the media before executing the Administrator logon, or you have the option to cancel the setup process as it resumes after logon.

- ***If you did eject the media before logon***, you receive a couple of prompts requesting you to provide the media to continue with BOSPREP.EXE.

o Close that prompt box by canceling, confirm that you intend to cancel setup with the prompt box that follows, and you have effectively interrupted the next phase of the SBS setup.

• *If you failed to eject the CD before the logon*, you will instead see a dialog box for the next step of SBS setup to resume. It will briefly indicate configuration of files into temporary folders. Wait just a moment and the setup will pause again at a dialog box screen showing the title "Microsoft Windows Small Business Server Setup" and with the headline text in the box that indicates "Continuing Microsoft Windows Small Business Server Setup." It's not too late, you can still stop here.

o You must choose **Cancel** here!

o Confirm you want to **Abort**.

o Choose **Finish**.

Note: *You will need to reinsert the SBS installation media during later steps. On any occasion you insert the media, Windows Autoplay feature will attempt to restart the SBS setup or present options for you to do that. You can cancel that immediately or as needed without causing a problem.*

3. **Do not activate the license for this server at this time!**—Even if prompted, you are recommended to wait until your final SBS Setup process is complete. Activating earlier is likely to create a license violation condition you will have difficulty resolving. You will probably want to wait until completing the full SBS setup and are ready to add the SBS CALS to activate the server. Just ignore any activation prompts in the interim.

4. **Verify Drivers and Set Server Configuration**—You many need additional drivers provided by your server motherboard manufacturer or other hardware device providers.

Perform the following minimum verification steps:

1) Inspect the Event Viewer to see if any error events are reported that require attention.

2) Open **Device Manager** to inspect for devices without valid drivers installed.

3) Ensure that NICs are connected with functional drivers.

4) As needed, install drivers for any other hardware devices that were not properly configured during setup.

5) On the primary NIC, assign a static IP that is available within the same subnet as the established LAN.

   ➢ If you are building the MigrationDC, you will be picking a currently unassigned IP.

   ➢ If you are building the SBSnameDC, you will want to choose the IP that the previously established SBS server is using to facilitate the transparent replacement of that server.

6) **On the primary NIC, assign the Primary DNS Server to be the IP of the DC hosting the AD instance you are about to join in the next section.**

   ➢ *MigrationDC requires unique available IP*

   ➢ *SBSnameDC requires original SBS server's primary LAN IP*

7) On the secondary NIC (if any), you can leave it with no IP assigned or assign an IP outside the subnet of the primary NIC.

8) Optionally, enable Terminal Services in Remote Administration mode.

5. **Ensure that DHCP Service is disabled or not yet installed**—This step is included to avoid complications with other DHCP Servers during the migration.

   o DHCP Server service is typically not installed by default to a new server by Windows setup. If you did chose to install it already yourself, disable the service before you connect this new server to the LAN with the production SBS. You can enable or add DHCP Server service back later if you ultimately expect to use it in your production environment.

o No need to uninstall the DHCP Server service it if you have it currently installed. Just open the **Manage Computer** console, drill down to **Services**, set the **DHCP Service** to startup type "**Disabled**".

o If you have a router or other device you prefer for providing DHCP Service to your normal LAN, you do not need to be concerned about disabling it or that it will impact the setup steps outlined here. The reason for discussing the DHCP Server at all is to ensure that you have the expected behavior of your server configuration. For that reason, you want to avoid conflicting DHCP Server operations.

Milestone

This is as far as you can proceed toward building this machine offline or in advance. You will need to connect to the established DC at this point to join the domain.

6. **Connect this new DC onto LAN with the Established Domain AD instance you plan to join and set a static IP**—The next steps require this computer to communicate with the existing DC for this domain.

o You should have set a static IP on this server in the same subnet as your local domain is using during Step 4 above. Because it's so important that this be done, I mention again here — the last point at which you can make a change without complications in the process as it is documented here.

o You should confirm that you can communicate to the established DC using the **ping** command.

> ➤ *If this is your MigrationDC*, connect the new server to the production LAN where your established SBS server is connected. Confirm that you set the IP to a unique address in the same subnet.

> ➤ *If this is the second DC you are building as the SBSnameDC*, connect the new server to the construction LAN where your cloned AD is held by the previously configured MigrationDC. Confirm that you set the primary NIC IP to the IP address previously assigned to the production SBS you are going to replace.

7. **Join the domain with DNS requests pointing at the opposite server**—Once connected to the LAN, you should be able to ping the existing DC to confirm basic network communication is available. Join the domain and reboot.

Note: You may find it convenient to disable any existing logon scripts configured for the Domain Administrator account you will be using with the new server setup from this point forward.

8. **Sync to Domain Time**—Log on as Domain Administrator; sync time of SBS 2003 server to SBS 2000 server.

   Net time /domain:[*your-domainname***] /set**

   Confirm with "Y" that you want to sync the time of the local machine to the domain time server (the DC you are connecting to).

9. **Time limit.** You now have a limited number of days to use this server installation before SBS-specific installation protection forces the computer to reboot every 100 minutes. This is not a standard Windows activation issue of the type you get 30 days to activate; rather, this is an SBS-specific setup installation enforcement. It wouldn't matter if you activated the Windows license or not (so don't do that). This limitation specifically forces that you to make a DC of any installation from SBS media within a specific period of time. Think hours, not days.

Technical Background

You will not be able to preserve any installation from SBS media in the condition of member server for an extended period of time. Technical blocks are built into the SBS server setup media to ensure that full installation of SBS designated as a DC is completed. Permanent use of a server installed from SBS Media outside this condition is not recommended. In fact, it's really not feasible. This limitation has no impact upon our process related to upgrade and migration steps other than forcing us to complete the planned DC promo steps in a timely manner. Immediately following completion of the first part of setup through Step 5 described above, you have a reasonable limitation of just under six hours of uninterrupted "grace time" to get past the DCpromo milestone. At that point, a forced server shutdown occurs. The forced shutdown now repeats on cycles of every 100 minutes. Note, the limitation is not to complete the entire SBS installation, just the next three steps that follow to complete DCpromo.If the server reaches the condition of a forced shutdown every 100 minutes, don't worry. This forced shutdown is removed by completing the DCpromo cycle of continuing normal SBS installation or the steps of DCpromo outlined in the next section. That time limitation is quite sufficient for a DCpromo in an SBS scale domain, since the steps can require as little as 15 minutes to complete, including replication time. Here are some details of the shutdown-related cycle:

- Event Viewer Displays the following related warnings:
  - **Source: SBCore with ID 1013** is a nag that you are required to complete setup.
  - **Source: SBCore with ID 1014** is a warning that the system will be shutdown soon
  - **Source: SBCore with ID 1001** is the notice explaining why a shutdown occurred

- After the initial four hours pass, you receive and Event Viewer Warning to complete the setup portion of making this server a DC.

- Forty minutes after the first (four-hour) warning, you receive an additional warning that the server will undergo a forced shutdown in 60 minutes.

- When the 60 minutes has passed, the system performs an automated shutdown without any warning to the operator.

- After the shutdown, you may restart the computer normally again, and you are provided an Event Warning to complete the steps to make this machine a DC. The server will now be shutdown in a 100-minute cycle each time you restart it, and similar events mentioned above will be posted to the Event Logo

- **You are strongly advised not to attempt to tamper with SBCore in any way, as you may end up rendering your installation unusable and unrecoverable.**

Step B. DCpromo to establish the server as a new DC in the existing Domain

Now we will perform the steps to move this server from a member server up to a Domain Controller. These are the DCpromo steps and related configuration.

1. **Install DNS Service**—If you have not already done so, install DNS on the new server now. (If you plan to install WINS, that is discussed below.) Leave the DNS queries (on your NIC configuration) pointing at the opposite server for now. Don't worry about configuring DNS forwarders.

   To install DNS Server, use the Control Panel option for Add/ Remove Programs:

   1. Select **Add/Remove Windows Components**.
   2. From the component list showing, highlight (but don't enable the checkbox) the **Network Services** option. Click **Details**.
   3. In the selection list, you should now enable the checkbox for **DNS Server** in addition to any other options already selected.
   4. If you inadvertently enabled additional options, you should cancel out of this operation and start over. It's important not to install services you don't need.
   5. Click **OK** to install DNS Server and then close out of the Control Panel.

      o In most cases, you do not need to be concerned about forcing replication or configuration of the DNS Server contents at this point. Replication will occur automatically in the next steps when AD replication takes place as part of the DCpromo process.

2.Run DCpromo on new server—Run DCpromo.

Note: You must be logged on as a Domain Administrator. You will receive errors and the process will fail if you are not currently logged on as a Domain Administrator enabled account.

1. Confirm that the scenario is accepting the condition, that a **Windows 2003 Server as DC is not compatible to communicate with Win95 and NT4.0 workstations**, and that your domain meets these requirements.
2. When prompted, change the default selection instead to indicate "**Additional domain controller for an existing domain**".
3. You likely will indicate the Domain Administrator account you are using as the account to execute the DCpromo action.
4. The default prompts for folder locations should be suitable for other prompted options.
5. When prompted to provide a Directory Services Restore Mode Administrator Password, you may wish to indicate the same password as the Root Administrator account. SBS Setup will force this anyway at the point you run SBS configuration on the final server. Generally, no significant security implications will result from having them agree in an SBS-based network due to the small scale and limited level of delegation of administrative authority.
6. Restart upon completion.

Notes:

3. **Establish Global Catalog Server Designation**—Make this machine a Global Catalog Server.

   To establish this DC as a new Global Catalog Server:

   1. On the domain controller where you want the new global catalog, start the Active Directory Sites and Services snap-in. To start the snap-in, click **Start**, point to **Programs**, point to **Administrative Tools**, and then click **Active Directory Sites and Services**.

   2. In the console tree, double-click **Sites**, and then double-click **sitename**.

   3. Double-click **Servers**, click your domain controller, right-click **NTDS Settings**, and then click **Properties**.

   4. On the **General** tab, click to select the **Global catalog** checkbox to assign the role of global catalog to this server.

   5. Restart the domain controller.

Technical Background

NOTE: Allow sufficient time for the account and the schema information to replicate to the new global catalog server before you remove the global catalog from the original domain controller. Fifteen minutes is typically sufficient on a small scale, single-segment network.Event 1119 may be logged in the Directory Services log in Event Viewer with a description that states that the computer is now advertising itself as a global catalog server.**HOW TO: Create or Move a Global Catalog in Windows 2000**http://support.microsoft.com/default.aspx?scid=kb;en-us;313994&Product=win2000

4. **Confirm that DNS Replicated from the existing DC to new Server**—You can compare the two server DNS entries from the Manage Computer console section for DNS.

5. **Reset the new server NIC configuration to point to self as DNS Server**—Later processes will be complicated if this server doesn't refer to itself as DNS provider at this point.

   o Inspect the DNS Forward and Reverse Lookup Zones to confirm that these are now populated with the same information from the previous DC/DNS server.

    o Once you are satisfied, reset the local NIC configuration on this DC to now point at itself only as Primary DNS Server. This supports the steps to follow when this server is detached and becomes the only server it can reach. It's not recommended to include the other DNS Server in the indicated Secondary DNS Server options.

6. **Configure WINS Server and Replicate (optional)**—You have the option to use conventional WINS Server Replication to migrate customizations in WINS database and settings.

    o Even though Microsoft states in many different references that WINS and Netbios resolution is not required for Active Directory operations using all AD compliant workstations and servers, it's misleading to leave that statement to stand alone. Many aspects of Windows Networking in fact still use Netbios, even if AD can operate without it. You don't get transparent operations if you don't provide support for Netbios, and WINS is what makes maintaining Netbios more obvious to the System Administrator.

    o If your previous SBS server used WINS, you have the option to directly transfer those records over at this point using the following steps:

- Using **Add/Remove Programs**, choose to modify **Windows System Components**. From the **Network Components**, select to install **WINS**.
- After WINS is installed, you can now configure a Replication Partner to pull a copy of the existing WINS configuration forward to your new server. Open the **Manage Computer** console, locate **WINS** under **Services and Applications**, and expand it to show the entry **Replication Partners**. Add the server you pulled the domain from (assuming it was the WINS Server) and indicate to pull the database over.

7. **Replicate, Shut Down, and Detach the new Server**—Detach the SBS 2003 from the production domain in order to complete the balance of the SBS setup offline from the production LAN. Make sure you allow time for any settings you wish to replicate to complete doing so, then shut down. Standard time delay to allow replication on an SBS domain with just the two DCs is about 15 minutes, unless your DNS configuration is flawed. You can use Reskit tools to do a technical verification as well.

Milestone (Phase 2: AD transfer completion)

The production SBS can now remain online—The method documented features a primary goal in the process, which is to allow for the option to continue using your production SBS during the majority of the remaining steps of building your new server. Let's review some of what is implied and the limitations this places upon us within the production domain.

- Details of this are discussed elsewhere in this chapter, both in the introduction sections and in the later steps as well.
- When it comes time to bring the new server online as the "only SBS server," we will need to synchronize the data and Exchange Databases. If your production server is well organized, that can be as simply as connecting the old drives, or restoring the data files and Exchange databases to your new server using comparable locations. The details of the data and Exchange transfer are covered in more detail in a later section.
- A critical point to make here, however, is that from this time forward, it will not be possible to synchronize the production AD configuration or the DNS settings with the new server we are building. Therefore, do not make changes to the AD information running on the production server from now on; otherwise, those changes will not be present in the cloned

AD version you will continue to work with offline from this point. An example of changes not retained would include add/remove Users/Computers, changes in User information, and even changes in User Passwords and security memberships. Any changes that must be implemented should be noted and re-created in the new AD clone context as well. This limitation is not really a major factor in a small domain, because the sort of changes that might occur are easily re-created. Just keep notes of what you need to do.

• While your Production Domain remains online and you continue to work offline on the migration DCs, you might be concerned about reversing the changes to your production SBS for some reason. I'm not recommending that you do this without symptoms of a problem pushing you to be concerned.

Step C. Root Domain Management Transfer/Seizure

All steps from this point forward are completed on the new server, with this server detached from the production LAN.

We will seize all five of the domain controller server roles over to the new DC in progress.

To accomplish this, we need to first install the Windows Server Support Tools included on the SBS Media Set, but have not been installed. We will use several of the tools provided in the remaining steps of our total process.

Additional Tools Required:
Windows Server Support Tools From the SBS 2003 media set, install the Windows Server Support Tools. You will need several of these. The installation resource folder is located on SBS media CD2: \CD2\support\tools\suptools.msi.

• **NTDSUTIL**

o NTDSUTIL is required to seize the Server Roles for the domain. It can also be used for removing domain controllers.

o To launch NTDSTIL on any domain controller, click **Start**, click **Run**, type **ntdsutil** in the Open box, and then click **OK**.

- **ADSIedit**
  o ADSIedit is required to view or modify the Active Directory database and structure and is specifically useful for addressing the needs to remove the Exchange Server configuration.
  o To execute ADSIedit, after installing the Support Tools, run the MMC item or create a shortcut to its location:C:\Program Files\Support Tools\adsiedit.msc

- For complete information on the complete contents of the Windows Server Support tools, consult the help file installed to this location: Start Menu >Programs >Windows Support Tools >Support Tools Help

Using NTDSUTIL, you can confirm that all server roles have been pulled to the remaining server. You can also use it to seize roles from other servers. Technically, when a server role is moved between two DCs that can communicate to each other, that process is called a "transfer." A "seizure" occurs when the hosting DC is unavailable to communicate, and the seizing DC declares itself as taking that role without an agreement with the previous role holder.

To seize or transfer the FSMO roles by using Ntdsutil, follow these steps:

1. On any domain controller, click **Start**, click **Run**, type **ntdsutil** in the **Open** box, and then click **OK**.
   Note: Microsoft recommends you use the domain controller that is taking the FSMO roles.
2. Type **roles**, and then press **ENTER**.
   To see a list of available commands at any of the prompts in the Ntdsutil tool, type **?**, and then press **ENTER**.
3. Type **connections**, and then press **ENTER**.
4. Type **connect to server** *servername*, where *servername* is the name of the server you want to use, and then press **ENTER**.

5. At the **server connections:** prompt, type **q**, and then press **ENTER** again.

6. Type **seize *role***, where *role* is the role you want to seize. For a list of roles you can seize, type **?** at the **Fsmo maintenance:** prompt, and then press **ENTER**, or consult the list of roles at the beginning of this article. For example, to seize the RID Master role, you would type **seize rid master**. The one exception is the PDC Emulator role, whose syntax would be "seize pdc" and not "seize pdc emulator". Execute the following commands:

> Seize pdc
>
> Seize domain naming master
>
> Seize infrastructure master
>
> Seize RID master
>
> Seize schema master

Expert Tip: *As you type each of the commands above, if the syntax is correct, a pop-up menu prompt asks to confirm the seizure. If you type an erroneous command, or make a syntax error, that is explained in the command window itself.One aspect of the display in the command window is confusing the first time you go through this process. It appears without a close reading that every command you are executing is failing because, in fact,* **an error result displays with every command each time when you do execute the command correctly**.*To understand why this happens, observe that before Seizing, the NTDSutil will first cause the DC to request transfer of the role from the DC that is the current role holder. The error indicates that this transfer request failed, which is to be expected. Since the server currently listed in AD as owning this is unavailable, the transfer request results in a failure, which is indicated as an error. Immediately after, the seizure step will next proceed. Therefore, don't be surprised to see errors reported. Expect them. What matters is that after executing the seizure on all five of the roles, you will confirm the success with a command to verify all roles.*

7. Each time the seize command is executed, the last response it pro-
    vides is a summary of role ownership as of that change. When the
    last seize command above has completed, that summary should show
    all five of the listed Server Roles are held by the new DC. That indi-
    cates you have accomplished your goal.

Section C: Additional References:

The steps above are outlined directly in Q255504. As indicated, to seize all
roles we use NTDSutil.

> Using Ntdsutil.exe to Seize or Transfer FSMO Roles to a Domain Controller
> http://support.microsoft.com/default.aspx?scid=kb;EN-US;255504

The following additional KBs are useful in documenting the process required
or alternative processes you could consider in different scenarios:

> HOW TO: Find Servers That Hold Flexible Single Master Operations Roles
> http://support.microsoft.com/default.aspx?scid=kb;EN-US;234790

The next KB method will not work unless the DC hosting the role currently is
still accessible to communicate with as the request for transfer is made. This is
fine if you are working in a larger LAN than with a typical SBS-based domain.
The problem with SBS is that since its role is intended to be unique in a domain,
transferring the server roles to a different server name essentially ensures that
you have taken the domain out of production already, because otherwise, you
are that point!Still, one useful approach for an orderly transfer of roles might be
to first create a drive image of the production server, and using that imaged
version, transfer the roles to the offline construction DC. In this way, the
production SBS is only offline for the time it takes to image the server, then
transfer the roles. You then restart the server using the production drives and you
have a more orderly transfer of server roles than the seizure provides, but it also
involves additional steps, and probably third-party software for the imaging steps.

> HOW TO: View and Transfer FSMO Roles in the Graphical User Interface
> http://support.microsoft.com/default.aspx?scid=kb;
> en-us;255690&Product=win2000

This next KB illustrates a technique that can be used in scripting the process of
domain controller creation.

Unattended Promotion and Demotion of Windows 2000 Domain Controllers
http://support.microsoft.com/default.aspx?scid=kb;
en-us;223757&Product=win2000

Step D. Perform Required Active Directory Cleanup

Review the following caveats. If one or more apply to your situation, please read the section in the "Before you Get Started" information of this document to determine issues that may affect your decision to proceed.

> **Expert Tip:** *The following steps make substantial changes to your AD information. This is a safe process primarily because you are working offline from the production LAN. Therefore, if a radical problem occurs, you won't to be in trouble because you can start over with the migration process. Doing these same steps to a production domain are normally only considered as part of a disaster recovery process in which you have no better choices for recovery steps. Therefore, this warning is to inform you not to take these steps lightly in a different circumstance, and to be sure you really are working offline in this case.*

Removing the Exchange Organization

Steps 1 through 3 indicated below are recommended for completely removing an Exchange Organization in the circumstances we are using. It will always work because it operates at the lowest level in AD to force the removal of the object. An alternative method is listed that does not require use of ADSIedit and therefore is more automated. However, it requires installation of additional Exchange tools and manipulation of the mailbox connections. And if it fails to work, you will need to use the Steps 1 through 3 at that point anyway. The recommended steps are not complicated, even if the tools could be somewhat unfamiliar to you. ADSIedit is a powerful tool that resembles the look of the AD Computer and Users console, but with fewer safety and security blocks built-in. You should be very careful in using ADSIedit in a production environment.

If you wish to use the alternative method, it's described at the bottom of this section.

The following steps are efficient and allow you to accomplish the tasks without installing anything more to the new DC. KB 279749 outlines the process, though it has an additional step—that we OMIT—which recommends running Exchange 2000 Setup with the **/forestprep** switch again. That will occur later during the final SBS Setup sequence.

Microsoft KB Reference:

XADM: ForestPrep Does Not Work with Error Message: An Invalid ADSI Pathname Was Passed 80005000

http://support.microsoft.com/default.aspx?scid=kb;EN-US;279749

The steps outlined below are the complete required actions. The KB is provided only as a background reference.

1. **Remove Exchange Server Organization using AD Sites and Services:**
   To completely remove Exchange 2000 from Active Directory:
   Click **Start**, point to **Programs**, point to **Administrative Tools**, and then click **Active Directory Sites and Services**.
   1) Turn on the **Show Services** node on the **View** menu.
   2) Double-click **Services**.
   3) Click **Microsoft Exchange**.
   4) Under Microsoft Exchange you will see Active Directory Connections and the Exchange Organization Object. Right-click your **Microsoft Exchange Organization** object, and then click **Delete**.

2. **Open AD Users and Computers to remove the Microsoft Exchange System Objects**
   1) Open **AD Users and Computers**
   2) Select a folder object. Right-click then enable **View|Advanced**.
   3) Locate the Microsoft Exchange System Objects item listed in the root of the AD tree below your domain. Dlete this object too.

This completes the steps required to remove Exchange instances from AD. You can skip the rest of this section if the steps above were successful. If you have difficulty with the last step and are unable to successfully delete the Exchange Object indicated, the following KB provides specific details that may be useful in resolving that issue.

Microsoft KB Reference:

XADM: You Cannot Delete an Exchange Server Organization in Active Directory

http://support.microsoft.com/default.aspx?scid=kb;en-us;325323&Product=exch2k

The steps outlined below are the complete required actions. The KB is provided only as a background reference.

The remainder of this section covers alternative methods of handling the process described above, as well as supplemental references. You may skip the balance of this section if you have already successfully completed the steps above.

Alternate Method for Removing Exchange from AD

The following KB explains an automated way to remove an entire Exchange Organization. It requires an Exchange SP2 or later install or SP disk. (You can use the SBS 2003 CD. However, to do that, you must install ADC on this DC and then delete the mailbox connections to all mail-enabled objects first.)

Microsoft KB Reference:

How to completely remove Exchange 2000 or Exchange 2003 from Active Directory

http://support.microsoft.com/default.aspx?scid=kb;EN-US;273478

Additional Detail Information

In order to remove the Exchange, you should use the AD Users and Computers to search for all mail-enabled objects and delete the mailbox. This will delete the connection between the mailbox in the store and the account that owns it. The mailboxes are not purged in this process, just the connection links. Once all mail enabled objects have been disconnected from the Exchange Store, you can proceed to delete the Exchange references.

1. From SBS 2003 CD2, add **Exchange Administrative Tools**. Choose **Custom install**.

2. Search for all mail-enabled objects.

3. Select **All**, right-click, choose **Delete Mailbox.**

4. From an Exchange 2000 Server Service Pack 2 (SP2) or later CD, or from the location where the service pack files are located, run **Update.exe** with the **/removeorg** switch. For example, type *d:***\setup\i386\update.exe /removeorg** at a command prompt, where *d:* is the drive that contains the Exchange 2000 service pack CD.

    Note: Exchange 2000 SP2 and later contains a command-line switch, **/removeorg**, that removes the Organization container and all sub-containers from Active Directory. You can run this switch from Exchange 2000 Server Service Pack 2 or later by using the following command: **update.exe /removeorg**. Additionally, you can run this command from any server in the forest, not just from an Exchange 2000 server. This command does not remove services, files, or registry keys.

5. Shut down the member server or domain controller where Exchange 2000 was   installed.

6. Restart the domain controller you were using to remove the Exchange organization. Allow sufficient time for replication to occur between the domain controllers.

Section D: Additional Resources

You may find that you need to manually delete the Exchange Objects in Sites and Services, as well as in AD Users and Computer with View Advanced enabled. You may also need to use ADSI Edit, with steps similar to this KB:

> XADM: How to Remove an Exchange 5.5 Server Computer from an Exchange 2000 Server Administrative Group Using By Using ADSI Edit
> http://support.microsoft.com/default.aspx?scid=kb;en-us;328668&Product=exch2k

> How to Completely Remove Exchange 2000 from Active Directory
> http://support.microsoft.com/default.aspx?scid=kb;EN-US;273478

> XADM: ForestPrep Does Not Work with Error Message: An Invalid ADSI Pathname Was Passed 80005000

http://support.microsoft.com/default.aspx?scid=kb;EN-US;279749

XADM: You Cannot Delete an Exchange Server Organization In Active Directory
http://support.microsoft.com/default.aspx?scid=kb;en-us;325323&Product=exch2k

XADM: How to Remove the First Exchange 2000 Server Computer from the Site
http://support.microsoft.com/default.aspx?scid=kb;[LN];307917

XADM: Reassigning Site Roles after Removing the First Server in an Exchange Site
http://support.microsoft.com/default.aspx?scid=kb;EN-US;152960

Step E. Remove Domain Controller entries: AD, DNS, WINS, DHCP

The steps below are required to purge AD of entries that refer to the previous SBS server. These entries must be removed in order to prevent AD from attempting to replicate to the missing DC. In addition, adding a new DC back into AD with the same name as the previous SBS would be blocked. Removing the DC entries solves both issues.

Microsoft KB Reference:

216498 How to Remove Data in the Active Directory After an Unsuccessful Domain Controller Demotion

The steps outlined below are the complete required actions. The KB is provided only as a background reference.

1. **Removing DC Role references**—We use NTDSutil to clean up the AD Metabase.
   Procedure
   1) Click **Start**, point to **Programs**, point to **Accessories**, and then click **Command Prompt**.
   2) At the command prompt, type **ntdsutil** and press **ENTER**.

3) Type **metadata cleanup** and press **ENTER**. Based on the options given, the Administrator can perform the removal, but additional configuration parameters must be specified before the removal can occur.

4) Type **connections** and press ENTER. This menu is used to connect to the specific server where the changes occur. If the currently logged-on user does not have administrative permissions, different credentials can be supplied by specifying the credentials to use before making the connection. To do so, type **set creds *domainname username password*** and press **ENTER**. For a null password, type **null** for the password parameter.

5) Type **connect to server *servername*** and press **ENTER**. You should receive confirmation that the connection is successfully established. If an error occurs, verify that the domain controller being used in the connection is available and the credentials you supplied have administrative permissions on the server.

Note: If you try to connect to the same server you want to delete, when you try to delete the server that Step 15 refers to, you may receive the following error message:

Error 2094. The DSA Object cannot be deleted0x2094

6) Type **quit** and press **ENTER**. The **Metadata Cleanup** menu appears.

7) Type **select operation target** and press **ENTER**.

8) Type **list domains** and press **ENTER**. A list of domains in the forest is displayed, each with an associated number.

9) Type **select domain *number*** and press **ENTER** where *number* is the number associated with the domain the server you are removing is a member of. The domain you select is used to determine whether the server being removed is the last domain controller of that domain.

10) Type **list sites** and press **ENTER**. A list of sites, each with an associated number, is displayed.

11) Type **select site *number*** and press **ENTER**, where *number* is the number associated with the site the server you are removing is a member of. You should receive a confirmation listing the site and domain you chose.

12) Type **list servers in site** and press **ENTER**. A list of servers in the site, each with an associated number, is displayed.

13) Type **select server *number***, where *number* is the number associated with the server you want to remove. You receive a confirmation listing the selected server, its Domain Name Server (DNS) host name, and the location of the server's computer account you want to remove.

14) Type **quit** and press **ENTER**. The **Metadata Cleanup** menu appears.

15) Type **remove selected server** and press **ENTER**. You should receive confirmation that the removal completed successfully. If you receive the following error message:

Error 8419 (0x20E3)

The DSA object could not be found

This indicates the NTDS Settings object may already be removed from Active Directory as the result of another administrator action removing the NTDS Settings object, or replication of the successful removal of the object after running the DCPROMO utility.

Note: You may also see this error when you try to bind to the domain controller that is going to be removed. Ntdsutil has to bind to a domain controller other than the one to be removed with metadata cleanup.

16) Type **quit** at each menu to quit the Ntdsutil utility. You should receive confirmation that the connection disconnected successfully.

2. **Removing the Computer account and Replication Reference—**
    Using ADSIEdit, we can inspect the Metabase for additional cleanup,
    as well as to remove the computer account and replication reference
    if it still remains.

    To delete the former DC computer account, follow these steps:

    1) Start ADSIEdit.

        a. Expand the **Domain NC** container.

        b. Expand **DC=*Your Domain*, DC=COM, PRI, LOCAL, NET**.

        c. Expand **OU=Domain Controllers**.

        d. Right-click **CN=*domain controller name***, and then click **Delete**.

            If you receive the "DSA object cannot be deleted" error when you try to delete the object, change the UserAccountControl value. To change the UserAccountControl value, right-click the domain controller in ADSIEdit, and then click **Properties**. Under **Select a property to view**, click **UserAccountControl**. Click **Clear**, change the value to 4096, and then click **Set**. You can now delete the object.

            Note: The FRS subscriber object is deleted when the computer object is deleted with normal administration tools because it is a child of the computer account. If ADSIedit or a scripted level tool is used instead, that typically fails to remove the hierarchy objects, including the NTFRS object. You can use the next step to delete that object as well.

    2) Use ADSIEdit to delete the FRS member object. To do this, follow these steps:

        a. Start ADSIEdit.

        b. Expand the **Domain NC** container.

    c. Expand **DC=*Your Domain*, DC=COM, PRI, LOCAL, NET**.

    d. Expand **CN=System**.

    e. Expand **CN=File Replication Service**.

    f. Expand **CN=Domain System Volume (SYSVOL share)**.

    g. Right-click the domain controller you are removing, and then click **Delete**.

3) Use ADSIEdit to delete the Site reference container for the removed server object. To do this, follow these steps:

    a. Start ADSIEdit.

    b. Expand the **Configuration Container**.

    c. Expand **CN=Sites**. Normally, you have only three entries below **Sites**. If the list includes different or additional names, inspect them for containers below that refer to the servername object you are trying to delete. The normal three entries are as follows:

       CN=Default-First-Site-Name

       CN=Inter-site Transports

       CN=Subnets

    d. Expand **CN=Default-First-Site-Name**.

    e. Typically you should see a container here named for the computer object you are looking for. It should read as **CN=*domain controller name* with the actual name of your server. Delete only the container (and its contents) named for the domain controller you are removing.**

4) Use ADSIEdit to delete the DHCP authority reference objects associated with the removed server. When you

reinstall DHCP Server later, you will recover this setting at that time. To do this, follow these steps:

a) Start ADSIEdit.

b) Expand the **Configuration Container**

c) Expand **CN=Services**

d) Expand **CN=NetServices**

e) Right-click the objects that indicate the class as "dHCPClass", and then click **Delete.**

Note: Even if a different server in your domain was associated with this object, there isn't any impact upon the DHCP Server configuration itself, only that the DHCP Server is returned to a non-authorized state. Once you authorize it again, it returns to original operations configuration.

3. **Removing obsolete IWAM_Servername and IUSR_Servername user accounts**—These accounts are created automatically when installing Internet Information Service, but run only against the local machine matching the Servername they were created for originally. Remove any IWAM_Servername and IUSR_Servername accounts in AD for which "Servername" portion matches a DC you have removed, even if you will be recreating a new server with that name. Leave the entries associated with the current server. If these accounts remain and you later create a new IIS Server with the same name, a password synchronization error occurs. In the case of SBS 2003, this will lead to non-functional service by the OWA, OMA, and similar services. The problem can be resolved if this step is missed, but it's simple to do at this point.

4. **DNS Records Cleanup**—Remove permanently abandoned DC entry instances from DNS, specifically the GUID-specific record in _msdcs.

As a result of this upgrade process, you will have entries remaining in DNS that no longer are valid. Depending upon the strategic migration plan you are following, you may need to remove DNS entries now.

Expert Tip: *Cleanup of DNS entries is required for deleted Domain Controllers that will never be restored to original by Disaster Recovery with a System State restore as the same GUID-based DC in the Domain. In our case, for any servers removed with NTDSutil, the GUID is already now invalid.*

Because of the GUID associated with the DNS _msdcs entry, these steps are required even if you are reinstalling later to re-create and SBS server with the same name on a new computer configuration. All other DNS entries for the previous SBS could be retained, but most if not all are re-created during the normal setup and installation of the SBS.

Even if you are not entirely familiar with all the DNS tree locations and their meaning, it's also reasonable to browse through the DNS tree to identify whether any additional miscellaneous references were retained for a permanently retired DC name or IP.

Here's a brief technical explanation, followed by steps for the details to accomplish this:

• You want to remove the cname record in the _msdcs.*root domain of forest* zone in DNS. Assuming that DC is going to be reinstalled and re-promoted, a new NTDS Settings object is created with a new GUID and a matching cname record in DNS. You do not want the DCs that exist to use the old cname record.

• In earlier steps, the NTDS Settings object has been deleted, so now you can delete the computer account, the FRS member object, the cname (or Alias) record in the _msdcs container, the A (or Host) record in DNS, the trustDomain object for a deleted child domain, and the domain controller.

> To complete these steps in DNS cleanup, from the Manage Computer console, locate the DNS section:
>
> 1) Use the DNS MMC to delete the A record in DNS. The A record is also known as the Host record. To delete the A record, right-click the **A record**, and then click **Delete**.

2) Also delete the cname (also known as the Alias) record in the **_msdcs** container. To do so, expand the **_msdcs** container, right-click the **cname**, and then click **Delete**.

3) **Important:** If this was a DNS server, remove the reference to this DC under the **Name Servers** tab. To do this, in the DNS console, click the domain name under **Forward Lookup Zones**, and then remove this server from the **Name Servers** tab.

   Note: If you have reverse lookup zones, also remove the server from these zones.

5. **Verify normal DC Operations**—At restart the remaining DC will confirm normal boot and DC operations on the remaining DC with the previous DC having been removed.

   Check for errors mentioned in the Event Logs.

6. **WINS and DHCP Cleanup**—Remove permanently retired DC entry instances from WINS and DHCP Scope Options.

   Both the WINS and DHCP Settings can be located in the Manage Computer console panel. Expanding each branch out to reveal the properties allows you to review table entries and settings.

   In some cases, static entries may have been added to the WINS table, though this is not common. You should browse the WINS list for entries you can remove that reference the retired DC or the IP it held.

7. Remove or revise permanently retired DC entry instances from DHCP Scope Options if the subnet is changing or if the new server will have a different IP.

   DHCP Options may also include references to the retired DC. This would include DHCP options that point to the SBS as the WINS and DNS Server or as a Time Server or Default Gateway (router) that should be shifted to the new DC when created. However, all of this only applies if the IP assigned to the new DC is not the same as the old one.

   Inspect both the Server Options and the Scope Options to ensure these entries are properly set or removed.

Milestone

This Domain Controller is now prepared to advance into the next phase. All references to all other domain controllers should have been purged as indicated from AD and DNS information. The remainder of this section includes information required to address removal of domain trusts that might be present only in a migration of a non-SBS domain. If your previous domain was an SBS-based domain, you can go forward with the next phase in your outline process.

Remove Trusted domains from (Non-SBS) deleted Domain Controllers

This is an unlikely condition with an SBS domain. However, it might occur if you are using this document to migrate from a standard Windows Domain that allowed trusts, but you are now migrating to SBS. In other words, this condition could not possibly have occurred in a domain that was an SBS, because Domain Trusts are not allowed. For that same reason, trusted domains will not be allowed in our final configuration.

Microsoft KB Reference:

The steps outlined below are the complete required actions. The KB is provided only as a background reference.

1. If the deleted computer was the last domain controller in a child domain and the child domain was also deleted, use ADSIEdit to delete the trustDomain object for the child. To do this, follow these steps: Start ADSIEdit.

    a. Expand the **Domain NC** container.

    b. Expand **DC=*Your Domain*, DC=COM, PRI, LOCAL, NET**.

    c. Expand **CN=System**.

    d. Right-click the **Trust Domain** object, then click **Delete**.

2. Use Active Directory Sites and Services to remove the domain controller. To do this, follow these steps:

   Start Active Directory Sites and Services.

   a. Expand **Sites**.

   b. Expand the server's site. The default site is **Default-First-Site-Name**.

   c. Expand **Server**.

   d. Right-click the domain controller, then click **Delete**.

Notes:

Phase 3: Transfer AD from MigrateDC to SBSnameDC
(Repeat of Phase 2 Transfer Sequence)

This section explains how to transfer Active Directory from the MigrateDC to the SBS nameDC.

15-8a and 15-8b

phase 3 tasklist and illustration

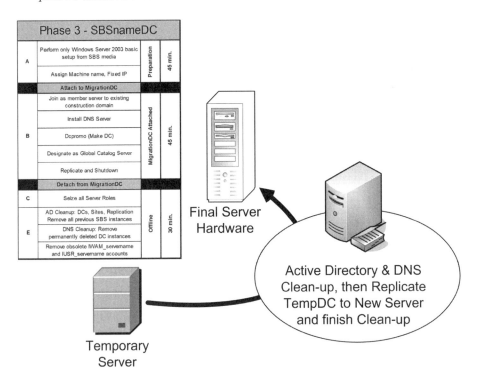

Previously in Phase 2, you perform Steps A through E on "MigrationDC" to build the MigrationDC. Now that MigrationDC has all the AD information, you want to build the final SBS server and transfer AD in the same manner. That means you repeat the steps, building another server. You should turn back to the previous chapter for details of the process as your guideline.

The only exception would be if you plan to intentionally and permanently change the name of your SBS server. If that's the case, you can move forward to Phase 4 and build the new SBS installation on the server you created with a new name under Phase 2.

Phase 3   Perform Steps A—E (omitting D) on "SBSnameDC"

From Figure 15-7b you will see that the list of tasks is just as you performed in Phase 2. Step D is omitted because there is no Exchange in AD to remove anymore.

Phase 4: Resume SBS-Integrated Setup Offline

This section explains how to resume the SBS-integrated setup offline.

15-9a and 15-9b
phase 4 tasklist and illustration

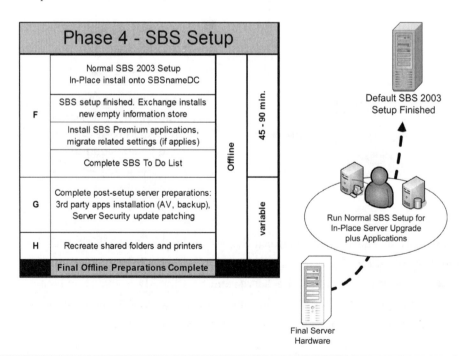

We now return you to your originally initiated SBS installation already in progress...

At point, we have completed the majority of the specialized upgrade process steps. In fact, the balance of the work is primarily the upgrade experience Microsoft originally intended for a routine install. We resume the installation process that was "interrupted" in Phase 1 when we prevented the SBS Integrated Setup from continuing.

The final part of our upgrade, which has several unique (yet still standard) options beyond those in the Microsoft documents, will follow the conclusion of the SBS Setup. We will look at that about the same time you normally start looking at the SBS "To Do List."

We can look at the Exchange Server Information Stores handling and the balance of the data files and shared resource information migration at that point, which is what we cover in the final phase, Phase 5, of this migration.

It's certainly possible that with the more critical parts of the upgrade problem solved, some folks will stay on the Microsoft documented trail for the balance. We have solved the most critical issues already, and we have the very same AD and an SBS server with the same name. That will mean manually recreating shared resources and related information, plus performing an Exmerge on the Exchange databases. However, these both equate to additional time invested in the upgrade and loss of continuity in the new server configuration versus what was present in the old server. It's your choice, but for now, the easiest part of the SBS upgrade begins. Resume the Wizard!

We pick up again with customized options in Phase 5, but now continue with Step F.

Step F.   Complete the Automated Setup for New SBS server

Before You Resume SBS 2003 Setup

Before you begin the installation, there are two possible conditions that might be of interest to you:

1. **SBS 2003 Sharepoint installation flaw**—The initially released media with SBS 2003 included a faulty DLL library file with issues caused if installation was begun after November 24, 2003. Later packaging included the media with a fix for this, but if you are reinstalling from older media, or just got unlucky enough to get some stale product from the back of a shelf, you might still see this come before you. You can be sure to solve this problem by either having media created after December 2003, or most easily by visiting Windows Update with this server in its current condition to obtain a patch related to KB832880.

2. **Manual Install for Custom Exchange Organization Namespace Option**—In earlier parts of this chapter, I discussed how you can resolve namespace problems using LegacyDN, assuming you have changed the server or domain name for you installation. One other possibility is that you attempt a "forklift" install of the production Exchange Stores, but you actually have a legacy Organization name, even though the server and domain name are the same. How could this happen, you ask? It happens if your installation of SBS 2000 was an in-place upgrade from SBS 4.5 or some previous Exchange version prior to 2000. In that case, the organization name probably isn't what Exchange 2000 or 2003 creates by default in a clean install.

    You have two options on how to address this. You could proceed with the SBS install and then use LegacyDN to tweak this, or you can go directly now to a manual install of Exchange 2003 on this server as outlined in the following KB:

    How to Create a First Administrative Group with a Different Name
    http://support.microsoft.com/default.aspx?scid=kb;en-us;271882&Product=exch2003

    I'm not going to describe the summary steps provided in that KB, because I don't think this is going to be a very common concern. However, I did want to mention it.

Resume SBS 2003 Install as Normal on Your Final Server

Now you can probably return to finish construction this machine by just inserting the SBS CD/DVD and let it run as you would normally do with a regular SBS install. We are ready to pick up where we left off when we interrupted the SBS

Setup on the very first DC. To resume the SBS installation, insert SBS 2003 Media CD1 (or browse to the CD1 folder on the DVD media). Either let Autoplay offer you the menu, or run the SBSsetup.exe. You will proceed just as outlined in the printed documentation you received with your SBS product, or using the normal white paper-based installation reference. At this point, we have no special conditions anymore up to the point of dealing with the Exchange Server data once the balance of the SBS server suite is installed.

One more point. If you are upgrading to SBS 2003 Premium Edition, you should complete the installation of those premium server components at this point as well.

> **BEST PRACTICE**: You should now have completed the entire SBS Setup process automated by Microsoft. Pay attention, though; you don't want to let Exchange go to work yet!
>
> Do not proceed with the To Do list items related to configuring the Internet connection if you also have Exchange Server operational to communicate to the Internet. In particular, do not allow the Exchange Server to begin processing e-mail unless you want to test it. Our next steps will be to bring over the production e-mail contents. You don't want to beginning pulling mail into the empty store if you are about to replace that store entirely, right?

Step G. Complete the Post-Setup Configuration for New SBS Server

Import the DHCP Server Database

One of the most common configuration options you will need to address is DHCP Server setup. If you plan to use DHCP Server assignment by the SBS to give IPs to your client workstations, you may have configurations you previously established on the existing production SBS server. Here's information on how to migrate those settings. Although you have the option to handle that manually if you prefer, it's not a complicated process for a small LAN.

> How to move a DHCP database to a computer running Windows Server 2003

http://support.microsoft.com/default.aspx?kbid=325473

For configuration and database exported from Windows 2003 Server or configuration export only from Windows 2000 DHCP Server:

netsh dhcp server export *C:\dhcp.txt* **all**

For a full database export from Windows 2000 Server, obtain DHCPexim.exe from the Windows 2000 Resource Kit Supplement 1, also available from this URL:

http://www.microsoft.com/windows2000/techinfo/reskit/tools/new/dhcpexim-o.asp

The results of the export above may be imported with this command on a Windows 2003 Server:

netsh dhcp server import *C:\dhcp.txt* **all**

Third-Party Applications and Advanced Configuration

It's pretty typical that you will have some additional server products to install now. This might include:

- Anti-Virus Management

- Data Backup Products

- Security Patch Management and Deployment

- Server Monitoring, VPN, or Remote Access Tools

You probably want to complete as much of this as possible before you move to the production LAN environment

Step H. Re-create Shared Folders and Printers from SBS Server

Import the Shared Folders Definitions

The following KB suggests a process that reveals what is possible, but it really doesn't go into sufficient detail to explain how much trouble this process could cause! Therefore, this KB is informative for what is involved, and I've created a tool to handle this process in a safe manner.

Saving and restoring existing Windows shares

http://support.microsoft.com/default.aspx?scid=kb;en-us;125996&Product=win2000

The following procedure is another method for handling the process manually, but documenting the information you need from the source server.

Open the **Manage Computer** console, expand the **System Tools | Shared Folders | Share** portion of the tree, as shown in the figure below. Click to select the **Shares** icon and that will display the shares in the right-hand pane. Now, right-click on **Shares** and choose **Export List**. You can export to a .csv or txt file, and this allows you to import to Excel or simply save the contents to review in Notepad.

Figure 15-10
   screenshot of manage computer Shares for Export

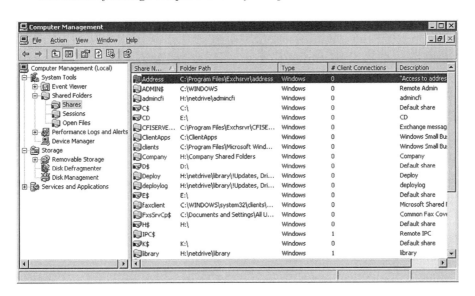

The information you have from that Shares | Export List feature is sufficient to re-create the shares again, but you will need to document the shared folder permissions by other means.

Re-create the Shared Printer Definitions

Shared printers should be re-created on the server in the normal manner you add printers. To assist in this process, a script to create a text file to document the printer information is provided at the back of this chapter. Some of these printers you may not be able to configure until you connect to the production LAN.

Phase 5: Finalizing the Migration for Exchange, Data, and Shared Network Resources

This section discussing finalizing the migration for Exchange, data and shared network resources.

Figure 15-11a and 15-11b
phase 5 tasklist and illustration

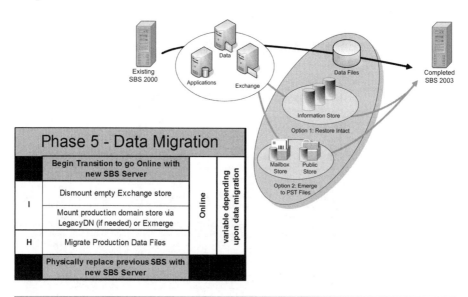

Phase 5 - Data Migration		
Begin Transition to go Online with new SBS Server		
I	Dismount empty Exchange store	Online — variable depending upon data migration
	Mount production domain store via LegacyDN (if needed) or Exmerge	
H	Migrate Production Data Files	
Physically replace previous SBS with new SBS Server		

Notes:

Step I. Final Exchange Server Configuration Issues

We're almost home now—just a little bit more of finalization left to do. The biggest issue is how we deal with the Exchange Information Store contents and configuration. The user mailboxes and related information is the last really technical process we have to address.

At this point, I want to remind you that you don't want this server connected to the Internet or to be available to user access with an e-mail client. Don't allow any e-mail to flow on this server until you have the permanent Information Store for Exchange you intend to keep. Otherwise, if you allow anything but test e-mails to flow, you will end up having to port whatever mail arrives over to the final store as yet another step in the migration you could otherwise avoid.

You have three options on how you can proceed now. Refer to the early part of this chapter for expanded details of the advantages and motivations you have in choosing the best solution for your migration.

- **Forklift an Identically Named Organization and Server**—The steps for this will be familiar to anyone who has done Offline Restores, so I offer no real details here, just a sample. Offline Restores for disaster can be complicated by many issues. For a planned migration, it's far less complex. I'll give a couple of simple examples that should work for a planned migration scenario.

- **LegacyDN: Solving Namespace variations**—There is only a subtle difference between the Forklift move of an Information Store, like an Offline Backup, versus the LegacyDN process. Therefore, use the same examples described below for the Offline Backup as your guideline. Details of how to use LegacyDN are presented in Microsoft KB 324606, or refer to SBSmigration.com for more information.

- **Exmerge**—I'm only providing the most basic outline of how to use Exmerge here. There are no SBS-specific issues involved, and the full documentation is self-contained with the Exmerge utility. I'll provide only a sample of how you can use it to export all your mailboxes. Don't forget to export your Public Stores to a .PST file using Outlook.

Though Exmerge is available from the SBS media, and LegacyDN is available from an Exchange 2000 SP2 or later media, you can also download a package of more than 30 Exchange tools, including these two, from the Microsoft website. It's a pretty cool set of tools, but it's also over 34Mbytes in size.

>Exchange 2003: All-In-One Tools Download
>http://www.microsoft.com/downloads/details.aspx?familyid=e0f616c6-8fa4-4768-a3ed-cc09aef7b60a&displaylang=en

>BEST PRACTICE: When you are ready to process the data from the new stores, if you stop the SMTP service, no new e-mail messages are delivered to the new stores while you are running ExMerge.

Option 1: Forklift Move (aka: Transfer Offline Backup of previous Server)

Perform an Online Backup at the Source Server before you begin
This is just common sense; I shouldn't even have to mention it! It helps simplify the transfer for several reasons, and it gives you some good options if you run into trouble unexpectedly. And yet, I know some of you won't want to take that time. But you should.

Simplify as Much as Possible in Preparation
Performing an Offline Restore on the same server as the previous database was run is generally pretty simple, assuming that the database was in good condition at the time of the backup. For the sake if this discussion, I'm going to assume that the Exchange EDB, STM and log files are all stored in a common location together, and that the folder name is MDBDATA. In fact, I'm going to encourage you to consider directing all these files to a common location before you do the migration of the stores, preferably to a drive letter and folder path location that is going to be the same location specified on both the Source and Target servers. This eliminates a possible complication in restoring Offline Backups of Exchange. If the databases are inconsistent, then the log files will include hard-encoded path references. It's a lot easier to not have to "recover" and repair

while resolving odd path changes as well as the server move. The simplest way to get all these files in a single location is to perform an Online Backup, which purges all the transaction log files, then redirect the transaction logs to where the EDB/STM files are held.

Another option would be to shut down the mail processing by the server as you prepare to shift the stores and perform an Online Backup. If no additional mail is being processed, you can now move these files and perform a "hard recovery" by relocating only the EDB/STM files and none of the log files.

Placing the Databases on the New Server

1. Shut down the Exchange Server Services (Some versions only require dismounting the store, but this always works.)
2. Rename the MDBDATA folder with the new (empty) Information Store to something like MDBDATA.mt (mt for "empty")
3. Create a new MDBDATA folder now in the same location as before.
4. Copy the Exchange EDB, STM and the transaction log files from the backup media (or the other server) into the new MDBDATA folder.

In many cases, if you have placed the databases already on the new server, but they are in a different folder on the same volume, you can use a "move" command in Explorer to shift the location instantly. From there, rename the folder if needed.

Allowing Offline Databases to Replace Newer Store

Before you can mount databases restored from an offline backup, you must configure Exchange to acknowledge that the database are to be "overwritten" during a restore procedure. In fact, you are not literally overwriting the previous database; rather you are replacing it with a copy that appears to be older. Follow these steps to enable this option:

1. Start the Exchange System Manager.
2. Expand **Servers**, expand *Server Name*, expand *Storage Group*, and then click the database that was restored.
3. Right-click the database, then click **Properties**.
4. Click the **Database** tab.
5. Click to select the **This database can be overwritten by a restore** checkbox.
6. Click **OK**.

7. To mount the database, right-click the database, then click **Mount Store**.

At this point, you could perform a number of consistency test and verifications, the sort of things you might do if you had a damaged Information Store and were recovering it. You might also decide to user Exchange tools to process all of the transaction logs. I mention this just to acknowledge that Offline Restores can have many other aspects I might be skipping over because I want this to be a simple illustration, and I believe that the database I just dismounted from the other server is probably in suitable shape to simply mount here.

LegacyDN Used Here, If Needed

Here is where we would introduce the user of LegacyDN. If LegacyDN was needed here, we would first need to restart the server. Continue on after the restart is complete. The Exchange databases attempt to mount automatically following this startup, so if you want to stop that, you have two simple options. You could disable the Microsoft Exchange Information Store service, or enable the checkbox for "Do not mount this store on startup" located in Exchange System Manager on the Database tab for each the Mailbox Store and the Public Store.

Mounting the Information Store

We are ready to try to mount the Information Store. If you previously stopped all the services earlier, you must restart them now, or the mount will certainly fail. With Exchange 2003, even with all steps performed correctly up to this point, you may still find that you receive an error on the first attempt to mount the store. This happens because if we didn't run the "patch" command, Exchange sees that it may need to be done automatically. You can just repeat the request to mount the store immediately, and in normal conditions it will mount just as expected. Hopefully, when you do your first production server or test system, this is just what happens for you.

If you have trouble mounting the stores, many issues could be involved. There is, however, one issue in particular specific to the migration process that you can address by planning ahead or making corrective changes (even at this point), but you quickly get into complications: broken path references. Make sure the databases and logs are in the same path location as before. If you didn't do this, and if you need to fix it after you shut down the old server or moved the databases, you do have a trick to help you. You can "move" the empty stores to matching folder locations, even if that represents splitting the databases or log files. Once you have Exchange expecting to find the right locations, you shut down the services and transfer the production store files to the various locations that match their original homes.

That's the last point I'll make here on troubleshooting the mount, so if it's not the issue you have with your offline restore, you need to go to standard Exchange documentation, or consult the Exchange Server chapter in this book to see if your issue is addressed there.

Reconnect the Users to Their Mailboxes

If the store mounted, you still have a last task related to the Exchange Databases: reviewing the mailbox connections and user assignments.

> BEST PRACTICE: After restoring the mailboxes, users with mailbox sizes larger than 175Megabytes are unable to send and receive properly due to enforced default quotas in Exchange 2003. You can remove the restriction or change the default values.

Inspect the Mail-Enabled Public Store Folders

Unfortunately, a frequently observed problem with a forklift of a Public Store is that some of the mail-enabled folders may lose their mail "proxyaddress" references or have folder security issues. This isn't entirely a problem caused by the forklift of the store as much as it is that the Public Store just has some stability problems that limit its flexibility to large-scale changes.

Notes:

You should be prepared to ensure your e-mail-enabled folders work by inspecting them individually from Exchange System Manager. Directly off the root of the Organization is the Folders Object, beneath which you find Public Folders. If the proxy address has been lost or corrupted, you will identify that by right-clicking and choosing Properties on a given folder. You receive a pop-up error with the error shown in the figure below:

Figure 15-12
    pop-up error message c1038a21

Correcting the mail proxy setting isn't hard. Close the pop-up by clicking **OK**. Now, right-click the folder, choose **All Tasks**, then **Mail Enabled**. Following a warning prompt, the folder will have the mail attributes restored. Verify that the mail settings and security are as you intended.

The error above doesn't occur with an Exmerge simply because no attempt is made by Exmerge to preserve either security or mail properties.

Option 2: Exmerge (Export/Import all mailboxes as .PST files)

Before you can run Exmerge successfully, you must grant the Administrator account permission to access all mailboxes with permissions not established by default. This step is required at both the source server and the target server.

Exporting Mailboxes from the Source Server

You will need to export all of the things listed below from the previous SBS server. Keep in mind that when you export the user mailboxes to a .PST, these files could be quite large. In fact, the total disk space required for all .PST files will almost certainly exceed the file size required for the original Exchange Information Store itself. This is because Exchange stores a single instance of e-mails and objects that are directed to more than one user. When exporting to .PST, each user mailbox exports out a copy of each object referenced. Therefore, an e-mail with an attachment sent to five different mailboxes would appear in each of the five .PST files.

Prepare all the following from the previously existing SBSserver:

- Export all your users' mailbox data to .pst files by using the ExMerge utility, and then export Public Folder data to .pst files on a Microsoft Outlook (MAPI) client.

- For each profile at each workstation, export Outlook Inbox Rules as well as export Offline Storage files (OSTs), if present

- Document all mailbox "alternate recipient" and "send as" permissions which were established administratively in the past for each mail-enabled user

- Document all Public Folder security permissions so that you can re-create them

Exmerge allows you to generate the individual .PST files for all users in one unattended process after you establish your preferences.

1. To start the ExMerge wizard, double-click **ExMerge.exe**.
2. On the **Procedure Selection** page, click **Extract or Import (Two Step Procedure)**, and then click **Next**.
3. On the **Two Step Procedure** page, click **Step 1**, and then click **Next**.
4. On the **Source Server** page, type the name of the server under **Microsoft Exchange Server Name**, and then click **Options**.
5. On the **Data Selection Criteria** page, click **User messages and folders** on the **Data** tab.
6. On the **Dates** tab, click **All**.
   Note: This option copies all the e-mail messages to a .pst file regardless of dates. If you want to specify a date range, click **Dated** and then specify a valid date and time range.
7. Click **OK,** then click **Next**.
8. On the **Mailbox Selection** page, select one or more mailboxes to extract the e-mail message from, then click **Next**.

9. In the **Default locale** list, select the appropriate language, then click **Next**.

10. On the **Target Directory** page, if you want to change the location of the .pst files, click **Change Folder**, then click **Next**.

    If you do not want to change the location of the .pst files, click **Next**.

11. On the **Save Settings** page, click **Next** to start the extraction process.

12. On the **Process Status** page, click **Finish**.

Importing Mailboxes back to the Target Server

Remember, you need to repeat the steps mentioned above to grant the Administrator account the required permissions to access every user's mailbox.

The next steps are quite similar to those we performed in the Export. You now want to Import all your mailbox, public folder data at the server. In addition, you may need to visit the workstations to configure any Outlook rules and OST files you saved earlier.

When you run the Exmerge, you again select the Two Step Procedure, but choose Step 2 this time. When you perform the **Import Procedure** tab, click **Merge data to target store**. The mailboxes will normally be empty to start with. This option checks to see if the message already exists in the target store. If the message exists, it will not be copied. The prompts that follow allow you to match the .PST file to the usernames.

> BEST PRACTICE: You might consider starting the Administrator's mailbox clean with the new server, particularly if it's the place where trouble reports and NDR notices go. No sense in having all the configuration stuff that isn't applicable cluttering the mailbox. However, it's not a bad idea to hang on to it. Therefore, you could choose from a couple different ideas:
>
> • Keep it as a .PST in the data folders
>
> • Import it to an Exchange Store mailbox but then reassign the mailbox to a different user you create for that purpose
>
> • Import the contents to a public folder

Step J. Additional Final Server Configuration Issues

Migrating Data Files

You can now migrate your data files by whatever method you prefer. This includes:

- Mounting the old hard drives in the new server or in a workstation on the LAN

- Restoring from tape

- XCOPY or ROBOCOPY

  Whatever method you like is fine, but the tape restore is the most reliable technical process. You won't need to be concerned about the NTFS permissions; they will still match if you restore them.

  One advantage of using the tape backup is that you can restore large volumes of folder trees and permissions using a familiar tool: your tape back program. It's possible to accomplish the same thing with XCOPY and the proper commands, but not everyone moves large blocks of files this way all the time. For a more complete discussion on file migration, refer to the Disaster Recovery Chapter.

Migrating Custom Web Site Content

I'm not providing any specific information on this process. If you figured out how to create custom Web site information, you probably should be able to figure out how to copy the contents from one server to the next. All kidding aside, this particular topic will depend upon the complexity of what you have done. There are no specific issues involved unique to SBS. I'm including this item here just as a reminder that you should address this move.

Migrating Shared Fax Databases

This isn't a very complicated process. You can refer to the old location you configured for the Shared Fax database and related image documents. In the management console of the previous SBS server, look at the Fax Server properties to identify the folder locations you were using. You can remove or replace the configuration files created by default on the new server by stopping the Fax Service, then transferring the files into the new location.

In some cases, if you previously had redirected the Fax configuration folders to a data drive partition, you may not have any work at all to do provided you make the same redirection configuration in the new server's fax configuration.

Is the Final Server Configuration Completed?

Hopefully, at this point, if you aren't actually finished with the migration of the server, you are close to where you need to be and have only familiar tasks left to conclude.

It would be impossible for me to try to document everything you might need beyond this point in detail. What I have tried to provide is the best review of the most unique and valuable information I have on performing a migration using the Swing Method. I've focused upon the aspects unique to the method and to SBS itself.

Summary

Months have passed since I completed this chapter, and so this becomes an epilog to that story.

I completed this chapter in time for a debut presentation of Swing Migration at SMB Nation 2004. That session was overwhelmingly well received. The positive feedback on the basic SBS 2000 migration to SBS 2003 concept *this* chapter covers was clear enough, but I was immediately swayed by requests to go even deeper, to outline other product scenarios and to automate the technical steps. Unfortunately, there's simply not enough room to add more detail in the book beyond this explanation! This chapter is the original, first generation project reference covering SBS 2000 to SBS 2003 migration. Production migrations were performed by many of the SBS-MVPs who helped "beta-test" this method before it was announced. Yet, the story doesn't end there.

To address requests from IT Pros who still wanted a similar documented path for migration from all previous Windows and SBS versions, I created a new website. I established www.SBSmigration.com as the permanent home for news on the evolution of Swing Migration and updated technical guidance for the long term. This is where you now can find migration guides across all Windows domains, plus more complex project scenarios, including technical transitions Microsoft provides no support to accomplish.

I didn't imagine that my desire to find a better migration plan for SBS 2003 for my own customers would lead to a new business. I am fortunate to be in the position to help many people who want an alternative migration path that is well documented, and includes support for getting the project completed. Saving the domain name and server name was the only priority for me originally, but I soon discovered other major benefits: "working offline, with nothing to undo, no workstation profile repairs and all with the weekends off" for IT Pros would become the key value of Swing Migration. I am now able to maintain a broad reference summary for all kinds of migration solutions to offer for scenarios when even Swing Migration isn't the best fit.

By the time you read this book in print, a more updated reference and related tools on Swing Migration will be offered through my website. Based upon feedback from IT Pros worldwide, I now maintain a full product option called a *Swing It!!* **Technician Kit** containing updated documentation, unique script tools, bundled with technical support for completing a migration project. My goal was to explain an idea that needed to be documented as an alternative to what was available at that time. I didn't see at that time how much more was left unexplained. I hope that this book chapter helps you to understand what is possible from my first idea.

Therefore, I encourage you to visit SBSmigration.com to see if any critical information is presented there to clarify issues discussed in this chapter. I will provide critical information there to ensure. I want to ensure that anyone choosing to working from the book can be aware of any errors that may be discovered in the book documentation that pose risk to their success with a Swing Migration.

Ideally, the latest Technician Kit itself will continue to be the route to obtain the most complete and tested migration project solution available. This chapter represents a great way to get insight into the total process. I must confess, I probably wouldn't have decided to investigate this project completely without the knowlege that my idea had a place in this book, a place I hope opens many eyes to what is possible with skills and imagination for SBS migration.

Appendix

Appendix A

SBS 2003 RESOURCES

This appendix will list SBS 2003 resources that will be useful in your quest to better utilize SBS 2003. Many of these resources have previously been listed in the book, but many new resources are added here as well. Bottom line: All the SBS 2003 resources you need to move forward in one easy, at-a-glance location.

Microsoft Windows Small Business Server (SBS) Sites

- www.microsoft.com/windowsserver2003/sbs/default.mspx

- www.microsoft.com/sbserver

- www.microsoft.com/sbs

- Microsoft Learning SBS course: Designing, Deploying, and Managing a Network Solution for the Small and Medium-sized Business (three day SBS course): www.microsoft.com/traincert/syllabi2395afinal.asp

- Exam 70-282: Designing, Deploying, and Managing a Network Solution for the Small and Medium-sized Business: www.microsoft.com/learning/exams/70-282.asp.

Microsoft Partners-related Sites

- Microsoft Partner's SBS site: www.microsoft.com/partners/sbs

- Main Microsoft Partner site: www.microsoft.com/partner

- Microsoft SBS Partner Locator Tool: sbslocator.cohesioninc.com/apartnerlocator.asp

- Microsoft Certified Partner Resource Directory (how to find a Certi-fied Partner): directory.microsoft.com/resourcedirectory/solutions.aspx

- Action Pack: members.microsoft.com/partner/salesmarketing/partnermarket/actionpack/default.aspx

Additional Microsoft or Microsoft-related Sites

- Microsoft TS2 Events: www.msts2.com

- Microsoft TouchPoint: www.connect-ms.com/mstps/ (or www.msbigday.com)

- Eric Ligman's Microsoft Small Business Channel Community site: www.mssmallbiz.com/default.aspx

- Microsoft TechNet: www.microsoft.com/technet

- Microsoft Office templates: officeupdate.microsoft.com/templategallery/

- bCentral small business portal: www.bcentral.com

- bCentral Technology Consulting Directory: directory.bcentral.com/ITConsultant/

- Great Plains: www.microsoft.com/greatplains

- Microsoft Visio: www.microsoft.com/visio

- Asentus: www.asentus.net

- Hands On Lab: www.handsonlab.com

- Granite Pillar: microsoft.granitepillar.com/partners/

- Entirenet: www.entirenet.net/registration

- Directions on Microsoft: www.directionsonmicrosoft.com

- Microsoft Solution Selling: www.solutionselling.com/mspartners/fusion.html

- Dr. Thomas Shinder's ISA Server Web site: www.isaserver.org

- Bill English's SharePoint Web site: www.sharepointknowledge.com

Third-party SBS-related sites

- Susan Bradley's Small Biz Server Links: http://www.sbslinks.com/ (and try www.sbslinks.com/really.htm for a really good time)

- Wayne Small's SBS Web site: www.sbsfaq.com

- Another SBS FAQ site: http://www.smallbizserver.net/

Newslists, User Groups, Trade Associations, Organizations

- SBS—Microsoft Small Business Server Support: http://groups.yahoo.com/group/sbs2k/

- Small BizIT "Small Business IT Consultants" newslist at Yahoo: groups.yahoo.com/groups/smallbizIT

- San Diego SBS User Group: www.sdsbsug.org

- CompTIA: www.comptia.com

- Network Professional Association: www.npa.org

- West Sound Technology Professional Association(Kitsap County, Washington): www.wstpa.org

- Adelaide Australia SBS User Group. For information, contact Dean Calvert: dean@calvert.net.au (also details at www.sbsfaq.com)

- Boston, MA, USA SBS User Group. For more information, contact Eliot Sennett: eliot@esient.com

- Cincinnati, OH, USA SBS User Group. This SBS group is a SIG that is part of a larger general user group. For more information, contact Kevin Royalty: kevin_royalty@yahoo.com

- Cleveland, OH, USA SBS User Group. For more information, visit http://www.gcpcug.org/ or contract Fredrick Johnson: fjohnson@rosstek.com

- Denver CO, USA SBS User Group. For more information, contact Lilly C. Banks: lilly@iSolutionsUnlimited.com.

- Omaha, NB, USA SBS User Group. For more information, contact Amy Luby: aluby@tconl.com. has started a user group in the Omaha, Nebraska area, 10 users

- Portland, OR, USA SBS User Group. For more information, visit http://pdxsbs.fpwest.com or contact Patrick West: patrick@west.net

- San Francisco/Bay Area, CA, USA SBS User Group. For more information, contact Ed Correia: ecorreia@sagacent.com

- Seattle, WA, USA SBS User Group. For more information, contact Steven Banks steve@banksnw.com

- Southern CA, USA SBS User Group. For more information, contact Donna Obdyke: DObdyke@prodigy.net

- Sydney, NSW, Australia SBS User Group. For more information, contact Wayne Small [wayne@correct.com.au] and visit http://www.sbsfaq.com

- Tampa/Palm Harbor/Largo, Florida SBS User Group. Rayanne M. Buchianico, rbuchianico@tampabay.rr.com, flsbsug@yahoogroups.com.

- Black Data Processing Association (BDPA): www.bdpa.org

Seminars, Workshops, Conferences

- SMB Nation: www.smbnation.com

- Microsoft TS2 events: www.msts2.com

- Microsoft Big Day/Business Solution Series: www.msbigday.com

- Microsoft Momentum Conference: http://www.microsoft.com/partner/events/wwpartnerconference/

- ITEC: www.goitec.com

- Guerrilla marketing and sales seminars: www.guerrillabusiness.com

- Who Moved My Cheese seminars: www.whomovedmycheese.com

- Myers-Briggs Type Indicator: www.apcentral.org

- Millionaire Mind / T. Harv Eker: www.peakpotentials.com

- TechMentor: www.techmentorevents.com

- SuperConference (accounting/technology): www.pencorllc.com

Business Resources

- US Small Business Administration: www.sba.gov

- Palo Alto Software for business planning: www.paloaltosoftware.com

- PlanWare: www.planware.org

- Outsourced accounting: www.cfo2go-wa.com

- US Federal Reserve Web site: www.federalreserve.gov

- Presentations: www.presentations.com

- CardScan: www.cardscan.com

- Plaxo: www.plaxo.com

Media

- Small Business Best Practices newsletter: www.nethealthmon.com/newsletter.htm

- CRN: www.crn.com

- SBS Maven Andy Goodman posts SBS-related articles at http://www.12c4pc.com.

- Small Business Computing: www.smallbusinesscomputing.com

- PC Magazine Small Business Super Site (www.pcmag.com/category2/0,4148,13806,00.asp)

- Mary Jo Foley's Microsoft-Watch: www.microsoftwatch.com

- NetworkWorldFusion SMB portal: www.nwfusion.com/net.worker/index.html

- Microsoft Certified Professional Magazine: www.mcpmag.com

- Certified Magazine: www.certmag.com

- Windows and .NET Magazine: www.winnetmag.com

- CRMDaily: www.crmdaily.com

- TechRepublic: www.techrepublic.com

- VAR Business: www.varbusiness.com

- Small Business Technology Report: www.smallbiztechnology.com

- Win2K News: www.w2knews.com

- SmallBizTechTalk: www.smallbiztechtalk.com

- Eweek: www.eweek.com

- ComputerWorld: www.computerworld.com

- Kim Komando Show: www.komando.com

- WinInformit: http://www.wininformant.com/

- Entrepreneur Magazine: www.entrepreneur.com

- INC Magazine: www.inc.com

- Fortune: www.fortune.com

- Bizjournals: www.bizjournals.com

- CNN: www.cnn.com

- Business Week: www.businessweek.com

- CBS MarketWatch: www.marketwatch.com

- USA Today: www.usatoday.com

- Money Magazine: www.money.cnn.com

SMB Hardware & Software Companies

- HP/Compaq: www.hp.com

- ConnectWise: www.connectwise.com

- Document Locator—Small Business Server edition: www.document locator.com

- TimeSlips: www.timeslips.com

- QuickBooks: www.quickbooks.com

Miscellaneous

- Geekcoprs—technology volunteers enabling communities worldwide: www.geekcorps.com

- Google search engine: www.google.com

- NPower, not-for-profit technology agency: www.npower.org

- eBay: www.ebay.com

- GeekSquad: www.geeksquad.com

- Geeks On Call: www.geeksoncall.com

- Soft-Temps: www.soft-temps.com

- Insurance for technology professionals: www.techinsurance.com

- Robert Half International salary survey: www.rhii.com

- AOL for Small Business: aolsvc.aol.com/small_biz

- eProject: www.eproject.com

Appendix B

FOOTNOTES

Chapter 6

1 "Bits & Bytes" column, *PC Magazine*, November 25, 2003, page 25.

2 *Internet Week*, October 25, 1999.

3 Eric A. Taub, "Ease of Paperless E-Mail Sidelines the Forlorn Fax," *New York Times*, March 13, 2003.

4 Brian Livingston, "The State of the Computer Industry," *Windows Secrets Newsletter*, September 14, 2004.

5 Ellen Messmer, "Symantec Report: E-Comm Attacks on Rise," *NetworkWorld*, September 27, 2004.

6 John Markoff, "Attacks on Windows PC's Grew in First Half of 2004," *New York Times*, September 20, 2004.

7 Ellen Messmer, "Symantec Report: E-Comm Attacks on Rise," *NetworkWorld*, September 27, 2004.

8 This was later superseded by MS01-027 in May 2001 that included this fix as well.

9 Scott Bekker, "Sobig Damage Estimated at $5.59 Billion," *ENT Magazine*, www.entmag.com/news/article.asp?EditorialsID=5931, August 26, 2003.

10 Ellen Messmer, "Symantec Report: E-Comm Attacks on Rise," *NetworkWorld*, September 27, 2004.

11 Jonathan Kim, "Spam's Cost to Business Escalates," *Washington Post*, March 13, 2003.

12 Sources: Eric Chabrow, "Spam Costs Escalate," *Information Week*, June 14, 2004, p. 22. Also Larry Seltzer, "How Much Is Spam Costing Your Company?," *eWeek*, June 9, 2004.

13 Cade Metz , "Slam the Spam," *PC Magazine*, February 25, 2003, p. 74.

14 Bob Sullivan, "Former Employee Charged with Stealing Subscriber List," MSNBC Article 5279826, June 24, 2004.

15 Andrew Conry-Murray, "Fighting the Spam Monster and Winning," *Network Magazine*, April 4, 2003, p. 24.

16 Andrew Conry-Murray, "Fighting the Spam Monster and Winning," *Network Magazine*, April 4, 2003, p. 24.

17 "How to Configure Connection Filtering to Use RBL and How to Configure Recipient Filtering in Exchange 2003," Microsoft Knowledge Base Article 823866.

18 Saul Hansell, "4 Rivals Almost United on Ways to Fight Spam," *New York Times*, June 23, 2004, p. C1.

19 Grant Gross, "FTC Won't Create Do-Not-Spam List," *InfoWorld*, June 21, 2004, p. 17.

20 "Offline Backup and Restoration Procedures for Exchange," Microsoft Knowledge Base Article 296788 .

21 "Chapter 2 – Back Up Exchange Server 2003," Microsoft Exchange Documentation.

22 "Chapter 3 – Restoring Exchange Server 2003," Microsoft Exchange Documentation.

23 "Description of the Isinteg Utility," Microsoft Knowledge Base Article 182081.

24 "The Database Files in This Storage Are Inconsistent," Microsoft Knowledge Base Article 327156.

25 "Running Isinteg – Patch Is Not Needed in Exchange," Microsoft Knowledge Base Article 240202.

26 Sources: Check.doc which is included with the MTACheck utility. "Performing an MTACHECK," Microsoft Knowledge Base Article 175495. "How and Why to Run MTACHECK," Microsoft Knowledge Base Article 163326.

27 "You Receive a Warning Message or You Cannot Start Outlook on a Computer That Is Running Small Business Server and Exchange Server," Microsoft Knowledge Base Article 828050.

28 "The Bad Mail Folder is Disabled in Exchange Server 2003 SP1," Microsoft Knowledge Base Article 884068.

29 "You Receive the Same Warning Multiple Times When You Synchronize the Calendar and Contacts List with a Palm OS Device in Outlook 2003," Microsoft Knowledge Base Article 821295.

30 Sources: "How to Reset the Nickname and the Automatic Completion Caches in Outlook," Microsoft Knowledge Base Article 287623. Also http://office.microsoft.com/en-us/assistance/HA011394511033.aspx.

31 Saul Hansell, "You've Got Mail (and Court Says Others Can Read It)," *New York Times*, July 6, 2004, p. C1.

Chapter 12

1 http://www.starwars.com/

2 www.cisecurity.org

3 1.2 The Evils of Features, Practical Cryptography, Niels Ferguson, Bruce Schneier, Wiley Publishing, Inc. page 5

4 http://www.microsoft.com/communities/default.mspx

5 In this context I am using the term "hacker" in the stereotypical view of today. Historically, hacker was not the "criminal" that it has come to be associated with.

6 Writing Secure Code/Michael Howard, David LeBlanc, 2nd edition. Copyright 2003 Microsoft Corporation

7 Writing Secure Code/Michael Howard, David LeBlanc, 2nd edition. Copyright 2003 Microsoft Corporation, page 83-86

8 http://msdn.microsoft.com/library/default.asp?url=/library/en-us/secmod/html/secmod76.asp

9 Discussed at the end of this chapter.

10 http://info.sen.ca.gov/pub/01-02/bill/sen/sb_1351-1400/sb_1386_bill_20020926_chaptered.html

11 http://info.sen.ca.gov/pub/03-04/bill/asm/ab_1901-1950/ab_1950_bill_20040929_chaptered.html

12 http://hfnetchk.shavlik.com/support/hfpro4help/HFNetChk_4_vs._WIndows_Update.htm. Shavlik has an excellent comparison of what is missed by Windows Update.

13 You can use an RSS feed reader and insert these bulletins into your own Sharepoint site. An example of a feed reader for Sharepoint can be found at http://www.smilinggoat.net/stuff.aspx.

14 http://www.microsoft.com/technet/community/scriptcenter/user/scrug74.mspx

15 239869 - How to enable NTLM 2 authentication: http://support.microsoft.com/ default.aspx?scid=kb;en-us;239869

16 299656 - How to prevent Windows from storing a LAN manager hash of your password in Active Directory and local SAM databases: http:// support.microsoft.com/default.aspx?scid=KB;EN-US;q299656&

17 http://support.microsoft.com/?kbid=829623

18 http://msdn.microsoft.com/library/default.asp?url=/library/en-us/dncode/html/ secure02132003.asp

19 http://www.microsoft.com/technet/community/columns/secmgmt/sm1004.mspx, http://www.microsoft.com/technet/community/columns/secmgmt/sm1104.mspx and http://www.microsoft.com/technet/security/secnews/articles/itproview point110104.mspx

20 http://www.hammerofgod.com/download.htm

21 http://msevents.microsoft.com/CUI/ EventDetail.aspx?EventID=1032255239&Culture=en-US

22 http://www.snort.org/

23 http://rss.softwaregarden.com/aboutrss.html

24 www.newsgator.com

25 www.intravnews.com

26 http://www.smilinggoat.net/stuff.aspx

27 http://blogs.msdn.com/aaron_margosis/archive/2004/06/17/157962.aspx

28 http://www.microsoft.com/resources/documentation/WindowsServ/2003/ standard/proddocs/en-us/Default.asp?url=/resources/documentation/ windowsserv/2003/standard/proddocs/en-us/windows_security_default_ settings.asp

29 http://www.microsoft.com/resources/documentation/WindowsServ/2003/ standard/proddocs/en-us/Default.asp?url=/resources/documentation/ windowsserv/2003/standard/proddocs/en-us/ windows_security_default_settings.asp

30 http://www.pcmag.com/article2/0,1759,1653326,00.asp

31 http://www.microsoft.com/technet/security/guidance/secmod129.mspx

32 "google" in this case is defined as going to the Google Web site and using both Web sites and "Google groups" to find past discussions on setting permissions that may help you in finding the right combination of registry keys to adjust.

33 http://www.sysinternals.com/ntw2k/source/regmon.shtml

34 http://www.pcmag.com/article2/0,1759,25126,00.asp. InCtrl5 is available in a bundle of tools to purchase for a nominal fee.

35 http://www.microsoft.com/technet/prodtechnol/sppt/reskit/c0661881x.mspx

36 http://download.microsoft.com/download/6/8/a/68a81446-cd73-4a61-8665-8a67781ac4e8/WF_XPSP2.doc

37 http://www.us-cert.gov/cas/techalerts/TA04-163A.html.

38 Draft at this time, you may need to find the updated link once it is finalized.

39 http://blogs.msdn.com/robert_hensing/

40 http://www.microsoft.com/resources/documentation/WindowsServ/2003/enterprise/proddocs/en-us/Default.asp?url=/resources/documentation/WindowsServ/2003/enterprise/proddocs/en-us/windows_password_tips.asp

41 http://www.rsasecurity.com/node.asp?id=1173

42 www.netstumbler.org

43 War Driving: Drive, Detect, Defend; a Guide to Wireless Security, Chris Hurley, Frank Thornton, Michael Puchol, and Russ Rogers, Syngress

44 http://www.microsoft.com/technet/security/tools/mbsahome.mspx

45 http://www.aicpa.org/download/trust_services/final-Trust-Services.pdf

46 http://www.isaca.org/Template.cfm?Section=COBIT6&Template=/TaggedPage/TaggedPageDisplay.cfm&TPLID=55&ContentID=7981

47 http://csrc.nist.gov/publications/secpubs/otherpubs/reviso-faq.pdf

48 http://www.insecure.org/nmap/

49 http://is-it-true.org/nt/atips/atips155.shtml

50 http://www.microsoft.com/resources/documentation/WindowsServ/2003/standard/proddocs/en-us/Default.asp?url=/resources/documentation/WindowsServ/2003/standard/proddocs/en-us/ref_we_logging.asp

51 http://www.securityfocus.com/infocus/1712

52 http://www.w3.org/Protocols/rfc2616/rfc2616-sec10.html

53 http://www.microsoft.com/technet/security/tools/mbsahome.mspx

54 http://www.sans.org/top20/

55 At this time, it is expected the updated SUS will handle patching for all parts of Small Business Server platform.

56 http://blogs.msdn.com/michael_howard/archive/2004/05/23/139987.aspx

57 http://blogs.msdn.com/michael_howard/archive/2004/06/16/157874.aspx

58 http://www.openwall.com/john/

59 http://www.atstake.com/products/lc/

60 http://www.hammerofgod.com/download.htm

61 http://www.atstake.com/research/tools/network_utilities/

62 http://www.insecure.org/nmap/

63 http://www.systemtools.com/somarsoft/ - It dumps the permissions (DACLs) and audit settings (SACLs) for the file system, registry, printers.

64 http://www.bindview.com/Support/RAZOR/Utilities/Windows/lsadump2_readme.cfm - This is an application to dump the contents of the LSA secrets on a machine.

65 http://www.securiteam.com/securityreviews/5DP0N1P76E.html

66 http://www.skype.com/privacy.html

67 http://security.web.cern.ch/security/software-restrictions/

68 http://www.ectaskforce.org/

REGISTER THIS BOOK!

By registering this book with SMB Nation, you'll receive discounts on future SMB Nation book, conferences and workshops. You will automatically be registered for our free SBS e-mail newsletter.

SPECIAL OFFER

When you register this book with SMB Nation, you will receive a <u>free PDF e-book</u> version of Advanced Windows Small Business Server 2003 Best Practices.

Complete the following information on this page and fax to 425-488-3646 or scan and e-mail to sbs@nethealthmon.com.

Name*_____

Address*_____

City*_____State*_____

Country*_____Postal Code*_____

E-mail address*_____

Second e-mail address:_____

(as a backup address)

Telephone:_____

How did you hear about Advanced Windows Small Business Server 2003 Best Practices?

__ Referral\Word of mouth   __ Advertisement

__ Newsgroup   __ Microsoft Web site

__ Other Web site   __ Search engine query

How did you purchase Advanced Windows Small Business Server 2003 Best Practices?

__ Online directly from SMB Nation

__ Online from book seller (e.g. Amazon)

__ Off the shelf, national retailer (e.g. Barnes and Noble)

__ Off the shelf, local book reseller (e.g. San Diego Technical Books)

__ **Follow-up.** Please contact me about SMB Nation conferences, workshops, books, writing for SMB Nation Press, complete a follow-up survey, etc.

* Required

Buy This Book! Buy That Book!

Small Business Server 2003 and *SMB Consulting Best Practices* provide the "bits" and "business" knowledge you need to be successful with Windows Small Business Server 2003. Both bring out the "best" of Brelsford's insights and humor.

Small Business Server 2003 Best Practices
ISBN: 0-974858-04-8
$59.95 USD

SMB Consulting Best Practices
ISBN: 1-887542-11-6
$59.95 USD

Visit the
SMB Nation site,
www.smbnation.com,
for purchasing
information.

PS – Don't forget our Small Business Server 2000 Best Practices book either!

SUBSCRIBE TO FREE SBS NEWSLETTER!

Join over 6,000 readers who want to stay in touch bi-weekly via the SBS newsletter, *SMB Technology Watch*. This newsletter presents both technical and business topics surrounding SBS and other Microsoft SMB products.

Now in its third year, *SMB Technology Watch*, seen in the figure below, has build a reputation for delivering the most current news on SBS. This includes breaking news announcements such as product alerts!

For your free subscription to *SMB Technology Watch,* visit the SMB Nation site at www.smbnation.com and sign-up!

Attend SMB Nation Workshops and Conference!

Plan on attending the annual SMB Nation conference that features SBS and other SMB technology solutions. In 2005, SMB Nation will be held in September 2005 in Seattle and Redmond Washington. You'll be able to interact directly with members of the SBS development and marketing teams, see the Microsoft campus and enjoy a day at Springer Spaniels Limited on Bainbridge Island for a retreat and concert! Good fun! Big fun!

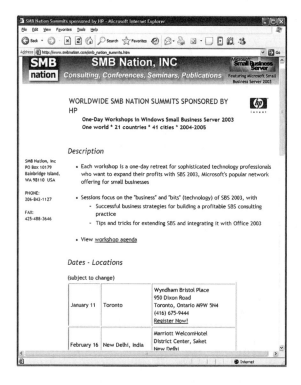

Visit the SMB Nation site to sign-up for the annual conference at www.smbnation.com

-AND-

Don't forget we have one-day SMB Nation Summits that travel worldwide! Information and sign-up at www.smbnation.com